BLOOD WILL TELL

girls we was all of us ladies
we was o what the hell
and once a lady always game
by crikey blood will tell.

—archy and mehitabel, XXXV,
mehitabel dances with boreas, by Don Marquis

Joseph Bosco

BLOOD WILL TELL

A True Story of
Deadly Lust in
New Orleans

William Morrow and Company, Inc.
New York

Library of Congress Cataloging-in-Publication Data

Bosco, Joseph.
    Blood will tell : a true story of deadly obsession / Joseph Bosco.
        p.   cm.
    ISBN 0-688-10889-X
    1. Myers, Janet Cannon.   2. Murder—Louisiana—New Orleans—Case studies.   3. Murder victims—Louisiana—New Orleans—Case studies.
I. Title.
HV6534.N45B67   1993
364.1′523′0976335—dc20   93-17770
                                                          CIP

Printed in the United States of America

First Edition

1 2 3 4 5 6 7 8 9 10

BOOK DESIGN BY LISA STOKES

This work is dedicated
in memorial to Janet Cannon Myers
and with love and hope to Ryan
and Sarah Myers.

Acknowledgments

A work of this nature is not possible without the assistance of literally hundreds of people. In the almost three years' gestation period for this book, several hundred people gave of their time to answer endless questions. Of these, some three hundred had enough probative or biographical information that a tape recorder was turned on at some mutually acceptable point and the conversations—I don't know what "interviewing" is—became archival material for this book. Since most of these people appear as characters within the text, their contribution will speak for itself. For those who didn't make it to the final draft, but whose assistance was, collectively, as invaluable as any of the most featured participants, you are too many to list here lest we leave someone out, so please accept our thanks en masse; you know who you are.

However, there are those persons whose relationship is of such a nature that their support transcends this work alone, and I will acknowledge them; very special thanks go to:

Sidney A. Cotlar, as fine a family attorney as he is a valued friend; Ralph S. Whalen, Jr., as topnotch a criminal defense lawyer as he is steadfastly a friend at any moment's notice; Ken Gaines, my "brother," my closest-friend-in-art, and the finest singer/songwriter America has but doesn't know about yet; and Pearl Bosco Reilly, who is always at the other end of the line when I need her muse to see me through.

At William Morrow, of course, there are many people whose labors go into the production of a book; we will thank three very important ones now: Adrian Zackheim, Vice-President, Editorial Director, who for the second time now has taken an editorial gamble upon the outcome of our work; Suzanne Oaks, Assistant Editor, she with the "down-home" voice to steady us, or gently nudge us when we were drifting too far from the channel; and Ted Johnson, copy editor, who deserves that art's highest compliment—he took a manuscript and made it better.

As always there is no thank-you adequate to say to my so understanding wife, Linda, and our son, Joe, for understanding yet again, and again, and again. . . .

But, in the end, this time, there is truly *one* person, singular, without whose efforts *none* of this would have ever been undertaken, much less her going so selflessly beyond the norms of her profession to ensure that it *would,* in *fact,* come to be a publishable book; she is Nancy Trichter, my agent, my rudder, my dearest friend. From my family to hers: love and gratitude.

Author's Note

In a few cases, a request was made for part or all of a person's name to be altered. In this litigious age, it is prudent to grant such requests when absent a journalistically compelling reason not to; these were granted. They are less than a handful, however, and the changes in no way diminish the standards of ethical journalism we attempted to uphold throughout the work.

Reader's Charge

Almost a decade ago, a most horrible crime was committed, exploding seemingly without provocation, motive, or even any logic, warped or otherwise, from the midst of a small circle of family and friends who were decidedly not of the criminal type: they were truly the boys and girls next door; they easily could have been models for any of Norman Rockwell's post-1960s illustrations. While they themselves were not of the rich and famous, and did not then grab the fifteen minutes of national fame Mr. Warhol prophesied for us all, the horrific central act of violence and its mystifying aftermath have become the stuff of forensic legend and seminars, being talked about and lectured about in law enforcement departments nationwide—cops of all stripes and insignia know it well. As do many lawyers, be they prosecutors, defense specialists, or jurists; it invariably comes up at their seminars and conventions, too. There is also an unusually large number of former jurors who know it well—after all, the case and its evidence have been presented to four sitting grand juries, two petit juries over the course of three criminal trials, and a number of "mock" juries privately empaneled by defense counsel.

However, even though the "system" finally exacted some measure of justice for the murder of a beautiful, bewitching, beguiling young mother, dancer, and poet, no one yet has been able to render a verdict as to exactly who did what to whom and why. It is now your turn to try. In the pages to follow, you will be privy to everything that is now known or has been circumstantially conjectured about the baseball bat murder. You will not be hindered in your deliberations by the rules of evidence, which, while absolutely essential to our system of American jurisprudence, can often be an obstacle in searching for absolute truth.

This story is actually two stories. One is a personal narrative of the lives of three people as related by their friends, their families, their loved ones; the other is a legal phenomenon whose unprecedented machinations have made it a landmark case in the U.S. criminal justice system for decades to come, as related by its participants.

Sift and mull it all carefully, because, when it is over, you will be asked to return a personal verdict which could mean a great deal to some bereft family members and friends who cannot let their wounds begin to heal without at least a decision one way or the other in the Court of Public Opinion.

Contents

BOOK I

"Don't be trying to confuse us with the facts, ya hear?"
—regrettably anonymous

1

Murder

To my little Ryan,

You're 12 weeks old today and I decided this journal waited long enough. I intended to start it before you were born, but time slipped away and I never did. Yesterday you discovered your voice, and it was then I refused to let 12 more weeks slip away. One day, when you're able to appreciate these written words, this book will be yours. I want to capture moments as they happen; I want to write to you feelings as they happen. Maybe through this you will have a better insight into yourself.

I should start at the beginning. . . .

—Journal of Janet Cannon Myers

*　*　*

1:40 A.M., February 24, 1984
Jefferson Parish Sheriff's Office Communications Division, Radio Room; "Operator 73"

Kerry Myers:	"Please! Somebody broke in my house and tried to kill me! I just stabbed him—2232 Litchwood in Woodmere! Please! Now! Hurry!"
OP 73:	"What's the problem there?"
Myers:	"Somebody broke in my house and tried to kill me!"
AT&T operator:	"Okay, wait, wait, calm down, calm down. . . ."
OP 73:	"Wait, calm down, sir. What's that address?"

AT&T operator:	"Someone tried to kill him, ma'am. They broke into his house and he stabbed him, okay?"
OP 73:	"Okay. What's the address?"
Myers:	"I got a broken arm and there's blood all over the place!"
AT&T operator:	"Okay, hold on, sir. . . . It's twenty-two what, sir?"
Myers:	"Thirty-two Litchwood Lane, in Woodmere."
OP 73:	"Okay, I got the twenty-two, twenty-two what?"
Myers:	"Twenty-two thirty-two—Litch—wood—Lane."
Dispatch trainer:	"Okay, someone broke in your house and you stabbed him?"
Myers:	"Yes!"
Dispatch trainer:	"All right, where's he at now?"
Myers:	"He just took off. I chased him out of the house down the street—"
Dispatch trainer:	"Okay, he's a white male or black male?"
Myers:	"—we been struggling for hours."
Dispatch trainer:	"All right, listen to me, white male or black male?"
Myers:	"White male."
Dispatch trainer:	"And do you know which way he was running?"
Myers:	"Yes! He was running down the street."
Dispatch trainer:	"Going which way?"
Myers:	"Towards the back of Woodmere. He had a car parked down the street."
Dispatch trainer:	"Okay, we've got an officer en route to you—now, just calm down."
Myers:	"Thank you."
Dispatch trainer:	"All right, listen to me. I need some information. What is your name?"
Myers:	"Kerry Myers. I'm scared! I need to pick up my gun in case he comes back."
Dispatch trainer:	"All right, you're gonna have to stay on the phone with me now until the police get there, okay?"

Myers:	"Oh! Get 'em here quick! I'm scared to death!"
Dispatch trainer:	"All right. . . . We need your telephone number."
Myers:	"340-3650."
Dispatch trainer:	"All right, and tell me exactly what happened— you just caught him breaking into your house and what?"
Myers:	"I came home at three-thirty this afternoon. I know the man. He's been despondent over his wife and [inaudible] . . . his wife and the kid, they left him. I walked in the door. He had my wife tied up! And he ambushed me with a baseball bat! I think my arm's broke! And he beat me over the head with the bat—and everything in my house he could find—and I been struggling with him—and trying to calm him and talk to him—and I just had an opportunity where he had a—then he tried to come at me with a knife—I took the knife away— and got an opportunity to—to—and just got him outa the house! And I stabbed him! He's got a—he's wounded!"
Dispatch trainer:	"Okay, can you tell me what he was wearing?"
Myers:	"Jeans and a blue sweater."
Dispatch trainer:	"A blue sweater?"
Myers:	"He's twenty-seven years old. Six-foot-two, got black hair."
Dispatch trainer:	"Where does he live at?"
Myers:	"He lives in . . . in . . . in, in Terrytown. I don't know his address. His mother also lives on Dunkirk—"
Dispatch trainer:	"Okay . . ."
Myers:	"—in Terrytown."
Dispatch trainer:	". . . do you need an ambulance or does your wife need an ambulance?"
Myers:	"Oh God! Yes! I need one!"
Dispatch trainer:	"Okay, we've got one en route to you, okay. What is your uh—all right, we're gonna get someone over there, okay?"

Myers:	"Now! Please!"
Dispatch trainer:	"Okay."
Myers:	"You want me to stay on the phone?"
OP 73:	"Yeah, you can stay on the phone with us."
Myers:	"Let me go pick up my gun."
OP 73:	"Okay."
Unidentified citizen male voice:	"Give me the Westwego Police Department—phone number?"
Dispatch trainer:	"How'd we get the Westwego Police on here?"
OP 73:	"I dunno."
Dispatch trainer:	"Oh, that was the operator, telephone operator. . . . You did call an ambulance?"
Unidentified emergency operator:	"Yeah." (Twenty-six seconds of static and background chatter and then the receiver can be heard being picked up again)
Dispatch trainer, away from phone:	"You got that code . . . ?"
Emergency dispatcher, in background:	". . . have an aggravated burglary, 2232 Litchwood . . ."
Myers:	"Okay."
OP 73:	"Sir, we have an ambulance en route to you."
Myers:	"Oh, please hurry—"
Dispatch trainer:	"Okay, we . . ."
Myers:	"—*please* hurry!"
Dispatch trainer:	"We've got an officer . . ."
Myers:	"How soon can an officer get here?"

Dispatch trainer:	"Just calm down and try to relax, 'cause it's only going to make it worse if you're all upset."
Myers:	"I just—"
Dispatch trainer:	"Just calm down."
Myers:	"—don't know if he may come back!"
Dispatch trainer:	"Okay, your doors are locked, huh?"
Myers:	". . . [inaudible] mad. Oh God! I got two small children—and one of them's stuck—and one of 'em hasn't even—one of 'em's seven weeks old! And hasn't even eaten since two o'clock."
Dispatch trainer:	"Are your children all right, sir?"
Myers:	"I think so! My wife's tied—he says my wife is tied up and wouldn't let me go in the room and see her! I need to go see about my wife."
Dispatch trainer:	"Okay."
Myers:	"Okay, hold on."
OP 73:	"Sir, did you check on your wife?"
Unidentified emergency operator, away from phone:	"340-3650."
Myers:	(In background) "Oh, God! God! Oh my God—oh God—oh God! Janet! Oh my God!"
OP 73:	"Get on the phone."
Myers:	"Oh, my God! I think he—*ohhh*!" (still in background)
OP 73:	"Get on the phone!"
Myers:	(Back on phone) "I think he killed my wife!"

Unidentified emergency operator:	"What's wrong with her?"
OP 73:	"Sir?"
Myers:	"Huh?"
Unidentified emergency operator:	"What's wrong with her?"
Myers:	"She's unconscious! There's *blood* all over her! He said he didn't hurt her—he *swore* he didn't hurt her!"
Unidentified emergency operator:	"Okay, we've got units en route to you. We've got an ambulance going to you."
Myers:	"I'm gonna kill him—"
OP 73:	"Tony?"
Myers:	"—if I find him. I'm gonna kill him. Oh, my God!"
OP 73:	"He thinks his wife is dead."
Myers:	"Oh! My! God! Oh!"
Dispatch trainer:	"All right, you stay on the phone with us, okay?" (Away from telephone) "He's armed."
Watch commander:	"Who is it who did it?"
Dispatch trainer:	"You know, sir?"
Myers:	"Huh?"
Watch commander:	"Who is it who did it?"
Myers:	"His name is Bill Fontanille."
Watch commander:	"Do you have any idea where he was going?"
Myers:	"I don't know! He may be going to try to see his son. His— they live in Aurora . . . Gardens. I mean not Aurora, Walnut Bend in Algiers."
Dispatch trainer, away from phone:	". . . [inaudible] he was running down the street [inaudible] Woodmere. . . ."

Myers: "The family's name is Mansfield—"

Dispatch trainer: ". . . [inaudible] he's stabbed."

Myers: "—I don't know the address or the street. Mansfield, in Walnut Bend in Algiers. And he may be trying to go ahead and see his son!"

Watch commander: "Does he have a car?"

Myers: "I'm sorry?"

Watch commander: "Does he have a car?"

Myers: "Yes, he does. It's a—I think it's about a '79 brown Toyota Corolla hatchback. I think my wife is dead! Oh, my God!"

Watch commander: "The ambulance is rolling as fast as they can, hear? We're gonna have help there. . . ."

Myers: "Think they'll make a call for me?"

Watch commander: ". . . soon as we can."

Myers: "Can y'all make a call for me?"

Watch commander: "Okay, who you want?"

Myers: "I don't want to get off the phone. I need to call my father."

Watch commander: "What's his address? I mean . . . ?"

Myers: "393-8609 is the phone number—"

Watch commander: "Okay . . ."

Myers: "—his name is Clifford Myers. Please call him and get him over here."

Watch commander: "Listen, what's his last name?"

Myers: "Myers."

Watch commander: "Listen, is your wife bleeding?"

Myers: "She's unconscious! She's been bleeding— 'cause the man's been here since three-thirty this afternoon—he probably did it since two o'clock this afternoon! She's unconscious! Full of blood! Oh, God! Oh! God! When can an officer get here? Hello?"

Watch commander:	"I'm still here."
Myers:	"When can an officer be here? I'm scared—I'm scared to death—I'm scared to death!"
Watch commander:	"Okay . . ."
Myers:	"He's hurt. The guy is hurt. I *stabbed* him in the side, and in the back."
Watch commander:	"You stabbed . . . ?"
Myers:	"Hello."
Watch commander:	"I'm still here."
Myers:	"Look, somebody's trying to call me. That's my call waiting on line."
Watch commander:	"Just—just stay on the line with me, hear? Don't worry about that. They . . . they can call back or they can talk to you later."
Myers:	"Oh, my God!"
Watch commander:	(Away from phone) ". . . just give me the police number."
Unidentified male authoritative voice on-line:	"Yes."
Myers:	"Please have an officer here right away! Okay? Please!"
Watch commander:	"Yeah—we have 'em on the way, hear?"
Myers:	"Oh! Ow—how long it's gonna take?"
Watch commander:	(Away from phone) "What is that ETA item [inaudible] . . . ?"
Myers:	"Hello?"
Watch commander, into phone:	"Yeah." (Then away) "Get an ETA on ambulance."

Myers:	"Oh, my God! I think my wife is *dead*—I hope to God she's not dead! Oh! Ah! Aa-aah-aaaa!"
Dispatch trainer, in background:	". . . Litchwood [inaudible] . . . we've got the man on the phone here."
Watch commander:	"Listen to me, how long has it been?"
Myers:	"He's been here he said since two o'clock this afternoon."
Watch commander:	"Since you saw Bill Fontanille, how long's it been?"
Myers:	"About fifteen—maybe ten minutes! The first thing I did was ran to the phone—after I chased him out of the house, I got—I made sure he left—and I made sure he ran down the street! He was walking. I screamed at him. But I got the chance to stab him! I was screaming at him down the street, and he left—he took off! About ten minutes maybe—as long as I've been on the phone with y'all."
Watch commander:	"Okay, you live at . . . ?"
Myers:	"Twenty-two thirty-two—Litchwood."
Watch commander:	"Litchwood?"
Myers:	"Litchwood."
Watch commander:	(Away from phone) "Litchwood."
Myers:	"That's in Woodmere."
Watch commander:	"Okay, and what's the cross street?"
Myers:	"Post is the first cross street. Coming right from the front of Woodmere you take a left on Post,

	it's the first street. And then Litchwood's the third street, you take a right."
Watch commander:	"Okay."
Myers:	"Please! Hurry!"
Watch commander:	(Away from phone) "Go up Woodmere, take a left on Post, the first street is Litchwood."
Myers:	"The third street . . . is Litchwood."
Watch commander:	"Litchwood."
Myers:	"Please have 'em hurry. Please have an officer here now! Oh my God! I'm scared he may come back! He's a—nuts! He's nuts. He's insane! He may be still trying to hurt his son and his wife—his—his ex-wife. I think he might have killed my wife! He had me here! He had me here! He said he would leave! He said he would leave and he kept lying!"
Watch commander:	"How do you know this guy? Huh?"
Myers:	"Guy was a friend of mine. He said he was out of town. He's—he's been hiding out from the police and everybody, 'cause they keep trying to pick him up for no child payments."
Watch commander:	"Uh-huh."
Myers:	"And he said he was in Florida working, and he showed up Monday at my house and everything was fine. And he stayed over for a while and then he showed up today and I guess my wife, you know, he was—he said he was gonna leave today, I guess my wife let him in to say goodbye. We been knowing him for years. He's a, you know, he's a friend. And they *did*—it looked like he hurt my *wife*! He clubbed her with a bat! With a baseball bat!"
Watch commander:	"Listen, where did you stab him? Where on his body?"
Myers:	"His side and in the back—I got the opportunity quickly—and I *stabbed* him—and he still was able to fight me. He got up, but I—I *hurt* him! I must have hit something 'cause I heard the—the—"

Watch commander:	(Away from phone) "Give that to [inaudible]...."
Myers:	"—the puncture noise—like air coming from his stomach or something. Oh, man! Oh, God! Help me!"
Watch commander:	"Look, how long ago did this happen?"
Myers:	"When?—what?"
Watch commander:	"How long ago did he stab your wife?"
Myers:	"I don't know if he stabbed my wife or not. I think he hit her with a bat—he hit her with a *baseball bat*—I say—I'm pretty sure 'cause she has *blood* all over her!"
Watch commander:	(Away from phone) "What?"
Myers:	"Oh, my God! I hope she's alive! Hu-hu-hn-aa! Aa! Aaa!"
Watch commander:	(Away from phone) ". . . [inaudible] possibly."
Myers:	"It was probably since about two-thirty or three this afternoon!"
Watch commander:	"Okay, when he left, he left on foot?"
Myers:	"On foot—but he had a car parked down the street."
Watch commander:	"Okay, the car's no longer there or what?"
Myers:	"No, he's gone—I ain't going out there to find out! I—"
Watch commander:	"Oh."
Myers:	"—after I chased him—made sure I chased him to the end of my sidewalk with the knife in my hand—and came back—"
Watch commander:	(Away from phone) "He left on foot but that car is his car and it was parked right down the block. Man doesn't want to go outside and see if he's still out there."
Myers:	"—I came back and picked up my shotgun—and put a shell in it—and that's when I called y'all—I'm waiting for y'all now—and I'm waiting on him if he tries to come back—I have a

shotgun—I'm gonna kill him if he walks in my door. Oh! My! God! Oh! Oh! Oh! My children and my wife! Hu-hu-hn! Aa! Aaa!"

Watch commander: "Are your children there?"

Myers: "I think they're fine! He didn't hurt my children—I have a little six-week-old baby who hasn't had any food or anything since two o'clock this afternoon—he swore. Every time he turned around he beat the hell out of me— then I got him to calm down—I grabbed the bat—and struggled with him—and got him to calm down. He's nuts! He's insane! I got him to calm down and talk."

Watch commander: "How old is he?"

Myers: "He's twenty-seven. I got him to calm down and talk. Then he swore he wouldn't hurt me anymore. And then he said he was going to leave. And when I got up he had a knife and tried to stab me! And then we wrestled with that—and we still had our hand on the knife—and we stayed on the ground for an hour—both holding on to the knife—and he finally let go—like he was exhausted—and I turned and stabbed him! I'll *kill him* if he comes back!"

Watch commander: "Okay, look, just stay calm, hear? When the officers get there they're gonna need your help for a lot of things."

Myers: "It's been ten minutes, where are they? This is an emergency!"

Watch commander: (Away from phone) "Check on that unit going to Litchwood."

Myers: "Where is he? Oh, my God! My wife! When I first walked in the door—and he attacked me—I didn't even see him, he was behind the— hah, somebody's knocking at the door but I gotta go make sure it's them."

Watch commander: "Hold on, hold on, wait. You got a unit—hello? You got a unit on Litchwood? Okay. Unit's 10-97, he went to answer the door."

Road deputy Chuck DeWilde would run the gamut of senses and emotions that early morning of Friday, February 24, 1984. The first was speed. He had been at Jamie Boulevard in Avondale when he'd taken the radio call. That was out of his beat; he remembers turning off the heater in his unit that cool deep-Dixie night so he could get all the horsepower his cruiser had to give as he raced east on the West Bank Expressway.

The next was confusion. "I knocked on the door numerous times, got no response. I radioed headquarters and asked them to call the complainant to answer the door. Then I heard at the door, 'Who is it? Who's there?' I told headquarters over my portable to 'disregard, complainant is at the door.' "

Then came fear. When the door opened, "it was a white male with a shotgun over the crook of his arm, and it was pointing at me."

Deputy DeWilde felt that sphincter suck of raw fear all cops feel often enough but will rarely admit to except when among their own. He felt it even though he could clearly see that the arm over which this weapon was draped had been broken. "I've seen broken arms enough. It had a big indenture, obviously misshapened, with the shotgun over it. I'm scared. I didn't know what was going down.

"The call came out as an aggravated burglary in progress. Then I was told en route the perpetrator had left. So when he met me at the door with the shotgun like that I didn't really know what to think—but to get it away from him."

Deputy DeWilde took the 12-gauge Remington 1100 without resistance and put it up against the wall just inside the door as Kerry Myers stepped back a pace or so to let him in and the two stood there in the foyer. Then came that sense of confusion again.

"My wife . . . I think she's dead."

"Where's the suspect?" DeWilde asked.

"He's gone. . . . I think my wife is dead."

DeWilde wondered what Myers meant. He didn't see anybody else in the house.

Confusion soon gave way to nasty beat-cop business. After pivoting Mr. Myers around and handing him to the EMT, Walter Cardin, who along with his partner, Patricia Murphy, had arrived almost simultaneously with DeWilde's cruiser and was waiting behind him on the small front porch, the deputy reentered the house. "I go back in. I start looking. I look over to the left after I pass the wall, over into the living room, then I see the body."

Or actually "a shadow on the floor." There was light coming from somewhere, some indirect light from some as yet indiscernible source.

He turned his flashlight on and "walked over to it." And "that's when I called in, I said, 'Send me Crime Scene and the Bureau, I have a signal 30.' "

At about that moment DeWilde became aware he was not standing over this lifeless female form alone. Sergeant Thacker, midnight patrol supervisor, his superior, had also arrived. Together and with purpose they took in the horror that all cops have to look at but, contrary to popular myth, never get used to.

Finally Sergeant Thacker said, "Go back out and try to get some information from the victim. I'll wait for Crime Scene."

DeWilde went outside to where Kerry Myers was then being helped into the back of the ambulance after having been sat down on his driveway for a while so that EMTs Cardin and Murphy could determine the nature and extent of his injuries.

"Sir, do you know who did this? Which way he went? What he looks like?"

Kerry Myers turned back over his shoulder from the ambulance deck and answered the questions with one of his own. "My children. I have two children. Where are my children?"

"I didn't see any children. What are you talking about?" DeWilde was back to confusion again, with an instant knot-in-the-guts anxiety for good measure.

"Where are my children? . . . They're in the house," Myers answered.

"Where are they in the house, Mr. Myers?"

"They're in the house. . . . Get my children."

DeWilde ran back inside, "Sarge, there's two children in here somewhere."

The whiskey-voiced sergeant's tone became truly a bark. "Where?"

"I don't know."

"How old?"

"I don't know. He says the children are here in the house."

They started searching. "We go to the first bedroom on the right, open the door, nothing. And neat as a pin. Second bedroom, same side, open the door, there's the infant. Just pretty as a picture, eyes open, not crying, sitting in one of those portable baby seats. Looked like she'd just been placed there for a minute while waiting to go on a picnic or something."

They took a few extra seconds to look under the beds in both those neat, well-ordered rooms. A quick look in the closets. Then the bathroom at the end of the hall. Door closed there, too. But nothing. Then they were in front of the last closed door, the bedroom in the northwest corner of the house.

Deputy DeWilde shrank back a little and said, "Sarge, I don't want to look in this one."

Thacker leaned around the deputy, turned the knob, and pushed. It didn't swing open. He pushed harder. DeWilde then lent his beefy shoulder. Whatever was there gave way, sliding across the carpet. DeWilde found the light switch. And there he was. What they had been pushing against was a young boy. To be precise, the "head and shoulder" of a young boy. He was bleeding from the ears and nose, a lot of blood, and was still as death, partially covered up by a disarrayed assortment of clothing tossed helter-skelter in the ransacked master bedroom.

DeWilde himself would later use the word "panicked" to describe his reaction. "I turned white as a sheet," he remembered. But what he did was run down the hall, into the foyer, and then a short left to the front door hollering to Pat Murphy, "Get in here quick!"

She came running and almost beat DeWilde back to the door of the strewn bedroom. The deputy was sick. He felt like throwing up. So pale and shaken was he that Murphy, after calling for Cardin to bring her an airway and before deciding that there was no time to wait for the emergency instrument and scooping up the limp, small body in her arms, momentarily looked at DeWilde and asked in all paramedic seriousness: "Are you going to be all right?"

He said he would make it. However, the big sandy-haired man wouldn't truly be all right for a long time afterward.

The ambulance raced off as more and more officers began arriving. DeWilde felt himself drawn back inside the house. Even though he wasn't a detective, perhaps he could chase away the nausea that threatened to embarrass him by acting as one. He only briefly glanced again at the slight but shapely thing with a vine of ivy around her neck and no face. Then he walked away from her toward the dining-room table in the short end of the L-shaped combination living room and dining room.

He was somewhat startled and surely further confused when he noticed a festive, uncut party cake, an unopened bottle of champagne, and two tulip glasses sitting atop the white fancy-lace tablecloth. He walked into the kitchen. Then the den.

"There was blood all over the place," he later recalled. "I had strong, conflicting emotions. What I couldn't understand was why he kept telling me, 'I think my wife is dead.' It bothered me from the very beginning. I mean, you either know a person is in the house or you know if they're alive or dead. Particularly this one. This one was very dead, and had been for hours."

And then there was that face that wasn't there. Not a mark of injury anywhere else but that face. In sixteen years as a cop, he'd never seen anybody beaten like that.

"There was a hole that you could put your hand into like this. Behind the ear you could almost put your whole fist in."

But what "tore me up the most was how could anybody do that to a child." And soon he was given more leisure to ponder that most horrific inhumanity. Sergeant Thacker had him stand outside and told him, "Don't let anybody in but Crime Scene or rank."

Except for the flurry of activity every time another cruiser or unmarked unit arrived and the unusually quick television news presence, there was very little else that Deputy DeWilde had to concern himself with. Certainly no crowds. Except for the neighbors on the north side, who were awakened deliberately by officers, no one stirred on the long block.

He held his post until his shift ended with the coming dawn. But even then he didn't go directly to the 3rd District station house to begin writing up his report. He first made a stop: the emergency room at West Jefferson Hospital, where he asked Deputy Fred Gonzalez about the condition and prognosis of the little boy, whose name was Ryan.

"It's pretty bad," Gonzalez said. "They don't know if he'll last the morning. The X-rays, man . . . the X-rays of his head looked like a plate of spaghetti."

DeWilde didn't go any farther into the hospital to see for himself. The people who surely by then were gathered around that all but lifeless grandchild had all the grief they could handle. They didn't need a stranger in a police uniform intruding upon their private shock and sorrow. How could they possibly appreciate or understand the bond he had forged with that child in those frantic seconds after he'd been found?

But he had. And Deputy Chuck DeWilde would continue to stop by the hospital every day for the next several weeks to inquire after Ryan Myers.

Clifford Myers, a New Orleans native, had been brought up the hard, old-fashioned way—*everybody* working for it. At sixteen he lied about his age just in time to join the Marines and see action in the Pacific during the last months of World War II. He had been a decorated and wounded combat veteran before he was old enough to drink 3.2 beer. And then he'd been ready to do it again when the Marines called him up during the Korean "conflict."

In between those two wars, he'd been an undersized end for the LSU Tigers when it was footballs and not bombs that were dropping from the sky. He'd seen a perhaps promising baseball career as a property of the Boston Red Sox come to an immediate, premature end when he tore up a knee in an exhibition game during his first minor league spring training.

But nothing in his life had prepared him for the phone call that raised him from his steady slumber within the two-story white brick Colonial at 796 Deerfield in Terrytown, one of the first and most affluent of the bedroom communities which had started springing up on the formerly rowdy rural bayous and "sticks" of Jefferson Parish on the west bank of the Mississippi River during the early 1960s after the completion of the Greater New Orleans Bridge had finally made the ferry system no longer the only way to get to and from "town."

"The phone rang about three in the morning, wouldn't you say?"

"A quarter to three," answers his second, younger wife, the patient, practical, pretty-faced Marva.

"Quarter to three," he agrees.

It had been Clifford who had answered the phone and heard, "This is West Jefferson Hospital. Are you Clifford Myers?"

"Yes, ma'am."

"Is Kerry Myers your son?"

"Yes, ma'am," again, though sharper, harder.

"Can you come to West Jefferson right away?"

"What's the matter? Has he been in an accident?" They were questions; they were also commands.

"I can't discuss it with you on the phone. I have to see you." The woman stood firm upon policy, though the ex-gyrene bullied and cajoled.

Finally, the father in him cried out, "Ma'am, is he dead?"

"No," she mercifully admitted. "But I can't discuss anything else with you now. You'll have to come up here."

"Yes, ma'am," came the clipped, resigned obedience to established order.

It wasn't long before Clifford and Marva were sitting in a little office just off the emergency room of the sparklingly efficient, modern parish hospital talking with the same nurse who had awakened and summoned them. Clifford was still thinking like most fathers who have worried through the teenage-driving years. "What's wrong?" he began. "Has there been an accident?"

"No," she said. "I can tell you this. Your daughter-in-law is dead. Your grandson right now has maybe a twenty to thirty percent chance of living. Your son, he's beaten up pretty bad, but he's going to be okay."

"My God! What happened?"

"I'm not at liberty to say." This lady was definitely by the book. It was then that Detective Martin Childs found them. "All we know is there was a bat, a knife, a gun, and a lot of violence."

They asked if they could see Kerry and Ryan. They were told their son was still being cleaned up, stitched, and evaluated; their grandson was too critical. With the initial shock abating at least a little, Marva's mind clicked upon her newest grandbaby. "Sarah! Where's Sarah? Sarah's not here—who has Sarah?"

They were informed that a neighbor had Sarah—would they go and pick her up? The only thing that either of them can really remember about fetching little Sarah is a fearful glance or two at the eerie, busy functionality of the scene next door before they hurried back to the hospital, where, eventually, they were told they could see Kerry, one at a time.

"Son, what in the hell happened?"

"Billy must've went crazy, Dad," Kerry Myers told his father. "I walked in the house when I came home from work and I heard my name and I turned around and Billy came from around the wall with the bat. He had the bat up like this, and he's hollering . . ."

"Son, why didn't you do something?" the combat veteran wanted to know.

"Dad, he's a friend, I thought he was just joking until he actually came down and hit me in the head with the bat. Then I put my arm up . . ."

Soon it was Marva's turn as Clifford held the baby. "I didn't know what to say to Kerry. I mean, I'm still like, 'I don't *believe* this.' "

All she said was, "Honey, how are you feeling?"

The doctors were still working on his arm; all Kerry kept saying was: "Mom, she's dead." Half crying, half talking, "Mom, she's dead."

Marva Myers just didn't know what to say. All she wanted was to get out, to get away from him; she didn't want to say the wrong thing. "I mean, what do you say?"

All she did reply was, "Your dad's got Sarah, I'm going to go back and take care of Sarah."

Then she and Clifford sat in this little room—Marva cradling her grand-baby—talking numbly, quietly, sporadically to each other until a nurse came and told them they could go and see Ryan.

Clifford went in first. He wasn't gone long. When he came back he stood in the door, dazed, sagging, empty, and said in a monotone, "You can go see him now."

Seeing Clifford Myers so affected, his wife felt the worst fear she'd yet felt that horrible morning.

"What's the matter?"

"He looks terrible. . . . The doctor said if he makes it to the morning he might have a chance."

Having never seen her husband in such a state, Marva Myers figured then that it certainly wouldn't do for her to go see Ryan; one of them must be able to stay in control, and she had Sarah to care for.

"No, I don't want to see him."

Soon they had to leave. Their fourteen-year-old son, Davin, had been left sleeping at home. They didn't want him to awake and find no one there and not know what had happened. Pediatrics fixed them up with about a dozen bottles of formula, diapers, and other supplies, to last until someone had the emotional strength to go shopping, or over to the house. It had been a long time since Marva and Clifford Myers had been parents to an infant.

After going home and seeing to Davin, the older couple went to Margue-rite O'Toole's house by the levee in Algiers. She was Clifford's ex-wife and Kerry's natural mother. Then it was on to Lorraine and Charles Cannon, Janet Myers's parents, to see what they could do to soften the telling.

Then it was back to the hospital as the vigil began again. It would go on for weeks—"hospital, come home, eat a hot meal, take a bath, and back to the hospital again."

* * *

Cissy Fontanille, as is her wont, had fallen asleep on the sofa with a book in her lap and the television on. Herman Fontanille had long before gone into his bedroom and fallen asleep.

There came a loud bang on the front door.

The noise brought her only partially awake; she wasn't sure if she had heard it in her dreams or if indeed someone was actually banging on her door at that hour of the morning. And she specifically remembers the hour, even after all these years, because the first things her eyes focused upon was the big clock the Fontanilles have in their den: it was 1:20 A.M., February 24, 1984.

By the time she was fully awake, Herman was already up and heading for the door. It was Billy—Cissy's baby, Herman's stepson.

"He was just standing there, kind of slumped over," she remembers.

"What's wrong? What's wrong?" she screamed; it was perhaps more of a squeal, a soft-throated, high-pitched Blanche Dubois trill.

"He's going to blame me for something . . . I'm going to be blamed for something," were the first words she remembers him saying at that dreadfully black hour of that morning.

"What are you talking about?"

"I don't know . . . I think he . . . I don't know what happened . . . but he told me he was going to blame me."

"Who? Who is he?"

"Kerry."

"Myers?"

"Yes, Kerry Myers. . . . I'm stabbed . . . I'm bleeding."

"Oh, my God!" she screamed as she watched her boy stagger into the living room doubled over and clasping his arms about his upper torso.

"I'm stabbed . . . I've been stabbed . . . I'm bleeding," he repeated, in a halting, disjointed tone which is forever etched upon her schoolteacher's memory.

"Why did he do it?" Herman finally demanded—a to-the-point question from a man of few words.

"I don't know . . . he's done something and he's going to blame me for it."

When Cissy got a good look at him she could see that "his sweater was just covered in blood."

She grabbed Herman. "We've got to get him to a hospital!"

As he stomped around dressing—she still had on her clothes—Herman asked, "Which one? Where do you want to take him?"

She reminded him that Jo Ellen Smith Hospital was the closest. Soon they were driving toward the river on Behrman Highway. Billy started talking again as he lay across the backseat of the van.

"I don't know what happened . . . I don't know what happened . . . I just know he did something and he's going to blame me for it."

"Blame you for what?"

"I don't know . . . but he told me he was going to blame me for it."

"Why in God's name did Kerry stab you?" she asked.

"I don't know . . . I don't know . . . I'm so confused by all of this, that this even happened . . . I don't know."

At about that time she "literally heard the blood coming out of him. Like a faucet. I heard it gush. From his chest. I panicked. I'll never forget how it felt in my ears."

Past the point where Behrman Highway turns into Holiday Drive and where it intersects General Myer, in their shock and confusion, they turned left. Jo Ellen Smith Hospital is to the right.

They drove several blocks toward old Algiers and the apex of the bend in the Mississippi River which has given "the Crescent City" its most lasting nickname before realizing their mistake. Herman made a U-turn.

When they got to the emergency room, they weren't allowed to accompany their son any farther. They took a seat in the waiting room. Cissy remembers "looking at the clock, it was five minutes till two."

A doctor came out and "talked very briefly with us. He said something about having to give Billy a blood transfusion." Then the police were there and wouldn't let them see their son.

John Taylor, a New Orleans police officer of some twenty-five years, assigned to the 4th District Algiers station, had been working an off-duty paid detail on the 11:00-P.M.-to-7:00-A.M. shift at Jo Ellen Smith Hospital that night of February 24, 1984.

It had been a slow evening. Weeknights usually were. At about 2:00 A.M., he had been by the nurses' station in the emergency room, drinking coffee and chatting, when the clerk up at the front desk called back and said they had a stabbing victim. A nurse went out to escort the patient back down the hall toward the triage room, and Officer Taylor got his first look at Bill Fontanille.

"His clothes were bloody, and he appeared to still be bleeding," Taylor remembers. While the nurse did have Bill by the arm leading him, he "was walking under his own power, and was calm. He wasn't gasping for breath. No sentence fragments. No hyperventilation. Never did he rant or rave that whole morning. I've seen a lot of scared defendants in my years, but he was not one of them."

Of course, at the time that fact did not appear significant to Officer Taylor. "I'm assuming he's a victim, not a perpetrator."

As the nurse was walking with him, Taylor remembers that Bill repeated several times, "I've been stabbed. My best friend stabbed me. He killed his wife and baby and is going to blame it on me."

Officer Taylor didn't intervene at first. He just stood in the doorway of the triage room and watched as a doctor and nurse started emergency procedures. A large-bore IV was inserted. Vital signs were checked—blood pressure was taken at exactly 2:05, according to the nurse's notes. A complete "hemodynamic assessment" was made. The wounds were examined for depth and proximity to vital organs.

After some few minutes, when he thought it appropriate, Officer Taylor asked, "What happened?"

According to Taylor, this time Bill Fontanille said, "My best friend stabbed me. He told me that his wife and baby were dead. He said he was going to blame it on me."

As Taylor listened and Bill Fontanille continued to talk, the officer heard the very first version of Bill's account of that afternoon and night. He'd gone over to pick up his baseball bat around four o'clock that afternoon. His best friend, Kerry Myers, had let him in and then had started stabbing him in the back. They had then fought back and forth the rest of the night until he'd finally been able to get away shortly before his arrival at the hospital. He several times said that the police needed to go over there, that during a stalemate of their last struggle his friend had told him he'd killed his wife and baby.

Taylor stopped this recital and asked, "Where did this happen?"

"Woodmere," was the answer. Not an address, just the subdivision.

Taylor remembers he then walked out of the triage room and went to the phone on the wall just outside the door and dialed the Jefferson Parish Sheriff's Office Communications Center. When the dispatcher answered he said: "This is Officer John Taylor, NOPD. I'm calling from Jo Ellen Smith Hospital. Are you working anything in Woodmere?"

"Do you have Fontanille?" was her immediate and breathless reply.

"Yes," is all he remembers getting out before she said: "Hold on to him. I'll get somebody over there as soon as I can."

She offered no further details, nor asked any. Officer Taylor hung up the phone, went back into the triage room, and saw that all of Fontanille's very bloody clothes were on the floor at the foot of the exam table. He went and got a plastic hospital admissions bag and put everything inside. Then, without any further conversation with the "subject," he stood at the door and waited. He left only once, and that was when he'd learned that the patient's parents were in the waiting room. He paid them a quick, inquisitorial visit. They knew nothing more than he did, which, of course, was nothing. There was, however, a thought, actually more a question, which tugged at his mind that morning and would continue to do so for years: why would a twenty-eight-year-old man, who had every reason to believe he was critically injured, drive almost directly past Meadowcrest Hospital in order to go to his parents' house before seeking medical attention?

* * *

Deputy DeWilde had requested Crime Scene and notified the Detective Bureau at 1:53 A.M. The first to arrive was Jefferson Parish crime scene technician Deputy William Vieira, almost simultaneously with the departure of the ambulance bearing Kerry and Ryan Myers to West Jefferson Hospital at 2:01 A.M.

"When I got on scene, there were only uniforms there, no detectives yet." DeWilde quickly filled Vieira in on the essentials and "showed me where the body was and stuff. He pointed out the shotgun, but said it didn't appear to be an element of the crime."

Crime scene technician Vieira then went out to his unit, got his camera, and started "loading up" preparatory to photographing the outside of the house, as procedure called for him not to start processing the actual crime scene until a detective arrived.

While he was standing at the trunk of his unit he saw Sergeant Thacker and Captain Roger Adams, night supervisor, run to the house on the north side of 2232 and knock on the door.

"They need a telephone," Lieutenant T. Wray, 3rd District Patrol Division, told him when Vieira gave a quizzical look. "The phone in the house is still off the hook, can't touch it. Be sure and get a picture of that, huh?"

"Right." Just what Vieira needed, somebody else to tell him how to do his job.

He was shooting the first exposures of the exterior when Detective Sergeant Warren Donnelly, Crimes Against Persons Division, arrived. The first thing the detective did upon realizing there was an infant girl still sitting "placidly" yet unattended in the middle of a very messy crime scene that was getting more hectic by the minute was to dispatch DeWilde to tell Thacker and Adams to also "ask the neighbors if they would take care of the infant for a short period of time."

When it was reported back that Steve and Gwen Faucheaux would be more than happy to oblige, and Captain Adams was about to scoop up little Sarah, Vieira, who was now inside with the rest of the burgeoning police, spoke up quickly; "Unh-unh! Wait a minute. Before you take her, lemme get some pictures, will ya?"

Consequently, after three shots of the exterior, the next half-dozen or so exposures on Vieira's first roll of film from that early morning were of the "Gerber Baby."

"That's exactly the way she looked. Eyes open, looking around, but not a peep out of her. In fact, she never cried once while I was on the scene. Chuck DeWilde told me she was yet to make a sound the whole time. It was amazing. From the looks of it, that house must've been bedlam for hours, not to mention when all of us started banging around in there. But her? Nothing. Like she'd been posed for a commercial or something."

Now that a detective was on scene—although not yet the homicide case officer in charge—Vieira could start in earnest completing the first of his several important responsibilities, namely to photograph every view of the house which he or a detective thought relevant to prosecuting the case.

According to William Vieira, there are basically two mind-sets you can have while processing a crime scene: a tense "cover-your-ass" abundance of caution and thoroughness, appropriate when there is no identifiable perpetrator; and a much laxer, more casual "Yeah, 'spect we oughta get that, help the DA fry his ass" attitude, appropriate when the perpetrator is a positively identified suspect.

Almost from the first moments of his arrival, Deputy Vieira remembers the process to have been very much in the latter category. Not only was there an identified perpetrator, the "suspect had already been apprehended." Open and shut.

While waiting for the arrival of the assigned homicide case officer, Vieira went about snapping his shutter at his own will, standard protocol: "You're basically on your own, unless specifically asked to do something by a detective."

One of the few times that a detective did ask for a shot was quite early on. Just as Vieira was starting the process of photographing what remained of Janet Myers from a dozen or so angles and viewpoints, Sergeant Donnelly and a number of other helpful voices called for his attendance in the kitchen.

"Look, sumbitch left the water running in the sink. And see them towels and shit. Fontanille must've been tryin' to wash hisself up."

"Looks like it."

"Get a picture of that before some yo-yo shuts the faucet off, huh? And them towels. And get the phone now, too. So we can use it."

"Right."

Having completed those, Vieira went back to shooting the body and the mostly unfurnished living room, then continued in a roughly clockwise pattern through the house: adjoining dining room, kitchen, den, hall, bedrooms, and bathrooms.

However, one particular image seized his thoughts, and several times he returned to it. Above and to the left of Janet Myers, stuck right into that Jackson Pollock pattern and expanse of "exploding" blood spatters upon the white textured Sheetrock wall, was a very distinct bloody left handprint.

So compelling was the image that he took several close-ups. Then he went back again and held his left hand up next to it; the handprint was considerably smaller than his own hand.

"I decided not to shoot it with a scale. It had to've been the little boy's hand, and he damn sure wasn't a suspect. Anyway, I knew I could explain its actual size if I had to, using my own hand as an example," Vieira would later try to explain.

"But I saw it. It was there. Sure as life. And strange, almost eerie-like, you know?"

He also remembers well the head with no face that was the source of that eruption of blood on the wall. "Twenty years doing crime scenes, and it was the worst beating I've ever seen."

JPSO CRIME REPORT SEC. A   ITEM: B/14695/84

OFFENSE R.S # & TITLE: 14:30   REPORTED: 2-24-84 1:41 AM

DATE/S & TIME/S OF OCCURRENCE: 2-23-84 4:00 PM--2-24-84 1:41 AM

LOCATION: 2232 Litchwood, Harvey, La.   ADDRESS: Same

VICTIM'S NAME: Myers, Janet

VIC. RACE-SEX-AGE-D.O.B.: W/F 10/29/58

DATE & TIME PRO. DEAD: 2/24/84 3:10 AM   CORONER NOTIFIED: 1:50 AM

INJURIES: Lacerations to head and face

51. SUSPECT ARRESTED? IF YES USE CODE "A" BELOW ON LEFT

CODE: A

NAME: Fontanille, William RACE-SEX-AGE: W/M 28 COMPLEXION: Fair

D.O.B.: 8/23/55 DESCRIP. HEIGHT & WEIGHT: 6'0" 190 lbs.

HAIR: Brown FACIAL HAIR: Mustache

MAY BE LOCATED AT: 545 Dunkirk, Gretna, La.

WITNESSES: See Narrative

On Friday, 24 February 1984 at approximately 2:00 AM Sergeant Robert Masson, Jefferson Parish Sheriff's Office Homicide Unit, was advised of a homicide at 2232 Litchwood, Harvey, La. The undersigned officer arrived on the scene at approximately 2:43 AM and met with Sergeant Warren Donnelly, midnight supervisor. The undersigned officer was advised by Sergeant Donnelly that the homicide victim was in the living room of the residence and that there were two additional victims at West Jefferson Hospital and a third victim at Jo Ellen Smith Hospital in New Orleans.

The undersigned officer observed that 2232 Litchwood is located on the west side of the street. The block is bounded on the north by Post St. and on the south by Patricia Ave. The front entrance of the residence faces to the east.

The front entrance leads into a foyer area. The foyer is bounded on the north by a wall and on the south by a half wall. On the half wall is a door which leads into the garage of the residence. An iron rail is located adjacent to the half wall on the south side of the foyer. The iron rail separates the foyer from the living room area of the residence. . . .

The undersigned officer entered the living room of the residence located near the southeast quadrant of the residence. The officer observed a potted plant along the east wall and situated in the northeast corner. . . . Proceeding south along the east wall, the undersigned officer observes two cardboard boxes. Adjacent to the two boxes and to the south, the officer observes the body of a white female. The white female is laying on her back face up. Upon checking the body, the officer observes the body is cool to touch and that rigor mortis is present throughout. Sergeant Masson observes no post mortem lividity in the body. The body appears to be that of a young white female. She is dressed in multi-colored pullover shirt, striped. The blouse is pulled up to just below the bosom. The female is dressed in blue gym shorts with a small white stripe along the side. Under the blue gym shorts the deceased is wearing a pair of maroon pantyhose or leotard type clothing. The deceased is also wearing a pair of white tennis shoes. A spot of red bloodlike substance is located on the right shoe. The undersigned officer observes that the head of the deceased is located along the east wall. The right arm is bent at the elbow with the hand pointing in an easterly direction. The left arm is also bent at the elbow with the left hand pointed in a southeasterly direction. Both legs are bent at the knee. The undersigned officer observes a large amount of red bloodlike substance spattered along the east wall above the head of the deceased female. A large amount of red bloodlike substance is also present on and saturates the carpet below the head of the female. A piece of broken ivy, green in color, is located underneath the body. Directly to the south of the female is located a three tier shelf. The shelf is knocked over on its side. . . .

    Sergeant Robert Masson

Bob Masson's memories of that early morning are characterized by a mixture of confusion and absolute certainty.

He had only a short while before ended a particularly tiring night shift as a homicide detective and squad leader working out of the Investigative Bureau located in Marrero on the West Bank of Jefferson Parish. He had in fact just settled into deep sleep when he was brought groggily awake by a phone ringing next to his head.

"Yeah."

"We have a 60:30 at 2232 Litchwood in Woodmere." The voice was one he recognized from the Radio Room in the Communications Center of the Jefferson Parish Sheriff's Office on the West Bank. There was little necessity for much conversation.

"All right. It'll be a while. I've gotta get dressed," he said, and then added before hanging up, "Be no traffic this time of night, though."

He shook his head hard a couple of times in an attempt to shake off the fog and lethargy he felt more than usual that night, and started dressing while consciously waiting for that adrenaline kick he was used to feeling upon notification of a homicide.

There still had been no glandular jolt as he went out and turned the ignition in his unmarked unit. "Damn," he remembers thinking, "luck be with me tonight." What he wanted most was a sure-thing collar on the other end of his journey from the East Bank of Jefferson Parish to the West Bank—which, of course, because of the convolutions of the mighty Big Muddy, isn't west at all. He thought about that incongruity of life in and around New Orleans for perhaps the thousandth time; it beat hell out of the nagging other thought that kept trying to intrude:

"A 60:30 in Woodmere? That ain't blacks killing blacks for a hit of crack or a fuck or a jug of wine, where the goofy fuckers always do their shit in front of a jillion witnesses and leave enough evidence behind that the good guys usually follow the cookie-crumble trail and are practically there waiting for 'em."

Nope. A 60:30 in Woodmere could definitely prove to be sticky. That thought now forced out all others as he came off the south end of the Greater New Orleans Bridge and hit the West Bank Expressway, pushing it hard now that a little of that adrenaline had been coaxed out. But only a little. Not nearly what he usually got. Or needed, sometimes.

His worst fears appeared to be what was waiting for him as he pulled his unit over to the side and parked it along with about a half-dozen others plus two TV news vans.

"Jeez! It was total confusion when I walked into that house. Uniforms walking all over the place." Such was his first remembered impression of what would shortly and for years afterward be known in south Louisiana as the baseball bat murder.

He passed DeWilde on guard at the door and then was immediately relieved when he almost ran over his friend Warren Donnelly standing in the foyer. There the two men stood at the intersection of the house and Detective Masson was competently brought up to speed on the known facts of the case by a relatively calm Donnelly while directed and misdirected chaos swirled about them.

Then he went to the body and did basic checks for death. As was his custom, after viewing the deceased, notebook in hand, he started off on a quick walk through the whole house, wanting to view everything in general before zeroing in on any particular elements of the crime scene.

That trip, however, and the subsequent more in-depth traversals of the scene, would not prove to be a smooth, continuous flow as they would appear to have been in his later typed report.

"Before I knew it, it seemed like every uniform man in the world came up and brought me another little piece of information. Or I'd get a phone call from somebody and have to stop what I was doing to go pick that up."

He stopped to talk to the crime scene technician, who might be on the other side of the house wondering if this or that was important.

"Of course, usually it's the other way around. It's always a fight to get technicians to cooperate with you, believe it or not. Only wanna do what's asked; sometimes they're real difficult to work with. You'll say, 'Need a picture of that,' and I swear, sometimes they'll answer back, 'Why?' Why? Because some jackleg defense attorney will ream you a new asshole on the witness stand because he'll be screaming that that one damn picture not taken, or evidence not picked up, is *the* thing that would've proven his client innocent. And boom, he's got reasonable doubt for the jury!"

That's what Bob Masson remembers he would've said to Vieira that night, but he's pretty sure he didn't. "What's the point?"

Not much on that night, apparently. Most of the photographs were taken before he got there. "Which can be a problem, because you don't know what's been taken. You ask a technician, 'Why don't you get a photograph?' 'I already have it.' But you don't know what angle he has or anything. So you rely on somebody like Warren Donnelly to tell you it's been done right. It puts further burden on you; you really have to watch not only what you're doing, but you also have to keep an eye on what everybody else is doing. Lot of confusion. That's what I remember most about that night."

At one point Masson remembers being in the ransacked master bedroom "going through the clothes and they wanted me on the phone, it was Deputy Gonzalez at West Jeff, he wants to tell me what's happening with the husband. When I hang up I go back and try to recollect where I was; I look down at my notes: 'Oh, already done clothes.' And you go on, but maybe you lose track. Man, I filled two and a half notebooks just like that one on this case."

He also had the public information officer coming at him every few minutes on what to give the press. For Bob Masson, that element of a crime scene is the "biggest pain in the neck" of all. It certainly was on that one. Right away:

"Give me what you have."

"I don't have anything."

"Come on, I've got to give 'em something."

"I can't give ya what I don't have."

Actually, though, all the confusion notwithstanding, Bob Masson knew quite a bit almost from the start.

Deputy Fred Gonzalez had called in several times with updates on what Kerry Myers was saying and on the conditions of Ryan and his father. Plus he was also continuing to get updates from Jo Ellen Smith Hospital concerning one William Fontanille.

So it really wasn't very long before Detective Masson relaxed some and stopped worrying all that much about not feeling at his sharpest. He didn't care that his energy level had never reached that rush he felt he needed for the tough cases.

In fact, he clearly remembers thinking to himself, "This isn't too bad. I've got a guy saying he came home, finds a guy he knows in his house who beats him with a baseball bat. There's this fight, he finally flings the guy off, the guy runs out, and he calls the police. Didn't sound all that complicated."

Of course, "You still try to pick up the evidence to get a conviction on him. It's not like nothing to it; you still go through the procedures."

And when Masson was told they were about to take Kerry Myers into surgery, he decided he needed to call for help. There was no way he was going to be able to get over there to talk to what was probably his only eyewitness before he went under anesthesia and then received pain medication. There was no indication that Fontanille would be going into surgery, however. Masson called homicide detective Martin Childs, who was on the day shift, and asked him to go to West Jefferson and talk to Myers.

Shortly thereafter, Detective Childs called with the results of his interview with Kerry Myers, who appeared to be a greatly beaten-up, forlorn, and bereaved father, widower, and victim.

While it certainly was bizarre—two longtime best friends fighting almost to the death for ten hours all the while the beautiful wife lies bludgeoned to death in the living room without the ambushed husband's knowledge of her or Ryan's horrific fate—after he had the basic gist of Myers's story, Masson became certain that the physical evidence in the house and the wounds ascribed to Bill Fontanille fit it like a glove. It was "completely plausible" to him.

In due time word arrived that Fontanille was about to be moved across the river to Charity Hospital in New Orleans. A crime scene technician was needed to go to both West Jefferson and Jo Ellen Smith in order to collect and preserve all of the clothes as evidence; headquarters wanted Vieira to go.

When Masson told Vieira that, the technician explained the obvious: "And who's gonna finish up here?"

It wasn't a bad question at all, since the coroner's investigator and driver, who had arrived some thirty minutes prior, were cooling their heels in the living room with the deceased as they waited for Vieira to finish his other work so he could strip her and they could go rolling on with theirs.

"Tell the deputies at the hospitals to get the clothes. I'll go pick 'em up when I'm done here," Vieira offered.

That was reasonable enough; Masson directed that it be done. Then soon enough came the last major work to be completed at the crime scene, the disposition of the corpse and its effects, which had to be precisely documented in part by Vieira and the coroner's investigator and in total by Detective Bob Masson, the homicide case officer in charge.

This work occasioned some discussion among them all as to their assessment of the damage inflicted upon the decedent, its extent, nature, and probable causal instrument.

Vieira was sickened by the severity of it—"Jesus, her face has fallen off the skull"—and he was certain that all of the damage had been caused by the quite bloody baseball bat which he'd photographed and processed from its discovered location, leaning barrel-down against the askew love seat in the den amid the shards of smashed crockery, glass ashtrays, table lamp, and various other shattered objects plus the literally thousands of blood smears, swipes, pools, drops, and splash patterns.

Don McIntosh, the coroner's investigator, agreed she'd probably been beaten with a "blunt instrument," but because of the particularly gaping rips and tears of facial and scalp epidermis he couldn't rule out some stabbing and slashing also, perhaps from the bloody kitchen knife that had been found, photographed, and documented at the far end of the kitchen counter next to the dangling wall phone. But whatever had been its cause, the effect had been especially "savage, some kind of incredible rage, no doubt."

Bob Masson grunted his dispassionate agreement to all views. But what he remembers thinking was that "it was brutal, all right, but not the worst I'd ever seen. I mean, it didn't jump into my mind like that. Didn't really grab me, you know."

He also remembers placing no significance in the fact that it appeared, as Vieira began to remove and document the clothing and accessories Janet Myers had chosen to wear on the final day of her life, that all of the blows or slashes had been to her face.

"Hey, if you're gonna club somebody to death, you don't go about hitting 'em in the ass or stomach, know what I mean?" Plus, "I didn't know if she mighta had any internal injuries or anything."

But as he stood and noted everything that Vieira and McIntosh did, mostly what he remembers is that he really didn't like having to send somebody else to the autopsy.

"Always like to go myself. But with Fontanille being transferred to Charity Hospital, I thought it was more important to go talk with him. He was the prime suspect—wanted to talk to him before he saw an attorney."

So, not long after Janet Myers was securely enveloped in a royal-blue body bag and had been rolled out into the night with the TV crews rolling tape and lighting up the yard, Bob Masson went back to the telephone and called Lieutenant Gus Claverie, commander of the Crimes Against Persons Division, to ask if another detective could attend the autopsy. The answer was affirmative, and Masson then quickly made specific requests concerning that autopsy, mentally checking each off as he went; he asked for vaginal swabs, hair sample, blood sample, photographs, and anal swabs.

Then something or someone, he doesn't remember which, had yet again directed his attention elsewhere. "Yeah . . . that oughta cover it, and thanks," he'd said to Claverie and hung up the phone.

Noel "Torchy" Adams was on patrol working Terrytown that night, "riding 207. I was a backup unit." He heard the call come out for the Woodmere area. It was an area he was familiar with, having worked it before during his then nine years on the Jefferson Parish Sheriff's Office force, when he'd been assigned to the 3rd District.

Deputy Adams listened to the increasingly frenetic comings and goings at the crime scene and West Jefferson Hospital on his radio until it became obvious that 3rd District was out of available units. That's when "I called my rank on channel 2 and asked if they wanted me to go to the hospital and interview the subject. They said, 'Yeah.' At the time I was at Carol Sue and Behrman Highway." From there it took Adams only minutes to get to Jo Ellen Smith.

He quickly huddled with John Taylor, who briefed him on what Fontanille had said thus far. Then Torchy Adams went into the triage room.

"The first thing I did, knowing there was a possible homicide involved, was introduce myself and advise him of his rights. I told him that he wasn't under arrest, that we were just conducting an investigation into a possible homicide. Then I asked if he had any problems with me asking him questions."

According to Adams, Bill immediately answered, "Oh, no. Not at all. Because I don't want to be blamed for anything I didn't do."

To Torchy the "subject looked to be troubled. His eyes were shaking. The pupils, the cornea was going back . . . he seemed to be nervous. He seemed to be excited. Yet he didn't look to be somebody that had lost so much blood in a ten-hour period that he was really sicko. I've seen people come out of minor surgery who looked worse than he did."

But Bill Fontanille didn't appear to be "scared of me at all. He came right out and said, 'I don't want to be blamed for nothing. And I want this for the record. I don't want to be blamed for nothing.' "

So Adams said: "Hold on, lemme try and get a statement from you."

But Torchy remembers that Bill then said: "Well, I just want to tell you."

"He didn't want me to write anything down, it seemed. And one of the homicide detectives had already told me that they were going to take the statement from him at a later time. That they didn't want to get it from him that night because of the scene and everything else the way it was, being so spread out and complicated. So, I let him tell me his story."

While it was the first time that Adams heard the tale, it was basically the same story that Officer Taylor, who was still in the room, and Dr. George Neri and nurse Gabriel LaMarche, who were coming in and out, had already heard—but not quite.

This time, after about the second or third repetition of "and he's going to blame me for it," Bill Fontanille paused just a moment and then said: "He's going to tell you we had a plan to kill both our wives but he didn't think I'd go through with it."

Whoa! What? "When I heard that, I knew something was out in left field." Torchy remembers thinking, "Why is he telling me this?"

And John Taylor heard it too. "Damn strange statement, without a doubt." Suspects don't often make statements that, while inculpating someone else, also implicate themselves. And this one was just "snatched right out of the blue," voluntary, not prompted by anything.

Bill continued on, apparently not noticing Taylor's and Adams's quickly masked reactions to his statement. He talked at length and in detail. About his marital problems—he was separated from his wife. About how he'd gone over to the Myerses' to pick up the baseball bat he'd left the day before, Wednesday. How, needing and looking for sympathy, he'd purposely gone there when Janet was alone. And how one thing had led to another and before they knew it they were making love. How he believed that Kerry was suspicious. He said that Kerry had come home early from work on Wednesday and, though they had finished their lovemaking, had probably seen them sitting close together on the love seat. But Kerry hadn't said anything. In fact, he and Kerry had gone together with a group of their friends and had played basketball Wednesday evening.

Afterward, when Billy had gotten his story out, Torchy asked if he'd mind him now making a few notes. Bill said he didn't, and repeated answers to specific questions where the officer's memory failed him.

Throughout it all, though, Torchy Adams, who was and still is a neighbor and good friend of Janet Myers's sister and brother-in-law, Joan and Wayne Switzer, knew "just as well as I'm sitting here that Bill Fontanille killed her. He would never look me in the eye when he talked to me. He'd look at me and start drifting. He'd blink. I just felt that he was lying. He had that coldness to him. We get gut feelings out here. I really in my heart believed he did it; that's one of the reasons I read him his rights right away. I didn't know this Bill Fontanille from Adam, but I could just tell he was lying."

Yet, all of that certainty in his mind and heart notwithstanding, Deputy Noel "Torchy" Adams still didn't really know what to make of that earlier statement: "He's going to tell you we had a plan to kill both our wives but he didn't think I'd go through with it."

"It was like a jigsaw puzzle with some of the pieces missing," is how Fred Gonzalez, a plainclothes vice officer, begins his memory of that night when he was still a road deputy. He'd been working another call when the initial dispatch had gone out. He hurriedly finished up and sped over to Woodmere, arriving at 1:55 A.M.; about six minutes later, Sergeant Thacker asked that he follow the ambulance to West Jefferson Hospital.

"There was something missing. The time spans didn't fit. I don't know. And then, while we were at the hospital, and I don't remember who said it, but somebody at the hospital knew them. They were West Jefferson people—it was probably a couple of nurses or a technician or something that knew Myers and knew Fontanille—but I heard somebody say, 'It doesn't make sense, that these guys would do something to each other. Growing up, these kids were like two peas in a pod.' "

JPSO CONTINUATION FORM   ITEM: B/14695/84

On the same date [February 24] at approximately 4:45 AM, Detective Martin Childs, Jefferson Parish Sheriff's Office Homicide Unit, proceeded to West Jefferson Hospital and interviewed Kerry Myers. Mr. Myers advised that when he returned to his residence at approximately 3:30 PM Thursday afternoon he entered his residence through the front door and as soon as he entered his residence he was struck with a baseball bat. Mr. Myers advised that he was struck by William Fontanille, whom he has known for approximately ten years. It was learned from Mr. Myers that he and Fontanille became engaged in a drawn out struggle and that Fontanille finally overcame him. . . .

Detective Childs observed the following injuries to Mr. Myers during his interview: a bruise over the right eye; cuts and swelling on the head and hair line on the right side in at least two areas. These areas required stitching; swelling and bruising on the forehead on the left side; scratches, cuts and abrasions on the right forearm, elbow and wrist; scratches and abrasions on the left elbow; a shattered left forearm; and a puncture type wound to the lower abdomen. . . .

Sergeant Robert Masson

"I'm always the last to be included in everything." Lorraine Cannon has a gentle, cultured, even overly polite voice—when she isn't shrieking. Then, and for years to come, she would do just that whenever that particular point was the issue.

"I'm her mother—you'd think people would have even the most common courtesy and call me first! But, no—and it's always like that. People trying to hide things from me!"

There was no way Clifford, Marva, or Marguerite O'Toole could soften that telling. Lorraine and Charles Cannon had already heard the early-morning news anchor on WWL-TV Channel 4 as they watched the video of their daughter's plastic body bag being carried out of the house at approximately 6:04 A.M.; indeed, it was the lead story, after the opening billboard and intro.

* * *

Anita Price is a genuine Southern belle, in almost all of that phrase's sundry senses. A South Carolina Southern Baptist wife, mother, and grandmother, she is still very blond and quite shapely. She is an avid golfer and bridge player, with a honey-dripping drawl and the affectation of correctness of manner, posture, and gesture for which Southern belles are so storied. She is a lady who believes that for her time has stopped. She and her retail manager husband, Thurman, she says, are "friends and companions" to their children and their children's friends.

She most definitely remembers every detail of that Friday morning. "The phone rang about five-thirty, it was Debbie Jordan, Curtis's wife, she was in hysterics. She'd heard it on the WWL-TV early-morning news. She told me to turn mine on. There was this picture of the open front door with Janet in a bag on a stretcher.

" 'Miz Anita, Janet's dead and Ryan's nearly dead.' " True to her type, Anita Price relishes telling a story and does it well, acting out the parts as she goes.

"At this point Billy's name hadn't yet come into the picture. The news lady had just said something about the suspect being 'the friend,' I think that's how she said it, 'the friend.'

"I said, 'Okay, Debbie, we'll be right over.' We got dressed, and I called Mike and then my two daughters and we all went to Debbie's. We were all talking, and upset, and crying, and all this kind of stuff going on, and Mike and Curtis called Kerry at the hospital somewhere around nine or so.

"But of course we'd already heard about 'the friend' before we spoke to Kerry. Because right away, Curtis had said, 'Billy Fontanille. I know it's Billy Fontanille.' I'm sure it was Curtis. We stayed at Debbie's for quite a while.

"And everybody felt like—I had heard the kids talk about it—Billy was on the razor's edge, so to speak. Billy had gotten really weird. But then he'd always acted weird. But now he was weird-weird-like as his marriage broke up. When he and Susan separated, Billy withdrew and was even more weird and crazy than before.

"So that's why when this happened everybody was scared to death. We were all afraid that he had just gone berserk. Some people got a little carried away. There was one phone call that morning, can't remember which one of the kids it was, but they said, 'Everybody look out, Billy's gone crazy and is killing babies!'

"And then when Mike and Curtis got Kerry on the phone at the hospital and he told the story about what Billy wanted to do, the story that we got in our mind was that Billy had really flipped out. Susan and Janet favored somewhat; so we just thought, 'Well, it's some kind of transference—Billy went over there and probably made advances towards Janet. She, being the excitable type, got hysterical. And they started running and fighting and we even went so far as to think that maybe Janet stabbed Billy in a fight. This is the picture coming to us. And then Kerry talking about walking in on this event . . . ?

" 'A friend'? What other friend did we have that was crazy?"

Tammy DuBuc will never forget when and how she first heard the news. Her husband, Clyde, who had grown up a close member of the inner circle of friends around Bill Fontanille—which later expanded to include a smaller, tighter circle around Mike Price, Curtis Jordan, and Kerry Myers—had just left for work.

"He'd just left, it was about six o'clock in the morning, he was going down by my mama's house." The blue-green eyes in that sunshine face darken and cloud and her utterly guileless but cover-girl smile, which is forever at wispy play upon her lips, hardens just a little even now, after all these years, as she recalls the events of that morning, the morning that changed her life so completely.

"The phone rang, and it was Curtis Jordan. He said, 'Are you listening to the TV?' I said, 'No, I just got up. I haven't turned on the TV yet. Why?' He said, 'It's about Janet and Kerry.'

" 'What about them?' He said, 'Somebody broke into their house and killed Janet and tried to kill Kerry.'

"Then he said, 'And we think it was Billy,' just like that.

"I said, 'You think it was Billy—Billy who?' I knew exactly who he was talking about, because that's the only Bill I knew. But he said, 'Billy Fontanille.' I was really mad when he said that.

"What makes you think that?"

"Because he showed up at his mama's house covered with blood," Curtis answered.

"What about the kids? Where's Ryan?" asked the professional mother and baby-sitter, who augments her husband's good income by taking in all of her friend's children plus those of the public at large in the day-care center she operates with her mother.

"I don't know," he said.

"Were they there at the time?"

"I don't know."

"Well, what about them? Were they there?" she demanded. "What did Kerry say?"

"Kerry never mentioned the kids." Then he said, "I'll call back and see if I can find out where they're at."

After Curtis hung up, Tammy called her mother's house. Clyde was still there, so he headed right back. But by the time he got there, Mike Price had called. He told her he wouldn't be bringing the kids that day; however, the first thing he said was, "Is your front door locked?"

"I don't really know," Tammy said. "Because Clyde just left."

"Well, go lock 'em," Mike said. "Because Billy's crazy, he might be going from all his friends' houses trying to kill us all."

Then it was starting to get to her, too. She put the TV on. "I'm like . . . going nuts. I'm screaming at my son, Chip—he was like about first or second grade then—to lock the front door. I was nuts."

Tammy and Clyde DuBuc, in short order, had burglar gates and bars installed around their comfortable suburban home.

JPSO CONTINUATION FORM ITEM: B/14695/84

On the same date at approximately 7:21 AM, the undersigned officer, along with Detective Childs, arrived at Charity Hospital, New Orleans, La., [and] met with William Fontanille. Mr. Fontanille was advised of his rights as per Miranda and he advised that he understood his rights. . . .

"He wasn't visibly upset about anything. This guy was just sitting there like . . . you know, nothin', no reaction."

When Masson and Childs got to Charity Hospital they found Bill sitting on a gurney in a hallway.

"I'm sitting there in the hall talking to him while Martin Childs was trying to keep people away—and it's almost like he's in this little dream world. Nothin'—he just kinda goes through his little statement."

The story Bill gave Bob Masson in that hallway in Charity Hospital, as far as he could tell from the telephoned or radioed synopses he'd already received, varied little from the versions previously told to Taylor or Adams.

Of course, Masson hadn't expected much variance. "I had Myers's story by then, too. So I expected Fontanille to give a statement denying the husband's, unless he just wanted to confess to it."

The only really significant new detail that Masson had not expected, but that Bill freely and seemingly out of the blue volunteered, was that on Thursday afternoon, when he'd returned to get his baseball bat, he had parked his car way down the block and around the corner on Patricia Street and then walked up to the Myerses' home some fifteen houses away. He said that he had parked his car in front of the house on Tuesday and Wednesday when he'd visited, but that because he had reason to believe Kerry was suspicious and might drive by, he had elected to park some distance away on Thursday.

Detective Masson also hadn't expected to find that Bill had other injuries besides the five stab wounds he'd been told about: cuts on the first two fingers of his right hand, which had required sutures, and numerous small cuts across both palms.

But then, as Masson said, "So? We knew there had been a hell of a fight. Over the knife, too."

                              *   *   *

W. J. LeBlanc was twenty-five years old and had been an attorney of good standing for exactly four months minus one day that Friday morning of February 24, 1984. When he had heard the news it was from his car radio as he was dashing to work a little before nine. W.J. (pronounced "Dub'ya Jay" and sometimes shortened to Dub) is a habitual late-nighter who opts for each last moment of sleep rather than catching up with the world's early-breaking news woes.

The work and place he was hustling to was Jefferson Parish Juvenile Court, where he was one of several fresh and talented young lawyers the District Attorney's Office had recently hired out of the Loyola or Tulane law schools that past year; W.J. had gone to Loyola. Of course, as in most professions, even clearly tagged rising stars have to start at the bottom, which meant the Juvenile Division.

Mostly what he remembers thinking upon first hearing news of the baseball bat murder is: "Jeez. I went to school with those guys." And then, like almost everybody else in the greater New Orleans area: "That's weird. Two guys, best friends, and one of 'em kills the other's wife? And nails the kid too? With a bat? We're not talking criminal types here. These guys could be your son, your brother, one of us." But to him, it was basically just another "senseless tragedy."

The parochial high school he had attended with Kerry Myers and Bill Fontanille was the prestigious Archbishop Shaw. Kerry was two years ahead of him and Bill three, and the two older boys had "run with a different group." W.J. didn't know either one personally, but they did share some acquaintances. W.J. reflects: "My impression was that Billy was more of a loner when he was at Shaw. Kerry I don't really remember hearing much about, I just knew he went there."

Cheryl Hickman remembers well her first association with the murder. She wasn't long out of Loyola University's Communications Department and was working radio news at New Orleans's king of the radio and television hill, the Jesuit-owned WWL radio and CBS-TV Channel 4. The initial news story she broadcast that morning had been read off news copy sent over from TV.

"I remember that first moment pretty clearly. It's just one of those cases that catches your attention.

"From the very beginning the word that has always been attached to this is 'bizarre.' From the very first day. I mean, here's these two guys blaming each other for this, and they're both telling the same story. This is weird. This is bizarre.

"I used that throughout. I had people coming up telling me, 'Isn't there some other word that you can use to describe this?' "

Final edition

Friday, February 24, 1984   *THE TIMES-PICAYUNE/THE STATES-ITEM*

Mom beaten to death, 2½-year-old in coma

By Richard Boyd and Joe Darby

West Bank bureau

   A young housewife was found bludgeoned to death and her 2½ year-old son beaten into a coma in Harvey's Woodmere subdivision Friday.

   Elsewhere in the same house in the quiet suburban neighborhood, the woman's husband and another man were found bleeding and scarred by knives, Police said.

   The men said they fought with baseball bats and knives and were unaware that Janet Myers, 26, lay dead in a pool of blood on the kitchen floor, police said.

   Late Friday, Eugene Fields, Jefferson Parish sheriff's chief of detectives, said no arrests had been made in connection with the incident at 2232 Litchwood. He said investigators still were trying to sort out what happened, even though police arrived at the scene at 2 a.m. Friday. Fields said a preliminary coroner's report shows Janet Myers had been dead at least eight hours when police found her body. . . .

   Fields said Fontanille, believed to be a former boyfriend of the wife, and Myers told investigators they fought each other with baseball bats and knives, but were unaware that Mrs. Myers had been killed. They also said they knew nothing about the beating of the child. . . .

The first newspaper story of the murder of Janet Myers appearing on the front page and above the fold, was reported and written in the main by Richard Boyd, the *Times-Picayune*'s West Bank court reporter, a veteran crime-beat journalist.

Even though he sensed "something big, something different" about the case that very first day, he never imagined that it would result in more than half a decade's labor on his part and in time would not only consume his intellect and passion but sweep him up in its wake and cause him to cross that fuzzy line between reporter and participant.

The next time Cissy Fontanille saw her son was late Friday afternoon, across the river in New Orleans at Charity Hospital; but first she and Herman had an encounter with another police officer.

Mr. Fontanille had called the Sheriff's Office to find out when they would be able to go and pick Bill up. He couldn't get any information over the phone, so they went in person. They found little sympathy.

"There's a woman dead and possibly a child," an officer had barked.

"But it wasn't my son who did it. You're looking at the wrong person."

Cissy Fontanille is no shrinking violet, and her tone matched his.

"How do you know? Were you there?" was the best retort the officer could come up with.

"I'd just as soon been there, because that's how well I know. *It was not my son.*"

On that he turned and walked away, grunting back over his shoulder, "Lady, go get your son."

When they got to Charity, Cissy found Bill lying on a gurney out in a hallway.

"Mama, what happened? What is going on?" are the first words she remembers him saying when he saw her coming down the hall.

"Janet is dead," she said in a throaty whisper when she reached him.

"Janet is dead?" She remembers his eyes got "about this big around." Then, "Oh, my God, Janet is dead! I can't believe Janet is dead!" He said it over and over again. "Oh my God, Janet is dead! Janet is dead!"

She remembers that the gurney was up against the wall, and that he leaned his head back against it. "My, God, is she really dead?"

"Yes, Bill."

Cissy distinctly remembers her son's next words for the chill they sent through her.

"God, she's the only one who could clear me of this, the only one. I can't believe he killed her. Killed Janet?"

JPSO CONTINUATION FORM   Item: B/14695/84

On the same date [Friday, February 24] at approximately 6:00 PM, the undersigned officer, along with Detective Martin Childs, met with Susan Mansfield Fontanille, white female, date of birth 11/2/60. Mrs. Fontanille advised that she is an employee of Texaco, located at 400 Poydras St., New Orleans, La.

According to Susan Fontanille, she was married on July 25th, 1981 and was separated from William Fontanille on August 11, 1983. She advised that at that time they obtained a legal separation. Mrs. Fontanille advised that she requested the separation due to mental and emotional abuse. According to Mrs. Fontanille, she last saw her husband a few months ago as he would come by to pick up the baby for the baby's visit with him. She advised the baby's name is Matthew. According to Mrs. Fontanille, she has known Kerry and Janet Myers for approximately two and a half years and that she met them through William Fontanille. According to Mrs. Fontanille, she last spoke to her husband approximately two weeks ago when he called for her and that she hung the phone up on him. . . .

If one knows Susan Fontanille and has cause to describe her, the words likely to be chosen are "very pretty." Then, if that phrase needs augmenting, will come "really cute," "sweet," "feminine," and occasionally, from perhaps a cop or ballplayer, "real looker" or *"fine!"* The blond, blue-eyed, shapely, bubbly former cheerleader looks *exactly* like the All-Dixie Miss Strawberry or Pecan Queen stereotype which so immediately comes to mind. Of course, she is also soft-spoken, proper, loyal, and flutteringly fussily vain.

Therefore, even though she was then in the final stages of legally excising Bill Fontanille from her family if not yet her life, Detective Masson wasn't surprised—only a little annoyed and pityingly condescending of her naiveté—when he found her to still be "kinda defensive and protective" of her husband.

"She wasn't crazy about getting back with him, don't get me wrong— and she did think it was a little crazy that he would sleep on the floor frequently instead of in bed with her."

Susan Fontanille was as cooperative as she could be with the investigation; Sergeant Masson learned a great deal.

He learned that after Matthew, their fourteen-month-old son, had been born with serious health problems, their relationship had steadily deteriorated to the extent that he would stop all communication with her "for three or four days for no reason"; that at other times, while Bill "never physically abused her . . . or the child in any way," he would "often become loud and angry"; that in the spring of 1983, Bill had abruptly quit his job at J. Ray McDermott Co. in favor of a position with another firm only to "quit that job after one month" without her knowledge and that he "drifted into a state of depression . . . worried about finances"; that after she left him in July 1983, he had "torn the house apart and thrown her clothes out," and that the house "was still in this condition and that recently the utilities had been shut off" while he was still living there; that on the occasion of Matthew's first birthday, December 23, 1983, Bill had kept the baby overnight and approximately twelve hours past the scheduled visitation and return time; that he had recently written her letters saying he had been converted to God and that "all he wanted to do was see God"; and that he had told her that he had "attempted to commit suicide on four or five occasions and that this was done with pills and with the exhaust from the car."

Yet, having divulged all that, she continued steadfast in her assurance that he wasn't capable of murder.

"She had that tone throughout, 'Yes, he did this. Yes, he did that. But . . .' Always a 'but.' "

Finally, "Well, you must've thought he must've been trying to do something with the baby if you were scared enough to call the police? Why call the police if he isn't any threat?"

But, nope. And the lady's logic was as simple as it was simply put: "Perhaps I don't want to be married to him anymore, but I *know* he couldn't do something this bad."

JPSO CONTINUATION FORM   ITEM: B/14695/84
    On 24 February 1984 at approximately 5:30 PM, Detective Marco
Nuzzolillo, Jefferson Parish Sheriff's Office Homicide Unit, conducted a
canvass of the area of the Myers residence. Detective Nuzzolillo spoke
with Marilyn Lejeune, white female, who resides at 2245 Litchwood,
Harvey, La. Mrs. Lejeune advised that at approximately 5:00 PM on
Thursday she observed a white male in front of the Myers residence.
She further advised that the white male was not the occupant of the
residence that belonged to the Myers. It was further learned that the
subject was carrying a baseball bat in his hand. Mrs. Lejeune further
advised that she did not see any vehicles belonging to the subject. It
was learned from Mrs. Lejeune that the subject was wearing a pullover
dark striped shirt, was approximately 5 ft. 10 in. tall, and approximately 30 years of age.

By that evening the Prices and Jordans had moved their fear and concern to attorney Ernie Barrow's house; from there eventually was placed
a phone call that would prove to be more than just a little fateful.
    "Ernie's wife is Lorraine Cannon's first cousin," Anita Price explains.
"And they were part of the social circle, too, sometimes, you know, at
barbecues and holidays and such. So it was only natural that when we
thought we ought to know what's going on legally, you know, that we go
over there.
    "We thought we had information the police needed to know about and we
couldn't understand why we weren't being questioned. Because Kerry had
told us that Billy was going to kill Susan. He'd said it over the telephone
when we called him that morning. And he'd said it to the kids at the hospital.
He said it to us many times that day: that Billy wanted the shotgun to get his
child and kill Susan. And Billy was still loose. Somebody said that he was
already out of the hospital. That he'd hardly been hurt at all.
    "Ernie and I talked about this and he agreed that there was reason for
us to be fearful. So Ernie called Bob Masson. He knew him. So he had him
come there and we talked to him.
    "When he interviewed me, he was objective. He had made no choice. He
was very objective that night. Because I told him what we knew about
Billy, and he said he knew he was crazy and all that. And he said his job
is to get the facts on both parties. I found him to be very objective, and
I didn't think that I swayed him, or the kids swayed him or anybody. I
don't think he made his mind up immediately, I think he was very open-
minded, and I don't think he had any ax to grind."

JPSO CONTINUATION FORM   ITEM: B/14695/84
    On the same date at approximately 9:35 PM, the undersigned officer
met with Anita Price, white female, 2169 Grape St., Gretna, La. Mrs.

Price is the mother of Michael Price, who went to play basketball with both William Fontanille and Kerry Myers on Wednesday night. . . .

According to Mrs. Price, she has known Fontanille for fifteen years and has known him to be a very good pathological liar.

After Cissy Fontanille had put her son to bed, she had thought he might want to talk some. But he had quietly told her to please just let him be for a while, that he needed to be alone.

Then, almost exactly twenty-four hours after that nightmarish weekend began, a percussive, impatient, arrogantly authoritarian banging sent Cissy again to her front door.

"Who is it?" her Irish Channel spunk had compelled her to demand in futile protest.

"Police," came the indignant answer—in chorus.

"My God. It wasn't just the police. They looked like they were going after a dope cartel or something," she remembers. "I never saw so many cars, so many people . . . plainclothesmen, uniform people. As I tried to close the door they pushed it open—they were so rude. The only reason I was closing the door was because I thought they were all in by this time. And all they're doing is coming to get one person? As if he's going to resist, he's in bed all stabbed up."

"Are you the parent of William Fontanille?" one of them had demanded.

"Yes, I am."

"Where is he?" Bob Masson had not been impressed by her attempt at dignity.

"I told them he was in the front bedroom, and oh, God, they went in there and yanked him out of bed, pulling on him and twisting him. I told them, 'God, he's just been stabbed, don't pull on his body like that!' "

Billy put up no struggle. His first word was just, "Oh."

"He didn't even argue with them. Then, as they put the handcuffs on him, very softly he said, 'You've got the wrong person. I didn't do this.' "
And then he was gone.

As far as Robert Masson was concerned, after his interview with Mrs. Price, he had all the facts and rationale he needed for an arrest. Even though he was yet to interview Kerry Myers personally or receive the autopsy or serology report, he was solid in his conviction that what he did have was a positive ID from a bereft and badly wounded husband who certainly, under any circumstances and particularly these, wouldn't be readily suspected of also brutalizing his son, and logic demanded that the assailant of Janet also be the assailant of Ryan.

"I've got a man who parks his car two blocks away—for the first time since he's been visiting over there. I've got a witness across the street who saw him in front of the house with the baseball bat before the murder—

and he's told me in his statement at the hospital, 'Oh, I went over there to get my baseball bat that I'd left the day before.'

"To me, hah!—that's the thing that got me. When I went to get the affidavit, I said, 'That's it, I've got him now. I've caught him in a lie.' "

JPSO CONTINUATION FORM   ITEM: B/14695/84

On the same date at approximately 1:40, Mr. Fontanille was advised of his rights as per Miranda. He signed the standard rights form and also the waiver of rights form. At that time a taped statement was obtained from Mr. Fontanille. A copy of that taped statement will be attached to and become a part of this report. [For transcript of statement, see Appendix.]

Robert Masson

At the conclusion of taking a formal, taped statement from a suspect in custody, it is standard police procedure to begin a period of the interrogation process characterized by the asking of "baiting questions" in either an intimidating, authoritarian fashion or a friendly, good-cop mode, depending upon circumstances and the individual style of the interrogator. It is also optional whether the tape recorder is left on or turned off. Sergeant Masson remembers that on that night he chose to use a mixture of both postures and turned the recorder off.

He remembers that at one point he had leaned in, cocked an eyebrow, and almost in a confidential manner said, "Well, Bill, we've got a little problem here. What would you say if I said someone saw you in front of the house earlier that afternoon with the baseball bat?"

To the sergeant's disappointment, this did not seem to rattle his suspect overmuch. In fact, Masson remembers basically no reaction. Just denial.

"I don't know who that could be. Because it's not true. Or else someone is mistaken," Bill Fontanille said.

According to Robert Masson, whichever of several tacks he took with Bill as he tried to impeach his statement, he was only a "little bit more upset than he'd been when I'd questioned him at the hospital, because he'd just been arrested. But even then, for a person arrested for murder, I found him relatively calm.

"Cold, actually. He sits there and tells me he had sex with the woman the day before—so he says. But everybody else? Is he the boyfriend or not? I don't know. That's only what *he's* saying. A woman who'd just had a baby? A woman who'd just been cleared by her doctor to resume marital relations? Whose C-section scar was still prominent and pink—she's gonna be all of a sudden jumping in the sack with one of her husband's ball buddies?

"Unh-unh, I've nailed him."

*   *   *

Ernie Barrow was raised just a little bit north of God's country—he mostly spent his youth in Pelahatchie, Mississippi. While that distinction gives him a most affable charm and a good-ol'-boy accent, he is in fact a big-city attorney.

"I went to the scene the day after the murder," he recalls. "I entered the scene about nine-twenty that Saturday morning; there was nobody on location. No security. No tape. No nothing. You got to remember, I'm an ex–assistant district attorney, I've prosecuted plenty murder cases—and I was shocked. Not only was I shocked at that, I was shocked to see that the door was opened.

"I entered the premises thinking there would be an officer on hand. Now, I wasn't by myself, I've got Janet's brother-in-law, Wayne Switzer, with me. So we walked on in and the first thing I noticed was a shotgun over against the wall with two shells on the little table there.

"About then I said, 'Wait a minute, we're in a crime scene, and there's nobody here. Something's wrong. Let's get out,' because I realized I was where I wasn't supposed to be. As we turned to leave, an officer walked in. I recognized him. Bobby Masson. I said, 'Scene's open.' He says, 'Yeah, I think we're finished.'

"I said, 'Is it all right if I look around?' He said, 'Yeah, come, I'll show you where they found her.' So at that point we moved into the living-room area and we saw the spot—it was like an explosion. On the wall. There was a large quantity of blood on the floor, too. Around where she'd been laying. I looked at that for a little while. Then I asked him if I could go into the kitchen. Because by that time I had heard Kerry's side of it. So we walked then back to the hall, walked down that hall toward the bedrooms, and then took a left into that little kitchen and den area.

"The kitchen was in unbelievable condition. There was dishes—I remember there was a frying pan with something in it that was in the sink—which was not like Janet. Janet had her faults, but she was a fairly good housekeeper. And did keep a fairly nice house. There were parts of food open on the counter. There was dirty dishes that appeared to be more than two days old on the counter. There was a ketchup bottle on the counter that was open. I thought that was strange—here's a ketchup bottle with the cap right there off like someone had just been interrupted. I'm looking for the oddities as a prosecutor. I'm looking for the odd piece that's gonna fit in the puzzle and make it work. And that ketchup bottle was really strange.

"Then I turned and I remember asking Masson, 'Have you printed the ketchup bottle?' And he said, 'No, I don't think.' I said, 'That might not be a bad idea.'

"We moved from there back to the bedroom where they'd found the kid, there was some spotty blood in there. Then we went into the room where the baby was. Nothing significant in there except for the clothes materials folded very neatly. Which was inconsistent with the way we found the kitchen. That was what I would expect of Janet, okay?

"Never will forget coming back out, though, and asking him about the shotgun and shells. I said, 'Has that been taken into evidence?' He said no, but it probably would be. He seemed to be surprised that it was still there.

"I didn't quite understand at that point in time who was conducting the investigation. It's always been my appreciation of the way these things is done is an officer is placed in charge of the investigation. He is the homicide detective in charge, and he directs whatever happens from that point in time on.

"So he and I talked outside in that little overhang there. I said there are some suggestions I'd like to make and you can do whatever you want to with 'em, but here they are. And I gave him a number of things that I had observed that I thought might be interesting to look into and to do. And he said he would. Then we left."

A most interesting story. Particularly since one of the things the Sheriff's Office had done quite well the night of the murder was to get a picture of just about every inch of that house. A number of those photographs were of the sink and counters in the kitchen. In those pictures there's not one dirty dish. No dirty frying pan. Not a scrap of food. And no ketchup bottle, open or closed.

On Sunday morning, February 26, the majority populace of the greater New Orleans area awoke to find bannered—front page and above the fold—across their copy of the *Times-Picayune* the headline "Family friend is booked in beating death," underneath which they found this lead:

> *While her family prepared to bury 25-year-old Janet Myers, and her husband and child remained hospitalized, Jefferson Parish authorities Saturday arrested the best man at their wedding and booked him with murder.*

Then, after some several paragraphs restating the who, what, when, and where from the first story, and since the Sheriff's Office "said it would release little information about the arrest," the article then went on at some length making full use of quotes from loquacious Myers family members, concluding with the report that "Myers is telling his family about feelings of guilt for not protecting his wife and Ryan, said the spokesman. 'He feels responsible. He feels he should have done more, but what could you do in a situation like that?' asked Switzer [Myers's brother-in-law]."

By February 1984, Pat Fanning, after a little more than a decade as a state and federal prosecutor and a short stint in a "silk stocking" law firm, had been in his own private practice as a criminal defense attorney for all of a month and a half. This was some years before he would become one of the more celebrated "hired guns" in New Orleans with a string of sensational cases and an association both legal and social with the *top* gun in Louisiana, Governor Edwin Edwards. However, his meteoric rise in public recognition would begin that very second month of going it alone.

It started in midmorning on Sunday, February 26, the third day of Carnival, when his brother, Michael Fanning, a Jefferson Parish assistant district attorney, whose wife is Cissy Fontanille's first cousin, found him amid the revelry of the Alla parade route and told him that his in-laws were in immediate need of an attorney.

"I left the parade, found my car, negotiated some serious traffic, and drove to the lockup."

Where he found his newest client, "with blood all over him, laying there obviously in pain, shivering, hadn't brushed his teeth or washed his face or taken a bath or anything since Friday night. He was seeping blood from his wounds. I almost made a complaint immediately and said you'd better get this boy to the hospital. I mean he belongs in a hospital, he doesn't belong here. But it's Sunday morning and I'm dealing with the lowest level of bureaucrats.

"He looked really bad. Like a drowned rat; hunched over in pain and blood and sticky hair and he smelled bad, he's barefoot and it's February. He was in a little holding room, concrete floor, no bed or anything. There was a little metal bench there; that's what he was sleeping on for two days. He looked really rough.

"And he was scared. If you ever go hunting and you corner an animal, and he's just quaking and wounded and scared, that's what he looked like. I said, 'If you haven't told them anything yet, don't.' He said, 'I already did. I gave a statement when they arrested me.' I said, 'First mistake.' "

Over the years, Pat has seen more than a few desperadoes, but "this guy certainly did not look or act like the typical jailhouse thug. He also did not look like a guy who was capable of being aggressive. He was a guy who looked to me like he had been through an ordeal. Like he was injured and wounded; and like he wanted to set the record straight on the one mistake that he'd made out of fear. I just never got the impression that the guy could've done what they said he did.

"The only real business we discussed that morning was getting that one thing corrected on his statement to Masson."

JPSO CONTINUATION FORM   ITEM: B/14695/84

On Monday, 27 February 1984 at approximately 4:00 PM, the undersigned officer met with Maureen Rilette, white female, 2305 Litchwood, Harvey, La. Miss Rilette advised that at approximately 1:45 AM on Friday, 24 February 1984, she was awakened by some unknown noise. She further stated that she heard a man yell in an angry voice,

"Get out of here," and she heard him say this twice. Miss Rilette advised she got up to see what was going on and at that time observed a white male running toward Patricia St. on the west side of Litchwood. Miss Rilette advised that the man was wearing blue jean pants that appeared to be dress pants, a white shirt with a collar and a black sweater. She further advised that she believed the man was wearing dress shoes but she could not be sure because he was running fast. Miss Rilette further described the man as approximately 6 feet tall, a fairly thin build, dark brown hair, unknown facial hair [and] that he appeared to be approximately in his early 20's. Miss Rilette stated that she observed no one else on the street and did not know who had yelled out, "Get out of here." She advised that the man running down the street did not appear to be injured at all and that his clothing appeared to be neat and tucked in.

As Detective Masson left Mrs. Rilette's house, he decided what the hell and walked on down to Marilyn LeJeune's and, just to be thorough—one can never be too thorough with a linchpin witness—followed up on Nuzzolillo's interview of the neighbor who'd seen a man answering to the description of Bill Fontanille walking with a baseball bat out front of the Myerses' house on the late afternoon on Thursday prior, the day of the murder.

"I'm glad you came," the stylish 1980s version of Mrs. Cleaver said to the detective at her door. "I was going to call you. I'm so embarrassed . . ."

"Why, ma'am?"

"I'm afraid I've made a mistake. It couldn't have been Thursday afternoon when I saw the man with the baseball bat."

"And why is that, ma'am?"

"You see, I had my husband's running schedule turned around. He jogs every Monday, Wednesday, and Friday. So it was definitely Wednesday, because I remember standing in the driveway with my little boy, you know, seeing Daddy off? And that's when I saw the man walking with the bat like it was a walking stick or cane."

"What time was this and which way was he walking, ma'am?" Bob Masson's professionalism was in command, externally anyway.

"On days that he runs, Earl comes home early, so it was about five or a little thereafter, I know it wasn't later than five-thirty. And he was walking that way, away from their house. Towards Patricia Street."

Detective Masson referred to his notes and asked enough questions to determine if she had any further alterations to the story of what she had witnessed. There were none. No, she had not seen the man get into or out of any car. He had just walked on out of sight and out of mind. He had been holding the bat at the top and placing it down in step as one would with a cane. Rather "nonchalantly." And, yes, she believed that the Myerses' cars were in their driveway at the time she saw the gentleman in question.

"Thank you, ma'am." Right.

Pat Fanning had been at the Detective Bureau first thing Monday morning to communicate his client's wish to make a change in his statement. It wasn't until "approximately six-fifteen" that evening, however, that he was able to speak with the man he needed, the homicide case officer in charge, Robert Masson, when Masson was back in his office.

"My man says you guys had him so shaken up he made a mistake and wants to change a part of his statement," Fanning announced.

"What part's that, counselor?" Masson asked and reached for his pen.

"The part about leaving his bat at the Myerses' on Wednesday."

"He wasn't there Wednesday?"

"Yes, he was. But he didn't leave his bat there then."

"So, when does he leave his bat?"

"Earlier Thursday afternoon. Then he goes back to get it between four and four-thirty . . ."

"He was at the scene twice on the day of the murder?"

"He went to his friends' house twice that day, yes. The first time was about one o'clock, leaving around three."

"Lemme get this straight. Your guy goes there one o'clock Thursday, stays till around three, forgets his bat when he leaves, then comes back to get it at four, four-thirty?"

"You got it—at which time he was then assaulted with deadly force by Mr. Myers."

"Wouldn't be anybody I suppose who your man might've been with in between these visits, huh? Somebody who saw him?"

"An alibi, sergeant? No, afraid not."

"Be anything else he might wanna change, huh, counselor?"

"That should do it."

And for Robert Masson's part, that surely did. "Now I *knew* he was *lying*. I had him changing a statement to fit an eyewitness's account, a *mistaken* eyewitness? Man, he's dirty. I had him."

2
Investigation

It was November 4th, 1980 when your dad and I went to the doctor to confirm the coming of you. It was the same day of the 1980 Presidential race: Ronald Reagan won. It didn't take Dr. Ferris long to confirm everything and your dad and I went home feeling a little numb, but happy. We wasted no time in telling everyone we could. And so our journey began. . . .

—*Journal of Janet Cannon Myers*

* * *

"Pat was absolutely convinced that this guy was telling the truth," Marion Edwards, first assistant district attorney, remembers those first few days of the case when it could be assumed that he and Pat Fanning, longtime friends, were on opposite sides of an adversarial scrimmage line.

"Pat is an old prosecutor and he doesn't labor under the delusions that a lot of defense attorneys create for themselves. He goes in with the feeling in most instances that his clients are guilty and does the best job he can. But, here, no, he was convinced that Fontanille was telling him the truth. And that impressed me."

Marion Edwards, a graying Dixie gentleman of distinguished manner, speech, and appearance, fond of wearing red suspenders, chooses his words most carefully, leaning back in his big leather swivel chair and forming his next thought.

"Masson, on the other hand, was absolutely one hundred percent convinced that Fontanille's action was pretty much as Myers had laid it out. And he's a good officer, had a very good reputation."

After more thoughtful silence, Mr. Edwards offers a concept he finds appropriate for the discussion at hand.

"It's amazing. Police officers that have been in this business for as long as Masson has—they'll be right nine hundred and ninety-nine times out of a thousand. But you'll run into the one case, like this one, when they may or may not be right. And it is very difficult, when you have been involved in this business that long, to maintain the kind of attitude that allows you to backtrack and say, 'Wait a minute, I might not have been right about this.' It is so hard not to adamantly maintain the views that you originally thought were correct. That's what happened here. I think."

"Thirty years I've been a policeman, twenty of them across the river in New Orleans, and I've never seen anything close to being like this case. Nothing as bizarre as this."

Jefferson Parish Deputy Chief Eugene Fields, then chief of detectives, had received his first impression of the murder of Janet Myers when he had been awakened at five o'clock that Friday morning by Captain August Claverie, homicide commander.

"We certainly never imagined just how strange it was really going to turn out to be when we talked about it that morning." In fact, "Even as bizarre as the particulars were, we thought it was a pretty cut-and-dried case. Fontanille did it. While there seemed to be some questions in the air regarding the physical evidence and how the crime scene was handled, I didn't think so. I felt good about it. Still do. Of course, Sheriff Lee, no. He wasn't satisfied with it.

"And then of course right from the first day we had the homosexual angle to look at. You know, just from the nature of the violence on the victim; the circumstances of here's two best buddies and a real, real dead wife. In fact, from the start the media people, not the reporters and all, but the camera people, the tech people, they were calling it 'that homosexual murder in Woodmere.'

"And Bob Masson's a very good investigator, very capable, very qualified. We'd never experienced any problems with any investigation of his. And Vieira is on a par with any crime scene technician we've got, and better than most, not lazy, willing—some of the guys you've got to push a little more than others."

"I told Billy, 'I'm going to put on my prosecutor's hat and I'm gonna make a case against Kerry Myers.' " Pat Fanning looks like Dennis the Menace might if allowed to age into his late thirties.

"I met with resistance from the Sheriff's Office—I say Sheriff's Office—it became quickly obvious that *Bob Masson* had made his mind up, he'd made an arrest, and now he had to defend it.

"Bob Masson is not the brightest guy to ever wear a badge. It's tough to be on the outside trying to make a case for the prosecutor when the law enforcement people are resisting and pooh-poohing everything you're bringing to them."

Pat speaks quickly, and restlessly, as if there is always something else he could be doing that might be more fun.

"Biggest problem first was that fucking statement. When people get arrested for murder or are under investigation for murder and they talk to the police, they uniformly, consistently, always, without fail, hurt themselves for later."

"Mirror image? What's that? What'd they expect Fontanille's gonna say? He's gotta account for the scene the way it was and for him being over there so long and his wounds. He can't say somebody from Mars did it. Here's a case where you'd expect conflicting stories."

Bob Masson is of medium height, medium build. He has graying sandy hair cropped military-style, and gray-brown eyes in a face one swears is familiar but cannot place. He almost never smiles or frowns.

"Here's a man that parks two blocks away. He comes over to visit his friend for what, past two, three days, and he parks in front the house every time? Then on this one particular day he decides to drive way down the street and park around the corner? I find that a little strange. A little odd. You know, such good friends with him and all? It didn't bother him the day before when he says he had sex with the woman."

A high school math teacher after leaving the Sheriff's Office, he is fundamental in his analysis.

"Why would Kerry park his car in front of the house, let the neighbors see his car? And the other man hides his car, then when he sees Kerry's car there, who he says he doesn't want to know he's there, why don't he just leave? What's he gonna say if Kerry asks where his car's at?

"I based my arrest on the facts I had. And I never did have any facts to accuse Kerry Myers of—and still don't. Only thing I had accusing Kerry Myers was Fontanille's statement. And I had absolutely nothing to back it up."

Tuesday, February 28, 1984   THE TIMES-PICAYUNE
Judge denies bond to Gretna suspect in beating death
by Richard Boyd

   William A. Fontanille, 28, made a brief appearance Monday in magistrate court and was told by state Judge Joseph Tieman that no bond will be set on the first-degree murder charge. . . .

   Kerry Myers was listed in stable and improved condition suffering from a shattered left arm, stab wounds and a fractured skull.

So began another morning's public briefing on the murder of Janet Myers. It went on to report that Ryan was still listed as "critical" and in a "semi-coma."

But real news from law enforcement authorities was still scarce, only two items: that Chief of Detectives Fields had announced that Bill Fontanille "apparently" wasn't under the influence of drugs or alcohol on the night of the murder; and that a new grand jury had just been empaneled and District Attorney John M. Mamoulides expected the case to be presented to it within two weeks.

On Wednesday morning, February 29, in the *Times-Picayune,* reporter Richard Boyd quoted Sheriff Harry Lee: "This is still a very open investigation. We are developing other information and continuing our questioning of those who may have knowledge of what happened." He called it "certainly one of the most bizarre cases I have ever run across." The sheriff "declined" Mr. Boyd's request that he "elaborate."

"At the wake—that's when everybody in the whole world knew Billy did it, right? There was no doubt. There was no suspicion on Kerry, at all. Nothing anybody had said. Nothing that anybody could fathom."

Chuck Cassard just might have had the single best vantage point from which to observe the characters and events which apparently came to such a nasty head the night someone took a baseball bat to Janet Myers's face—though he has done precious little testifying.

Chuck had known Bill Fontanille and his family before they even moved to Terrytown. Then, in the "D Section" of Terrytown, he, Billy, Russell Ardneaux, and "Uncle" Ted Blanchard had been the nucleus of a group of adolescents and then teenagers who in time came to be known as the Ratters. Chuck had been at Shaw High School with Billy and Kerry. He had been there when the two circles, Billy's and Mike Price's, merged to play ball. He was there in Thibodaux, Louisiana, attending Nicholls State University, when he and Kerry shared a trailer and where Kerry first met and started dating Janet Cannon. He was also there to share an apartment with Billy in Terrytown—Billy's first venture out of the nest—shortly after he left Nicholls State.

Subsequent to that, Chuck married Connie Burmaster, a cop's daughter, and also a lifelong member of the Billy circle. He then enrolled at Southeastern Louisiana University in Hammond, Louisiana, just across the lake from New Orleans, which his wife and Billy were also attending. He then became a Jefferson Parish sheriff's deputy. He still is a deputy as he sits with Connie, in the home they bought in Terrytown, talking, at least a little, about those years and that event.

"Kerry's sitting in the funeral home, his arm's in a cast, and she's laying in the casket—which I couldn't believe it was open, I mean, her head looked like a pancake.

"I didn't really want to talk to him about it, because I hadn't seen him in a while. But I walk over to him and I shake his hand—I didn't say anything, I just kind of put my hand on his shoulder—and he said, 'He went berserk. He just went berserk.' That's what he was saying. 'He went berserk. I just kept asking him, "Why? Why?" '

"I said, 'Kerry, don't worry about it—don't think about it. Just forget about it.'

"And he's sitting within spitting distance of the open casket. If he did it, the son of a bitch deserves an Oscar. Because there ain't no way in hell I could've sat there and been so straight-faced and lied."

For many of those whose lives were much affected by the baseball bat murder, it will always be the impressions and images from Janet Myers's wake and funeral that linger the longest. Those very impressions and images, however, are sometimes quite different for each, almost diametrically so, for people who often do not disagree on much else.

"What I can't understand, at the funeral, how they put her back together," Connie Cassard says.

"I just remember her head looking like a pancake," Chuck shrugs and adds.

"The open-casket decision I'll never understand," Connie continues. "Kerry said, 'Go look at her, go see her.' We went up and when we came back he said, 'Doesn't even look like her. Did you see her? Look? It looks nothing like her.' And then he said that Janet's mother wanted him to remember Janet not the way he last saw her. That's why she insisted the coffin be open. Kerry said she didn't want him to remember Janet laying on the floor full of blood like he saw her last. That's what he told us at the wake."

"Now, don't say 'us.' I didn't hear that one," Chuck offers up with some emphasis.

"No. I was with Carrie Lynn and Lisa."

"I went to the wake," Chuck insists.

"I know, but we weren't standing with you. I remember he was sitting there and he just kept saying, 'Why me? Why me? Why'd he do it?' I thought he should be more emotional than he was, but everybody tried using the excuse of the drugs, 'He was on drugs. They drugged him up with painkillers, that's why he's not emotional.' But I felt he wasn't emotional, period. He didn't shed any tears. He just sat there."

"He showed me a lot of emotion," Chuck says, and it is obvious this discussion has taken place on other occasions.

"Like how?"

"Like he kept saying—he kept telling me, 'Why did he do it?' "

"I remember him saying that, but it wasn't . . ."

"He said, 'He just went berserk. He just went wild.' "

"I remember that. But he was just sitting there . . ."

" 'I just want to know why?' "

"But he was sitting there like this, it wasn't an upset person . . ."

"I said, 'Kerry, it's not doing anything to figure out why. There's no answer to "Why?" ' "

"But the emotion wasn't there—I remember him saying all that—but he just sat there, and he just kept staring, and saying that. And when I questioned why he wasn't emotionally upset, I was told, 'Well, you know if they put you on drugs and they drug you up and all,' that's why he wasn't emotionally upset."

" 'Course he was on something for the pain—his arm was in a cast."

"But, still—well, you had to be there."

"I was there. I don't know. Maybe he trusted me. Maybe he understood that I understood him and her. That I knew 'em. Maybe that's why he opened up to me. But I saw emotion, a lot. In fact, I was getting kind of uncomfortable with it, because he was getting a little loud, and I was saying, 'Kerry, just calm down. Don't worry about it. They got him. They'll take care of it.'

"But, yeah. Without a doubt I thought he was sincere. Without a doubt. If he was lying, it was one hell of an act."

Peggy Cowan grew up on the same block in old Gretna with Janet Cannon. Until Janet went to River Oaks Academy to begin the eighth grade, Peggy considered their relationship to be that of "best friends." While they remained after-school neighbors with close family ties, it wasn't until both were married with a toddler on their hands seeing the same pediatrician that their friendship rekindled.

Peggy and all her family members attended both the wake and funeral. Her vivid memories of those days are bitter indeed.

"The wake and funeral were absurd. Kerry's behavior was very cold-hearted, no remorse, he sat there like he was waiting for someone to come and get him. When they closed the coffin—Kerry never went to it. Never shed a tear.

"His cousin even commented about this. But she was told by his dad and the rest of the family, 'Oh, he's in shock. He's in shock.' His cousin said he wasn't in shock—she said, 'He was *scared!*'

"Anybody, really, who can open their eyes and take a good deep-down look at the whole situation and really picture back at that wake—he was not in shock. He was petrified. He was scared to death that someone knew the truth.

"When they were closing the coffin, Janet's dad almost had a heart attack. They had to give that man nitroglycerin. Kerry never cried, never shed a tear. His dad stood right behind him and they both walked past the coffin like nobody was in it.

"I mean, I looked at my mama—my mom and dad were with me—and it was like, 'What the hell is this about?' We're boo-hooing and crying—I mean, uncontrollably—and this son of a bitch walks past like nothing? And then a week later I see him at the Spur gas station in his car with a woman snuggled up to him! Unh-unh. No way."

Thursday, March 1, 1984   THE TIMES-PICAYUNE/THE STATES-ITEM
Husband a suspect, Jeff Prosecutor says
By Richard Boyd
West Bank bureau

Kerry Myers, whose wife was bludgeoned to death in their Harvey home last week, is a suspect in her slaying although there is no conclusive evidence of his involvement, a prosecutor said Wednesday.

Authorities said they expect to get the results Thursday of laboratory tests to determine if Mrs. Myers' hair and blood are on the clothing of her husband or Fontanille. That could help answer some of the questions in the bizarre case, they said.

"The investigation is still open," Chief of Detectives Eugene Fields said. "We are keeping an eye on Kerry Myers."

. . . Judge James Cannella denied a request by Fanning that [Fontanille's] $200,000 bond be reduced.

JPSO CONTINUATION FORM   ITEM: B/14695/84

On Thursday, 1 March 1984 at approximately 7:30 PM, the undersigned officer, along with Detective Martin Childs, arrived at 796 Deerfield, Gretna, La., in an attempt to interview Kerry Myers. The undersigned officer at that time was advised that Myers was at the hospital visiting his son. Sergeant Masson was advised that Kerry Myers at this time was being represented by Mr. Robert Broussard, attorney at law. Arrangements were made with Mr. Myers' father to have Kerry meet with the undersigned officer and Mr. Broussard in the Detective Bureau office on Friday, 2 March 1984.

"Getting an attorney—that was my idea, because of all the stuff I was reading in the paper," Clifford Myers says.

"I remember how surprised Masson and Childs were when they came here. Masson said, and he was upset about it, too, 'You don't need an attorney, Cliff. We're your attorney.' I said, 'Did you see the paper?' He said, 'Don't worry about the paper, they don't know what's going on. We have the evidence. We know what's going on.' I said, 'Yeah, but people read that paper.' And then I said, 'They shouldn't be allowed to write things in there like it's a "mystery" and all, "baffling." ' And he said, 'Well, It's no mystery to us.' And you could tell he didn't like what was going on.

"When that came out about them having to say that Kerry was a suspect, too? As far as the detectives were concerned, the way Masson told me—I said, 'If you find Kerry was involved in any way I'll help you put him away'—but Masson said, 'Everything Kerry says fits the scene of the crime and I know Billy's lying.'

"I said, 'I hired Bobby Broussard because I don't trust Jefferson Parish politics.' I knew this boy, through the Fannings and all, had some pretty good pull.

"Now, I might've known a few people fairly well, but I never worried about trying to pull any political strings. Try to go to anybody I knew and ask 'em to give me any help or nothing because the detectives were satisfied Kerry was innocent.

"And Kerry swore to me, you know, what had happened."

JPSO CONTINUATION FORM   ITEM: B/14695/84

On Friday, 2 March 1984 at approximately 4:15 PM, the undersigned officer met with Mr. Robert Broussard and Mr. Ernest Barrow, attorney[s] at law. Mr. Broussard advised that he was presently representing Kerry Myers in this incident.

On the same date at approximately 4:57 PM, the undersigned officer, along with Mr. Broussard, Mr. Barrow, and Kerry Myers, proceeded to the Correctional Center. Arrangements had been made previously with Mr. Broussard to obtain a sample of blood from Kerry Myers, as well as samples of hair and saliva.

On the same date at approximately 6:15 PM, the undersigned officer was contacted by Mr. Patrick Fanning. Mr. Fanning advised at this time that Janet and Kerry Myers were at a Halloween party approximately two years ago and that Janet Myers was wearing some type of revealing clothes and became engaged in an argument with her husband.

"She was very pretty. Very petite features; someone you would think would be a model. And she was. She had a nice figure, but extremely thin and tall, maybe five-seven. Beautiful hair, long straight hair all the way to the middle of her back, and bangs," Sue Durgin LeBlanc remembers her former classmate and fellow dance-team member at River Oaks Academy, a small, private first-through-twelfth-grade prep school in Plaquemines Parish, an all-white institutionalized response to forced integration of the public schools.

"Her features were so petite, she had the tiniest little nose, but it was beautiful—just very different. The features that make a good model. Delicate.

"Fragile, also. Maybe her expressions made you feel that way, her little hand gestures and all. She had a flair for dancing too with her hand gestures. Like ballet, fluid, graceful.

"But I remember she dressed really arch-conservatively for the times. I definitely got the impression that her parents were overprotective of her. The hovering types; parents very involved with her life," says Ms. LeBlanc.

"I went to Marion immediately, 'Listen, case law is that you can't just use the grand jury as a tool for the prosecution. If you're gonna put all that shit in there, why don't you just put our side of it in, too.' "

It is obvious that Pat Fanning is fond of remembering and recalling the early days of his first famous case, those days when he was playing detective as much as defense attorney.

"Of course, he didn't know *where* to put the most plausible and popular theory in town: what Marion called the 'deviant sexual angle.'

"I mean, when you first see those pictures of her like that? Motherfuck, it's like, 'We've got psychosexual murder at least, whether it's homo or not.'

"See, when you get these sorts of crimes of passion that are aberrations on the part of the people—like, Kerry Myers has never murdered anybody before, never been involved in any violent activity before, other than probably knocking his wife around; and Billy Fontanille, of course, doesn't have that kind of criminal history—but for people to get that aroused, I mean, that kind of fire in the belly is only brought out by sexual activity.

"This case is definitely a crime of passion. This case reminded me of cases I've seen in the past, mostly as a prosecutor. Gays, lesbians and homosexuals, when they have it in for each other? I mean, they do some bad things. They cut each other up, body parts and stuff. I mean, they do those kinds of things. And when I saw what was done here, I said, 'Some sumbitch was *really* mad. We've got a passionate endeavor here.' "

On Monday, March 5, Bob Masson returned to the crime scene. He wasn't alone. With him were Ronald Singer, director of the Jefferson Parish Crime Lab; Carol Dixon, senior biologist of the Crime Lab; and crime scene technician Jerry Stapler.

Detective Masson takes credit for that initiative. "I did that. It was my idea. I went to Singer and said, 'Ron, I wantcha all to come and take a look at this thing, just to make sure I didn't miss anything.'

"Now, we spent hours there. And Singer looked at the scene and told me, 'From the way it looks, the guy was right-handed that did it. Her head was here, he stood here, and the bat swung like this and came down.' And he told me, 'The guy that's got the blood on his right pants legs is the guy that beat her.' And he said, 'You see the sweeps up on the ceiling? That's probably cast off from the bat.' He said, 'It's gonna come down to the guy that's got the blood on his right shoe and his right pants leg—that's the guy that killed her.'

"And I brought up the fact that, 'Hey, Myers is left-handed.' Martin

Childs came back, 'Yes, but he plays golf right-handed.' And I said, 'But he's predominantly left-handed. And I would think—you get into that type of situation—you're gonna go with your strong hand.' "

JPSO CONTINUATION FORM   ITEM: B/14695/84

On Wednesday, 7 March 1984, the undersigned officer arrived at the Crime Lab and met with Ron Singer and Carol Dixon. The following was learned:

(1)   Janet Myers had type A blood
(2)   Kerry Myers has type O blood
(3)   William Fontanille has type B blood
(4)   Ryan Myers has type A blood

In the two weeks or so since the murder, Marion Edwards, first assistant district attorney, heard at least an epoch's worth of theories concerning its execution and happenstance.

"Masson's theory was that it was an act of Fontanille. And that part could be true. But there were too many side issues left unexplained. And the deviant sexual angles were just too striking not to pursue all the way out.

"But, even with all the circumstantial uncertainties, I fully expected us to get the lab results back and that would settle it clear and simple—bizarre, for sure—but solved. Explained.

"Because of the stories themselves, at the point where they diverge, it would seem that the type and quantity of blood found in that den area should have told us who was telling the truth. And when the lab reports came back as totally inconclusive, I was amazed, I didn't expect that.

"I was about as familiar with the case as anyone at this point. I had a great intellectual curiosity about it, apart from the purely tragic elements. I had early on been contacted by the attorneys involved. Pat, of course, Broussard, and then Jack Rau when he came in, and I knew Ernie Barrow from when he'd been here as an assistant DA.

"Long before I went to the grand jury the first time, I'd had more than one meeting with each of the defense attorneys. And prior to those meetings, I'd had preliminary but fairly extensive discussions with Masson about several aspects.

"I looked for drugs; but nothing. Not even casual use in college. The only common thread that ran through the whole group was softball. They were softball nuts, they played it year-round.

"However, all the oddities aside, whatever evidence we had then did in fact weigh in on Fontanille. Plus there was a lady now dead who I had known and respected for years who told me that she had known Billy all of his life and that he had jumped out and attacked people with a baseball bat when he was younger on more than one occasion.

"So it wasn't something that I was looking for—predisposed to believe that Kerry was involved. As a matter of fact, I believe the first thing to truly strike me as not making sense about the case were the lab results.

"Totally inconclusive? That amazed me."

Bob Masson remembers receiving the serology reports with an entirely different interpretation from that of Marion Edwards.

"The information I had *exonerated* Myers. I didn't have any of Janet's blood on Myers. Carol Dixon told me 'none.' You know, that was *significant* to me. To me that was the most damning evidence against Fontanille that there was.

"She told me there was only 'trace-blood,' on the T-shirt, of type A. That's why I asked Myers if his wife ever wore his clothes. Because Dixon had told me that Janet was a secreter and that her perspiration would account for the trace of A blood. It was such a slight trace—in fact, there was no blood, just her type showed up.

"Now, if he'd said, 'No, she never wears my clothes,' then you do have another monkey wrench to throw in the problem. But Carol Dixon gave me nothing damaging on Myers at all.

"But on Fontanille? Extremely damaging. The thing ya had on Fontanille was that *his* blood was on *Janet*. Here's a man telling me he never saw the woman, he never talked to her. Now I say, 'Well, fine, you might explain the fact that her blood was on you from wrestling with Myers—'course now Kerry doesn't have *any* of her blood on him according to Carol Dixon, so how do you get her blood on you wrestling around with him anyway?—but second, how does *your* blood get on her?'

"Oh, I had an open-and-shut case. It was cut-and-dried after the lab reports."

Pat Fanning particularly relishes recalling the circumstances of Bill Fontanille's and Kerry Myers's first appearance before the grand jury, Friday, March 9.

"When we went to the grand jury, Kerry Myers went in first. Marion had him in there for an hour and a half or something like that. Then they broke and were going to lunch.

"I'm sitting there waiting—Billy's still in custody—and Marion pulled me on the side and said, 'I know you believe your guy, and I've got problems with this too, but still, after hearing Kerry testify, I believe if your man goes in there now and testifies he is going to get indicted anyway. And you're gonna have to live with that.'

"From a defense attorney's perspective, the absolute safest thing is don't put him in the jury. But I was still convinced that Bill was very convincing. So I'm thinking these lay people in there can't possibly look at this boy's testimony with any more scrutiny than I have, and they're not going to be able to shoot holes in it, number one. Number two, he's already made extensive statements to the police department and his testimony is going to be consistent with everything he's said up to now.

"So, in this instance, I didn't prescribe to the theory that you're giving them your whole case, because they already had our whole case.

"And I really believed that Marion—in spite of what he's saying about how he's made up his mind—I believe that he is still open-minded enough that after he hears Billy he can be dissuaded.

"And so in forty-five minutes in the lockup, we decided to go forward. And we came back and we went forward. And Marion came out afterwards and said, 'I don't believe it. As convincing as the first guy was, this guy is every bit as convincing and in exactly the opposite direction. The stories are diametrically opposed to one another, and I just don't know which one to believe. So we're not going to do anything.'

"Of course, I felt much more comfortable about our position. Plus I'd been vindicated, sort of," remembers Pat Fanning.

In Jefferson Parish, assistant district attorneys are allowed to maintain and conduct a private law practice in conjunction with their public office so long as their representation excludes criminal defense work, and most do so.

Consequently it is not improper, only fortuitous, that, along with his Juvenile Division caseload, W. J. LeBlanc, always ambitious and never lazy where his career is concerned, had undertaken working for Marion Edwards in the latter's private practice. He was with Marion during the whole of the period when his double-time boss was taking Janet Myers's murder to the grand jury.

W.J. would clear Juvenile usually by midday, and he and Marion would have lunch together. "I wasn't making a hell of a lot of money and Marion was kind of carrying me, he'd usually buy my lunch. Then we would go up to the DA's Office until quitting time. Then we'd hit the tennis court."

" 'Come on, boss, I know you can't talk about what goes on in grand jury. But, I mean, you don't have *any* idea who the hell did it?'

"And he goes, 'As stupid as this sounds, I believe the last one I hear. When Kerry Myers tells his story, that's it, it's Bill Fontanille. But then Fontanille gets on and tells his story, that's it, it's Myers.'

"But really Marion's gut feeling was that Kerry did it. Even though that was going against the tide—he definitely felt it was Kerry."

" 'If you *had* to pick one, who would it be?'

" 'The husband.' "

JPSO CONTINUATION FORM   ITEM: B/14695/84

On Sunday, 11 March 1984, the undersigned officer met with Sandra Giardina, white female. Miss Giardina advised that Janet Myers had been employed by her at Zee Medical Service from July 1, 1980 until October of 1980, a period of approximately three months. She advised that Janet Myers spoke to both she and her husband about Kerry Myers beating her. She further advised that one morning her husband, Jay Giardina, came to work and Janet Myers was present. She advised that there was an injury to the face, eye, cheek and nose and that Janet Myers told her that this was the result of a fight with her husband Kerry Myers.

Mr. J. T. "Jay" Giardina's memories and impressions of the very personable, attractive young girl with extremely blue eyes—"I've never seen blue eyes like hers before"—who had worked so briefly for him all those years before are still deep and readily plumbed.

He particularly remembers the first time he asked Janet about the "bruises and stuff" she occasionally came to work with. He and several of his employees were gathered around the office's lunch table at the time. "I wasn't really thinking anything and I asked her what had happened. I'll never forget it, she said, 'Oh, my husband and I had a fight,' just like that. Then, 'But I don't take that shit from anybody. I fight him back.'

Notwithstanding that offputting incident, Jay Giardina says: "I liked her, a lot. I felt comfortable around her. She had a certain way of doing that. And always immaculately dressed. Makeup just right. Wore her hair down."

He definitely remembers her last day of employment at Zee Medical. During a brief absence by Mr. Giardina, apparently an argument over a less-than-two-dollar procedural error in the petty cash drawer had started between the firm's bookkeeper and Janet.

"So I'm walking in the door and there's this big fuss going on between her and him and I had to try to calm it down," Jay Giardina remembers. "But she's storming, you know, '*Nobody's* going to accuse *me* of stealing!'

"I said, 'Well, wait, I don't know if anybody's accusing you of stealing.' But she wouldn't even listen. That's when I realized she had a pretty foul mouth and pretty explosive temper. We're talking gutter language—fuck, motherfuck, cocksucker.

"She showed a really fiery temper. I was shocked. I'm not comfortable around women that curse. I mean, I curse but I don't like to hear women curse. I soon saw that I couldn't calm her down and I told her, 'Janet, you're going to have to step outside. I don't like this kind of language being used in my office.'

"She said, 'Well, I'm calling my husband.' I said, 'Go ahead, and you can go on and leave then.' She sat outside and waited for him. He came right by and picked her up."

JPSO CONTINUATION FORM   ITEM: B/14695/84

On the same date, the undersigned officer spoke with Curtis Jordan, white male. Mr. Jordan advised that he and William Fontanille were close friends, as they were with Kerry Myers. He further stated that on the previous night [to the murder] they had gone and played basketball together. . . . Curtis Jordan further stated that he has known both Kerry Myers and William Fontanille for approximately eleven or twelve years, and that during that time he has never noticed or observed any abuse of Janet Myers by Kerry Myers. He further stated that as far as he knew there were no arguments. When questioned about an argument that took place on Halloween night in 1981, Curtis Jordan advised that it was true that Kerry and Janet Myers did have an argument outside the residence but at the same time William and Susan Fontanille were in another part of the house arguing with each other. Debbie Jordan advised that Janet had told her that she and Kerry were having marital problems and that Janet told her Kerry had hit her about four or four and a half years ago and that she had some fear of Kerry. Mrs. Jordan advised that this had taken place some time ago and that recently everything appeared to be calm between all parties other than the Fontanilles, who were separated.

Curtis Jordan can be described as a St. Bernard with a small burr under his collar. A big, playful, rumpled, basically good-natured man who doesn't really give a rat's ass about anything too substantive, but who is always just a little irritated and irascible about one thing or another which he never actually addresses or defines.

He grew up in Terrytown and knew Kerry Myers since before even Mike Price, whose family hadn't moved into the neighborhood until 1969, which was a couple of years after Kerry, at the age of eleven, along with his older brother and sister, left his mother's house in old Algiers to live with Clifford and Marva in Terrytown.

He had also known Janet Cannon before she ever met Kerry Myers. Before Kerry transferred into Nicholls State, her first love and passion had been for and with the roommate of one of Curtis's close friends at Nicholls.

By the time that Kerry and Janet became a pair in the second semester of her sophomore year, Curtis had left school to go to work. He did, however, remain very much a part of the circle whenever its members were home on weekends or summers. There are those who think that Curtis and his wife, Debbie, have what is perhaps an especially revealing vantage point from which to observe the relationship of Kerry and Janet Myers—close, yet with a certain distance in space and circumstance to lend objectivity.

"Sure they argued; but just verbally. I've never seen any violence between them. I'm not saying it wasn't there. I've heard the stories. I'm just saying I didn't see it.

"But what you have to understand is that Janet basically was a very unstable person, and Kerry wanted to have the perfect family. You know, a wife, two kids, a two-car garage, a boat—he didn't want all the trouble he got.

"There were times when Janet would step out of bounds or something like that—I'm not saying Kerry wouldn't blow up and put her back in her place. But she was the type where she—she could really get on a tangent, get on your nerves. She could bring the worst out in you. I mean, she did. She did bring the worst out in Kerry. Kerry wasn't a violent person. *And* Billy wasn't a violent person.

"Now, Janet knew if they came over here and started that crap I'd bounce 'em out. I explained it to Kerry. 'When you're in front of me and my wife you're going to behave like two adults, not like children.' I told him, 'I don't want to see any of that fighting crap when I'm around.' It must've worked. When they came over to our house they acted like adults. We'd have people over and have barbecues, and they were always polite, showed affection to each other.

"And something else, Janet never showed me any kind of hard feelings, never gave me any trouble, any kind of rip at all. She'd come over and we'd talk just like normal people. Her and my wife were close. Her, Janet, and Miz Anita would do things together. She and Kerry respected Debbie, so they didn't do all this crap like everybody talks about.

"But now, understand me, I didn't think she was all that sane either; I didn't say she *wasn't* crazy. I think I said she was just a couple of DNAs away from being a baked potato.

"But then Billy wasn't quite sane either. As many lies as he's told and put together? He can tell you something right out of the blue and be sharp as a nail on it and then you'd find out later he's lying. It'd be like nothing to him, like water off a duck's back.

"But you've gotta understand I've got other thoughts about all this because Fontanille shows up at *my* house two days *before* this happened. That Tuesday night he went to Kerry's? He came to my house first. Why? I hadn't seen the guy in two months. He hadn't contacted me, hadn't called, hadn't done anything. As far as he's concerned, I'm supposed to think he's working in Jacksonville with Pepsi-Cola.

"And he expects—now all of a sudden out of the blue on a Tuesday night he shows up knocking on my door? You don't know how many times I've kneeled to thank God that my wife wasn't home. I might be in Kerry Myers's position. He came to my house *first*. Goddam! This is what I look at. A friend of mine was parked out in front waiting for me to get home. Billy walks up—he didn't *drive* up—he walks up from three houses *off* the corner, from *around* the corner? My friend says, 'They're not home.' Billy goes, 'Oh. Oh, okay,' turns around and walks off—and he walks back the *other* way? After this thing happened? I'm wondering what the hell's this?

"Then the basketball game the next night? I didn't get to the gym until late, I had to work. They'd already been playing for a while when I got there. Billy was sitting up in the stands. I said, 'Billy, you don't want to play?' 'No, no, I don't want to play,' and I went on out on the court and someone said, 'Yeah, he said he hurt his back or something.'

"Then he told me that he was waiting on a ride. Someone 'might come pick me up.' He said he 'might be leaving early.' But he's acting real nervous-like. He'd keep going over by the door, I guess looking for when his ride was gonna come.

"Now, his car is back at Kerry's house. So if someone's gonna pick him up, they're going to have to take him back to Kerry's. Mike and I have talked about this often. We're playing ball, some sumbitch is gonna pick him up and he's going back to Kerry's house? And the guy we thought was gonna pick him up was that Chuck Cronin guy? And that's another strange thing. When Billy got married, out of the blue—here we are all friends and everything—and all of a sudden bang, 'Here's my best man, Chuck Cronin.' We're like, 'Who is this guy? Cronin?' We'd probably seen him, but he wasn't really from our neighborhood. He lived in Terrytown, but he wasn't from the D Section.

"Anyway, Billy was going back to Kerry's. Now, whether he was going back to Janet, and then what his motive was for wanting to go back, I don't know. It's just something Mike and I've talked about. Just like why he had come over to my house first on Tuesday night.

"There's a sequence of events here. Here's this guy Bill Fontanille, who is definitely, by this time, in my opinion, off his rocker. All right? And now he's shown tendencies for violence from what he's done to his house. You know, with the baseball bat? Now he's going nuts, beating things and shit. There was even the incidence going around, true or not—but told to me—that he tried to commit suicide by putting himself in his car in his garage, and then chickened out.

"Then there's this matter of the big job lie. He told me in November that he was going to California and then I see him Thanksgiving Day. I remember all this because that night he told me, he said, 'I'm going to California.' I'm getting dressed for work and I said, 'Oh, yeah? Whatcha going to California for?' 'I'm going to be a bottling plant manager trainee for Pepsi.'

"I said, 'Really? That sounds pretty good. How'd ya land that?' He said, 'I was reading in the paper and I called this headhunter thing, this national headhunting thing. I sent my résumé in and they called me back and wanted me to go for an interview.' I said, 'Here locally or something? Right there on Pepsi Street, that's right by my office?' He said, 'No, I had to go to Fort Wayne, Indiana.' I said, 'Oh, Fort Wayne, we've got a transport plant there.' He said, 'Yeah, I flew in there yesterday.'

"This is on a Monday night, because I have this part-time job working Monday, Tuesday, and Thursday. So he said, 'Yeah, I flew in there yesterday, interviewed this morning, and got back this evening.' I said, 'Well, that's good.' He said, 'Yeah, I gotta be out there by Monday. I'm leaving Friday.' That's when I told him, 'Look, Wednesday night'—Wednesday was our night out—'we're going up here to the bar, why don'tcha come on and we'll celebrate your job.' He said, 'Okay, I'll consider it.' Yeah, that's how Billy talks.

"So he comes and we sit there drinking pitchers of beer and joking about California and wishing him well and all and that's it. Supposedly he's gone west. Right?

"But two weeks after that, it was Thanksgiving morning, I was driving up to the store and I look to the side and there he is walking. He didn't see me. I passed by and I said, 'Look at that.' I just kept going, but I said, 'That lying son of a bitch.'

"I really wasn't surprised. I told Debbie when I got back with the wine, 'I just saw fuckhead walking down the street.' 'I thought he was in California?' 'Yeah, well, I thought he was too.' But what the hell, he's told lies before; what the shit, it doesn't surprise me.

"Then, just two or three days before Christmas, I came home to change clothes for my evening job. There's a knock at the door. It's Billy with the baby. I told him, 'Look, I've gotta go to work, I've gotta get dressed. But come on in and we can talk while I do.' He came in, I said, 'Whatcha doing in town?' Just to see what he'd say, you know. He goes, 'I'm passing through on my way to Jacksonville, Florida. I'm being transferred—you know, it's closer to home.' I said, 'Yeah, I'd rather live in Florida than California.' And he said, 'Yeah, I'm going to be taking over a plant,' and blah-blah-blah.

"By that time I'm dressed and the phone rings, it was my wife. She said, 'Whatcha doing?' I said, 'I'm talking to Billy.' She goes, 'Fontanille?' I said, 'Yeah, he's here with Matthew.' 'He's there with that baby?' This is on her end, I can hear but he can't. I said, 'Yeah.' She said, 'He's not supposed to have that baby.' I said, 'Well, yeah, I know that.' And Debbie goes, 'Do you think Susan knows?' I said, 'I don't know.' She said, 'I'm going to call her.' I said, 'That's a good idea.'

"So she called and Susan told Debbie, 'Oh, yes, I know, it's all right. He's bringing the baby for a little visit with his mother, it's okay, it's okay.'

"Well, I worked. I came home, it's about nine-thirty, we get a phone call from Susan, 'Have you seen Billy and Matthew?' Debbie asked me, and I said, 'No, they were here earlier but they only stayed a little while and then left.' 'Did they say where they were going?' 'No, they didn't say.' Debbie says, 'Is everything okay?' 'Yeah, yeah, I guess everything is going to be okay,' and she hung up.

"Then they came to the door. They were looking for Billy and the baby. Susan and her father. By this time there's a bit of panic in her. The real thing. Calling the police and everything.

"But then, shit, a little later when all this happened and came out?

Nothing. Nothing was hardly even said about it. You know like, 'What were you doing?' But no, she *defended* him. She thinks he's innocent. Da-de-da. 'He was the perfect father.' I mean, come on, the guy—the guy was totally off the wall. He was going bonkers.

"That's why I say—you've got to look at Billy Fontanille's history for the six months before and all of a sudden, like Mike said, you throw these three together and boom. It just blew up. But it's definitely strange. And if you look at it from Mike's shoes and my shoes and all the others—you know, the stuff that happened? It's really weird. Really, really weird."

"Kerry was a good employee. He did a pretty good job. If we had problems with Kerry, we had personal problems with Kerry, you know, head problems." Aside from the odd jobs Kerry Myers had held as a teenager and as a college student, Jake Hahn, executive vice president of Air-Dreco, an engineering sales firm specializing in pneumatic and hydraulic components and systems, is the only real boss he's ever had.

"We had problems with Kerry and Janet as a group. When I was branch manager we would set goals. One time I said, 'Hey, if we hit four hundred thousand dollars in sales this month, you guys pick the restaurant, company pays for it, we take the wives and we go out and eat.'

"Boom, we hit the goal. 'Where you guys wanna go?' 'We wanna go to Chris's Steak House.' I gulp and say, 'Ohh-kaayy, this is gonna swallow the apple here,' but I said what I said, I gotta back it up. So we go. We have like a room at Chris's, upstairs. And I remember Janet coming in, she had a great dress on her, she looked stunning. And that's where my solid opinion of her stops.

"She bitched about the drinks. She bitched about the food. She ordered lobster! We're at *Chris's Steak House,* you don't order lobster, you order steak! She frustrated me so badly. She sent everything back. You know, she'd whine, she'd mope, she'd nyak-nyak.

"I walked away and I said, 'I'll never do this again.' I'm spending five to six hundred dollars of the company's money as a good gesture?"

Mr. Hahn shakes his head hard at the memory and continues.

"It seemed like every time I turned around she was on the phone, she had Kerry upset. He was yelling and screaming. You could hear him through this wall. Just flip the button and he was off. And I'm sitting here going, 'He's gotta be putting this on, he can't really react this way.' But it was a sincere reaction because it happened over and over and over.

"Janet at first was extremely immature. Always making accusations about affairs. One time—I'm not in the office. When I come in I'm confronted by one of the guys here: 'Man, we don't need this. Gwen is all upset. She left.' Lord, she was having marital problems enough, she didn't need any more.

"It turned out Janet had called, then even come by the office and accused Gwen of having an affair with Kerry because they were both away at lunch at the same time. She called and screamed. She came and screamed some more. That was that immature, emotional stage that we went through with Janet, where it was really off the wall.''

On Wednesday afternoon, March 14, Bob Masson took a taped statement from Kerry Myers. The formal statement was taken at the Detective Bureau. Jack Rau, Myers's now sole attorney of record, was allowed to be present during the process and in fact was even allowed to participate briefly in the questioning. (See Appendix for transcript of statement.)

On Friday, March 16, Marion Edwards brought more witnesses before the grand jury. All of them were Fontanille witnesses found and supplied by Pat Fanning: Chuck Cronin, who was a lifelong friend of Bill's but had not been a part of either of the two eventually overlapping circles; Joseph and Sandra Giardina, Janet's former employers from Zee Medical; and Sandra "Perky" Allan.

The Giardinas were important witnesses as to a pattern of behavior, but they were "old news"; what they saw and testified to had happened some three years before the murder. And those from the Myers camp, while admitting there had been turbulence in the marriage early on, were telling the grand jury that it had ended and everything had become harmonious after the birth of Ryan.

"However, Chuck Cronin potentially was one of the most important witnesses of all," Pat Fanning explains. "I mean, a guy, if he's off to commit a murder, doesn't stop to visit with an old friend, the old friend's sister and mother, and tell them where he's going, who he's going to see, and what he's going there for. Right?"

The story Cronin tells is indeed crucial. And the fact that it appears to have *two versions* perhaps makes it even more so.

One of them goes as follows: "Bill came over Wednesday, the 23rd, late in the afternoon. He said he had a job in Jacksonville and that he was working for a trucking company. He asked to borrow ten dollars and I said I didn't have it but I would see if I could get it.

"He also told me that he was going to play basketball that night and he wanted to know if I wanted to go over there and watch him play. I said no, but later told him I'd try to meet him there and he gave me directions.

"He also told me he was having an affair with a married woman, but he wouldn't tell me who it was.

"The next day, he came over around ten-thirty. I was in the shower and when I got out, he and my sister were watching *The Young and the Restless* on TV. We laughed, we joked, Bill was in good spirits, and we went outside. I smoked a cigarette, because I can't smoke in the house.

"When we went, I asked Bill again who he was seeing, did I know her. And he said, 'Yeah.' He finally told me it was Janet Myers, Kerry Myers's wife. And I told him that it wasn't a good idea to be doing that. He agreed. Then he said he was going over there to break it off.

"He left a little after one. But it was around one that he told me."

Perhaps the story told by Perky Allan, the south side next-door neighbor to the Myerses on Litchwood, is a particularly representative indication of the dilemma Marion Edwards and the grand jury were facing during those confusing days of March 1984.

Ms. Allan would be a relatively important witness if the prosecution attempted to convict Kerry Myers of the murder of his wife with wholly circumstantial evidence—because she could only testify to something she heard, and then give a layman's opinion of what it was that she heard:

"Janet was three or four months pregnant with Sarah, so it must've been late summer of 1983. Anyway, I was sitting in the hot tub by myself, it was around eight P.M. or nine, and I heard arguing. Now the hot tub is at this end of the pool, up by the house and right next to the fence. So I listened and I could hear curse words; I couldn't catch sentences, but I could understand words. And they were both spitting them out as vulgar as the other one, so it was not one-sided. It was a full-fledged argument.

"I got up and I stood up on the side of the hot tub and looked over there and didn't see anything. So I sat back down and tried to see if I could hear any better, but really all I could hear were the loud curse words. Then I heard something hit the wall—now I assumed, because of the sound, it sounded like a body: it wasn't like a vase, or a—it was a thud.

"Something solid hit a wall with some force. Like maybe a bowling ball without the crash—usually their fights were like bowling balls with the crash and scatter of the pins, you know. Then nothing. No noise. Silence."

While Perky would estimate that she had heard all told between six and a dozen disturbances at the Myerses' house during the time they had lived there, there was another one she distinctly remembered and told the grand jury about.

"I heard them arguing. My window was up, so I went and looked out. Janet was standing—it must've been in the garage, because I didn't see her—and Kerry was standing at his car door. They argued for a minute and then he got in the car and pulled out of the driveway real fast and peeled off down the street.

"Then—it couldn't have been more than ten or fifteen minutes later—he came back very quietly, got out, and went in. And again, nothing.

"But one of the things that really stood out both times, all of the times, really—she was so mousy and shy, yet I remember thinking to myself, 'I would never have imagined that those words could come out of that girl's mouth.' I was just shocked at the violence and the viciousness."

Saturday, March 17, 1984   THE TIMES-PICAYUNE/THE STATES-ITEM
Grand jury can't decide in Jeff slaying
By Richard Boyd
West Bank bureau

A Jefferson Parish grand jury Friday refused to indict or clear a suspect jailed in the Feb. 23 beating death of a Harvey housewife. . . .

The grand jury, after hearing six witnesses, took no action in the case. District Attorney John Mamoulides . . . and his first assistant, Marion Edwards, said . . . [they] will go back to the grand jury with more evidence. [But] they will . . . confer with Jefferson Sheriff's Office Detective Robert Masson . . . and have detectives look into a couple of other matters before deciding when to take the matter to the jurors again. "We will continue. It is still an open case. It is the most baffling we've had in a long, long time but we keep trying to resolve it," Mamoulides said.

Sheriff Harry Lee said he doesn't know what other evidence can be produced for the grand jury. "But we will go over everything we have up to this point and make certain we have thoroughly investigated every item that has come to our attention," he said. Lee said detectives are still uncertain who killed Janet Myers. "At this point, we still think Fontanille and Kerry Myers are suspects," he said.

"It's bad enough that it happened. I mean, it's bad enough that Janet is gone and the kids have to be without their mother. But then to have Kerry accused of it? Like these aren't bad enough, we're going to slap you in the face with a little bit more."

Marva Myers still bristles when recalling those days when it was being insinuated publicly that her victimized, widowed stepson was a wife murderer.

Clifford, on the other hand, is certain the entire nightmare is a conspiracy and political cover-up.

"They had it in the *paper* that Lee thought the husband could've done it! Then we find out real quick from my cousins about Mike Fanning being the one who was screening the evidence for the grand jury, and Pat Fanning, his brother, is Billy's attorney? Which just happened a day or two after? I got real suspicious then.

"Then when the District Attorney's Office released the same statement, you know, 'one of the most baffling cases,' I said, 'What in the hell?' After the detectives are saying they had the evidence and all? You know, the detectives are telling me one thing, yet their boss Lee makes his stupid statement.

"Nobody wants to admit it, but Bob Masson told me, 'If I said everything I know, they wouldn't come after me, they know better. But they would

go after my family, kinfolks, find some way to get something on them.'
" 'They play dirty,' Bob said."

Monday, March 19, 1984   THE TIMES-PICAYUNE/THE STATES-ITEM
3 weeks taken to post bail after pal's wife is slain
By Richard Boyd
West Bank bureau
   William J. Fontanille, accused of killing a close friend's wife, was freed Saturday night after posting a $150,000 bond. He reportedly has now gone into seclusion with his parents. . . .

"My brother mentioned that he'd seen Bill walking in the neighborhood. Just hanging his head and walking. Bill was a walker."
   Assemblies of God pastor Jonas Robertson remembers the first time he saw Bill Fontanille shortly after his release from the Jefferson Parish Correctional Center.
   "A week later, I saw him walking across the street by the church. I'm coming home in my car and I pulled into the parking lot of Christ the King Church where he's walking and said, 'Hey, Bill, how ya doin'?'
   "You could just see the weight of everything in the world pushing him down—you know, he knew that everybody knew what was going on. And there is nothing worse than that for Billy. What people think of him is something above all else.
   "Basically my intention at that point was witnessing to him. Sharing Christ with him. Reaching out to him. I explained, 'Bill, I believe you're innocent. I believe that you didn't do it. My brother and I've been talking about it.'
   "Oh, man, lemme tell ya, you could just see the relief pass over him. 'Jeez, man, I'm glad *somebody* believes me. Because I feel like the whole world's against me. Everybody is blaming me for what happened.' I said, 'Look, why don'tcha come over and I'll introduce you to my wife and my family. I'm livin' right there.' He said, 'Yeah, I'd like that.'
   "So we went over to my house and we spent about an hour and a half and he shared some of the story with me, not in specific detail, and I suggested to him that, 'Maybe Kerry thought you were having sex with his wife.' And he adamantly denied that. He said, 'No. I don't know how he could have. There wasn't anything going on.' He told me he'd just walked in and got stabbed. That he didn't know why Kerry stabbed him.
   "So, he lied to me even then; but I understood why," says Brother Jonas. "But Billy started coming by fairly often, two, three times a week, and we'd talk. I'd tell him about the Lord. See, he knew me in the olden days. He knew I'd been totally nuts and lost. I'd punch people out. I was hostile.

I was bad news. But he saw the change in my life. And he was looking for some help."

JPSO CONTINUATION FORM   ITEM: B/14695/84

A request was made to have Mr. Fontanille submit to a polygraph examination. Mr. Fanning advised that he would have to talk to his client and discuss the possibility . . . but at this time he was inclined not to have his client submit to [an] examination.

On Thursday, 12 April 1984, the undersigned officer spoke with Mr. Jack Rau, attorney representing Kerry Myers. Arrangements were made with Mr. Rau to have Kerry Myers come to the Jefferson Parish Sheriff's Office Detective Bureau at 6:00 PM on Tuesday, 17 April 1984, and submit to a polygraph examination reference to the death of his wife, Janet Myers.

It should be noted that the request for polygraph examination of Kerry Myers was made by Mr. Marion Edwards, First Assistant District Attorney, Jefferson Parish District Attorney's office.

Robert Masson

"Now, there's polygraphs, and then there's polygraphs. And I've played the polygraph game at the highest levels—with clients who the FBI has made go to Washington to have the head of their polygraph unit test 'em because they didn't want anybody else doing it, they were such sensitive cases and such." Pat Fanning can wax positively swashbuckling upon the subject of polygraph tests.

"Lawyers react different ways when they hear 'polygraph.' And there's all sorts of ways to do it, and I don't know that anyone has had more experience dealing with these damn polygraphs than I have. Polygraphs are only as accurate as the operator is, and whenever it's a law enforcement officer acting as the operator, there's a built-in bias. And that's not a personal knock at Officer Churcherillo, their guy over there.

"Here's the way you deal with polygraphs. If you're gonna consider letting a client take the box, you go to Mississippi, or Florida, or north Louisiana—I wouldn't use a local polygraph examiner—and get a guy in private practice. If he passes, put the results in my pocket and show up at Churcherillo's desk. And if Churcherillo bombs him, says, 'Unh-unh, Churcherillo,' as I'm reaching into my pocket. 'That just goes to show how you guys jerk around with these tests.'

"Now if he fails it? You shred it. You swear the private examiner to secrecy. Tell him you're going to sue him if he tells anybody else and you come back and say, 'I don't believe in polygraphs. We're not taking the test.'

"The way they posed it to me was, 'Myers is taking it.' I mean that becomes a no-brainer to me: 'Well, let's see how he does.' "

* * *

"I went to the hospital to see Ryan several times," Monique Price, Mike's wife, is saying, "And Kerry would be there—but somebody else was always doing for Ryan, and that bothered me.

"He didn't go over and put his arms around him and hug him and kiss him and say 'Darlin', Daddy's here' and this kind of thing. I expect in life-and-death situations that people either crawl into a shell and they can't let out their emotions, or they get hysterical and let out all their emotions—but blank? I don't know. You'd go to the hospital and here's this motionless, lifeless child lying there who's been beaten and you don't want to retaliate? You don't have to go out and do it, but I mean you *say,* 'I could kill this man for what's he's done to my baby and the next time I see him I might!' Something—I mean I kept waiting for something, and *nothing* ever happened.

"I really felt like he was scared. I can't tell you why I felt that way. I sometimes wondered if he was afraid of Ryan remembering or like maybe what his first words were going to be."

Tuesday morning, April 17, Bob Masson was told by Marion Edwards to cancel the polygraph examination of Kerry Myers which had been scheduled for that evening. For the official, chronological case narrative, Sergeant Masson then wrote:

> It was . . . learned from Mr. Edwards that Mr. Patrick Fanning had contacted the District Attorney's office and advised them that his client, William Fontanille, did not wish to submit to a polygraph examination at this time. . . .
> Due to the fact that there is no additional follow-up to be done at this time, and that all leads at this time have been exhausted, the undersigned officer requests that this case be closed.
> Sergeant Robert Masson

Marva remembers Ryan's first words. "Kerry would like read to him, nursery rhymes and children's stories and things, you know. And one day he was reading something with animals as the characters, and all of a sudden Ryan echoed him, said 'oink, oink.' I don't know what story it was. But those were his first words, 'oink, oink.' "

"We had this big meeting in the District Attorney's Office. And I'ma tell ya what my impression was: 'How can we get Fontanille *off* and how can we get Myers *into* the hot box?' But, ya gotta remember that Fontanille is a relative of an ADA." Bob Masson tilts his chin in, lifts an eyebrow, and nods his head as he then pauses to let that tainted question hang there just long enough, then:

"You wanna know how unusual it is to have a meeting like that? It's *never happened before in my career*. Sure, there are times when you're going to trial you'll meet with a couple of assistant DAs.

"John Mamoulides went around the table and asked everybody what their 'gut feeling' was. Marion said the husband did it right off the bat. I guarantee you that day it wasn't like he was going back and forth. It was 'The husband did it.'

"Never got an opinion from Mamoulides. He just wanted to get it over with, like, 'Hey, this sumbitch isn't going away, get somebody. Get this shit off my hands.'

" 'What's your gut feeling?' I said, 'I don't base it on gut feeling—I base it on fact. And the evidence I've got says it's Fontanille.' And I told 'em, 'I'm not saying Myers isn't involved—but I guarantee you one thing, Fontanille *is*.'

"Yeah, there were definitely two camps. And everybody was curious about the case. But, how do we minimize Fontanille's involvement and maximize Myers's—that was the definite tone or agenda I felt.

"The Myers-did-it people kept saying, 'Listen to the tape. Listen to the tape. It's obvious it's fake.' It wasn't obvious that it was fake. I got the tape about a week after it happened. My first impression was he was plenty scared—I didn't find anything that was completely out of line with it. I mean, I don't know how I would react if I walked in and saw my wife laying there dead, you know? I don't know. Does any of the circumstances leading up to that have any effect on that?—in other words, the fact that he was beaten, the fact that he was bleeding, the fact that he's in—I don't want to say 'state of shock'—but it's something, he's in pain for sure. So what effect would that amount of pain or that amount of anxiety have on it? I don't understand how you can even make a study of that. I certainly wouldn't base my case on it.

"But all I know is that when I went into that meeting I had Fields, Claverie, Dixon, Singer, and myself for sure saying it's Fontanille. And that's exactly the way it was as Mamoulides went around the table. The last vote—or opinion—he got to was Sheriff Lee. He sort of leaned back, had his fingers together across his big Buddha belly, thought for a bit while he twirled his thumbs, and then said, 'The husband did it. Only a spouse can have that much rage.'

"Immediately Chief Fields goes, 'Yeah, you're right.' Then Claverie, 'The sheriff's got a good point there.' Bang—there went their votes to the other side.

"At the end all I had was Carol Dixon, Ron Singer, and me."

"I seem to remember at least two meetings in Mamoulides's office—the infamous round-table meetings. Harry Lee was certain the husband had done it. Me? I swear, whichever I heard tell his story last was the one I believed that day. I've got to admit that straight up. They are both *very* convincing."

Marion Edwards, while perhaps somewhat grayer in the hair since the events he methodically reconstructs, retains a presence and manner which one can imagine would be very effective in the setting of a grand jury proceeding.

"However, there were two or three basic areas where I believed Kerry just had to be lying, although doing it very well.

"After seeing the house it struck me as being impossible that at some time prior to making that phone call he hadn't seen the body. In the dry reports you think initially that maybe there could be enough space there from the door that maybe . . . ? But it's just not possible after you go see it.

"The 911 call always bothered me. I must have listened to it a hundred times—and at different speeds. My first impression and what stuck with me all the way was that it was staged. At that point in time there were a lot of people in the Sheriff's Office that were just as convinced as I was; probably more so.

"Yet there were things I wanted to have done that we just didn't get done. I don't know if they would've led to a different conclusion or not. At several meetings I requested that they make arrangements to have tests of that phone made—see just how far away it would pick up and see if we could determine based on that tape using that phone where he was when those sounds were coming across the phone.

"I'd already presented it twice before that first grand jury when I asked Masson to do two things specifically before going back in. One was the telephone check. And I wanted him to go and try to retrace the steps that Kerry Myers had made during that day and see if he could confirm that the clothes Myers was wearing during the day were the same clothes he had on when he went to the hospital that night.

"Also there always seemed to me to be some significance to the time discrepancies, like when Myers was first asked about it he told them that Bill left his house sometime earlier than the time indicated by his arrival at Jo Ellen Smith.

"The thing that came to my mind immediately when I first realized there was this discrepancy—I felt that Myers knew there was a discrepancy but that he'd sort of lost track of the time and didn't know how much time he'd lost. Like you'd been busy doing something and was very much afraid that five minutes had felt like an hour. And he was trying to fill that in and account for it as best he could.

"But for every obvious untruth that you could see on one side, you could see them on the other side too. It was obvious that Fontanille was lying when he was talking about how he passed in front of the house, didn't see Kerry's car and went all the way around and hid his car on the other street and walked back just to get his baseball bat . . . et cetera, et cetera.

"The only thing I was absolutely convinced of was that both were lying. And that Bob Masson was dragging his feet—in sand."

"Marion Edwards came up with, 'Why don'tcha go over to the house and take a phone call from headquarters and go stand in the living room and yell with the phone off the hook,'" Bob Masson remembers. "Which I thought was ludicrous, personally, okay? And I refused to do it—and I *didn't* do it. 'Cause I didn't think it was gonna serve a purpose, in all honesty," Bob Masson says with his indignation still showing.

Saturday, June 16, 1984   THE TIMES-PICAYUNE/THE STATES-ITEM
West Bank slay case going to grand jury
By Richard Boyd
West Bank bureau

Still struggling to determine who battered a young mother to death in her suburban West Bank home, Jefferson Parish prosecutors next week may ask a grand jury to decide between her husband and his best friend . . . First Assistant District Attorney Marion Edwards said Friday. . . .

"Obviously, we don't have enough evidence to book Kerry Myers with the crime, but some things we have re-examined point to him. We are just going to let the grand jury decide," said Edwards.

Richard Boyd's reporting went on to quote Deputy Chief Eugene Fields as to why little Ryan had not yet been questioned: "We are not pushing that because he is so young and we don't want to cause him more problems."

Mr. Boyd concluded with the tidbit that "Fontanille's attorney, Patrick Fanning, said his client is working and passed a lie detector test to get the job. He told job examiners he had never been arrested or involved in a crime and passed the lie detector exam."

"I made sure the paper got that about the polygraph for a job." Pat Fanning grins just like Dennis the Menace when he's duped Mr. Wilson again.

"Bill needed a job. He applied at a Chevrolet dealership as a salesman. They required a polygraph as a condition of hiring, and when Bill asked me I said, 'Hell, yeah.' Hey, if he fails it, nobody knows the difference; no harm, no fault. But if he passes it, telling lies about a criminal record and ever being arrested, that just further sullies in the public's mind the validity of the box.

"Of course, as soon as that hit the paper the dealership let Bill go, but then we knew that going in. All in all, I think it served its purpose."

*   *   *

In Louisiana a grand jury sits for a minimum of four months and a maximum of eight. So it was to the same panel that Marion Edwards again presented his two principals' stories on July 13 amid the humidity of a Deep Delta summer. But this time he took a different approach—reversing the order that Bill and Kerry testified in. Billy testified for about two hours, then Kerry spent an hour on the stand.

On July 27, Marion Edwards went back again with a really full plate: included among the thirteen witnesses stacked toward the Myers's camp were both sets plus one of grieving parents, and grandparents and friends, including Russell Ardneaux, a big man, well over six feet tall, solidly yet trimly built, brown-haired and handsome, with an engaging, forceful, analytic manner.

Four years younger than Bill Fontanille as they grew up together in the D Section of Terrytown, the then overweight, bumbling, underachieving, vulnerable, yet always game Russ was, from the first memories of adolescence, a full-fledged charter member of the Rats, as the circle with its sun as Billy would, in their teenage years, "officially" name themselves.

Russ also was a schoolmate of Janet Cannon at River Oaks Academy, graduating in 1977, one class behind her.

And, when the Bill Fontanille circle and the Mike Price circle merged as young men and formed a sports alliance under the Christ the King CYO banner, a grown-into-his-frame Russ was a valued asset who occasionally hit the long ball on what was basically a banjo-hitting, good-fielding club that won a lot of games by only a run or two. He had also married Carrie Lynn Cassard, Chuck's sister.

"They called me and my wife. We both got a subpoena. And when I got into the grand jury—the questions they asked me? I just wanted to turn around and tell 'em, 'You know, what are you wasting my time for and your time?'

"Like the question that really threw me—and I was so darn mad that I had to watch my temper, because I don't know law and I was afraid, what the heck, they could get me for contempt of court or something—the damn lawyer, or whatever the heck he was that was running the whole show, actually asked me, 'Who do you think did it?'

"I turned around and I said, 'Sir, I don't have a lawyer representing me, but that's an opinion!' And I said, 'I'm not gonna give my opinion in front of people that can make the decision of whether one of these men are gonna be tried for murder.'

"I said, 'I'll tell you the truth—you want my opinion?' I said, 'I don't think *either* one of them did it.' I said, 'I wouldn't've hung around with someone that I thought was a murderer, I'm just as shocked by this as you are or anybody else.' I said, 'Whatever happened that night and whoever did it, there's a lot to it and they cracked seriously.' I said, 'Because I can't believe that either one of those guys were capable of just murdering somebody.' I went back to it again, 'I wouldn't've hung around with 'em. Why would I wanna spend my time? Billy? I've been knowing Billy for twenty-six years, since I was six years old.'

"Lemme tell you something they asked me in the grand jury, and I think I threw 'em for a loop, 'cause I remember the look on everybody's faces. For some reason they asked me, 'Billy Fontanille, did he bat right-handed or left-handed?' My reply was 'He was a switch-hitter.' "

Clifford Myers remembers that the grand jury "wanted to know if I'd ever seen bruises on Janet and if I didn't why not? They even asked Marva if I was violent. She said, 'God no.' And there was this one muscle-man type on the jury who kept wanting to know why Kerry didn't try to do something to save his family."

"They even said, 'You didn't want to question Ryan because you thought that Kerry was guilty?' " Marva remembers her stint with the grand jury. "I said, 'No. It's because the doctors didn't want him to be questioned.' They actually asked me that—had I ever questioned Ryan? I said, 'No, I haven't questioned Ryan.' I said, 'Ryan doesn't remember right now what happened to his mother, and I pray to God that he never does!' " Marva Myers almost never ever raises her voice, but on the last sentence she does, just ever so much, and she also almost sticks herself with the needle she's using to sew little Sarah's dance costume.

Mike Price got into a verbal brawl with Marion Edwards. "It got into a real yelling match," Mike remembers. "I told him he was an asshole. It got real hairy. He threatened me with contempt or something and I told him he was contemptible. It was ridiculous—I went in with a grudge to bare, I went in to *get* Billy Fontanille. He was guilty. He needed to go to the electric chair because he killed Janet."

Curtis Jordan also provoked a contempt threat from Marion Edwards while heaping all of Billy's "oddities and propensity to lie" upon the grand jurors. At one point Curtis had shouted down "those idiots" with an outburst along the order of: "Do you want me to lie? To tell you, 'Oh yeah, he beat the crap out of her,' when I never ever saw that? Well, I'm not going to and I'd like to tell you where you can stick this grand jury!"

Charles and Lorraine Cannon were profuse and unwavering in support of their son-in-law during their testimony.

Joan Switzer was vitriolic and fawning in her condemnation of Bill Fontanille and her support for her sister's "loving, considerate, devoted husband." She also made a point to get it officially and forever on the record that Bill had been "only an usher" and *not* the best man at her sister's wedding. And many on the grand jury refused even to believe that; eventually documentation had to be presented before they would accept the fact that Bill Fontanille was not Kerry Myers's best man.

* * *

Marion remembers that even though it could be fairly perceived that he did have a belief that Kerry Myers was involved in the murder, there were some troubling things he was being told about Bill Fontanille that continued to confuse him.

"I talked to Susan Fontanille a couple of times; I really got the feeling that she maybe thought that Bill had done it and if so that she was responsible for it. That he was transferring it. She told me all kinds of stories of how she had humiliated him and he had never raised a hand to her or even raised his voice. That he got on his knees and begged her not to go out of town with her friends. She said, 'I'm going,' turned on her heels, and walked out."

"I leaned pretty hard on Billy," Pat Fanning remembers of that summer of '84. "And I had a lot of background, I spent a lotta, lotta hours with this guy—both in my office and at his mother's home and in jail cells talking to him. And I can't tell ya how many times I said, 'Billy'—and I just laid it on him—'I'm not so sure about your story. It is just so unbelievable that it could've happened the way either of you say it happened. I'm not calling you a liar or anything, but I'm just gonna say this to ya: if, in fact, something else happened, and you believe that you have to stick to your story because it's your story and you've already testified to it under oath, that's not the case. If you tell me—if this is not what happened, what you've been saying all along—even if you tell me, 'I did it,' and there's nothing we can do to change that and you killed the girl and Kerry came in and it's as he said, then there's no harm done because that's a privileged communication. That's confidential between you and me and it'll stay right here. And when we go to trial they'll put your statements into the record and we won't put you on the stand. But, now, if he did it but you were there and watched him, and didn't stop him, maybe even lied to help him cover it up, and you're afraid of the exposure that that gives, then you should tell me that. Because if you did *anything less* than personally and alone beat that woman's face off, there's a deal we can make. Anything less. I can do something. And even if you did it all, I think there's something there for us.'

"But nothing. He told me he was innocent and whether it made sense or not that's what happened and he wasn't taking a plea for something he didn't do. He told me to tell them to make that offer to Kerry. He was the one that killed his wife."

JEFFERSON PARISH SHERIFF'S OFFICE INTERDEPARTMENTAL TELETYPE MESSAGE:
To: All Districts and Divisions
Subject: Transfer, Lt. Vincent Lamia
Effective August 1, 1984, Lt. Vincent Lamia, Commander of Robbery,
is transferred to Commander of Homicide.

On September 27, 1984, Kerry Myers underwent a polygraph examination requested by the state and administered by Officer Sam Churcherillo. Marion Edwards was there.

"When we polygraphed Myers, he was almost too calm. I mean, he was very, very unemotional—of course, he really was all the time," Marion remembers. "And on all of the salient questions he showed deception—clearly, unequivocally, no question in the operator's mind about it.

"When Churcherillo came out and told me that, he said, 'You want me to tell him?' And I said, 'Yeah, tell them.' And he told Myers with Jack Rau there, and I know his attorney was shocked. Because Jack at that point in time really believed that he was innocent. But Myers was absolutely unconcerned, he just shrugged his shoulders and said, 'Oh, well.' That was in my presence.

"No concern. None."

Anita Price remembers, "Kerry always told us that he was always willing and anxious to take a lie detector test, and when he did take it, he couldn't wait to tell us he had passed it 'with flying colors.' Of course, we believed him. I mean, why shouldn't we?"

"What really burned me up was I found out about the polygraph by accident." It is obvious that Bob Masson is still burned up about this particular point.

"I happened to be in the courthouse one day, going down the elevator, and Marion Edwards was in there and said, 'Oh, by the way, your boy Myers flunked the polygraph.' I said, *'What are you talking about?'* "

On Monday afternoon, October 23, 1984, the grand jury refused to indict Bill Fontanille—which meant that he was no longer charged with first degree murder.

"When they no-true-billed the boy I was elated that we had made the right decision." Pat Fanning is smiling the same way he had for the TV cameras back then. "Because usually, effectively, that's almost like it's all over. They don't often go back to a later grand jury and try again. *But—*" And with that the smile is gone.

"What happened was Mrs. Cannon—she just kept push-push-pushing. 'Conspiracy! Conspiracy!' Yet what made the constant talk around town of this cover-up shit so really silly was that at the same time the Myerses and Cannons were running off at the mouth, Mrs. Fontanille was constantly railing to me about how unfairly the Sheriff's Office and the DA's Office were persecuting *her* son: a cover-up attempt because they'd botched the investigation so badly. And I'm having to *defend* the DA's Office! I was put in the untenable position of defending the prosecutor to my clients, who're paying the bill."

Pat relaxes some and the smile returns, one of his better mischievous ones. "But, look, Kerry was represented by Jack Rau, who—may his soul rest in peace—was a very nice man, but he just didn't have the defense and prosecutorial school of trench warfare that I'd been through."

Wednesday, October 24, 1984   THE TIMES-PICAYUNE/THE STATES-ITEM
Parents beg to keep dead daughter's case alive
By Richard Boyd
West Bank bureau

The grief-stricken parents of a Marrero housewife killed eight months ago pleaded with two top Jefferson Parish officials Tuesday to keep investigating the baffling bludgeoning death.

Charles and Lorraine Cannon, parents of slain Janet Lynn Cannon Myers, met with District Attorney John Mamoulides and Sheriff Harry Lee.

"We didn't know what else to do," Lorraine Cannon said, her voice breaking. "We went to see them. We are so frustrated and still have so much grief." She said Mamoulides and Lee assured the couple that the case is not closed. . . .

"We were told Tuesday that our son-in-law is still a suspect also," Lorraine Cannon said. "That just can't be. We know him. He loved our daughter and he loved his children. He just was not capable of doing this horrible thing. If I ever learned that he did it, they could just put me in my grave; my life would be over." . . .

"I want to believe the district attorney and the sheriff when they said the investigation will continue," Lorraine Cannon said. "But I just don't know. I am very skeptical now. I used to believe everybody, and I guess I was naive. They are just politicians and I don't know if I can believe them, even when they look me in the eye and shake my hand."

Shortly after Christmas, Bill Fontanille, using his real name but not mentioning any of his recent difficulties, answered a classified-page advertisement for someone with shipping management experience. The firm was Eckard Drugs, a large regional chain of full-service drugstores, which had just built a large shipping warehouse in Hammond, Louisiana, just across the lake from New Orleans and where Billy had gone to college. He was hired on the spot, and soon moved into an apartment there in Hammond and set about salvaging what he could of his old life while mostly building a new one, since so much of the past held only closed doors for William Fontanille.

3
Growing Up

Being pregnant was not all that bad. It had its ups and downs. I never had "morning sickness." I was just tired a lot. At the time I was substitute teaching at Livaudais Middle school in Terrytown. We lived in a one bedroom apartment in the Ballinger Oaks apt. complex, but we knew we'd be moving to make room for you. You were due on June 15th, 1981.

On January 21st you kicked me for the first time. I remember how I would sit an hour at a time just feeling you "roll around." That alone was wonderful!

—*Journal of Janet Cannon Myers*

* * *

"The girl in the window," Peggy Cowan says softly, as if from a distance, musing, as she looks out at the winter sunlight and reflects upon the days when she and Janet Cannon were children growing up together on Stafford Street in old Gretna.

"You would see her watching from her window: everybody else outside playing. And there were times when we just *knew* she wanted to be out there playing, but she never came out.

"Later she'd tell you, 'I'm writing a story about you. That's why I can't come out and play. I'm writing stories about y'all playing.'

"We were close, we all played together—when she was allowed to. There were four or five girls at that time on the block that all bummed around together. Myself, Janet, Janelle, Patty and Beth and Carol, and I'm surprised I can still just rattle off the names like that. We were all within three or four years of each other. We were inseparable friends. You know, you were together constantly, especially when summer came along.

"We always went bike riding. It was a very quiet neighborhood. An older neighborhood. Not a lot of cars going around, so we always rode bikes, we were always out in the street and all. But not Janet. I don't remember her ever coming out and riding bikes with us. I don't remember if she ever even had a bike.

"The main thing that I really remember is her always being inside. Homework and reading. That was the main, main thing. When she did come out every once in a while, you know, sit outside? She always had a book.

"It was something she enjoyed. I always pictured her to go off to be into a lot of bookwork, having some type of profession in books and writing. She didn't talk about it; she wasn't the type of person to open up and want to talk about things like that. She just wasn't a talkative person. I mean, she had her times. But not about—and this was kind of strange: you *never talked about what went on in her home.* You know, things that families did and stuff like that?

"That made an impression on me even then. Because everybody, when you're a kid, you'll talk about, 'We went to the zoo,' or, 'We did this.' You'll talk about what you got for Christmas. What you did for Easter. You'd talk about things. But not from Janet. Never anything like that from her. She would always sit there and say, 'Y'all did that? That must've been fun.' "

"You cannot stay married just for children. At one time society pushed you to, but it's unrealistic—you have a life, and you can't stay married for children."

Cissy Fontanille's hands flutter when she talks. It's not so much a nervous reflex as it is a style; while the movements are quick, they are small, graceful.

"If you're married to an alcoholic like I was, you certainly cannot stay married to that alcoholic who never held a job, whose brother went out there on the limb and got him a good job and then he'd leave vehicles parked on the sidewalk where the company would have to come get them.

"No one had to live this life but me—and my poor mom, bless her heart. Thank God Bill was very young at the time and didn't know anything about it. The only father Bill knows is Herman Fontanille. And on his birth certificate it has Herman Fontanille as his father. He's legally adopted. His birth certificate has been changed. Legally amended.

"Point-blank, my husband is my son's father. I don't want him thought of as a stepfather. It would upset Herman very much, and it would upset me—my life—I'm a very private person."

Cissy Fontanille's hands are aflutter, mostly in the vicinity of her throat and bosom, as she confronts these memories.

"His natural father has never ever given one red penny to support this child. So he's very legally a Fontanille. Of course, I am a Daigle. But there's not many of us left."

*　*　*

"We were managing. Let me put it this way—I had just gotten Marva a new '66 Mustang, white. Remember that one with the blue leather?" Clifford Myers is remembering when he married the almost-twenty-years younger Marva, and then shortly thereafter when Clifford's three children came to live with the newlyweds.

"We'd just gotten that, because we had some extra money and all of a sudden we've got the kids. What the hey, I'd been supporting them anyway. I had to borrow the down payment to even get this house—but three kids, and my mother came with us, all of us in a two-bedroom apartment just wasn't going to cut it.

"I was working for Interstate Electric when we bought this house," Clifford continues. "Then I went over to Westinghouse. Twenty-nine months later, the guy that hired me, a friend of mine, we swapped places. I became manager and he was a salesman working for me. So we were going up. We were both working. Getting all the bills straightened out. We had two cars and we're starting to come up in the world a little bit. Even after getting the kids, we're working everything out. We had to both keep working because they all went to Catholic schools."

"If she was allowed to go out and play, she was not allowed to go inside anyone's home. That was 'No.'" Still within the warmth of the sunlight through the sitting-room window, Peggy Cowan continues her memories of growing up with Janet Cannon.

"As well as they knew my parents, when she rode back and forth to religion classes at St. Joseph's—you know, my mother would pretty much chauffeur the neighborhood kids—her mama would walk her to our front door and wait until my mama was out and in the car and ready to leave. She'd watch us leave. Then she knew what time they would get back home and she'd be waiting on the doorstep to get her. She could not just walk herself.

"And when she could come over and play, we could sit in the front yard and play, but if you said 'Come on, let's go inside and get a drink' or something, she couldn't. It was just common neighborhood understanding—she wasn't allowed to go inside anyone's house.

"Her childhood was completely different than the rest of us. I remember many a time—Barbie dolls were the big thing, and that's what we always played when we got together—but I always had to go to her house, and we had to do it outside. She could not play in her house, and I was not allowed in her house.

"It was just a rule. All parents set rules; you didn't discuss it, you didn't worry about it, you just left it be that that was the way it was. That they were just very quiet people who were different and more or less stayed to themselves. And she was the same way.

"Although her sisters were *not* raised the same. They were older, they were in high school already, dating, working, you know, the normal things, coming and going freely. But when Janet was a teenager it was still 'No.' She didn't have the same freedoms Joan and Jane had had. She could be fifteen, sixteen years old—the minute it would start getting dark, she had to go in. I mean she *had* to go in.

"The only place she ever went and did things was right next door at her grandma's. She could go there and do stuff. She could spend nights by her grandmother's. But as far as her spending the night by a friend's house, or a friend spending the night with her, 'No!' "

Russell Ardneaux, who has a good job working for a local utility, bought a home in Terrytown. He and his wife are growing older in the same neighborhood where they grew up. It is there that Russell talks of his childhood with Bill Fontanille.

"Typically, he was a bully—you know, like he would push and torment the littler ones. And Billy was the rebellious type. I think he also felt sorry for himself a lot of the time. He always wanted to be the main picture. I think that goes back to lack of attention at home. He really felt that there was more attention shown Angela than him. He was always jealous of her. Billy always held it against Angela for not being a little boy. He wanted a brother, not a sister. He really resented her.

"Look, Billy's family life was *bad.* I keep coming back to that, but it was. The boy did not feel at home. He hated Herman; he hated Herman with a passion. Him being adopted I think was the biggest effect on Billy's life.

"Now there's something I've heard, and I've heard it from many, many people. And Billy has never denied the story, either. Like I said, remember Billy really wanted a little brother? Yeah, well, he *put Angela in a garbage can when she was a baby.* Threw her away because she was not a little brother, she was a little sister. 'Course, somebody discovered her before anything happened. But that's how resentful he was."

When they could afford to, Chuck and Connie Cassard also bought a home in Terrytown, in D Section. While Chuck's being a cop has changed much of their lives from the days when they "Ratted" and "Miced" with Bill Fontanille and their other friends on those same suburban streets, just as much has also stayed the same.

"One day, I had already eaten, and I went over by Billy's house," Chuck remembers. "We were sitting in his room and we were getting ready to go somewhere and he had a box of Popeye's chicken. He said, 'I gotta go throw this away and then when I get back we'll go.' Right when he walked into the kitchen he threw the garbage away. But at that very moment, his father comes home. The first thing Mr. Herman says—now, I'm nineteen or twenty by this time, so Billy's twenty-two—'Whatcha hiding from me? Every time I come home, you're throwing something away. You're hiding something!'

"And all he was doing was throwing away chicken bones. 'Course, that don't mean Billy *wouldn't* hide something. But that's the mistrust in that family. It wasn't the house you go visit."

"It's still happening," Connie Cassard says. "Right now, this evening, you go by the A&P and there she'll be in the parking lot in her car just sitting there reading a book until she knows Mr. Herman's left—only then will she go on to the house. She's moved into Billy's old room—it's like they live together separately. She'll climb through the window if she has to get in and he's not gonna be leaving. That's what Billy grew up being a part of."

"I always felt that there was something strange about her upbringing. You almost never saw her away from school."

Claire Firestone Pasqua remembers when she, Janet, and Karen Attardo Stone were the "Three West Bankers." The three met their first day of transferring into Plaquemines Parish's River Oaks Academy. It was the fall of 1971. The beginning of eighth grade.

"We were in the pep squad together at first. And we became good friends, but school friends, we didn't hang around together after school. But I remember meeting her parents early on. They were a much older couple. Which I found unusual. They were *much* older. It was like a separate family almost. Because they had the two older girls and then Janet.

"Janet seemed to be overprotected or something—or just wasn't explained a lot of things, maybe? Just about life. I remember it was ninth grade, we were on the bus coming back home from an away game, Buras, I think, and Janet asked me if I washed my hair during my menstrual cycle. And I was like, 'Well, *yeah.*' I mean, we're perspiring all the time, and we both had long hair, and it was like, 'What is this child being told or rather what is she *not* being told?' I know I'm a doctor's daughter and all. But this is something that is part of being female. It was either she was not being told anything, or was being told a bunch of old wives' tales.

"When she asked me that it was just like, 'Something's different here, but I'm not quite sure what.' It was just very strange. Her immaturity was striking for her chronological age. Silly and naive. Even for a thirteen-year-old.

"Her mother didn't allow her to dress in style with the times. She was a goodie-two-shoes to the limit; and she was even more restrained when her parents were around. Which they were. A lot. An almost eerie hovering presence; whenever you think of Janet, they're there.

"She never drove in high school. The Cannons were a very backwards family when it came to what the women were allowed to do—almost like the Amish people. I never remember seeing Mrs. Cannon drive.

"Janet had a thing about her hair. It was something that she felt was very important, very unique about her appearance. She wore it like a badge. She wore her makeup like a china doll; she was very pale to begin with and tended to keep herself that way. Very fragile, like she could break.

"She didn't have any real boyfriends in high school. Not like you think of the so-called typical high school boy and girl thing. But there were at least two guys I know she liked. Crush or what have you. B. J. Perez was first. And that was more like a crush. Then Mike Daigle, he was a year behind us. He had the crush on her. And he was convenient and safe. But they didn't actually date. They would hang around at school together. Eat lunch together. Janet wasn't allowed to actually date date.

"She could be very catty, at times. Kind of a back-stabbing person. Would never get in trouble for it, though. Wouldn't risk it. That's why I think she was so catty and tacky to Lee Ann Cousins, the principal's daughter. She was jealous that Lee Ann seemed to have everything and could've gotten away with anything she wanted to but didn't, which seemed to make Janet dislike her all the more."

"How can I put this in words? Let me tell you this—when Bill became frustrated and angered with Herman, there were times I did not blame him, okay? There were *many* times that I did not blame him."

Cissy Fontanille's hands are somewhat stiller now as she in turn becomes more forceful, more intensely determined in tone and manner.

"Because Herman was *not* the easiest man in the world to live with. It's very hard right now living with Herman. No one lives behind these walls but *me*," Cissy says. "He's an old-fashioned man. Herman wants your opinion to be his opinion. Small things—when Bill didn't want his crew cut anymore, Herman couldn't understand this—because the man *still wears* a crew cut.

"Another thing he had a problem with is—Bill would outsmart him. Oh, and Herman could not take that. He could not take the idea that Bill was smarter. More educated. Bill had a brain, and there was the *problem*. Herman could not contend with the idea that Bill was very intelligent. Bill's a man of strong opinions of his own, and Herman, of course, does not think people have a right to have this opinion if it's not his opinion."

"With Kerry's dad, it was, 'You ain't no good. You're not as good as Cliff. You'll *never* be as good as little Cliff.' "

Mike Price has almost kinky, short-cropped sandy hair, a trim, athletic build, and a brisk manner. He speaks quickly and exuberantly, yet also is somehow always just a tad away from seeming sly, as if there is always something more beyond or beneath what he is saying.

"And it wasn't just Cliff Jr. he had to live up to, it was Cliff Sr., too. If Kerry came home and said, 'Dad, I hit three home runs today,' his dad would sit down and proceed to tell him how *he* hit fifteen home runs in a row. It didn't matter what the story was, his dad did it bigger, better, and first, and then Junior did it *better* than that. Kerry's just never going to be as good.

"But Kerry? Unh-unh. *Cliff* wanted Kerry to play pro ball," Mike Price says, a thought from before popping back into his memory. "What he *really* wanted was Cliff Jr. to play pro ball, but while he was all-everything in high school and later at LSU, that never happened. So Mr. Cliff rode Kerry hard.

"I mean, I hated Cliff, and he's a nice guy. I mean, Cliff Jr. is a *nice guy*. Really a nice guy. But I hated the guy and I hardly knew him, because of what it was doing to Kerry. I mean, how can you live up to a legend?

"And he was so always trying to make Mr. Cliff happy. He wanted his dad to be proud of him. He wanted his dad to say something nice about him."

"Janet was not your normal girl," begins Penny Price Fox, Mike Price's younger sister, who graduated from River Oaks Academy with Janet Cannon Myers. "She was nice, but a little crazy, she had a temper. Her mother—when you say ditzy, or out in left field, Mrs. Cannon is like that. And Janet was a *very* different person. She was *not* the normal kid in high school.

"She was a 'good girl,' she was in the band; she was on the dance team, Pantherettes. But you know how you always have the 'in crowd,' and then you have the 'bad crowd,' and then you have the crowd that never fits in—Janet was always in the crowd that really never fit in. No matter how much she wanted to. She had her friends—but the people she was really friends with were the other people that really never fit in.

"She liked scenes. She liked a lot of attention focused on her. She was obsessed with dying. She had a heart murmur and told everybody she was dying from it. When we were marching in parades, she always had to be picked up by the paddy wagon because she was hyperventilating or something like that. Anything to draw attention to Janet. She used to write about death in her poems. She used to talk about it. She *predicted* her death. She always said she was going to die when she was twenty-five years old, and she said it was going to be a violent death and by a man's hand. I mean, that's so accurate it's *scary.*"

Kenny Betbeze has done well enough to buy a home in Terrytown, planted firmly in his roots. An affable, well-adjusted realist with a touch of the muse within him, Mr. Betbeze is very thin, not much over five-eight. He's a wiry bundle of enthusiasm and energy as he sits in his living room and remembers those days when he lived just a few houses down from Bill Fontanille, when he was one of the best friends Billy ever had, even if Bill was never aware of it or appreciated it.

Kenny Betbeze sits in silent reflection, but only briefly. Then: "You know, I didn't know that Billy was adopted—not until after the murder. And we were close! My whole life. My parents are still close friends of Miz Cissy and Mr. Herman. They never knew either."

Another pause, then, "Billy won your confidence, knew everything about you, because you grew up with him. So when something would happen he could always pull something out the closet that maybe you only told him one night when you were laying on the sidewalk just kinda looking up at the stars, bullshitting, you know? And he had a great and long memory.

"I'd like to romanticize it and say he was loyal, but he wasn't. Only to a degree; it depended on what he was going to get out of it.

"But through everything, I always liked Billy. He'd mess you over from time to time, two or three days later you'd be back bumming around with him. I don't know. Nobody else did that to everybody else. Or could get away with it. But Billy could. And you'd still want to be his friend.

"I remember Billy asking one time to spend the night by my house, and I was outside, but the window was open and I could hear Miz Cissy telling him, 'He's three years younger than you. You need to hang around people your own age.'

"And Billy says, 'Yeah, I know, Mom, but it's just one night.' And when he came out he said, 'You heard that? Fuck her. Don't even worry about it.' "

Another pause. The smile hardens a bit. Then: "Billy Fontanille could be your best friend or your worst enemy all wrapped up in the same person. Intelligent, good-looking, conniving. Behind your back without a doubt. Pure Bill."

"Mr. Cliff and Marguerite's breakup was probably the most shaping factor of Kerry's life. He told me about it when we were older. It was a pretty intense thing too when he finally told me."

Mike Price, Kerry Myers's champion, apologist, longtime spokesman, and the loyalest truest-of-blue friend any man in a real jam should be so lucky to have, looks back.

"But I realized there was something wrong real early. In those days you didn't see very many fathers with custody of their children. I knew that there was something drastically wrong in that family to begin with. And we were always mindful—even kids are intuitive enough to understand that she had to be a pretty bad mother to have lost the kids.

"We never knew the whole dynamics. But when he finally told me at least parts of it, it didn't come as a surprise.

"It affected his whole relationship with girls. When he dated somebody he was their husband. He didn't think about other girls. I mean, when you're sixteen, seventeen years old and your hormones are racing, you might be dating a girl and be totally in love, but the next little girl that comes along and lifts her skirt, you're jumping into bed with her. Not Kerry.

"He didn't really date a lot. But when he'd meet a girl and they'd date, whoever it was, he dated her and only her for what was long periods of time for that age group.

"Like take this. Bobby Riley actually paid Kerry money to take his sister out one night, Kay Riley. She was dating this guy we knew, a real jerk, and Bobby hated him. So he paid Kerry three dollars to take her out on a date. We're fifteen or sixteen years old.

"So he takes her out on this bet, this deal. And bam, he dates her for six months. He was going steady with her for six months! I mean, this was a girl that was there all the time. I mean, she'd been there forever, and then all of a sudden this happens and he's talking about *marriage.*"

"Ironically, in many ways, even as unhappy as he often seemed to be, you'd have to say that Billy was spoiled," Kenny Betbeze says over a cup of coffee in his living room, which has most of one wall filled with expensive audio equipment.

"Billy's grandma I think had a little bit of money. She had an antique store or something like that on Magazine Street. I don't know whether she passed away or she just gave him some money. But he got a brand-new Pinto, 1973 or '74. It might've been a graduation present. But none of the rest of us had anything like that. Even later.

"Of course, before that Billy had this old VW that we painted with a spray can. Used to never be able to turn the engine off once you got it started. He, Timmy, and I used to go bowling. Come out the bowling alley, he'd always beat us out to the car to get it started, and then he'd ride around the parking lot in a circle with the door open. We had to jump in when it was driving 'cause he couldn't stop the car. Well, he'd kill hisself laughing, of course.

"But he got the Pinto his senior year. Now we're all from working-class families, even though it was a Pinto, that was a big deal. It didn't have air conditioning, but it was a brand-new car.

"He always had nice clothes. And he always got the girl. But, you see—and at the time I realized it—the crowd we ran with, most of the girls were younger, so, naturally they're going to be drawn to him. He was the first one to drive. He would buy us liquor when we were all a lot underage.

And we drank like fish when we were teenagers. He was our *supplier.*"

Kenny laughs a bit before he continues: "Billy needed to feel needed. He also wanted to feel that he was in control of situations. Situations where people are going to look up to him. Which is not necessarily a bad thing. We all would like that—we're just all not in a position to be. Billy was. He made sure of that.

"Billy squandered his career. My opinion the boy has—he was good, you know. He was good. And he knew it. He was confident. I don't know if that's from hanging around with people he was older than or what. But to me, he had what a lot of us wished we could've had. Except to do it. And he could've done anything he wanted to, but something stopped him. He was a dreamer.

"When he was a teenager—we were all TV nuts, watched Johnny Carson religiously, watched *Laugh-In,* this was before *Saturday Night Live.* Billy would sit down and write a script—shu-shu-shu, just like that—we'd do our own parody of *Star Trek* or of *The Brady Bunch* or something. He'd come with pages, dialogue, written like a movie script, and he, myself, and Timmy would sit there on a tape recorder and act this whole thing out on a cassette. Those were some of the best times of my life! We did this from about twelve to fifteen—Billy sixteen to nineteen.

"And Billy to me—it kinda fits, like—he was either gonna be destined to do—he *was* gonna be in the spotlight, whether it was gonna be for something great, a cure for cancer or whatever. Or something like this. It shocks me, but it kinda fits.

"You know, Chuck Cassard said something to me after all this happened, he said, 'Billy always had a scheme. Always something.' "

Kenny Betbeze, when asked to explain a "Billy scheme," as an example goes on to offer an account of the circumstances which led up to the two circles becoming one.

"It was the CYO. Billy realized, 'We can have a team. They can buy us jerseys.' You know? We always played ball in the streets, 'Now we can—heeeyy!' So Sunday after church we're all in a CYO meeting. There was an old lady running it—but we all came in and took it over. We fixed the elections, we controlled the treasury. When Connie and Chuck and them wanted to go to the beach—Connie was the treasurer—'Let's go to the beach.' Zip, it's on the CYO, 'It's Beach Night.' Nobody could go but Connie and Chuck and a couple of other couples? Go on the CYO. I went to Disney World for twenty-five dollars on the CYO—my parents couldn't afford to send me, so Billy and Tony had some bogus lottery for the 'CYO member who helped us out the most,' and my name was the only one in the hat. Whoop—'Kenny Betbeze.' I went for a week with the whole crew for a twenty-five dollar bus fee or something.

"Anyway, so we figured out, 'Man, they can buy us jerseys and stuff.' So Billy got me and Timmy and Louie and Russell and we all just came in and took it over. Tony Bordelle was the president. Billy was the minister of state. Whatever state he wanted.

"It was great. We did what we wanted, when we wanted, and we told everybody else what to do as well—we controlled everything. We had a blast. And then from that evolved the infamous 'softball team.'

"When I was about eighteen or nineteen and Billy was twenty-one or twenty-two, I just started dating outside the circle. And about this time through a guy named Danny Bush, Billy got the Price group to merge for a better softball team, they were starting to get serious about playing more softball. I wasn't that interested, so I drifted away.

"It's strange the way things turn out. Billy got notoriety, which is what he always wanted, but it was for a bad thing, not a good thing. A very bad thing, about as bad as you can get. And everybody knew about it, and Terrytown and the West Bank are pretty small—for Billy, it doesn't get much worse than that."

"So with this family deal, it was kind of like Billy was off by himself. And he was always kind of a loner—he's the kind of guy who wouldn't let you get real close to him."

Louie Valdin, who has a squat, bulldog appearance, is the only one out of the two circles to make his living in athletics. He is an assistant football coach at Jesuit High School in uptown New Orleans. It is the most prestigious of the parochial high schools that dominate the New Orleans area athletically.

"Even though Billy was in a group he was always—he never told you exactly what he was feeling and stuff like that. He kind of liked to be the mysterious type. Every now and then he'd kinda, you know, drift off, and want to be by himself and all. Every now and then he'd just do some kind of off-the-wall-type deal—I don't know whether to get attention or whatever.

"He always thought he was a lot smarter than a lot of people. And he couldn't be in the background. He didn't like that at all. He had to be in the spotlight. Anything to draw attention to himself. And everything with him had to be just so. I don't know, it was almost like he was scared for someone to think he wasn't perfect.

"No one really totally trusted him. He was a nice guy, every one liked him, but—I mean, you just—well, you knew he was conceited. You knew he didn't really care about you that much.

"No one ever thought of Billy as a 'good friend.' I mean, you wouldn't trust Billy with your girlfriend or anything like that. And if you were in a money jam, he wouldn't loan you any.

"There's something you've gotta realize . . . I'm gonna tell it 'cause it seems that nobody else wants to talk about the truth. Billy's big thing was—he'd kind of look and wait and hear that you're having problems with your girlfriend, you're breaking up or something, then he'd go in. He'd sneak in around the back door. That was pretty common. In other words, he was like a buzzard—he'd be sitting around waiting for the relationship to die and then he'd swoop in. Oh, yeah. Without a doubt. Everybody knew it. He did it twice with Connie: the first time when it was me and Connie, and then with her and Myers. It was his pattern."

"Kerry had always been a quiet and withdrawn kid. Not one to dominate a conversation. Very unaggressive. He wasn't going to call you," Mike Price explains.

"He finally got to where he'd call or come visit me, but most of the times I'd go see him. He just doesn't take the initiative. And I was never comfortable in that house.

"We all slept over each other's houses and everything—but I never slept at Kerry's. Never. I don't know of anybody who ever went over there and spent the night. He'd stay at my house. Or we'd stay at somebody else's house. Never Kerry's. To me, being in that house five minutes makes my skin crawl.

"There was always a sense of sadness over Kerry, we felt sorry for him. I mean, basically, for all practical purposes, Kerry is defenseless. He's helpless—he's naked and vulnerable to the max. Listen, I could walk up to Kerry and punch him in the face, and Kerry would've turned his back and the next day he would've been back over at my house, 'Hey, what's going on,' and we'd go on. I could do it a hundred days in a row, and still the next day he'd come over to the house, 'Let's go out and do something.'

"He was totally accepting for a friend. Not only accepted it, but expected it. He clung to people. He craved affection so much, he craved this camaraderie or affection or closeness with another human being so much, that he would cling to you. Because he didn't get it at home. We always got the feeling that he needed somebody to take care of him."

"Billy came from a badly broken-up family. Billy was very resentful about his real father across the river. But he almost never mentioned it," Connie Cassard says, remembering those days when she lived just a few lawns down from Bill Fontanille.

"You know, Billy *was* a junior. Yes, but not for long. When Mr. Herman adopted Billy, they changed his middle name to Adam so he wouldn't be a junior. Billy never did like that man Herman. He called him Dad. But it was bad. I can remember so many days sitting outside and hearing big commotions and the next thing you knew Billy would come running out the door. They'd just had an all-out fight.

"Billy picked a lot on Angela. I'm surprised she still talks to him to this day—he was so cruel to her. I remember one day Angela used his toothbrush—with his germ fetish, can you imagine what that did to Billy? We were sitting on the grass outside in front of his house. His daddy was in the house, they were fighting. His daddy pushed him through a closet door and Billy came running out. He'd hit Angela over the head with a vase." (According to Angela, it was a ceramic piggy bank.) "Billy was in a rage. I mean, he was just flipping out. All because she used his toothbrush.

"Billy told us the whole story. He said, 'She used my toothbrush and my daddy's trying to kill me. He threw me though a closet door!' But it happened so often, the actual incidents blur together.

"And Miz Cissy the supermom? Hmmph! Billy used to climb in and out his bedroom window; his mom never even knew when he was home and when he wasn't.

"And what Louie said about Billy, it's true. Billy was always there when somebody's relationship was going down. It was like that all the time. It wasn't just like that with me. Billy always came around when he knew there was a chance of a breakup. Billy always squeezed in. I mean, this was when we were in high school, when we were a close group. Billy was a real snake.

"It wasn't a coincidence, Billy was like that. That's why so many of the guys hated Billy, for that. Because he was like that and they knew it."

"Definitely, Billy was in love with himself, you can say that," Russell Ardneaux says.

"I think he loved himself more than he did any girl," Louie Valdin says in clarification.

"But this 'gay' shit?" Russell Ardneaux continues. "Billy Fontanille? That's the one thing that if you had to be jealous about him, it was he did have a touch with the girls. If there was one girl, and she was gonna like somebody, it was gonna be Billy. You know, he did well. So what the hell, they're gonna go around now saying he's gay?

"One thing, though: Billy liked to see confrontations between other people. He loved to instigate shit. Man, did he love to instigate the problems. Instigate, instigate. He loved doing those things. He likes to start shit and then stand back and watch it.

"He could hurt ya, now. This one friend of ours didn't have a father. And Billy was actually making fun of the boy for it. I mean, ridiculing him. Just push and push to where this boy wanted to kill Billy. I couldn't believe he could be that cruel.

"Anything he could do to belittle you, particularly in front of girls. Definitely. He loved to belittle you in front of girls. It's the same old thing. He belittles you in front of the girls, makes him like the big guy, he picks up on the girl.

"And he was *good* at it. *Damn,* he was good at it. He did it to me. But ya gotta understand, I like Billy, still. As many problems as I had with him,

I grew up with the boy, we were friends, we really were. And the boy's just got something about him. You can't help but like Billy."

"Billy drank back then, just like the rest of us," Chuck Cassard is saying. "The only thing was, you never shared his drink. You don't drink after him. Nobody. You wanna ruin his day? Grab his beer and drink some of it—'You can have the whole thing!' We used to do that to him all the time, just to aggravate him. I was on double dates with him, watched him kiss a girl and not drink after her. But Billy's girls, have you noticed? Everyone of 'em's young. A lot younger than him, 'cause girls his age could see through his bullshit.

"Oh, yeah—Billy's out for number one. And everything with him had to have a scheme. A racket. That was Billy. Billy was the idea man. Without a doubt. He made shit start. But he was older than everybody. That's the deal. That's why. And there were guys in the neighborhood who were his age. Timmy's brothers, right across the street, were his age. And kids at school. But manipulation is easier on the younger. The only one his age in that first group was 'Uncle' Ted. The close group; the Ratters.

"But you know how you hear that Kerry was boring and a wimp. And to some extent, depending on how you're looking at it, maybe to a large extent that's true. Spock, that's what we called him, those ears are weird, man. But personally, I believe Kerry's codependent. He needs somebody to push him. No new ideas generate from inside his soul.

"But Billy? Full of ideas and full of bull. Full of Billy. So maybe boring and a geek, I'd still rather be friends with Kerry. He wasn't that bad. I can understand his insecurities and things. And he never really did me anything. Never plotted against me or anything like that. But Billy? You wouldn't know where you stood with him day to day. How're you gonna be friends with somebody like that? You can't trust him. You can trust Kerry.

"But you know, there's something Timmy Arnold said to me once before, this was before all of this even came about. There were qualities that you liked in Billy, you couldn't put your finger on 'em, but a lot of his schemes were fun. And it was good to do 'em. But you never invited him anywhere, he'd always just show up. He'd just be there. Somewhere down the road, there would be Billy—with an idea that sounded good, so let's do it. Always scheming. But fun. Kerry was a follower.

"Make something out of this. You know how Billy won't stand and fight nobody? Absolutely chickenshit, never putting himself in a position where he might get hurt—and I mean never. A confirmed coward, no doubt, and everybody knows this, right? Even him.

"Well, I'm driving down Belle Chasse Highway about ninety. We're all drinking. They got that curve there by the high school? I'm driving, I guess the curve came up on me too fast. I never lost control, but here's the curve, here's the side of the road, it's like *ride* the side of the road the whole way around the curve. Light poles going right past, two or three of 'em, if anybody's elbow's out the window it's gone. The car's full of people. I had a big Impala. Got three people in the front seat, four in the backseat. Billy was sitting in the middle up front.

"So, I'm driving. I straighten it back up, nobody says a word. About thirty seconds later I look over at Billy and say, 'I almost lost it.' And he said, 'Nah, you had it all the way.' Now, most of the time you put Billy in jeopardy of getting hurt, he wouldn't like it. But he wasn't frightened of that. But I think as a group back then we were more cohesive, more of a conglomerate, that we really felt nobody could hurt us. And that we'd be like that forever."

4
Indictment

On February 6th, 1981, we moved into a 3 bedroom townhouse in Harvey. Being slightly pudgy in the belly, moving wasn't exactly easy, and the day we moved in I came down with a stomach virus that landed me in bed for a week. But you and I came through it okay.

It was April 1st that dad and I started our pre-natal training class at Baptist Hospital. Every Wednesday for the next four weeks we went to class and then dad and I would sit up and read all the booklets and information we would get from class. Usually during this time you'd really give some strong kicks and rolls. It was about this time that sleeping comfortably became almost impossible. But, every night I'd go to sleep holding my belly and loving you. . . .

—Journal of Janet Cannon Myers

*   *   *

"Deputy Chief Fields, Captain Claverie, Masson, and I started ongoing discussions pretty soon after they no-true-billed the boy."

The then lieutenant Vincent Lamia, the new commander of homicide, is a tall, blond, ruggedly handsome man who looks like he should be playing quarterback in the NFL instead of being the intelligent, articulate, well-read, well-groomed, sensitive, new-breed detective that he is. He is also now a captain as he reflects back on his early participation in the baseball bat murder.

"I'd read the file by then, had familiarized myself with the case as much as possible, while also breaking in a whole new job. I remember there was a fairly sizable pile of what we call 'dead file cases.' The unsolved crimes. And even though there had been an arrest made on the case, and was technically a closed case, it really wasn't. So, I got myself involved.

"Mostly what we're doing is, 'What about this?' And, 'Maybe this could've happened?' We were pretty much at an impasse, actually," Vince remembers.

But not long after the first of the year, Vince Lamia picked up a book at an airport to read on a flight to interview someone on another case. The book was *Fatal Vision,* by Joe McGinniss.

"I'm reading this and all of a sudden I start thinking, 'Since blood is the most relevant thing to solving the Fontanille-Myers puzzle, then reconstruction of the scene by blood would have to be where the answer lies.'

"I went to our criminalist and said, 'What we need is a blood spatter expert.' Singer mentioned Herb MacDonell as the 'best in the country.' Normally we would go through the FBI. But as soon as he said it I recognized the name. MacDonell had just been used to get an acquittal on the Aaron Mintz case in New Orleans. This wife was shot in bed and the defense claimed it was suicide, and it was the battle of experts and the state's expert lost.

"But I called the FBI anyway and they said, 'Yeah, Herb's the guy. He wrote the book on blood spatter.' "

JPSO CONTINUATION FORM   ITEM: B/14695/85

In speaking to First Assistant District Attorney Marion Edwards about the possibility of bringing in Mr. MacDonell to examine the evidence, he (Edwards) agreed that MacDonell's expert opinion could strengthen the case and possibly result in an indictment.

Lt. Vincent Lamia

In the pecking order of the District Attorney's Office in 1985, Bill Hall was a bit above the midmanagement notch. As a supervisor in Felony, the highest category of attorneys working for the DA, he was assigned three of the then fifteen divisions of state court, each with an assistant district attorney. He would assist them with difficult cases and give them authority in plea-bargain situations. If he had a problem he would go to Bob Pitre or Marion Edwards, the two supervisors of the supervisors. Anything bigger than that would go to John Mamoulides. By 1985 Bill had been with the DA's Office for fourteen years, a supervisor since January 1982.

Sometime early in the winter of 1986, Bill Hall began his role in the saga of the baseball bat murder.

"The case was just sitting around and it was personally bothering me. So one day I'm at lunch with Mamoulides and he's talking about the case, I said, 'John, look, this case worries the shit out of me, too. If you need some help with this damn thing, if you want me to get personally involved, I'll do it. I know it's a real can of worms, but I'll be glad to spend some extra time on it.' Should have known better—I was in the Army, never volunteer for anything. Because John went and took me up on it. So I started reviewing everything that had been done. The prior grand jury testimony. The police report. The entire record."

"I'll love Kerry Myers till the day I die," says Penny Price Fox, eyes straight on, without even a blink, but they're soft, liquid, glistening blue-green heart-and-soul window eyes, hiding nothing. Asking everything.

"I seriously considered marrying him after Janet died. I love him so much, I could not bear his heartbreak. Gerald and I had divorced and I wasn't interested in meeting anybody else. And I knew that Kerry would provide for me and I knew that he would be a good father. I considered it for a long time. He would take me and Ryan and my two boys out to dinner.

"I had never had a crush on him when we were younger. I didn't even notice what he looked like then. I just liked Kerry as a friend. He was my friend. I never considered dating him.

"It was around the fall of '84 when we started seeing more of each other. It was before the holidays and just before or after the grand jury didn't indict Billy.

"He would come by the endodontist's office where I worked. He used to come by and ask if he could take me to lunch. My boss, who I was friends with, would laugh and say, 'Are y'all going to bring the bat or is he going to pick it up?' You know, it was humor, but I didn't appreciate it. I mean, I didn't think I needed to be scared, it's not like Kerry would hurt *me*. But people were always making these really sick jokes.

"Mostly we went places to eat. I was strapped for money. We used to joke with each other about marriage. 'Let's get married and the hell with 'em all.' Wanting to be in love. Wanting somebody. If I'd given him more encouragement I'm sure he would've fallen in love with me like all the rest. And maybe he did.

"But I know like at times when my heart was broken and my life was in turmoil and I was scared to be alone and I just wanted somebody to take care of me, it was like, 'I just think he's so nice, and he didn't kill Janet. He's been through so much and somebody should just take care of him.' That's how I thought about it. And I did think alot about it.

"But when it came down to it, it would've been like kissing your brother—we were *friends;* he was far more of a big brother to me than Mike ever was."

JPSO CONTINUATION FORM   ITEM: B/14695/85

Lieutenant Lamia consulted with Captain August Claverie and Deputy Chief Fields concerning the matter. Both agreed that MacDonell's expert opinion could strengthen the case. Lieutenant Lamia was authorized to contact Mr. MacDonell and arrange a consultation.

On 1 July 1985, Lieutenant Lamia contacted Mr. MacDonell and after providing some basic details about the case, he felt that a possible conclusion could be reached concerning the perpetrator of the homicide.

"Kerry's lawyer did nothing for him, but Kerry did nothing for himself," Jake Hahn of Air-Dreco is saying.

"You know, you see grandstanding on TV all the time, you see it in almost all criminal trials. You can convince a whole bunch of people when they put the camera in your face and you say, 'They don't prosecute him? I'm gonna kill him!' Then everybody believes this guy is mad. He is pissed off that this guy's killed his wife, and if the jury don't get 'im, he's gonna get 'im. I mean, you'd have everybody on your side going, 'I hope they burn him.'

"But we saw nothing. I saw a guy walk in front of the camera with just no emotion. Or smiling? You know? We're all going, 'Man, don'tcha think you'd get a press conference or do something where you'd say, "Not only do I want justice, I want this guy burned, I want him in the electric chair." ' I mean, some real anger.

"But we didn't see any of that. What we see is Pat Fanning going on TV and saying all this, and we're saying, 'Man, you'd better get'—we're telling him here—'you'd better get in there!' Yet it's like he's *disengaged*."

"Yes! Kerry was angry," Penny says, as if she would have accompanied it with a stamp of a foot if both of hers weren't tucked demurely and quite fetchingly beneath her on the sofa in the living room of her upper-middle-class suburban custom-deluxe.

"When I was with him he said he wanted to *kill* Bill. He said it several times, 'I want to kill him. I just want to get him.' He said it hundreds of times; but first he wanted to ask him, 'Why?' He couldn't think of a motive either. 'Why? Why? Why? Why did he do this to us?' He would say it over and over again.

"When we talked, and it never failed, he had a new plan or idea of ways—something they could do—to get something going on getting Billy. Proving his innocence. And Billy's guilt."

JPSO CONTINUATION FORM   ITEM: B/14695/85
Sergeant Masson made arrangements to meet with Mr. MacDonell in Corning, New York on 6 August 1985. Sergeant Masson was to obtain the evidence from the Clerk of Courts Office, all reports and scene photographs concerning the Myers homicide.

Sergeant Masson also made arrangements with Mr. Bill Hall and Henry Sullivan, Jefferson Parish District Attorney's Office, to accompany the former to Corning, New York. Hall and Sullivan would provide the scene photographs and case report.

On 5 August 1985, Sergeant Masson arrived at the Clerk of Courts Office and obtained from Deputy Clerk of Courts, Paul Boudreaux . . . articles of evidence.

On the afternoon of August 5, 1985, Sergeant Masson received a telephone call from Mr. MacDonell, who then informed the detective that the appointment scheduled for the following day would have to be postponed until the last week of the month.

However, Lieutenant Vincent Lamia would have to take the place of Sergeant Masson, because Masson resigned from the department effective August 17. Masson left the force on his own accord. But it was widely speculated that if it hadn't been for the baseball bat murder he probably would have remained on the force. According to one veteran cop, Masson "looked like a man who's had the rug pulled out from under him."

"I took a lot of abuse over this. But I sleep right at night. Lemme tell you, I told Ernie Barrow and Jack Rau both, right in front of Kerry, 'Hey, I don't have any evidence against Kerry, but I'll tell you what, if I find something, I'll do what I can to get him in the electric chair, too.'

To say that Bob Masson, who eight years after the murder teaches math at one of New Orleans's larger Catholic high schools, is defensive on the subject is an understatement. However, to say that he is insincere is a lie.

"I told Kerry that right up front before he gave the statement to me. Jack Rau was there then too. I said, 'If you're lying, and we find it, I hope you burn.' But we never found it. Not while I was there."

JPSO CONTINUATION FORM   ITEM: B/14695/85

Lieutenant Lamia made arrangements with Mr. MacDonell for the consultation to take place in Corning, New York on 27 August '85. Lieutenant Lamia contacted Mr. Hall and Mr. Sullivan and arrangements were made for them to accompany the former. . . .

On the morning of 27 August '85, Lieutenant Lamia, Mr. Hall and Mr. Sullivan met with Mr. MacDonell at the latter's lab. . . . Beginning at approximately 10:00 A.M. (Eastern Daylight Time), Mr. MacDonell was briefed relative to the incident. He was shown a rough sketch of the scene, and allowed to view the case photographs.

Mr. MacDonell then examined the following articles of evidence (in order of appearance):

Article #26—Fontanille's blue jeans
Article #29—Fontanille's shoes
Article #25—Fontanille's shirt
Article #24—Fontanille's sweater
Article #23—Kerry Myers' shoes
Article #20—Kerry Myers' pants
Article #18—Kerry Myers' shirt
Article #16—Janet Myers' leotards
Article #15—Janet Myers' shorts
Article #14—Janet Myers' blouse

The examination by Mr. MacDonell was with both naked eye and microscope. Based on the evidence examined by Mr. MacDonell, the following results were noted. . . .

At the end of the examination which took approximately seven (7) hours, Mr. MacDonell gave Lieutenant Lamia a preliminary opinion as follows: If the areas of blood like spots mentioned above (and highlighted by Mr. MacDonell) are in fact the victim's blood type, then Fontanille (or someone wearing Fontanille's clothing) was in close proximity to the victim at the time of impact.

Lt. Vincent Lamia

"John Mamoulides kept up with this case more than most," remembers Bill Hall, who has much the appearance and manner of an Air Force Ground Officer—sandy, close-cropped hair, squared face, medium height, medium build, officious.

"One thing about Mamoulides, he is tight as far as money goes. He won't even put hubcaps or whitewalls on his car because of that; he does not give raises. But this case? Whatever we wanted. He said, 'Whatever it takes, do what you've got to do.' This case bothered him on a personal basis, he was troubled by it. The fact that we weren't moving, weren't getting a resolution of it. On a human level."

JPSO CONTINUATION FORM   ITEM: B/14695/85

On 9/23/85, Lieutenant Lamia received from Ms. Dixon the serologist report which was dated 9/17/85. According to the report, the reexamination of the evidence revealed the following:

Article #24—(The blue pullover sweater belonging to Fontanille.) Human blood was present on the sweater. Further analysis proved to be inconclusive.

Article #25—(The white pin-striped shirt belonging to Fontanille.) Human blood was present on the shirt. The stain is consistent with ABO type "B" activity. (Fontanille's blood type is "B.")

Article #26—(The blue jeans belonging to Fontanille.) Human blood was found to be present on the jeans. In addition to type "B" blood being present, there was also discovered type "A" blood. This type "A" blood was found below the front, right knee area. It should be noted that the victim's blood type is "A."

Article #29—(The tennis shoes belonging to Fontanille) Human blood was present on both the right and left shoe. The stains on the right shoe were consistent with type "B" activity. The stains on the right shoe (rear aspect) were consistent with type "A" and "B" activity.

A copy of Ms. Dixon's 9/17/85 Serological Report will be attached to and should be considered a part of this report.

After living with Clifford and Marva for about a year and a half following the murder, Kerry Myers, who was not having to make rent or mortgage payments or pay for utilities, groceries, or day care and was earning a good deal more money than he had when Janet was alive, was able to make a hefty down payment on a modestly palatial home on Breckinridge, in a newer and ritzier development across Lapalco from Terrytown.

He brought Ryan with him. He did not bring Sarah.

"I was really upset about Sarah," Tammy DuBuc says. "Kerry just totally rejected this child—still to this day you never hear anything about Sarah, it's all Ryan. And the last time I saw Janet, just a few days before she was killed, she came over to make sure I had a place for Sarah because she was looking to go back to work soon. She said she wanted me watching her little girl. And I promised her that there would always be a place for Sarah and Ryan here with me. I promised her that. It was the last thing I said to her.

"Why is he rejecting this baby? Ryan for a long time referred to Sarah as 'my friend Sarah.' He didn't even realize this was his sister. He'd say, 'Can we go visit my friend Sarah?' I'm thinking like, 'Your friend? that's your *sister*.' That really upset me, Kerry treating her like that. Why? So you get to thinking . . . ?"

JPSO CONTINUATION FORM   ITEM: B/14695/85

On 27 December '85, Lieutenant Lamia received a preliminary report from Mr. MacDonell. The report indicated that additional information would be necessary before a final conclusion could be determined. In particular, Mr. MacDonell needed to know the exact location of the victim's blood on Fontanille's blue jeans (Article #26 above) and Fontanille's tennis shoes (Article #29 above) to determine if a pattern was present. Mr. MacDonell also sent twenty-eight (28) 3½ x 5″ color photographs of Article #26 (Fontanille's blue jeans) and two (2) photostatic copies of Article #26.

A copy of the preliminary report dated 12/19/85 will be attached to and should be considered a part of this report.

Penny continues her memories of Kerry in those days and of the story he stuck to. "Most people were afraid or too polite, I guess, to ask Kerry questions. Not me. I asked him about the murder and the case everytime we were together. Every time I was with him I asked.

"I'd say, 'Kerry, what happened when you walked in?' And he consistently, always told me the same thing. He walked in. He turned around to shut the door and he heard Billy say, 'Kerry!' He turned, put up his arm, he hit him with the bat. The next thing he knew they were in the den fighting. They fought off and on and he heard Janet moaning. He asked, 'Where's Janet?' Billy said, 'She's tied up in the bedroom.' He said, 'Where are the kids?' 'They're in their rooms. Ryan's tied up.' He said Billy was hitting him over the head with things. He said, 'I heard Janet moaning for a long time.' But he didn't know how long.

"I said, 'Well, do you think it was like hours? And he said, 'I don't know because I kept going in and out of consciousness.'

"He told me that every time he tried to get up to check on Janet, Billy hit him. And he kept hitting him. He said, 'I was in pain. I broke my arm. I knew it was broken.'

"I didn't push too hard, because when he talked about it he cried. He would start crying, then I would start crying. He cried. We cried together. We would just start talking about it and he would sit there and he'd go, 'I don't know why. I just don't know why. I just want to ask Billy why.'

"He never talked about suspecting Janet of having an affair. And Kerry never would've cheated on her or anybody. He's a one-woman man."

JPSO CONTINUATION FORM   ITEM: B/14695/86

On 7 January '86 at 9:05 A.M., Lieutenant Lamia received the Serological report from Ms. Dixon which was dated 1/3/86. The report answered all questions submitted by Mr. MacDonell as per his 12/19/85 preliminary report. In addition to the report, Lieutenant Lamia received numerous 8″ x 10″ color photographs of Articles #26 and 29 which help document and support the 1/3/86 lab report. Lieutenant Lamia also signed the Chain of Custody report and received Articles #26 and 29 from Ms. Dixon.

A copy of the serological Report dated 1/3/86 will be attached to and should be considered a part of this report.

"Kerry took me to the house before he moved in," recalls Penny. "And he told me, 'This is going to be Sarah's room.' I said, 'When are you going to bring Sarah home?' He said, 'I don't know. I'm just not ready.' And I said, 'Kerry, she's not even going to know that you're her father.' He said, 'Oh, I visit her almost every day.' I said, 'But visiting her is not going to let her adjust to you being her father. She's going to want to go back to your parents' house.'

"It was weird the way he constantly took Ryan everywhere he went, but yet never Sarah—you never saw him with her. There was never any real emotional contact between he and Sarah. I never saw him pick her up and hug her or kiss her. Never. I know one time we went out to dinner with he and Ryan and I asked him how come he didn't bring Sarah? And he just said, 'Because I didn't want to.'

"That's when I started thinking about just who that child's father really is, you know."

JPSO CONTINUATION FORM   ITEM: B/14695/86
On 5 February 86, Lieutenant Lamia received a report from Mr. MacDonell outlining his opinion based on the analysis of evidence and information provided. Mr. MacDonell concluded that William Fontanille, or whoever was wearing his (Fontanille) jeans, was in the immediate vicinity of the victim's head when she was beaten. The victim's blood on Article #26 was the result of impact spatter completely consistent with the beating the victim sustained.

A copy of the report of 1/29/86, will be attached to and should be considered a part of this report.

"They asked me if I'd mind getting off the case and letting Bill Hall present it to the grand jury. That maybe I'd gotten too close to it. They thought I was convinced that Myers did it," Marion Edwards explains without a trace of rancor.

"Which wasn't the case. There were just a lot of unanswered questions as far as I was concerned. Frankly, there were so many that I believed you couldn't get a jury of any kind to come to a consensus about it; grand jury, petit jury—there just wasn't any way. Because the things that were obvious to me were going to be obvious to anyone."

"I'll tell ya what I think bothered me the most and is maybe the first thing that gave me any real doubt at all," Jake Hahn announces after moments of reflective silence.

"Kerry didn't seem to give a shit about this little girl. Never talked about her. And I would ask. I remember telling him one time, I said, 'Boy, I'm out of line here maybe but, Kerry, Ryan lives with you?' 'Yeah.' 'Why doesn't

Sarah?' 'My grandmother's taking care of her.' He never answered my question. This is his daughter, the last part of his wife, the last—why wouldn't you . . . ? I got a divorce, and I *wanted* my kids.''

As it had been apparent for some weeks that something was going on with the case, what with the flurry of activity at both the DA's Office and the Sheriff's Office, Jack Rau informed Clifford, and then Kerry, that because of his close personal relationship, both social and professional, with several of the higher-ranking people at the DA's Office, it would be best that he withdraw from the case.

"That didn't bother me any," Cliff Myers says. "As far as I was concerned, Jack was just part of the *same clique*—God rest his soul.

"So, I'm thinking let's start looking for a hotshot from New Orleans, too. I suggested several names. But Kerry didn't want to listen. He wanted this guy Wiley Beevers. A friend of ours works over there at the courthouse and Beevers handled a case for some of the employees of the courthouse against the judges so they could be put on civil service, so she mentioned it. And she told Kerry the name and everything else. Kerry, I guess, decided he was just going to go with him. I went over there with Kerry the first time—I didn't think that much of him. He was bragging about how many murder cases he'd handled and everything else—he used to be a big-time federal prosecutor or something like that.

"But at the time I said, 'Well, hell, if Kerry likes him, wants to stay with him.' I mean, they weren't about to indict Kerry or anything like that, so where's the harm?''

"In a case like this you really get a lot of calls, mostly cranks," Chief Fields explains.

"But about the time in '86 when they were taking the case back to the grand jury, there was a lotta news coverage, I got more than one anonymous phone call suggesting that the baby girl was Bill's. One in particular was from a white male, young, sounded like he knew the people in this circle pretty well. I thought that call wasn't a crank, that it was significant. But what of itself can the police do with something like that? Get a court order to determine the parentage of the daughter of the accuser? On what grounds? DA'd hit the ceiling and a judge would probably laugh you out of court.''

The DA's office also gets its share of phone calls from the citizenry at large—the vast majority of them also cranks. However, Peggy Senat, who lived across the street from the Myerses on Litchwood Lane, is by no stretch of the imagination a crank. And after waiting two years for someone from either the police or the District Attorney's Office to come and interview her, Mrs. Senat decided to take the initiative and made a phone call to the DA's Office. When she told a receptionist the nature of her call, she was patched through to someone who identified himself only as an "investigator for the District Attorney's Office, what can I help you with?" and who then, after listening for only a few moments to her story, said: "Ma'am, we appreciate your calling, but we know all about their fighting. All couples fight. But I have your name and number and I'm sure someone will get back to you."

"When I went into that grand jury," Bill Hall says, "based on Herb MacDonell's representations to me that the man wearing those jeans was the man who committed the murder, and they were Fontanille's jeans, I had enough evidence based on everything else. And the fact that we had nothing to point to Myers. I went in there with the idea that we *are* going to get an indictment. I went in there as a tough prosecutor, and put it on that way. No nonsense. 'Watch what I'm gonna show you.' And that grand jury didn't bat an eye. I played the tape for them. We had MacDonell do his thing; get on one knee and demonstrate how the spatters hit the leg, hit the wall, and obviously it was a right-handed guy."

"All Herb really would say, though, was that the *person* wearing these jeans was in the *vicinity* of the impact of the bat against Janet's head," adds the always rock-solid and correct Assistant District Attorney Art Lentini in a display of "abundance of caution."

"Typical expert," Bill Hall agrees. "Has all the shit in his head and knows he can do the job, but he won't lay it all out to you. He just asks a few questions, bullshits around, and has another glass of wine—and the next morning we're wondering if this guy is even gonna come in. He did. He came into that grand jury and just zapped 'em. Came across as *the man.*"

It should be noted that in the vast canon of legal literature there is an anonymous quotation which has survived since at least 1933, and is today used in lectures or seminars on the effective use of grand juries by prosecutors. It is: "A grand jury would indict a ham sandwich." Legal scholars have guessed that it is attributable to "a disgruntled defense attorney."

On Friday afternoon, May 16, 1986, the grand jury deliberated less than an hour after hearing two days of testimony and indicted Bill Fontanille for first-degree murder. The fact that he was also indicted on two counts of attempted murder (for the assaults upon Ryan and Kerry) provided the "special circumstances" necessary for the State to seek the death penalty, which it stipulated it would do.

"The day they did the indictment, it was like 'Hit the air-raid shelters!' Assistant DAs were taking four-hour lunches and getting sick—nobody wanted this piece of shit to try," says Pat Fanning with a certain combination of glee and ruefulness.

"Now, they might all sit around the hallways and tell ya, 'Aw, man, fuck Fontanille—he got arrested, his statement doesn't hold up, there's some evidence against him, it's a horrible crime, charge him.' But then when it's 'Okay, you try it,' 'Ahh, now wait, I'm a little busy this month.' There were people bailing out. Hitting the lifeboats."

"It's my division, I've got it," says Paul Connick, first cousin to Harry Connick, Jr., this generation's legitimate boy wonder of the music world, and the nephew of Harry Connick, Sr., the district attorney for the City of New Orleans.

"It wasn't like it was routinely assigned to Division K, though, I seem to remember. Like maybe it was supposed to be assigned to another division—I don't know, I think maybe Chuck Credo should've gotten it or had it there at first or something.

"But I remember them saying to me, 'You want this case? It's going to be a pain in the ass.' 'Yeah, I'll take it.' So we're rolling along and then my supervisor, Mike Grosz, said he didn't want it to stay in his division—I mean, *nobody* wanted it."

"I thought I was going to get stuck with it," Bill Hall says with a laugh. "I told 'em, 'Look, I'm kind of busy over here.' "

"So I talked to Art about it, and Art said, 'It sounds interesting, I'll get in and help you with it a little,' " continues Paul Connick, who is also in private practice with Art Lentini.

"So we start working together, and when Art got in a little bit he got sucked in all the way. Which I knew he would. Then we just handled it like any other case. We get into it. There were some preliminary motions and discovery with the defense. Started interviewing witnesses. Lining them up. It took a long time to bring it to trial; scheduling expert witnesses was a big problem."

"My problem was when Richard Boyd came out in the paper with what I thought was a chickenshit hatchet job about my brother being in the DA's Office and maybe Fontanille's getting 'special consideration,' " Pat Fanning says as he starts to bristle again.

"I got really irritated about it. Because the DA's Office then took a hard line on it. And a very unfair hard line. They said, 'Look, Pat, any conversations we have from now on we're gonna have to have witnesses there, and be on the record.'

"And I said, 'Man, that's bullshit, why can't we handle our business like we handle any other case? Nobody's done anything wrong. I've never asked you for any special considerations. You haven't given any special considerations. It's a nutbuster case that everybody's struggling with and doing the best they can, and fuck Richard Boyd and the *Pica-yune.'*

"Well, their attitude basically at that time was that Harry Lee still thought he needed to avoid doing anything to stir up the *Picayune* against him any more than they already were.

"The next time I saw Billy, I said, 'It looks like me representing you is going to have a negative effect on you. The Sheriff's Office is tightening up, and you're not going to get the concessions from the DA's Office that you would if you had another lawyer—and when I say concessions, I mean they are not going to do the routine things for you that they would do for anybody else because I'm your lawyer. They're afraid it might look bad, so instead you're gonna start getting unfavorable treatment if I stay on.'

"He was a little upset about it, and I said, 'I really don't think I oughta stay on the case.' He and his family said, 'No, you gotta stay on the case.' I said, 'Look, I know we've developed a relationship and you people have confidence in me and I understand that and I appreciate that you think I'm a good lawyer—but if I am, I'm not the only one around. I'll certainly see to it that you get someone who does well by the case.'

"I didn't do it lightly, and I really didn't do it that willingly, because it's a scary situation for a guy who's now facing a murder one indictment and the chair to suddenly have to break in a new relationship with a new attorney and facing trial soon. But I said it's just really better for me to get out. And there was some money to be made in the case at that point—I mean, nobody knew it was going to drag out like it did.

"What I believed this case needed was a special kind of bulldog. I sent 'em to Nick Noriea. Nick and I had been officemates when we were prosecutors. He's just a tough little son of a bitch. Nick and I tried a lot of cases together, and I had a lotta, lotta respect for him. He hadn't been doing too much criminal work since going into private practice. Yet I just knew that Nick was gonna get immersed in this up to his ass and really fight for the guy; and that's what Billy needed."

Put expensive, conservative charcoal pin-striped suits on a bulldog, give him an encyclopedic brain with microchip recall, a rapid-fire, street-smart, impatient, I-want-it-yesterday bark with a vocabulary to match any level of society at will, a Price-Waterhouse accountant's thoroughness for detail, send him off when he's coming of age to play football for Bear Bryant at the University of Alabama as a defensive back with the competitiveness to eat fire and the combativeness to spit it back, and then send all of that to a pretty good law school, and you've got Nick Noriea, a full partner well before he turned forty at Gainsburgh, Benjamin, Fallon, David & Ates, one of the largest and most prestigious of New Orleans law firms.

"Me and one of my law partners went to visit Bill over in the JPCC. I wanted to take Irv Washauer, because he had prosecuted and he had a good feel for whether or not somebody is telling the truth.

"We spent probably an hour, hour and a half, and recorded Bill's first conversation. Irv believed him, and so did I. There were a few things that we questioned. That kind of didn't make sense, but then again, too, I've never been stabbed in the back four or five times. I don't know what I would do in that situation. There's an old saying, 'Money makes people do funny things.' I guess getting stabbed in the back can make you do funny things too.

"So, not ever having been in a hostage-type situation or stabbed in the back, some of the stuff that didn't sound completely accurate that Bill told us I kind of let go—I didn't *not* believe him, but I wasn't completely convinced. But then never having been in that position, who am I to say? Human nature's a funny thing.

"But Irv and I both agreed that Bill's story was basically the truth. And obviously we both agreed that if he said what he said it was consistent that he would act the way he did, which wouldn't make sense to somebody that wasn't stabbed or wasn't held a hostage."

"I've got to say it in his defense, we discussed the area of plea-bargaining this thing, but Mr. Noriea wasn't interested. And, candidly, Paul Connick wasn't interested. He kept going up to New York to see this blood-spatter expert. The problem was we didn't have enough blood."

Judge Alvin Rudy Eason, now retired, is a tall, imposing man, completely bald. He has a wooden leg, because of diabetes, and various other ailments, all of a serious nature. In the last few weeks of his almost two decades on the bench of the 24th Judicial District Court for the State of Louisiana, some seven years after the murder of Janet Myers, with his wooden appendage propped up on the big desk in his most commodious office, Judge Eason talks about his lengthy participation in the baseball bat murder case. It is the case he chose to mark in his retirement feature story as the single most memorable and intriguing—and still puzzling—case of his career.

"Nick's a fighter," the judge says. "He never gives up a fighting hope. I don't think Nick Noriea would allow himself—if he felt that way, that his man did the killing, I think he would've gotten out of the case. He's basically so honest.

"I believe that Nick is just that sincere. 'Course, that may be sincerity born of his self-esteem, if not egotism, but we've all got to have that."

"By putting certain things in motion, that momentum will carry forever. Bob Masson decided very early that Fontanille did it. This is a nightmare of a crime scene," says Nick Noriea in his twenty-eighth-floor corner office in the Entergy Building in downtown New Orleans. Two walls are nothing but plate glass, revealing a spectacular panorama of the city and the crescent of the Mississippi River.

As Mr. Noriea continues, the sarcasm drips until it's a torrent.

" 'It's early in the morning, I want to go home. I don't feel like traipsing through any more blood. I don't feel like looking at a body bag. And the asshole, the violent bastard that did this, we've got cold in the emergency room. Hooray! For me.

" 'Now, if we really had to work this one up? Man, can you imagine—we'd have to take the Sheetrock out, we'd have to remove all the carpet and vinyl tile in the house and would have to mark and label every garment wherever it is. Golly, that's a thousand pieces of clothes in that thing! Also, we really oughta take out the kitchen-sink trap and see what was washed down the sink. And the same for the bathrooms. And we really oughta see if anything's in the washing machine. Golly, look at all the work we have to do if we'd have to figure out. Aw, boys, take it easy, Uncle Bob's got it straight—Fontanille did it. Let's go home. Take the yellow tape down, let's go.' " The crescendo. And then the end piece:

"He's a big hero. 'Masson's smart. Case closed.' Talk about saving the department time so they can go out and investigate one of these really unsolved crimes that comes on Channel 6's *Unsolved Mysteries* every night. Masson's a genius. He's got this one under control. Now we can look for a real complicated murder scene. We can spend our time there and solve crime in the Parish.

"Once you paint yourself in a corner, you're not going to get out unless you walk through wet paint. Nobody likes to walk through wet paint."

Wednesday, July 3, 1986   THE TIMES-PICAYUNE
Suspect: Unaware woman was dead
By Richard Boyd
West Bank bureau

Two men fought, rested and watched television, talked about domestic problems, then fought again while the wife of one lay beaten to death in another room of her home, the family friend accused of her 1984 slaying told authorities.

William A. Fontanille, 30, formerly of Gretna . . . in a statement released by prosecutors to his attorney, said Kerry Myers attacked him with a knife when he arrived at the Myers home, and that they fought for hours. Fontanille says he did not see Mrs. Myers during this time, and did not know she had been killed.

The prosecution handed over the statement Tuesday in District Court in Gretna in response to a defense motion. . . .

On Tuesday, Judge Alvin "Rudy" Eason denied a defense motion for a bond hearing for Fontanille, who has been held without bond in

*the Parish jail since May 21. But Eason ordered the Indigent Defender
Board to spend up to $1,500 for the services of Judith Bunker of
Orlando, Fla., the defense's blood-spatter expert.*

*The Orleans Parish district attorney's office called Bunker as its
expert in the murder trial of furniture store executive Aaron Mintz,
while the defense used [Herbert] MacDonell.*

"I can't remember how many times I went to Orlando," booms Nick
Noriea.

"But I remember the first time I went down there—I'd spoken on the
phone a couple of times with Judith, she was somewhat delighted to be
able to—quote-unquote—'testify against Herb MacDonell' again because
she felt she got the raw end of the deal when Aaron Mintz was found not
guilty. So that kind of inspired her a little bit to *want* to help. Which is
what you really needed because you've got such a short period of time
between May of '86 and an October trial date.

"And time's getting on. We had to get the photographs—the crime scene
photographs. We had to pay the Sheriff's Office a thousand bucks for that.
I don't know what the normal procedure over there is, or if it's even legal.
But I needed the photographs—one thousand, one hundred and eighty-six
dollars. It wouldn't do me any good to go to Orlando, Florida, to meet with
Judith Bunker, probably on a very short list of maybe two people who are
the best blood spatter and crime scene reconstructionists in the country
who ain't a prostitute—first thing she's gonna say is, 'Lemme see what
you've got.' Why it wasn't part of routine discovery, I don't know. A *lot*
of odd things happened in this case. But I did get 'em with the fifteen
hundred from the Indigent Defender Board (IDB), I thought that was a
nice touch.

"Anyway, Judy told me, 'Nick, you're probably going to need a serologist.' I said, 'You got any suggestions?' She got me Ray Grimsbo, who used
to be the head of the Oregon State Police Lab, but he's in Portland, Oregon.
So Judy kind of coordinated the two things. She gave me a crash course
in blood spatter, she teaches the Florida State Police.

"She studied with Herb MacDonell. He's supposed to be the 'father of
blood spatter.' But now she's outdoing the teacher, a lot of people say.

"But Ray Grimsbo said, 'Nick, you oughta talk to Dr. Henry Lee in
Connecticut. Henry would *really* be good.' He gave me some of Henry's
articles. Some heavy-duty high-tech stuff, like distinguishing thirty or
forty different things with one drop of blood. But after we got all the lab
reports from the DA's Office, it was almost as if the three bloods *were
different colors*—one was A, one was B, and one was O. So Ray said, 'You
don't really need a lot of in-depth enzyme analysis to see who's who and
what's what. Is this your B or is this my B? This is a serologist's dream.'
So Ray said, 'You don't really need that, but Henry's the best there is and

he's a straight shooter. He might have some insight to the case that you might not get from Judy or I.' But we never could hook up schedule-wise; kept playing phone tag. It just wasn't meant to be."

"It's funny, right after I got the case, I run into Ernie Barrow, and he says, 'Watch Kerry, he lies. For no reason, he'll lie,' " Paul Connick says, and then adds, "I'll always remember that."

Then a pause, a glance at his partners, and, "There was something about Kerry Myers that was not right. And there were some things we didn't feel comfortable with, but there wasn't anything glaring that we could point to. We talked to people who said—I mean, we had people calling me—we had the roommate at Nicholls State saying Janet came in with black eyes and that kind of thing. And we'd say, 'Man, this doesn't sound right.' "

"But he always denied it," Art Lentini says.

"And the time she fell and broke her nose," continues Paul. "It was, 'Oh, she tripped and fell.' You know, 'Man, something's not right.' He put her out of the car on the highway. All of these things were just there, and he would always have an explanation."

On Wednesday, July 31, upon a motion by Nick Noriea, Judge Alvin Rudy Eason ruled that the State must provide the defense a copy of the 911 tape.

Nick was also successful in his media management. Richard Boyd's story of the 911-tape ruling included the insight that Nick "wants the tape to show that the incident could not have happened as claimed." And that the tape "implicates the victim's husband."

"At the time, one of the paralegals that was working here was a nurse, Lydia Shumock," Nick Noriea is explaining.

"We were doing medical malpractice cases, and you've almost got to be a doctor or a nurse to read hospital records. I said, 'Here, look through this. I wanna know, number one, if there's anything in any of these records to indicate or would be consistent with Fontanille being stabbed at four or five o'clock in the afternoon and not getting to a hospital until two or three in the morning. Number two, I wanna know if there's anything in the records that indicates somebody had a scratching fight with Janet Myers; or conversely, did anyone *not* have a scratching fight with Janet Myers. Number three, I wanna know how bad the kid's hurt.'

"She took all the records, it was three volumes, the State produced them in discovery; she came back and said, 'Kerry's all scratched up on the forearms. Bill's not scratched at all.'

"I even remember telling her, 'I will *kill you* if there's one word in the record that indicates Bill was scratched. I mean, just *one* word in *any* of his records.' I don't want *one word* that fits the description of scratch, abrasion, or whatever.' We got Webster's plus a couple of medical dictionaries and got *every* word that *any* doctor or nurse could *possibly* say was consistent with a scratch or abrasion.

" 'Lydia, not *one* word. Or else we're in big trouble.'

" 'Nick, it's not in there.'

"I said, 'Well, that's good.' And then she said, 'I know an emergency room doctor that I'll talk to about these records.'

"She came back to me and said, 'His hematocrit being this, taking into account the fluids he got at Charity, it's consistent with him being stabbed at four or five in the afternoon as opposed to thirty minutes before he got to the hospital.' *'All right!'* "

5
Preparation

By the beginning of May, the "up" feeling that I had experienced for the most part started to disappear. I started to get uncomfortable. It was difficult to breathe, the weather was getting hot and I really started to "blossom" in the belly area.

Through the next couple of weeks I fixed up your nursery. During this time your dad was refinishing my baby chest for you. At times I had to push him, but I wanted it to be finished when you arrived.

—Journal of Janet Cannon Myers

* * *

"It was always she'd throw the first blow," Paul Connick remembers. "He'd hit back just to protect himself. That's basically what he said. Kerry didn't deny that with us. We asked, 'Look, were there any other incidents where you would beat her?' And we talked to his friends about it, and anybody else that would call we'd try to follow up—'What do you know?'

"Most of it was, 'I can't say for sure, but . . .' Stuff you couldn't use in court. All hearsay and not supported by evidence. I heard about them driving on the interstate, she's punching on him, and he put her out. I asked him and he said she was causing a dangerous situation, his little brother and a nephew were in the backseat, he told her to get out knowing that one of the other cars would pick her up.

"We heard she was the type that would jump him. If something would go wrong, she'd start popping him. These were his friends and they obviously wanted to testify for him. So we tried to look at it from the angle 'Did he beat on her regularly?' We'd talk to him; and of course he'd deny it. He said there would be fights, and there would be physical stuff, but most of his was more restraining her attacks on him. That was what he told us. And nobody—not even Nick—could ever find anybody that could say they actually saw Kerry beat the hell out of her.

"And him, he said, 'It was the best the marriage had ever been.' The best relationship they had was the six months before the baby was born. The baby kind of brought them back together. That's what he told us.

"And we had no one to refute that. The friends all agreed that while there had been turbulence in the marriage, it had greatly improved over the last year or so."

In the summer of 1986, Madeleine Landrieu was a law clerk at Gains-burgh, Benjamin, Fallon, David & Ates, heading into her last year of law school. At which time the daughter of Moon Landrieu, the highly regarded liberal, reformist former mayor of New Orleans and member of President Carter's cabinet, would be going into the Law Clinic, a pro bono legal shop; the Loyola Law School is one of the few in the country that allows law students to actually handle tough cases, even murder cases. Which was why the sister of Mary Landrieu, the current secretary-treasurer of the State of Louisiana, was assigned to gain criminal defense experience work-ing with Nick, thereby beginning her first association with the baseball bat murder. It would prove to be a fortuitous happenstance, even if it at times it would also prove to be exhausting and apparently endless.

In those early weeks, one of her more important roles was that of buffer between the very focused, often abrasive Nick Noriea and everyone else.

"You know Madeleine's a Landrieu and her heart's in the right place when it comes to the downtrodden. I'm not being critical or complimen-tary, it's just a fact. Madeleine gave good balance to the whole thing, because she was a good translator between Bill and I.

"I really didn't need to deal that much with Bill after hearing his story. I had to deal with these experts, because this was an experts' trial. It wasn't an alibi case where I had to go and check him out."

That was, of course, not Ms. Landrieu's only duty that summer. She began researching and building a fat file on Speedy Trial precedents. [The 1978 Louisiana Speedy Trial Act calls for a defendant charged with second degree murder to be tried within two years of original indictment; three years if first degree murder.] She also participated in the medical research. It was there that she ran smack into one of the darkest, most repugnant, yet little-known facts of the baseball bat murder case: the additional injuries to Ryan. The medical records clearly indicate there was bruising around Ryan's kidney area and lower lumbar region, and the contusions were not minor. In fact, at West Jeff that first early morning after the murder of his mother, a kidney specialist was brought in on consult for Ryan. Of less significance, but also unexplained, were the abrasions to both of Ryan's knees.

"As horrible a thought as it was, what if any even sicker element it added to the crime," the very personable, warm, genuine, and quite at-tractive Ms. Landrieu explains, "*nobody knew what to do with it.* Because nobody could answer the question. It's a bad move for a lawyer to bring up an issue he can't answer.

"We thought the State might bring it up to show that only a nonparent could have done such a thing. But they also had the same problem: what did it mean? How did it happen? Is it a part of the crime scene? They didn't have an answer either, so if they're asking a question they can't answer, it just might be a Pandora's box they'd rather leave locked too."

"Anything bad about Ryan, I didn't want," Nick says abruptly, looking up from the dozens of files and scattered papers on his overflowing desk.

"I wanted it to look like Ryan had bumped his head walking under the dinner table," Nick continues. "The biggest doubt that Kerry did it was that a father wouldn't do this to his kid—just as there was a maxim that only a husband could do this to Janet. So anything bad about Ryan, I completely ignored . . . I didn't even know if the State knew."

The law firm Nick is a partner of, because of its size and assets, has more resources at its command than would normally be available to most criminal defense efforts. One of these would be its retainer of psychologists who conduct jury surveys and also complete mock jury studies. However, in this instance, there was only time for Nick to have a psychologist do one jury survey using a total of thirty-six panelists. Small as this statistical sampling was, it demonstrated two strong currents:

"On Bill, every man voted guilty; every woman voted not guilty or guilty of a lesser charge. *Everybody* would've convicted Kerry. I would give them the facts in a light most favorable to Bill, and the facts in a light most favorable to Kerry, and ask, 'Who did it? You figure out who did it.' When they decided who did it, I'd ask 'em, 'Would you give 'em the death penalty?' And the people that said Bill did it, 'Aww, no. I wouldn't give a life sentence for this.'

"So the study indicated that Bill, just by being in the house, he was either gonna get convicted of something less than first degree murder or it was gonna be a hung jury."

"A nurse at Jo Ellen, not one there at the time, but she's looking at the chart for me." Paul Connick is explaining the circumstances of the State's biggest break in the case after Herb MacDonell. " 'No blood given to Fontanille, that's strange. And also his hematocrit level was normal.' A flag goes up and we think we're on to something.

"So we go track this Dr. Neri down, the emergency room doctor who treated Bill. I said, 'Doc, what can you tell me about this thing that I should know? Will you talk to me?' He said, 'Fine.' He's at Victory Hospital in Brooklyn. So we go on up. My initial questions were on a sort of simple level—basically if Fontanille said he was stabbed at four o'clock and he got to the hospital after midnight, describe the wounds for me, were they closing up? Did they look like they were fresh wounds? Can you tell me which came first? That kind of stuff.

"He said, 'If somebody would've asked me right after this happened I could've told you. But nah, I can't remember.' But he remembered the case. He goes, 'I know it was strange. It was just kind of weird. I remember packaging the clothes off. . . .' And then I said, 'What was his hematocrit level? Do you remember anything about that?' And he said, 'You know, that I do remember, it was the same.'

"I said, 'Okay, and what's the significance of that?' He said, 'If he'd've been stabbed in the afternoon, his hematocrit would've been different.' It's the ratio of red platelets to white platelets after a loss of blood. When your red goes down, the body produces more fluid to counteract any drop in the blood pressure. A balancer, more or less. Six to eight hours after you've been stabbed, your hematocrit level should be reduced, the norm in a man is like forty-seven or something.

"Neri says, 'Go see Dr. McSwain over at Tulane Medical. He's a trauma expert.' Bam, we send the records over there. And soon he's on the phone telling me something's wrong, 'His hematocrit should be in the thirties based on what I've seen.' Man, we gather up the whole file and we're in his office.

"This Dr. McSwain, I mean, he tells you basically what they had to drink, how much water, whether they had to go to the bathroom—remember where they said they had one glass of water? The doctor, he didn't know anything about the water drinking in the statements—and he was telling me things that fit with what Kerry said. 'Son of a bitch, this guy's right on!'

"This is when I start feeling good, where we finally feel a little more comfortable with Kerry, after this was discovered."

Judith L. Bunker's professional integrity—some attorneys would call it her annoying, ultraconservative propensity for using the word "inconclusive" or the maddening criminalist's phrase "It is consistent with"—as a forensic expert might best be illustrated by her turning down a case: that of Jeffrey MacDonald, the Green Beret doctor, of *Fatal Vision* fame.

Upon examining the physical evidence at the request of MacDonald's defense team, headed by Bernie Segal, which hoped that she might lend her credibility by testifying at the Army captain's last trial, Judith Bunker had said, "No. My testimony would only hurt your client." Ms. Bunker said this even though there was big money to be made off that case.

While her first report back to Nick Noriea upon her analysis of the physical evidence in the baseball bat murder case was preliminary because of the time constraints involved, it is nonetheless of no small import, because it set in motion the direction the defense subsequently followed throughout:

CONCLUSIONS:

Janet Myers received multiple blows to the head while lying on the living room floor. All evidence indicates this assault originated in the living room.

This subject was turned to her left, head resting upon her left arm when trauma inflicted to the right side of her head. Arterial spurting occurred as a result of this wounding, with blood projected onto the carpet and the *east* wall, *south* of the body. A plant stand lying next to the body was also a target for this projected blood.

This subject then turned to a supine position, her right arm in motion, forming a semicircular transfer pattern upon the carpet. Another blow was inflicted while her right arm was above her head.

The major force of these blows is directed *north* to *south,* with the heaviest concentration of impact spatter above and to the subject's left. The location and direction of this spatter suggests an assailant located on the subject's right while administering multiple blows. There is, however, a cast-off pattern observed on the *south* which suggests an assailant located on the subject's left when at least one blow was delivered, using a right overhand swing.

Type A blood was isolated on carpet taken from the master bedroom. There is photographic evidence of pooled blood on the carpet in this room and could indicate Ryan's location. There is evidence of a moving blood source across the carpet in this area. This could have occurred during removal of the subject from the floor. It could also indicate movement of the subject, prior to removal. There is also evidence of blood drops and transfer stains on clothing near the *north* side of the bedroom door opening. This indicates a blood source above floor level and suggests a bleeding person, walking in this area. No blood is observed in the "ransacked" area.

There appears to be bloodstaining on the carpet in the hall and on hall doors. Though no serological identification was accomplished on these stains, they are consistent with statements of a struggle during bloodshed. A framed picture seen on the floor and shoe indentations in the walls further support this premise.

The foyer and den contain bloodstain evidence indicating the movement and directionality of people and objects during the following bloodshed. However, due to the absence of detailed photographs with scale and the limited number of stains collected for serological examination, a total reconstruction of the chain of events is not possible.

Certainly, it is clear that one or more persons moved through these areas while bleeding. The most predominant area for bloodshed is seen near the *west* wall of the den. The floor behind a recliner lounger is stained first by one or more objects moving across the floor in several areas. Secondly, circular blood drops occurred from a bleeding source well above floor level. The greater accumulation of drops in this area suggests an origin for the additional inflictions of wounds.

When determining whether the defendant's clothing was targeted for spatter produced during the beating of Janet Myers, many factors were considered:

1. Position(s) and location of subject during bloodshed.
2. Location of objects surrounding the subject.
3. Location and directionality of impact spatter.
4. Arterial projection from right side of head.
5. Cast-off stains on south wall.
6. Serological findings.
7. Stains on blue jeans and tennis shoes.

COMMENTS:

Type A blood was not isolated on the blue jeans or tennis shoes. Nor was it isolated on the bat. However, Type A blood was isolated on the carpet in the master bedroom, living room, and on a white handtowel found in the kitchen sink.

Note:

No attempt was made to isolate Janet's blood type from that of her son, Ryan, who also shed blood at the scene and had Type A blood.

Of all blood stains examined on the blue jeans, only 12 spots were found to include Type A activity. While 12 spots could represent a *partial* pattern of medium velocity impact spatter, this limited number of spots is totally inconsistent with the degree of blood spatter observed on other objects and surfaces in the immediate vicinity of this beating.

Considering the degree of spatter produced during the assault on Janet Myers and the minimal number of spots in question, along with the equivocal serological findings, neither the manner in which these stains were deposited nor their origin can be concluded.

NOTE:

There is evidence that the defendant was in the immediate vicinity of the bloodstained bat during other forceful events.

ADDENDUM:

The left hand print seen on the living room wall above the right side of Janet's head, further supports the evidence of the assailant positioned here.

After receiving this report, Nick remembers talking with Ms. Bunker:

"Whoa! I go, 'Does that mean what I think it means? That it wasn't all one beating? And that she was beat from both her left side and her right?' I mean, this is just about the way I'm reacting. Because, God almighty, if that's the case, we're talking about something out of a horror movie—one of those B-grade chainsaws and axes shit! Something pretty sick, you know?"

Yes. That was exactly what Judith Bunker was saying. The same thing—and one of the few things—that every expert criminalist who has studied the autopsy report and the crime scene photos of Janet Myers's murder have all agreed upon: that Janet was beaten for at least one series of blows, then left alone, almost certainly still alive, for some period of time, and subsequently struck again.

"What in the hell do we do with that?" Nick asks rhetorically for maybe the dozenth time. The answer is always "Nothing."

All of the attorneys and investigators who have worked on the case for years on both sides agree—it was something *no one* wanted to deal with, neither the defense nor the State. "It's just too heinous to present to a jury. It would sicken them and from then on you'd never get 'em to focus on anything else. And the ramifications of it don't serve either man well, and it opens up some pretty ugly doors which nobody knows what's behind. Unh-unh. You don't touch that with anybody's stick." That is a fair sample of thoughts on the matter by folks on all sides of the issue of the death *and torture* of Janet Cannon Myers.

Playing the "scenario game" is the essence of any in-depth participation in the baseball bat murder. It is done constantly, even by those who know all too well the maddening futility of it and have heard and thought about it all, because somewhere there must be *the* scenario that will fit both the physical evidence and the circumstantial and behavioral elements.

Nick Noriea plays the scenario game as well as anyone—he's been at it the longest. At the moment, he is recalling how playing with scenarios was also how he worked on an opening statement and overall trial strategy.

"Listen, now. It's the key to understanding it. *Bill never tries to kill Myers.* But Myers does Bill. At some point in time, Kerry realized the only way he could really get away with this was by killing Bill," Nick says.

"Now, getting stabbed in the back is one thing. But when Bill gets stabbed in the chest and it goes right through the nose spray bottle in his pocket, I don't care how superior of a negotiator you are, at some point in time, you've gotta realize, 'If it wasn't for this nose spray bottle, I'd be *dead.*'

"So there ain't no more negotiation here, 'I'm gonna have to just leave my bat here and just hope that somebody believes me.'

"That's the straw that broke the camel's back as far as this negotiating.

'I've got a nut on my hands and I'm in big trouble and I can't do anything else but take a chance that they'll believe me. Because if I stay here too much longer he's gonna stab me someplace where there ain't no nose spray and it goes straight into the heart and then it's sayonara.' "

Tammy DuBuc really wanted to believe Kerry, if only for the sake of the children. She'd been almost a second mother to Ryan, and she was going to start keeping Sarah as soon as Janet went back to work.

"For a long time I did everything humanly possible to block out all the negative things I was thinking about Kerry doing it—'Well, Billy must've snapped, he had to.' But I never could. Even with Kerry calling over here at different times telling me the story. Making sure that I understood what he said had happened that night. At the funeral I even kissed him."

Tammy shivers and blanches at the memory. "When I think about the things I did to try to support him . . . ugh!

"But then, not too long before Billy's trial, I have a dream. Two weeks in a row, every night the same dream. There would just be this voice saying, 'You're making a mistake. You're making a mistake.' Sometimes it wasn't even a voice, it would just be the letters, the words, like on a sign but all over, 'You're making a mistake.'

"Every night I'd go to bed thinking I was going crazy. Till I just couldn't stand it anymore. I made up my mind to follow the feelings I'd been having for a long, long time. I started going over every little detail of information I could get and put it together in my own head.

"I just couldn't see myself keeping supporting him when I didn't believe him."

"I've got a problem with blood spatter experts," Pat Fanning is saying. "Before [the Mintz trial], blood spatter analysis was something kind of new, at least around here, anyway. Mike Fawer first brought MacDonell down here. He was defending Aaron Mintz, you know, more money than God, right? So it was MacDonell versus Bunker.

"But lemme tell ya something, in the legal profession you talk about experts—Edwin Edwards says, 'An expert is any fool more than fifty miles away from home with a briefcase.' And it's true. It gives credibility to a guy if you brought him from New York or from Orlando as opposed to somebody from St. Charles Avenue or Poydras Street.

"And experts in legal proceedings, I think, are very often whores. It's the only testimony that can be given that does not have to be based on fact and can be opinion—and the expert is very much immunized from perjury prosecutions because it's his opinion. It doesn't have to be true or false, it's his opinion.

"Back when I was still on the case, I was on the phone with Michael Fawer about some other business and I said something about this case, and he said, 'Lemme tell you what to do. Go get this fucking Herbert MacDonell, man, he's a real whore.'

"Far too often I think they're prostitutes, they take a fee and assume a position."

"From the very beginning I've always told Bill, 'There's some things in there that I and a number of other people don't believe,' " Nick Noriea is saying while he's doing at least two other things involving the telephone and the clutter on his desk.

"But I also told him, 'There's big problems with Kerry's 911 statement— getting anybody to believe that.' I figured Kerry and Bill's testimony would cancel the other and the rest of the stuff would make the difference.

"So I always told Bill, 'The most you can hope is to negate Kerry.' But in a case like this, you never know what a jury's gonna do—they just might convict.' I always made him aware of that. But what are you gonna do, plead guilty to the death penalty?"

Saturday, October 26, 1986   THE TIMES-PICAYUNE
Trial may unravel puzzle of slaying
By Richard Boyd
West Bank bureau

If bloody baseball bats could talk, many people would know what prosecutors hope to start proving this Monday: Who killed young housewife Janet Myers in her Harvey home in 1984.

"We feel confident," Jefferson Parish District Attorney John M. Mamoulides said. "We think we have a provable case. We have done all we can do. We have spent more time and more preparation on this case than any since I've been chief prosecutor here."

Mamoulides said it is "the most baffling, puzzling case I have ever encountered . . . it is, in many respects, our 'Fatal Vision.' " . . .

Officers and prosecutors almost immediately began bickering among themselves about who committed the slaying.

"I wrote Joan, Janet's sister, a letter," Tammy says. "She gave it to Kerry. It was right when the trial was fixing to start. Because I baby-sit for Joan, too. I had her little boy for quite a while. I felt like we were pretty close, and I wanted her to understand that when the trial started I wasn't going to be there with Kerry."

In closing her letter, Tammy had written: "You don't know the things that went on between Kerry and Janet the way their friends do. If you want to know, I will be glad to explain, but I don't want to write them on paper. Joan, you can reach me during the day at my mother's house. . . ."

"So Kerry freaked out and called Mike Price. And Mike jumped all over me for writing this letter. I baby-sat his three kids from the time they were babies until they started school. And through the whole thing, since the beginning, all I ever heard was Mike telling me 'Billy did this,' 'Billy did that,' and 'Kerry didn't do this.' That's all I heard. But I just didn't believe it."

Tammy's letter did indeed cause a bit of an uproar within this almost unnaturally entwined circle of friends. And the invitation to meet with Janet's family for further, specific explanation was accepted. However, it would take the Cannons almost four years and another letter to get around to it.

6
Trial

*We were so excited about watching, we forgot to ask what you were. Dr.
Ferris informed us that you were a boy. . . . Meanwhile your dad was in
the family room being overwhelmed and finally he cried. Everyone was
so excited. At 11:00 p.m. they got ready to wheel me to my room. Everyone was still in the hall. They said good-bye and dad walked with me to
my room. I got all settled in and dad and I took a deep breath. It was all
over. One phase ended; one began.*

*Dad left and took grandma & grandpa Cannon home. Before he left the
hospital he stopped in the chapel and gave thanks for everything. . . .*

—*Journal of Janet Cannon Myers*

*   *   *

Only moments after nine on the Tuesday morning of October 28, in the
24th Judicial District Court for the State of Louisiana, the Honorable Alvin
Rudy Eason addressed the standing-room-only crowd filling his courtroom:

"Ladies and gentlemen, we're having a trial here that is concerning first
degree murder. Mr. Fontanille, if he is found guilty of this charge, may be
facing the death penalty. Accordingly, I will not have anything but the
most complete decorum during the course of this trial. . . . I do not abridge
your right to freedom of speech—but if you want to stay in this courtroom,
you must be very quiet so that Mr. Fontanille will have the benefit of all
the justice he's entitled to. . . ."

Soon the jury was brought in, and Judge Eason addressed them:

"Ladies and gentlemen, once again I remind you that Mr. Fontanille, as
he sits there, is presumed to be innocent, and it is the duty of the State to
prove his guilt beyond a reasonable doubt. If the case was stopped now,

then Mr. Fontanille would have to be acquitted, since there has been no evidence against him."

Then, shortly: "Ladies and gentlemen, my name is Art Lentini. I'm an assistant district attorney in Jefferson Parish. And I want to take you right now to a house on Litchwood Lane in Marrero. The date is February 23rd, 1984.

"Now . . . living in that house is a young couple, Kerry and Janet Myers, and two children, Ryan . . . two and a half years old . . . at the time, and Sarah . . . six weeks old. She'd just been christened the Sunday before. This is a Thursday. . . . Kerry Myers got up that morning, the evidence will show, kissed his wife goodbye, and went to work as he had done a hundred times before. He worked almost a full day . . . he was a sales engineer . . . he was at a customer's. He was going back to the office, the evidence will show, and he decided to stop in on his family. He pulled into the driveway, walked up to the front door, crossed that threshold into his home.

"At that point, the State's evidence will show that this man seated over there next to his attorney came at him with a bat and shattered his arm, shattered the arm of Kerry Myers, and he shattered his life also because at the time Kerry didn't know it, but his wife lay dead in the house, his two-and-a-half-year-old son lay near death in the house, both bludgeoned with the baseball bat."

The so earnest Mr. Lentini proceeded to give the jury a blow-by-blow, bloodletting-by-bloodletting, hour-by-television-watching-hour recitation of Kerry Myers's version of those at least ten incredible, fatal hours. He also explained that a blood spatter expert would be instrumental in corroborating Kerry Myers's story.

He finished strong, putting a literary metaphor to effective service: "You're going to hear physical objects that the State contends will speak to you, even though they don't testify. What do I mean by that? There's a line from a famous play: 'Murder, though it has no tongue, will speak.' I'm speaking of the blood . . . the baseball bat and the knife, the clothes of the victim, the clothes of Kerry Myers, the clothes of the defendant . . . it will speak to you, in fact this murder will cry out to you; it's going to tell you what happened.

"And after we have presented the evidence and the trial is concluded, Paul and I are going to ask you to return a verdict of 'guilty as charged of first degree murder.' "

Then it was Nick's turn. "This is the kind of case that fills the annals of our courts and police departments that typifies error. In this case the error has been fostered and compounded since February of 1984. But today we're going to examine the evidence that the State puts on, and I ask you to examine the evidence that we put on. And we're going to determine if that evidence is credible, and in looking at the evidence, we should also ask ourseleves, Is there any evidence that's *missing*?

"Are there any test results that are inadequate? Is there evidence that was *not taken* in the investigation? And is there a commitment to the idea that once the Jefferson Parish Sheriff's Office takes a suspect into custody, that they do *everything within their power to make the charges stick*?"

Nick's close was also designed for maximum impact. His strong suit called for no fanciful metaphors, but rather was a questioning of fact regarding the physical evidence which went right to the essence of this case based totally on circumstantial evidence: "If Bill is stabbed in the hall at the end, if Kerry chases Bill out of the hall, *how does all of Bill's blood get in the den?*"

Cheryl Hickman was no longer doing radio news in the fall of 1986. She had moved up in the world, even if the move itself was only to a different part of the almost block-size compound on North Rampart Street in the French Quarter that is home to the New Orleans media monolith WWL. She was now a very young television reporter, not quite twenty-five.

The baseball bat murder was her first trial. There had been some discussion of whether she was experienced enough, but she had already done a follow-up story on the case and was at least as familiar with it as anyone else, and, young or not, she was good.

But just a little after twelve o'clock on Tuesday, October 28, Ms. Hickman, who wasn't altogether sure herself whether she was up to the task, was given little time to ponder the question as she was switched electronically from the steps of the courthouse onto Channel 4's midday Eyewitness News:

"The defense and prosecution have wrapped up their opening statements before the jury of six women and six men. It is a bizarre case. . . ."

Her first live broadcast of the baseball bat murder was bland indeed. But the prospects of capturing video dynamics from almost any attorney's opening statement have always been exceedingly slim.

Things would, however, change in a hurry—in fact, only minutes after court convened from its noon recess.

Wednesday, October 29, 1986   THE TIMES-PICAYUNE
Jeff jurors relive tragedy of woman's death on tape
By Richard Boyd
West Bank bureau

The hysterical moans and screams of Kerry Myers filled a Gretna courtroom Tuesday as he told a Police operator about finding the battered body of his 26-year-old wife, Janet.

Spectators jammed into the courtroom of state Judge Alvin Rudy

Eason who sat in silence as the jury listened to a more than 10-minute cassette recording between Myers and the police operator shortly before 2 a.m. Feb. 24, 1984.

"It was a bold stroke for Paul and Art to put the tape on first thing," W. J. LeBlanc says. "Before anybody had a chance to question Kerry Myers's version of events, they could take it for what it is, a frantic 911 call. While there are obvious problems once you know some of the facts before and after he dialed that phone, at first listening, it can generate strong reactions from a lot of people. It's dramatic; that's why you have to lead off with it—before any of Myers's credibility is trashed."

But in truth, the State couldn't just bring in a tape recorder, set up some speakers, say, "Listen up, folks," and let the fourteen-minute tape rip. As with anything introduced into evidence in a criminal trial, a predicate, a standing for it, has to be established. Therefore, the very first witness to ever be called into open court to testify about any aspect of the baseball bat murder case was, fittingly enough, someone who had been anonymously involved with it from its very first moments, Joseph Koehler, Communications Division platoon commander for the 10:00 P.M. to 6:00 A.M. watch the night of February 23, 1984.

For the State's purpose, all it needed and all it elicited from Mr. Koehler, who had left the force and was currently working offshore in the oil industry, was an explanation of how the Communications Center worked at that time, the circumstances of that particular call, and how he himself had decided to make a cassette recording of it immediately, when it was still readily available from the huge master tape, which would run continuously for weeks at a time.

Nick, however, had a little something extra he wanted the jury to know. "Now . . . the Jefferson Parish Sheriff's Office keeps time cards, and when these calls come in, they're punched into a time clock, are they not?" Nick asked.

"Yes, they do." Joe Koehler shifted his weight from one asscheek to the other in search of a suddenly desired comfort zone.

"Do you have that time card so we can see when this call came in?"

"I don't have that. Those are . . . every night . . . are turned in to Records and Identification and are held by them."

"But those time cards that punch the exact time are kept by the Jefferson Parish Sheriff's Office, are they not?"

"Yes, sir."

"But you don't have that card, do you?"

"No."

"Have you seen that card?"

"I saw it on the night that it happened, but I haven't seen it since."

"Do you know where that card is?"

"No, I don't."

Shortly thereafter, transcripts of the tape were passed out to the jury, and then Kerry Myers's voice stunned, horrified, titillated, and confused all those within Judge Eason's courtroom.

While there is no doubt it was the playing of the "911 tape" (actually a misnomer; Jefferson Parish's state-of-the-art 911 system wasn't on line until six months after Janet Myers's murder) that grabbed the emotions and headlines that first day of the trial, those who were best aware of known and unknown facts in the baseball bat murder would gladly have traded away any number of Kerry Myers's hyperventilating oh-my-Gods and calm-as-an-air-traffic-controller's vocal attitudes when directing police to his house to know *exactly when* the call was made.

In other words, a lot of folks would have loved to have gotten their hands on that police operator's punch card. However, when it was requested, even by the prosecution, it was "not available." Then it was learned that not only was it missing, but it appeared nowhere on the microfilm record which is made each morning of the previous night's stack of cards.

All of the calls in the range of time within which it is reasonable to assume that the call came in, before and after, are there. But, other than the sound on the cassette tape, there was no physical record that the call had been made.

Knowing exactly when that call was made is extremely important. One of the most obvious reasons is to determine whether Kerry was in that house alone with his dead wife and critically injured son at any time before he dialed zero and asked for the police.

This is true even though two witnesses soon to take the stand would present their timing of events, which when factored into the equation should permit a relatively accurate conclusion concerning when Kerry called 911.

Maureen Rilette took the stand after Koehler and testified that her digital alarm clock read 1:45 A.M. when she was awakened by "an angry voice yelling, 'Get out of here! Get out of here!' " and then she went to her window and saw the man jogging toward Patricia.

Then Chuck DeWilde testified that he had logged and entered into his report that it was 1:41 when he first received the dispatch to proceed to the scene and that he had arrived on scene at 1:49. (Actually, it is almost impossible to get from Jamie Boulevard in Avondale to the middle of Woodmere in eight minutes; and in any event the fact that Chuck did not is proved by the tape, which is some fourteen minutes long from the opening sentence to DeWilde's knock on the door.)

However, the third, and probably most reliable, timing evidence comes from the nurse's notes: "BP 2:05 A," meaning that the ER nurse at Jo Ellen Smith took Bill's blood pressure, glanced at her watch, and duly noted the time. Since this is an important routine for nurses, it can be considered the most reliable time constant from which one can count *backwards* when placing events into a time sequence. And if Kerry Myers did call the AT&T operator at 1:40 (as the prosecution accepted, based upon it taking about a minute for a call to come in and then be dispatched to a unit or units), then there is a *big* problem with time, since it is hard to imagine—and impossible to demonstrate when tried—that Bill could've gotten to his car, driven to his parents' house, waited for Herman to dress, made the wrong turn on the way to the hospital, and been there in time for his vital signs to have been taken at 2:05.

As much as some investigators and attorneys would have traded a goodly amount of Kerry Myers's shrill, unsettling, raw, and obtuse caterwauling for that Radio Room punch card, they would've given even more for the last witness of that first day of the trial to have been more expansive or at least more thorough in the performance of his duties at the crime scene that early hour of a winter Friday morning.

Crime scene technician Deputy William Vieira endured more than ninety minutes of abuse during his time upon the stand—which in theory was solely for the purpose of the formality of establishing the chain of custody for and the identification of the items of physical evidence which he himself had collected.

Nick Noriea conducted a relentless cross-examination designed to draw for the jury a clear picture of police bungling at a crime scene. While Nick is quite skillful at it, he also had great ammunition to work with:

Of the "thousands" of "clumpings" of bloodstains on the floors and walls throughout the house, only six samples were retrieved and preserved for testing. And one of those was contaminated by water after it had supposedly been sealed into its own plastic bottle and was therefore rendered useless for typing. In the den, where the floor in at least half a dozen places was all but covered with blood, and where most of that evening's activities obviously had taken place, and with four people known to have been bleeding in that house, Deputy Vieira took only three blood samples, all of which were Bill's, Type B.

Vieira took 140 or so photographs that night, but not once did he place a ruler next to the evidentiary item in question. Of the trails of blood drippings on the tile floor, he had not used his tripod for shooting exact 90-degree-angle exposures for the later establishment of a "grid" to determine the direction of the trails. Nor did he pull up and preserve any of the tiles.

The bloody handprint on the wall above Janet's head had fascinated him, but he had not tried to raise a finger or palm print off the Sheetrock—much less cut it out and preserve it for possible laser identification—and did not take a single photo of it that would enable scaling the size of the handprint.

Of the phone, knife, water glasses, and baseball bat, he dusted none for fingerprints.

Perhaps the most damning admission Nick got out of Officer Vieira concerned the various patterns of bloodstains behind the recliner in the den, where the largest concentration of multi-deposit stains in the den were found:

"You selected one of these spots as a representative for the entire blood clumping on the floor," Nick asked. "Is that a fair statement?"

"Yes, sir," Deputy Vieira answered.

"Are there any particular rules or methods or procedures that you use to select the area that you're to remove to retain as a sample?"

"The only rule I use is if there's a . . . it's the *easiest* area to obtain a sample."

Except for the orthopedic surgeon who operated on Kerry Myers's "closed fracture of the left ulna bone," which Paul Connick had the doctor further explain was "typically the type of fracture also known as a 'night-stick fracture,' " all of the eight witnesses the State brought to the stand on the second day of the trial were law enforcement personnel. Three were crime scene technicians who identified the scaled drawing of the floor plan of the house, the autopsy photographs, the hair and body-fluid samples taken from William Fontanille and Kerry Myers, and the photographs of both men's injuries.

Through cross-examination, Nick was able to further document JPSO sins of omission, particularly the neglect of all involved to have fingernail scrapings taken from the person of what used to be Janet Myers, even though it was testified to that the procedure was and is routine in the investigation of violent crimes in which the victim is female.

Then Detective Martin Childs took the stand to identify each article "that was in the bag of the clothing I collected from" the nurse at West Jefferson Hospital, clothing that was taken off Kerry Myers and that he in turn had given to Vieira. Nick elicited that the clothes had been "all bundled up together in one plastic bag" when Childs received them and that they had remained in that condition for some hours before being released into the custody of Vieira.

Two more police officers testified and were cross-examined toward the chain-of-custody prerequisite on the admissibility of the clothing worn by Fontanille, New Orleans Patrolman John Taylor and JPSO Deputy Noel Adams. Similarly, Bill's clothes had all been put together into one plastic hospital bag for some three hours—including an undetermined amount of time spent on the "hot floorboard" of a police car—before being turned over to Vieira.

However, while Nick was again forceful in his show-and-tell with the jury of another instance where bloody clothing was not handled in accordance with the Sheriff's Office's own crime lab procedures, what was remarkable about both officers' time on the stand to those who were in the know on the case was that no one breathed a word about the several really strange statements Bill Fontanille made to Taylor and Adams that early morning—statements which Torchy Adams had duly noted in his report and were therefore well known to both sides, and which were denied by Fontanille only hours later in his statements to Masson and in all of his subsequent grand jury testimony.

Years later, Paul Connick will say: "We weren't about to make an issue out of the 'We had a plan' statement, we didn't even want to open that up. And Nick couldn't use it, because while it accuses the other guy, he's also pointing to himself. It was just a strange thing sitting there."

On the second afternoon of the trial, Carol Dixon, the former senior forensic biologist at the Jefferson Parish Crime Lab, came to the stand. It seemed as if she stayed forever. Perhaps even longer. It is bad enough to give a rambling, overly techno-jargonistic, boring scientific lecture which literally put at least two jurors to sleep and the others into a state of confusion, but to also do it and get your science wrong!

But then perhaps the Jefferson Parish Sheriff's Office shouldn't be putting someone with a B.S. degree in "marine science biology with a minor in chemistry from the University of Tampa, and an internship with the North Louisiana Crime Lab in Shreveport" in a position to put an individual into the electric chair based upon her expertise with a test tube and a microscope.

Judge Eason, in time, instructed the jury: "The witness is certified as an expert, ladies and gentlemen. And you will be given the same admonition. She can give us expert opinion, opinion testimony, but the weight of her testimony goes into your own little computer, in your minds, what weight you attach to it."

Then, much as the day before, the State's attorneys played pitty-pat with what they knew to be one of their weakest areas. And Nick Noriea, with his newly acquired "crash-course" knowledge of forensic science in general and the finer points of serology in particular, ate their lunch and served them a bitter dinner with what was left of the credibility of their bartender-turned-senior-forensic-biologist-turned-bartender-again-while-waiting-to-join-the-Army. At one point she actually referred to the components of blood as looking "like jujubes."

Then, in her own words, and on the record, Nick cajoled out of her the following admission, which serves well as epitaph to both her short career as a forensic scientist and her performance in the first degree murder trial of William Fontanille: "Well, that is not necessarily what I said . . . *I got myself in a trick bag, I guess.*"

With Carol Dixon's testimony not concluding until 6:25 P.M., it wasn't until the 10:00 P.M. Eyewitness News that Cheryl Hickman was able to file her full story of the day's proceedings, including a taped interview with Nick that, of course, had him succinctly, with almost perfectly timed sound bites, review his points on the sloppy police work and again tell the news-conscious populace that it was Kerry Myers who had killed his wife and not his client.

Nick Noriea remembers driving back to the Holiday Inn not long after giving that interview, and saying to himself, "I don't think Bill will get the death penalty. He could still be convicted, but—from a professional standpoint, the first thing you wanna make sure is that your client doesn't get the death penalty. The second thing you wanna do is make sure he doesn't get convicted of guilty-as-charged. The third thing you wanna do is, if he's gonna get stuck, you let him get stuck with manslaughter, which is twenty-one years as opposed to life for second degree or first degree without the death penalty. And of course the fourth is not guilty. After Carol, Bill still had some problems, but the biggest problem, step one, had been completed."

"He's *cavalier,* all right." Paul Connick is commenting on how he and Art Lentini spent that Wednesday evening after their more than just grueling day in court: entertaining expert Herbert MacDonell rather than preparing him for testimony as they had planned and wished to do.
"Yeah, remember how positive he was that night at dinner?" Art agrees. " 'No attorney can shake me.' We're saying, 'Look, we have this problem.' 'Don't worry,' he said. 'Let's get the salad. Twenty questions—that's all and we'll put it to bed. Twenty questions. Let's have a good time tonight. Don't worry about it. How about another bottle of wine?' "

Thursday, October 30, 1986, was perhaps one of the most pivotal days in the entire saga of the baseball bat murder case. It certainly was one of the most eventful.
Dr. Gutnisky was first up, and his stay upon the stand was shortened considerably because Nick, knowing the doctor well both professionally and socially, immediately stipulated that he was indeed qualified "as an expert in the field of neurosurgery."
Art Lentini went quickly to the facts: "All right. Were you able to evaluate the child and tell what was wrong upon your examination?"

"Yes. The boy was comatose and had multiple bruises and hematomas and blood coming from the ears, and he was basically comatose."

"When you say comatose, would you tell the jury . . ."

"Basically not responsive to any . . . verbal stimuli."

"Would it be safe to say, or, in your opinion, was the child close to death at that time?"

"I would say yes."

After eliciting a detailed explanation of the treatment of Ryan, the three separate surgeries, and the complications involving fluid to the brain, Art held up the bat and asked Dr. Gutnisky:

"Would you be able to form an opinion as to whether or not the child's injuries were consistent with being inflicted by this type of an object?"

"I believe it would be consistent with any conundrum object. I don't know exactly if it was a baseball bat or whatever, but he was obviously hit in the head with something."

"With a blunt object?"

"I would say a blunt object, yes."

Soon it was Nick's turn: "When Ryan came into the hospital, there were no blood clots on his brain, correct?"

"That's correct."

"Matter of fact, you did a CAT scan, and it showed that there was only a mild depression of the skull. Is that correct?"

"Yeah, that's correct."

Nick then addressed Kerry's initial condition, whereas Dr. Gutnisky had consulted on the head wounds. Specifically he wanted the doctor to confirm that narcotic pain medications, as a rule, are not administered to a patient who is suspected of having suffered a concussion or recently "was not conscious as a result of some episode" because it "is going to disguise a neurological problem."

"That's absolutely right," Dr. Gutnisky answered.

Nick then asked him to read a section from the West Jefferson Hospital records for Kerry Myers: " 'Demerol . . . fifty milligrams . . . to seventy-five milligrams IM Q three hours PRN.' "

The autopsy testimony of Dr. Richard Tracy was so gruesome that even the court reporter gasped audibly at one description of the chopped meat which had once been Janet Cannon Myers's face.

"All right. Now . . . doctor, I'd like you to look at wounds five and six on the right side of the victim's head and explain those to the jury also," Art requested.

"These two wounds were on the right forehead, temple and ear. One was about three inches long through the right temple. . . . And the other extended across the top of the right ear, partially removing the ear from the head, so that the ear was hanging down."

"Now . . . doctor, were you able to penetrate wound number five through to wound number six? Were you able to stick your finger through the cut that appears at five and have it come out at six?"

"These three wounds on the right side of the head and around the ear tended to run parallel to each other along the length of the face and communicated with each other beneath the scalp, so that the three wounds kind of ran together in the deep tissues."

There was a reaction in the courtroom when Dr. Tracy explained that the "reddish or brownish colored spots" on the knuckles and back of Janet's hands were areas "where the body was nibbled by cockroaches."

Also certainly horrific but of some probative value was Art's eliciting from Dr. Tracy that the partially digested blood in the stomach, which was there because "the victim, lying unconscious, was by reflex swallowing some blood," and the "prominently swollen black eye . . . intense shiner" on Janet's left side indicated, in his expert opinion, that she had survived for "at least twenty minutes" to "an hour or two" after the initial beating.

Along that same ghoulish vein came the first public awareness of the actual cause of Janet Cannon Myers's death: "The immediate mechanism of death was air embolism. These gaping wounds which cut into the large veins of the face allow air to get into these open veins, and this air, then, gets into the heart and fouls the pump and that's what happened in this case."

During Nick's turn with Dr. Tracy, he had quite congenially solicited and received all he wanted on three medical issues without having to use a witness of his own later, understanding that a State's witness intrinsically carries more weight with a jury than does one for the defense.

"Show you the State's exhibit 77. That depicts Janet's fingernails on her right hand, does it not?" Nick asked.

"Yes."

"Are those fingernails capable of creating abrasions?"

"I would think yes."

"Show you the emergency room report of Kerry Myers. Would you look and see if there indicates the presence of any abrasions?"

"I have . . . this is a report from West Jefferson Hospital emergency room. I haven't seen this before, and what comes to my attention is the first sentence . . . 'multiple contusions . . . or abrasions . . . over the entire body.' "

"Thank you, doctor," Nick said. He had the doctor peruse Bill's records from both Jo Ellen Smith and Charity hospitals, taking all the time he needed, and then asked, "In any of these other records at Jo Ellen, did you detect the presence of any notings of any abrasions whatsoever?"

"No such note in these records."

The long-ballyhooed appearance of the "blood spatter expert" turned out to be anticlimactic and, for the prosecution, not up to its advance billing. Even Herb, whose ego is as large as his celebrated appetite for good eats and fine wines, later apologized for having given the State admittedly "not one of my better days."

After a wrangle, provoked by Nick, over whether the witness was qualified as an expert in bloodstain analysis—which brought out and displayed for the jury a defensive, petulant, quite subjective scientist—Professor MacDonell left the witness box and stepped to an easel upon which there was a stack of large color photographs of the crime scene. Once there he began a long, highly technical, erratic, and rambling classroom-style lecture upon bloodstain pattern interpretation in general and his opinions and conclusions on the baseball bat murder in particular.

Consequently, what the jury, the judge, and the courtroom at large learned through Paul Connick's examination of MacDonell was problematical at best. Perhaps the only truly revealing exchanges did not come under direct, but rather during Nick's devastatingly well-scienced cross.

Nick wanted to know where Professor MacDonell would place the assailant with respect to Janet's body. The answer eventually forthcoming was that he had to have been on the right side because the heaviest concentration of impact spatter on the wall was "over the victim's left shoulder." In other words, *away from* the one swinging the bat.

"You're assuming the person's standing, though, correct?" Nick asked.

"No, no, not at all."

"Well, if the person . . . well . . . you assume the person's kneeling?"

"No, they could be either. I'm just not assuming. Either one or the other."

"Okay. Well . . . let me ask you something. Were all the fatal blows delivered before this hand reached that location, or can you even say that?"

"I don't know. I can't . . . I . . . frankly I don't know which blows were the fatal blows. I'm not sure that the autopsy identifies which was the fatal blow."

"The autopsy . . . this lady died because after a period of time air got into her heart. That's what killed her," Nick told him.

"Air embolism," said Dr. MacDonell as if making a diagnosis after some newly rendered fact suddenly became clear to him.

"Now . . . what is the more likely position of the assailant to deliver these blows?" Nick went back.

"Again . . . I don't know which blows. The blows that cause spatter are the ones I'm addressing myself to. Which specific blows they are I don't know. The right ear, as I recall the autopsy, was split. Now . . . she's not lying in a position that I would expect her to be beaten at the time most of this blood spattered on the wall, if the majority of the wounds are to the right side of the face. Usually turn facing away . . ."

"But isn't it . . ."

". . . consciously or unconsiously."

"Isn't it a fact . . ."

"What?" asked MacDonell, visibly distracted from his train of thought.

". . . that this woman was struck with a bat after her hand lay in that position?"

"I don't know the basis of that. I couldn't conclude that . . ."

"Wait a minute." Nick found and then handed to MacDonell one of the crime scene photos, and said, "Look on the underside of this lady's sleeve and tell me if that's not medium-velocity spatter."

"There are spots there. They certainly could be."

"That indicates that at least one blow was delivered after this arm had arced up to that position. Correct?"

"It would certainly indicate it, but it's . . . as I said before . . . it's only apparently three spots. If I could look at the blouse again, I think that would be helpful."

Nick fetched him Janet's blouse, and soon Professor MacDonell was fingering the greatly bloodstained blouse that Janet Myers had worn for her appointment with death with a tenderness that one would think should not be present in a man who has spent a lifetime studying the effects of carnage.

"It is, however, rather heavy with blood spattering . . . you can feel it . . . which indicates that there's been clotting. So this blow, whatever caused these spots . . . may very well have been delivered three minutes to six minutes after the first blood was clotted. That's the approximate length of time of clotting."

"I didn't ask that," Nick quickly said and added, "Is that medium-velocity spatter?" MacDonell had gotten far too close to revealing the possibility that the clubbing of Janet Myers's face was not all one frenzied, raging event, and he wanted to avoid that dehumanizing, maniacal element of this crime scene.

"It certainly could be . . ."

"Okay. Well . . . that's fine. We agree. All right. Now . . . so that means that when the impact, the several blows, multiple blows that were administered during that period of time, this arm moved from what appears to be her stomach . . . this area . . . and made an arc around that way. Correct?"

"I don't know that it started in the stomach because both hands are equally stained with blood, but certainly blood got on her stomach from some source. Could have been either hand, but it does come around in an arc, yes."

"So . . . if this girl's arm moved in an unbroken arc while the blows were being delivered, the assailant would have to be back far enough from her so that her arm was not stopped in its movement in that arc. Is that correct?"

"Correct."

"Do you know how far this girl's head is from the outer portions of that arc?"

"Within three feet, but I don't know exactly."

"Would you expect that someone would stand up and stay that far back and try to reach with a right-handed swing?"

"They might. It depends upon their size, the lift of the instrument, and at what time the swinging occurred."

"Wouldn't it be easier to deliver a right-handed swing like this . . . to reach your target?"

"I think it's . . . in my experience . . . more common to reach over the person. They . . . the person doing the beating addresses themself to the object, and reaches right over them, and in this case, I think the concentration of blood certainly shows that they were to the lower left. As you look at the body, to her right side."

"But they got to get out of that arc of her arm to prevent it from being broken. Correct?"

"At that particular time, yes, but I don't . . ."

"Okay," Nick said, not really wanting the professor to elaborate at will on that particular point. However, MacDonell did.

". . . know when the person moved the arm or the arm was moved, so I . . . when the arm slid across the carpet, obviously no one is standing in that area or kneeling in that area. That's all I can conclude from that arc."

In about the same spot where the most unathletic Dr. MacDonell had been when he'd demonstrated for Paul Connick how a semi-kneeling batsman could hit Janet and also drop a spot of blood on the heel of his sneaker, Nick had gone to the floor as the athlete he had been, kneeling on his right knee, left leg bent and braced and the bat raised up and back, cocked to strike at a prone figure within reach of the "sweet" part of the barrel of the bat.

"And you . . . you agree that the position I'm in is a position that one would swing with a right-hand, overhand swing that produced the cast-off patterns that you saw further down the wall."

"It could be, or you could be kneeling on the other knee or both knees."

"And if I'm kneeling on both knees or this knee, how can I get blood spots under my shin here, where Fontanille's pants have blood on them?"

Ooops!

"It would be very difficult . . . it'd be easier if you're kneeling on the other knee."

"I have no further questions," Nick said as he rose to his feet, believing it not even necessary to explain that it would be ludicrous to imagine that anyone who had ever been any kind of an athlete would be on his left knee raising and swinging a bat across the balance of his weight—back across his body—greatly dissipating whatever power the "bat man" might have.

Paul Connick was quickly up for redirect, to make whatever attempt he could to "rehabilitate" the damage done to his expert witness's testimony.

"Professor MacDonell, if the person administering the beating was in this fashion . . ." Paul was now on the floor, kneeling on his left knee, right leg bent at the knee and braced, with the bat across his body, grip held up high behind his head with the barrel dipping low behind him—what in baseball is commonly referred to as "wrapping" the bat. "Would that account for the drop of the victim's blood on the back of the left shoe?"

"The way you swung it just now, yes, it certainly could."

"And could it also account for the . . . blood spatter pattern of the same type on the defendant's jeans?"

"No, not the way you swung it."

Paul was definitely having a bad day; his highly paid, internationally renowned expert witness was *contradicting* him. While taken aback, he did manage to ask, "Can you demonstrate how it would?"

"From the impact you could get spatter going back to the pant leg, but swinging it over your shoulder, knowingly or not, you swung it right back to your heel. Now . . . that is the left heel. The blood spot that was checked for A blood is on the right heel in back. So there is going to have to be a reversal . . ."

"Of the leg."

". . . to have that done."

"Right," Paul said and then added, "That's all I have."

There were those that afternoon who expected to watch the utter annihilation of a once well-respected cop. They were wrong.

Art had Robert Masson up there only briefly, for the ex-detective to verify his recollection of the crime scene that night by showing him pictures and asking if that indeed was the way the scene appeared when he arrived. There was also the verification of some evidence gathered, and identification of the pictures of William Fontanille that were taken after his incarceration depicting the wounds received.

Then Nick had him. But Nick knew that after the grilling of Vieira and Dixon, the same was not necessary with Masson. Badgering Masson might be perceived by the jury as unfair to a cop who had chanced upon a career-ending nightmare of a case and therefore would probably be counterproductive. Nick kept him on the stand for only a few minutes, primarily eliciting one line of thought, that the master bedroom was in disarray similar to how one would expect it to be after a burglary.

"It's not uncommon to have all the drawers pulled out at burglary scenes, is it?"

"It's not uncommon, no, sir."

                              *   *   *

"State will call Chris Richier," Art announced.

Mr. Richier's stay on the stand was also short. However, what he had to tell was of no small import. Richier testified that Kerry Myers, who was instrumental in having Blaine Kern Artists begin to use pneumatic cylinders to animate its Mardi Gras floats, was with him at the float den the Thursday afternoon of the murder "between three and four o'clock" because of a problem with a pneumatic device the day before the first Carnival parade.

Not only was this almost as good an ironclad alibi, given the distances and driving time between Blaine Kern Artists in old Algiers Point and Woodmere in Harvey, but it was also effective in going to Kerry's "state of mind" on that afternoon. Because, according to Mr. Richier, Kerry Myers had not acted troubled, nervous, or in any way out of the ordinary. In fact, as they had parted after Kerry's "about twenty, twenty-five minute" visit, they had been quite jovial and had talked about seeing each other that weekend on the parade route because "we were using the first animation. I wanted him to be there just to see it, and he said he'd be there."

Chris Richier came across as so earnest and believable that Nick made only a cursory and polite cross-examination. Then, after a brief bench conference, Judge Eason announced:

"I understand that the next witness will be . . . Mr. Kerry Myers, so we will take a little break now because we believe that his testimony will be a long time."

"I went to every day of that trial," Mrs. Peggy Senat is saying, with a goodly amount of the indignation she felt then still very much present. "And they were making Mr. Myers look like a Mr. Goody-Two-shoes. That was *really* getting me upset.

"It was during a break or something during Kerry's testimony, and I walked over and tapped Mr. Noriea on the shoulder, and I said, 'May I please see you out in the hall, I need to talk with you.' And that's when I told him, 'I must've spoken to the wrong people.' I said, 'I'm *very* upset, because I told the DA, but it looks like they've already got this cut and dried and really and truly the picture that he's giving up there is not the right picture of this man.'

"I said, 'Mr. Noriea,' oh, I was really upset, I said, 'I don't know your client, neither do I know Mr. Myers other than living across the street from him, but what this man is saying is all a bunch of lies!'

"I was talking a mile a minute. By that time I was *really burnt up*. I said, 'I'm quite upset because what they're letting Mr. Myers paint a picture of is just a *farce*.' I said, 'Because he is really not that type—you know, like he comes home and he checks on his kids and all that kind of stuff; like it was a loving marriage, and it *wasn't.*

"I just told him that I was very, very upset. I mean, after the DA telling me, 'Oh, we know they fought and all.' But yet they put him up on the stand and let him make it sound like everything was hunky-dory? And his saying, 'Oh, the police never came to the house on Litchwood.' I said, 'That's a *damn* lie! My husband and I both saw it.' I mean that was a *lie,* yet the DA had said to me. 'Oh, we know everything about it.' "

When Peggy Senat had slowed down enough to let him talk, Nick informed her that he was very interested in what she had to say, but that since she'd been sitting in on the trial, it would be very unlikely that she could testify. But he said, "Just in case I need you, will you testify?"

"Yes, I will," the feisty little lady said.

At 3:15 P.M. on Thursday, October 29, 1986, as Kerry Myers stepped into the witness box to tell his story publicly for the first time, Cheryl Hickman wrote the words "thin, pronounced nose," and Judge Eason addressed the courtroom at large:

". . . this will be a very serious and difficult part of the trial. So I will not allow anyone to make any noise or emotional outburst. I don't want anybody sighing or shaking their heads . . . if you're overcome, please leave the courtroom."

It would appear the witness thought the judge's strictures were for him. Kerry Myers's recitals of the events of that night have never strayed far from his statement and grand jury testimony; neither has he ever gotten emotional over the task. That afternoon upon the stand in open court was not an exception.

Paul led Kerry through his story, which he said began when Bill attacked him with a baseball bat as he walked into his house that Thursday afternoon.

"I don't know how to describe it. At one point he could have killed me; he could have continued; he could've killed me if he'da just continued. Yet it seemed like screaming at him brought him back to some sort of normal calmness or . . . whatever . . ."

"At the time that you were stabbed or that knife fight began, do you recall what happened to the bat?" Paul asked.

"All I know is that when he made me get up, he had the bat . . ."

"Up un . . ."

". . . when he told me to get up, up until that time. The next thing I know he touched my shoulder; he tried to stick a knife in my back, and I don't know . . . I don't remember anything about the bat at that point."

"Up until that time, had you seen the knife?"

"No. That was the first time I saw the knife."

Then Paul went through the evidence with Kerry. Soon: "Is this your wife's shirt?"

"Yes."

"Is this the shirt you saw her wearing when you last saw her?"

"Yes."

"Is this the same shirt you saw her in when you found her body in the living room?"

"Yes."

A powerful, poignant piece of judicial dramaturgy: the reverent knight of justice, the bereft widower, and the very bloody death shirt of many colors. However, since God isn't a playwright, this show couldn't fade to black on a two-count and the curtain be brought thundering down; Paul had several more articles to be brought forth for a very unemotional husband to identify.

"Mr. Myers, do you recall exactly the time or as best you can recall the time when you stabbed the defendant?"

"It was late. It had to be after midnight. The exact time . . . I don't know, but it had to be after midnight."

"Was he stabbed immediately before he ran out of the house?"

"Yes. That was . . . that was the only chance I had to get him out of the house. That . . . that whole night . . . that was the first opportunity I had to . . . that I thought I could do anything . . . without risking myself any further or my family any further. That was the last thing that happened."

Paul Connick reflects on Kerry's performance on that so critical, perhaps so pivotal Thursday in the baseball bat murder saga: "I thought Kerry held up well. I mean, he looked cold—the problem was, Kerry handled the questions well, his answers, but he just didn't get emotional. He was scared to death, I can tell you. He didn't show remorse—not remorse, because he wasn't on trial, but in effect he was because Nick was going for him. Of course, a tear or two would've been better. I mean, for Christ's sake, he asked Leslie Hill for a date!"

"I felt a little uneasy with Kerry's testimony," Art Lentini says. "It wasn't what he was saying—but he just looked like he'd done something. Just the way his eyes were. You look at both of them, though—Bill's eye had not sunken in, but he just sat there, too."

When it was the defense's turn, Nick came at Kerry like a buzz saw: "As of this time, were you bleeding yet?"

"Yes. When he started to hit me, I was definitely bleeding."

"Where were you bleeding from?"

"From the face and the head area."

"What did he hit you in the head with to cause you to bleed?"

"Apparently it must have been one of the things on the . . . on the counter."

"Where was the baseball bat?"

"In Billy's hands."

"What hand was the baseball bat in when he was picking up things off the counter?"

"I don't recall."

"Was blood running into your eye?"

"It was running all over my face, at that time."

"And you were standing here by the love seat?"

"I was in that general area. We started struggling there, and we stumbled back over towards this area."

"Now . . . as of this point in time, was Bill bleeding, or did you ever injure Bill up until that point in time?"

"No, I didn't."

Then: "Over here, what did Bill do to you?"

"Well . . . when we got into struggling in this area and I was screaming at him, 'Why?' He could have continued to kill me at that point, if he'd have just kept it up, because at that point I don't think I could have stopped him, and I was screaming at him to stop it . . . 'You're killing me! If you don't stop it, I'm going to bleed to death!' And I yelled that I can't . . . 'I can't stand up any longer!' Then he stopped hitting me, and he let me down on the ground."

Then: "The blood was falling to the linoleum?"

"I don't know how bad I was bleeding at that point. I just know that I had a lot of blood in my face."

"Before that point in time, was the blood running down your clothes?"

"I don't know. I know I was bleeding."

"So you sat on the floor in this area?"

"Yes. And I pulled myself up . . . my back up against the sofa."

"And where did Bill sit?"

"In the recliner chair."

"Right here."

"Yes."

"What happened after that?"

"Well . . . he sat there with the bat, and said if I moved, he would kill me."

"So he sat over you."

"Yes."

And Nick moved on: "When you opened the front door, what did you do with your keys when Bill struck you?"

"I . . . had my keys in my right hand 'cause the door was on the right side, the door lock. I don't know."

"Did you drop 'em? Did you put 'em in your pocket?"

"I don't recall."

"You don't know what happened to your keys."

"I don't recall."

"How did they get in the corner of the den?"

"They must have flew out of my hand."

"Did you have the pens in your pocket that day at work?"

"Probably."

"How did they get on the coffee table?"

"Might have taken them out."

"Were you bleeding before or after you took 'em out?"

"I'm sure I was bleeding before."

"Did you place the pens on that table?"

"I don't remember doing it.

"Do you know that the pens were placed on the table?"

"I'm sorry?"

"Do you know the pens were placed on that table?"

"I did have knowledge that they were on the table."

"How did they get from the pocket to the table? Or do you know?"

"I don't remember. I must have done that, but I can't actually remember the act of doing it, 'cause usually they're in my pocket."

"You don't remember anything about the keys."

"No, only that I opened the door with it."

"By the time you got to that corner of the den, your hands were bloody."

"What corner?"

"The back corner, where he hit you in the head with the lamp."

"I'm not . . . I can't say that my hands were bloody. I don't know. I know I was bleeding. I don't . . . I couldn't . . . I can't tell you where the blood . . . I wasn't paying attention. I was more worried about staying alive."

"Did the baseball bat have blood on it?"

"At what point?"

"At any point did you notice blood on the baseball bat?"

"I know it had blood on it when we were struggling."

"Pardon?"

"I'm pretty sure the bat had blood on it when we were struggling."

"Where . . . where . . . where was that struggle taking place when you noticed blood on the bat?"

"In the den."

"Did you ever notice blood on the bat in the foyer?"

"No, I didn't. When somebody's swinging a bat at you, you . . . the bat looks like it's about six feet in diameter."

"Is that the corner where you sat?"

"Yes."

"And you sat on the floor."

"That was at first, yes."

"When did that blood get on the floor?"

"I don't . . . I'm sure it got on there during one of his fights."

"Well . . . were you sitting in any blood?"

"I know my . . . the side of my . . . I know my shirt had some blood on it. I might have got some blood on . . . on my left arm. I know my face had blood on it."

"See all that blood smeared on the floor?"

"Yes."

"That's the area where you were sitting?"

"That's probably where my legs were. I was leaning all up against the arm of the sofa."

"How'd all that blood get back there?"

"I had said earlier we . . . we went from this side of the room over there. When he picked up the lamp, we were behind this furniture."

"Were there blood droppings all over these baby books in the middle of the floor?"

"I don't remember. It was dark."

"You never asked to turn a light on?"

"No, I didn't. I . . . I was more worried about my family and myself dying because . . . whether a light was on or not."

"I'm going to show you State's exhibit 70. You see that blood?"

"Blood?"

"On the floor."

"Yes."

"Is that your blood?"

"I don't know."

"Were you bleeding at that point?"

"I . . ."

"It's by the television set."

"And it's the entrance. Only thing I could say is my arm must have bleed . . . been bleeding as soon as he hit me, but I don't know if that's my blood or not."

"What caused your arm to bleed . . ."

"I don't remember that."

"What else bled?"

"My head, when he hit my head, with the . . . with the objects."

"Is that your blood on the floor?"

"I don't know."

"All throughout this whole altercation in here Bill never was bleeding. Correct?"

"The only time . . . first time I saw him bleeding was when he sat down in that chair and his . . . his fingers were cut, 'cause when he went to get a towel, he wrapped it around his fingers."

"That was minor compared to the bleeding you were doing, though. Correct?"

"It seemed that way."

"Was he bleeding when he ran out the door, do you know?"

"I am sure he was bleeding somewhat. I had just stabbed him."

"How can you account for Bill's blood being in the den?"

"His finger was cut. I know that."

"You told this jury that you stabbed Bill, and you chased him out of the hall, out of the foyer, and it all took about two minutes, correct?"

"That's correct."

"And all of this blood that got on your clothes, Bill's blood on your clothes, in a two-minute period of time is from his finger?"

"Possibly, yes. It's the only . . . I have no other . . . I'm telling you the story as I know it, Mr. Noriea."

Then: "When you called the police, what were your first words to them?"

"All I could remember is getting the police on the phone and saying, 'Somebody's gotten into my house, and we need help, an ambulance, and I think he's killed my wife.' I don't remember exactly."

"You recall telling the operator . . ."

"I was pretty . . . I was pretty upset at that time."

"You picked up the phone right after Bill ran out the house."

"I . . . that's the next thing I did. I went back in, straight to the phone."

"First words were, 'Somebody broke in my house and tried to kill me. I just stabbed him.' Is that correct?"

"If you're reading from a transcript, it must be correct."

" 'Somebody broke into my house and tried to kill me.' You recall making that statement?"

"Not word for word, but if you're reading from a transcript, it must be correct."

"Why did you tell the police that somebody broke in your house?"

"Mr. Noriea, I was pretty upset when . . . he was in my house, where he shouldn't have . . . shouldn't have been. How did I know how he got in there? I was just upset. I was in panic. I was . . . I had just been through eight or ten hours of somebody trying to kill me, not knowing where my family was, not knowing if my wife was alive or dead. I . . . I couldn't tell you half of what I said."

"Why didn't you go look for your wife and kids before you called?"

" 'Cause the first thing I could think of was just to get help 'cause I knew we would all need help."

"Why did you wait so long to ask the operator about going to check on your wife?"

"I don't remember it being that long. It seemed like just a few minutes. They kept . . . kept telling me to stay on the phone, stay on the phone, give them information, give them information."

"I've got a direct quote from an operator, asking you, 'Did you check on your wife?' Do you recall that?"

"No, I don't."

"After that you went to check on your wife. Correct?"

"I don't remember the exact sequence."

And: "You sure you didn't stab Bill in the back with this when he walked in that door?"

"I am sure."

"You're absolutely certain of that?"

"I am telling this story. It is the truth, as I've told it ever since this has happened. I am sure."

"Then how can you explain Bill's blood being here and here?"

"I'm not an expert," Kerry Myers said probably for the first and only time in his life.

"He had been so positive over drinks, but then on the stand he started crawfishing on us," Paul Connick remembers.

"All Herb would say really was that the person wearing these jeans was in the vicinity of the impact of the bat against Janet's head," Art Lentini explains.

"But we had never realized until the middle of the trial just how totally Carol Dixon had botched it; she fucked up so bad," Paul says.

Indeed, Paul and Art had a bad day, and by late afternoon it got worse. "We get a message to call Dr. McSwain. Bam, his father is dying in Carolina somewhere, he's gotta go," Paul says. "But not to worry, he says his associate Dr. Morris Kerstein can do it.'

" 'Oh, shit, this guy doesn't know anything about the case!' I'm saying, and Art's getting that look on his face again. This guy hadn't even talked to McSwain about it yet. So we go to his house that night—our biggest witness. But damn, he was right in line with what McSwain had said. Even a little bit more detail. This guy knew his shit! So, it's 'Shwoo, everything's all right again.' "

Nick knew he'd had himself a good day. Yet, after patiently making himself available for all of the metro and regional press who needed an interview or statement, as he was heading back to his hotel to tell his panel of experts that, thanks in large part to their tutoring, they would not now be needed to take the stand, he had gotten everything he needed from the State's experts, Nick spent not a moment's energy savoring or even much expounding upon his "team's" prowess or apparent success.

Yes, after Carol Dixon's glaring ineptness and now Herb MacDonell's testimony attempting to put the bat man in a position that would've *precluded* the impact spatter that *was* on Bill's leg from getting there, Nick felt reasonably sure that "Bill was not going to get even first degree without the death penalty. Hurdle number two was behind us."

But Nick still was not in a charitable mood toward the system that had brought things to this state:

"It took me two or three months of reading and studying to learn something about blood spatter. Here's a jury that gets a class in thirty-five minutes and they can't appreciate the full impact of what he's saying.

"Herb confused them; and that's good for me. But if they're confused, then they're gonna end up a hung jury, because no one juror can take over and say, 'No, you should change your vote of guilty to not guilty because of this, this, and this.' And that's good so far, but it's not good the rest of the way. Because what you really wanna do is convince one or two jurors strongly so that they can continue your jury argument into the jury room. But the State's evidence was so confusing that they couldn't even do that.

"I mean, 'It's gotta be Fontanille's handkerchief because he's got the goddam nose spray in his pocket!' That's what the jury probably thought. That's what I had to go up against because of the inadequate investigation."

By Friday morning, when the State promptly announced it was resting its case, Cheryl Hickman, after almost a week of covering a gut-wrenching murder trial, had become more and more observant of and fascinated by some of the audience members and those who had to sit their vigil out on the hall benches, almost as much as by the dynamics of the murder itself.

"It was really interesting to talk to the friends, these really closely interwoven, overlapping circle of friends now having to choose sides. I mean, these were normal people. Good people. And obviously both men had maintained long friendships through the years, had grown up with these people. And these people knew them—knew them very, very well, and knew them before and after the two guys met, knew what they were like as friends, and what they were like separately. And they were all still very shocked by it. Their lives still very affected by it, you know, 'What happened here?' They couldn't fathom it."

The baseball bat murder case also had a direct impact on Ms. Hickman herself: "I felt that my standing in the newsroom had changed. I think they recognized that something was different. I think they were glad I threw myself into it so much. I would go back to the newsroom at the end of the day and they would say, 'Give me more details about this.' They wanted to gossip about it, they wanted to talk about it.

"It was very much a phenomena of people *wanting* to know about this case. 'Did they do it? Who did it? How did this happen? Did they really have sex the day before? And the baseball bat, what kind was it? How big was it?' All the little details. These are *professional* news people, TV people. Angela Hill, Bill Elder, I mean they *wanted* to know about it—they wanted all the grisly details. Other reporters were listening in, 'Tell me more about this.'

Just a tremendously morbid, gossipy kind of interest. Are we finally going to have this explained? 'Okay, so what are your gut feelings? Do you think these guys did it?' They wanted to know beyond the facts.

"In your reporting you lay out the facts, and you give a little interpretation in a story, though you don't want to go too far, you try not to convict in the press, and that's difficult.

"But afterwards? When your day is done, the last story filed, it's like, 'Oh, yeah. He's guilty!' "

Nick Noriea didn't think he needed a parade of high-powered impact witnesses; of the eight people he put on the stand that momentous Friday, October 31, 1986, only one could be considered an expert on anything relevant to a murder trial or investigation and perhaps not just a John Q. Citizen who might live next door. On the defensive roster, in order of appearance there were Susan Mansfield Painter, Charles Michael Cronin, Beverly Cronin, Sandra Cronin, Joseph T. Giardina, Sandra Giardina, William Adam Fontanille, and Patrick Fanning.

It is also of note that the first six witnesses were up and out within an hour and thirty-five minutes. And that though brief, all were very credible and—aside from that of the Giardinas, who were there only to trash Kerry—their testimony absolutely supported the story that Bill went back to the Myerses' house the afternoon of the murder for no other reason than to pick up the baseball bat he'd left earlier when he'd gone there to "break off the affair" with Janet.

At 10:35 A.M. on October 31, 1986, William Fontanille took the stand in defense of his life. After a series of establishing questions, Nick soon asked: "What transpired—when did you next see them? Did you go over there Wednesday and Thursday of that week?"

"I went over there Wednesday around noon."

"Tell the jury what happened when you were there Wednesday."

"I went over again looking more for a sympathetic ear than anything else. I talked to Janet about what had happened between me and Susan. And Janet and I began to talk about different problems we both shared. Uh, she told me . . ."

Up came Art. "Your Honor, I object to hearsay of the . . ."

Judge Eason was already up to Art's speed and didn't bother ruling on the objection—before Mr. Lentini had even finished, the judge was addressing Bill directly: "Don't tell us what she said."

"Try, if you can," Nick said calmly, "to tell us what you said and what you did as a result of what she said as opposed to telling the folks on the jury what Janet said to you, if that's possible."

"I'll try. We had more or less the same marital problems. I was led to believe . . ."

Up went Art. "Same objection."

Bill looked to Judge Eason and said, "I'm sorry, I don't know how to say this."

"You *can't* say it," Paul Connick challenges Billy, who's got Paul by about three or four inches and maybe thirty-five pounds of muscle. "It's hearsay."

"Now wait, wait, wait, thank you, Mr. Connick. I'll give it a try if you just give me the chance," the judge said, dismissing Paul. He turned again to Bill. "Just tell what your impressions were without saying those magic words that I was this, that, and the other."

"I'm sorry, Your Honor," Bill offered again.

"Now, Mr. Fontanille, it's very important that we—I'm not going to interrupt as you go along. So please bear that in mind."

"Yes, sir."

"Because if I interrupt you, then I interrupt your train of thought. We want to give you as fair a hearing as we possibly can."

"Try to do as best as you can," Nick encouraged with a reassuring, protective tone.

"Right. Because of what I was told, I felt a close binding for Janet at that time based on what I was telling her. And later that afternoon we had sexual intercourse together."

"What happened after that?"

"After that we went into the master bedroom and she asked about . . ."

"Objection, Your Honor." Art again.

"Sustained," went Judge Eason.

"After that," Bill tried another route, "I went to Wendy's and got lunch for Janet, myself, and Ryan, her son. She told me . . ."

Art and Paul both were up. Art said the regular: "Objection, Your Honor." Paul went for the rationale: "Your Honor, some of this he recalls the victim we can't deny . . ."

"I have done all right so far, Mr. Connick," Judge Eason admonished. "Just give me a chance."

"I apologize," said Bill again. "It is very difficult."

"I understand, sir. I understand in the normal tone of conversation that is the type of things you ordinarily say," the judge told Bill. Then, to the jury and the court at large, "Ladies and gentlemen, the reason we have such a strong feeling about hearsay evidence is that in years past there was no hearsay rule and witnesses would say, 'Somebody told me that so-and-so stole a horse,' and real witnesses who saw the thing never came in. In those days they used to hang horse thieves. So that's why we have the hearsay rule. So we can't tell a tale of a tale or what somebody else tells you. All right, let's proceed."

"Based on what I was told, I parked my car down the block when I came back from Wendy's and walked to the Myerses' residence."

"How long did you stay there?"

"By that time it was probably three-thirty, around four o'clock Kerry came in the house. Janet and I were sitting on the love seat together, she had her legs across my legs, and Kerry walked in and she immediately moved her legs off of mine."

"How was she dressed at that time?"

"She had a pair of white leotards on and, uh, I believe a pair of shorts over it."

"Okay. Continue."

"Uh, Kerry came in and looked at us and, uh, he turned around and walked into the garage, because of what she said I followed him into the garage."

"Did you eventually leave there that afternoon?"

"Yes, I did about forty-five minutes later."

From that point on, Nick led his client through his version of the events of the following day and evening which ended in the murder of Janet Myers.

There was not the same roteness in Bill Fontanille's retelling as in Kerry Myers's, yet there is nonetheless very little in his story of that night which is newly probative or at substantial variance from anything he'd said previously. Paul Connick then led the cross.

"Mr. Fontanille?" Paul began by addressing Bill with the back-lilt of a question, as if to imply that even his name was a lie.

"Yes, sir."

"Do you want to take a drink?" Paul then asked, another strategic effect. From the giddy-up, Mr. Connick was attempting to show Bill and the courtroom who was in control and that this was going to be one of his better days.

"Yes, please." Then, soon, "I'm ready."

Immediately Paul began eliciting a series of confessions, bringing out each of the many bogus job lies; the damage Bill had done to his house after he discovered Susan had left him, and that he'd thrown her clothes out; that he'd been severely "depressed" and avoiding his friends, "hiding out"; and that he'd even boycotted his son's christening and sundry other oddities, including still lying to his closest friends that Tuesday evening even after he'd "decided I wanted to see my friends and that it was silly to go on pretending that I was working when I wasn't."

Then: "When was the last time you saw them?" Paul asked.

"Approximately noontime Wednesday."

"And you go over there . . . for what reason?"

"To talk to Janet."

"To talk to Janet, why?"

"Again, it felt good for me to discuss Susan and our situation."

"The situation that you're *not* over and *not* depressed about anymore?"

"That is correct."

"And . . . tell us what happened?"

"She started . . ."

"Just tell us the facts. You don't have to say what she said. You made love to her, allegedly."

"That is correct."

"And where did you make love to her?"

"In the baby's room."

"And who was home?"

"Ryan and the baby."

"Ryan and the baby. Where was Ryan? How old is Ryan?"

"Uh, at the time, two and a half, three. I don't know."

"Two-and-a-half, three-year-old child. Mother's home, baby—six-week-old baby she just had, do you know if she was released from the doctor for a cesarean yet?"

"I did not know, I didn't know she'd had a cesarean until then."

"Well, where was Ryan?"

"I know at the time, she was preparing to give him a bath. It may be a bit presumptuous of me to say he was in the bathtub. I doubt it. He may have been in the bathroom."

"Did you ever tell Sergeant Masson that he was in the bathtub?"

"I may have told Sergeant Masson that. Again it may have been presumptuous of me."

"So she was prepared—she was running the water preparing to give him a bath . . ."

"Right."

"And then she says, 'Wait a second, Ryan, let me go make love with this man that I haven't seen since November in your bedroom. Stay there, son. And don't get into the tub, okay, because you may drown, you're only three years old.' Is that what happened?"

"No, not at all."

"Is that what you want this jury to believe?"

"It didn't happen like that."

"It didn't what?"

"It didn't happen like that, Mr. Connick."

"What happened? You tell me *how it happened*," Paul demanded. "You tell me how I can believe that you went to this woman's house, saw her the day before, she invites you to dinner, her husband's there, you walk in this house, you go in there, she's getting ready to bathe her baby, and then she goes—which room again?"

"We were in the back bedroom."

"Right there. Where? In the bed?"

"No, on the floor."

"On the floor. Why on the floor? Why on the floor?"

"She wanted to be in the bedroom so she could hear Kerry coming up."

"That's a good idea, because he might pull up and you know it could get pretty bad for you, right? So she was—where's the bathroom? Here?"

"That's right."

"The door opened or closed?"

"It was opened."

"The baby's in there. And she's going to go with you—what was this, was this door opened or closed?"

"I—it may have opened, I think it might have been closed, because . . ."

"Yeah, because if you come out of that bath he can see you . . ."

"That's correct."

". . . and his—and his mother making love, right?"

"That's right."

"Yeah? *That's wrong!*" Paul was in his face.

"That's right." Bill may have appeared emotionless to many, but he did hold his ground.

Soon, Paul asked, "So, you're finished making love to Janet."

"That's correct."

"What happens next?"

"We went into the master bedroom, where she changed into some clothes, and I then left to go to Wendy's and buy lunch."

"And you went through her drawer at that time, right?"

"I went through to get some money out, correct."

"So you went to Wendy's. When you arrived there that day, where did you park your car?"

"In front of the house."

"Did you have your bat with you?"

"Uh, yes I did."

"What did you do with the bat when you arrived there?"

"I—I assume I brought it with me."

"And when you were making love to her, where was it? Did you have it with you?"

"No, I don't think I did."

"Where was it?"

"It may have been in the den."

Soon Paul was saying, "And his mother is going to sit in front of a two-year-old, three-year-old child, with a strange man that she hasn't seen since November, and drape her legs over your legs in front of that child?"

"That is what happened."

"That's what you're telling these people?"

"That is what happened."

Then, quite some time later, Paul was saying, "The three statements. An oral one to Deputy Adams, two twenty-five A.M., shortly after the murder,

another oral statement to Masson at seven twenty-one A.M., shortly—
hours after the murder, and then one Saturday night the day after the
murder. Three statements in close proximity with the time of the event.
And in each statement you say, 'I left my bat there Wednesday.' "

"The only statement I recall is the one I gave Sergeant Masson that
Saturday morning in his office and the next morning I told my attorney
please go back and tell him that I left out—I omitted that I was there at
one o'clock."

"Isn't that because he told you that a witness had seen you in front of
the house on Thursday with the bat? And you thought that if you were
with the bat on Thursday you couldn't have left it there Wednesday so you
have to say you were there twice Thursday and left the bat the first time?"

"That's incorrect."

"That's incorrect."

"If Sergeant Masson had told me that, I would have corrected myself at
the time."

"Did you lie to him to protect yourself? Didn't you? And then later
thought better of it and came back through your attorney and told the
truth. Right?"

"I was very scared."

"I understand."

"I was handcuffed, I was just—I had been stabbed twenty-four hours
earlier, I was in a policeman's office arrested. He was telling me all types
of things, that I was going to jail for the rest of my life. I was very nervous,
very scared."

"So the next morning you changed your story."

"I didn't change my story. I added it. There was—it had happened."

"You say you originally told them you went there one time on Thursday
and left the bat on Wednesday."

"Correct."

"And then you came back and said I didn't leave the bat there on
Wednesday and I came twice on Thursday. That's a change, isn't it?"

"I had left out the part where I came there at one o'clock on Thursday."

"But that . . ."

"I was very scared what Sergeant Masson was trying to do to me."

"You think Janet Myers was scared?"

"I—didn't—yes, Mr. Connick." Bill had not spoken his interrogator's
name plaintively. Or questioningly. But as a superior would to an inferior
who is in the process of being embarrassingly stupid.

"Please, I'll ask the questions and you can respond when I—and you can
answer them. So you go there at one o'clock, you have the bat with you."

"Yes I do."

"Walk up to the door, ring the doorbell. 'Janet, I've got to break this off,
it was wrong.' Right?"

"It wasn't done with that callousness, sir."

"You were being sweet about it, right? *Right?*"

"With as much decorum as possible."

"As much decorum as possible. How much decorum did you use when you swung this bat against that woman's face?" *P'thang!* is the sound of that aluminum Easton bat as Paul slammed it against the floor.

"How much decorum?" *P'thang!!* Paul was giving that floor hell, and scaring the bejesus out of the whole courtroom and surely every rodent throughout the edifice.

P'thang!!! again as he demanded, "Are you still haunted by the sound of that bat slapping that woman's face?"

P'thang!!!! "Are you?"

"I'm not even going to answer that."

"If you do answer it . . ."

"There is no way I could have killed Janet Myers with that kind of rage and that kind of anger! *There is no way.* Our relationship was not that kind of relationship."

"Relationship?"

"I could not be filled with that kind of rage and that kind of anger towards Janet Myers. It's impossible. The type of anger that could have done that to that girl could not have come from me!"

"The type of anger that was required to tear up a house with a hammer, sinks, walls, stereos. Could that have come from you?"

"That is the extent. I have never hurt anyone in my life physically."

"Until February 24, 1984, is that correct?"

"That's incorrect."

While everyone within sound of that bat crashing against the courtroom floor was now wide awake and on the edge of his seat, that thunderous, ringing, reverberating noise in such an officious place meant that there would now be no going back with the same attention to the nuances of the verbal chess game that was the cross-examination of Bill Fontanille. Everything after that was just so much grist for the legal record mill. And a good deal of it was important for triers of fact hearing it for the first time. However, with Bill, the accused murderer, being the only person who had not jumped or flinched to those bat blows and with Paul's frustration at having his most dramatic moment spent too soon, it was ensured that the prosecution would never regain control of the cross-examination.

"Why didn't you give her a call, just to tell her, 'Janet, look, I don't think this is a good idea,'" Paul would ask about the visit to "break it off."

"I thought it required more than a phone call."

"Did you park your car in front of the house when you came that first time on Thursday?"

"No, I believe that I had parked it down the street."

"How far down the street?"

"Down at the end of Litchwood."

"And this is the first time you went back?"

"At one o'clock on Thursday. Right."

"And then you left the bat there. And then you left the house. And then come back, right?"

"Yes, I did."

"Why did you come back?"

"To get the bat."

"And before you came back, you called."

"Yes, I did."

"What time did you call?"

"Around three-thirty."

"Around three-thirty you called. And you talked to . . ."

"To Janet."

"And she says, 'Sure, come over and get your bat, everything is fine.' Right? No problem."

"Uh, no, that's *not* what she said."

"Okay, you arrive at four o'clock. Janet's alive and well at three-thirty. You arrive at four o'clock."

"Right."

"You walk in. Where did you park?"

"At this time I parked on the corner of Patricia and Litchwood."

"And you parked there because you didn't want Kerry to catch you at his house."

"That's correct."

"Objection, Your Honor," boomed Nick. "He is parked there as a result of hearsay testimony that he is not permitted by this court to give."

"That's what really convinced me," Mrs. Peggy Senat says. "When Bill picked up her clothes—I mean, he fondled them almost, you could see a tear come to his eye. Myers grabbed them like they were old dishrags."

"I can be absolutely certain that he was changing his statement about the fact that he had been to the house earlier that day," Pat Fanning said in answer to a question from Paul. The last witness for the defense and the prosecutor were wrangling around the sticky area of purported statements of Janet to Bill being ruled beyond the scope of the "dying declaration," the only exception to the hearsay rule regarding statements of the victim in a murder trial.

"But when you ask me now whether the reason was to retrieve the bat," Pat continued with appropriate emphasis, "that's not why he said he went there earlier in the day."

"Right," went Paul.

"He told me why he went there earlier, but it wasn't for that reason."

"Did he tell you that he had lied to protect himself and then wanted to straighten it out?"

"No, he told me that the police officers were accusing him, that they were being harsh with him, that they made statements to him that he knew to be untrue, that could not have been true, and that he felt intimidated by them, he felt panic, and that during the course of the statement he did not tell them that he had been there earlier that day."

"Well, if I told you he made three statements to that effect, prior to him changing his story, do you recall whether or not he told you that all three separate instances he was intimidated by the police?"

"Mr. Connick, I think it's a fair statement to say that from the time that Mr. Fontanille first came in contact with the police after Kerry Myers made the telephone call, they immediately began accusing him of committing the crime without even really getting into the investigation—and because of that he felt intimidated."

"Do you waive polling at present, gentlemen?" Judge Eason said.

"Polling waived," a most disgruntled Nick Noriea barked.

"Yes, Your Honor," responded Paul Connick with all the glee of a man who knows he's sitting in the catbird seat.

"Do you have a rebuttal witness, sir?" the judge asked.

"Yes, Your Honor," Paul Connick announced. "The State calls Dr. Morris Kerstein to the stand."

"Aw, man, it worked perfectly," Paul Connick remembers. "Nick had Billy on the stand saying, 'I bled profusely, I was bleeding the whole time, *blood everywhere.*' So then his hematocrit level should've been *down* when he got to Jo Ellen, and it *wasn't*. So that's how we got Kerstein in—and that just blew Nick away. He got pissed off."

"On rebuttal? That was *wrong.*" Nick Noriea gets mad all over again, banging his hand down on his big, cluttered desk as he talks of the State pulling "their rabbit out of the hat" with Kerstein.

"It's over for me. I can't do anything after that. That's why they put him on in rebuttal. I mean, they had a judge that they obviously knew would let 'em do that.

"I knew enough about hematocrit to where Kerstein was cross-examined. But Kerstein is not a credible witness. He said he's *never* been wrong!"

"Bill did a good job on the stand," Pastor Jonas Robertson assures. "From the talk in the hall, the consensus was that you could tell Kerry was lying, and that Bill did a great job.

"But when they put the doctor up there, you sensed the moment. Like these cold chills that run down, and you get this hot flush, you're about to pee on yourself? It was such an emotionally charged moment—the *prostitute doctor* on rebuttal.

"And then after Nick challenged him? 'But, wait, Mr. Noriea, that's because they gave him two units of protoplasma, not real blood,' and Nick goes, 'I have no further questions.' When Nick said that, just surrendering, you could hear a gasp in the courtroom.

" 'Ninety-nine point nine percent degree of medical certainty'!

"I mean, you could see they had built their entire case up to that one statement—when they proved that Bill didn't get stabbed at four o'clock, that was it, forget about the evidence. It was *the moment.*"

"The artist that we hired," Cheryl Hickman is saying, "he got up in the jury box and was getting a drawing of Billy, a three-quarter face, an excellent drawing, by Lou Graff. This was right after closing arguments.

"He said, 'Boy,' at one time he looked at Billy, and Billy had this half-smirk on his face, like, 'I'm outa here. I've won this.' And then suddenly he realized that Lou was looking at him and he sealed his face off. Immediately changed expression. And Lou said at that point he knew, 'The bastard *did it.* This guy's *guilty.*' He said it was a really creepy thing. That made perfect sense to me, just based on what I had seen of Billy's performance throughout.

"Billy's smile—it never reaches his eyes. The expression in his eyes doesn't change at all."

The jurors began deliberations at 6:55 P.M. At 7:30, they sent out a note requesting the 911 tape. Judge Eason, as per Louisiana law, denied that request. At 10:00, the judge called the jurors into open court, told them to break for the night, and sent them to their motel.

"I felt we had a real shot," Art Lentini says. "I remember we went back to our West Bank office to wait for the jury to come back. We felt we had a real shot at it.

"But twelve zip, that's tough," Art concludes, referring to the fact that for first degree murder the jury verdict *must* be unanimous; second degree only needs ten.

"It was a *tough* case. From the get-go," Paul Connick muses. "The problem was—when you break it all down—we were prosecuting Fontanille and defending Myers. Noriea was prosecuting Myers and defending Fontanille. They have essentially the same story. So you're telling a jury, 'Please believe Kerry and not Bill.' Well, 'Why should we? Why is Kerry's story believable and not Bill?' That's the biggest problem with the case."

Nick called it "a wash. The points I was going for were the scratching, the fingernails, which I got early on, and the fact that Ryan, even though he was knocked out and in a coma, didn't take that hard of an impact to do what it did. Then Herb not really hurting Bill; and Carol Dixon and the other police coming through with testimony that indicated they were a bunch of buffoons.

"I always just hoped that Bill would cancel out Kerry and use the other stuff to make sure Bill wasn't convicted. And hopefully found not guilty."

Sunday, November 2, 1986   THE TIMES-PICAYUNE
Fontanille murder case ends in mistrial
By Richard Boyd
West Bank bureau

A mistrial was declared in William A. Fontanille's murder trial Saturday, leaving unanswered the 2-year-old question of who killed Janet Myers.

Following five hours and forty minutes of deliberations Friday night and Saturday morning, the jury . . . declared itself hopelessly deadlocked with six members voting for a first-degree murder conviction and six for acquittal.

Fontanille, who has been held without bond in Gretna since his indictment in March, showed little emotion during most of the six-day trial. After the verdict was read, he turned and smiled at relatives. He visited with them briefly before being returned to parish prison. . . .

"In my judicial heart I knew they were both lying about something." Judge Eason, in his retirement, reminisces on the outcome of his most famous case.

"But this guy the spatter expert?" the aging jurist continues. "Everybody wanted to believe him, he had the greatest credentials. But he got kind of out in left field.

"By the time he got to that kneeling-down demonstration with the ball bat, he was so far into left field, my feeling was, candidly, I'm not sure that I wouldn't have to be the thirteenth man if they found him guilty. Especially if they come back first degree. Because I just didn't feel like the showing was clear enough—and that's entirely backwards, of course, because if you're not clear enough then you oughta find him not guilty in the first place.

"The thing was just plain bad police work, of course . . . 'God, with all this blood, and they don't have any samples to amount to anything? They never got a print of that bloody hand?'

"The most dramatic thing I think that could've been shown, her hand sliding down the wall—*in your mind's eye you could see her trying to stand up with all her strength, then fading as she just sort of slithered down the wall.* But we can't even prove that was her hand!"

BOOK II

"There's a piece missing. There's something they're more ashamed of letting the world know of them than being the murderers of a wife and mother. Something worse. That's one of the only arguments that does make sense."

—Marion Edwards

7
Conspiracy

And there I was . . . alone in my room . . . drinking apple juice and eating crackers in the dark. It was very quiet. Only the babies crying across the hall in the nursery pierced the quiet. And suddenly I felt alone. You . . . who had been a part of me just a few hours ago . . . were across the hall. Dad was going home. No more kicking or rolling. No more snuggling with Dad. Just me, the darkness and the crackers. But while I felt alone, I was overwhelmingly happy. The moment I awaited was over. I laid there for hours reflecting on the past, on the moment, and the future. And then the epidural started to wear off. The aftershock was painful. They gave me Demerol shots and I slept until it was time for the next shot.

—*Journal of Janet Cannon Myers*

*   *   *

"To Herb MacDonell's credit," Paul Connick is saying. "As soon as the trial was over, I said, 'Herb, I need a first-class forensic biologist. Give me the best guy you know.' Herb said, 'You need Henry Lee. Henry Lee's your man.'"

Friday, November 7, 1986   THE TIMES-PICAYUNE
2nd trial in killing likely in January
By Richard Boyd
West Bank bureau
    William A. Fontanille will stand trial for a second time, possibly in January, attorneys involved in the case said Thursday.
    Assistant District Attorney Art Lentini, who prosecuted the case with another assistant, Paul Connick, said Thursday night that he understands District Attorney John M. Mamoulides will retry Fontanille.

"Here's what was really going on, not what was being released to Richard over at the paper," Paul Connick says. "We'd just tried the case. There were a lot of motions going back and forth. Nick's coming in, 'Are you going to drop the case?' He talked to Mamoulides. There was a lot of indecision, 'What are we gonna do? Are we gonna go back again or are we gonna shit-can it?'

"Mamoulides asked me what I thought, and I told him, 'The best shot we had to convict one man in the case was with Kerstein. Now we don't have any surprises. It's going to be very difficult to get a conviction now. The *easiest* way is to put both men in the pot—but for that reason alone we can't, you've got to have evidence to do it.' And at that point we had no evidence against Kerry other than this, '*Maybe* I think he did it.' Nothing hard to put your teeth into.

"So some time passes with that discussion going on. And Nick was holding off, he wasn't going to file any more motions until Mamoulides made a decision. Are we gonna reduce it? Are we gonna do this or that and all that crap? Would he plea? Just a lot of hashing it around. No real direction yet.

"That's this case, man, the whole time, nowhere to go. Nick was looking for us to drop the thing. Never gave any sign that he would deal at any level."

Tuesday, January 6, 1987 THE TIMES-PICAYUNE
Fontanille will be jailed until slay retrial
By Richard Boyd
West Bank bureau

William A. Fontanille will remain in jail awaiting a second trial on a first-degree murder charge, a judge has ruled.

State Judge Alvin Rudy Eason Monday denied a motion to set bail for Fontanille, who has been held without bond in the Jefferson Parish Correctional Center since May 1986. . . .

Later Noriea and Assistant District Attorney Tom Wilkerson conferred over a possible trial date. Noriea said the trial may be held in March. The date is expected to be set later in the week. It hinges on the availability of Herbert MacDonell. . . .

"It was only bullshit about MacDonell; Dr. Lee was the man," Paul Connick explains. "Right around Christmastime it started to be obvious we were going to go ahead with it. We started gearing up again, coordinating schedules and all.

"Right after the first of the year, I contacted Dr. Lee. We missed phone calls for a while; finally got to him maybe a month before the scheduled trial.

" 'Too busy. Too busy. Got too many cases,' he's going. I said, 'Look, do me a favor, just review the transcript of Dixon and give us some ideas as to how we can get it ready for the next trial, because the other side has somebody.' "

After more phone tag and time passing, "Finally Dr. Lee says, 'Okay, okay, I'll look at it,' " Paul continues. " 'Thank ya, Doc, thank ya.' So, 'Mike, get on a plane!'—Mike Maunoir's my investigator by this time—and I mean that afternoon. Shoom! He's flying out.

"So Mike's up there and soon I'm on the phone with Henry Lee, and he's saying, 'You got problem.' "

"With me I took Kerry Myers's brown leather shoes, the dress slacks, the baseball cap, and something else, I think, but I'm not sure." DA's investigator Mike Maunoir is remembering the event which was his first active participation in the baseball bat murder case.

"They had somebody pick me up at the airport and I went right over to the lab. I sat in Dr. Lee's office while they ran around trying to find him. He comes in the door and he grabs the transcript—Paul'd already sent him a copy of Carol Dixon's testimony and report, hoping he'd get interested—so, he's waving the transcript and says, 'I read serologist's testimony. If you want me substantiate serologist's theory, no can do. Theory all wrong.' And he says, 'I don't know about her results because I have not test any evidence—but her theory all off.' He said, 'I cannot go there and back up serologist at this point.'

"I explain to him the pieces of clothing I'd brought with me, the things he and Paul had talked about. The first thing he does is unwrap Kerry's pants and he puts them under this large magnifying glass which had some kind of a round fluorescent light, like a ring around it, and—you know, you look at these dark brown-gray pants with the naked eye and you really can't see anything—all of a sudden blood was showing up like little pieces of chipped bicycle reflector, almost in the fiber itself. You could see the pattern of the fiber, and the blood was actually down in there. He said he thought he could get enough off the pants to be able to type it, said he wanted to do extensive testing on them.

"Then he looked at the dress shoes and he said some of the preservatives they use in leather can give you a false reading on the blood so he'd have to work with that, but said he saw plenty enough that he thought he could do something with it.

"I said, 'Let me try and get in touch with Paul and tell him this.' "

"I said, 'Leave the stuff up there, Mike.' We grabbed a coupla more pieces of evidence and we're flying up—we cross in the sky—Mike's coming back, and me and Conn Regan are flying up. Art's left the office to run for sheriff," Paul Connick remembers, and explains, "And Conn volunteered.

"We sat down and basically said this is what we have, this is what we need, and we're within a month or two weeks of the trial by this time.

" 'Whooo! Yeah, problems. That serologist? *No jujubes,*' he goes. He's talking, and, aw man, I'm just sitting back listening and he says, 'Hmmm, this interesting case.' So he keeps going on and he says, 'You can't use this. Other side see this? Too many things in it—I did not say what she did wrong, it the way she explain herself—the other side, if they get expert serologist, big problem.' "

Wednesday, March 25, 1987   THE TIMES-PICAYUNE
Murder suspect loses attempt to get out of jail
By Richard Boyd
West Bank bureau

   William A. Fontanille lost another attempt Tuesday to get out of jail—where he has been since last March—even though his first-degree murder trial in November ended in a hung jury.

   District Judge Alvin Rudy Eason denied a motion to set bond for Fontanille. . . .

"We had to continue the case so many times because of how bad Carol Dixon had fucked up on the first trial," Paul is saying.

"Finally, Dr. Lee had thought about it and he calls me, 'Look, you cannot use this woman.' He said it was so bad, totally off the wall, and they were gonna tear her to shreds. The good news is that he's interested, he's decided to take it, *he's hooked.* In Henry's words, 'Serologist's dream.' He says, 'You pull up vinyl floor, you cut out Sheetrock,' if you do this, if you do that, you can reconstruct the whole scene just by the blood. *Like connecting the dots.*"

Debra Blakely, a divorced mother with one child and a cocktail waitress at Cannons Restaurant in Oakwood Mall, flirted with Kerry Myers as he was eating with Mike Price and Curtis Jordan, primarily, she later says, because she liked the white slacks he was wearing. "It was the last week of March 1987. I remember exactly, because our first date was April 1st, April Fools' Day," she explains.

Mike Price had encouraged Kerry to "go for it." Ms. Blakely's apparently less than virtuous reputation was known to Mike, and he felt it was exactly what Kerry needed. Mike even wrote the mash note for Kerry on one of the suggestion forms some restaurants use. In short order a date was arranged.

* * *

The 24th Judicial District judge for Division O had been ill for almost a year and there had been an ad hoc sitting in. Ad hoc jurists usually prefer not handling the tough trials. Consequently there was a backup of serious cases on the docket: a multitude of murders, aggravated rapes, crimes of other assorted violence and such.

"Welcome to Felony," Supervisor Jim Maxwell had said with some ruefulness to Assistant District Attorney W. J. LeBlanc.

Dub decided for the first trial week in April 1987 for his first felony trial, he might just as well take on a murder case; he had a number to choose from, plus the powers upstairs are always anxious for movement of any manner on all jail cases.

They got it.

The jury was out thirty-five minutes; second degree murder. Life without parole, Errol Carlin.

"Dr. Lee looked at the hat and a couple of things, and the handkerchief, the nasal secretion," Paul Connick is saying. "We always assumed it was Bill's but our lab couldn't tell us.

"All along I'd been saying, 'Why can't we test this?' And all I'm hearing is, 'There's no way.' Yet Henry tested it, found it had Kerry's type, not Fontanille's. Then he found some things on other items that were different from what Dixon had found—where she found inconclusive, he found something.

"I said, 'Whoa.' I went to Mamoulides, we sat down, this is maybe a week before the trial. I said, 'We've got a problem here, 'cause now it's looking like we have some stuff on Kerry. We've gotta do something.'

"Mamoulides immediately said, 'Stop the presses. Let's go talk to Rudy.' And that's what we do. We tell Judge Eason what we've got—and that we've got to get to the bottom of it.

"*Every* item of evidence, every result we had, was suspect now. We have to redo it. From top to bottom. Pitch Dixon and start all over. We were hampered there because once you take a blood spatter out of those jeans, it's gone. Forever. So you've got a nice little pattern here for the first trial, but you've got to go again? I mean, we'd already lost the B spot on the leotards that way, going from Dixon to Herb."

"I couldn't believe it," Mike Price says. "But then again, knowing Kerry, I should've seen it coming from a mile away. Here all I was doing was trying to get him out of his shell. You know, get back in the saddle again—for crying out loud, she was a cocktail waitress! Just the thing, right?

"Wrong. Big-time wrong. They hadn't gone out twice before he's talking 'love.' *'What?'* 'Yeah! The real thing.' And I mean just like that—they're inseparable. This was like in April, and before summer she's moved into that big house and brought along her whole strange family."

Tuesday, May 5, 1987   THE TIMES-PICAYUNE
Evidence twist might help out slay suspect
By Richard Boyd
West Bank bureau
   Prosecutors said Monday they have uncovered evidence that might be favorable to William A. Fontanille, charged with the 1984 murder of a young Harvey mother of two.
   Assistant District Attorney Paul Connick Jr. made the announcement before jury selection would have begun in Fontanille's second trial for first-degree murder. . . . Jefferson Parish prosecutors also reduced the charge against Fontanille from first-degree to second-degree murder. If convicted of the lesser charge, Fontanille would spend the rest of his life in prison but the state can no longer seek the death penalty. . . .

"Nick is screaming. But we did it because we found stuff that was brand-new to us," Paul Connick says, remembering—with more than just his usual level of animation—that eleventh-hour bombshell dropped on the defense and public at large. "We were shocked. I said, 'Look, we knew that Dixon had screwed up. We just didn't know how bad.' Henry told us how bad. He also found some things."

Indeed, Dr. Lee did find "some things" in just his preliminary analysis, such as:

The handkerchief with Janet's or Ryan's type A blood also contained a rather large mucus stain deposited by an individual who is a secretor of antigen H, more commonly known as type O, in the body fluids. Kerry Myers is a secretor; he is also type O.

On the dishtowels, where Carol Dixon had found types B and O, Dr. Lee found A, B, and O.

On a piece of amber glass that was once part of the shattered ashtray and was retrieved by Carol Dixon from the den area on her March 5, 1984, visit to the crime scene, the piece she had determined to be inconclusive regarding the blood of human origin upon it, Henry Lee found type A blood.

Six or seven dozen medium-velocity impact spatters with a telltale pattern on the upper left thigh of Kerry Myers's dress slacks were type A bloodstains.

On the baseball cap on which Carol Dixon had determined that there was blood of human origin but that it was inconclusive as to type, Professor Lee found both A and B bloodstains, some spatters and some transfers—and not only on the outside but *underneath* the bill of the McClean Trucking hat which had been found lying upright on the carpeted floor of the hall just past where the linoleum ends from the foyer.

Just the above was enough to raise considerable doubt about the State's victimized, bereft, and widowed star witness's oft-repeated version of the events which took place that Thursday evening of February 24, 1984. To say the least. It did not, however, do much toward determining which of the two men was lying—or rather which of the two men was lying the *most.* Which, while it may be a contradiction in legal logic, is perhaps the only appropriate approach available, since just the preliminary work seemed to suggest that *both* of them were lying about *something.*

Tuesday, May 12, 1987   THE TIMES-PICAYUNE
Court sets 30-day deadline for slay trial
By Richard Boyd
West Bank bureau
   A Terrytown man charged with second-degree murder in the bludgeon slaying of a Harvey housewife must be tried within 30 days or be released from jail without bond, the Louisiana Supreme Court ruled Monday.

In May 1987, W. J. LeBlanc prosecuted one Jerald Daisy for aggravated rape. Mr. Daisy had picked up a woman hitchhiking on the West Bank Expressway and raped her at about four o'clock in the morning at knifepoint. Guilty as charged; life without parole.

Wednesday, June 10, 1987   THE TIMES-PICAYUNE
Jeff murder suspect expected to be freed
By Sandra Barbier
West Bank bureau
   William A. Fontanille is expected to be released from jail without bond Wednesday although second-degree murder charges against him in the slaying of a Harvey woman have not been dropped. . . .

Pastor Jonas Robertson, who now had his own fundamentalist church established and prospering within the building and grounds of what used to be Woodland West Country Club, was preparing the way for Billy to come live with his family and join the flock of the Church of Abundant Light.

While preparing a back room for Bill in the quite impressive home only a thousand yards or so from the church, the good reverend was also preparing his true believers to accept the most famous possible murderer in Louisiana since young Dr. Weiss either did or did not assassinate Huey Long in 1936.

One of Brother Jonas's flock, Allan LeMoine, eight years younger than Bill, would soon become one of the more important persons in his life.

Thursday, June 11, 1987   THE TIMES-PICAYUNE
Trial delay frees slay suspect
By Sandra Barbier
West Bank bureau
   A smiling William Fontanille on Wednesday walked out of the Jefferson Parish Correctional Center in Gretna where he has been held more than a year after being indicted in the killing of a Harvey housewife.
   District Judge Alvin Rudy Eason ordered Fontanille's release without bond in accordance with a state Supreme Court ruling. The release contains no restrictions such as limits on where Fontanille can travel, Nick Noriea, his attorney said. . . .
   Fontanille paused a few seconds on his way to a waiting car to answer reporters' questions. Asked how he feels, he said, "Like the French when Lindbergh landed." He said there were "about 30 things I want to do," but added the first thing was to go home.
   Fontanille is still facing a second-degree murder charge in the slaying of Janet Myers. . . .

Jonas Robertson is recalling a day and a conversation about which he still has regrets. "When we pulled up after he got out of prison, I turned to him and said, 'Now, Bill, in that back room you'll notice there's a bolt-lock and a key-lock which locks you in there. You'll have total privacy. It's yours to come and go.'

"Then I told him, 'But, listen, Bill, the only thing I'm going to ask you to do—you're welcome in my home, I love ya, I want to help ya—but when I'm not home, I'm gonna ask ya not to come up front.'

"That kind of like stuck a knife in him. At that point he went overboard not to be around us because he felt I didn't trust him. He pouted. For the entire three years—he'd come in for the occasional meal, and we'd have to go knock on his door to answer the telephone and he'd have to come in the house. He wouldn't get a phone. We had a jack back there for him, but he wouldn't buy a phone.

"This statement really affected him and our relationship, our friendship," Jonas continues. "But it wasn't from a sense of mistrust. It was from the appearance of evil—how does it look for a man to be in the house with my wife and I'm at work? It wasn't a lack of trust."

In June 1987, W. J. LeBlanc not only took on and put away another murderer for life, he also forged an alliance and soon a close personal friendship with his kind of a cop, a relationship which would serve both of them well. With the assistance of commander of homicide Lieutenant Vincent Lamia, in a tough investigation of a tough case, Dub got another "guilty as charged" to second degree murder from a jury, this one against a John Kirk Richard.

"The jury came back after three hours, about seven P.M.," W.J. remembers. "I took them all out for a few beers. We went to Copeland's. I always talk to juries after trials, I learned that on my first case. They can give you valuable insight on how they viewed the presentation of the case, the defense as well as the prosecution."

The next day was a Saturday, and since the case had ended so late the evening before, W.J. went into the District Attorney's Office to get his paycheck and he heard activity in the grand jury room. When he poked his head in he saw Robert Pitre, Paul Connick, Wally Rothschild, "and this incredibly interesting Chinese guy going through this slide show on Fontanille-Myers."

Dub sat in and listened, asking only a very few questions. Then he went with them out to the house as Dr. Lee studied the crime scene. W.J. even got to play a role—lying down here or there in the house at different times representing Kerry, Bill, and Janet as the scene was reconstructed and scenarios played out. He was immensely impressed with Dr. Henry Lee.

"I was hooked by that slide show—this was my first substantive look at the case. I just sat there and listened. Right from the start it grabbed me, and I seemed to just have a grasp of this case as if it were déjà vu or something, like I'd had the case from the beginning or something.

"It was the mirror-image aspect that grabbed me the most, which was almost brilliant, in a sense. I was fascinated: very attractive woman, two guys I knew a little, fellow Shaw grads, in this bizarre, seemingly motiveless crime, each pointing the finger the other way, and no conclusions could be drawn from photos of the scene, so it was just . . . bizarre."

"Bill came to church and seemed sincere in his conversion. The first time we actually met was at the church when Jonas and Bill were working out with weights," remembers Allan LeMoine. He joined in.

"That's all he wanted to do then. Get his body in shape. That was the main common ground between Bill and I originally," says Allan.

"We mainly just worked out. But from what I could see he wasn't socializing. The very first thing we ever did together socially was a Wednesday night we went to a movie at Oak Ridge. After the movie I remember I prayed with him. He was crying. There were tears in his eyes. He goes, 'Boy, you must've been practicing.' He was incredibly moved by it. No doubt in my mind that he was sincere."

Within a week Bill brought the case up. "He told me that when he was out in public he would run into people who would come up to him and say, 'Hey, I know you didn't do it.' Complete strangers.

"I had more respect for Bill than any of my three older brothers, even my dad in a way. Nobody ever told me to read a book. None of my brothers, in just conversation, ever told me about the greenhouse effect. Things like that. Bill would explain things to me.

"He was brilliant. He told me he had taken the test to get into LSU Law School and had passed it. He said he'd scored two points less than the highest possible. I believed him. I had no reason not to. From the way he carried himself. The books I always saw him reading.

"He was constantly reading a newspaper. When the stock market crashed in October of '89, he explained it all to me. A brilliant guy. Nobody ever explained things to me like that before.

"His books overtowered the bookcases. He had books stacked on the floor, bookcases weren't big enough. This guy totally amazed me."

During the third week of June 1987, W. J. LeBlanc was visiting at the home of a longtime family friend. She was reading the details of a particularly disgusting, soul-numbing murder in the newspaper and remarked to the young prosecutor, "Gee, wouldn't it be something if you had to try these animals."

Those "animals," Charles Gervais, Michael Phillips, and Thelma Horn, had tortured and killed one André Daigle, already a prosperous residential builder and renovator while still in his early twenties, picked at random so that they could "practice" at murder in preparation for taking over an organized prostitution and drug gang in Texas. After almost a week of frenzied panic by the Daigle family, young André's remains were located and three killers were captured and confessions obtained, indisputably, by all accounts, due directly to the intervention of a psychic some 2,500 miles away in California at the time.

And, as fate would have it of course, the case file did find its way to W.J.'s desk.

Friday, September 18, 1987   THE TIMES-PICAYUNE
Man facing retrial in slaying of Harvey woman
By Richard Boyd
West Bank bureau

A Terrytown man may go to trial for the second time on Oct. 26, charged with the brutal 1984 bludgeoning death of a young Harvey housewife. Assistant District Attorney Robert Pitre said earlier in the week that Oct. 26 has been tentatively set as the start of the retrial of William Fontanille, 32. . . .

Earlier this week, prosecutors said they are still awaiting a written report of the analysis of the evidence. . . . Pitre said that Oct. 26 was selected because an important out-of-state prosecution witness, Herbert MacDonell, is available that week.

On September 28, 1987, a three-volume report from the Connecticut Division of State Police Forensic Science Laboratory, prepared by Dr. Henry Lee and his staff and totaling seventy-three pages, finally arrived at the Jefferson Parish District Attorney's Office. It was the culmination of a great deal of activity, comings and goings, stayings and leavings, fuss, bother, conflict, success, ethical controversy, and the beginning of lasting new friendships and the diminishing of a few old ones, and most of it had also somehow managed to remain relatively secret.

In the late winter and early spring of '87, Wally Rothschild returned to the Jeferson Parish District Attorney's Office after a stint of prosecuting at the U.S. Attorney's Office in New Orleans. Soon thereafter, John Mamoulides asked him to oversee the Fontanille-Myers case. While Wally Rothschild's efforts and theories turned the baseball bat murder case 180 degrees, the true extent of his role was virtually unknown to the public. Perhaps that is due to his unassuming, non-grandstanding style.

"I had prosecuted a number of conspiracy cases in federal court. This case appeared to me to fit the bill for a criminal conspiracy." Mr. Rothschild—whose nickname is Uncle Wally because he looks and sounds like he could be anybody's favorite uncle—explains how he came to be involved in the baseball bat murder case and, in truth, would play the single most pivotal role in its long, twisting, greatly disputed, and hotly contested history.

"I read Myers's testimony, and it was incredible. As was Fontanille's. But the difference being that when they came in one of them said the other one did him something. When it ended one of them said the other one did him something. Other than that you could almost overlay their testimony and statements. So it was obvious to me just reading this alone that these guys were involved in it *together.*

"Reviewing the 911 tape, it appeared to me that the guy was acting, the husband. I had contacts with the FBI and I asked the FBI lab to look at the tape. We had to do this with some urgency because the case was getting older and older and there was a lot of attention on it. We had to make a decision on which way we were going to go."

Mike Maunoir was sent to take the 911 tape up to the FBI technical lab outside Washington. He remembers that "somebody from the U.S. Attorney's Office had put Wally onto this guy up there. The question we were asking was did Kerry really leave the telephone when he's yelling 'Oh my God, she's dead, she's dead' or is he just holding the phone away. It didn't sound quite right.

"I went up the night before, stayed in a hotel, and met the guy the next morning at the lab. We walk into a room about three times the size of this with nothing but this tape-type equipment. Floor to ceiling. There's this long table in the middle of the room and there's a guy sitting at it with a portable recorder listening to something with headphones on.

"So we're in this space-age, high-tech audio room. The guy I'm with puts the tape on, listens to it, and says definitely he was in another room, or outer room from where the phone was, because he could hear the echo in the background. Then he says, 'Did this guy ever have any drama experience?'

" 'You got me. Maybe in school.'

"He said, 'This isn't really my expertise. But I listen to thousands of tapes a year, and this guy is acting.'

"Now, the door's over here, and in walks somebody else and my guy goes, 'Come over here and listen to something.'

"So this guy listens to the tape and says, 'All right, what's your question?' I say, 'When the guy is yelling, "Oh, my God, she's dead, she's dead," is he away from the phone?'

" 'I think I can answer that. Let me check.' He puts the tape back on. 'Oh, yeah. There's the echo. He's in a hallway or another room not much bigger than where the phone is.' Then he says, 'But this guy's acting.'

"Now the guy at the end of the table finishes his tape. Bring him over, he plugs in and says the same thing. 'Yeah, he's left the phone. But, hey, this guy's acting.' "

"So that, of course, is evidence," Wally Rothschild is saying. "It's not evidence you can use, but it certainly bolsters the impression that he had some knowledge of her death inconsistent with what he was telling us.

"Paul Connick made contact with Henry Lee. We went to Henry Lee with the idea of replacing Herb MacDonell, because Herb's testimony was wishy-washy to say the least.

"And Henry Lee said there was information—there was hard evidence that suggested that the husband was in close proximity of somebody swinging the bat with the blood source being her head.

"Based upon their stories, it was inconceivable that her blood could have gotten on the husband in any other manner than him being present while she was getting killed. So with that in mind and some other information in hand—Bill's statements at Jo Ellen, which in my opinion were conspiratorial—we had real good strong evidence of a conspiracy.

"I knew all along that you're not going to be able to convict Fontanille using Kerry Myers as a witness. It's impossible. That was proven by the first jury . . . I thought from the first moment I looked at the case that both of them did it. It was just a matter of sifting out the facts the way they came down and seeing whether you had enough to support any sort of charge, and it was my opinion that the conspiracy charge was the most viable. See, you can charge a conspiracy and you can also charge a substantive violation. A conviction of the conspiracy is separate and apart from a conviction on the substantive violation, so you can have both.

"So very easily you could've convicted both of them of conspiracy and one or both walk on the murder. And the opposite is true. The jury could've said, 'No, we think they committed the murder, but not the conspiracy.' So I figured that conspiracy is the linchpin.

"But the most important thing is to get the dual indictment. Because once you get the indictment, any jury—and I feel very strongly on this—any jury that hears those stories alone is going to convict both of them."

On September 19, 1987, W. J. LeBlanc prosecuted one Edna Gibson, who claimed self-defense in a rather blatant case of spousal murder. Guilty as charged, second degree murder, life without parole.

"This is the point where I didn't feel comfortable," Paul reflects, and his discomfort is obviously still with him. "They started switching to this conspiracy theory. I just didn't see it. And we went up to Connecticut. Wally and I were flying up. Art got out and Wally got in. I get out, too, but I stay on as a special prosecutor for just this one case.

"We were going up and they were talking about this conspiracy theory. This is after Henry's report and we're going up for a review of it. On the way up, Wally and I are talking about it. And he's saying 'conspiracy, conspiracy'—look, one of the problems with this case was you had so many people putting their two cents in over at the DA's Office, but very few people actually read everything, Art and I had of course, yet everybody had an idea, but invariably they're always missing one little thing, because if you really know the case you can always come back with 'Yeah, that's great. But what about this? What about that? How do you make that neat little fact fit with all this other stuff?' So Wally's really pushing this conspiracy at me.

"We get up to Henry Lee's. We met for a couple days, going over everything. When we finish up I said, 'Henry, let me ask you, do you think we have a conspiracy?' He said, 'I don't think we have enough for conspiracy.' Henry just never felt comfortable with the conspiracy. On the way back on the plane, Wally said, 'Yeah, I guess you're right, we don't have a conspiracy.' "

One of the things that always struck Mike Maunoir as being most odd about the baseball bat murder case was "Kerry not burning Billy with his statements or on the stand in the first trial. I read all that and I asked Paul Connick about it, I said, 'What kind of witness did he make?'

"And Paul said, 'I don't know. Man, he really didn't—I don't know, something's wrong.' But man, anybody who had gone through as much as he'd gone through, not even knowing if his son's gonna live, and all: 'You're goddam right there was blood all over him and that bat when he came at me when I walked in. That son of a bitch had just killed her! He tried to kill me! He tried to kill my kid! When he left, I chased him out the house, I found my wife dead. You're damn right he killed her!' But there was none of that. Instead, both of them went out of their way to say they didn't know she was even dead, much less who killed her."

"You know, Billy always talked about the good times with Kerry," Allan LeMoine recalls. "He talked a lot about spending time on a boat in the lake—and that boat oddly enough was Kerry's dad's.

"One time when he brought it up, I asked him how he felt about seeing Kerry in court. I said, 'Do you ever look at him?'

" 'Sometimes I do,' he said. 'And sometimes I wanna run up to him and strangle him, but then on the other hand I want to hug him and tell him I love him.' I remember that as clear as day.

"When I first met him I was very much into church. I was faithful, I was sincere in my relationship with the Lord." Allan LeMoine continues to explain and remember. "Then Billy and I started hanging around together more and more. At first it was just going to movies during the week. And what wound up happening was we became good friends. Now, he was going to church and all, but as far as his real commitment? I don't know.

"So we start hanging out a lot, going to the Mississippi Coast, to the beach a lot, and what started happening was—I hate to say it—but he drew me away from the walk I had with the Lord and the envelopment of the church, because, to be honest with ya, I seen the *influence* this guy had on *girls*. It just fascinated me. I've never ever seen anything like it.

"You know why he got into reading the *World Almanac* every day? To pick up girls. He said girls are fascinated if instead of immediately hitting on them you let them start conversations and no matter what they say, you can talk intelligently on it. Throw some neat piece of trivia or detail about something they're interested in at 'em.

"I tried it, and it *worked*. This girl said, 'Gee, you know a little bit about everything.' I said to myself, 'Look at this!'

"And, oh yeah, *The Dead Poets Society*? He *loved* that movie. And it reminded me a lot of him. I mean, the character that Robin Williams played, his class, I mean, just totally looked up to him. And then he got taken away from them. I was crying at the end of that movie because I knew that one day Bill was going to be gone.

"Bill totally identified with that movie. He had this mentor thing, the prophet and his disciples. He was up at this level and we were down here looking up admiring. Especially around girls. When it was just Bill and a couple of guys, like the pastor and me, working out or something, it was just good ol' Bill, you know. But when an incredibly attractive girl just happened to be present—it became what I called the Billy Show.

"That's when I would just be quiet and watch Billy-boy take over. And he would do it at anybody's expense to get the girl. Belittling somebody for his advantage. I remember one time we were out by the swimming pool at the apartments where I live and I was talking to this girl and the Billy Show came on, and she went up to her apartment for a second and I said, 'Unh-unh, Bill, she's mine.' And he goes, 'Don't be so insecure.' Yet that's what he was doing. He wanted the same thing I did. Her.

"To me it was like if he went to bed with Kerry Myers's wife, it was nothing for him to try to get somebody else's girl.

"He loved Bart's. The phony people. Club Fontaine, that was his next favorite bar. But he wasn't out to drink. I've never seen Bill the slightest bit drunk ever, he'd nurse a drink forever. He hated disco, but still he would go to City Lights. And he would create these different identities to fit every occasion. Aliases. Different schools he'd gone to. Different states he was from. He would use Bill as his first name, but not Fontanille as the last. And employment? His phrase was 'independently wealthy.'

"The Billy Show—all he had to do to pick up girls was to stand there looking sad or thoughtful or distracted or just intense and different from all of the other guys hitting on the girls in these 'meat markets.' He never approached them. They *always* came to him. I never ever saw him approach a girl. It was always them coming over to him. Girls would come up and ask him if he was a model. Or why did he look so sad? They'd want to buy *his* drinks. My sister was in love with him. Whatever the occasion or circumstance, he would create a character that every woman would fall in love with.

"We described them as 'statistics.' He'd be talking to a girl and I'd be talking to one and we'd go to the bathroom or something and he would say, 'Oh yeah, she's going down in the books. She's going to be a statistic.'

"He was incredible, he kept a list of girls he'd done. Now, I don't know if this was for his whole life or just those three years, but towards the end he'd put real numbers to our stock statistic line, like, 'Oh, yeah. She's gonna be number 116.'

"But almost always it would only be girls from out of town, either new to the area or a tourist. He never wanted to run the risk of a girl knowing who he was. That he couldn't handle. And there were maybe less than three or four exceptions to that—you know, him making a 'statistic' of a girl who knew who he was and what had happened."

"We took Dr. Lee out to the crime scene and he suggested dressing a model up, same height, and laying her out on the floor and letting the jury see," Wally explains. "And that's exactly what I planned to do when I go to trial.

"Then we made several trips out to the house with the grand jury, let them look around. After that we came back and showed them the photographs. Based on Kerry's statement—regardless of under what circumstances, staying in the house for ten hours, running up and down the hallway, with Fontanille coming at him from that living room with a bat, yelling at him so that he would've had to look in that direction—it was inconceivable, even if you allow for the shaded condition of the room, because the drapes were closed, for him not to see that body. It's just impossible. Especially the way she was laying, with her head against the wall, and her feet stretching out into the room.

"With that, the physical evidence, Dr. Lee, and the statements, we were able to get an indictment charging both of them with murder and with conspiracy."

The grand jury included in its October 8, 1987, bill of indictment the charge that the two old friends also *conspired to kill Bill's wife, Susan, at the same time.*

There were, of course, any number of comments being bandied about in and around the greater New Orleans metropolitan area disparaging and mocking the fact that the same District Attorney's Office that had used Kerry Myers as its star witness was now trying to convict him of that very same murder.

To Paul and Art's credit, they have not remained silent in the face of their detractors and armchair quarterbacks.

"In my mind I could not say, 'I know he did it,' " Paul Connick explains, and not at all from a defensive posture. "Ninety-nine point nine percent of the time, when you prosecute a case, you know you've got 'em. You just know it. So you go after them. But this case? I didn't know. I didn't have that feeling. Against Fontanille I did.

"Even after going up to Dr. Lee's, there was no way I was going to try this case—even if I'd stayed in the DA's Office—because I could not in conscience go against Kerry. Now, I can't say I'm the judge, I'm the jury, and he *didn't* do it. But in my heart I couldn't go after him and do my job because I said, 'I might put the wrong man in jail. Because I don't *know.*'

"What haunts me," says Art Lentini, "what happens if Kerry was there, in the vicinity while this guy is killing his wife and has hurt his child? And he's trying to do what he can but he's really not doing enough in his mind, but he's getting spattered because he is in the vicinity, and then Billy tells him, 'I'm gonna blame this on you. You've got her blood on you, too.' He gets scared. He's a wimp. He's ashamed and so he starts making up little stories, changes this and that, maybe even alters evidence, I don't know—

but does that mean he should be charged with murder? That's what bothers me.

"Because neither one of us is going to put a guy we don't *know* is guilty on trial with someone who *is* guilty just to get a conviction."

Friday, October 16, 1987   THE TIMES-PICAYUNE
Myers case hearing is scheduled
By Richard Boyd
West Bank bureau

   A year and four days after facing William Fontanille in a courtroom and accusing him of killing his wife, Kerry Myers will stand beside him on November 3 for arraignment on murder charges.

8
James Hearing

Thursday morning they wheeled you to x-ray. My heart broke. It was a hectic day. The doc told me if everything was okay, we could go home Friday. Although your test results come back okay, you developed "baby jaundice" and they would have to watch your blood count. We planned on going home Friday. Dad brought things home Thursday night and Grandma & Grandpa Cannon were scheduled to pick us up in the morning. Dad arranged for his vacation to start. And they all came Friday morning, but during the night your jaundice count rose. They said I could go home and you could stay. No . . . I came to have you . . . I wasn't leaving without you.

—*Journal of Janet Cannon Myers*

*   *   *

On a morning in mid-November 1987, while coming out of the elevator onto the first floor of the Jefferson Parish Courthouse, W. J. LeBlanc, his mind much distracted from the mundane, almost ran smack dab over a young woman who had often waited on him at Cannons Restaurant, a favorite watering hole of some within the criminal justice system in Jefferson Parish.

Being somewhat surprised to see her in that setting, he innocently inquired as to the nature of her business there and if in his capacity as an assistant district attorney (along with being the Gretna city attorney) there was anything he might be able to help her with.

His mild surprise immediately turned to incredulity when she answered that her fiancé had been indicted for murder and only if he could undo that grave injustice would he be of any real service to her.

"Get outa here!" was how the gregarious Dub registered his amazement. Basically, he thought it was a joke and was waiting for the punch line when she floored him by naming the individual she was about to become the wife of—Kerry Myers.

"But Debbie, he killed his *wife*!" It was the best rejoinder the flabbergasted W.J. could muster at the moment.

"But he told me he didn't do it, W.J.," said Debra Blakely.

Dub shook his head in sadness, quickly wished her a hollow "Good luck," and then got the hell away and down the hall shaking his head in his wonderment at just when the ever-increasing circles of overlapping relationships within the world of the baseball bat murder case would come to an end.

"Damn!" Dub said to the world at large once he was out of the building and heading toward his parking spot. Later that afternoon he mentioned it to Mike Maunoir.

"Think we oughta send a wedding present?" Mike asked.

"What?"

"Yeah. Buy her a batting helmet. Whatcha think?" a barely straight-faced Mike said.

Against a consensus of advice and pleas to the contrary, Ms. Debra Blakely *insisted* upon becoming the new Mrs. Kerry Myers, and was married in festive fashion on November 26, 1987, a full six weeks *after* the groom had been indicted for clubbing to death the first Mrs. Myers.

"I think she got off on the idea, myself," says Mike Price.

On a late November morning, W. J. LeBlanc, with his notes and files and the always present volume Louisiana Code of Criminal Procedure, was pumped and ready to proceed with the business at hand: sending Charles Gervais to the electric chair for the murder of André Daigle.

But then, well before the bailiff was due to announce "All rise," Wayne Walker approached Dub and said he wanted to plead Gervais guilty to avoid exposure to the death penalty.

"He said he just had to convince his client. I ran upstairs—I knew what the policy was, but I convinced Pitre to let me make a further condition of his plea that he testify against his codefendants in any future trials.

"Gervais wasn't crazy about it, but he agreed."

Guilty as charged: first degree murder; life without parole.

"Lemme tell ya why Wally wanted a conspiracy," Nick Noriea booms. "Wally says, 'Easy, let's try 'em for conspiracy. That way we can put both of 'em on trial at one time and use Fontanille's statement against Myers, and Myers's statement against Fontanille, because any statement made by a co-conspirator is not hearsay and you get it in.' *Great* idea. *Great* idea. Get both in court with both the statements and all three charges and tell the jury, 'Look, y'all figure out what we screwed up and what we can't figure out and take the political heat off of us, because if you mess up, so what?' "

"Not only that," Madeleine Landrieu joins in. "Let me tell you the terrible conflict put on a juror. 'Juror, one or both of these men committed this crime, there's nobody else in the world who could have but them, can you let them both walk if the State doesn't prove its case beyond a reasonable doubt?' I mean, it's fact, one or both of these two men killed her, period. No other choices. Lot of pressure on a jury to convict one or both."

"They're both getting convicted," Nick says with the undramatic finality of a person looking out of the window at a cloudless day in Arizona and remarking that there will be no rain today.

"I file motions to sever," Nick says, returning to his narrative of those confusing legal days when different criminal charges and different strategies were changing with the rapidity of the weather in this Gulf Stream squalls-and-hurricanes part of the world.

"The judge grants it—separates the two murder charges. But they're gonna go to trial together on conspiracy. And that was the charge that really worried me. That really bothered me. Because they're gonna get convicted. Fontanille's gonna get convicted of conspiracy as sure as I'm sitting here."

In late January 1987, W. J. LeBlanc, for probably the first time in the history of post-colonial American jurisprudence, put a psychic on the stand as a fact witness in a criminal trial for the purpose of testifying for the prosecution about supernatural events which are entered into evidence. She is one Rosemarie Kerr, the little old grandma who just happens to have, well, this gift, of sorts. Whatever it is, she is the only "forensic" psychic that the FBI works with routinely. Together, she and W. J. LeBlanc convicted Michael Phillips of the murder of André Daigle. Guilty as charged: first degree murder; life without parole.

Wednesday, March 2, 1988   THE TIMES-PICAYUNE
Joint trial is set in slay plot
By Richard Boyd
West Bank bureau
   . . . State Judge Alvin Rudy Eason on Tuesday set May 1–6 for the trial in Gretna for both on conspiracy to commit murder charges. Eason has granted defense motions for separate trials on the second-degree-murder charges. Eason said the separate trials are proper because in Fontanille's 1986 trial, Myers was a key state witness accusing Fontanille of committing the baseball-bat slaying of Janet Myers.

Assistant District Attorney Robert Pitre said Tuesday they will be prosecuted first on the conspiracy charges. . . .

On Monday, April 27, Nick and Wally were in agreement that a continuance of the conspiracy trial scheduled to start that day should be granted since all involved were "awaiting the outcome of . . . new tests."

Judge Eason granted the delay and suggested that they try for an October trial date.

In May of '87, Madeleine Landrieu, having finished law school and being admitted to the bar, came back to Gainsburgh, Benjamin, Fallon, David & Ates as a full-time associate, and immediately rejoined Nick on Fontanille-Myers, except this time as his second chair.

When W. J. LeBlanc left Division O, Andrea Jantzen, one of his dearest friends, was brought in, so she had a lot of cases that Dub had already begun the preparation for.

"One of those was John Wieland for first degree murder," Ms. Jantzen remembers. "Because Dub had been involved with it from the beginning, we prosecuted it jointly.

"We worked hard, got a conviction of first degree murder, and then the jury returned a life sentence as opposed to the death penalty. We kind of expected that. I was not disappointed. W.J. was.

"But the boy was seventeen years old at the time of the offense. He was barely old enough to be prosecuted as an adult. He had had an awful, miserable childhood himself and he probably deserved life in prison."

"Bullshit!" is still W. J. LeBlanc's comment to that philosophical difference between him and Ms. Jantzen. "There are millions of kids who come out of a terrible home life, childhood or whatever, but they don't stab a guy fourteen times over a buck seventy and a few joints of weed!"

Guilty as charged: first degree murder; life without parole.

Wednesday, October 5, 1988   THE TIMES-PICAYUNE
Former pals set for trial on conspiracy
By Richard Boyd
West Bank bureau

Two men, once softball team buddies, go on trial together Wednesday, accused of conspiring to kill their wives in 1984.

Several motions have to be resolved Wednesday before jury selection can begin. One of those involves the jury itself. Fontanille is asking for a jury trial; Myers, through his attorney, Wiley Beevers, wants a judge trial. . . .

Noriea and Beevers have joined forces on requests to block the state

from using statements made at anytime to anyone by Myers. They
argue that as a codefendant, Myers cannot be forced to testify and if
any of the statements pointed to Fontanille, they would not be able to
cross-examine Myers if Myers refused to testify.

"If there's one ruling that I *needed* to win, it was the ruling on the
conspiracy," Nick Noriea says. "You know why? Everybody, I mean everybody, would've convicted Bill on conspiracy. *Everybody.* Whether he said
a word or not.

"The only ace in the hole I had if I didn't win was that Beevers had
already committed himself to waive a jury. Which I loved. Because I knew
Eason wasn't going to find Kerry Myers guilty of conspiracy. And if you
find Kerry Myers not guilty of conspiracy, you can't find Fontanille guilty
of conspiracy because you can't conspire with yourself and there's no
unnamed unindicted co-conspirators like you have in a federal case.

"But you think I'd've told Eason that? Eason would've found Kerry
Myers guilty and given him a month's probation just so Fontanille would
hold up on appeal. That's how little confidence I had in Eason being fair
with me vis-à-vis the State.

"Then, on the morning of the conspiracy trial, Eason said, 'Before we
have motions and make two hundred jurors sit all through the morning
and not get sworn in until this afternoon, let's voir dire as many as we can
for cause and let those people leave.' We didn't ask for a change of venue,
but the judge knew how much publicity there had been, so he said, 'Look,
let's start preliminarily going through some of them so we don't have to
go through all those questions.' You know, 'What'd you read in the newspaper? What ya saw on TV? Is there anything that you've seen or read,
da-de-da.'

"So we did that in advance. He had thirty-six jurors there to start with,
so we went through the thirty-six to find out what impact the publicity
had on the case. Ya call that voir dire for cause. Not a test group. The ones
that knew about the case and had their minds made up wouldn't be
brought back for the general voir dire."

"It was an amazing process for Bill to sit through." Madeleine joins into
the narrative of that most peculiar day. "We're sitting there in this room,"
she continues. "A room no bigger than this, the judge, Wally, Kerry, Bill,
Beevers, Nick, me, Howie, the court reporter, and the jurors would come
in one at a time and sit in a chair right inside the door . . ."

"They could barely fit in the room," Nick offers.

"Judge Eason's old office. You know." Madeleine places the scene. "Bill
and Kerry were sitting on the sofa, next to each other—and do you
remember what Eason said? That was one of the most amazing things
to me."

"Oh, yeah. Yeah!" goes Nick.

"As we're waiting for the first juror," Madeleine continues. "As the bailiff is calling off the names, Eason looks at Kerry and Bill and says, 'Y'all look so solemn. You look like a funeral. Reminds me of a cartoon where it says, "Don't worry about it, it's just your life." ' Nick and I looked at each other. Their life *is* on the line! Then, when the jurors started coming in, they were saying they didn't know anything about the case . . ."

" 'Oh, no, haven't heard anything about it,' " Nick jumps in. "And I said, 'Okay. What about the baseball bat murder? Remember that?' 'Oh, *yeah! Oh, yeah!* I remember about that. Aww, they're *both* guilty.' "

"Initially they were asking, 'Do you know Kerry Myers or Bill Fontanille?' Madeleine explains. 'No.' 'Do you know anything?' 'No.' But as soon as Nick called it the baseball bat murder, 'Oh, of course, I know *that*—yeah, they *both* did it.' "

"I said, 'Aww, jeez, here we go. We've got a problem,' " Nick remembers.

"It was a frightening experience for Bill," Madeleine says. "He was shaken. We explained to him that people like that would be excused for cause and we would end up picking an impartial jury. But it was the first time Bill had sat down with strangers and heard how many people in this world thought he was guilty of this crime."

"They wouldn't have served on the jury," Nick says. "But guess what? If twenty out of thirty-six jurors think they both did it just based on what they've heard, and if that's your sample? Whatcha think the jurors that's gonna hear about it in the courtroom are gonna think? 'They both did it.' That's the sum and substance of it."

"We walk out and Bill says, 'We're gonna lose.' I said, 'Yeah,' " Nick remembers. "He was positively shaken at the lunch break. He's sitting back there saying, 'How are we gonna win?' I said, 'We're not. You're not gonna beat the conspiracy.' I said, 'You're probably gonna be convicted of it, and the only hope is on appeal. I don't want you to mention a word about this to anybody, but I'm positive Eason's gonna find Myers not guilty, and I'm not sure but I don't think you can conspire with yourself and the indictment doesn't name any unindicted co-conspirators. If they'd have done that, then we've got a problem.'

"So we come back, and before we start picking the real jury, the judge says, 'I'm gonna take up that pretrial motion first.'

"Well, that's the so-called James Hearing we'd been asking for, to make them show they had a prima facie case which would allow the admissibility of the statement, and Wally and Howie had been saying, 'No, no. We don't do that now.'

"But he wanted to do these jurors in the morning and I never could figure that out, so coming back he says he wants to do the motion, to have your witnesses there. So I figured, 'Hey, I finally won one with Rudy.' "

Thursday, October 6, 1988   THE TIMES-PICAYUNE
Appeal sought in rejection of Myers evidence
By Richard Boyd
West Bank bureau

   Jefferson Parish prosecutors will appeal a ruling that rejected evidence they say is vital to prove that two men conspired to kill their wives in 1984.
   The state 5th Circuit Court of Appeal will be asked to let prosecutors use statements made to police in an attempt to prove that Kerry Myers and William Fontanille conspired in early 1984 to kill Janet Myers and Susan Fontanille. The statement under contention was made by Fontanille concerning the death of Janet Myers.
   Late Wednesday, after hearing almost four hours of testimony, Judge Alvin Rudy Eason threw out the Fontanille statement and ruled that the state had not proven enough of a conspiracy case to present the evidence to a jury. . . .
   After prosecutors Walter Rothschild and Howat Peters told Eason Thursday they planned to appeal, the judge dismissed the prospective jurors.

"I was absolutely amazed, and actually went over Nick's head when the judge ruled in our favor," Madeleine says, chuckling at the memory.
"He'd never ruled my way," Nick explains. "I wanted to argue with him a little more."
"Nick is standing up and the judge says, 'I don't think there's a prima facie case,' and Nick kept talking. I grabbed his pant leg and said, 'We won.' Nick just stared at Eason and then looked at me like I was out of my mind, because, of course, we don't win, we never win with Eason."
Nick laughs. "I was in such a state of defensive posture, I guess I just kept trying to argue with him and didn't realize we'd won. Even after he told me what he'd said, I thought he was joking, I was waiting for, 'What's the matter, Noriea, you thought you won? Ha ha.' "
The prosecution was at least as shocked as the defense.
"I guess Wally *was* shaken," Nick booms. "He'd been told in chambers a week before that, 'Oh, yeah, you've got enough for a conspiracy.' He was visibly shaken. And then he says he wants to try Fontanille for murder right now. I said, 'Wait a minute. The murder case is not set for trial.' And the judge said, 'Right. It's not.'
"So lo and behold the murder once again falls back into the background. I told Madeleine, 'I can't believe this.' They take Eason's dismissal to the fifth circuit, then the supreme court."

"I think he was confused," Wally, remembering that morning, says with no mirth at all in his voice. "I really do. You know, maybe his medications or something. We thought we were on solid ground. Howie and I felt strongly about it; both of us have been federal prosecutors. We both knew the conspiracy law pretty well. I mean, I would've never asked the grand jury to return an indictment I didn't think I could prove.

"We went into the hearing thinking we put on more than we actually needed. We put on John Taylor, Masson, introduced the taped statement of Kerry Myers, plus the hospital records—we felt we put in more than we needed. And then the judge, I mean, just said, 'I find there's no prima facie case of conspiracy,' shoom, he's off the bench. To say that we were flabbergasted is an understatement.

"But we were definitely ready to go with the murder case. We had Dr. Lee scheduled, the time blocked out for him to be here. And Nick was aware of this. So Howie and I went and huddled. We came back and said, 'Screw this, we're not going to let them get away with this.' Regardless of what the judge says, we have a good case even with the murder cases.

"So, 'We'll go with the murder cases. Right now.' We went into court and I made the announcement. 'Judge, it doesn't make any difference, let's go to trial right now with the murders. Fontanille first.'

"The defense went crazy. Nick said he was prepared for a conspiracy trial, not a murder trial. Which is ridiculous, one is the other. But they didn't want that. They wanted to continue as much as they could. And the judge, I guess in the interest of what he thought was fair, continued the case for them."

"They came up with what I thought was a weak case of conspiracy," Judge Eason drawls, and reflects. "I was not convinced that they put the facts together, Myers's and Fontanille's statements primarily, to support a conspiracy. In fact, everything attendant showed that definitely there was *not* a conspiracy.

"Bill Fontanille, when he went to the hospital, was the only thing they had indicating that there may be some kind of a conspiracy, and this didn't prove that to me at all. That he told the cop there, 'Listen, there are two dead people there,' and I think he was talking about the child, which indicated to me that he had knowledge, but not conspiracy.

"Now, I felt like certainly after the fact they had gotten together."

Saturday, October 8, 1988   THE TIMES-PICAYUNE
'84 murder a puzzle after second trial
by Richard Boyd
West Bank bureau

  Who killed Janet Myers?

  Since February 1984, when the 26-year-old mother of two was found beaten to death in her Harvey home, the question has gone unanswered. . . .

Kerry Myers' taped statement was played in the courtroom Wednesday for the first time. His statement was not produced in 1986 because he was a state witness against Fontanille.

Robert Masson, former homicide detective for the Jefferson Parish Sheriff's Office, took the 30 minute statement from Fontanille on Feb. 25, 1984, the day he was booked with first-degree murder in the death of Janet Myers. Masson took a 50-minute statement from Myers on March 14, 1984, after he had recovered from a broken arm.

The two statements dramatize what has long baffled the public and the police. . . .

BOOK III

"It's not crazy to try Bill Fontanille for the murder of Janet Myers, it's crazy to try Bill Fontanille with Kerry Myers as your star witness."

—W. J. LeBlanc

9
College

And so we came home and another phase began.

The next six weeks were a little rough. You developed a colic problem and we were at the doctor's office a lot. You were eating every 2½ hours 'round the clock. At times dad and I didn't know who was more tired. Sometimes I'd cry right along with you. I was tired and I felt I couldn't take good care of you. . . .

Now you're sleeping just about 10–11 hours a night and eating on a good schedule. On September 27th you discovered your voice and you've been singing ever since . . . you do so many cute things that you melt my heart every day. Dad and I know that we'd be empty without you. More later . . . mom

—Journal of Janet Cannon Myers

*   *   *

Claire Firestone Pasqua remembers the fall of 1976 when she was staying home and entering the University of New Orleans as a freshman, and Janet Cannon was "going off to college" at Nicholls State University, some seventy miles southwest of New Orleans in Thibodaux, Louisiana, the heart of sugarcane country.

Claire remembers being "surprised that Janet was allowed to go to college," let alone leave home to do so. There also "seemed to be a great deal of concern over the finances of her going to college. But I remember her telling us that because her father was on disability there were scholarships and grants she could get to go to school.

"As I look back on it, that was the reason she got to go to college—it didn't matter that she wanted to go, or had the intellectual ability to go, above average at any rate. But it was like, 'Well, if you can get this, then you can go.' It was something for nothing, can't pass that up. That's more what the scenario was like to me," Claire recalls.

* * *

Lee Ann Cousins Buras and Laura Denise Miller, classmates and fellow Pantherettes with Claire and Janet of the River Oaks Academy Class of '76, also enrolled at Nicholls State that fall. They were in for a surprise one late August morning, their first day of college.

"Laura and I go to check in the dorm and we say, 'Who are our suite-mates?' 'Janet Cannon and Lynn Lonadier.' I mean, no love between the four of us, right?" recalls Lee Ann, the slender, patrician, overachieving, all-everything principal's daughter.

"Janet and I had had our problems; for some reason I was the only person Janet ever really directed her dislike toward at River Oaks. I was a too easy target for her; I had everything she wanted. And Lynn was one of the nobodies, charter member of the ugly-duckling clique that Janet was kind of the hero of," remembers this new breed of Southern belle, Lee Ann.

"Those two had been friends all the way up. Well, we were shocked. We laughed and joked about it. 'Can't *believe* they *asked* to be *our* suite-mates.'

"So we went up, we talked to them, and we were friendly enough. The next morning Lynn comes over to our side and wakes us up.

" 'Oh! Y'all get up! Get up! Janet didn't come in last night. She had a date and didn't come in!' Laura and I are going, 'This isn't like Janet.' She wasn't the type.

" 'Well, Lynn, what do you think? Where did she go? Do you know the guy's name?' Lynn knew—'Gary Landry.' Janet had met him the day before in line at registration.

"Laura and I said, 'Well, when people get away to college?' You know. 'Maybe she ended up staying with the guy.' Lynn convinced us: 'Janet's not like that. Y'all know Janet.' And my heart started beating fast and I said, 'Something could've happened to the girl, Laura.'

"By this time we're getting close to missing class. 'What are we gonna do?' I go down the hall and wake my big sister up. Carol Ann comes down. She too said, 'Lynn, are you sure? We don't want to look stupid here when we call the police.' Well, we did look stupid, because we called the campus security and they thought it was funny because they're used to this. So they come over and finally agreed to check it out, just to humor us. Lynn went with them, and sure enough they found her at Gary's apartment.

"We'd gone on to class, but I was nervous about it, and when I got back I asked Lynn, 'What happened?' 'Oh, it was nothing.' 'What do you mean, it was nothing? You get us up at six in the morning. What's the end of the story?' 'Well, she was feeling *sick* and had to sleep over.' Come on, give me a *break*. I mean, even at eighteen!

"My summation is that she went kind of wild when she went off to school."

* * *

"Janet started off as a home-ec major, and I didn't have any contact with her until she started dating Gary pretty steady and hanging around the radio and TV station," remembers Bob Blazier, who has been teaching in the Nicholls State Communications Department for almost two decades.

"I expected the two of them to get married right after they got out of school. They gave every indication that this was serious, the real thing," he says and then shuts the door to his office.

Bob Blazier is a big man with an Abraham Lincoln beard who is fond of wearing jeans and work shirts.

"She was not secretary of the station yet, she was Gary's girlfriend. At first she was real quiet, she stayed over out of the way. But the eyes, man—because she watched Gary all the time. They would watch the news together. Gary wanted to be so perfect. He was focused—enough to stay around an extra semester for a course he felt he needed. Gary had one thing, he *wanted* to be a star. And he did go on to win a couple of national awards and he was noted as a good reporter. And now he's a bigwig in the Republican Party of Florida—go figure. So they were together almost all the time.

"But when I first met Gary Landry he could not look you in the eye. Gary was the repressed one. Gary was the one that I figured could be a psychotic somewhere. Gary was a real pretty boy. Nice hair, well-manicured, kind of a wimp. Not really talented. Just worked hard at it. Tenacious.

"Janet was the quintessential power groupie, like up at the legislature. And that's why she would flirt with me, like if she could get close to me she could plug into the power. I probably should have."

"I knew a lot of Billy's friends because we were all the same age. But I wasn't into sports," says Ron Dupuy, who, despite growing up in Terrytown, was never a part of either of the two and sometimes three overlapping circles around Bill Fontanille and Mike Price. He perhaps knows Billy Fontanille better than many who were. Their bonding, while apparently as long-standing, was more cerebral than athletic.

"I was considering going to college. I wanted to go to a small school, so he talked me into going to Southeastern. He didn't want to go to a big school. He felt like he'd get lost; he didn't want to go to LSU. And he didn't have the money to go away.

"So there weren't too many options, it was either Nicholls or Southeastern. And I think he had the idea that Nicholls was a backwoods, redneck kind of school. Southeastern is the more traditional old-buildings-and-ivy, rah-rah type of college. He wanted that atmosphere, the whole deal, all the things you see on TV and hear about. But he also wanted to stay at home."

Southeastern Louisiana University, in picturesque Hammond, Louisiana, while just across Lake Pontchartrain from New Orleans, is still about a fifty-five-mile commute, each way. Which is exactly what Bill Fontanille did for all of the almost six years he attended.

"Now I asked him a million times why he didn't just stay there," continues Ron, a small-framed, soft-voiced, pleasant, and erudite young man.

"One reason was finances. The other I never could figure out. But I think he didn't like to be by himself. He liked being around his friends. Part of him wanted to get that college life and part of him didn't want to break away from what he had back in the neighborhood.

"He was having problems at home—at this time he was extremely moody. We'd talk on the telephone, 'Yeah, let's go.' Then, when you dropped by to pick him up, he'd often come to the car all down and wouldn't go.

"Billy would sulk. That's the best word for it. His shoulders would go up, his head would go down, his lip would stick out, the whole thing. You could tell a block away what kind of a mood he was in. Either he would be up, you know, straight, looking good, bouncy, or he'd have his look on him. And you knew what to expect from that point on for the rest of the day. If we were going somewhere, I could tell in the first five minutes what he was going to be like that day. For some reason I think he enjoyed being in that mood. He got something out of it."

"I remember Billy first, but it was all about the same time. Connie and I'd been close friends since nine, ten years old," begins Lisa Comeaux Grubic, who has traveled back to New Orleans from her present home in North Carolina, partly in order to talk publicly for the first time upon the history she shares with the principals in the baseball bat murder.

"Throughout all the grand juries and trials and everything else, I managed to stay in obscurity. Nobody knew where I lived. Nobody knew what my last name was. And I tried to keep it that way." She smiles at her candor; her words, even when they are on grave matters, have a bounce, as she sits in the den of her girlhood home in Terrytown.

"I used to spend the night at her house and we would be outside and the guys would come around. We would go to the CYO dances and we'd see Billy, Kerry, Chuck, Louie, and all.

"My earliest personal memories of Billy were when he was going with Carrie Campbell. I was in class with her. I know she was the one girl he never got over. He really was in love with her. And she didn't want any part of him after a while. It wasn't just her father breaking them up. She'd get back together with him and then she didn't want to see him anymore and then she'd be seeing him again. And then she broke up with him for good. He was the one that didn't give up, and he was the one that was so torn and hurt. She pretty much went on with her life and was dating other people. I was fourteen.

"Billy used to come over here a lot. He knew I was in class with Carrie and he would ask about her. Sometimes I thought the reason he wanted her back so much was because maybe she didn't want him anymore.

"He would mope around and get real quiet; but he was pretty aloof, anyway. He would come and sit here and just kind of mope. At the time, I was just *amazed* that he was here talking to *me*. I couldn't believe he would be here talking to me, so I was kind of like—no matter what he had to say I was going to sit here and listen because I was always *crazy* about him. At that age I wasn't allowed to date; and he never really asked me. He used to just come over. Chuck was the first person I really dated; but they all knew I liked Billy. But I was a freshman and he was in college.

"Connie and I used to get in the car and go—he worked at Sears in the appliance department—we used to get all dressed up in our sundresses, and we used to go there just to go look and talk to him—it wasn't her, it was me.

"But he would come and he would just sit here. The phone would ring and then it would hang up. Then all of a sudden there would be a knock on the door and he would be standing there with a smile on his face. I'd open it and let him in and he would just sit here. Sometimes he'd talk, and sometimes he wouldn't say a word and he'd just sit here for two hours and do nothing. He continued coming over once I was dating Chuck.

"He was just the weirdest—I don't know if you can call it friend—it was weird. I don't know, I guess it was a crush. Yet I couldn't figure out *why* he was there. And I *wanted* to find out."

"There was never any doubt that Kerry was going to LSU," Mike Price remembers. Other aspects of his late teens were also right in character for "dull" Kerry Myers.

"It was during that first year of college, Kerry was at LSU and I was at Nicholls State, when he started dating Marcella," Mike Price recalls. "She lived right around the corner from our house. She was a beauty queen and had been going with a guy, a quarterback, of course, for years and years, all the way through high school, and then broke up with him. That's when Kerry started dating her and totally fell in love with her.

"He came home from school one weekend and told my mom and dad he was going to ask her to marry him. He went back up to school and came home the next weekend to pick her up for a date and she's *married*. She'd gotten back together with this other guy and gotten married!

"That's an example of how Kerry saw a different world than other people. He thought up until that moment that Marcella was going steady with him. Was in love with him.

"Every girl he ever dated he wanted to marry. But he was delusional about it, he really was. He could manufacture this *Gone with the Wind* romance in a heartbeat."

*   *   *

After the fall semester of 1976 at UNO, Claire Firestone Pasqua transferred to Nicholls State Nursing School for the coming spring.

"I'd already gotten wind that Lynn wasn't going to be there, that she had
dropped out. So I applied and found out I was going to be with Janet and
was all excited because at least I knew my roommate."

That was to be short-lived.

"Covetous of what other people had. She was. That was maybe why I
was treated differently by Janet and her parents than some of the other
girls, because I was a doctor's daughter. They were impressed by things
like that. Big cars and titles and things. I can remember on several occasions Mrs. Cannon was always, 'Well, hello, *Dr.* Firestone,' " Claire says as
she sits at the island bar in her and her policeman husband's large, airy
rancher in Zachary, Louisiana, a small town all but spitting distance from
being a suburb of Baton Rouge to the northwest, where the doctor's
daughter is now an RN.

"You would *never* be invited in, though. When we'd drop by to pick
Janet up, I'd stay at the door and wait for her to come.

"Janet dressed like they didn't have enough money. And, of course, very
conservatively. When I started off to college my parents had bought me
these beautiful sweaters. Janet would ask to borrow them, and having no
boundaries myself, I said, 'Sure, Janet, you can do that.' And so she'd
borrow them—and she used Charley perfume. I remember the whole place
would reek of it after she put it on. My clothes were beginning to smell like
Janet. I finally had to tell her, 'No, you can't do that anymore.' She got very
hurt and upset, and that was when things kind of parted as far as the two
of us.

"By that time she was already seeing Gary Landry, and being very
controlling and manipulative of him. You can split that semester in thirds.
First third, the relationship with Gary wasn't particularly tempestuous.
The last two-thirds it got that way.

"It seemed like she clung to him a lot. She was always over at the radio
station talking to him. Here he was, he was in school, this was part of his
schooling, but he was also trying to run it—and she'd be there in the
middle when he was trying to work. He was trying to pull back a bit, and
she clung to him, got more and more smothering.

"Her sexual relationship with Gary surprised me. There were nights
when she didn't come in. And I remember a conversation between Janet
and Gary that got my attention. I had never realized Janet did this—but,
if like she was wearing pink that day, she made sure she had on pink
panties and all the other stuff. One day she asked Gary what color he
thought she had on underneath, and he answered that it was whatever
color she was wearing that day. And I remember thinking, 'Well, how does
he know that? How does he know they always matched?' But I never
asked.

"I mean, all of a sudden doing this—going from a 'nun' to a . . . ? I found it strange. From Janet it just wasn't expected."

"I first became aware of Janet in October of 1976. She was Gary Landry's girlfriend at the time and I had heard that they were planning on getting married."

Hurst Bousegard, now living in Texas, speaks with the refined articulation of a trained broadcaster—which he was. But there is also a certain and quite gentle range of sensitivity in modulation and imagery which one can often hear from one who has "a touch of the poet," which he does.

"I first laid eyes on her in Gary's office and I was literally blown away. I recognized her immediately as my soul mate. And when I found out she was Gary's fiancée, I said, 'No way is this going to happen. This is going to come to an end and we're going to be together.'

"She knew of me because I was a disk jockey at the radio station; she knew my name, she found it interesting. But I just let it go. I didn't initiate anything. So I found it pretty amazing that three or four months later, she was approaching me.

"I also knew that her and Gary's relationship at that time was deteriorating. It was a public deterioration."

Margaret Dubisson, the popular nightly news anchor for WVUE Channel 8, the ABC affiliate in New Orleans, went to grammar school with Kerry Myers and was a communications major at Nicholls State with both Kerry and Janet.

It is shortly after the second of her three nightly newscasts has wrapped and she is speaking of her personal connection with the baseball bat murder. She says, "I remember Janet much better. Because I knew Gary well. I knew them as a couple. It was embarrassing.

"Fights in public. Her crushed. Crying and slamming doors. Scenes, unpleasant little things that made you uneasy to be around them. She would just not let go, and he was ready to move on to something else. She'd *cling* to Gary. That's the word!" Margaret Dubisson nods her bright blond head and face with emphasis upon the insight.

"What's odd is that Gary didn't seem like the kind of guy that would be real public with stuff—but a lot of it happened in front of people. Of course, it only takes one person to have a scene in public. You can laugh and walk away, but people heard."

"By this time she had also met George Knight, he was crazy about her," remembers Claire. "And it was apparent to me that she used him.

"In one semester, there were three men in her life. Hurst was more of the nurturing-type person—and they did seem like they were very close. Really, like sweethearts, best characterized as; more normal, or traditional or something. But when I heard that Janet was getting married, I said, 'George or Gary?' 'Kerry? Who's he?'

"Janet was never without a boyfriend. Even when she didn't date in high school—she always had a boyfriend, from B.J. to Mike Daigle to . . . whoever.

"She would be openly very affectionate with Gary. I can picture her sitting in Gary's lap in his office. A demure adoration-type attitude she had. You know, she just sucked him in, is about the best way to describe it. You didn't see her openly affectionate with George.

"But George was just enmeshed—really adored her, almost worshiped her, that's the type of relationship they had. It was like when she had attention from Gary, 'I don't need you anymore,' and he'd go off like a whipped dog. And then Gary wouldn't pay her attention and she'd go and find George again.

"I'm a Christian, okay?" Sitting in the kitchen of the rustic, sprawling country manor the land and construction baron George Knight and wife Yvette call home in Baker, Louisiana, another small and rural outpost of Baton Rouge, George, a positively bubbling, gushing sort of man, tall, thin, dark-haired, earnest, and gawky, begins the story of him and Janet Cannon.

"A lot of the problems that Janet and I never could get together were because of my beliefs spiritually. And I'm going to tell you the side on it that I believe the girl was—she had a lot of—there was a lot of oppression from the spirits.

"First of all, it was weird, because you know the saying 'hung by the tongue,' spiritually? Well, she would confess that she was gonna die.

"Our relationship developed from a little before Mardi Gras '77, through Lent and into the hot summer months and frequent trips to the Coast. I was between Gary and Kerry.

"Our relationship was in three phases. The first is me realizing our life-styles were greatly different. During that early dating period—I came to pick her up in our family Mercury Grand Marquis, a big car. I remember I had my cowboy hat in the back window, and I remember her saying, 'Oh, I feel so rich! I feel like a rich Texan.' I never will forget—I think she thought I had money. We're not hurting, but we're not—anyway, that excited her. And her family really liked me. Maybe, kinda, I think because they perceived I was from wealth.

"I think she was embarrassed about her house, because I remember her telling me, 'Now, our house, we're not finished with the brickwork on the side.' And their bathroom sink didn't have any plumbing. The water would go into a bucket under the sink. And it was like it had been that way a long time. Take a couple of bucks to fix it. Why?

"Later I learned her sister had told her, 'Gary, no. George, yes.' The sister had said, 'He's going to give you a better life-style.'

"I'd come in and stay at my brother-in-law's on weekends. Dinner and a movie was a date. Four or five dates and it's like, 'Hey, I'd like to see you on Sunday, too.' But I'm going to go to church on Sunday—I was born and raised a Catholic—I guess I'm kind of sheltered, because I thought *everybody* went to church on Sunday, you know? 'Okay, well, I'm gonna be staying at my brother-in-law's and I'll come by and pick you up for church.'

"It was like, 'What? Go to *church*?' I said, 'Yeah, we'll go to church.' So I took her to St. Louis Cathedral at Jackson Square, it's where she told me to go. When we were there, I said, 'Where are all your friends?' you know. I got the picture that apparently the girl didn't go to church. And that bothered me, that was a mark against her in my opinion.

"One of the casual things we'd do was go to Mardi Gras parades when I first dated her. I'd drink beer on the way there. Good Catholic drinking beer. And I'll never forget her saying, 'I love the smell of beer on the breath of a *man*.' I'm kind of woozy and I'm trying to make a good impression on her parents! Wow!

"We're dating, and towards the end of spring her parents let me take her to my uncle's beach house on the Coast. 'Sure, George.' We jumped into the Mercury and went. At the beach, Janet said, 'God, we didn't get to stay in places like this when we'd go to the beach. You go down to the public beach and that's where we stayed.' She felt like they were poor, and that really bothered her, I guess. She would bring that up every once in a while—about how she felt that they needed more money.

"She slept at my sister's and I brought her back that Sunday and made her go to church. 'I don't want to go to church.' She went, but she didn't like it."

"It was spring '77," Hurst Bousegard remembers. "Right after the Easter holidays; I'd stayed in when just about everybody else had gone. Me and my roommate were on the front porch of our apartment and everybody was coming back into town, and Janet and Claire drove right by, right in front of us down our street, and they saw us. We waved. Janet was driving her white Mustang. She turned around, pulled up, and they came in and we had a great time just talking. This was late afternoon; they'd been there a couple of hours. It got to be dinnertime so we offered to cook, for them to stay and talk some more; so they did.

"After dinner it had gotten dark and we decided to go for a drive. We went in my roommate's car, he had a hatchback Vega, maroon. He and Claire were in the front seat, Janet and I were in the back, and we went down these dusty old roads on the other side of Thibodaux. It was very dark, there were thunderstorms in the distance. We watched the lightning, there was a nice breeze, Eddie left the hatchback open while he was driving to let the breeze in. Janet and I spent time just looking at each other and looking outside at the lightning, communicating with just our eyes. Not saying a word, not a single word. One of the most incredibly romantic experiences I've ever had in my life. We came back to the apartment later. The girls went home. I've never been so happy in my life. And nothing happened. Except in the spiritual sense.

"After that first afternoon and evening, Janet and Claire came back for another evening of dinner only days later. Janet came in upset about something with Gary. Again. She cried for at least an hour. We put dinner on the table and we were eating, and during this whole time she was on the sofa still crying.

"After that it was just chance meetings and so forth. Then one day I had gotten sick at school and I went to the doctor and he gave me an injection of Dramamine for nausea; I went straight to bed. Later on that evening, the phone rang. Eddie answers. It's Janet. He tells her I'm sick and I'm in bed and everything. As a joke, Janet asked him if I needed a nurse. He said, 'Hey, Hurst, Janet wants to know if you need a nurse.' And I said, really sick now, 'Yeah, I do.' And I drifted back off to sleep. About an hour or so later, I wake up to the sound of my bedroom door opening and Janet comes in carrying a toy doctor's kit. She came and sat on the edge of the bed where I was laying and soon she starts rubbing her hands on my chest. I just laid there enjoying it, and we just kept looking at each other, not saying a word. She's caressing my chest and finally she leans down to kiss me for the first time. And never in my life will I ever feel that kind of sensation again. It was all-powerful, consuming; the most passionate kiss I've ever had; there's no way I can ever experience that again.

"From then we started seeing each other, but at the same time she and Gary had not broken off. Within the week, me and Eddie went to visit Janet and Claire in their dorm room on a visitation night.

"While we're there in her dorm room, the phone rings and it's Gary; he's downstairs waiting for her, to take her to a movie. I'll never know if she did this on purpose or not. It seemed like it was a surprise to her at the time. When the girls leave the room, we have to go with them to sign in and sign out. Gary didn't know what to think, and I was a little embarrassed. But I wasn't really worried about it.

"I have always felt it's entirely possible she set it up to happen that way. Janet initiated the invitation to us. But she made it look like it was just a friendly get-together with no romantic intentions, being that she was inviting Eddie also.

"Then one day Janet asked me to go with her to the library to study for final exams. We didn't have any classes together or anything, she just wanted to be with me—so she said. So we're there and then boom, there's Gary walking up. I didn't know what to do. I didn't know how to react.

I was embarrassed and shocked that he was there. It was obvious he hadn't just chanced to be there at that time.

"We sat at a table. We talked sporadically; but it was mostly a very uncomfortable silence. And then Janet started to cry, quietly. Gary and I tried to ignore it; because I know damn well we both knew what the problem was. She stopped after a few minutes; but the situation got so uncomfortable, we started to separate. Gary left first; then Janet. When I went out to my car I found a note on my windshield from Janet saying, 'This isn't going to work. We shouldn't see each other anymore.'

"The next day I called her for an explanation. She explained to me that she set this up in the library to purposely get us all together just to see what would happen—just to see how I would react and how Gary would react. She wanted to see a reaction from Gary and I. And basically she didn't get it.

"By around that time it was understood she and Gary were just about over with. And that I'd come in at the right time. She was telling me she was going to leave Gary. And that's when she started telling me the stories of his being verbally and physically cruel and abusive to her.

"I don't know how she ended it, or if there was any specific action that brought it about, but before the semester ended we were together; because near the end we have the end-of-the-year banquets. I attended two, one for theater and one for student government. She was my date at both. In fact our first really romantic evening together was right after.

"There was, however, one disconcerting moment about that night at the theater banquet. Being a college student, I certainly didn't have a lot of money; I had five dollars with me. We went up to the bar. I knew I had enough money for one drink, and the rest of the food and soft beverages were free for the banquet. Janet wanted a Brandy Alexander. I had never heard of a Brandy Alexander. So I ordered two and it cost four dollars for both. She wanted another one and I told her we couldn't have another. She said, 'Well, that's that.' She was disappointed that she couldn't have it. When the bartender brought the drinks, he'd said, 'Yep, this is the Cadillac of them all.' And she was impressed by that.

"She did covet the best things. During the time we were together, it was my impression that she was spoiled. She was used to having what she wanted, no matter what it was. No matter what it was—somebody would provide; whether it was me, her parents, or another boyfriend, whatever. Whatever Janet wanted, she somehow got."

"She'd be very excited, and then she'd be very quiet, almost want to say depressed. Looking back now, knowing what I know as a nurse, she was certainly manic-depressive to some degree," Claire explains.

"For my sanity; that's why I left," Claire continues. "Janet was just very,

very needy. Constantly keeping things stirred up in her life. With the three guys. Borrowing clothes. Her up-and-down mood swings—everything was always in a whirl.

"One night Laura and Lee Ann told me, 'We're getting out of here. We're moving to another dorm next semester. If you want to come with us that's fine—it's a way out.' At that instant it was like 'I'm outa here!'

"I was very hesitant to tell Janet. To be honest, she intimidated me. I was afraid she was going to have a temper tantrum. But she took it in stride. Of course, there was a strain between us from the time I told her till the end of the semester.

"I remember even the last day, moving out, was a big ordeal. Slowly, toward the end of the semester, you start bringing things home. Every time your parents come or go you throw a few things in so you don't have to get a U-Haul.

"But Janet had too much, we couldn't fit any more in my mom's car, so we just had to let her call her parents to come up from Gretna to get some of her stuff. Pragmatic she was not. Driving away looking at her like that all I could feel was 'What a relief.' The weight was off. I could breathe.

"I saw her for the last time that next fall semester. She came by our new dorm to visit one day—I remember being very on guard with her, very uncomfortable. What is going to happen? What is she going to do? With Janet there was always the possibility of something happening."

"As far as boys, the only guy we'd ever known she even liked was Danny, my brother," Peggy Cowan remembers. "We used to tease him all the time because she liked him from itty-bitty. She would kind of follow him around and stuff. They were the same age. First crush. Oh, yeah! They went to catechism together.

"All the guys in the neighborhood thought she was attractive and they all talked about maybe at one time they would've liked to have taken her out. But nobody asked to take her out because you just didn't cross those boundaries with her parents."

"Billy had these real high aspirations and wanted to be right at the top and walk right into it and didn't want to put in the groundwork to get there. I think he felt that he *deserved* a lot of things," Lisa Comeaux Grubic remembers.

"He never had any trouble with having a girlfriend, or women or anything—I think he amazed a lot of them, he kept them captivated. I've talked to a lot of women who have just seen him in interviews or in the trials and everything and they're just dying to meet him. To date him. It's truly incredible, but I understand it, all too well.

"The other ones would come over and tell you you were pretty and ask you out and everything and then here is one who would just come and sit on your couch and just kind of stare into space or something—you couldn't crack him, you couldn't figure him out. And so there was this mystery.

"Let's face it, Billy's different. I mean, he has these little idiosyncrasies. He won't drink behind anybody. He will sit and kiss you for two to three hours and then won't drink behind you two minutes later. I know it, because he did it with me. Billy was also squeamish about blood, body fluids and things—he didn't want to talk about that kind of stuff. He was the kind if they'd been drinking and somebody threw up—he's gone.

"However, the really weird things, in retrospect, were the hanging up on the phone and parking around the corner and showing up at the door but never calling me and telling me he was coming. He also *always* had his baseball bat with him, too.

"The phone would ring, I'd pick it up, nobody there. Then I'd go open up the curtains and wait; I'd already have the door open. There was supposed to be this suspense or whatever and you're supposed to be there waiting and everything and he just stands up there and he's just kind of leaning this certain way—he doesn't have to say a word, it was the expressions. He would look at you with his head cocked the other way. He'd stare at you, but not directly, he'd have this sheepish grin on his face and would look at you sideways. I'd say, 'Come on in. You want a hamburger?' And I'd go put hamburgers on the grill.

"The phone call would never be mentioned. He knew that I knew—I'm sure he didn't think I just stood at the door for six hours a day. And his car would *never* be here, there would never be any evidence that he was here. It was a game, though; he liked to play games with your mind, with everyone. I liked it too. It was different.

"A conversation with him *is* a mind game. It's like playing a game of chess—him always being one move ahead and you not knowing what's coming next. You never know—you see his eyes, you know there are certain people that when you look into their eyes you can see into their heart and into their soul and you know that everything they're saying is sincere—and then there are people where it's all rehearsed, it's all set and there's a stage, the lights are up here and there's a curtain behind it and they can be whatever they want to be at that moment—that's Billy.

"I've met several people in my life like that and I've been attracted to most of them. And that scares me about me. It's an intellectual allure. It's not his looks—I mean, for some girls, it is—but, to me, it's this aura. There's an air of danger there. But then they feed into that. You never feel like your feet are on ground. You never feel like you're sure when you're with somebody like that. Because no matter how far you get, they're always a step ahead; it's not like a normal relationship where there's give and take.

"When you're fourteen years old and you've never been around too many guys or anything, you maybe figure that's what everybody does. You don't have any experience to relate it to—now I think it was pretty weird and I was pretty weird to let it happen."

"What we used to do—one of the best summers Billy and I ever had—we went to a different college about every two weeks and we'd pretend we were somebody else," says Ron Dupuy with obvious nostalgic glee as he continues his remembrances.

"We'd both research information on that area—and we'd say we were from Florida, we'd say we were from Texas; one time we were from Arizona, California, we were from different places. Billy decided that women loved to meet people from other places. I thought it was a good idea. He'd pull his 'lost puppy' routine; then we'd start talking to some girls and it was a big play, it was a big act the whole night. We were different people. And we enjoyed the hell out of it.

"Billy's a *very* shy person. Billy is an extreme introvert. So his strategy of just standing in the corner didn't start out as a strategy, it started out because he was scared to talk to people. So he'd be standing in the corner at a bar or party looking lost and hangdogged, and it worked. So he kept at it.

"He *needs* people to accept him. And if you *don't* accept him, that tears at him deep inside so he's *got* to, he's got to stop that. You can't reject him. Any kind of rejection whatsoever—and rejection is the key—if you reject him as a person, that's unacceptable. So he gets obsessed with it, and he'll do whatever he can to try to turn it around. How he is perceived is the be- and end-all for Billy Fontanille—period."

"He went up there sowing his oats," Marva Myers says.

"He had an IQ that was like one point from being a genius and we used to always kid about it being hard to tell a genius from an idiot. Well, Kerry goes up to LSU and he plays around and makes a 1.90 GPA and got on probation," Clifford Myers explains.

"He played around up at LSU for two years and he came back and talked himself into a job at Leson Chevrolet," adds Marva.

"Kerry was going to marry the first girl that said yes," Mike Price assures. "If she didn't break mirrors, and she was willing to have kids and be married and faithful to him, that was all he wanted, he'd take care of the rest."

"I didn't really get to know Kerry until my high school years," Connie Burmaster Cassard begins.

"He started coming around with the group. We didn't start dating right away. That's when the two groups were kind of getting together. I remember it was Easter, '77. Kerry came by the house after he went and dropped the boat off and we started talking. Right after that, we started dating.

"Right away he took me to meet his mother—his real mother, Miz Marguerite. She was very nice. Kelly, his half sister, took to me right away, and Grandma Mac did, too.

"When he worked at Leson Chevrolet, we saw each other all the time. He was very sweet. He was very nice, very friendly. We didn't date a long time; only from July till November of 1977. I was still in high school. It was the summer between my junior and senior year of high school.

"Kerry's very vocal. And he would do anything for you. He was very loving—you know, he was the polite type that opened the door for you, shut the door. Kerry was one that—oh, you *had* to wear a seat belt every time you got in the car.

"Kerry took a possessive attitude right away. When he went away to school, I'd get maybe three letters a week. And it was always about him and I. Weekends we were together. He came in on Friday and picked me up from school. We'd sit around the house, go visit his mother, or whatever. And we'd eat together. He'd go home every once in a while and eat supper with his family—but for the most part we were together constantly.

"It was really pretty much like a married life, looking back on it now. Go visit Mom on weekends, you know. Sit around watch TV. Once in a while go to a show. And Kerry used the 'L word' a lot. That and marriage. Constantly saying 'I love you.' As a reassurance of some kind. Marriage was a foregone conclusion; that it was going to happen in the proper scheme of things. No rush. And sex was never an issue with him.

"I can remember when Kerry came to me one day—I'd had dinner with the family and all—and he told me, 'Connie, I want you to know this, I'm proud of you. Because my mom and dad, they really like you. They said you're the sweet Catholic girl that they always wanted to see their child with.' And then—I think that made Kerry cling to me even more, because it was something his parents accepted. Kerry wanted his parents' approval so bad—his daddy's especially.

"But Kerry had his mood changes. One minute he's as happy as can be and the next minute he'd be mad at me. I can remember, we'd go off somewhere and all of a sudden he just starts screaming. I'm like, 'Wait a minute, you were happy just five minutes ago?' He was also very jealous. But he never ever raised his hand to me, he used his voice. He was soft-spoken until he got mad, and then he would just start his—he was a screamer. And a crier.

"Kerry was always a father image. Because Kerry always stood up to you, you know. He never wanted you to do anything.

"He was possessive of my work; he wanted me home where he could watch me—that I was with him. His biggest fear was that—he never wanted anything like what happened with his mother.

"We held hands a lot. He liked to hold hands."

"By the end of spring '77, Gary was out and I was in," Hurst Bousegard continues his rendering of the Janet Cannon portion of his life.

"I remained in Thibodaux to attend a summer session; she went home to Gretna. June of that year was the most creative month in my life—because of her. I wrote more good poems than at any time before or since. We would talk on the phone, I would drive to Gretna to see her when I could.

"She never spoke unkindly about her parents, other than the fact that they would slap her on occasions. Whenever she did something that was wrong in her parents' eyes, she'd get slapped. She didn't tell me what she had done to get slapped. That was just how she had been disciplined. Slaps to the face. They made the rules, she followed them.

"Now Gary was a different matter. Definitely, she told me about his violence. She was repulsed by it; it was the reason she was leaving him. According to her, his violence and his meanness toward her is what broke them up. Not because she didn't love him. I'd drive a hundred miles to go see her and have a good time and she'd be depressed, and say, 'I still love Gary.' "

"The air of mystery about Janet was one of the things that attracted me to her," George Knight explains with a guileless gusto that is almost unsettling in its naive candor.

"She was hard to get, and I liked that. She still liked Gary, and she would never open to me at first. I was the rebound man. I remember one time she said, 'It's an insult when a guy doesn't want to kiss you.' She was directing that on me. And so we started developing more of a romantic relationship.

"Her parents allowed me to stay in their house to sleep. They let me sleep in that back room where the TV was, and I'll never forget, I was sleeping on the sleeping bag I'd brought, and I had my shirt off and I was in my blue jeans and she came up to me and said, 'Oh, you're so sexy. I could jump your bones right now.' I'd think that would be my job to say—but she definitely, after a little bit of time, started being sexually aggressive towards me.

"I remember her saying that and me saying, 'Look, I'm a human being, okay? I have certain values, but I'm human.' And then that Sunday evening her parents had to go to the sister's house and they left us. I was getting ready to leave and like, 'It's time for me to go, Janet,' and like, 'Lemme kiss you goodbye.' And we're sitting on the sofa watching TV and she really came on hot and heavy.

"Now, I was brought up that guys want to do it and girls don't. And I realized that maybe this was a reversed situation here. Man, we started kissing on the sofa and then we laid down—and it's like shooom! I've got a hot potato, here. Sometimes your animal instincts get going, but I said, 'Your parents are going to be coming back. We've gotta stop. I've gotta go. Because *I don't do this.*' Here I am trying to establish a relationship with someone to marry!

"One time I went into her bedroom with her and Miz Lorraine said, 'Janet, y'all keep that door open!' Her mama was very protective. I liked that. I want a girl to have parents with those values. To keep her daughter pure for the man she's gonna marry. But it really ticked her off that her mama was always nosing in there. I got the feeling she was going to do things to show her parents.

"In that time frame of getting to know her, she started opening up to me—she opened up to me sexually about her prior boyfriend, Gary. Right at the end of the semester she told me about catching his eye the first day of school and them going out and her staying overnight with him on the first date and making love.

"You know the song 'Torn Between Two Lovers'? That was my song, she would tell me. Me, 'I don't *care* about you and Gary.'

"One time she had Gary's name on a button—I'm dating this girl, I'm getting emotionally attached to her, and she's got Gary's name on her dresser!

"My understanding of it was—'I fell head over heels in love with the guy. Everything about the guy. We had sex. I loved him, and I wanted to have sex with him.' And then the guy just threw her for a loop. It was a tragic event, it really was, in her life.

"She said, 'It was Gary that opened me up and I liked it.' And that's what made me mad about him. She said Gary brought her into the room and she had never made love, she didn't know anything about it, and she said she experienced this for the first time and it was incredible. She said she liked it so much that when she woke up, he didn't want to do it but she was ready to continue, she wanted more.

"She would tell me about going into Gary's office and hanky-pankying. That intrigued her. She was very open about Gary. What she said was that Gary used her like an old rag and threw her away. To this day, I believe that Gary was the downfall and the tragedy of her life.

"And I was struggling between the virtue I was brought up with, and my sexual passions to try to go to bed with this girl. Which was overwhelming me; it was to the point where it was consuming me. Because she would talk openly about sex, about their exploits, and so I was—I had to deal with—it was the spirit of lust in me. That's all I can say. You've got to get into some kind of spiritual thing to explain it; there was a *spirit* of *lust.*"

* * *

"When you grow up with somebody that long, you don't really consider them your girlfriend much anymore," Peggy Cowans's brother, Danny Carr, explains.

"But I guess she still had the crush, and to me it was like, 'I'm your friend.' I was working on a car with my father on the side of the house and she brought her car over because it was running hot and she told me when she gets out of school she would like for us to get married. That's always been her dream. She's always loved me ever since we were kids. And she would like for us to get together.

"I just blew it off. It was the summer between her first and second year of college. She said she wanted to introduce me to her new friends.

"All we did was just talk on the side of the house and she was dreaming about her and I getting together and raising a family and being happily ever after—like in a fairy tale. I told her, 'I don't feel it would be right. I like you as a friend, not as a girlfriend.'

"That's when she got upset and started crying. She said, 'Maybe things will change.' She said she wanted somebody that would stand up and fight for her. 'This is mine. Don't touch it. Don't look at it. Don't do nothing with it'—I was always the jealous type.

"Then the wheels started turning in the brain. So like a week or two later she come back in and I seen her pass in back the house and she said she was in for the weekend and I told her we were going to go out on Saturday night, 'I'll pick you up at eight.'

A chance conflict of scheduling occasioned Danny to break that date and claim a raincheck. Janet threw a tantrum the likes of which he, who'd known her from birth, had never seen. He was more than a little surprised.

"She flipped out on me. She started crying, wanting to know why I did her this. That I really broke her heart—the only one that she really cared for. You know, ever since she was a little bitty kid.

"Never did call her back. Never did talk to her again until she called me about the accident."

"The first and most lasting impression when I think of Janet—was Halloween. She was still going with Gary, fall '77," muses Bob Blazier.

"Up until this point I remember her as being very pretty but always really high-necked and everything else. Then for this party, I'm at the radio station and she comes in in a black leotard, and lemme tell ya, it's hard being on a college campus and seeing all this stuff. She was made up like a cat, and I had to look away, it was just too much. I mean, the girl looked fine.

"Gary wasn't going to the party because he was working on a news show. She was heartbroken, because she had gone to all this trouble to get ready. It was an important party for her. And it wasn't to him. She stayed up there till about seven-thirty, eight o'clock.

"That night she sort of threw everything up to Gary—she was trying to do anything to get him to take her to this party. She brought up this heart murmur condition. She went on to explain to me, with him listening, that she had this condition and that Gary was the only guy who knew what to do when she was having an attack. She was one determined young lady.

"She had definitely discovered the better things in life, by that point in time. But she was not promiscuous; because, believe me, *everybody* took their shot."

"In the fall semester of 1977, we were forced to pay more attention to our individual problems and spent little time together. I was tied up between working nights and spending time in the TV studio while she struggled with many personal demons which continued picking at her insecurities," narrates Hurst Bousegard in the memoir he self-published as a gift to his mother.

"That's when things started to go downhill," Hurst is now explaining at his home in Texas. "She was having trouble with her family. I don't know any specifics. I just knew there were fights with her parents. And she had some disagreements with her sisters.

"We still dated, but the passion which had existed the previous spring was put on hold. I got the impression she had gone back to seeing Gary.

"It was attitude also. Shortly after the fall semester started, I had gone up to visit her in her dorm room during the visitation time. She was in a bad mood. She was grilling me about my activities during the summer. And then, just like that, she turned it around on her roommate about Gary. Janet accused her of contacting Gary and trying to get Gary.

"The girl denied it. The argument went on till Janet slapped her. It was the first time I saw her in that kind of light, and it took me by surprise. But then I remembered she had also accused Claire of going after me in the spring of '77.

"We occasionally dated that semester, but it wasn't the same; it was the beginning of the end."

"She was so good-looking," Professor Blazier says. "I assumed she was a cheerleader and all-everything in high school. She was always the center of attention. From the time I knew her, she had this air about her where she just drew people's attention. And she started dressing a lot more attention-getting after Gary. During Gary she was still mostly the home-ec–looking type."

Bob Blazier pauses, goes to silently stroking his beard and looking out at a bayou late afternoon slipping by, and then offers: "If she had once gotten as far along as both Gary and Kerry were at that time, skillwise and being a marketable person—that gold ring she was always looking for somebody to give her? She'd've got on her own.

"She was looking for it from these guys, yet she had it in *her*. But she never let herself get to the point where she could have done it. I am fully convinced if she and Kerry both would've graduated, they probably would have split up because she would have been the center. We're proud of Margaret here, but Margaret was not as good at reading copy as Janet. Oh, Margaret's a better writer, a better news person and everything else, but Janet was *not trained*. She was just a baby at her craft.

"And when she read copy? With those eyes? Boy, she had those eyes that just saw right through you. She'd look at that camera, and the camera was *so friendly* to her—she could've gone a lot further than Gary or Kerry, and Gary's done pretty well for himself.

"She was a good enough writer that you could just tell her what you wanted to say, and she could put it into dandy letter. She was around when we redid an application for the FCC which required some long narratives, and she gathered a lot of the information and put that to-gether.

"I saw a beautiful piece of clay. Not real smart, not real dumb, but real attractive, good at manipulating people's feelings, which you need in the broadcast news business, and she *wanted* the best. All the ingredients for a 'star.' "

"That's like saying what if Amelia Earhart had a 747. She *didn't* apply herself. That was her personality." Steve Richier, assignment editor for WVUE-TV Channel 8 News, who, like his co-worker Margaret Dubisson, is a successful product of the Nicholls State Communications Department and also was there at the same time as Janet Cannon, is addressing Bob Blazier's projections of how far she could've gone if she'd tried.

However, with that said, the quietly self-assured, boyish-faced veteran of the broadcast trenches pauses for a long moment, then says:

"I was program director or assistant station manager, I can't remember which, when she started her shift—and it was daily, afternoon drivetime four to six P.M. It was a treasured spot for me, because that was where I had started. I felt like she was a good replacement for me. She played a very consistent show. But she played—as we all did—her own certain sound. She played mostly love songs, rock love songs. Particular tunes, too. Where I would buy . . . say, a Journey album and play the songs that were normally not the top-forty stuff, she would play the top-forty stuff if it was a song she liked, and keep playing it—not the same shift—but I'd hear the same show. Which was actually good for a radio person.

"So maybe Bob's right. She was consistent; and creative doesn't make it in the business unless you make it big, and then they let you do whatever you want.

"There are certain tunes, all I can think of is Janet." Steve Richier quickly re-creates on his home sound system a facsimile of a typical Janet Cannon radio shift from the late '70s and then, with the music under, he continues, in a musing vein, "Always very melancholy stuff. She was a true romantic. Obviously . . ."

There is only the music for a while, until, "When Janet was doing her show, Kerry wasn't really in the picture yet. This was when Gary had moved from his apartment in town into a trailer at the same place where my roommate and I were renting one. Gary was in essence my boss.

"But Janet often rode back and forth from school with me. It was always a pleasant event. "We'd listen to music and talk. It was something I looked forward to.

"Janet was fun for me. A fantasy in my mind. You know? Hell of a lot of fun as a conversationalist: she liked to talk about music; she liked to talk about life; she liked to talk about love; she liked to talk about sex. There were no limits to her conversations. She was open to everything. Her ideas were all pretty sharp, too.

"It wasn't like what you would've thought would have come out of that repression as a child. I had met her parents by then. And it seemed very—well, like—'Gee, why are you living with your *grandparents*?' And I thought *my* parents were fairly strict."

"Lorraine Cannon is the daughter of my mother-in-law's sister, so Lorraine is my wife's first cousin. Janet is my wife's first cousin once removed, to be perfectly correct on that," explains Ernie Barrow, the prominent West Bank and Jefferson Parish attorney. After his salad years as a prosecutor, for the better part of two decades now, Ernie has had a lucrative private law practice in the sphere of civil and domestic law; he is also general counsel for the Jefferson Parish School Board.

Aside and apart from his good-ol'-boy "networking" and social and political prominence, the Mississippi-raised Mr. Barrow is something of a Renaissance man—he and Janet shared and critiqued each other's poetry over the years—even if he does reveal such aspects of himself only among close friends and some family.

"I always felt like Janet had great potential and that she could've gone a long ways in either modeling or some part of the music industry, or publishing.

"She was a good dancer; and she had a good voice, too. She was a *beautiful woman*. She could easily have been a high fashion model, easily.

"Janet had the greatest potential of the whole group. I mean, from an intellectual standpoint—*and* from an emotional sensitivity point. She was more sensitive emotionally; an artistic temperament, what other generations called bohemian or the beats.

"What she did with it or would do with it, I don't know, but I think eventually Janet would have emerged somewhere along the line *some-where* in the arts, either in music or literature. Modeling wouldn't have been enough for her for long.

"She was a most unusual and extraordinary girl."

With his resources for resistance all but expended in the tug-of-war between his virtue and his glands, George Knight remembers he survived that summer of 1977 with his virginity technically and only barely intact, but he lost the girl.

"She said, 'George, you need to find yourself a good girl, I'm not a good girl.' Then she said, 'I'm a used car, George.' Sex controlled her. Demonic possession," George says with a nod of agreement to his wife, Yvette, before continuing.

"I was consumed by lust. But that wasn't the end of it. What was strange about her was she kept me guessing. I felt like I was falling in love, but she would tell me, 'I don't know if I love you. Because if I fall in love with somebody, I fall into love hard, deep. And I don't know if I'm ready after Gary.'

"I said, 'Janet. I'm not going to do that to you.' The sex part of her was exciting and intriguing and I didn't understand it and it bothered me about virtues, that's what broke us up eventually, but she was fun—I didn't see the dark side of her.

"So, we're back at school and she started talking about Gary, and I said, 'Girl, you are not going to treat me the way you have been.' She started crying. I said, 'I mean, I'm serious. I'm starting to develop a love for you. A relationship that's consuming me and not you and now you're starting to talk about Gary again?

" 'It's either you're not going to prick-tease me like that and we're gonna casually date and go have a dinner and go to a movie and you can date other people and I can date other people—but when you get into the sex part of it, I'm not going to share you with nobody else. Last semester you talked about Gary and everything, but man, I am not going to have you start talking about Gary, now. I can't handle that. Okay? At all!' And I said, 'I want to end it right now. Because you're gonna drive me nuts.'

"She really cried. Enough to make me feel like I'm the one that ended this thing. And yet I felt like if she really loved me, she would come back. But she never did.

"I remember in my dorm. It's lonely. And it's like maybe I should—oh, I can't tell you the times I felt like calling her and trying to set something up. But I said, 'I'm not going to do it. I'm not going to let that girl control me—with her sex.' "

"Kerry came home one day and said, 'Dad, I think I missed something.' I said, 'I know you did,' " Clifford Myers is saying.

"He said, 'I want to go back to college.' I said, 'Okay, Kerry, I'll tell you what. You're gonna pay for your first semester, and if you show you're serious about it, I'll take over from there.'

"His first report he had a 3.5 or 3.6. He was doing great—then he met Janet."

"It was really hard to see Kerry with his daddy, because his daddy was really too tough on him," Connie Burmaster Cassard, a cop's daughter and a cop's wife, reflects.

"I can remember Kerry going to college and I remember his daddy always getting on him the Sunday before he'd leave. That would hurt him so much.

"Mr. Cliff was forever screaming at him and fussing. Just different things. Like with the food; we'd go to the grandma's house and Grandma would load him down with food every Sunday, but that's just how she was. He'd keep telling her, 'No, Maw Maw.' And I think Mr. Cliff felt like Chuck was using Kerry because they lived together, that was why all the food and all, but he didn't know Chuck's side. And he never gave Kerry a chance to ever say anything or to explain. He was always harping on him.

"He'd just sit and talk about how he wanted the perfect family; naturally, I dreamed the same *Brady Bunch* life. Kerry would say to me, 'When we get married, I want just the perfect family. I'm not going to end up like my parents.' That was the one thing that bothered Kerry the most, he brought that up a lot. He always told me he *would not* be divorced. We would go visit his mother . . . that's all he talked about, it really affected him that his parents broke up like they did. We'd be sitting and talking and he'd just come right out and tell me about this man that was his stepsister Kelly's daddy.

"Miz Marguerite talked about him a lot, too; he was only around from what I understand until Kelly's first birthday, if that long, and then disappeared. Miz Marguerite told me that she had Cliff Jr., Dawn, and Kerry with her after the divorce from Mr. Cliff, but that she just couldn't afford to keep them. She always talked as if Kerry was the one that was special to her, of the children she and Mr. Cliff had.

"It upset him to see his mother living like that, you know, Kelly not having a daddy. He started telling me how he felt sorry for Kelly, because he knew what she was going through and he wanted to be the daddy that Kelly never had, which is what he tried to do. We took Kelly a lot with us. And that brought it all out when he started talking to me. He blamed his mother. But he still really loved her. Hated what she did but loved her. He loved his mother to death, he told me that. We went over to Miz Marguerite's every Sunday, we didn't miss a Sunday to go see her.

"But, you know, I can see a lot of the similarities in our relationship and his and Janet's. The possessiveness, the control. Except Kerry never used any physical violence with me. He did use verbal abuse. That's one of the biggest reasons our relationship broke up. Kerry used to always tell me I was getting fat. And my mom used to say, 'Connie, why do you put up with that from him? You're not fat. You're far from fat.' I mean, I weighed ninety-eight pounds.

"In public, he'd scream, 'I hate you!' When we broke up, I told him, 'Kerry, it's over with.' And he said, 'I'm still giving you a Christmas present.' I said I didn't want anything. And he went and sold his camera to buy me a Christmas present. It was a diamond necklace, a V necklace, I never did get it, I never would take it.

"But he couldn't deal with the rejection, I guess. There was a Christmas party or something and I tried to get him to stay home, I told him I didn't want him to come, but he insisted on coming anyway so he just followed with us, followed right behind us. And it was like I totally ignored him. But he still stayed, and then he insisted that he was definitely giving me a Christmas present. That he'd already bought it and he wanted me to have it. So he hung around for Christmas and New Year's; it wasn't until after New Year's that I could get him away from me.

"Right before we broke up, I knew there was a girl interested in him at Nicholls State. I can remember Kerry saying there was a girl over there, but it was more like him telling me, working on me, like, 'But, see, I'm not interested in her.' "

"Kerry was extremely sensitive about his appearance," Mike Price explains. "He is extremely insecure about how attractive he is to women. He was always afraid of losing a girlfriend, that someone better-looking may come along and take her away.

"He was desperate when he broke up with Connie. It was during final exams of the fall '77 semester. He would come home on weekends because she was still here in high school. When he came back up Monday morning—God, he must've drove that car at a hundred miles an hour and spun into the parking space between the two trailers—his driveway was right between my trailer and his. He skids to a stop and backs up and skids to a stop again, and I went outside and snatched him out of the car telling him if he didn't turn the damn thing off I was gonna take the keys and shove 'em up his ass.

"That's when he tells me, all broken up, 'I'm sorry, I broke up with Connie.' 'Jesus—there are six thousand girls here on campus, just pick one.' But he sulked over her until Janet."

Hurst found it necessary that he resign from the university for health reasons before the end of the fall '77 semester. He reflects on his goodbye to Janet.

"She said, 'Wow, you're really leaving, huh?' I replied, 'I've got to. I need to rest up and get myself back.' She seemed disappointed but not terribly broken up about it."

"Kerry immediately got involved in radio here," Bob Blazier says. "First as a volunteer disk jockey, then he went before a committee and he was selected by twenty people to serve in one of the paid staff positions. Of the group of people he was with he seemed to be one of the most conservative, straightest I knew."

"It was Kerry, me, Jimmy Jordan, and Chuck." Mike Price is remembering an afternoon in December 1977. "Kerry and Chuck were roommates; Jimmy and I were roommates. We were all out in front of the trailers throwing a football and squirting each other with water pistols. Somebody was barbecuing. I don't remember who.

"We're out there playing and we hear a ruckus going on in the first trailer—Kerry and Chuck lived in trailer two, and Jimmy and I lived in trailer three. The trailers were only ten feet apart, just wide enough to park your car. And so we hear this ruckus, we're all watching—then we see this girl and we hear, 'Get the fuck out!' And all this, 'Get out of here and don't come back!' Gary Landry, a guy we knew a little from around school, lived in that trailer; anyway, he either threw her or she fell down the steps and lands all in a pile. She jumps up, she's banging on the door, 'Ooo!'—crying and all this stuff. Then she walked off a little and stopped and just kinda looked around so helplessly, you know. The tears and everything.

"Well, it didn't escape any of us that she was *so fine.* I mean, she looked *good*—and obviously she was now available. So we kind of swooped in and tried to help out the 'damsel in distress.'

"And it was that fast. Kerry—I mean, we all had designs on her; believe me, any one of us would've taken that girl in the trailer right then and taken care of the whole business—the thing is, Kerry, he went into his swoon. I mean, instant—we were all having such a good time, and all the air was gone because Kerry . . . I mean, he ain't even talked to her yet and he loves her!

"We were all offering her a ride back to wherever. Kerry ended up taking her back to her dorm; but we were all trying to help out. Actually, we were all trying to get into her pants. But he was more successful at that. It turned out that Kerry knew who she was. Seems they'd had a communications class together the first semester. That's why it worked out that way—she at least had something in common with him to let him take her back.

"It was instant—just add water. Kerry came back from taking her and *he was in love.* There were no ifs, ands, or buts, and he told us, he verbalized that, right away. And Chuck said, 'Aw, fuck!' "

                              *   *   *

"She would pick enough—it's hard for me to imagine Gary getting violent, but anybody can. I was at the trailer park any number of times," Bob Blazier says.

"The cat costume came that first semester of '77. He was trying to break it off. They were being verbally very cruel to one another, and doing it in front of me added more to it. She taunted Gary that night. Like she asked me to go with her, and I was tempted because she was looking good. I don't know why I didn't . . . there was something deep . . . but she wasn't doing it for me, she was doing it to dig him because she knew he had respect for me, we had our friendship. And if you really want to hurt somebody, you fuck their friend. That's probably why I didn't do it. But it was crushing to her when they broke up."

"She cut her hair. Her beautiful long hair," George Knight remembers. "It blew my mind. I saw her on campus, and she said, 'All the guys were attracted to me for my hair. I'm *sick* of guys.' I said to myself, 'Ah, man.'

"Then I saw her with Kerry at the trailer. Penny's brother Mike and I took off somewhere and we ended up going to Kerry's trailer. Janet was there, I saw them together. I thought, 'Well, she must've linked up with somebody else.'

"Then I remember seeing her on campus . . . she said, 'He told me to shut up about Gary.' She gave me the impression—the gist was, 'Janet, shut up about Gary. I'm in control. I don't want to hear a word about Gary. You're going to love me. Period.' I felt, after her and I had this conversation, that if I would've been more solid, okay?—more directional, and told her to 'shut up about Gary, I don't want to hear it anymore, Gary's history, girl,' then I would've straightened her act out."

"At first I thought she was going out with Kerry just to twist the knife into Gary," Bob Blazier recalls. "And I got on her for it. That was when I began to realize she might really care for Kerry. That it wasn't just a passing thing. But Kerry just did not seem her type.

"That's why I chastised her when she started the thing with him, because Gary and Kerry worked together. And they had a relationship. It wasn't very close, but they had to be with one another a lot. Had to be in the same rooms.

"But that was my impression of the beginning of that relationship that ended up in marriage—that she was doing to Kerry the same thing she had tried to do to me that night: use him to get to Gary. And Kerry was younger, probably hornier, and he didn't find himself with as many limiting factors as I had.

"I wasn't sure until Gary left to go to Lafayette and she didn't follow him—and even then I wasn't absolutely sure that she *still* wasn't using Kerry to get at Gary."

"A few months in Grand Isle got my health back and I wanted desperately to strengthen our alliance. So once the fall semester ended in December, I decided to call Janet at home to make a very special dinner date," Hurst Bousegard writes.

"What I had felt she wanted that summer—no, what I *know* she wanted from me then, because we had talked about it, was some form of commitment for the future," Hurst says now, and the pain is still very present after all these years and the changes they have borne.

"Unknown to her, I was going to ask her to marry me as soon as I could accomplish some type of job security."

So Hurst made reservations at Brennan's in the French Quarter and called her up. Love, happiness, and poetics would then surely thereafter reign all the days of his life. But when he mentioned the dinner date, Janet said, "I don't think it would be right, now. I'm seeing someone else. But I still want us to be close friends."

"It was as if having my chest slashed open with a sword and then given a Band-Aid to make it better," remembers Hurst.

"But, our relationship, there was never anything mean about it. There was no viciousness involved, she never tried to get at me for something I did or anything like that. It was just a loving, caring relationship. Even when it was over, you know, I was angry and bitter in the beginning because I lost her, but by the time I got back to school and she and Kerry were together, I accepted it, the atmosphere was very friendly.

"But, you know, she didn't light up like she was in love with Kerry. That's what struck me funny about the whole thing. You see, the reason I was being so friendly and cordial to both of them all the time was for selfish reasons—I knew that this would not last and I was waiting for that. Even when they were married, I knew it couldn't last, and I waited.

"I heard her have one argument with Kerry; I was totally unaware that their relationship had gotten to that point. It was during spring '78, I was going to the radio station, I think it was because I knew she was there. I was just stopping in to see her. But right as I stepped in the door, I heard all the yelling and screaming behind the door and I took off."

"Her roommate, Claire, liked me," George Knight says. "And Janet hated that.

"I got the feeling that she felt like I was stupid sometimes. That she felt she was a lot smarter than me. That she was a lot more worldly—she would try to belittle me, about the way I talk with a country accent. I'd use a big word, and she'd say, 'Listen to you. Listen to you coming out with these big words, you Country Jake.' She made fun of the Baker Roller Ranch being the only thing to do in Baker, Louisiana. 'You're really a hick, George. Even your roller rink is called a *ranch.*'

"She said she liked poetry and music. She wanted to write a book and I'd be the artist. She wanted to have two children and name them Andy and Mandy. I'd talk about my expectations of being in business, she'd say, 'Ooh, I'd like to make a lot of money.' I think she was attracted to me because she felt like she would make a lot of money. But then I think she was tormented by past histories of Gary, and that situation there and that she really loved him.

"She really did have a way of making me feel inferior and putting her on a pedestal and having me to shine up to her."

"Miz Marguerite called my house to ask me not to break up with Kerry, to stay with him," Connie Burmaster Cassard remembers. "She said they liked me, that I was good for Kerry and to please take him back. I told her I just couldn't.

"Kerry would go over to my older sister Beverly's house and actually cry real tears that I broke up with him. She used to just sit there and listen to him and he'd go on and on. I could have understood his taking it so bad if maybe we'd been going out for years. I could understand if maybe you've become so attached to someone. But it wasn't the case here.

"When I was trying to break it off, he would come to Maison Blanche where I worked and harass me. This one time I was working and he just wouldn't leave the department. He wouldn't leave me alone. He kept crying and begging and just kept going on and on with me, getting louder and louder and nastier until finally it got to the point where I was really getting scared so I picked up a pair of scissors and told him I would call security if he didn't get out. Finally he left.

"Soon after that I started getting phone calls from Janet. She'd call and curse me out and tell me I would never have Kerry back. That no matter what I did, I wasn't getting him back. She would even call me at work and do the same thing. The calls would just come out of the clear blue, on a weekend usually. She'd call and just curse and scream and holler and then tell me how Kerry was never going back to me.

"Now, nothing between Kerry and I was ever said about it. I wasn't seeing Kerry. Oh, he called a few times, still trying to get me to go back with him. I would just say, 'Kerry, it's over.'

"But Janet would call two or three times a day for several weeks. She'd just start hollering and screaming. In the beginning I tried to talk to her, explain to her I didn't want Kerry. It got towards the end where I would just hang up on her. Because it was always the same thing over and over again. Half the time Lisa was there and I'd give the phone to her and she would listen. Whoever was there got to listen to the phone calls. She didn't know who was on the phone, she was screaming so much."

"I got dressed for my senior prom with Kerry sitting on my deacon's bench crying the whole time," Lisa Comeaux Grubic says.

"Connie was going with this guy Kevin to her senior prom and Kerry still wanted her back. This was *May* 1978. Months after him and Janet were together . . . ?"

"That winter of '78, we were all on staff together, I was station manager, I think Margaret Dubisson was news director, Kerry was program director, Janet I think was music director, and Richier might've been assistant station manager," remembers Logan Banks, formerly a reporter for WDSU-TV Channel 6, the NBC affiliate in New Orleans and another of Bob Blazier's success stories. Banks is now back at Nicholls State in an executive position.

"At first glance you'd think Janet and Kerry were a normal couple. You'd see them walking around the quadrangle holding hands. But as you got to know them, as time wore on, you realized there was some kind of strange psychology to their relationship. It started to become apparent that it wasn't what it appeared to be. Frankly, we used to always make jokes about their arguments. They would fight right at work. She would nit-pick, but he was very jealous and also had a violent temper. He was *really* jealous of her.

"Later, as things went on, these arguments would get started and they would go off into one of the vacant rooms at the radio station and you'd hear this"—he bangs his fist on his desk three times. "Pounding and screaming and pounding and 'Urggha! Urggha!—Nnhh! Nnhh! Nh!—Urggha! Urggha!' Violent argument tones. His gorilla and her high-pitched Minnie Mouse."

"We had a trailer park that was at the end of a dead-end street in the backyard of a big house on LA 1 in Thibodaux," Steve Richier explains. "It was a big house with a big yard, so they went and cut it in half and put these six trailers on it. Brand-new. It was nice. Eventually it became seven when they put in a used one. I was in number six, I had the biggest yard.

"Kerry moved into trailer number two with Jimmy Jordan. Jimmy had been living with Mike Price. I used to go and visit with them occasionally. We were all college buddies. Jimmy was a nut about his VW. And my brother and I both had one.

"When Mike moved next door, Kerry moved in. I didn't care for the guy immediately. Then when Janet started dating him, Jimmy would tell me about their fights. One day I saw the glass broken on the front door and

I said to Jimmy, 'What happened to your door?' And he said, as if it was nothing, 'Oh, Kerry and Janet had a fight. Kerry threw her out the trailer door, over the steps, onto the shells, she landed hard, picked up some rocks, crying and yelling, threw the rocks at the glass window, and broke it—and how is your car?' "

"From day one they fought," Chuck Cassard explains.

"It became commonplace, their violence. It was just that that's how they got along. If I had to feel anything, I felt really embarrassed for both of them, because it was so childish, I just didn't get involved with it. 'Here they go, they're at it again. Just leave 'em alone.'

"Nothing ever came of it. It was always just the way they were. It was pretty loud at times. But it was never anything that caused me any concern. Maybe the first time, but when you see it every day, you don't care. It's just how some people relate to each other.

"It wasn't just one, they both argued. I remember one day they were arguing because Kerry had gotten a lower grade than she had gotten on something, and Kerry had blamed her for flirting with the instructor—whether she did or not, who knows? Who cares? If it works, do it." Chuck laughs.

"I remember one time, I don't know what in the hell they were arguing about, Jimmy and I were sitting there listening to an album that he'd brought down called *Crack the Sky*. I don't even know why I remember that. But we were listening and they came home arguing and screaming and they were right next to the refrigerator and for some reason the argument got a little bit more than normal and she kneed him in the groin and he grabbed her by the neck. I looked at Jimmy and I said, 'Come on, let's get out of here, we can't listen to this. They're making the damn needle jump up and down.' So we got up and Jimmy said, 'Y'all are ridiculous!'

"So we went outside and Jimmy loved his car and he was showing me something he'd done on his little green Volkswagen. And they come out a couple of minutes later and say, 'Y'all wanna go with us? We're going to go get some ice cream.'

" 'No. Just go.' "

"Yet, you know what I think about? I'm the one, really, that was close to 'em when they were in the period where they should've been on their *best* behavior. Early in their courtship. So what in the hell happened when I left?"

"All that we saw took place over less than a semester. The four of us only lived next door to each other in those trailers for a very, very short period of time. Maybe a month, maybe two," remembers Monique Price.

"So the half-dozen or so fights we either saw, heard, or saw the aftermath of—was many in that time frame, because it was at least a once-a-week occurrence.

"The one-word answer is denial. Every episode that I would ever try to talk to her later about—she'd act like it never happened. She would deny that it happened. She would say you were lying if you said otherwise.

"Of course, it depended on which stage of a fight you caught her in; if she thought you didn't see it, or there wasn't any evidence of it, it was denial. But she had no problem telling me that Kerry broke her nose, or Kerry bruised her arm. She had no problem telling people when she had injuries that Kerry did it.

"Initially it would be kind of like Kerry was only trying to restrain her; trying to keep her off of him. But inevitably it would turn into mutual knock-down, drag-out fights. And she mostly gave as good she got. Of course, being that he was a man and she was a woman, I guess he could've always killed her, or totally knocked her out. But he didn't do that. It was more like *two women* fighting most of the time. It was a lot of scratching, clawing, slapping, hair-pulling, hissing, and screeching.

"There were a couple of really big fights . . . the broken-vase-and-knife fight, the head-banging-into-the-hood-of-the-car fight, or the trying-to-shove-her-into-the-car fight."

"Their fights could be about anything; normally it was totally trivial," Mike Price remembers, reluctantly and with obvious difficulty, and it is clear where he still places the blame.

"She was so bizarre, and her thought processes were so foreign to me, you know, if you just looked at her wrong—one time they got in a fight because a cockroach crawled across her while she was in bed in the trailer and they started yelling and screaming and the next thing you know they were fighting all over the place.

"Most people build up to a fight. The thing about them was there wasn't enough time between fights to build up. It was one continuous fight interrupted by momentary peace treaties.

"One time after they had a big fight Monique and I were driving her up to the radio station. I said, 'This is crazy. Y'all need to stop this and start getting along or break up.' And Janet said, 'We don't fight *against* each other, we fight *with* each other.' That's when you give each other a knowing glance that says, 'Let's get this load out of the backseat real quick, because this is nuts.' "

"She could punch Kerry's buttons. Never seen him go off on anybody else like that, not at all," Chuck Cassard is saying. "I saw Curtis go off one day on him. And Kerry just stood there and took it. If he'd yelled at me like that I'd've popped him. I never remember Kerry being one to start a fight—except with Janet. And she would start most of the physical ones; I think she would swing first. I mean, the ones I saw—maybe three I can remember. And when he'd hit back, it wasn't like you'd think—you know, because I hit you, I'm looking to take your head off. It was more like a wake-up shot.

"But then five minutes later they'd jump into bed. I never paid any attention to it. I just went about my business. This is their version of foreplay.

"Knowing them, *anything* could happen—as long as the bottom line is they don't break up."

"I remember when Kerry got engaged to Janet," Connie Cassard says. "He made sure he came by to show me her ring. He'd bought the complete wedding set.

"I can also remember when she was dating Kerry, his parents did not welcome her. They hated her. I remember all of that going on. Kerry's parents would not let her near the house. They did not like Janet at all. They saw the fighting."

"There was another time where we heard all of the commotion but it all stayed inside the trailer," Monique Price recalls. "And then a little while later she came and knocked on our door; she came in and she was cut and bleeding, sort of like scratches or small cuts. She was crying, of course her hair was a mess, and the cuts bothered me and I remember looking at her, it was the middle of the night, and saying, 'My God! Janet, what have y'all done now?'

"In her raving state of mind she was in—I mean, she'd just stepped out of a fight—she said something about fighting with a knife and a broken vase. She wanted to use the phone to call someone to come and get her. She called somebody. Then Mike and I tried talking to her again about this craziness. The next thing we know she goes back into the trailer and stays all night long. That was a very typical, common occurrence.

"Normally, if you'd catch her in the fight, she couldn't deny it. So, she'd start saying it was all Kerry—'Kerry did such and such.' I do know if you got Janet where there was physical evidence, such as a cut or bruise, she would claim it was all Kerry—as if she was an innocent bystander.

"In Kerry's defense—even though he partook of all of those fights, and he didn't just walk away and say I'm not going to be a part of this—but in his defense, every fight I ever saw, Janet was the antagonizer, the instigator, the start, the reason.

"And I never knew what Janet was mad about. No one knows what triggered her—that's the whole mystery to Janet, is that nothing would trigger it. You'd be sitting there and everything would be calm and cool and the next thing you know she'd be totally out of control.

* * *

"One time I went with Billy up to Southeastern, I wanted to see the campus," Connie Cassard remembers. "We drove up there and he had me write a note for him, because he was graduating—I wrote a note saying I was his mother—I can't believe I did this—and that his grandma died and that he couldn't graduate onstage. It was the only way he could get out of it. He did *not* want to graduate on the stage; he refused to graduate on the stage. Now this is a guy who was an honors student—I mean, Billy was so smart. It was so bizarre that he wouldn't get up onstage—and his mother really wanted him to graduate onstage. But he would not do it; so I wrote the note and they said okay.

"I never did know why."

"The worst part was they could have a fight like that and, I mean, twenty seconds later they're in the bed and the trailer is rockin' 'n' rollin'," Mike Price says.

"And what was really strange about that was that Kerry had never been as sexually active as the rest of us. He was more of a romantic. It meant commitment to him. He wasn't able to separate love and lust—his sexual activity was more on the lines of a female than it was a male.

"So I can't explain it. Other than her being *that good.* I would think she was anyway. Yeah, I would think she was *very* good. It was an intriguing possibility—I wasn't brain-dead. There was no one out of our whole group that didn't think she would probably have been the best fuck of all.

"But the fighting and sex? I think she got off on it. I think that was her only way—I think really and truly that was her favorite time to have sex. Almost as if she had to make sure she was punished for enjoying sex. Kerry as much as told me once, kind of like, 'Yeah, but it's great, I'm telling ya.' "

"Dating Billy was totally different from what one might think," Connie Cassard explains.

"The odd thing is that I didn't find Billy sexually aggressive at all. When we dated we just went out to the show and that was the date. We'd come home and that was it, it'd be over with. It never really led to anything. We'd sit around and watch TV.

"It only took one time for him to try to push himself, and as soon as I told him no, that was it. But a talker? Oh, he's got the words; he's a silver tongue.

"Yet anytime anybody talked about Billy, that's all you ever heard—'Billy has a one-track mind: sex.' Billy had this car and he loved it because the seats laid down in it, everybody said. And he used it quite often, to hear the stories; I mean, Billy would find a girl somewhere. He was strictly that way. I mean, he lived out of his car half the time—he had clothes in his car all the time. He lived out of that car."

*   *   *

"Billy told Louie that he had been sleeping with Connie," Russell Ard-neaux remembers. "He said that the way he did it was that he made promises to her that they would get married someday. And every time he played that up, he was able to score. That was to hurt Louie. Billy knew how crazy Louie was about Connie."

"Billy went on a job interview not long after he graduated and he asked me to take a ride with him," Connie Cassard recalls. "I said, 'Okay, I'll take a ride with you. I don't have to go to work till eight.' We went across the river—it was Dun & Bradstreet. I stood out there and waited for him. It was a job agency that sent him. They told him—now this is what he told me—that he would probably have to go on six to nine interviews before they would hire him. He walked out and he had the job; he impressed the people that much. And do you know, he was there, what, a week or two, and then quit.

"He was just so excited when he got that job. It was, 'I got it on one interview!' We went back over to the agency and he was just so proud. They couldn't believe it, that he got the job on that one interview."

"Billy is so smart that he can come across really well. He can fool a lot of people because of the way he is."

10
Cases

We've been so busy little one. You've been keeping me on the run. In the last month you've learned to roll from your back to belly and belly to back, you've found your feet and you're now laughing out loud. It has been a busy month. On Nov. 6th you made 4 months old. You were 15 pounds, 4 ounces and 26 in. long and very healthy.

At this time you enjoy your swing, you really like bath time and eating is very special. You and I giggle alot, and I try to teach you new things. You're really beginning to teeth, and soon your first tooth will be out. . . .

I want you to have a background on your family, especially me and dad. So often children don't realize that their parents are "people" too.

Your dad and I met at college . . . Nicholls State University in Thibodaux. December of 1977 is when we first met . . . no, actually it was August of 1977. We were in a journalism class together. At the time he had another girlfriend and I was on-off with someone else. We went the entire semester without saying a word.

It was in December when I was visiting a friend in the same trailer park your dad lived that I talked to him. I had always thought he was cute but "TAKEN." We became sort of "friends." And then the Christmas holidays came . . . I thought a lot about your dad, but figured he didn't remember me. And so came our Spring '78 semester. I walked into a classroom that had alot of unknowns in it, so I went and sat by your dad. We started to talk about last semester Journalism, and he remembered me. At the end of that week I needed a ride home, so I mustered up the courage to ask him . . . Of course he said yes.

When I was waiting that Friday for him to arrive at the dorm, I watched out the window. When he crossed the street I thought how cute he was . . . During the ride home I discovered he broke up with his girlfriend. I was delighted, but didn't know why!

—*Journal of Janet Cannon Myers*

* * *

" 'Janet stabbed Billy.' "

W. J. LeBlanc remembers and repeats those three words, approaching almost the same mixture of blazing insight and excited, zealous conviction which gripped him almost two years before when he first heard them in December 1989.

There is almost a little-boy bounce upon the big leather chair before he catches back his exuberance, restrains it. Then he leans back with only a trace of that little smile of his in the big comfortable chair framed by the floor-to-ceiling French windows of the elegant National Landmark old home smack-dab in the middle of old Gretna which he and his partner, John Molaison, chose to be as the offices of their recently established private law practice.

"But, no doubt, that was it. That's when everything started making sense. The pieces of the puzzle now had a place to be put. Obviously, they didn't totally fill up the puzzle. But at least we had the outline of it. And that had always been the problem. Not only did we have so many missing pieces—and still do, of course—but we didn't even know what the puzzle was supposed to look like. And that's really whistling in the dark."

W.J. chuckles—and then sighs deliberately before leaning forward and saying with that certain sense of finality which is the trademark of his pronounced thoughts:

"With that I had a baseline against which all the physical evidence, behavioral inconsistencies, circumstantial evidence, and plausible scenarios could be measured."

W.J. adds, "Of course, I guess it really started with my finally getting the case."

Even though he was peripherally involved with the baseball bat murder ever since that Saturday morning in '87 when he walked in on Dr. Lee's slide show, and thereafter had often let it be known that he wouldn't mind being assigned to the case, the elements which culminated in that happening certainly were not diminished by the prosecution of Thelma Horn for second degree murder in January 1989—she who was the "bait" in the André Daigle case.

The Horn victory was a "masterpiece," a prosecutor's "career win," against all odds and practical jurisprudence probabilities. It was that hardest of hard cases—totally, 100 percent circumstantial.

Initially, the prospects of prosecuting the pitiable Ms. Horn seemed to be a lock after her two codefendants agreed to testify against her. Just another photo for Dub's sequential rogues' gallery, which prominently, uniquely, and some say inappropriately adorns the pegboard in the small office he shares with John Molaison within the district attorney's complex.

However, when both reneged and refused to testify, Dub was left holding an all but empty bag.

Almost invariably, when a purely circumstantial case is won (and later dissected), it is learned that the verdict was in large part swayed by voir dire technique and the prosecution's closing argument.

W.J.'s uncanny knack of making a panel of jurors trust him took care of the first prerequisite.

Then, when the defense rested and it was time for the State's final thrust, W. J. LeBlanc rose, walked to his favorite position for closing argument—up close to the rail and dead center of the jury box—and pointed back at the defendant:

"We are here today because of what Thelma Horn did," said W.J. "If not for Thelma Horn, we wouldn't be here and, more importantly, André Daigle *would* be. . . . Thelma Horn did not hand the killers the hammer. Thelma Horn did not hand the killers the electrical cord. Thelma Horn handed the killers their victim."

Guilty as charged, second degree murder, life without parole.

While the sobriquet of "Luck" had already been whispered or muttered by some within the DA's Office in W.J.'s wake or absence, the derision became more entrenched and widespread afterward.

At the same time, Wally Rothschild again left the department to return to the U.S. Attorney's Office across the river in New Orleans, and Howat Peters became titularly responsible for the seemingly moribund Fontanille-Myers prosecution.

W.J. went to his friend Howie and asked if anybody else had offered to help with the case which now had almost a complete hold upon Dub's intellectual fancy and his prosecutorial soul. The answer was no. W.J. then asked if Howie was still looking for somebody. The answer was an emphatic yes. "Well, you know where to find me," Dub told him. "Yeah, I know," Howat Peters replied.

And so the baseball bat murder case just sat there. A fat, seductive feast of either gourmet bounty or suicidal poison—with the smart money coming in heavily on the latter. Which was why the line forming behind Howie was nonexistent after the exclusion of W. J. LeBlanc.

So W.J. waited. As long as there were no takers, he figured that sooner or later the job of finally exacting justice for the murdered Janet Myers would be his, if only by default.

In April 1989, W. J. LeBlanc and Detective Vincent Lamia flew to Huntsville, Alabama, to meet an FBI agent who drove them to interview an informant they needed to testify in an impending first degree murder trial—an interesting case of mistaken identity that would be known as the Good Samaritan Murder.

However, on the plane that April morning they weren't talking about what was officially called the McCullough case. The topic of that flight was the baseball bat murder, then five years and two months old and counting. Dub, sure that his time would come, that it had to, asked Vince, "Look, if I get it, do you want in?"

"You call me. *I want in.* We can do the same thing with this that we did with the Richard case," Vince answered in less than a heartbeat.

"It was the first time we'd spent any significant time together since the Richard case, almost two years," recalls Dub, sitting at his desk in front of those panoramic French doors.

"That had been only my third case. And over those next two years I had come to recognize just how rare a job he had done. But hey, stupid me, I'm thinking all detectives are like Vince Lamia—and boy, was I sadly mistaken."

One thing W.J. does with all his case officers is get the officer's home phone number and ask what is the latest he can call him at night. Vince remembers his answer had been "Anytime, day or night, just *call* me," because "W.J. is the first ADA to ever really give a shit about one of my cases."

Vincent Lamia has a passion about his cases, and he'd hooked up with an ADA who approached his job the same way.

"Vince was very open-minded." W.J. is again speaking about that flight to Huntsville. "Even though he had been the man most responsible for getting the Fontanille indictment off a dime. He'd had a chance to reflect upon Dr. Lee's findings, and he was also excited by my belief that we could get both these guys; that they were both dirty.

"I wanted somebody who could live this case with me. Somebody I could call up at midnight because something was bothering me and to go through it all. I wanted somebody who was going to be as thorough as I was going to be. Because it was going to take that kind of effort."

"The supreme court eventually ruled our way on the conspiracy, but I didn't know if Howie was going to still try the conspiracy case or not, because all the court did was say they couldn't use the statements." Nick Noriea works, hunts for things on his desk, and talks on the telephone even as he remembers and rat-a-tat-tats.

"I knew the murder charge was sitting out there in the back, and I knew the *original* indictment was May of '86, and I knew the reindictment was November of '87, and I was trying to get past three years from the original indictment because the law says you've got three years under the Speedy Trial Act.

"Now it's May of '89. I told Madeleine, 'We've got three years. We're gonna lose between thirty to sixty days because of suspensions for pretrial motions.' I took the average, forty-five days. I said, 'We've got till the Fourth of July. If we make the Fourth of July, we've got it.' And I knew the rules of court said you need fourteen days' notice for trial, so I figured the Fourth of July would give me until the 18th and that would make the forty-five become fifty-nine . . . that's close enough.

"Now, I'd done the first trial with one contact lens in and one out, and I'd kept putting off the second eye operation to let the three years pass. I had a civil case, representing a doctor, that was scheduled for trial the end of June. I figured right after that I'd go ahead and have my cornea transplant.

"Then there was a delay with finding a donor for the transplant, so it wasn't until the 7th that I went into the hospital. That was Thursday. Operation Friday. Let me go home on Sunday. I can remember laying in the hospital thinking, 'These people over there—it's too *late.*'

"I was clapping each morning that another day passed before they fixed this thing for trial. I was celebrating with the passage of each day."

Wiley Beevers's favorite way of passing time on the baseball bat murder case—when he took the time—was to routinely drop by the DA's Office and ask of everyone and anyone, in his exaggerated Mississippi drawl, "When y'all gonna lemme 'n' my cly'yunt he'p ya put that wife murd'rer behin' ba's? We got th' ev'dence an' th' proo'uf."

At one point Beevers had even sent a certified letter to Howie Peters offering his and his client's assistance. Just to make sure there wouldn't be any trapdoors involved, Howie sent him a reply by certified mail declining his offer: "Please be advised that your offer to cooperate is being turned down, your client is every bit as guilty and will be tried accordingly."

During the Winter of '89, Howat Peters was assigned a high-profile case of a missing little girl; her remains were eventually located and her father was then charged with murder, which completely galvanized the populace of the greater New Orleans area. However, Mr. Peters, with his docket now overloaded by the singular crusade to avenge the murder of little Melissa Estrade, was *not* relieved of the Fontanille-Myers case.

Consequently, spring turned into summer without notice and time marched hot and humid onward until about the second week of August 1989, at which time Howie Peters, upon encountering W. J. LeBlanc in the hall outside the fifth-floor elevator, grabbed him by the elbow and asked: "Hey, are you still interested in doing the Fontanille case?"

"Yes!" Dub replied.

"I'm up to my ears with the Estrade case," Howie told him. "If you want it, I'm gonna talk to 'em. I'm gonna tell 'em I need help in a jam and you're the guy."

"Yeah. Yeah, do it. Good," Dub answered.

About a week later, on a Friday afternoon after the weekly supervisors' meeting, Howie caught Dub again and reported on his conversation with Mamoulides.

"What'd he say?" Dub prompted, wanting to cut to the chase.

"He said, 'If he's got the time to do it without taking away from his docket, then fine.' So you're on it if you still want it, okay?"

"Yes!" After his expression of gratitude to Howat, Dub immediately went and found Mike Maunoir and asked him to be the DA's investigator on Fontanille-Myers.

"I'd love to, Dub," Mike answered. "But I don't know if I'm still assigned to it or not. It really hasn't been in a working stage for a long time now."

Dub then went to Robert Pitre's office. "Bob, I'm working on the Fontanille case with Howie now . . ."

"You know it's a loser."

"Well, we can't just dismiss it. I wanna get started on it. Can Maunoir be the investigator? He's been involved with it in the past."

"Yeah, sure."

W.J. went straight back to Maunoir, told him it was official, and asked, "Mike, where's all the stuff?"

"In that little area, you know, off from the grand jury—it's locked up in there."

They then went and got a key from Mamoulides's secretary and "opened it up." They moved everything down the hall and put it in the first vacant office they found over by Screening. From that moment on the office became the baseball bat murder command center.

"It was a shambles; we got the case in worse condition than it was originally, in terms of organization. There was shit everywhere. I mean everywhere, in all kinds of boxes, that we had to go through. Once we found the transcripts of the first trial, I loaded 'em up in the boxes, loaded 'em in my car, and took 'em home."

During that short drive through the streets of old Gretna, W. J. LeBlanc was fully cognizant that what was in the box beside him on the passenger seat of his black Porsche was a major lifetime milestone for him. What he felt was determination:

"It was truly a challenge: to me there was no doubt as to who did it; we had to figure out a way to *prove* they did it, the ultimate challenge for a prosecutor. It was an entirely circumstantial case. Totally baffling. I felt I might never see another case like this again.

"Also, it really stuck in my craw to think that these guys would get away with it. You had a woman bludgeoned to death with a baseball bat inside the house; it's either one guy, the other guy, or both. Period. Those are the only possibilities. And these clowns may just walk away from it? That really bothered me!" Dub's voice has come to a crescendo; as he realizes it, he falls silent and there is only a mockingbird out past the veranda to be heard for several moments.

Then: "So I start reading that Friday night. Making my notes, writing down my questions on my legal pads like I would do for any case, and then I stopped. I'd brought myself up to speed; but there were decisions that had to be made now—as to which course the preparation was going to follow for trial.

"At that point I'm just sitting back and waiting in a holding pattern."

Catching the harried Howie in the hall one day, W.J. told him, "Look, I've read the transcript. I know you're busy on Estrade . . . ?"

"I'm gonna do that, too," Howat distractedly cut him off. "But I've got to finish . . ."

"I understand," Dub cut back, with some delicacy, "but when you get a chance . . . ?"

W.J. really wasn't surprised that Howie, who had been on the case since before the conspiracy trial, hadn't had time to read the entire case record—it was a monstrous amount of work: all of the grand jury transcripts, the trial transcripts, the complete police file.

"My game plan was to make the effort and know *everything* there was to know about the case. . . ."

That might've been the game plan, but the game itself continued to be a nonevent.

"Labor day came. In September I went to Lake Tahoe, just to get away," Nick Noriea recollects. "Then there was a Louisiana Trial Lawyers seminar in San Francisco. Got back to New Orleans about the 17th of September and I said, 'Gee whiz, another month has passed!' Because I was kind of counting off the days from the original indictment, every time a 16th came, that was another month knowing they had to give me two weeks.

"Nothing's a sure thing, but I had a good error on appeal, because I knew that Eason was going to deny it—but each day that passed makes it easier and better for me to convince an appellate court that they waited too long. Each day I rejoiced because that gave me an extra day to argue on appeal.

"My contact with Bill was, 'Bill, we got another week past. We've got three years and two months. I'm going to get my eye operated on next week, so we're gonna have two months.' Then, 'Bill, three months.' Then, 'Bill, four months.'

"At one point he actually said, 'You think they might just let this thing go?' I said, 'I have no idea.'

"But I kept telling him, 'Bill, I don't want you to tell anybody. Not Jonas, not your mama, not your sister—I don't want anybody at the DA's Office even thinking I'm counting time. Because if they know I'm counting, they're gonna know what I'm counting for. So you never repeat this to anybody.' "

11
Marriage

The next week was focused on classes. I saw your dad, but we were just friends. The following Friday your dad brought me home again. The following Tuesday your dad asked me to "get together," so I cooked for him at his trailer. I also baked chocolate chip cookies and burned my finger. But I had a nice evening. The next Thursday your dad invited me to go watch T.V. with him at his trailer. So . . . I did. I remember we started at each end of the sofa and ended up in the middle. We joked and laughed and even got in a kiss. It was sweet . . . He asked me for a date that next night which was a Friday. It was a Mardi Gras parade (Cleopatra, by Grandma Rodriguiez's). Of course I accepted and we had a good time. We even got caught in the rain. It was that night I met aunt Dawn, Poppee and alot of Mommee's family. Mommee was in the parade. We later went to Spanky's disco. It was great. I knew then I was "falling." And the rest of the weekend we had dates. By that Sunday we had become quite acquainted.

But within the next two weeks something happened. Your dad wanted to go back to his "old" girlfriend. And I surely thought that was the end of that. I was miserable. He still brought me home on weekends and we remained friends. Whoopee!!!

On Valentine's Day that year I baked dad a cake. While studying together at the library he gave me a Valentine card (to a good friend).

The following week your dad came to me at the dorm to tell me he had once again "broken" up . . . hope restored. The next night we went to a movie and right in the middle of the movie your dad said he loved me. And from then on we've been inseparable.

—Journal of Janet Cannon Myers

* * *

"They stood right at this kitchen counter and it wasn't a surprise to Marva and I," Clifford Myers remembers.

"They said, 'We've got something to tell you—we are going to get married.' And I said, 'Fine, finish college first.' And Janet said, 'Well, I may go back after we're married.' "

"She's the one that pushed the marriage. She definitely wanted out of that house," Marva adds.

"The Cannons didn't like the idea, and I didn't like the idea," Cliff says.

"I think they both wanted to get her out of that house." Marva continues her line of thought. "That's my idea. He felt obligated to get her out of that house and away from her family. Because I don't think Kerry is so stupid that he didn't realize that he didn't have enough money to get married. I mean, he did some foolish things as far as money is concerned, but I don't think he didn't realize that."

"He said he was going to go back and finish up. But Marva and I knew damn well he wasn't going to go back and get that degree if he left," Clifford concludes.

"There was a very, very big unhappiness about the pending marriage," Peggy Cowan says. "Because I do remember there was a scene, what I would call a *big* scene. We were all outside in my family's backyard, probably having a crawfish boil or something, and Janet came running down the street in one of her rages—running behind our house, her mother, on foot, chasing her, screaming, 'Janet, don't leave! Don't leave! Come back home!'

"A guy—who the guy was, I don't know, but it wasn't Kerry—pulled up and opened the car door, Janet got in, and that was it. And her mother went back home *crying*. Her aunt came out and said, 'What was that about? What's going on?' She wanted to know if we had heard or seen anything. My mother said, 'I don't know.' All we could tell her was what we had seen and heard.

"To this day nobody was ever told; and you didn't go to her parents and question afterwards: 'What happened last night?' Like someone would've come over to my parents and said, 'What in the world's going on with your daughter?' or something like that. But with her parents, no. With her family you just didn't get involved."

"Curtis and I told Mr. Cliff, he wanted to talk to us about it and we told him, 'Kerry loves her, she's gonna be his wife, then we have to accept her—but only because of that,' " Mike Price says. "Otherwise?"

"They were going out together and they had an argument about something and Kerry came home," Clifford begins.

"No, they had an argument," Marva corrects, then continues. "Kerry came in the house, never said a word about it, he'd gone out and come back in, kids that age do that.

"He sits down and him and Cliff are watching television, a ballgame, the doorbell rings. I was upstairs. Cliff gets up and he opens the door and Lorraine starts screaming at him—I'm talking *screaming,* okay? I'm not talking just talking loud. Well, when I heard the screaming, I came down the stairs, and I was on the third step and Kerry is standing behind his daddy's shoulder a little bit, behind and to the side."

"She's screaming, 'The wedding's off!' " Clifford picks up the narrative. "There's no way that they're going to let their daughter marry him. Janet's standing behind her mother hollering, 'Kerry, don't let her take me away!' "

"Janet's crying and carrying on, 'Mr. Cliff! Don't listen to her, Mr. Cliff! Don't listen to her!' " Marva says. "And Lorraine turned around to Janet—she had the child by the wrists the whole time—and she turned around and she slapped her across the face—"

"Slap *hell,* she *punched* her," Cliff interrupts.

"—I mean, like *wham!* Well, when she slapped her—"

"She punched her right in the mouth."

"—she fell."

"I turned my lights off on my front porch, I said, 'I don't want my neighbors to see this in my yard.' "

"When she slapped her, Janet fell—"

"She more punched her, she had a closed fist."

"—and she grabbed her by the hair and by the arm and pulled her across the lawn to the car. And Janet's yelling, 'Kerry, don't let her take me! Kerry, I love you, don't let her take me!'

"We're all standing here, and nobody—I'm gonna tell ya, and this is a terrible time to make a joke, but when Cliff can't open his mouth to say something it's a shock—and he could not say a word."

"All I told her, when she said the wedding's off, I said, 'That's fine with me!' I did tell her that, I said, 'Fine, Lorraine.' "

"But this was the craziest thing I've ever been involved in in my life," Marva says.

"Maybe fifteen minutes later, we're all sitting here still in shock, we don't know what to say to one another. I said to Kerry, 'Yeah, that may not be a bad idea.' By this time Cliff's kind of coming around, and he's trying to talk Kerry out of it, too; and Kerry doesn't know what to say, because he doesn't know how to explain the scene that just happened. 'I still don't *believe* what happened,' you know, 'Am I awake or did I fall asleep and I'm dreaming this?' Because I don't believe people act like this.

"All we know is that she and Kerry had an argument. And when they got mad—I mean, she would get mad too, because Janet could go into a rage like that—but Lorraine said something like 'Kerry drove off—he took off and he almost ran over Janet!' And Janet's hollering, 'That's not true, Mr. Cliff!' That's Lorraine, you see."

"*Charles was sitting in the car.* Didn't say a word. Didn't make a move," Cliff remembers. He continues: "Anyway—fifteen minutes later the doorbell rings. I opened up the door and it's Janet. She got Jane, her sister, to drive her back over here. She's crying, 'Mr. Cliff, please let me in. Don't let what happened stop anything. Please let me in. I love Kerry. I want to talk to him.'

"I felt sorry for the child. Jane stayed in the driveway until I let her in. And she and Kerry talked. The phone rang, 'Your daddy's in bad shape, he's having a heart attack, and if he dies I'll never forgive you!' "

"You could hear Lorraine shouting over the phone," Marva says. "But Janet also told us what her mother said."

"I told Marva afterwards, 'What in the hell is Kerry getting into?' "

"I don't know whether she was brought up in that type of fighting and then making up—because that's all the two of them seemed to do," Monique Price says. "Fight and then roll around in the bed together.

"They *would;* immediately afterwards. Almost like a turn-on. That's right. I've seen that. After a fight—you could not talk to them, you couldn't take one of them home, they'd be back in that bedroom in two minutes and stay in there all night long, it was sickening.

"I believe it became part of the sex act. Because that's basically what it was with them. You know, a normal person, if you have a fight like that with somebody, you want to get as far away as possible—but you could not drag either one of them away from that trailer after one of their physical fights—they'd be back in that bedroom in two minutes and there was nothing you could do about it. It just disgusted everybody."

"If he'd've married a sane person, none of this would've ever happened. I really believe that," Mike Price says.

"Well, remember the night we sat there—under the carport the day before the wedding, drinking those little Miller ponies in the ice chest," says Curtis.

"Drunk," answers Mike. "Remember his dad begging me to take him away?"

"Uh-huh. And we told him right then, 'This is a bad idea. It's going to turn out bad.' And it did. This was a freight train."

"You're right. I think once they got married—it's like that old joke, once they got married, everybody else was just going home and really appreciating their wives and kids, because they'd never seen a train wreck before—I mean, the rest of us were just relieved. There were problems from the minute they met each other."

* * *

"What ticked me off was that we were informed that it was the groom's responsibility to pay for the flowers for the wedding," Cliff says with a hard shake of his head. "I mean, we knew better, but I said, 'Okay, I'll buy the flowers.' "

"The day of the wedding? It was like a premonition," Marva says. "We got into the car here and I started crying—and I don't mean just tears running down, I mean *crying*. I had calmed down enough to walk up the aisle and I sat down. And then I ruined the wedding because I was sobbing so loudly nobody could hear the service. And I kept thinking, 'I don't know why I'm crying. I don't know why I'm crying.' Was God trying to tell me something?"

"There were a *lot* of things bothering me," Cliff says. "We were late for the wedding; you know why we were late for the wedding? Because I was in Kerry's room trying to talk him out of it while he was getting dressed."

"Let me tell you what an actress she was," Marva says. "She said, 'This is my wedding day and I'm going to be happy.' She had made up her mind she was going to be happy and nothing was going to spoil it. And she walked around that whole time with this little smile on her face—it was a phony smile, it wasn't a genuine smile. It was like, 'Nothing and no one is going to spoil this day for me.'

"I looked there and I thought, 'This is all a show for her, this is not what's it's supposed to be, this is a big production.' "

"This is the Leslie Westerhouse and Billy story," Ron Dupuy announces after some thought.

"She was from Terrytown, lived on Wright Avenue. Billy had known her before, but started dating her when she was going to LSU. He got involved with her; he liked her a lot, a pretty girl, bright, outgoing. She thought he was wonderful, thought he was everything, did everything she could for him.

"He was going to marry this girl, they were engaged. I liked her more than Suzy. See, Leslie was Susan's roommate. Blond hair, typical LSU-co-ed-looking girl, sorority-looking girl, real friendly, real nice. I liked her. She was more outgoing, and Suzy was real quiet—I thought Leslie was perfect for Billy, myself. I really thought that would be a good couple.

"Now, whenever Leslie wasn't there, Billy got to know Susan by talking to her on the phone when he called. Then he started calling just to talk to Susan. And she would sometimes go places with him and Leslie. And he decided he started liking Susan more than he did the one he was going to marry. So Billy started fooling around with Susan on the side, discreetly. But eventually Leslie found out.

"They weren't just roommates, they were best friends. It really messed this girl up. She couldn't believe it—she didn't want to lose Billy; she put up a little fight.

"He juggled them both for a while. He was testing to see if he liked Suzy enough to drop the other girl. There was a time there when Leslie really wanted Billy back. Her and Suzy had some pretty intense fights over that. It was 'How could you do this to me?' sort of thing. And she absolutely hated Susan from that point on. But it didn't seem to bother Susan; Susan wanted Billy more than she wanted the best friend.

"Billy thought Susan was the absolute best-looking girl he'd ever seen in his life, okay? You know, she had the lily-white skin, the whole thing. Billy was attracted to her looks more than anything else."

"Billy never really knew what he wanted," Mike Price says. "But he really loved Susan. I've never in my whole life seen Billy as excited as I did the night he introduced Susan to us. He was glowing. When Billy is telling you something and he's not positive or he's unsure, he looks down, he looks away. But when he brought Susan to our house, he was positively radiant, his eyes bored holes in mine. But over and above his feelings for her was his pride in having this beautiful girl.

"Oh, yes. It meant as much to him that she was beautiful—it meant *more* to him that she was beautiful than that she loved him.

"What really became so strange about it was, they weren't married but a matter of a few months before he started picking at her appearance."

"Well, Susan and Billy's marriage has always been somewhat of a mystery to me, too," Miz Cissy says.

"But, I think they were hooked on each other's looks. Billy thought he was God's gift and Susan thought she was a God's gift. I think that had a lot to do with it: which one was more vain than the other.

"I also think Susan modeled her life after her mother and father's," Miz Cissy says. "Her mother never did work. Her mother was a homemaker who raised the children and probably never worked a day in her life after marriage. But this is a different time completely. Nowadays men and women both have to work to make it. And I think Susan truly wanted to stay home, have children, and have a housekeeper.

"I think that's exactly what was wrong. And, of course, Bill never made enough money for that—because no one these days makes enough money for that," Miz Cissy concludes.

"So they ate out just about every night," Angela adds.

"I remember standing there when Billy got married and we were talking about how pissed off Mr. Mansfield looked," Chuck Cassard says.

"I remember looking at Curtis and him saying, 'Whattaya expect? His daughter's marrying Billy Fontanille.' "

"Her parents weren't happy, I remember that," Connie agrees.

"They were ticked!" corrects Chuck.

"They were, seriously. And they did not try to hide it."

"Nooo. Unh-unh. It was funny. I remember Curtis saying, 'How happy would you look if your daughter was marrying Billy Fontanille?' "

"I don't think Mr. Mansfield would've approved of anybody," Miz Cissy says. "Susan desperately loves her daddy. Her daddy was the perfect man. The day of the wedding—I'll never forget it, in all my life I'll never forget it—she said, 'Look at my father, isn't he handsome?' This is something you say about your new *husband*! You know?"

"I tried to tell him you don't get married in debt," Cliff is saying. "You start off in debt, and it'll be a long time before you climb out of it. But you can't tell Kerry nothing. They were in love. They wanted to get married.

"That's why I suggested—I said I'd never let 'em live here. But you know how that goes . . . ? My oldest son, and now Davin, they think I was wrong. They said, 'You shouldn't have let 'em live here. You should've made them get out.'

"Even after they moved out, anytime he was in a jam, or he needed somebody to supplement his rent—he'd come to Daddy. 'Well, we're gonna move into this house but the rent's gonna be a little more, can you help me for a few months?' It was always—come to Daddy. And the other kids know all this now, and they figure I shouldn't have done it. I should've made him stand on his own two feet. When the other ones got married, they stood on their own two feet. And they just figure that—you know, maybe he'd've been a little more responsible for some things.

"I say, well, maybe I did wrong, maybe I did, you know. To keep pulling him out of these financial jams. Even before he got married. Maybe I should've made him get out on his own. But the other ones didn't need me.

"I'd say, 'Kerry, you're not going to be able to do this.' 'Yes, Dad, I can do it.' Well, he'd finance it, then 'Dad, uh, I can't.' You try to tell Kerry, 'Everything don't work out like that. Everything just don't fall into place the way you think it should.' "

"But Kerry was not realistic enough to think that," Marva says. "If that's the way it was supposed to work, that's the way it was gonna work. That's Kerry's biggest fault."

"To the nth degree, he's idealistic," Cliff says. "When he left that last semester, I don't know why, but he had said, 'Well, we have to have at least one hundred and twenty dollars and probably we'll have enough to get married.' I remember he had this job with a paneling company. It wasn't much of a job—but at least they were going to be able to get married."

Marva explains, "They were getting married and he didn't have a job. Cliff and I kept saying, 'Kerry, you need to have a job if you're getting married.' I mean, 'How are you going to support your wife? You're taking on a responsibility, do you realize?' 'Yeah, yeah, I do. I'm going to get a job.' And I remember he got this little job, and I remember Janet bragging because he got this job. Because everybody was on their case because Kerry didn't have a job.

"Not only us. But her parents were on her too because he didn't have a job. And I remember when he got this little job, she came over here and she was just all elated, because now—it was like, 'Now he's got a job they can't tell me that anymore.' "

"Back when all of us first got married," Monique begins, "we were all still in college or finishing up college and none of us had any money. Janet was always sort of a braggart but never really had anything to brag about. They had these fancy cars, they had that big Lincoln or LTD which they smashed up but didn't have any insurance. She was always bragging about that car.

"And bragging about the money they got out of the lawsuit. She was always bragging—this was sort of a point of contention, when we would all buy our first home—she was always bragging about she was going to have a home first. They were going to buy this home. They even took us one time and showed us this house they were going to buy; of course they never did. But that was her big thing: Kerry was going to buy her a house. Somehow. Anyway.

"So there were *lots* of lawsuits. I used to think and comment that it wasn't that she wanted to work for the money—because she didn't want to work. It was okay for Kerry to work and it was okay that she stay home—I know of three different lawsuits that she told me about, and they were all bogus, but that was going to be her way of getting money.

"Kerry sued for a knee injury that he'd had long before the car accident. They sued and got some money. This was while they were still in college. He had already had this knee injury. Well, with the money they got from that they bought that car. Then they smashed it up and all she talked about was how they were going to win *this real big* lawsuit.

"But they didn't have any insurance. I remember thinking how funny it was, that here they were, they'd bought this car, but couldn't afford insurance on it. She told me this big story when I asked why they didn't have insurance, it had expired, they didn't notify her, all this stuff, and I remember telling Mike, 'What is it, they scraped together the money to get the car, to make the car payments, but couldn't afford the insurance?' 'Yeah.'

"All she talked about was they were going to win a big lawsuit. Then it turned out they never could find the people and couldn't get anything. So they had to continue paying off that car without having it. I was telling Mike, 'What goes around, comes around.'

"The third lawsuit was when she so-called fell and broke her nose at the

Myerses' house, and they figured—she told me—the way they were going to buy their house was they were going to sue the homeowners insurance and use that money as a downpayment on a house. So they sued Kerry's father's insurance company. She wanted these things, but her way of getting them was to sue somebody.

"When we bought our house and they still did not have their first home, it became sort of, 'Well, we're going to buy a bigger one. A fancier one.' She had been very obsessed with being the first one to buy a house.

"Even at Litchwood, she was trying to tell us that they really owned it because they were really on a lease-purchase plan and all this stuff; but we knew they were just renting. You know, it just got to where you didn't question Janet. Rental cars? They wanted to tell you they owned 'em. It doesn't matter, if that's what they want to say and you know otherwise, it doesn't do any good to confront them.

"A lot of things you knew they lied about and you just kind of over-looked it, I guess."

"They weren't married two weeks when she got mad at Kerry and broke a vent window of the car, parked her TV set by the door, called her daddy and said she was going home," says Cliff. "That lasted a day and then she was back again.

"It galled Lorraine that they were living here. She couldn't understand that they didn't have no damn money to get an apartment. If it wouldn't've been for *me,* they'd've been out on the *street.* Janet didn't want to live with her mother and daddy.

"I supplemented their rent when they first moved outa here and into this apartment off of Manhattan; I was still supplementing their rent for a while when they lived in the place on *Woodmere.*"

"Billy's used to having women tell him how good he is and do everything for him and just be there for whatever he wanted," Ron Dupuy explains.

"But Susan was a quiet girl; she wasn't that type. She didn't give him—she was good-looking, so he liked that part, he liked being seen with her, it made him feel good—but on the intellectual side and the adulation side he didn't get what he needed. And he never tells other people compli-mentary things. So she didn't get that from him, he didn't get that from her—I just didn't think they belonged together. They were a good-looking couple. Plastic-wise, with the 'Joneses' they were a beautiful couple. That's what Billy liked.

"He felt it was time to get into the married thing, it was that point in time. He wanted to be the perfect couple. The kind you see on TV. The old sitcoms. He wanted to be that, so he had to have the pretty wife. She had to fit into that little story. He got the nice house. The good job. The pretty wife. It looked good. *The problem was it didn't work.*

"He realized that after he married her but he was looking more for the superficial. That's what he wanted, it looked nice."

"He was doing manual labor, putting up paneling, and he was an electrician's helper, not making much at all, and him so sharp and all? But that's all he could get right then," says Clifford Myers.

"Yeah," Marva agrees. "But Kerry had a good job offered to him at a TV station in Lake Charles, and Lorraine got onto Janet about leaving—"

"She raised so much hell with Janet that they didn't go," Cliff prompts.

"Maybe this wouldn't have happened if they'd left, who knows," says Marva. "That's what Kerry went to college for."

"He could run the whole damn television station," Cliff adds. "Janet told me that one of her sisters' husbands had a good job in Virginia, big home and all, but Lorraine wouldn't hear of it—'You're separating the family. You're leaving.' "

"Now, she was very proud of the fact that she was the only one in the family that went to college," Marva says. "She also told me that they did not want her to go to college. She said, 'But I was determined.' She said, 'First they didn't want me to go, now they're mad because I didn't finish.' "

"Supposedly, when Bill and Susan first got married, when he was in between jobs, he'd send her off to work on the bus, while he sunbathed and kept the car in case he had something he wanted to do. Her father, of course, had problems with that," Tammy is saying.

"But then it wasn't long before he had a good job at McDermott and they bought that really nice house on Northbrook before everybody else, except for Clyde and me and Curtis and Debbie—and they paid over eighty thousand dollars for that house, back then, so you know they were doing well financially."

"Mike and I were playing Monopoly over at their house one night, it was wintertime and Susan was pregnant," Monique remembers.

"The four of us are sitting on the floor. The first thing Billy did was open all the doors and windows, the glass sliding door wide open, it was the middle of winter, it's in the thirties, so we were all freezing. Of course, we're company so we're not saying anything. Susan's saying, 'Billy, don't open those,' of course he opens them anyway. Then she starts saying, 'Billy, close the doors and windows, we're all freezing.' He wouldn't close them; he just acted like he didn't hear her. So she kept on begging and pleading, 'Please, close them, Billy. We're freezing and we have company. Please, close them.' He just ignored her.

"So she went and got blankets for the three of us, and we sat around with the blankets on, that satisfied us, so it was quiet for a few minutes.

"He gave no reason or even acknowledgment. He didn't say, 'No, I'm hot.' He didn't say, 'No, it's stuffy in here,' he would not acknowledge her speaking to him. We didn't say anything, we took the blankets and we said nothing. When he's ignoring her like he was, there was something else going on and we didn't want to get involved.

"The next thing—he reaches over and nudges her and says, 'Get up and move places with me.' She said, 'Billy, all my stuff is here.' He said, 'Get up, move places with me.' 'What's the matter?' 'Get up and move with me.' You know how when you play Monopoly you put all your money under the side of the board and everything laid out, she had to gather up all of her money and move from one spot on the floor to another. She got it all set up, and as soon as the game started again he said, 'Now, move again.'

"Now you realize there's four sides to the board, and he's making one person move, guess who else has to move? The entire board. So we'd all take our money and we'd get up and move again. That continued until we kind of rotated the board and we said, 'That's enough.' I remember we finished the game and we never went back over to their home again. He never made a single explanation.

"Susan talked to Billy almost as if he were a child. 'Billy, come on, Billy, it's cold in here, close the window.' You know, then it'd be, 'Billy, everybody's going to have to pick up their money and move.' And, 'Billy, there's nothing wrong with where you're sitting.' She didn't lose her temper. Neither did he. He was apparently just trying to aggravate her for whatever personal reasons that had started before we got there.

"That was how Billy was when he was upset about something in his marriage. Not anger, just an odd kind of defiance, childlike. But I liked Billy, even after that. We did things together. He was a nice fellow. We saw less of him than we did the others. I think it was because when we were going out as couples he wasn't dating anyone.

"You do know I was the only person in the group who didn't believe he did it from the first day?"

12
Bluff

Since the day your dad and I realized that what we had between us was extremely special, we've had some very difficult times. Most of all, we've had some great times. We attended Nicholls State together until December of 1978. It was then I decided to "postpone" school for awhile so I could work. But, I'm jumping ahead. . . .

It was in February (the nineteenth) of 1978 that we declared love. In May of the same year, we decided to plan on getting married. Actually, the first time dad brought it up was after we had been to a party. He'd had a little too much to drink and asked me to run off and get married and let no one know for a year. I really didn't take him seriously. The next day, when he called, the part about running off was dropped, but the part about being married stayed. So, I thought about it, a couple of weeks later we went "ring hunting." And on June 14th, 1978 at "The Point" by the Lighthouse at the Lakefront I received my ring, and it was all official. We set the date for April 6th, 1979.

—Journal of Janet Cannon Myers

*   *   *

In late September 1989, W. J. LeBlanc prosecuted one Angel Baro Pedrosa for second degree murder, a domestic violence case in which the defense was heat of passion: guilty as charged, life without parole.

Then, during the first trial week of October, while down in Division B in the midst of a motion docket, he was abruptly replaced by a fellow ADA and summoned upstairs to the office of Robert Pitre, supervisor of Felony.

"What are you doing on the Fontanille-Myers case?" Pitre asked.

"Nothing. I'm waiting for Howie. I'm assisting Howie. I've read the transcript, I've made my notes. But I'm waiting on Howie. He's running the show."

"Well, we've got a problem."

"What's that?"

"I think the case prescribes pretty soon, maybe in November."

"What the hell are you talking about! How'd this happen?"

"I don't know. You'd better go down and get with Research and check it out."

"You've got to be fucking kidding me. What is this prescription shit?"

"Look, Research is down there. They've got the record, go see what the deal is," concluded Mr. Pitre.

Barron Burmaster, then a law clerk working in Research and now an assistant district attorney, had discovered the problem by accident and brought it to Pitre's attention; it had been a random quirk of fate that Barron had chanced upon it.

W.J. hustled on downstairs and was soon huddled with young Mr. Burmaster and Steve Grefer, Judge Joe Grefer's son, also then a law clerk working in the Research Department. They showed him how to compute days in regard to the Louisiana Speedy Trial Act of 1972—not an easy task, leaving one to wonder why such matters are routinely part of the apprenticeship of becoming a real lawyer.

It was readily apparent there was plenty of time left on Myers, but prescription on Fontanille would toll pretty damn soon.

W.J., getting more concerned and exasperated by the page, said, "Look, just give the bottom line to me. How many fucking days do we have?"

After careful perusal and cross-referencing of dates among the plethora of Fontanille defense motions with their applicable suspensions, the young legal scholars came up with their best estimate:

"You gotta try him by November 14." Five weeks hence!

Dub spun on a heel, shagged upstairs to his cubbyhole, and immediately tried to get Dr. Lee on the phone. He got Barbara, Henry Lee's stalwart secretary. The doctor was out of town. W.J. proceeded to explain the dire nature of this latest crisis and then said: "Look, I need a day. I don't care when it is—I just need a day, any day between now and November the 14th."

"But, really, Dr. Lee doesn't have anything open until January," Barbara replied more than once and as best she could, with some patience.

"No. No. You do not *understand,* the case *prescribes* November 14, I've got to get it tried before then!" Dub had said.

With much effort and rescheduling she came up with Thursday, November 9. Which meant the trial had to be set for that prior Monday, November 6. Once Dub had a date, he went in to Mamoulides's office and explained the problem. The boss was not pleased. After all, he did have an election coming up in a year and the political fallout from the most famous murder in Jefferson Parish history going unpunished because of a technical faux pas by the DA's Office could all too easily be imagined.

"Set it for trial," Mr. Mamoulides said after several expletives.

"There ain't no way I'm gonna be ready," Dub almost choked. "That's just not enough time for me to be ready. I don't think I can win the case if I have to go this quick. For one thing, I'm waiting on Howie . . ."

"It's your case now. You call the shots. Howie will assist you if he still wants to work on it."

"Yes, sir."

"Just get it tried," John Mamoulides said.

"I'll do what I can," Dub said as he exited the big office and hurried to call Barbara back and tell her to block the day out for Dr. Lee.

"I'm in a position where I could work almost twenty-four hours a day from then on until the trial date and still not have my shit together. And I'm very, *very* upset at that," W. J. LeBlanc says through jaws that clench tighter by the syllable even now as he reflects on his humbling brush with his worst nightmare, being naked in front of twelve jurors, "unprepared."

"I'm really sweating this out. I don't have the time to get it done. I've *got* to get it continued. But I know I can't continue it because time keeps running if I continue it. But I've gotta get something because I *know* I'm gonna lose a case I'd been screaming to get for three years.

"So the question is, I need to set a trial date quickly, but I have to set it late enough that they will be tempted to file a motion to continue. I need to create a sense that time is too short for them, that 'Oh, shit, the DA's right on top of it and I don't want to be rushed.' But I can't wait to where it's too short. Because then the judge can say, 'No, I'm sorry, you've just got to pick another day, whether you've got prescription problems or not.'

"So I notify the clerk of court to set the case for trial November 6, but I don't call Noriea or Beevers, piss on 'em. Because I'm hoping one of 'em's gonna get me off the hook, okay? Get me the time I so desperately need!

"I wait another week, and then have Mike hand-deliver the subpoenas to Beevers's office and Noriea's office letting them know the case was set for trial. Then I ask the judge to call a status conference for like the next day or the day following.

"Normally the DA controls the first setting of the case—somebody gets arraigned, pleads not guilty, DA picks the trial date—beyond that it's the court's call. And I really don't know Judge Eason very well. I'd never been in his division; never tried a case before him yet. So I don't know what Rudy's gonna do. All I know is that by reputation he's known as being somewhat unpredictable.

"So I walk into his chambers for our first status conference like gang-busters. I'm the last one to get there, Nick and Wiley are already sitting there, and the judge says, 'Okay, gentlemen, what do we have here?' "

"I go, 'Judge, I asked you to call a status conference because we need to set a trial date.' Then, before anybody can say anything else, I go, 'The date is Monday, November 6th,' just like that. Well, then, boom! The shit hit the fan.

"Nick starts, 'Wait. Wait. Wait a minute here. What are you talking about—the date is November 6th?' And Wiley's going, 'I've got cases I hafta . . .'

"All this yamming and jamming is going down, and I said. 'Look, Dr. Lee is available at this date. It's the only date this year. So that's the date. If you don't like it, continue it.'

" 'Unh-unh, I ain't continuing this case,' Nick goes. 'But what the hell's happening here? Paul used to . . . judge?' He quits talking to me because I turn my back on him. 'Judge, I don't understand this. We used to get together—Paul Connick used to call . . .'

"Eason said, 'Now, Mr. Noriea, you can continue the case. If you need the time, I'll certainly understand.'

" 'No . . . unh-unh, no, judge . . . that's not the case. But I've got people from out of town, experts and things like that just like the State does, you know. And I may need the time.'

"I say, 'Hey, I ain't worried about that. The case is set. That's when it's going to trial. If y'all're not ready, that's y'all's problem.' I go, 'I'm ready. The State's ready, we're gonna be there. If you can't be, you know what you can do.' I mean, I'm bluffing my ass off.

" 'I ain't continuing it, not me,' Nick says. And I just keep baiting him. 'You don't like it. File for a continuance. And 'Unh-unh, I'm ready,' Nick keeps saying. 'I just don't know if I can put on a defense.' And they're still bitching, 'Nobody called us!' And 'In the past, Paul Connick called us and we got our calendars together and we'd all pick a mutual date . . .'

" 'Look,' I tell 'em, 'I ain't Paul Connick. Paul Connick has nothing to do with this case. Dr. Lee's available that week, that's when we're going to trial. That's it. If y'all can't be ready in that time, continue it.' I'm playing hardball, and they're not used to that on this case.

"Wiley says, 'We're ready to go. Whenever y'all're ready, we're ready. But this ain't . . . !'

"And Judge Eason goes, 'Well, then, that's when we're going to set it, gentlemen. If y'all have additional motions to file, y'all file 'em.'

"Nick's just grumbling and Beevers says, 'We're ready. We've been ready for trial.' You know his 'We'll always be ready for trial.'

" 'Fine, let's go,' I say. And then the waiting starts—to see what they're gonna do."

"When I get the subpoena setting the trial date for November 6, I immediately calculate how much time they had let pass past the three years and I figured we were in decent shape," Nick Noriea recollects.

"I don't care if D.J. or P.J., whatever the hell it is, is prepared or unprepared. Because I know it don't make a bit a difference. I immediately think how much time have these people let pass beyond what I perceive to be the cutoff day. And what I'm thinking as I go into that status conference is, 'You're about five and a half months overdue; you waited five and a half months *too long.*'

"But hell yeah, I'm arguing up a storm. I'm trying to get three more. I'm thinking, 'I've got five and a half in my pocket, can I squeeze another three months out of him?' I'm playing his little game, I'm letting him go, 'Man, we can't do this . . . !'

"Because my whole thought is, 'I have five and a half months, what can I do, without asking for a continuance, to get more?' If I can't do nothing, I'm still in great shape for appeal. From May 16 to the end of October, I know I have that. And anything beyond that is gravy. But this kid ain't asking for a continuance. This kid's going to the last minute letting them think I'm stupid.''

"It was obvious—especially with Noriea—that they want to go to trial. So I am really, really under the gun.'' W. J. LeBlanc shakes his head, leans forward in his chair, and continues:

"I know that outside of something extraordinary—in my opinion, a bad move by a couple of pretty good attorneys—I'm going to trial in less than three weeks. And there's still five or six boxes of grand jury testimony alone to go through; obviously I can't waste my time doing the type of background work I needed, because my back is really up against the wall timewise. So it's a question of what is the best use of my time. And the best use of it is to go through the present as opposed to digging through the past.

"In that regard, there are two primary things I have to do: concentrate on Kerry Myers's statements and testimony, because he's the variant from the first case; and I *have* to get the murder charges put back together. Therefore, as I'm going through my notes from the transcript of the first trial, and realizing just how many things *do* have to be checked, how many things have to be verified, at the same time I'm making notes for a motion to consolidate.

"Ever since Wally had gotten them both indicted, it was generally conceded that the best shot at getting a conviction was to have them tried at the same time—physically in the courtroom at the same time.

"For one thing, these two guys are ice men. I mean, these guys sit through proceedings like they're sitting through an insurance seminar. Very, very little emotion.

"We just felt like that's contrary to what people expect. If any one of our individual lives had been totally destroyed like this by supposedly a friend—it should literally be a powder keg. You ought to be able to cut the tension between them with a butter knife. I mean, getting up after every recess ought to be very structured, because one of 'em's got to stay exactly where he is until the other one's completely gone and vice versa. But nothing. It's like they didn't even know each other; like they never even met.

"Some of that was evident at the first trial. Then it was very glaring at the aborted conspiracy trial. And early on, in various pleadings and at discovery motions and whatnot, I can see it and I think, 'Oh, man, if we get this thing back together!' Because that's just a little subtle thing that I know is not going to be lost on the jury—simply because juries take note of everything.

"Steve Grefer was my Fontanille-Myers research man; whenever I had a problem or question that needed to be researched in regard to the law or an evidentiary point, I always had Steve do the [legal] memo. So first thing I get him working on is consolidation, I've given Mike [Maunoir] a list of things I need done, things I need verified. And, hey, it's just Mike and me. Howie's involved up to his eyeballs with Estrade; and Vince is on hold in the unlikely event I get a continuance and have the time to do this thing the right way."

On the same day that W. J. LeBlanc asked Judge Eason to set the first status conference, the State filed a motion to consolidate and a memo in support of same.

"But, man, what I need—*I really need is to get this fucking thing continued.* I mean, I just do."

"I remember I got something in the mail from the State saying something about Bill's murder count and Kerry's murder count was gonna be consolidated," Nick Noriea is saying at about thirty thousand feet, somewhere in the skylanes between Lake Charles, Louisiana, and Houston, Texas.

"Well, the State can't ask for a consolidation, only the defense can do that, so I knew that wasn't gonna fly in that form, number one; but then I thought to myself—'Well, now I know what they're gonna do: they're gonna do exactly what the supreme court said they shouldn't do.' The supreme court had said, 'The State is apparently planning to put both of the defendants before a jury and let them decide who committed the murder.' In other words, 'We can't do nothing, y'all figure it out.'

"I always figured they would try to put them back together. I just didn't know what method they would use. I knew there wasn't any strictly legal way they could do it, but then that's Jefferson Parish, where they ain't real big on making that sorta distinction."

On October 19, 1989, Wiley Beevers, on behalf of his client, Kerry Myers, filed a motion to quash indictment for failure to timely institute prosecution.

*   *   *

"I never did understand that," W.J. says as he actually scratches his head, which is uncannily similar to that of the young Napoleon Bonaparte. "I mean, Beevers isn't even in the ballpark with his prescription deal. His man ain't even close; it's not even an issue of case law and interpretation. It's a joke!

"It also doesn't help me one damn bit. I have all the time in the world to try Kerry. It's Fontanille that's busting my balls. And all that's coming outa Nick is, 'We wanna go to trial.' "

"Whatever Beevers did was a nonevent as far as I was concerned," Nick all but barks.

"I didn't care what Beevers did. I knew Wiley. I wasn't dependent on Wiley to do anything. On the brief to the supreme court for the conspiracy, Wiley didn't write a brief! He didn't do anything. So Wiley was just excess baggage as far as anything was concerned with me. Furthermore, Wiley had a different prescriptive period running for him than me, his man came in late."

"Technically it should've been a motion to vacate prior judgment of severance, because the State really can't 'consolidate' cases, that's only upon motion of defense," W.J. explains. "It's just a question of semantics, basically."

And he's right; but then semantics notwithstanding, the fact that the State would work so hard researching the applicable statutes and case law on the issue of putting back together that which the same court had once definitively set asunder and then not know what to call its motion after it had spent more hours than Steve Grefer and Barron Burmaster care to recall writing a brief in support of the State's position suggests the relative rarity of such an occurrence in state or federal jurisprudence.

"We feel like it was wrongly severed in the first place," Dub begins anew.

"Look, the State is entitled to try codefendants together, unless there's a *Bruton* problem—a U.S. Supreme Court case which dealt with the admission, in a trial of two codefendants, of one codefendant's confession which implicated the other codefendant. *Bruton* essentially says that you can't take the incriminating portion of one person's confession and use it as substantive evidence against another person, which is what it all boils down to.

"So they're saying, 'Classic *Bruton* problem.' You know, 'I didn't do it, he did it.' And the other, 'I didn't do it, he did it.' Okay, well then you just throw it all out there and let the jury decide on who's guilty. *Bruton* basically says, 'No, you can't do that. They are antagonistic defenses.'

"However, our argument is that they are not antagonistic. That they are *silent* on the issue of the murder. That, at best, you could say they are passively antagonistic. The only thing they say is that they accuse each other of attacking the other and deny *any* knowledge of what happened insofar as the murder's concerned. Well, that's not antagonistic."

On Wednesday, October 25, 1989, the State filed a motion to vacate the previous judgment granting severance.

On Friday, October 27, Nick Noriea filed a motion to quash indictment for failure to timely institute prosecution.

"I file the motion to quash the last day before the pretrial hearing Eason's scheduled for the coming Monday. Which I'd planned to do all along," Nick explains. "You have to file a motion to quash to exercise your right to a speedy trial—Louisiana Code of Criminal Procedure says that is how you're supposed to do it. If you don't, then you waive it.

"And I ain't gonna waive it."

"This is what I need. I'm trying to push them in that direction; I'm trying to get them to continue the trial. But this is just as good," W.J. remembers.

" *'Upon denial of motion to quash, the State shall have no less than one year from that point to institute trial'*—it's very, very clear in the code. Of course, I'm not home free yet—almost—but Rudy's gotta deny it and we've gotta lose that Monday November 6 trial date."

Wednesday, November 1, 1989   THE TIMES-PICAYUNE
Judge OKs dual trial in slaying
By Richard Boyd
West Bank bureau

   Two West Bank men accused of killing the wife of one of the men will go on trial together next week, a state judge ruled Tuesday.

   State Judge Alvin Rudy Eason denied a defense motion to quash an indictment against William Fontanille, 33, and Kerry Myers, 32, both charged with second-degree murder in the slaying of Myers' wife. . . .

   Eason ruled that, in an unusual procedure, the two men will be tried together on Monday, but one will have a jury trial and the other will face a verdict by Eason. . . .

   Fontanille's lawyer, Nick Noriea, and Myers' lawyer, Wiley Beevers, said they will appeal both of Eason's rulings but did not ask for a delay in Monday's trial. . . .

"Listen to this," Nick booms before he starts rat-a-tat-tatting. "This is in the morning, in chambers, before we go out into the courtroom. It's Halloween, I'll never forget it. I go, 'Judge, what happened from the time that you granted a severance till today?' He says, 'Mr. Noriea, in case you forgot, we had a trial.'

"I go, 'What trial? Who won? I wasn't anywhere around—who won? Tell me what happened, judge, was it a good trial? Did I do good or did I do bad? What was the verdict?' I mean, I can't believe this.

"And he just cannot explain to me what had changed to make the defenses nonantagonistic. He says, 'Well, *something* changed.' "

For the record, out in the courtroom that morning, the following occurred and was said:

W.J. stood and addressed the bench: "Your Honor, I believe we are here today on the court's ruling on a motion to consolidate, and to set aside the previous judgment granting severance."

Judge Eason, taking his sweet time and with that north delta lilt, said, "I have seen the brief of Mr. Noriea and have researched the law, in this particular situation. I would like to hear some explanation before why we should not . . . some argument of counsel why we should not put these cases back together. As far as I can see we have been through this thing a multitude of times. I can't see any conflict in their positions. I don't think anybody has accused the other one of doing it."

To which Nick replied, "We filed a motion to sever a couple of years ago. The court granted it . . . ?"

Judge Eason cut Nick off. "At that time I was of the opinion, Mr. Noriea, that there was conflicting positions and that it would be antagonistic to one another, but having gone through this thing and having Mr. Myers appear in the trial—during Mr. Fontanille's first degree charge it appeared to me, at that time, that Mr. Myers didn't have anything to say except the story that has been said and repeated in these long-drawn-out statements before the grand jury, which have been read into the record and the previous statements that have been before us, I don't see anything that is accusatory or counter-accusatory from either side."

With surprising patience, Nick said, "Judge, you knew that when you severed it two years ago."

"No, I didn't know that," the judge answered. "I was under the impression, at that time, that there were other things that would be said and done. . . . Mr. Beevers, you have some remarks, sir?"

"Yes, Your Honor," Wiley Beevers said. "The consolidation will take place only by taking the trial . . . the same mode of trial. It had been indicated by Mr. Noriea that he is going to go with a jury trial and I have indicated that I am going to go with a judge trial."

"I understand that, Mr. Beevers," Judge Eason then said. "But let me say this to you in that regard. That position can be changed by either of you at the very inception of the trial and for that reason, the court is going to vacate its previous order, severing these defendants."

"Your ruling," Nick began, "is that you are going to put Fontanille and

Myers together for the first degree murder and conspiracy . . . ?"

"Second degree murder," Judge Eason corrected Nick and then offered, "The conspiracy is over as I understand it."

"Wait, judge," Nick said quickly. "Don't say that, because you don't know what is going to happen next. But the conspiracy is severed from the second degree murder charge?"

"Yes," Judge Eason said. "This only involved the second degree murder."

"Note an objection to the court's ruling," Nick responded.

"Note my objection, same, Your Honor," said Beevers.

Shortly thereafter, Judge Eason summarily denied both motions to quash based on prescription. Nick and Wiley announced their intentions to take writs to the fifth circuit.

"Actually, there really wasn't as much hue and cry and bombast as I'd expected," W.J. remembers. "It was more incredulity on the part of Nick, 'How can you do this?' That sort of thing.

"I thought they would've gone nuts over it. Probably one of the reasons why they didn't was that we were able to attack it on the two-prong fashion: one, that that was the case to begin with, that they were not antagonistic defenses; two, they had different triers of fact—that was in the alternative—which effectively severed them and cured any possible *Bruton* problems.

"Now, the weakness in that strategy is that the defendant is entitled to a jury trial at any point up until we actually start picking a jury. All he has to say is, 'Judge, if you find that that's the only reason why you're going to grant the consolidation, then we're going to go for a jury trial.' And practically speaking, the judge, any judge, would almost have to sever them right then and there. Beevers can drop that shoe on me at any time up until jeopardy attaches, and he damn well knows it."

On Wednesday morning, November 2, Wiley Beevers filed writs with the fifth circuit on motion to quash and requested a stay of the pending trial. On Thursday, November 3, Nick filed writs to the fifth circuit on motion to quash and did *not* request a stay.

"In the application for writs," W.J. explains, "the party seeking the writ declares whether or not they're seeking a stay of the proceedings. The fifth circuit sees two briefs. Boom. Boom. One for Myers. One for Fontanille. Wiley is seeking the stay. But Noriea is saying, 'We don't want a stay. We're gonna be ready for trial.' Which is sort of pissing me off. But there's nothing I can do about it.

"So I'm still sweating some. Because theoretically we can go on to trial and during the middle of the trial the fifth circuit can rule. And if they quash it, then it's over with, even though we might be three, four, five days into trial and all that court time and expense is for nothing. So there wouldn't be much sense in doing it that way from a judicial economy standpoint, which is one of the criteria in these situations—that it really doesn't make much sense. But they *can* do it. And have before."

"I'm either gonna win, or I'm gonna lose," Nick says. "If I win, it's all over. Bill's free. Can't be charged. Can't be tried. Like he was never indicted except he's got one hell of a civil action.

"I told the judge, 'Look, we can start the trial.' At that point in time, I didn't care what they did. I didn't care whether they were prepared or not prepared. I could've gotten my people here. I had commitments from all of these experts that they would bend the world to get here. And I knew I had lead time because it was gonna take the State three or four days to put on their case. And I had good, good experts that were very committed to Bill's situation.

"So going to trial then or later didn't really make much of a difference to me. At that point in time, by filing a motion to quash, my time stops. And I either have won or lost with the five and a half months. I move my stuff into the motel. I'm ready for trial. Because my hope—what I'm *really* wishing for is that the fifth circuit will stay Beevers and let me go to trial, which in effect gives me my severance."

On Thursday afternoon, November 3, 1989, the fifth circuit issued an order fixing the time for the State to file writs in response to the defendant's appeal writs as Wednesday, November 8.

With the trial to start on Monday the 6th, and the return date order for the State being the 8th, two days *past* the scheduled start of trial, the fifth circuit had effectively granted W.J. exactly what he needed: time.

"Mamoulides says, 'Fine.' I go, 'It's still my case?' He says, 'Yes.' I say, 'Can I go to Harry about getting Vince Lamia assigned here? It really needs a lot of work.' I say, 'Now that I've got the time to do it, I can do it *right.'* He goes, 'Do what you gotta do to get it done.' "

Dub then went to see Sheriff Harry Lee. "I tell him I need Vince. Harry says, 'Well, I don't know, this case is very important to me, but I've given Vince time off from the Detective Bureau'—because of the burnout problems his wife was experiencing with Vince spending so much time away and the stress—'so I don't know if Vince . . .'

"Well, I know, because I've just called Vince again telling him, 'Look, I'm going to see the sheriff, do you still want in?' 'Oh, yeah. Absolutely.' He says, 'Get it and I'm there.' "

After getting Vince on the phone and verifying his wishes, Sheriff Lee said to one of his most favored and effective officers, "Look, this is a very important case to me. I want you to do everything you can. You know you've got a blank check as far as doing what's gotta be done."

13
Husbands and Wives

I was in school until December, 1978. Then to help pay expenses, I decided temporarily to quit. So I got a job and your dad went back to NSU without me. At first I missed the "school life" and going back and forth to school in dad's rust colored Toyota. But, after I got settled at work and your dad got into his routine of school and work, it wasn't so bad. The weeks went by fast, and we wrote letters to each other every other day.

In the meantime, plans for the wedding weren't going so well; finances weren't the best. Because of family pressure on both sides your dad and I argued some. Because of this many people were skeptical about this wedding. Your Grandma Cannon canceled the wedding a few times, but what she didn't realize is that she could cancel the reception, but the marriage would take place.

It got to where circumstances caused us to move the wedding until June 8th, 1979. And through all the hassle . . . the wedding went great. . . .

—Journal of Janet Cannon Myers

* * *

"One morning my husband called me at home. He said, 'You're not going to believe this. Janet just came in to work with a black eye.' " Sandra Giardina has very clear memories of that hot delta summer of 1980 when Janet worked for her and her husband's firm, Zee Medical.

"Then there was this other time that I thought was really strange, too. One afternoon, around three o'clock, the phone rang. She answered it and then I heard her sobbing—from my office—and I looked and she was crying and crying, really upset, and I thought something terrible must've happened. She cried for one solid hour. I watched the clock, because I usually have to go home early, and I couldn't leave because she was on the phone. She got off at four o'clock—she'd been crying all that time. I went up and asked her what was wrong, had somebody died? And she said, 'No, our house loan wasn't approved.'

"Gracious. I just couldn't believe it. That's when I said to myself, 'Gee, this girl has got to be spoiled.' That wasn't just crying, that was an hour-long temper tantrum. She couldn't get her way. She wanted something and she was probably used to getting everything she wanted and this was her temper tantrum.

"You'd see Jaclyn Smith. That is who I think of. And you'd see sweet and quiet—until she started talking. She was abrasive.

"Kerry would fix her lunch to bring to work, did you know that? Yes. And sometimes he'd bring her lunch. And sometimes she'd say, 'Oh, why'd you fix me this! You know I don't like this!' And I said to myself, 'My God, how many men would fix their wives sandwiches in the morning to bring to work?' "

"Billy and I were area traffic coordinators at McDermott together. I handled South America, West Africa, and the Caribbean; Bill handled Dubai and the Middle East." Ron Ackerman, a pleasant, convivial man pushing fifty, an obviously well-educated man, is talking about when he and Bill Fontanille worked together at the only adult job Bill stayed with for any length of time.

"We handled all rig supplies and material and project equipment. We purchased the transportation for the materials to be shipped overseas, to make sure that everything was documented properly. We would receive goods from all over the world and have it crated and shipped out.

"I started in June of '82. Bill had already been there about a year. For that position you need business management skills, knowledge of accounting, knowledge of economics, some computer knowledge, the ability to schedule and plan, and general knowledge associated with the particular fields of transportation that we have. The job required some previous knowledge of transportation. Bill had worked for Roadway Trucking prior to McDermott. He had been an assistant terminal manager for them when he left. His salary at McDermott was in the mid to high twenty-thousand-dollar range.

"Bill was a diligent employee. He was knowledgeable about what he did. Very efficient. He put the hours in, came on time, and stayed late when he had to. He worked with the minimum amount of supervision, which spoke well for his personal discipline.

"I'm a gregarious sort of person; Bill was, initially, sort of hesitant to mix, I guess. He's not as outgoing as I am. Over the course of a month or two we finally drew him out. We both lived on the West Bank—difference of ten years in ages, of course.

"After getting to know him, he was very personable, very friendly, with a good sense of humor. He was more organized than I in that he seemed to have more plans for his life . . . Bill was more of a person who had an idea where he wanted to be and what he wanted to be doing at thirty-five than I did. In general he handled his life like that. He planned his budget and he tried to live within it as opposed to a lot of us who just try to make as much money as we can and spend it. He had a good sense of responsibility.

"And all that's why I've always had difficulty reconciling what happened with Bill—how his life seemed to fall apart over the course of six months or so—from the Fontanille I had observed and formed these opinions about."

"I hired Kerry as inside salesman," Jake Hahn says. "I was branch manager then and had more day-to-day contact." As an executive vice president of Air-Dreco, Mr. Hahn now has dominion over five branches.

"Kerry had more of a telephone personality than a face-to-face personality. Which hurt him later in outside sales, but again the technical part carried him—wherever he failed in being personable he could talk product or business and do okay."

"It was when they were still in that apartment off Whitney, after they moved out of here, and not long before they moved out of there because Janet said a bullet came through the window—"

"Which bullet nobody ever could find, by the way," Marva Myers throws off quickly. "She just wanted to move."

"Yeah, well, with her sense of what truth was, who knows," Cliff says. "But that's what I was getting to. One night, I think we were about ready to go to sleep, the phone rings. It's Janet. And she's screaming, 'Help, he's killing me! He's killing me!' "

"I could hear her and I wasn't on the phone," Marva confirms.

"Anyway, we jump up and get over there, she's still a little hysterical, but not a mark on her. And when the police get there right after we do, she's calm as can be. They didn't even have to come inside. You know, we were there and told them it's all right. But it was. He hadn't touched her. And within minutes she's like they're on a honeymoon."

"With Janet, you never knew—everything was a big deal. Very dramatic. I remember Cliff telling her more than once about the little boy who cried wolf too many times," Marva sums up.

"I did do that," Clifford Myers adds.

"I can remember Janet calling him—this is after midnight, we'd already gone to bed—a dozen times, no, *dozens* of times. He'd say, 'I've gotta go, It's late. I've gotta go.' Finally I got fed up, I told him, 'Hang up the phone.

Tell the woman to get off the phone and don't call again, because I'm trying to get some sleep!' "

John Johnson, Air-Dreco's office manager, is recalling a sales retreat for the company's inside salesmen held in Houston during which he and Kerry roomed together.

It was during "Kerry's first year here. It was a two- or three-day trip. They hadn't been married long. He was reticent about going—about having to leave his wife by herself for the first time in their marriage. He went because it was a command performance—'You will go. Here's the tickets.'

"I'm talking dozens of times. He'd hang up and she'd call right back. But he never lost his patience with her. Continued to be doting. It wasn't like he was angry—he wanted to get off the phone, okay, but it was like, pick up the phone again, we know who it is."

"She was just *hysterical*. I was trying to calm her down. 'What's the matter, Janet? What's the matter?' She said, 'Is Mike there?' I said, 'No, they've all gone to the game. What is the matter?' " Monique Price is remembering a phone call.

"I was at Mike's parents' house—they were gone for the weekend, and there was a softball tournament going on. I had gotten a call that my grandmother had died, so Mike went to the game and I stayed at the Prices' house.

"She's crying, she's hysterical, and she said, 'Can you take me to the game?' I said, 'Janet, I really wasn't planning to go to the game, I just found out my grandmother died. What's the matter? You sound so upset.'

"She was just crying and sobbing and goes into this 'I need Kerry. I'm hemorrhaging, I need to go to the hospital.' I said, 'My God, Janet! Why didn't you say so—I'll come and get you and I'll take you.' Because she was saying that there wasn't anybody at the Myerses', that's where she was. The Myerses' house is right around the corner from the Prices'. I said, 'I'll be right there.'

"I get in my car, go around the street real fast, pull up in front of the house, I go to the door and knock and nobody answers. So I walk in and start yelling, 'Janet, Janet.'

"And from upstairs I hear, 'I'll be right down.' And she comes running down the stairs—and I remember it to this day—in a pair of white hot pants and little tank-top thing and I knew right then I'd been *had*. I knew that there had probably been a fight or something. That Kerry had left her and she didn't go and it was going to be the same old thing, just get her to the game.

"I'm saying, 'My God, Janet, I thought you needed to go to the hospital.' She said, 'Oh, it stopped. Let's just go to the game.' So I took her out to the game, where she continued to prance around and have a good time, and that was the last heard of the hemorrhaging."

"That night at the Halloween party," Monique Price is saying, "I did not see that fight. I heard about it from Mike and the people outside who saw it—they'd gotten in a fight and Kerry pushed her down and dragged her by the hair across the lawn or something. And when Mike took Kerry for a ride to settle him down, she came inside, and that's when I ran into her and she told me about it. I just said, 'Come on in, Janet. Calm down.'

"Then she runs and grabs Bill and takes him into the bedroom. Miz Anita came up to me later and said, 'They're in the *bedroom*. What are they *doing* in there?' I said, 'I don't know. They've been in there awhile.' Then I said, 'You walked in on them, what were they doing?'

" 'Talking.'

"There were two separate Halloween party incidents, actually, two different years. One I spent counseling Janet and another counseling Susan," Monique remembers.

"The one with Susan was all about Lisa Comeaux. Billy sat off in the corner at Curtis's and talked and flirted with Lisa in front of everybody. I remember saying to Mike, 'If he sits there another five minutes, I'm gonna go over and say something to him.' In fact I remember telling Mike, 'Why don't you go on over and say something to him, that his wife's upset.'

"They sat by the fireplace, right there in front of everybody, him and Lisa, for what seemed like hours on end, totally ignoring Susan, until I found her in Debbie Jordan's bedroom crying. I went in, closed the door, and started talking to her. And she was telling me about his flirting. A lot of things about the problems in their marriage. She was pregnant at the time. She was dressed as a pumpkin.

"She was just very upset and she went into a lot of things about their marriage and things that Billy had been doing and she was just totally confused as to whether she should stay in the marriage. They weren't major things, she never talked about any arguments or violence; she just thought that Billy didn't want her or didn't like her because, 'Why would he flirt?' And I'm like, 'You're just blowing this all out of context—Lisa's a flirt, I got upset with her flirting with Mike.' But she started going, 'No, there are *other* things.'

"She told me that on many occasions they'd be getting ready to go somewhere and she would come out ready to go and he would tell her that she was ugly, to go wash her face and do it over. Or that he didn't like what she was wearing, to go and change clothes. She told me he makes her exercise because he says she's fat.

"And I said something to the effect—I was trying to calm her down, you know—'Oh, in marriage, you can't take little comments seriously.' And she says, 'No, it's not little comments, it's *all* the time. He *makes* me exercise. He sits and watches me—makes me.' And she said, 'One day a package came in the mail, it was in brown paper. Anonymous. No return address. It was a Marc Eden Bust Developer. And he makes me use that—every night, he watches and makes me do that.' "

"I think Billy felt he needed to totally control Susan," Ron Dupuy says as he attempts to explain Bill's odd, if not unseemly, treatment of Susan.

"See, once he married her, he was starting to fall off the edge. So she never got to know the real Bill. He let out his frustrations on her, too. That's what she was for. Before, his parents used to dump on him, he'd fight and argue; but Susan wasn't that type, she'd just take it. The more she took, the more he gave.

"The marriage broke up because they were incompatible. He has to have somebody who adores him. I mean, he *has* to. That's an integral part of his core. If you follow his past, there's always been somebody there, or a group of people there, always. And it wasn't at that time. His old friends were grown up and married, so he didn't get it from them; and she wasn't giving it to him."

"After he and Susan got married, it seemed she got to where she was kinda scared of Billy," Louie Valdin remembers.

"One time I saw her walking in the rain and I picked her up and brought her home. She was saying things like 'Boy, Billy will really be mad if I do this . . .'

"It wasn't a physical fear. It was an emotional fear. I couldn't picture Billy putting a hand on her. I think Billy would be scared to hit her, because he'd be scared her old man would beat the shit out of him."

"The one thing that jumps out in my mind about Bill Fontanille is he would never ever look at you when you spoke to him," remembers Sydney Kornick, now a forty-something but still hell-on-wheels dusty-blond divorcée who worked with Bill Fontanille for the entirety of his tenure at McDermott.

"It used to aggravate me. There were times I can remember saying, 'Would you look at me!' Even if he had something to tell you, he would always look at the floor; even if he was in a group.

"Even though I was only a few years older than him, I always looked upon Bill as a little boy. Very lonely, scared, starving for affection, but not knowing how to go about getting it or handling it.

"I can remember in Metairie when we were in the office on L&N Road, there's a foyer with a sofa up front by this little waiting area. One day he was sitting next to me on the sofa, and he said something about he was thinking about going back to school to get his master's. He was sitting next to me and I kind of put my hand on his knee, and he *flinched*, really. It was like I patted him to say, 'Oh, gee, that's great,' and he moved away from me. I thought, 'How odd.' I just thought it so completely odd. I felt terribly sorry for the man; well, I felt terribly sorry for the *boy*.

"But then it goes from that to me having trouble with Bill Fontanille—*sexual harassment* trouble, really. It was weird. I wasn't any friendlier to him than I was to any of the other people I worked with—and I kind of felt sorry for Bill, he just seemed like the odd one out, the underdog, he always felt like everybody was against him. I didn't want to mother him, but I guess I did.

"One day, it was before Susan was pregnant, I was in my office by myself. It was during lunch—sometimes if we're real busy, we'd eat at our desks. Just about everyone else had gone off for lunch. And Bill came into my office, walked behind my desk, and *put his hands on my breasts,* from behind.

"I turned and said, 'Are you crazy? *Are you losing your mind?*' And he just kind of—it was weird, he was a weird person; really weird, I mean that came off the wall. And I thought, 'My God, is my niceness and friendliness being taken the wrong way?' He pulled his hand away immediately. He wouldn't look at me. His head was down. He shrugged, you know, like I think he tried to make it seem like, 'Well, I had to give it a shot.' You know, if it turned out good, fine, if it didn't, well, okay. He threatened to call the big boss and say he had been intimate with me. . . . I finally said, 'Look, I'm in the middle of a divorce. And you start any of this bullshit with me, I'll bring sexual harassment charges against you.' That cut him off. He went away as meekly as a lamb."

"It was bizarre," Ron Ackerman recalls. "Bill's wife was pregnant and she was going along fine up until when the baby was born. The umbilical cord wrapped around the baby's neck at the last minute. When they delivered, this doctor came in and told them the baby had massive brain damage and that he probably wouldn't live and they had him on a respirator.

"A couple of weeks after that—during this period you could just see the anxiety and the torturous situation that Bill was going through over his child; not knowing if the child was going to live or if he did live if he'd have any normal brain function at all or whatever—and they took the kid off the respirator after a couple of weeks and he was breathing on his own.

"Then a couple of months later they came in and had a test done on the child and he had normal brain-wave activity and it appeared that there was no substantial brain damage to the child—so they went through all of this *for nothing.* Some doctor just came in and laid this on 'em and it was a real horror show to have to go through.

"I remember that very distinctly—I remember all of us at work how angry we were that someone would be put through something like this so unnecessarily. He was just totally devastated by this thing. They went through this for several months. This naturally would have to place a tremendous strain on the relationship at home and everything."

"I had to call Billy to even find out the baby was born," Mike Price remembers. "I hadn't seen or talked to him in days and we knew she was due anytime and we kept expecting to hear. But nothing. Finally I call him and he tells me, 'We had a boy. He was born with the cord around his neck. He's brain-damaged.' He's saying this terrible news but it's like he's telling me the moon is shining—no emotion, a monotone, flat, *weird.* And I'm going, 'Ah, man, God! I'm so sorry,' and all and it's like, click, he hangs up."

"That sexual harassment thing kind of passed over," Sydney Kornick continues. "And so we were work friends again; and I always did just feel kind of sorry for Bill. Then his wife got pregnant. I remember we were getting ready to leave for the Christmas holidays, Susan was due any day; the last day of work before we left I told him, 'As soon as she has the baby, I want to know what she had, call me.'

"He called when the baby was born. It was at night. Apparently there were problems. He said, 'I have a little boy.' I said, 'Oh, that's wonderful. How's Susan?' 'She's doing fine.' 'How's the baby?' 'Well, we had problems with the baby,' and he told me the whole thing.

"He was distraught; it sounded like he wanted me to feel sympathy and invite him over for a shoulder to cry on. But I just knew that he would probably try to turn it into something sexual. So I just said, 'I'm terribly sorry, if there's anything I can do, if Susan needs anything,' you know.

"Then he didn't call me again for a long time."

"Kerry was a hot-tempered man—short-fused."

Gwen Benitez Landry started working at Air-Dreco in January 1980 and left in September 1981. For the almost two years she was the receptionist-secretary and sole female employee, Kerry Myers was the inside salesman.

His anger would come all of a sudden, she remembers. "If there was a snag in anything he was doing, what he had planned, how he thought things should go, that's it. That's all it took and he'd be mad. He would raise his voice. Slam a phone, a desk drawer. Rifle a catalog, throw a pencil."

Then came a day Gwen will never forget. "He flipped the desk! A metal office desk. He was on the telephone, it was a personal call. His voice had been getting loud. Then he slammed the phone down, stood up, and flipped his desk over.

"One thing I definitely noticed, when Janet got pregnant, his moods got worse. I don't know if he didn't want her to get pregnant or what. But she was happy; he wasn't as happy as she was."

"The infamous christening—it's true he stayed in the bedroom," Tammy DuBuc says. "But you have to know Billy's personality to understand it.

"Janet and Kerry were there, Debbie and Curtis, me and Clyde. Ryan was there; that was when Janet asked if I could start watching him. I didn't think Billy was home, because we came in late, and Billy was nowhere around. The kids were sitting on the floor playing and I asked, 'Where's Billy?' Janet said, 'Shhhh,' like this, like to keep me quiet. I'm thinking, 'What did I say wrong?' Susan's off sitting in the corner and Janet whispered, 'He's in the back.' 'What's he doing back there?' 'Him and Susan's dad had a fight, so he's staying in the room, doesn't want to come out.'

"It had nothing to do with the baby not being perfect. Their marital problems had more to do with Billy's casual attitude about keeping a job. Her father didn't think much of him as a provider. He had a good job, but he talked like he was always about to leave it, that he wasn't happy at McDermott.

"Now, all the guys went in the bedroom with him. But he didn't tell them what the problem was."

"It was one Friday afternoon, I don't know whether Susan was out of town, just as a gesture, I said, 'Hey, if you're not doing anything, we're all going to the Hilton for a couple of drinks, stop by.' You know, he just seemed so alone," Sydney Kornick remembers.

"Everybody in the steamship business would go to the Hilton Hotel after work, because the International Trade Mart is right there, and they'd have drinks at the Rain Forest upstairs. So Billy said, 'Yeah.' My girlfriend Tammy was meeting me there with a couple of her friends. We had maybe two or three drinks, and he met us there.

"After a couple of more drinks, I was getting ready to leave and he said, 'Would you give me a ride to my car?' I said, 'Sure.' I brought him to his car, it was a short distance away. And *he asked me to give him a blow job.* But he was not looking at me. Just said it flat out. No emotion—I don't think he does have emotions. He used those words—it was either a 'blow job,' or no, it was 'Would you suck on me?'

"But he was *not* looking at me. He was looking straight ahead. I said, 'Bill, I think it's time for you to leave. Maybe you've had too much to drink.' I said, 'Now get out. Now!' And he did. Meekly."

"That was Janet. Sometimes she'd have a tube top on that covered maybe three inches of her top, and she'd have the shortest pair of short pants that covered the essentials," Monique Price says.

"In the summertime it was tank top, tube top, and short shorts. Standard summer wear of Janet. But that was the late '70s, that was the style. She wasn't unusual. She was maybe a little on the skimpy side sometimes. She dressed more that way than anybody else.

"She was proud of her body, and that was just her personality. Yes, she was a flirt. I think she dressed like that for a purpose. If you've got it, flaunt it."

"I think it was more the way she carried herself," Tammy DuBuc says. "Her personality, she was very confident of herself."

"Sensuousness—it was probably more of that," says Monique. "Because she always left that—that always sort of came through, this confidence, 'I'm here, I'm available,' kind of thing—whether she was or not, nobody knows. Or I don't know, let's put it that way. But she exuded that type of personality—'I'm here if you want me,' what a guy likes in a woman, I guess.

"Every Halloween party we would have conversations like, 'What can she come in this year?' Because it always seemed to be something in a black or white skimpy leotard. Except when she was pregnant. Always something as skimpy and revealing as it could possibly be. A cat or a bumblebee. It was funny. It got to be a joke—'How many things can you come in a leotard as?'

"But I never saw her as gorgeous or beautiful," Monique continues. "But Mike and all the guys did. *Every guy who ever saw her says that,* you know. Maybe she's a man's idea of gorgeous but not a woman's."

"We were gonna play basketball, the guys. It was a planned thing. I'm taking the truck and I'm picking up some of the guys," Mike Price says.

"Kerry was one of 'em. I'd just talked to him on the phone. 'I'm coming to getcha.' 'Right.' So I pull the truck up to their apartment complex and hit the horn. No Kerry. 'Oh, shit, what's the deal this time?' I say and get out and go up to their door.

"Well, the door isn't closed, it's ajar. I knock. Nothing. I push the door on open and step in calling him. I'm standing there for like a moment or so and then Janet steps out of the bathroom with just a bath towel around her head and another one around her, and I mean just barely covering the absolute essentials, and she acts just like—well, like Janet—and says, 'Oh, I needed something from the store. I had to send Kerry. He'll be right back.' With the cutest, most innocent little smile, like, 'Oh, what a surprise, I was just taking a shower, excuse me.'

"She did that on purpose and nobody will ever convince me differently. She knew exactly when we were coming."

"Oh, yeah. Janet was flirty." Chuck Cassard says it as if it's gospel. "Because when they first said that Billy and Janet had had an affair, I thought to myself, 'Well, I don't doubt that at all.' The reason I don't doubt that is Billy's a slime. He'll go after anybody's wife. Janet, she's two-faced to me, she'll do what she wants to do. So I don't doubt that at all."

" 'Danny, how ya doing? This is Janet.' 'Janet who?' She said, 'Cannon,' and then I knew who it was," Deputy Dan Carr remembers. "I'd handled an accident that Kerry was involved in. He backed out onto Terry Parkway and a car caught him in the rear end.

"She'd called the district that night and wanted to talk to me. She'd left the name of Janet Myers; never rang a bell to me, so I didn't bother calling. Then she called back and said it was in reference to an accident her husband was involved in; that's when I called. She wanted to know the details."

Soon Janet asked if he was married and did he have any kids; she told him about Ryan.

"Then it was like, 'Can you come by and talk to me?' " Danny continues. "Like maybe we can rehash what might've happened back then but never happened. And I sat there and I figured, 'I'm married. I got my little girl. I'm not looking to do anything now.'

"Now, before the accident, I didn't know Kerry Myers from Adam. But he was upset. He was pissed because his car had a dent in it. He was mad at everything. It was like the end of the world to him. He started getting loud; that's when I told him to go sit in his car. I had to tell him to calm down.

"I started thinking how practically the last time I'd talked to her, that summer of '77, she'd said she wanted a strong man who would dominate her, and I couldn't believe she married this little bitty skinny jerk."

"It started when my son was about six months old," Peggy Cowan remembers. "Ryan was six months older. July of '82. My brother worked Kerry's accident on Terry Parkway, he told me, 'Boy, her husband is a *psycho*.' Then he told me about her calling and catching up on old memories and how she seemed so glad to talk to him again.

"About two weeks after that accident, I also happened to meet Kerry pretty much for the first time. I went to the pediatrician's office to bring my son in for a checkup; Janet and Kerry were both in there with Ryan.

"She introduced Kerry to me—I think I'd met him maybe once or twice before that, but this was really a meeting—and she told him, 'This is Peggy. You hear me talk about her a lot, the girl I grew up with.'

"He said, 'Her brother's the policeman.' Really snide, with what I would later, after the murder and funeral, call the 'evil eye.'

"I said, 'Both of my brothers are policemen.'

" 'Well, I've had the *privilege* of meeting only one.'

"I noticed Janet had a black eye. She had makeup—she was wearing heavy makeup—but you could tell she was covering a black eye and a bruise on her arm.

"Now, what popped into my mind at that moment was, 'Gee, I hope this didn't occur out of the jealousy of my brother.' That's something that has been on my mind to this day. That she got a beating because of Danny.

"She got my phone number. To be honest: they went in, Ryan was checked before my son, they left, Janet claimed she had forgotten something in the doctor's office and came back to get it. He stayed in the car, and she got my phone number and gave me hers.

"Not even my husband knew that Janet and I renewed our friendship—it was hush-hush. It had to be. My husband knows Kerry, and it might've slipped out accidentally. And she did *not* want it to get back to Kerry.

"He didn't want her to have any friends of her own. He didn't want her involved with anybody—he wanted to pick everyone and everything for her.

"So a couple of days later she called me, because she knew my little boy was sick—we talked about that, and that's when I asked, 'Gee, were you hurt in the wreck?'

"She said, 'No.'

"I said, 'Where did you get the bruises from?'

"She giggled about it. 'Well, you know, everybody has a temper and everybody loses his temper once in a while, and somebody ends up with bruises sometimes.'

"I said, 'Well, who lost their temper and put bruises on you? It had to be your husband.'

"She said, 'Well, yeah, but you just wait until you're married a few years, you'll see what kind of things happen.' "

"After Janet and I were ended for sure, I never made any effort to contact her," Hurst Bousegard says with much pain still evident in his voice after all these years. "Even though she wanted to remain friends if that was okay with me, I didn't. Emotionally, it took me years to get over it. So I did not keep in contact with her, she kept in contact with me.

"It was after Ryan was born, he wasn't quite walking yet. Janet had continued to write and call me on occasions, and I had an opportunity to go visit at their house one day. She'd invited me. Kerry wasn't home from work yet. Janet seemed happy; just adored Ryan, loved watching him grow. This was fall of '82. I was in town on business.

"Ryan was crawling around on the floor; I held him in my lap for a while. The mood between us was very nice, it was like we were two very close friends coming together after a long time of not seeing each other.

"Not long after that, Kerry came home. He greeted me; I was very nervous being there with him, the tension showed. Not long after he got home I left and decided I'd never go back.

"But the phone calls and letters continued; usually once a month, sometimes a couple of months would go by. It would be either a phone call or a letter. She *always* called me. I never called her. Basically just small talk, catching up, in the beginning.

"Then a lot of depression started showing through, but no details. She'd only speak in generalities."

"We used to have a nickname for him: the Shadow. Kerry would come in the office, do a little work or whatever, and before you know it he'd be gone. You'd say, 'Where'd he go?' 'I dunno.' He never told people goodbye," Mark Francis remembers.

"Usually we just thought he'd gone home early. Middle of the day sometimes. We were never sure how much Kerry was working even before the incident."

Mark joined Air-Dreco as an outside salesman in 1981 while Kerry was still inside; in 1983, Kerry was moved to outside sales and given a territory. "His income doubled—from fifteen, sixteen to thirty, thirty-five grand the first year," Mark says.

Gary Guidry, Air-Dreco's perennial top salesman in the first years of Kerry's move into outside sales, who later, from 1986 on, was Kerry's direct supervisor, remembers difficulties with the shift.

"Kerry had a hard time making the transition. When you're in sales, generally you want to go in and talk to a customer and warm them up a little bit. But Kerry always had a difficult time doing that—in fact, he always had a hard time with anybody just saying hello and goodbye. It was a personality flaw that was pretty evident—and if you're a salesman, that's a disadvantage."

"As outside guys, we'd come into the office on Mondays and Fridays, bustin' butt with a lot of paperwork to do, and Kerry'd be propped up," Mark Francis says. "He'd handle a couple of calls from his three customers and then read his newspaper. Most of his time on the phone was either with Janet or talking about sports, not business. But you see, he was getting most of his business from only two or three customers; and everybody had anywhere from one hundred to two hundred customers on their account sheet."

Gary Guidry continues, "I think in the beginning maybe he did work hard. For the first year or so he probably was making a lot of sales calls. But then it got to the point where he'd been around his territory once or twice and met everybody; he selected the accounts that accepted him and maybe brushed past the ones that didn't. Or lightly brushed over them, and by that process of elimination had less work for himself. At that point it was maybe two, three o'clock he'd go home or do whatever."

"Kerry was like the Nutty Professor. He could pick up anything and describe it to you intricately," says Mike Lessard, currently an inside salesman at Air-Dreco. He started work about a year after Kerry did.

"He understood every working part—but he seemed to see *everything else* in a different perspective than other people."

"Kerry had that gray void," Jake Hahn remembers. "He had the ability to just separate himself from things he didn't want to deal with.

"Everybody here is extremely sports-minded, and we'd start talking about a particular game and it'd be like Kerry watched a *different game.* We'd look at each other and say, 'How could Kerry come to that conclusion?' We'd even ridicule him—'Kerry, why don't you come over to my house and watch the game so that we make sure you're watching the same game we watch.' And he took that kinda harassment fairly good, because he took a fair amount of it."

It was the same thing with ball games that Kerry played in. " 'It wasn't my fault, I didn't get doubled up. Unh-unh! I went three for three,' " says John Johnson, quoting a typical Kerry rejoinder. "There was Kerry's softball game, and then there was the real game. There was only his perception of things. That was it. He saw things differently than everyone else."

Gary Guidry adds, "Kerry wore blinders; he didn't see things other people saw. It became a standing joke: 'Whatcha hitting?' 'I'm hitting .650, just a little behind Kerry.' That was fairly typical."

"He had a type of one-mindedness," John Johnson continues. "He would be on a thought pattern and you or somebody would bring something else up and he would continue his thought pattern as soon as you finished talking. Everybody knows him for that. He was like, 'Huh?' That's the way it was. He had that one-track mind, and unless he emptied it all out, he was not done."

"Probably half the time you couldn't get a word in edgewise if Kerry wanted to talk," Jake Hahn explains. "It would be, 'Kerry, hold on a minute.' You'd have to stop him. Never had a problem interjecting at meetings. Discussing problems. He seemed to be able to vocalize about things. But you take that and you put it into a personality of that void.

"If I would come down on Kerry for something he would respond to it mostly with—as we put it—the Navajo Indian look of like, 'What?' Like, 'No way.' And, 'Huh? You're in left field, Jake.' And once you got that look, you knew, 'I'm not getting through to this guy.'

"Cut from a different mold. . . . You know how when people talk about their family, or what they've been doing, this and that, you really don't pay that close attention. Well, especially with Kerry, because he talked so much, and his stories? You know, everybody else, 'What'd ya do this weekend?' 'Ahh, I cut the grass and na-na-na.' *Kerry went to Mars.* His stories were always—you know, and you'd go, 'Uh-huh . . .' and tune him out."

*   *   *

"Kerry was jealous of even her past," Peggy Cowan says.

"We talked on the phone a lot. There were times she would call me all upset, they'd been in an argument, they were having problems. She suspected he was running around, fooling around. She said she wasn't sure but she suspected it was due to just the ways he was acting. Working late, not eating home. Also softball—that was the thing, he was always involved in ball. 'Ball, ball, ball, ball!' And she didn't believe it was always ball.

"She said Kerry was always doing what he wanted. But he wouldn't let her go places, she was very isolated. She still had her dreams. She wanted more out of life.

"She would also tell me how violent he was—that he was the type to pick up, break up, throw things. Hit her. But she never indicated she was the type that did it too. There were times she would tell me, oh, he picked up like a little figurine or a picture frame or something and threw it, or threw a glass at her or something and it'd break. And I'd say, 'What'd you do?'

" 'I moved out the way.'

"My attitude was, 'Why didn't you pick up a frying pan or something and throw at him?'

" 'Well, what's that gonna solve? Other than a bigger fight.' And she would always ask me, 'How do you have such a good marriage? If that's the way you are?'

" 'Because I speak my piece and he speaks his piece. You can't have a marriage if it's only one person's way.' And I used to tell her that over and over and over again. 'Whose marriage is it? Yours between the two of you, or his?' You know, 'What are you to him? Just someone to yell at and punch around?' "

"It's not the kind of thing people want to witness, it's not the kind of thing you want to do at work."

Gary Guidry had a desk next to Kerry for several years and heard the "frequent phone fights with Janet. It could be anything. And then loud profanity. Slamming phones. At least one a week. But as soon as it was over it was over. Like nothing had happened. If you asked him what was wrong, 'Nothing.' Cooled down immediately. After a while you get tired of asking so you just look at him after one of those things and then it was back to business."

John Johnson had several "experiences" with Janet while Kerry was under him as inside salesman.

"If Gwen and Kerry were gone at lunch at the same time, that was it, two plus two is four, he's having an affair with her. She would call and ask, 'May I speak to Kerry?' 'Well, he's not here, he went to lunch.' 'Where did he go?' 'I don't know.' 'When did he leave? When will he get back?'

"... and a white picket fence." Kerry and Janet Cannon
Myers on their wedding day

"The perfect family" that never was: Susan, Bill, and Matthew Fontanille in 1987, *after* Bill was released from his 14 months in prison and more than three years *after* their divorce and the murder of Janet . . . when Bill almost had Susan beguiled into remarrying

"I never saw anyone take to mothering like that girl did. . . ." Janet and Ryan, in the spring of 1983

"The Circle" onstage, drunk, singing at Janet and Kerry's wedding reception: The Jordan brothers, Jimmy and Curtis, on the left flank; Mike Price, as always, out front and center stage; Greg "Diggie" D'Argonne; and then, all but cheek-to-cheek, Billy and Kerry

Last Christmas . . . 59 days before the murder: Kerry, Janet (pregnant with Sarah), and Ryan in the living room at 2232 Litchwood, only a few feet from where Janet will come to die

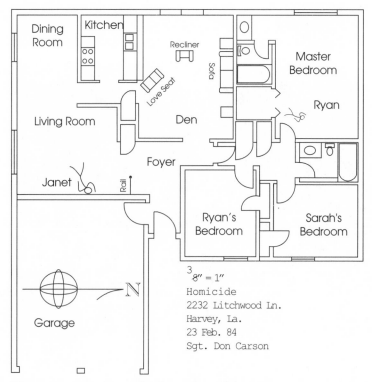

Diagram to a murder . . . the floor plan of the Myers house used at trial

"They did indeed fight, we know that." . . . What appears to be the indentation of a hard-soled shoe heel in the Sheetrock at the end of the hall just outside Sarah's bedroom and across from the master bedroom

"There was blood everywhere. . . ." The multiplicity of types of blood deposits in the west end of the den behind the recliner and sofa

A burglary? "Somebody broke into my house. . . ."? The ransacked master bedroom

The closet in the master bedroom . . . From the look
of it, was someone hiding in there? Does the soiled
and streaked condition of the mirror suggest the fas-
tidious Janet, or a very depressed wife and mother?
In the foreground is the mixture of blood and vomit
on the carpet where Ryan was found.

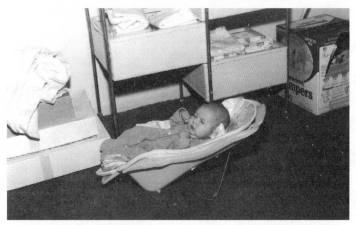

"The Gerber baby": Six-week-old Sarah, photographed only
minutes after police arrived on the scene

The Killing Wall . . . after Janet's body has been removed. Note the bloody handprint, upper left of the "explosion" pattern of many, many different types of blood deposits.

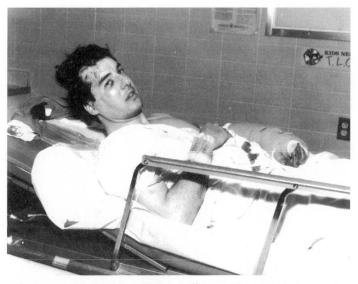

A beaten-up Kerry Myers at West Jefferson Hospital that morning

"The Bill Show" . . . Bill with yet another "statistic," an unidentified, forgotten stewardess, less than two week before the last trial

The final prosecution team outside the law offices of Molaison & LeBlanc: *(from left)* Mike Maunoir, W. J. LeBlanc, Howat Peters, Vince Lamia

"Earthmother" . . . Tammy DuBuc

For the defense of Kerry Myers . . . Wiley Beevers

For justice . . . First Assistant District
Attorney Marion Edwards

For the defense of Bill Fontanille
... Nick Noriea

For the prosecution of Bill
Fontanille for first-degree
murder ... Art Lentini

For the prosecution of Bill Fontanille for first-degree murder . . . Paul Connick

In victory for *The State of Louisiana* versus *Fontanille and Myers* . . . W. J. LeBlanc

The bat . . .

The law . . . The Honorable Ernest V. Richards,
Judge, 24th Judicial District, State of Louisiana

Janet Cannon . . . 1976 River Oaks Academy
senior annual

'. . . Janet, at one o'clock.' And that would be it, she'd hang up. Then in a little while I'd hear somebody else talking to her on another phone, she'd call back again.

"There were also times when you'd answer and it would be a blank phone—you'd have to assume that was her calling to get another opinion on where Kerry was, because she was really neurotic with that.

"She was frequently in accidents, too," Johnson continues. "There was always something going on. She fell and broke her nose; he was in an accident and demolished his car and she was hurt; then she got pregnant—Kerry found himself uninsured. Yet he blamed it on someone else: the company because they didn't give him the necessary forms to be filled out so his wife could be covered under the family plan; or the insurance company because they allowed his insurance to lapse. You know, cast the blame over here, because it wasn't his fault.

"There were always hints of violence," Mike Lessard remembers. "Kerry would come around here with a black eye and I would just think he'd walked into a door, he was that kind of a guy. He would never explain.

"He came to work once with a patch on his eye, said he had a scratched cornea or something. The way they would argue over the phone you could tell she was feisty. He didn't just dominate her."

"Janet talked to me a lot over the years, at various times, about problems she and Kerry were having," Ernie Barrow is saying as he begins to tell the tale of a series of events which will be more than a little pivotal in any final disposition of the Fontanille-Myers prosecution.

"They were having troubles, financial troubles. And that seemed to really touch Janet off. She really could not handle not having enough money to pay their bills. She expressed that to me on more than one occasion—basically, she just said that he was lazy and didn't get off the dime. Of course, if I remember right, he gave me a litany of places where he'd applied and things he'd tried to do and the whole smear, you know.

"There was this one time they called and they wanted to talk. She'd been in an automobile accident; she'd been struck by a Vietnamese. We'd spent a lot of money trying to find the guy. To no avail. Janet was hurt, she was injured fairly bad. She broke her pelvis and had a bad back strain. So she had a cause of action. And they had spent some money on medicals, and rental cars, and I was trying to get some kind of line on this thing for them. They didn't have insurance for some reason.

"That was one of the things we discussed that day. Then after that they started talking about some of the problems they were having. And they got into a little argument—they were sitting side by side across the desk from me—and they got into this little argument and one word led to another and she reached over and rapped him upside the shoulder and neck, and it was getting fairly serious—he bristled up with his fist like that, and she bristled up, and I said, '*Wait a minute!* Both of y'all sit down or I'm gonna run the hell out of both of y'all.'

"What was really unusual about it was her instant resort to violence—and his reaction was a little surprising to me. I mean, he immediately drew back and had that fist cocked and if I'm not jumping up hollering 'Wait, now! Y'all hold on here a damn minute,' I don't know what he might've cold-cocked her a good one. But, man, it sure looked as though they had done this sort of thing before."

According to medical records, in March 1982, Janet Cannon Myers suffered a miscarriage.

"I knew about it because I was watching Ryan at the time," Tammy DuBuc says. "Janet and Kerry went to Mississippi for the weekend. It was very strange. She calls me Monday morning and tells me she'd had a miscarriage. That she'd been either riding a horse or a motorcycle. Why would a pregnant girl get on a horse or a motorcycle? Of course, she wasn't big yet, but still. I just assumed that they got into a fight, always did think that.

"Everybody else did, too."

"She was a hell of a good mother. As far as taking care of the kids," Clifford says. "Boy, I'll tell you, when I went into that house after all this happened, Sarah's little clothes, they were in the locker hung a certain way, Ryan's, everything clean, neat . . ."

"She was a very orderly person," Marva says. "It was like all the little blue shirts were together, all the little red shirts were together . . ."

"She liked things organized," Cliff echoes.

"She was the only young girl I've ever seen who took to mothering like she did—myself included," Marva continues. "With a new baby it's like, 'What am I gonna do?' You know. Not her. It was as if she had twelve before Ryan. Just a natural mother."

"I don't think we were on the hit parade at that particular time, but it was not a very stable environment," Ron Ackerman is saying.

"The situation we had at McDermott was one where the company was cutting back and laying off people. I mean, literally every other week they came through at payday handing out pink slips. So that was the general circumstance for Bill's job-hunting.

"This fellow, Victor Noe, who was the terminal manager for McClean Trucking in New Orleans, he called and asked if I was interested in a job. I told him no I wasn't, he asked if I knew of anyone who might be, and I gave Bill a real good referral.

"Bill met with him, interviewed, and was offered the job and accepted. He was there about three months and then quit.

"It was unfathomable to me that he quit without another job waiting or without a reason. I finally got him on the phone about a month later, and I said, 'What happened? Why'd you quit? Was it that bad?' He said it was just a lot of stress and he quit—other than that I have never heard anything about the circumstances of him leaving McClean. During the time he was at McClean, I talked to him every two or three weeks and he'd call me at the office sometimes.

"This was a person that I had grown to have a personable relationship with. We talked every day, I rode him home from work, and we'd go out and have a beer together once in a while. And after this thing with the baby—well, that was just like a disaster. You could see, there was just like a cloud over him.

"Then I heard later on that he had split with his wife."

"Billy had a hard time telling people he wasn't working," Tammy DuBuc says. "He'd make up these jobs so people would stop asking him. Billy can't have people thinking he can't hold down a job; same thing about his marriage. When his marriage fell through a lot of people didn't know about it for quite a while. He's Billy, he can *do* these things.

"And all of that is part of the reason I know Billy couldn't have killed Janet. No way he would be able to let people think he's a murderer. He would've killed himself or run away, not go to the hospital. He couldn't live with that. He wanted people to think *only* the best of him."

"Billy disappeared there for awhile after Susan left him, just dropped out of the world," Mike Price remembers. "Then I see him in his car, he's driving on Carol Sue. I honk my horn at him and he looks right at me but doesn't acknowledge me. He goes on, I keep beeping and follow him. I'm thinking he's going to pull over at this little neighborhood grocery where we used to hang out in front of and drink beer.

"But no. He just keeps on going and drives to his house. Now I'm right on his tail all the way. He pulls into the driveway, gets out, goes right inside, and I'm just seconds behind him knocking on the door. No answer. Man, I'm knocking and saying, 'Bill. Hey, Billy, it's Mike,' you know. But nothing.

"Then I look and see him peering out at me from behind the blinds. No expression. Like he doesn't know who I am and furthermore doesn't care. He never comes to the door. After a while I just go on. But I'm worried about him; this is unusual for even Billy. And that look he gave me? Unh-unh. Something's wrong. Big-time."

"We were at the Halloween party at the Jordans'," Penny Price Fox is saying. "Janet was pregnant with Sarah, she was dressed as a ghost with this white bedsheet. We were all talking, and I went up to Billy, who I really wasn't friends with, but he and Susan had separated and everybody knew how down he was, so I felt sorry for him. I said, 'Bill, you have lost a lot of weight, you look really bad.'

"He turned and said, 'So what? I'm gonna die anyway.' I said, 'What are you talking about?' Then he told me, 'I hear 'em knocking, I hear 'em coming over; but I don't let 'em in.'

"I said, 'Who are you talking about, Bill?' And it was like a conversation where you want to kind of just back off. But he was holding my arm, and he was just repeating, 'I hear them knocking. Mike and Curtis and Jimmy, I hear 'em knocking, trying to get me to come out of the house—but I don't come out.'

"I said, 'Never?' He said, 'Nope.' I said, 'What do you eat?' 'Crackers.' I said, 'Any particular kind?' I was being real sarcastic. He said, 'Sometimes I just drink water.' I said, 'Well, what do you do in the house all day, Bill?' He said, 'I watch TV. I watch soap operas.' Then he got lighthearted, so I said, 'Oh, what soaps do you watch?' Just trying to make a light situation out of something real tense. Then he started talking about the soaps, and when I tell you he knew every detail of every soap opera—I don't know how any person could watch so many of 'em. He said, 'I just flip the channels all day long.'

"And he was real crazy about Erica on *All My Children,* okay? But wait, then he started calling Susan Erica and Erica Susan. I said, 'Who are you talking about?' 'Erica.' 'On *All My Children*?' 'No, Susan.' Then he was just like in and out of the soaps, doing the characters and all. I said, 'Bill, how do you have time to watch all those? Aren't you going to get a job?' 'No.' I said, 'Well, what do you do?' He said, 'I don't sleep. I don't eat.' I said, 'You don't ever sleep?' 'Sometimes.' Then he told me how he got rid of all his furniture and he lived in that house with a recliner and a TV.

"I told my husband, 'Something's *wrong* with him.' That was the weirdest conversation. I even told my mom, and Debbie, and all of them, 'Something's not right with Billy. He's *hallucinating*.' "

Louie Valdin remembers the same October 31 evening at Curtis Jordan's house. "It was the first time I'd seen Billy in a long time. He kind of poured his soul out to me. He was telling me how bad off he was, how he didn't have anything anymore. His wife was taking everything and he wasn't going to see his son. And then he kind of hinted around that, 'Well, if she's gonna take everything, maybe I oughta just not leave her anything to take.' You know, 'Maybe I oughta just go smash the house up.' The only other time when he was like that was when he was dating Carrie Campbell.

"I remember thinking that whenever Billy needed to talk to someone, he'd always kinda latch on if he found someone he could talk to, and he'd be around all the time: I remember mentioning it to my wife. I said, 'Look, if Billy knocks on the door, I'm not home, because he's looking for somebody to listen to him and I don't want him over here every night aggravating us.' "

"At first, just out of the blue she'd call," Peggy Cowan says, remembering what she knows of the last eighteen months of Janet's life.

"I mean, for a while there it was once a week, and then all of a sudden it would seem like forever before I would hear from her. But she always resisted advice—from anyone. If you said to her, 'Go back home to your mama and them'—'No!' At times I thought, 'Gee, that doesn't make sense.' Her parents had a home with plenty of room, there was nobody else there.

"She told me she was planning on leaving him after Sarah was born, but you'd heard it so many times before . . ."

"Billy had a real problem with Matthew's birth. He had a hard time accepting that," Tammy says. "And he also was jealous of the attention that Susan gave to Matthew and not him.

"But he had accepted Matthew's condition. 'Well, I always said I dreamed of having a quarterback for a son, now a linebacker will be fine,' he said. That's when I realized he'd accepted him being a slow learner. And he was good with Matthew. He said that the day he took Matthew for his birthday and kept him; he was taking him to all his friends."

"She told me she went to see an attorney. She told me that in person, on the phone," Hurst Bousegard is remembering. "She said she'd thought about divorce. But she said the lawyer told her, 'You live in a nice house, your husband makes a good living, you have a wonderful child. You'd be silly to get a divorce.' From what she was telling me, she'd decided to accept that and try to work things out.

"She then blamed her ill feelings of her marriage on her pregnancy [with Sarah]."

"I typed up résumés for him and had some run off at school. He was looking for work, he wasn't locked up inside that house." Cissy Fontanille is very adamant on this point.

"Bill was getting out. He used to use my car—he didn't have the money for gas or anything for his own car; he'd use my car, it stayed parked at school all day anyway—use my gas. But, no, he was going out trying to find a job; because he just had this idea that if he got a job, everything would be all right again. But at that time, you have to remember, half this nation was out of work."

"He avoided only 'the circle,' " Angela helps her mother explain. "He was embarrassed, he wanted to stay away from them until he had everything together."

Miz Cissy continues, "Sometimes he'd go over to his house and stay there and sometimes he'd come to my house and stay. He'd be back and forth, just depending on if he wanted to be alone for a little while, then he'd go over to his house. Then maybe the next night he'd come back and sleep at my house."

"He was seeing people other than 'the group.' Chuck Cronin and Keith Kline were around with him then," Angela says.

"I know Bill was looking for work," says Monique Price. "He applied at an employment agency where I was working at the time. Executive Personnel was the name of company. So I knew he was looking for work during the 'black hole' months. I told everybody that Bill was not working off somewhere, that he came in the office today applying for a job.

"I went and told the guy he'd interviewed with what I knew to be some of the problems with Bill and that he'd better look at the résumé and application a little closer. 'Oh, that's not the story he gave me,' I remember Bob said.

"Billy saw me, spoke to me. He looked good. He was dressed up in a suit. Not this hermit guy I'd been hearing about. He was Bill."

"She told me she went to see an attorney," Peggy Cowan says. "I knew that when she was pregnant with Sarah—I had a feeling just by talking to her that she had pretty well planned that once she had the baby, recuperated, got back on her feet and all that, that she was going to get out of the situation. It was an impression, but it was an impression *given* in so many words."

"It got especially bad right after she had Sarah," Mark Francis of Air-Dreco is saying. "Right after she had Sarah, she couldn't seem to handle parenting. That's what it sounded like, the way Kerry was describing it. The kids, both Ryan and Sarah at home, the baby crying, maybe Ryan crying or whatever, the two at once. You know, she'd call Kerry to complain about it, 'You've gotta come over here and help me.' And Kerry'd slam the phone down—I mean, they'd be doing some serious arguing; he'd be yelling, man, at the top of his lungs. And we're trying to talk on the phone with customers, I mean. . . .

"Janet came over to the office with the baby, Sarah; must've been a coupla weeks before she got murdered," Mark Francis continues. "She was dressed in shorts, she had an old T-shirt on, her stomach was still kind of bloated, just kind of strange—you know, she had the baby in one arm. And I thought she looked a little sloppily dressed. I thought it was a little unusual for her. I don't think she even had a bra on. She was standing out by the warehouse, she didn't really come out into the front.

"We'd been out with 'em before, office parties and stuff, and she was always *meticulous*."

* * *

"I get another phone call at work—and this one really scared the hell out of me," Sydney Kornick remembers. "Bill called me up and said he was in his house, the house he and Susan had bought—that the house was empty, all the furniture was gone, he had spent the night in the house, he was crying hysterically, he was drunk. I asked him if he was taking drugs, I didn't know whether he was drunk or whether he was on something, because he was not coherent at all. He was just out of control. He was crying. Begging me to meet him. I told him no. In the meantime I had put him on hold, I said, 'Would you hold one minute, I have somebody coming in my office.' I put him on hold and I ran and got Joe Camet. I said, 'Joe, you're not gonna believe this, Bill Fontanille is on the phone crying and threatening to commit suicide if I don't meet him after work.'

"I told Joe that Bill had told me he would hang up if anybody else got on the phone. I said, 'Joe, I don't know what to do.' He said, 'Let's try and find his mother's phone number'—because we knew his mother was a schoolteacher. Joe Camet grabbed a phone book, and he started hunting while I got back on the phone with Bill.

"It was winter, he said he'd spent the night in the house, the empty house—you could like hear him shivering. He said his life was over, that he couldn't see his son still, and that he really had to see me—and believe me, there was nothing for him to think that I would have met him after work, especially after those incidents that had happened, I couldn't understand why he wanted to see *me*.

"I remember him telling me that the house was empty, there was no heat, because the utilities had been turned off. He kept telling me, 'I'm so cold.' And I said, 'Bill, what have you taken?' Because of him talking about suicide—I thought maybe he'd already taken an overdose. And this was like the phone call for help. He said no, he had drank a fifth of something— he mentioned whatever it was but I don't remember—and he said the night before he had thrown his guts up. I could just picture him in that empty house all alone, cold and sick.

"He must've kept me on the phone about forty-five minutes, but I was afraid to hang up because Joe was gonna try and get in touch with his mother on another phone, to tell her where he was, what was happening, to please have somebody go get him. I was even going to call the suicide hotline—but then he just said, 'I have to go,' and he hung up."

"This was the week before the murder," Cliff is saying. "I went over there to pick 'em up that time they had the flu—they all had the flu, except the baby. And I said, 'If y'all want me to take ya to the doctor, get dressed.' She said, 'I wanna go and get well.'

"I said, 'Honey, you'll go to the doctor and he's gonna give you a shot, and you'll probably feel better, but this type of flu—you're not going to be well when you walk out of his office. It's gonna take a while.' I was trying to be as nice as I could about it—but, 'You mean you're telling me it's not going to do me any good? You just don't wanna be inconvenienced.'

"I said, 'I didn't say that.' Well, that set her off, I don't know why. And I had Marva's mother with me, she'd been going over there every day to help them with being sick and having the kids and all. Janet got real nasty with her, saying stuff like she hadn't asked for any help.

"So we left. She was throwing a tantrum, and you know Kerry, he's upset right back. And they're at it.

"A day or two later I asked Kerry to come by the house alone, that I needed to talk with him about something. And we were ready for him. It was little Cliff, Marva, and I, and we sat at this table and told him about the lies, and stuff. I said, 'Kerry, son, we've had enough of it. Her and her tantrums,' I said, 'and the lies.'

"Kerry defended her, Clifford—you know, he kept talking—and little Clifford said, 'Kerry, you're a damn demagogue.' Kerry said, 'I'm not.' He says, 'Yes you are. You've got one idea and one opinion—yours and nobody else. You don't want to hear anybody else's. We're not trying to tear you down. We're just trying to explain to you.' What the heck, even if the truth hurts sometimes, you don't have to lie about these little things, and make up all these excuses defending her."

"He still does that," Marva says.

Clifford continues, "Little Cliff told me, 'I admire him in one way, the way he defends his wife. But in another way, I feel sorry for him because he won't face the truth.' He said, 'He's gotta know it and he won't admit it.'

"I told Marva, I said, 'You know what, that seems to work two ways. If you're around somebody like that long enough, you're gonna start lying yourself.' I said, 'He's lying now to protect her. It's already starting.' "

"He couldn't explain it; he wouldn't admit it," Mike Price says. "You can't explain something that doesn't happen. And we talked. Believe me, I talked to him a lot of times about it. But you can't get past go if you say, 'Kerry, y'all gotta quit fighting,' and he says, 'What fighting? We don't fight. We've *never* fought.'

"He used to make excuses for her, you know, about, 'It's her mom's fault. Her mom's crazy. Her mom's this. Her mom's that.' That the two sisters 'are just barely on the fringe of humanity.'

"He always made those excuses—and *they* made those excuses, I mean, she was open about it, she'd always say that her mom made her like that. They would even rationalize out this whole scenario that they weren't really fighting, they were trying to 'get through these problems that her parents caused.' She was 'so fucked up because of her parents'—she verbalized that to me several times. And she'd say, 'But we weren't fighting. That wasn't fighting.' "

"The day of the christening," Cliff begins, "she said, 'I've got my family—I've got my boy and girl, the two kids.' She was as happy as could be, 'cause I even commented about her dress, I said, 'Girl, you got your figure back already?' And she said, 'You like the dress?' I said, 'Is that a new one?' She said, 'Yeah, my husband gave me that.' That was Sunday, and the following Thursday she was killed."

"It was after Sarah was born; she'd sent me a birth announcement, the last thing I received from her by mail," Hurst Bousegard says, recalling his last contact with Janet.

"Then she called me after the baby was born, but it was a few weeks after the baby was born, she talked about being excited that she was going back to dance class. In figuring it out with Joan later, I realized the phone conversation was two or three days before the murder.

"The conversation was bright and cheery. She was looking forward to dancing again. I asked her about her feelings of wanting to get out of the marriage, and she said, 'No. No, I was just emotional with the pregnancy and I wasn't involved with a lot of activities. *Inactivity makes me think too much'*—those were her exact words. She said everything was fine, now.

"*But*—I definitely got the feeling she wasn't telling me something."

"She called. She was thinking about going back to work and wanted to know if I had a place for Sarah," Tammy says, remembering her last conversation with Janet. "She was in a good mood. She was happy. She was ready to get back to work. She seemed fine."

"It was the week of the murder, either Monday or Tuesday," Peggy Cowan says, remembering the last time she saw Janet alive.

"She called me and told me things were rough, that she still suspected that Kerry was having an affair, that the situation at home was very rough. I went over there to visit her—which was a first, that's how desperate she seemed—and that's when she was telling me that his temper had gotten just unbelievable, how violent he was and things like that.

"There was something else she wanted to tell me, she alluded to it. But we were cut short on time. She didn't want Kerry to come home and see me. I didn't press her. I knew she would tell me next time. But there wasn't a next time."

*   *   *

February 23, 1984, the night they all went to play basketball, the night before Janet Myers was clubbed to death with a baseball bat, Mike Price remembers "picking 'em up at Kerry's house, Billy was happy, up, 'We're all getting together again, it's old times.'

"We went to the gym and we started playing, and we played thirty minutes, maybe forty-five minutes, and then Billy just walked off the court. He didn't say 'I quit,' he didn't say 'I'm tired,' he just walked off.

"In truth, I was very jealous that Billy had gone to Kerry's house—that he had decided to come out of hiding after all these months and that's where he ended up, at Kerry's instead of maybe coming to my house.

"And then a little later he said that somebody was supposed to pick him up, he was supposed to go do something. Chuck Cronin, he said.

"We kept playing basketball—I mean, it pissed me off that he wasn't playing, but I thought, 'Okay, fine. No big deal.' Then he started complaining about his back hurting. So we finished playing and we got in the truck. We were driving back home and stopped at a Time Saver to get something to drink. We all got out. I think it was me, Kerry, and I think just Billy in the truck—Curtis was in his car, and it was either three or four of us in the truck, but Kerry and Billy and I were definitely in it—and I said, 'Let's go in and get something to drink.'

"And Billy said, 'No.' 'What do you mean, no?' He said, 'No, I'm not getting out.' I said, 'Come on, Billy, we're just gonna sit around and shoot the shit.' And he said, 'No. I don't want to get out. I'm not getting out,' and he was just so insistent on it.

"When we got out they were talking about, 'Man, he's acting weird.' I said, 'I wouldn't joke about it.' I just felt like at that point he was so tightly strung, that there was so much heaped on him, so much stress, that he just wasn't able to handle it—I just knew in my heart that he wasn't going to be able to handle the pressure anymore, he was ready to snap.

"I said, 'That sucker's gonna kill somebody.' "

14
Murder

Circumstances and finances had it that the first 3 months of being married we lived with Momee & Popee Myers. It worked for awhile, but eventually it was feasable for dad and I to get our own apartment. We thought it was the best place on earth. We had one bedroom, kitchen, living room–dining room, study, and one bath. We lived there until I became pregnant for you.

We had our good and bad times there. Overall, we were happy. Financially, for awhile anyway, we did okay. Your dad got his job with Air-Dreco in September of 1979. I had a good job at Baker CAC. That is until the car accident; the one that turned our lives upside down. After that, I lost my job with Baker and it was difficult finding a job while under a doctor's constant care.

—Journal of Janet Cannon Myers

*   *   *

"From the minute that the phone call came to my house at five-something in the morning, whatever time it was that morning, until the funeral, I was in a daze." Mike Price is remembering that morning.

"I know Curtis and I went to the hospital first, the wives were all still gathering, but we just had to know. I remember going to the hopsital, I remember trying to hold Kerry's hand, but it was all bound up, and I remember telling him that I love him. I also remember the first words out of his mouth when he started telling us what happened:

" 'Billy must've went crazy. I came home at two o'clock and he attacked me.'

"Then, I know it was the same day, and there's a lot of people in the room and Kerry and Mr. Cliff are telling the story, mostly Cliff, and it's now four o'clock when Kerry came home. He never ever said two o'clock again.

I even remember about a week or so later, I asked him about it. He said, 'No, it was four o'clock, you must've just heard me wrong.' I said, 'Yeah, guess I did.' "

"The first phone call I got was my dad calling me. He said, 'Penny, I have some bad news.' I said, 'What?' And he said, 'Somebody broke into Kerry's house, they killed Janet, and Ryan's dying.' I said, 'A burglar broke in?' He said, 'Yes.' 'You mean somebody just broke in and killed Janet and Ryan? I mean, why? Why wouldn't they kill Kerry?' That was my first—why just Janet and Ryan? And my dad said, 'I don't know, but I'll call you when I hear something else.' I called work and told them I couldn't come in.

"Then three minutes later my dad calls back, and my husband was getting ready for work, and my dad said, 'Penny, it was Billy who broke into the house.' I said, 'Why did Billy break into the house?' My dad said, 'I don't know.' And then my mom hollered to him, 'It wasn't Billy that broke in, it was Billy that *killed Janet*.' So where she got that from— probably from Debbie, who got it from who knows."

" 'If she's dead, *he did it*.' " Monique Price is recalling her first words to Mike right after he'd hung up the phone the first time that morning and told her someone had broken into Janet and Kerry's house and that Janet was dead, before there had been any mention of "a friend" or any suspect on the newscasts.

"Mike, of course, wouldn't even *hear* of it. And he's not one to listen to anyone when he believes something. But then, he'd known these people most of his life. I'd only known them through Mike, perhaps I could be more objective than others—not that anyone listened, and not that I pushed too hard. I mean, when you hit a brick wall, you stop. Maybe you can go around it or over it with a big fight, but you can also slowly chip away at it without hammering away and ensuring resistance."

Monique had not completely held her tongue later that day as everyone gathered at the Jordans' house. At one point amid the rampant paranoia and panic over Billy's "rampage," Monique had looked at Mike and said, "You *know* Kerry did that."

"I used to try to talk to everybody about it. I used to ask them, 'Why would you choose to believe that instead of a husband—who everybody knows fought violently with his wife—that some friend that's back in town went over for a friendly visit and then suddenly just battered this woman to death, his other friend's wife? Why would you choose to believe that? I don't believe it, and you aren't going to get a jury of people in this land to buy this story.'

"Part of it was by the time they'd told and retold that story of him staring at Mike through the blinds, they had Billy out to be a lunatic,"

Monique continues. "His hair long, unshaven, living in an abandoned house for a year and capable of doing something like that—but that was *not* the Billy I knew. I've never even seen Billy yell at anybody. Even back during the ball-game days, when Mike was throwing bats and kicking dirt in umpires' faces and spitting and yelling and climbing over fences and the other guys would all be the most poor sports, Billy would get up there, you know, kind of cross himself before he took a bat, and just as quiet as anything if it was called against him or something. But the others would be lunatics out there, he was always quiet."

"The morning of the murder I was on a helicopter to Alexandria on another story," Logan Banks of Channel 6 and Nicholls State remembers.

"When I got back, I was listening to the news on WWL radio. There was a tease, 'Bizarre murder in Woodmere.' I knew they lived there, and I thought, 'Oh, no.' Then, 'Nahhh.' WWL went to a commercial and then came back and said, 'A Marrero housewife was killed in a bizarre case, Jefferson Parish sheriff's deputies say . . . was beaten to death,' and then they said the names and it was like *pow!*

"And the first thing that popped into my head was, 'Oh, no. He's gone over the edge and he's fucking killed her.' I said it out loud to myself. I was driving over the bridge."

"I'm so sorry. I'm so sorry. I know this can't be true," Susan Fontanille said on the phone that morning to her soon-to-be-ex-mother-in-law.

Later that same day, sitting out in the yard at the Fontanilles', Susan had told Miz Cissy, "I hope you understand how I feel—you don't just lose your feelings for a person so easily."

"I know what you mean—I understand. Just show your emotions. Don't be afraid to show them," Cissy Fontanille replied.

"He was arrested on my birthday, February 25, and I was thankful," Sydney Kornick is saying. "This was like no more than two weeks after he'd called from the empty house. Because I told my parents that I was petrified after it came out in the news. I know when I saw the TV that night, I thought, 'My God,' and then I started thinking about the last phone call. And the first thing that clicked in my mind was, 'He did it.'

"I remember I told my parents, 'You know the guy that I told you called me and everything? He was on TV, they have him in jail for murder, oh, my God.' "

"When I saw him he was sitting up talking just as calm as can be. Of course, by this time he has this whole entourage around him. They even catered in sandwiches to the hospital room." Monique is remembering how her lonely doubt was only amplified by the time she and some of the other wives had gotten to West Jefferson Hospital that Friday to see Kerry Myers.

"To begin with, we were told that he had a severe concussion, and was beaten badly; that he was in shock. Well, when I got to the hospital, that wasn't what I saw.

"He had some blood in his hair. And his arm was in a cast. He had a catheter in. But I remember thinking that this doesn't look so bad."

"We saw it on the news that Friday morning," Ernie Barrow says. "Of course, everybody started telephoning back and forth.

"Cliff called me. Said Kerry was in bad shape. He asked to come over and talk. So he came. He told me the whole horrible story. Then we made a couple of trips to the house. The second one was to get some things for Kerry, some clothes for the wake and funeral . . . which was surrealistic, it really was. First of all, I was shocked that they would open the casket. And I was really a little disturbed by the attitude about opening it. Not that I voiced any objections. It was just the way Cliff handled it . . . unusual. He was apologetic about it. He would bring it up and then he would apologize for it, then he would ask the questions, and then he would answer the questions . . . he went through all the gyrations. He went full circle.

"Kerry—was no emotion. Clifford did all of Kerry's talking for him, exactly: that's the first time I got the least inkling of suspicion, but I passed it off. I said, 'Nah, they're just upset, they're shook, and Clifford's this and Clifford's that.' "

"When they closed the casket," Marva begins, "and everybody is going through their own pain, Lorraine grabs Charlie, 'No, Charlie! Not here! Not here!' and she's hollering like this in the funeral home. They're bringing Charles to the room in the back and she's screaming, 'Janet, don't take him! Don't take him! Janet, don't take him!'

"They laid him down on the sofa. And she's leaning over Charlie yelling, 'Janet! Please don't take him! Janet! Please leave him here! Janet! Please don't take him!'

"I was embarrassed, I really was," Cliff says.

"I went into the room only so that nobody outside could see me," Marva admits.

"Me too."

"I mean, that was just too much," Marva continues. "My mother, she told it like it was—she said, 'Did you ever see anything so crazy in all your life as those people!' "

*   *   *

"At the wake, his dad followed him, his dad stuck by him, Kerry never spoke one word," remembers Peggy Cowan. "But his dad sure as hell talked. He spoke for him—he could tell you exactly what happened, blah-blah-blah, Kerry's mouth never moved. His dad knew—what Kerry had been through, what had happened. How the hell does he know? He wasn't there."

"Later, it all started feeding back on me," Ernie Barrow is remembering. "And when you go all the way back, you go back even to the discussions we'd had only hours after the murder—it was a three- or four-party discussion and Cliff is leading the way.

"About a week after Janet was killed, Cliff came over again, except this time he's with Kerry, and we sat down and we talked. And I would look at Cliff and wonder, 'Why in the hell's he doing this? Why doesn't he let Kerry say what happened?' "

" 'It's horrible, it's the most gruesome thing I've ever seen.' That's what the deputy said to headquarters on the phone when he used it."

Steve Faucheaux is remembering the first few minutes of the baseball bat murder case, when Deputy Chuck DeWilde knocked on the door asking if the police could use the Faucheaux's phone "to operate out of. He was extremely upset, very emotional."

"Then there was a lot of action," Gwen Faucheaux remembers. "Police coming and going. The baby Sarah. We also had a house guest, Father Jack, a priest, and I remember right after the officer first used the phone, and he said that, Steve turned to me and Father Jack and the first words out of his mouth were: 'He finally killed her.' "

"Here's the really strange part," Mr. Faucheaux, a pharmacist, says. "For three nights I did not sleep; I had to take sleeping pills for the first time in my life. But it was the only way I could go to sleep, because I'd close my eyes and there was a terrible turbulence in our room, and I mean turbulence."

"Our bedroom is right next to theirs and upstairs. We had the split-level model," Mrs. Faucheaux explains.

"So every day—we both work at West Jeff—we'd check on Ryan." Steve Faucheaux continues his strange story. "Then they put the shunt in and he started to improve, he was going to come out of it. From that moment on, *perfect peace.* Never had to take another pill. People say, 'Maybe you were just scared for what happened.' But it wasn't. It was something different. I felt something. Oh, yeah. I felt it. I felt an evil. Definitely. When I closed my eyes it was like a big tornado going around the room, like, shwoo-shwoo-shwoo-shwoo."

"He thinks it was Janet hanging around to make sure that Ryan was all right," Gwen Faucheaux offers, but not condescendingly.

"That's what I think, just personally," Steve says with no hesitation or embarrassment. "I mean, I have my own beliefs about it. But that's what I felt. And I had never experienced a spirit before, or a ghost or whatever you wanna call it, but *something* was going on in that room."

"Just looking at his eyes you could see he was looking right through us—he wasn't hearing what we were saying." Gary Guidry of Air-Dreco is remembering his first contact with Kerry after the murder, when both he and Jake Hahn went to the hospital that morning.

"He was all beat up and looked very distraught. He asked me, 'Did you hear anything about Billy?' I said, 'No. But I did hear he was involved.' I said, 'What happened?' He said, 'Man, I just don't remember.' I said, 'Well, what was the situation?' He said, 'All I know is I walked through the door and then I got hit in the head with a bat. From there my memory of everything is real fuzzy and my head still hurts. My skull's been fractured.'

"Mike and Curtis were there. They were scared. They talked about Billy coming after their wives. They seemed more concerned about themselves than they did Kerry.

"Kerry came back to work within three weeks," Gary Guidry continues. "I for one was encouraging him—'I don't want you back here too soon, but at the same time you really need to get back to work. You know, get your life going again.'

"Again, no rage. His demeanor was, 'Time to get back to work.' There was very little mention of what had happened.

"You'd think there would be *something* in his voice that would let you know that something tragic happened in his life. It wasn't there, it really wasn't," John Johnson says, recalling his first visit with Kerry shortly after the murder.

"What we were told by Cliff was just to get him in here, to get him out of the house, get him around people and get his mind on business, something analytical. And really, he just basically jumped back in. Business as usual."

Mark Francis remembers, ". . . I'm going, 'What's this guy doing here? This guy should take two months off, not two weeks!'"

"One day a group of people in our department went out to lunch," Sydney Kornick is saying. "They came back at one o'clock and told me they had seen Bill Fontanille across the street from the building, our building, walking up and down, like looking to see who was coming out for lunch.

"I was getting ready to go and I thought, 'Oh, my God, I'm not going outside.' I even called and told my mom and dad, and they lived in Mississippi. The only reason I felt afraid—he had never threatened me—

was because I had received that other phone call, and you know, 'Why me?' I kept saying . . . 'Why me?'

"Later that afternoon, maybe three-thirty, four o'clock—now this is maybe three weeks or four weeks after the suicidal phone call, so he must've just gotten out on bail—the phone rang and it was Bill. I remember my blood just ran cold. He said, 'I want you to know I didn't do it.'

"I said, 'Bill, they put you in jail.'

"He said, 'Kerry did it.' I mean, he went through the whole story. He told me that he was having an affair with this woman. He said, 'Syd, Kerry found out and was waiting there for me.' He said, 'I was able to tell the police about a scar she had that unless you were intimate with her, you wouldn't've known.'

"He said that he was over there to get his baseball bat and 'to end it with her.' So if it was a one-night stand, he wouldn't have had to go over there and say, 'Hey, it's over with.' My definite impression from the story was that it was an affair; and he told me that Kerry had beaten Janet before.

"I wanted to believe him. I said, 'Well, Bill, I have a question to ask you. Some people saw you today . . . ?' He said, 'Yes, I was downstairs waiting for you to come out at lunch. I wanted to see you.' He didn't want me to think he was a murderer, that's how it came off to me."

"We pretty much stood behind him as a group," Gary Guidry is saying. "There were quite a few people who didn't, but the majority of the people said, 'Boy, what a horrible thing to happen to somebody.' We wanted to believe. I wanted to believe that Kerry was not involved."

"My wife was deathly afraid of Kerry; she kind of had an inkling that way from the beginning," Mark Francis remembers. "She said she didn't like the way Kerry looked at her after the murder.

"From the very beginning, almost pretty much through the office, if you'd gone through and asked all our wives, I'd bet ninety percent of them would say, 'He had something to do with it.' Or 'He did it.' Whereas it was just the opposite with the guys; probably almost a hundred percent 'No way.' "

"I always felt it was something they did together, Kerry and Fontanille," Sammy Pessin says. "Just a personal thought."

Mr. Pessin joined Air-Dreco as an outside salesman a month after Janet's murder. In his early days of learning the product line and the nature of the business, he rode with Kerry.

"I made a couple of trips on the road with him—to Morgan City. In Kerry's car. When we'd get back I'd tell the other guys that as we'd be traveling down the road, you know, looking over my shoulder at this guy and wondering if he's gonna pull onto the side of the road and do me in or whatever. You know, I was with the guy alone and I didn't trust him," Sammy Pessin says.

"He never went into detail about the case. Just one time he came out and said on the drive, 'If I ever see him, I'm gonna kill him.' I hadn't brought it up. I didn't know how he would react. Nobody ever really openly talked to him about it. So he just brought that statement up out of the blue. But it wasn't anger, it was just a statement . . . to try and cover himself; that he knew I was wondering."

"It was more so after Janet's death. I mean, we were very close friends before," Mike Price is saying, "and he's one of the five or six guys that I would call my best friends. . . . You see, part of the social dynamics the group had was me defending everybody. If anybody got into a fight or a jam, I jumped in and we stomped on to victory—the knee-jerk reaction from me was 'I'm gonna jump in and take care of it.' And I did. I mean, I took care of it.

"Kerry was so shattered initially by the whole thing, to me the fight in the house wasn't over; until he's better, I'm *gonna be there*—it's me against Billy and them with Kerry behind me."

15
Reinvestigation

In October of 1980 we tried to buy a house in Terrytown. It fell through because of the car accident. That devastated dad and me. But, on November 4th, 1980, we found out we were going to have you and things got brighter. . . . On the day of your Christening, we realized we needed more room. Your Christening party had everyone jammed. . . .

Your dad, through alot of looking and calling found us a house to rent. Money was still tight and getting tighter. Utilities were high, rents were high; there were bills. Sometimes I'd cry because I'd wonder how we would literally make it through the months. I still cry.

—Journal of Janet Cannon Myers

*   *   *

As preoccupied as W. J. LeBlanc had been with the procedural bogeyman of prescription, he nonetheless found the time and the inclination to place two phone calls early on in those frenetic weeks. They were, regardless of the personal motivation for each, absolutely strategic.

The first was to Rosemarie Kerr, of Harmony Grove, California, an entirely enchanted community nestled in the most beguiling little valley among the hills right outside Escondido.

Since that phone conversation was recorded, we know that in the main, upon the matter of the murder of Janet Myers, it went like this:

"Rose. You know that big case you said I was gonna get this year?" W.J. said.

"You got it," Mrs. Kerr answered.

"Yeah, how'd'ya know?" went W.J.

"I'm psychic," and then the full, jolly laugh from Rose.

"Right," laughed Dub back.

"So?" Rose asked.

"It's a *very* interesting case. I was wondering if you'd like to—I've got pictures of the three people who . . ."

"Stop! And yes. But you know how it works. No names. No details. Nothing. Okay?"

"I know the routine, Rose. . . ."

Of the second phone call, it can be said with certainty that there was nothing familiar or jocular about it, much less remotely pleasant; it was, in fact, very painful on both ends of the line. The call was to Lorraine Cannon.

"I called her, number one, as a courtesy; I certainly didn't need her to testify or anything." W.J. is remembering his first contact with the victim's family. His voice is somber, and his manner uncharacteristically humble.

"And I called her because this had to be unbelievably intense for her to have to go through. So I'm also trying to feel the Cannons out, trying to see what they're saying and where they're coming from. Their position is well known; I'd been told not to expect any cooperation out of the victim's family at all. It is just a sad and another bizarre but known fact that the family has closed ranks around Kerry.

"But I'm just trying to see where they are now, whether I feel there are any cracks in the armor. It's obvious that they were either ignorant of or chose to ignore the marital violence."

W.J. introduced himself and told her that he would keep her informed as to court dates.

"She said, 'I really appreciate that,' " W.J. continues. "I said, 'That's no problem at all. I don't want you picking up the newspaper and finding out that the trial's on. When there's a date set, I will call you.'

"Then I told her I really would like to meet with her, and talk with her and her husband about the case. She said she didn't know. That she had to check with her husband. I said that's fine, and told her I'd be calling back.

"She said she wanted to be able to sit in on the trial. That was her big question. I said that as far as I was concerned, she could. But that I couldn't promise that she wouldn't be subpoenaed by another party, and if that happened, I'd have no control over it. Then she wanted to know if that happened, would she be able to get a copy of the transcript. I said contact us after the trial. There would be copies because of the appeals process.

"Then she said, 'You just don't understand what it's like not knowing.' And you could just feel the sadness and the grief pour out of the telephone. You could just feel it. And this was six years later. I was very, very sensitive to that. There was no anger. Not anger at all, in no way.

"She said, 'The terrible things are just not knowing and never having it end.'

"That's when I said, 'I will make you two promises. One, it is going to end; and two, your daughter's killer is gonna be punished. That I can promise you.'

"She didn't say anything back. I said, 'Look, please talk to your husband and I'll get back to you.'

"Then she told me something that I feel is still very strange, she said, 'If I thought that the father of my grandchildren had done this to my daughter, I don't know what I'd do. I really couldn't cope with the thought that he had done this. I don't think my mind could stand it. I *cannot* comprehend it.' "

"The two biggest problems we had to overcome from the start were"— Dub is now leaning back at his desk, the usual snap and animation having returned—"one, *putting the bat in Billy's hands;* two, *negating the 'happy marriage' syndrome.*

"Wiley's fond of telling everyone that his client's innocent. That they had a happy marriage. It was the perfect life—that's always the thing with Wiley. Every chance he gets, 'This beautiful family that this murderer destroyed.' That's obviously going to be their defense. And we need to find the smoking gun to indicate that there was in fact true domestic trouble.

"And of course we're facing a conspiracy of silence from the Myerses and Cannons' camp, steadfast to a person that they were volatile in the past, but everything's fine after Ryan—*nobody's* willing to come forward to dispute that.

"That's the big thing they're hanging their hats on. They're gonna parade a zillion people up there to say what a great marriage they had after a rocky start. After Ryan was born. So there's no motive. According to them, no motive for the killing.

"Yet I know it had to be a battered-wife deal. Had to be. Based on the fact that I was sold from day one on the conspiracy, and in this conspiracy, what is Kerry Myers's motive for eliminating his wife? It's not money. It's *got* to be misery. So if there's misery, there's gotta be evidence of misery out there somewhere.

"With Bill it was a whole different deal. We've got a real big problem with motive. But to me the ultimate thing is, we *know* Bill is lying about *something.* So, 'Hey—what reason did he have to lie unless he's guilty, unless he's *involved?'*

"But it's not enough to just prove that they are lying—especially in Fontanille's case. Because it's like, 'Yeah, he was in the wrong place at the wrong time, he was scared, he panicked, he lied . . . does that mean he's guilty of murder and can go to prison for the rest of his life because he was scared and he lied?' No. So that he's a liar is not all we have to prove. It goes a long way. But is it enough?

"There are now plenty folks who say no, it's not. That it was goofy to even try Bill the first time. But it isn't crazy to try Bill Fontanille—it's crazy to try Bill Fontanille *with Kerry Myers as your star witness*. And that's the difference.

"And that's also the problem. Why does Bill Fontanille want Janet Myers dead? Much less where does Bill get all this *rage* to kill Janet that way?"

There was a third rather consequential conversation W. J. LeBlanc had early on. But it was in person right there at the courthouse, with Richard Boyd, from *The Times-Picayune*.

Upon hearing that W.J. had gotten the case, during an idle moment between docket motions, Richard suddenly said, "You know, I'll never forget, during the first trial, there was one of the cameramen with one of the news stations and he said that Kerry Myers was running a 'fuck club' out of a trailer at Nicholls State and Janet was involved in it."

"You gotta be kidding me," Dub said.

"No. No, I'm telling ya true."

Consequently, as W.J. explains, "The day I get Vince, I put him on it. Because I really feel it's a strong lead."

"The first thing I do after reading the complete file—again—is get into the Richard Boyd information," Vincent Lamia remembers.

"The name of the game is to win the case and present something to the jury that they can grasp onto, that they can say, 'Yeah, that makes sense.' That may not have been what happened, and yet it makes sense, 'Yeah, I can buy that.'

"And that's what I feel we have to do to win the case. And there are some things that we feel Eason has a problem with. One is he doesn't believe that these two guys in that short amount of time, in that three-day period, would've developed this plan—what would've been the motive for that? Now, if we could prove that they had met prior to that, that there was an ongoing relationship during this time, well then that would go against what they say. And that would make it more palatable for the judge. We could say, 'Look, judge, you've got a problem with this, hey, they did meet.' "

On the second and third pages of the school-size notebook Vincent Lamia will use throughout his reinvestigation of the baseball bat murder, there are two lists:

Why Fontanille committed the murder

1. Font. enters life and two days later Janet is dead! (lacks symmetry)
2. Font. goes to Janet's house for baseball bat! (sex)
3. Font. parks car 2/10 mil. from residence (concealment)
4. If Kerry's home, Font. wouldn't have gone in residence.

5. If Kerry killed Janet, why let Font. in?
6. If Kerry wanted to kill Font. why not use the shotgun?
7. Why would Kerry kill his wife in that fashion & endanger kids?
8. Janet killed w/bat Font. allegedly goes to the residence to retrieve.
9. Dresser drawers pilfered.
10. Myers children placed in rooms other than their own.
11. Blood transfer & spatter.
12. Font. changes story to meet circumstances.

Why Myers committed the murder

1. Lack of Myers blood in den area?
2. Myers ink pen neat on table?
3. Myers came home in part to pump up low tire with "foot pump"?
4. Transcript & 911 tape—Bullshit?
5. Incoming call while on phone w/911
6. Arrangements w/friends to find body?
7. Prior history of violence w/vic.?
8. "Sex club"
9. Myers keys across the den.

"It was very obvious to me that no one had ever read through every one of the grand jury transcripts," W.J. explains.

"While Vince is running down the sex club and other leads, I'm poring over every scrap of grand jury testimony, looking for inconsistencies, things that were maybe overlooked.

"But I'm also focusing on the 911 tape, because I feel that is very important. It was obvious, after I'd listened to it several times—the forced hyperventilation. Real excited, then very calm. The slowing down to give directions I thought was unbelievable, it's almost a normal conversational tone.

"And the sequence is interesting: he starts off with, 'Somebody broke into my house and tried to kill me.' And then it's 'I know the man.' And then finally it's 'His name is Bill Fontanille.' The really interesting part of that is he doesn't say his name until he quote 'discovers' the body. And then he comes back on the phone and says it's Bill Fontanille.

"I don't know if that was by design or whatever, but I think that's a point in his favor, I find that's almost like, 'Hey, he really has just discovered the body.' And this is when it's like, 'Oh, he lied to me, that son of a bitch, so I'm spilling the beans on him.' So I don't know whether that was by design or not. It's not something I'm spending a lot of time worrying over, because I don't think anyone's gonna pick up on it. But I find it incredibly interesting. If you look at it from the standpoint that Kerry is telling the truth, that would've been just the way it would've happened.

"The other thing that is mind-boggling to me is the thirty seconds he's away from the phone when he goes to get the shotgun, and you know the smallness and the closeness of everything in the house—what the fuck is he doing for thirty seconds? You could run around the house ten times in thirty seconds! Remember his taped statement, his testimony, 'All I kept asking him was to let me check on my wife, let me check on the kids.' It's incredible enough to think that you're gonna close and lock your door and not go check on your wife who you've heard moaning. But your kids? You've got a six-week-old who hasn't been cared for in ten hours or a two-and-a-half-year-old who you know that's just been foot-tapping on the door—you've *got* to go check on those kids at that point; if not, there's something very wrong there.

"And then you put down that phone and you're gone that long—you can't tell me you're not going to go check on *somebody*. That was another real big problem.

"His saying 'Yes, I need an ambulance' in answer to 'Do you or your *wife* need an ambulance.' A full minute later he puts down the phone and *still* doesn't check on his wife.

"So ultimately, the 911 tape is one of *the* most damaging pieces of evidence against Kerry Myers. But there are a lot of people who believe it if they don't know the facts and sequence.

"And that call-waiting at one forty-five A.M. A coincidence? Could be. But how many times has your phone rang at that time on a crank call during the past year? Or two years? Coincidental? Yes. But *highly* coincidental.

"I think it was a confirmation call. Remember the last thing they did was fight. Bill's calling back to find out what is still the operative story? 'We can still pull this off' kinda thing."

"I'm *very* worried about Vieira and the processing of the scene, the fact that you only had six blood samples," W.J. is saying.

"It's the first disagreement Howie and I have. He wants to concede the shoddy investigation. And I don't. If we start backing up, there would be no stopping it. His theory is, 'Even though the police didn't do a bang-up job, there's *still* more than enough here to convict.' Not that it was really botched, just that they didn't do the best job possible.

"And really it's a subtle distinction. But I want to say, 'Look, anybody can play Monday-morning quarterback and say ya shoulda done this and ya shoulda done that. But based upon what he had at the time, what he did was proper.' But I'm still *absolutely* concerned. That's something I obviously have to address with Dr. Lee.

"I'm also at this time making my notes on Vieira's testimony from the first trial, looking for problem areas with his testimony that we can work with him on the next time around.

"Carol Dixon? I think my note on her testimony pretty well sums up what I'm thinking: 'Carol Dixon, hope we don't need this woman.' "

On November 13, Vince spoke with Richard Boyd and noted that the journalist remembered the conversation as having been with "a cameraman" who "had been a student at Nicholls State," with the gist being that "Kerry Myers . . . ran a 'Fuck Club' w/Janet & other co-eds" and that he "ran it out of a trailer in the woods"; that it was "supposedly pretty common knowledge & cards were printed & distributed."

It isn't until November 20, however, that Vince's calling of all the local TV stations pays off with a lead on who this "cameraman" might be. Mr. Philip Nye, station manager at WVUE-TV Channel 8, the ABC affiliate, suggests that it might be Ray Roy, who no longer works at the station, but is still in television, he just doesn't know where.

On November 21, Vince, with information obtained from Records and Identification, is able to contact Mr. Roy's mother locally, and learns that he's employed at Channel 13 in Tampa, Florida, but is currently on vacation in Key West through Sunday, November 26.

On the afternoon of November 21, Vince went to 725 Fielding in Terrytown, the last known address of Chuck Cronin. Finding no one home and the house up for sale, Vince subsequently entered into his notebook what he learned from a neighbor: that Cronin's mother, a widow, was probably in Atlanta visiting one of her two children and that Chuck had not been seen in the neighborhood "for couple of years."

The next afternoon, the computers at Records and Identification delivered, and Vince noted the following, in part:

Charles M. Cronin (AKA: Charlie), w/m DOB 7-17-58 *Born in Georgia* 6'0 - 180 lbs.—Bro/Blue (1916 Springcreek Ln., Dunwoody, Ga.) private tele. #

Hitting that obstacle, Vincent called the DeKalb County Sheriff's Office in Georgia and spoke with "Invest. Cohen" regarding access to the unlisted Cronin phone number. Not long thereafter, Cohen called back to say that the request to the phone company "was refused."

Vince then speaks with "Capt. Durks of the patrol division [who] will make dispo. check & have Cronin call collect (2:45 P.M. request made)."

Later that afternoon, back in his office at the Detective Bureau, Vince called Special Agent Judd Ray, FBI Behavorial Science Unit, Quantico, Virginia. Agent Ray informed his friend that he would be in New Orleans the following week and would be only too happy to meet "to discuss the case. He will call upon his arrival to set date."

* * *

In the evening of November 22, when Vince joined W.J. and Mike in the Fontanille-Myers command room for the daily debriefing and yet another round of the scenario game, and told Dub of his continuing difficulty in locating Cronin, W.J. was disappointed and a little frustrated. He still had nothing of any presentable evidentiary value toward his two principal objectives: "Knock *recent* holes in the 'Happy Marriage' "; and "putting the bat in Billy's hand."

"This is why Chuck Cronin is so important," W.J. begins to explain. "One of the problems the State has always had is him testifying at the first trial that Bill tells him he's going over to Janet's house the day of the murder. You don't have a plan to kill somebody and then go place yourself at the house. Actually, on Bill, this is probably the biggest problem we've got. It was a big part of their defense in '86; do you tell somebody openly, 'Hey, I'm going over to Janet's to break off this affair I feel so bad about'—in front of Chuck, his mother, and sister, he's happy go-lucky—and then brutally murders her? It doesn't make any sense. Right?

"However"—Dub bounces and grins as he brandishes a yellow legal pad—"that *ain't exactly* what Chuck Cronin told the first grand jury!"

Indeed, in Mr. Cronin's grand jury testimony of March 19, 1984, he said that Fontanille told Cronin that Janet "called *him* up to come over that Wednesday! That she was throwing herself over him!

"That's markedly different, major discrepancy," W.J. assures. "If someone had read the grand jury testimony, he could've put the fear of God into Cronin on the stand.

"Since Bill's the odd man out when it comes to motivation, particularly this rage kind of killing, if we can prove he's lying about these rather significant details, then we go a long way towards proving he's in it.

"We've also got to establish circumstantially that he was very unstable and was capable of doing almost anything at that time—whether it's totally against his nature or not. The weirder I can make Bill Fontanille appear to a jury the better.

"For Kerry, I need concrete evidence of recent domestic problems. I don't need that much of it, because I think there's a very fine line between domestic violence which is just verbal abuse, and taking it to the next level, just crossing over that line to the physical abuse, which might be a slap, an isolated slap. Then I think it's a very fine line going from a slap to a punch. And I think there's a very fine line going from something like that to a really brutal beating. Just like with child abuse. It's the same thing. It's an escalation. And you can show that to a jury. They can relate to that and make the logical assumptions.

"But even with as volatile a relationship as they had at the beginning— the Nicholls State days—there isn't anybody willing to go on the record to talk about any problems of violence in the marriage—especially recently.

"We have the 'bowling ball crashing sound' comment from the neighbor in the grand jury, but nothing real recent. Everything else we've got is very old. Putting her out on the interstate, that was 1978; the broken glass door on the trailer, same thing; the Zee Medical, 1980; and the Halloween party, before Ryan was born, and everybody says everything got better after Ryan was born.

"So, unh-unh. Need something recent to the murder, and it's gotta be out there where Vince is working, or in that stack of boxes I'm digging through."

On the Monday morning of November 27, early, Vince Lamia tooled his unit west on old Highway 90 toward Raceland and then wound his way up Bayou La Fourche to Thibodaux and Nicholls State University, where he began his first visit on campus with Mr. Dale Guillot, head of security, who remembered "a 'prostitute' ring at about time he took over as head (1979.)" Other than that the ring "worked out of a trailer," Chief Guillot could not "provide specifics."

Vince made the drive back to Gretna and the courthouse with some excitement for the evening debriefing with Dub and Mike.

After another frustrating and tedious day of rummaging and reading, W. J. LeBlanc was also excited about the "first hot lead in the case in years."

"Finding the 'fuck club' would be important because, in a sense, that would tie in the conspiracy," Dub explains. "It's a very important issue, to me. In my mind, it's like if we can establish this kinky sex angle then Billy is *in.*

"Also, I want to check the time of the 911 call for maybe a delay by Myers in calling the police. I put Mike on it, trying to locate that Communications Center time card, or some record of it somewhere," W.J. says.

"From his earliest statements, Bill had always said he thought he'd left the house around one-fifteen. He only went with the later time based on DeWilde's report and the testimony of Mrs. Rilette who said her clock had it at one forty-five when she saw the man running down the street.

"But, with all the other factors, it really is questionable that Bill could've gotten to his car, gotten out of Woodmere, stopped somewhere to make that call-waiting call, go by his mom's, and been taken to the hospital in less than twenty-five minutes.

"Man, if we could show a jury that Kerry was alone in that house for any length of time after Bill left, he's a cinch principal to murder: what's he doing in there, washing up? We got the water patterns on his shirt. Is that when he ransacks the bedroom to make it look like a burglary? Is that when he gets those clothes on top of his—in his mind—'already dead son'? Is that when he 'doesn't see' his dead wife?

"You get that idea firmly planted in a jury's mind, ah, look, Kerry's a gone pecan."

* * *

"There it is!" W. J. LeBlanc says with exuberance—wielding a yellow legal pad.

"I'm reading through the grand jury and I hit upon Peggy Cowan! There's the *recent evidence.*"

On the legal pad, under the note heading "Grand Jury, July 27, 1984, Peggy Cowan," W.J. had noted more than enough ammunition to sink the "Myerses' love boat."

"Right *there* in the grand jury!" Dub is still animated, but he's no longer pointing at the Peggy Cowan entry.

On the same afternoon, noted on the same page of his yellow pad, separated by two other witnesses in order up from Peggy Cowan, W.J. found the second of the four true bombshells he would eventually have in his arsenal when he brought Bill Fontanille and Kerry Myers together before triers-of-fact: it was contained within the testimony of none other than Charles Cannon, the father of Janet, and quite arguably Kerry Myers's most dug-in zealot.

On Tuesday morning, November 28, Vince Lamia spoke with Captain Mike Elsinor of the Terrebonne Parish Sheriff's Office and noted the following:

—does not recall anything relative to sex club or prostitution ring in trailer.

—did advise that Taylor's Trailer Park goes "way back" in the woods.

—will check w/Sheriff Larpenter & get back if info. available.

At ten-thirty that morning, Vince called Ray Roy at his residence in Tampa and left a message on the recorder. He also called WVTV Channel 13 and left a message for Mr. Roy to call collect, which he did only shortly thereafter. Unfortunately, other than remembering being at Nicholls with Kerry and Janet and that she was "a looker," mentioning the other New Orleans media people Vince should contact, and his opinion that the whole thing could've been just "initiation rights involving prostitution with fraternities," but that in no case had the comments been made by him, Mr. Roy was a dry hole regarding the "fuck club."

Later that afternoon, Vince received a call from Investigator Cohen of the DeKalb County Sheriff's Office, who, as the result of a subpoena, was able to give him the unlisted phone number of a Sandra E. Cronin of Fulton County, Georgia. Subsequent calls to that number over the course of the day, however, went unanswered.

On Wednesday morning, November 28, Vince Lamia met with FBI Special Agent Judd Ray. Right from the start, without giving any of the details, Vince slid across the table to Agent Ray crime scene photographs of the horribly, but precisely, bludgeoned Janet Myers and asked:

"What kind of a killer do we have here? What's the profile?"

Agent Ray studied the several photos briefly before answering with conviction: "Organized personality, homosexual or deviant sexual activity."

"All right," Vince asked. "Now, what about if I tell you there are two and *only* two possible perps, both guys?"

Agent Ray immediately slid the photos back and said, "Then all bets are off."

"I never approached the State for a deal on manslaughter." Nick Noriea is answering a question which many have wondered about yet never asked. "Because the only time even a hint of it was raised with Paul Connick, I was told, 'Your man's the *bat man*.' Also, when I made my offer to Mamoulides to help 'em prosecute Kerry, his words and attitude were also colored by 'Bill's the bat man.' All of this gave me the assumption that there was nothing there for Bill, so don't even bring it up."

At a time when it seemed the reinvestigation was chasing puffs of smoke, a sure bird-in-hand was also worrying W.J. no end.

"Peggy Cowan's a very important witness; obviously, at this point, besides Dr. Lee, she's the most important witness. *But,* she doesn't wanna talk; when I call her on the telephone, she's very, very reluctant. Seems her family is still close, if not supportive, to the Cannon family; some of the family still lives next door to relatives. Plus she says two of her brothers are on the police force and she thinks it might be a problem for them. Basically, she's scared and doesn't want to get openly involved. And, under the circumstances, one can't really blame her. *But I've gotta have her.*

"So I ask Vince to check out who her brothers are. He finds out she's Danny Carr's sister. I know Dan, hell, we went to St. Joseph's catechism together. Went to Gretna Two together. So I call him and tell him what it is, 'Look, you need to talk to her, you need to tell her that I'm straight and I'm not going to do anything to hurt her, but I've *got* to talk to her and she very well may have to testify. Like it or not.'

"He understood."

On Wednesday, November 29, Vince interviewed Margaret Dubisson at Channel 8 TV and Logan Banks at Channel 6. While he learned more than he thought he needed to know about the sordid sojourn of Janet Cannon, Gary Landry, and Kerry Myers at Nicholls State, both interviews tapped up as more dry holes in the search for the "fuck club."

* * *

On Monday, December 4, Vince called the number of Sandra Cronin in Dunwoody, Georgia. "Spoke to Sandy Cronin (sister of Chuck Cronin) who advised that her brother left approx. 3 weeks ago for job in North Carolina. Hasn't been heard from since, but he should be in town soon." Vince gave her his office and home phone numbers and asked her to have Chuck call him collect.

The following morning, Vince drove to Baton Rouge and pulled up a photo of Ray Roy from the files of the Department of Motor Vehicles.

He then immediately turned around and made the eighty-mile drive back to Gretna and met with *Times-Picayune* reporter Richard Boyd at the paper's West Bank office. Richard couldn't make a positive identification, but the veteran crime reporter did feel that Roy was probably the person who made the allegation.

Vince then drove to the house of Tammy DuBuc, the author of a lengthy, well-informed, well-reasoned letter the District Attorney's Office had received containing strong circumstantial elements which tend to support Bill's version of events over Kerry's.

During Vince's visit with the so guileless, so decent, and beautiful wife of Clyde DuBuc, a lifetime member of the Bill Fontanille circle, he filled three pages with notes.

Not a single story of the many Vince heard and noted that afternoon will ever be shown to be loose gossip; not a single fact will ever turn out to be groundless: as a social historian of the interlocking circles of the baseball bat murder, Tammy is peerless, even if her objectivity is occasionally at question. When Vince finally left the DuBuc home, he knew a great deal about the personalities, backgrounds, and relationships within the rippling parameters of the Fontanille-Myers case.

However, while there were some real investigatory nuggets Vince will take with him, there was absolutely nothing of the "recent, smoking gun" variety for W.J. to present to a jury.

It was in that first week of December 1989 that W. J. LeBlanc made perhaps the most momentous decision in the history of the baseball bat murder. Based upon a series of phone conversations with Rosemarie Kerr, Dub decided her physical presence in Jefferson Parish was required.

However, as Dub says, "I *don't* like to be laughed at. So this boy ain't goin' to the boss saying we need expense money to bring in a psychic!"

This is true even though Dub's rationale concerning the use of the paranormal in criminal investigations is fairly well planted in its pragmatism.

"She's an investigative tool. The way I look at it, whether you believe in it or not, whether you're religious or not, you'd be stupid not to take advantage of something that could provide you with some insight in solving a crime. Particularly when I know she has done it in the past.

"You treat it like an anonymous informant. You can't put an anonymous informant on the stand, because you don't even know where the hell this anonymous informant gets the information. But what you do is you look at the information the informant gives you and you decide whether or not it's valid and how to follow up on that investigatively. So why not?"

Indeed. Now all he had to do is persuade the other members of the prosecution team to all chip in and pay her way there plus room and board—Rosemarie accepts no fees for forensic work.

While Howie was more than a little skeptical of the whole idea, he *was* needful of some help on the monolithic Estrade case. Therefore, without too much resistance, Howat Peters signed on at least intellectually and financially, with Mike and Vince never being any doubt.

The date is set for her to arrive the second weekend in December, with work scheduled to start Monday morning, December 11, 1989.

It turned out that Danny Carr's intercession with his sister Peggy on W.J.'s behest was only moderately successful.

"I follow up with a phone call a little while later," Dub remembers. "And then go over to see her and she's very apprehensive. She clearly *does not* want to get involved in the worst way, but will in fact do her duty when the time comes.

"I'm already thinking trial strategy: I'm thinking maybe I'll give an unhappy marriage as the motive during my opening statement. Now, I don't have to prove motive, okay? So I don't have to put on any testimony about motive if I don't want to, because that is not an essential element of the crime.

"*But* what if I supply them a motive and watch the grin on Wiley Beevers's face as I say it and then let him parade one family member after another up on the witness stand to talk about this happy marriage, 'Especially since Ryan was born. Yes, there were rocky times early on but then everything couldn't have been better.' *Then* I put Peggy Cowan on the stand in rebuttal. And, really, with one witness, take *out* his defense."

". . . again I'm coming to the back of the head area strong on her."

The voice is fast, and familiar, even though it's not; the accent is Brooklyn, the cadence is second-generation Italian-American tempered by some two decades of living in linguistically quirky Southern California, the resonance and authority is middle-aged: it is the voice of Rosemarie Kerr as she recorded her very first impressions of the contents of the package she received from W. J. LeBlanc at the end of October.

"Now let me go to . . . Kerry . . . who I haven't read yet." There is the sound of paper against paper as Mrs. Kerr removes the last of the three photographs from the envelope and then there is the unusual yet unmistakable sound of fingertips being rubbed rapidly, repeatedly upon slick paper.

"Okay, now I'm working on . . . Kerry—*he could tell a lie so convincingly!* He's got it down pat. He could look you right in the eye and lie, no problem. *Cold,* very cold. Very cold-blooded.

"Okay, it's like I'm seeing him put things in a bag, a plastic bag or sack, to remove them so that nobody can see them. For some reason one of these articles looks like it's either a purse or a folder that would look like a purse, but the color changed from green to brown. He either destroyed them or hid them but I see him being very stealthy about it, getting rid of it.

"Something is hidden! I want to find out what! Spirits see a black bag with bones in it which is symbolism for something missing." The exasperation is real, common, someone who's lost something important just as she's ready to walk out the door.

"Did anyone notice in the house if there were any pornographic books around? I don't know why this keeps coming into it, but, pornography. It's the first thing I picked up on the other fellow, too. It's all around them. Something pornographic: photographs, books, films."

Then, all in a rapid, tumbling, twisting flow: "Was Kerry having other problems—does anybody know if he was having problems at work, too? Again, I'm trying to go backwards in time and pick it up—because he's so confident that nothing's gonna happen: 'There's no way you can pin this on me.' I find other females around him than his wife. I don't know if anybody has established in his background—I'm finding it *not pure.*

"I don't know why I keep seeing a paycheck around him, or a pay stub around him either. Around the time of the tragedy. You'll want to find out if Kerry was having financial problems.

"And again—I don't know why this comes in again now—I'm on his picture but I feel broken female fingernails.

"And I have no idea why I'm seeing a pair of men's brown shoes but I have to give you that, too. And the other thing, were there any bloody rags that you found? And if you didn't, why not?

"We find the husband with the knife—we find the knife in the other man's hand, too, but we find it in the husband's also. So it could've changed hands or it could've been that the other one was trying to fend him off. We don't find the knife in the wife's hand, and if her prints are on it, they were put there.

"On her death . . . I feel suffocation—breathing injuries?

"Boy, I've got between the husband and William a lot of the same makeup—so, if you saw them you'd think one was more subdued than the other but I don't, I find an anger around each of them. And I find that they both feel the world owes them a living, or they're missing out on something, in other words, crybabies.

"Don't overlook the possibility maybe they had a mutual girlfriend someplace. The other man's wife, would the color of her hair be light brown to blond? Because I keep picking up somebody like that.

"Neither one of them should be walking free—and *I want to know what happened to a square purse of hers*, could've been brown or green in color. A square purse, I have no idea why spirit keeps showing it to me—put in a black bag; either discarded or hidden.

"A lot of the evidence is not there."

"Today is December 11th, 1989, Gretna, Louisiana."

It is the same voice, but on a different tape recorder, and Rosemarie Kerr's rapt audience now sits around her as she first starts with a Catholic prayer and then, for official purposes, the date and location of the "reading." With her in the small office which is the command center for Fontanille-Myers a little after midday of a Monday are W. J. LeBlanc, Vincent Lamia, and Mike Maunoir.

"This woman was *scared* during her life, so she had—she had fears around her. She probably did not voice them out but she did—she had a lot of fears around her. Now—give me her name again?"

"Janet," W.J. offers very quietly.

"She also had a lot of anger inside of her and a lot of problems in her life—also I don't know if there'd be anyplace you can establish it at any time, because I'm picking up something around her, it could've been before or after the murder—problems with her hand . . . I'm picking up around her that she did suffer grief at her husband's hands at different times in the marriage—does she have a mother or father or somebody close to her?"

"Yes." It seems at this point only W.J. has the temerity to speak, and he isn't all that rambunctious about it.

"Is her mother angry with anyone? Okay, that's a rough road, question, but what I'm picking up—I'm picking up her mother's vibrations for some reason."

"She's not pleased with the DA's Office," Dub says.

"Okay, so that's the angle. Thank you." The thank you is not for Dub. "She's resentful—she's sarcastic and angry.

"I keep feeling suffocation—again, we're going to the throat area—suffocation around her. Questions? Whatever you want to ask."

"Hand me the schematic." W.J. looks to Vince. When Vince wordlessly hands it over, Dub gives a copy of the prepared drawing of the Myerses' house to Rosemarie and then asks the first question of what must certainly rank as one of the more unusual interviews to ever take place within that courthouse. "Can you pick up anything as to what room you find this suffocation occurring in?"

"*Oooh, boy,* I'm right in *here*! I really remember, boy, I'm in here some-place," Rosemarie's reaction is instant startle and instant cognition, even though her eyes are closed and she as yet has no idea what it is her right index finger is tapping hard upon. Which impresses the bejesus out of both Vince and Mike, because it is the living room.

". . . when I first came in I went from whatever this room is, over to here, and I'm finding the suffocation coming in here. I want to say I'm being subdued in here, too—feel free, you can break in on me and ask questions, go ahead."

"That particular area that you were covering was where you felt like the suffocation—" W.J. begins a question.

"But it's like, too, it's almost like somebody's chasing me first, or walking behind me, however you want to put that. What happened over in here? There was furniture, had to've been picked up—there was, because we see stuff that was down but we feel it being picked up. Is this a bar area?"

"Yeah. There's a bar there," W.J. says as Rose taps around the dividing wall and walk-through between the kitchen and the dining room/living room. "Because we feel things around here that were down, they had to be picked up before you guys got there. Had to be."

After Dub hands her a blown-up version of the scaled floor plan, Rose-marie says, "I'm feeling the woman grabbed, but I'm feeling the fight between the men."

"Was that how Janet was supposed to die? Was it supposed to be suffocation?" W.J. asks.

"In the bedroom, somebody came in—there's gotta be a sliding glass door here, or a big window right here," Rose says, as her fingers sightlessly tappy-toe out to the west wall of the den where the sliding glass door *is.* "And it would look like it was done through a robbery. This should have been found jimmied or pried—or *left unlocked.* Yes."

"What room was she in when she first got hit?" W.J. asks his very special "informant."

"I find a lot of it in here—but I find her running through the rooms, you should have found blood in more than one area. Did you?"

"But they weren't all typed," Dub says.

"Oh." Rose acknowledges the loss, and then is off into stream-of-con-sciousness:

"I find, okay, for some reason, I find the menace coming in through the front door. But there's one outside and there's one inside. We find her in the bathroom, running into the bedroom. Again I keep finding a pillow suffocation, hand suffocation over here and her running out into this area. And again, in this area, I keep finding something overturned, a chair, *a high chair.* And then it had to be picked up. I find an altercation between the two men, it's like the woman's out of the way, the baby is—I want to say he's down, I don't know where—but I find the two men—before we go to the two men, again, we see the knife going back and forth—did she have any bruises on her anyplace?"

"No, she was—" begins Dub.

"Because why do I keep going—?" Rose continues.

"—her face was beaten badly," W.J. finishes.

"This right arm is *really* doing a job on me. Questions?"

"Did Janet Myers ever have possession of the knife?" W.J. wants to know.

"We don't find her having possession of it—she has fingerprints—it's because they were put there. We don't find that she fully had possession— we find—let's *rephrase* that! Because I've got *two* people here, okay? It's like I'm looking at a doorway and here's this man—Fontainebleau, or whatever his name is, he's over here. Here's Janet, and her husband is over here, and what I'm feeling, her hand—I'm feeling *more* than one person with that knife. I know that doesn't make sense . . . I'm seeing two people wielding that knife, which could be both her and her husband wielding it—because he's behind her, and this other man is over here. So do ask it again, because, again, he's over—give me Fontainebleau's first name?"

"William." As yet it seems only W.J. has the comfort level to engage this so ordinary yet so extraordinary grandmother.

"Here's Bill over here, and I find the husband behind her and there's an altercation going on, the knife is changing hands in here. Is this a kitchen knife?"

"Yes."

"The knife is changing hands, again. Ask that question again, because I've still got two hands on that knife."

"That makes sense to us."

"Okay."

"Did Janet ever, ever stab anybody? Janet herself, as opposed to just handling the knife. Did she actually stab anybody?" Dub really wants to know.

Rosemarie says: "Yeah, she got one stab in. So she did have the knife in her—"

"*She* had the knife?" W.J. is on that like a horn-shell snapper.

"Yeah, she *did* have the knife in her hand. And she—did you establish, is she right-handed?"

"Yeah."

"Because—the knife was taken from here, here is where I was, you remember? My thumb was pulled back and it hurt?"

"Uh-huh."

"Okay, and it was taken . . . when you say stab, I don't want to say stab, I want to say superficial, not anything deep, just like a—surface—"

"Do you have a time as to when that stab may have occurred? If we gave you a picture of Bill's wounds, would you be able to determine which ones—?"

"I could try. And what I'd like to do is do them with my eyes closed, too."

Vince hands W.J. the photographs of Bill's wounds taken after he was arrested; Dub places them under the hands of Mrs. Kerr.

"Now, am I in the picture? Okay. No, she would've been straight on to him, not in the back. Is this not superficial, maybe?" Rose asks, as her hand moves over and is tapping on the frontal shot of Bill, the one showing the two upper-left-chest wounds, above and below the heart; her finger is on the one above.

"Yes."

"Okay. Who would be here? I'm not finding—I'm not finding her there so much. I'm finding her over here. She's facing him. I'm not finding her ever behind him. I'm finding the two men and her facing—him."

"That's okay, that's fine."

"*Boy,* maybe you don't have anything else on him, but lemme tell ya, this guy is *not clean.*"

"He's not what?"

"He's not clean. Now—and again, I'm gonna have to give you what I picked up someplace else, I don't know what it is but there's some type of pornography. Whether it's just him himself, or other people, but—"

"Is that Fontanille or is that Myers?" Mike Maunoir asks.

"I've got it on that one there, too," Rose says as she gestures with one hand back to Bill's photo as the other hand is rubbing Kerry's. "But lemme tell ya, I *don't* like this vibration, really."

"Where was—?" W.J. begins another question.

"Oooh!" Rose exclaims in some distress, and her breathing is suddenly quite labored.

"—Kerry when Janet was being struck?"

"Okay," she manages to get out. Then a deep breath and a loud exhale.

"Where was Kerry when the suffocation was going on?" W.J. continues his gentle but firm probing.

"Okay." Rosemarie has caught her breath somewhat, enough to continue. "I've gotta go with the first one you gave me—was there a baby walker? Anything, any kind of baby deal in this part of the room, over here? I don't know what room I'm even in—"

After some moments of confusion, Vince corrects everyone as he regains his direct, powerful voice: "This is the dining room."

"Anything in there that belonged to the baby?" Rose still wants to know.

"Yes—was like a slide there . . . wasn't there?" Dub asks of his partners. "Check the pictures."

"Okay. This baby crawled?" Rose asks.

"Either crawls or walks, wouldn't you say?" Dub, the confirmed bachelor, asks Vince and Mike, both fathers and husbands.

"Because I find the baby here—" Rose continues.

"There's your high chair," W.J. says as he looks at the pictures of the living room/dining room.

"That should've been down. Okay, over here, I keep going over into here—" Rose says.

"That's where you're looking," all three men confirm.

"This is where I find the baby when this is going on. But then later I find him moved, which I'm sure I told you that already. I don't find him there."

"That's the infant as opposed to Ryan? There are two children involved," W.J. asks.

"Okay, I'm finding the baby over here—"

"We're talking six-week-old and two years old," Dub explains.

"Okay, I find him better in—" Rosemarie is tapping on the schematic, wanting the word for what she sees in her mind.

"In the high chair?" W.J. helps.

"Yeah—okay—this would have to be the two-year-old that's walking—he's not confined—this two-year-old should be able to tell you things! *Definitely. And I wouldn't discredit it either.*"

"No, I'll bet that—" W.J. begins.

"I wouldn't discredit it and I'm getting strong confirmation that if his mind is blocked that it can be opened. Definitely."

"Where was Kerry when the suffocation was going on? When the first attempt at suffocation—" W.J. asks, and Rose immediately moves her hand and taps on the den.

"Where was the first blow struck with the bat?"

"Okay, we're still going back, we're in the—"

"Hall. Hall and foyer," Dub says.

"Yeah. We're in here and again we're finding movement, and we're finding blood in more than one place."

"Was Janet struck with the bat before or after she stabs Fontanille?" W.J. asks.

"I can only give it to you the way I'm getting it. First I'm feeling—and again, I have *two* suffocations in here—we're finding her—were there wounds on the back of her head? Or neck up in this area?"

"Yes, there was," Dub says.

"Okay. And we find the knife that's here coming down like an automatic reflex, I don't find strength behind it—and here is where my hand is hurting me again—this knife is being taken out of my hand, and I'm rubbing this part of my hand because it's really pain now, like somebody pulled your thumb back—and it's over here, this is the husband—the *husband's got that bat, too!* It looks like I'm looking at him and he came first—because it's coming from behind as Bill is over here and she's getting hit from behind over here."

"With the bat?" W.J. asks.

"Uh-huh. She's here, he's there, and there's somebody striking her from behind—also that little boy should be running around in here or hiding in here—during the struggle I find the little boy—he's holding his mom's leg and he got hit right in the middle of it all when he wasn't supposed to get hit."

"Who hit him?" W.J. asks.

"Should be Bill."

"Bill?"

"Yeah."

"Where was Kerry when the child got hit?"

"He was right there in the area, but it happened—again, it wasn't supposed to be when he got hit . . . what I'm looking at is like four people together all yelling and screaming and the bat's being wielded and then Kerry, the husband, let go of the wife—Bill has the bat and as he's going this way, he hit the child—I'm not finding him hitting him on purpose, but that's why the husband went nuts."

During the almost three hours that Rosemarie is in the office with the tape recorder running, the prosecution team asks many questions and receives her answers to many; but, because of their lack of definitive knowledge of most aspects of the crime scene, she and her spiritual hosts also ask just as many, for which the prosecutors have no answers.

". . . there was another woman involved also on the husband's part. Again I come to another woman, and I keep seeing these men with another woman between them, which I've been trying to establish were they both with this one or just belonging to the husband."

"Was Fontanille or Myers at the house first?" W.J. asks at one point.

"Oh, boy, give it to me again, because I heard one name and saw somebody else."

"Was Bill at the house first, or was Kerry at the house first?"

"Kerry. Bill came in the front door."

"Is there anyone other than Kerry or Bill—"

"No."

"—that has direct knowledge or involvement in this?"

"Okay, spirit says, 'No, not direct, but there is knowledge around in somebody else's hands'—again I'm seeing that attaché, whatever it is, it's gotta be around someplace. Black, it's got something in it. It could be a purse. It could be a checkbook. But, yes, there is knowledge floating around."

"Are they lying about the times?" Vince wants to know.

"Oh, definitely. They took time to do things before—again, I keep finding things moved. Nobody went through that closet? Should've been books, photographs, something? Never went through it?"

"No," the police captain and detective admits with great distaste, even though he hadn't been on the scene.

"What time were the drawers pulled out?" W.J. asks.

"Afterwards."

"What did Myers and Fontanille discuss after the murder and before the police arrived?" Vince asks.

"Everything that they were going to say on how it took place. They also discussed what not to say, and again that mutual bonding here, that if either one gives evidence without the other, how they will go down together. So we have feeling here on both sides, really. And I feel both of them have something on each other. I still keep seeing something . . . this has something to do with pornography. *And I keep going back to that*."

"Did Kerry Myers have any involvement with a sex club of any sort?" W.J. asks.

"He was involved with some type of pornography, I don't know if you'd call it a sex club, but, again, pornography *is* involved in here."

"What do you mean by pornography?" Vince asks. "Do you mean like kinky sexual habits—?"

"That's right. And we see pictures and/or movies being made. In other words, not normal—abnormal."

"Was Janet involved in this?" Vince has to know.

"Janet was on the fringes—there should've been some pictures of her."

"Do you see this back when they were in college?" W.J. asks.

"I see other people around him like that in college. I can't verify in her, it could be—but there are others around him so I can't verify just she."

"Could that have been involved in the reasoning for the motive?" Vince asks.

"Give me that question in a different phrase."

"Did they want Janet to become involved in this type—?"

"*That's it*. And she didn't want to become involved. She wanted *out*. Again, they had a lot of problems in the family before this took place—she also was keeping some kind of . . . keeping a diary, notes or something that is tangible. There's got to be something someplace."

"Could that be the cleanup, the hiding—?" Mike is asking.

"Yeah. But I still find something—there's still something around. I don't find that it's all completely gone."

"Do you see any location on this stuff?" asks W.J.

"A box. You already asked that. A box, a brown box."

"And where is the brown box located?" W.J. again.

"It's packed away. In storage. Her mother should have some of her stuff. Can you verify if her mother has some of her stuff?"

"I'm sure she does," W.J. says. "But we couldn't verify. We wouldn't have any real probable cause to go in looking for anything. Can you give us the name of anyone having information relative to the case that we don't know about?"

"That girl that's a waitress or was a waitress that had dirty-blond hair we talked about—tell me, is there any girl that's been verified with the letter M in her name anyplace?"

"Not a woman," W.J. says, and then offers pointedly, "We have a man, with the letter M."

"What color is his hair?"

"His hair is blond."

"Okay, I'm seeing the hair—curly, almost kinky—and the letter M—yes, would have some knowledge."

"If I told you the name?"

"We could try."

"Mike Price?"

"Okay, when you said Mike Price—is there anybody else around him that has dark hair? Female? I'm trying to make sure I'm picking up Mike. Would you know?"

"I really wouldn't know," answers W.J., as none of them have ever seen the proper, pretty, petite, and raven-tressed Monique Price. "But I think that Mike Price is probably the blond. He's Kerry's best friend."

"Notes, words, maybe just scribblings, something, there's *something*."

"Janet's?"

"Yes."

"Is Fontanille's wife withholding information?"

"As to his whereabouts and what he does, yeah—she's afraid of him."

Somewhat later Vince begins a line of inquiry: "What do we have for why Janet was killed? Was this a spontaneous reaction—in other words, to try and initiate her into some sexual or some . . ."

"We don't find it, no, we don't find it spontaneous. We find that they had talked about doing it. The time that happened wasn't planned right; we don't just find it spontaneous. It had more than one reason behind it. One, to get her out of the way. She was interfering, she wouldn't cooperate. Two, there may have been some money involved. But three, we keep finding another woman in the picture."

"Was there an affair between Bill and Janet?" Vince asks.

"Again, when we go into this, we don't call it an affair, we find it on his side mostly being the pursuer. And what we did find in there was a false affair—which I want to call rape."

"Did this happen in close proximity to the murder?"

"It would have to be, if not within the same time as the murder, within a few days of it. She hasn't blown the whistle on them yet. She has

something on them—there's got to be, again, someplace just sitting
around. In a brown box."

"Was Janet attracted to Bill?"

"When you say attracted, it was not an attraction, physical attraction
for life, but I wanna say physical dis-like. I don't know if you understand
this, but it goes the opposite, not that she liked him for what he was, but
an attraction because of what he wasn't, meaning—call it the bad-boy
thing, whatever you want."

"Who initiated this plan?"

"They both talked it over when they were drunk, it came out like, oh,
more or less something just boasting about, 'Yeah, I could kill my wife,' this
and that. It didn't start out as being a plan, it started out as just being
talked about and 'If I could.' And then it became a plan."

"Where were they when this plan was conceived?"

"In a bar."

"Anything on a name?"

"Okay, I feel like a Western bar—two bars, two people over here, the
door is—I see two doors, one is that—and one is that way."

Rosemarie quickly sketches a crude floor plan for what would seem to
be a large nightclub. Then:

"We see a pool table or something there—but something square, could
be a square light fixture. I keep finding an R in the name of the bar. I feel
it could be that it's a Western name or a logo. I also see like a bucking horse
and I heard wrangler—and there should be a telephone in there too."

"Should we suggest a name to you? Does that help?" Mike asks.

"Sure."

"How about 'Bronco's'?"

"Does it have a logo of a horse—uh, this way?" Rose makes a gesture
which she wants to convey as that of a rider pulling back the reins on a
bucking horse.

"It's got a cowboy," W.J. offers.

"Okay, because I saw it. I'm getting very good verification on that. I
wanna go with that. Because I just went head to toe with that name."

"Bronco's?"

"Yes—and, also, maybe one of the neighbors may have seen Bill standing
across the street, or looking at the layout of the house. Somebody has got
to have seen him—not going to the door—but being in the neighborhood.
And on his car, or any car around him, were any of them colored tan or
anything like that—we keep picking up that vehicle."

"He's got a brown Toyota."

"Brown or tan, okay. For some reason I keep seeing that car coming in
and out. And I'm trying to find out why. Would anybody know, did any of
these people doodle in any way? I know that's a crazy question, but for

some reason something significant—on a *napkin*! Okay, they *sketched it out on a napkin*."

"That's me," Vince says sheepishly. "I doodle on napkins."

"You doodle on napkins? Okay, and they also sketched *this* out on a napkin—like a floor plan. Of course we don't have that napkin, that's long gone. I don't find it around."

Shortly thereafter, Vince hands Rosemarie an aerial photograph of the Litchwood Lane section of Woodmere, with row upon row of neat but seemingly identical houses and yards. "This is the initial photograph I was going to show you," Vince says.

"Gee, I wouldn't want to come home drunk here, I'd lose my house," quips Rosemarie the psychic.

"Here's the house," says Vince.

"Show me, I'll see if I was right. Okay, I was right over in here—is that it?"

"Where were you?" Vince asks in mock surprise as Rosemarie is tapping on a different house from the one he had indicated to her.

"Right in here."

Vince grins and says, "You've got it right."

"Okay!"

"Fooled ya, huh?"

"You showed me there, but I was picking up—testing the spirit, huh?"

Everybody laughs and no one more than Rosemarie herself at another of the inevitable gimmicks of skeptics.

"If we can, Rosemarie, can we recap a little bit? We're going kind of fast." Vince is back to serious business. "Let me see if I can get a scenario of what you're feeling so far. The murder did not occur the way it was supposed to occur? Correct?"

"That's correct."

"But, if I can interrupt you just on that point," W.J. says. "But it was supposed to happen on that particular day?"

"Yes."

"Just not the way that—?"

"It just didn't go according to the way they had it set up."

"And the way the murder did go down—the brutality of it," Vince probes. "Was that more of a reaction to the change in events that happened?"

"Yes. Again, I don't find that the child was supposed to be part of it."

"Is the child a pivotal point in what transpired between Kerry and Bill?" Vince continues to probe.

"Yes."

"So the whole thing was falling apart, but the fact that the child got hit changed the complexion entirely as far as Kerry and Bill becoming adversaries?"

"Yes."

"Okay. The particular brutality of the murder, with the weapon that was used, was that—who actually swung the bat?" Vince is the one to finally ask *the* question.

"We find two people swinging the bat. Because it changed hands, both Kerry and Bill."

"Okay, now, do we see two people swinging the bat at Janet?" Vince asks. "Or do we see maybe the bat in the possession of somebody swinging it at each other? Does it necessarily have to be both people swinging the bat at Janet?"

"Let me give you what's coming in—I think you'll understand from the question—we see the bat hitting Janet from behind once, and Kerry is behind her. And then we see the man over here after he's hit with the knife, getting possession of the bat—I don't know if Kerry dropped it—all of a sudden it's changed hands. But we find him coming from another direction, so we find him hitting the front of Janet, and somehow the little boy is over here in the vicinity and he's getting hit. There's four people—again the child is one—and what I'm seeing is such a hodgepodge right now with the yelling and screaming . . . in cleaning up there were some things that were moved—there *should* be some cameras in the house. Because I'm picking up some type of camera, movie camera or projector—there's something black in the form of a camera that was in that closet.

"You know, the neighbors *should* have heard or seen or known *something*. Because I *don't* find these people as a normal couple. They may have been on the outside, but they weren't on the inside—and the neighbors should have some feedback."

"There was an initial altercation that involved the wife and then the son getting hit—is the son hit in a different location than where he's ultimately found?" W.J. asks.

"Yeah, because for some reason I find him in their location, but then I find him moved."

"Who moves him?"

"The father, I feel the father moving him."

"Now after that they calm down, there is a point at some distance in the future after that, that we believe there is a second altercation which ultimately led to Fontanille being driven from the home—what triggered that second, later altercation?"

"Again, when the father noticed the baby again it hit home, 'This is not what was supposed to be,' and that's what I'm finding there, that he realized, but it was too late. So what he's trying in essence to do is put it all on Bill, 'You did this.' By him going after him, chasing him out, it looks like, 'He did it. I'm not involved. Look, I chased this man out because he did it.' "

"What made her get that knife?" Vince asks.

"They were after her. She was running. I find her movement starting in the bedroom and then going out and into the kitchen. For some reason I found a lot of stuff which I haven't been able to break it down, but I saw four of them right in the foyer. Right in close proximity to it. Somebody *should've* heard this woman yelling—*everybody* should've heard this woman. I hear the woman yelling, 'Oh my God!' She's the one that doesn't understand what's happening—that *aggravates* me—I want to find that portfolio, or whatever that leather thing is, and that brown case—somebody had to've heard her that day and maybe is afraid to say anything because they don't want to get involved."

"You picked that up, or is that Rosemarie?" W.J. asks.

"No. I'm picking that up, that's not Rosemarie. Did anybody ever go through anything in these rooms? Does anybody know? To look for anything? I'm finding that she's either got photograph albums, diaries or stuff, papers in something brown."

"I don't think anybody went through anything." W.J. answers the truth.

"I find her alone in here, going through the rooms."

"Was that a happy bedroom?" Vince asks.

"*No!* Not a happy bedroom. And again, there's something hidden in that closet. *That's it.* Hidden in the closet. You know what that is? *Not* hidden *in* the closet, it's hidden in the bedroom. *Not shown.* Do you get it? I'm getting a catchphrase in here. Not hidden in closet, it's hidden—not known, because it's not normal. The bedroom isn't a happy place—and it's where they don't want things to be found. In other words—give me the words for it. Things not normally found in the bedroom, thank you. In other words, this is *not a normal bedroom, plain and simple.* And again I'm seeing what looks like a camera, a brown box which could be film and/or photographs in it. There are still some in existence! Whoever this hat belongs to, they had to have back problems."

"Yes."

"This is wrong. The chair should be over. I find that little rocking chair down. See the photograph album. Is that a photograph album?"

"Looks like it," W.J. answers.

"Was that ever picked up?"

"No."

"It keeps coming up, it keeps coming up. Photographs. And I keep hearing, 'overlooking.' Overlooking what? There's more. Did anybody find anything else around the body—a ring?"

"Is it a button?" asks W.J.

"Could be, it's round and small."

"Dr. Henry Lee said if you can find Kerry Myers's button off of his shirt he'd solve the case," W.J. tells her.

"Could be—do we know anything about Kerry's background? If you do, just say yes or no, don't tell me."

"Yes."

"What I'm picking up on him is though he may have the strength for a lot of things—the spirits saw him as a wimp, plain and simple. I don't know if you could verify that."

"That's been the general description of Kerry. In fact, 'wimp' is the word that is used," W.J. says.

"Okay, that's what I'm picking up."

"You're on him," Dub assures.

"Let's release this, let's release this. We don't want to accept. Okay, I've got him standing there—do you know anything about her background?"

"We know a little bit about her," W.J. says.

There is what is for Rosemarie a very long pause as the only sound is her fingertips rubbing a photograph. Then:

"She's gonna work with ya to get 'em, she wants them. She really does. . . . *She wrote down something that's incriminating and all we have to do is find it.* It's gotta be. It's someplace—did she scratch anybody?"

"Not that we can prove," Dub has to admit.

"What I'm hearing—this is to her husband—calling him an SOB because she's gonna get him. And again, we're looking that way." Rose looks and points straight up. "I sure hope her husband is superstitious."

"Why's that?" Vince bites.

"Because she *told him* she was gonna get him." There is laughter all around.

"She lived—that's the hard part, the bad part, that's why it's very rough coming into her vibrations—because she's seeing and she knows and she's terrified for her kids. *Nobody should have to die like that.* Let's release, thank you. Okay, what I'm hearing around her is, 'Why are you doing this to me?' This is before her mouth couldn't talk—but, but—release this please, *please* release this.

"I'll tell you what's happening to me now—it looks like I'm blocking off part of her. Because one part of me is really blocking out what I'm looking at. I'm trying to work up to a different level so I can look and keep my eyes open—it's very difficult right now.

"I've gotta go back and work with her, because she's the whole key—I'm gonna have to really psych myself up to another level, go into her consciousness and pick up; and I'm really going to have to go deeper—all I need is one or two, I don't need all the pictures. It's very hard for me to look out of her eyes, let me put it that way, it's very difficult."

In short order comes: "I'm running scared, I know that, I'm running out of time. I'm gasping for breath. In the head area. My arms are being pulled back, my hands pulled back—she was concerned for the children because she knew what was happening to her. She should've had a broken nose, too, lot of facial damage." Rose groans, and her face and hands are writhing in pain.

"Who's beating her at that point?" W.J. has to know.

"I'm finding—I want to say a large man—I don't know how large he is but I feel weight behind him, beating her—but I do find the presence of another man in the room—and let's *release all this, thank you.* Again, what I'm trying to do is come into her vibration and see through her eyes. But as I'm seeing—because the body is going in different directions—let's release this! If we can have it without all the feeling. Thank you. I'm seeing and I'm knowing, but the concern is not me, not for herself, it's for the children, because I hear a child yelling or screaming in the background and somebody screaming, 'No,' which is she. I'm picking up great disbelief at what is happening."

Rose's groaning is more pronounced, her breathing is labored. "Let's release this, *let's go through it without the pain, thank you,* please release. Let's release, thank you. Okay. I'm seeing her afterwards, laying down, okay, with the eyes up and two men standing over her looking. And it's like the child is over here and somehow in this whole scuffle he has gotten hurt—is down, something has hit him too."

"At this time?" Vince asks.

"Yeah, it's like it's all happening together—everything at once and there's so much movement with the two men there and the child is there and I find that the child—he's doing some moving around, but he's in the area. *My head is just driving me crazy,* I'm trying to pick it up without the pain and I'm trying not to look at the picture . . . I'm in more places than one because I'm running back and forth—I think I'm running because I may be picking up the child's vibration and running with him. Can we go to the next picture?—I'm having such bad headaches on this one."

"Well, that's *exactly* where she was," W.J. says.

"I felt the little boy—it feels like maybe they were chasing him. Hnnn! *You don't get used to this.* Ahhh! Again. The only thing I'm picking up right now—and, spirit, you take over, please, release me from this, I don't want to feel this pain. Thank you. Release all pain, everything. Thank you. What I'm feeling now and I'm picking up—give me the lady's name again, please?"

"Janet."

"I'm picking up Janet and what I'm seeing around her is disbelief—the agony, 'If this is happening to me, what about my children?' Because she knows it's more than one person and the person she relies on and loves is doing this to her. As she was being hit in the head area, I didn't find her going unconscious right away, I found that she still had sensibilities around her—*this is premeditated murder, no matter what anyone says.*"

"Is it a left-handed or right-handed person who did that?" Vince asks.

"Do you see?" W.J. prods.

"I'm picking up two people. Still picking up two people in here."

"Even at that point?" W.J. asks.

"I guess I have to look to find out what I'm pulling them on. I'm finding it difficult looking at this, I think you know that. I'm trying to get my senses. I've gotta clear my senses, let's release, please, let's release this, we don't want to accept. Without the feeling, thank you. Tell me, are her eyes open or closed because I can't look?"

"Closed."

"Okay. Before this, her eyes had been open. Because as I'm laying down looking up, I'm seeing the man that was stabbed standing over me—but *he doesn't have those stab wounds on his chest now,* so know that."

16
Baseline

So here we are . . . you, me and dad . . . in our house (a very nice house) trying to survive.

Dad and I have our problems. Sometimes we don't understand each other. Sometimes we just get depressed because of money and bills and life in general. We do love each other, but "life" gets in the way. One thing to remember: don't ever let business, or money, or bills, or material things come before love. That has happened to dad and I, and that has caused problems. But, we're happy. We've come a long way from Nicholls State.

And you make it so worthwhile. Things can look so bleak and then you smile at me. . . .

—Journal of Janet Cannon Myers

* * *

"Nobody really knows what happened, but I feel like I know what happened because I have an inside source." W. J. LeBlanc is standing behind his desk, framed and highlighted by a flickering light and shadow show produced through the old leaded glass of the French windows by a low-hanging sun and a late-summer breeze through the oak branches outside, sounding just a little bit like a stump preacher.

"There are as many theories as stars in the sky, but all I have is one. Everybody's got their favorite idea and favorite theory of what happened. But as far as I'm concerned there's only one—by which all others are to be measured."

Now sitting, W.J., reining in his remembered excitement, says, "On tape Rosemarie talks about seeing something black covering Janet's face, like a pillow. Which was right on the money, 'It's supposed to be a strangulation'—that's when everything started falling into place.

"Richard Boyd tells us about a 'fuck club' and Rosemarie sees pornography? It's always the first, middle, and last thing she sees? *It's got to be there.* 'Go run it down.'

"We can't put Rosemarie on the stand. Everything she gives us has to be corroborated with admissible evidence. She's not a fact witness as in *Daigle,* she's only an investigative tool.

"What it does is steer my investigation—my way of examining and analyzing people's testimony and the evidence from that point on. It gives me a baseline on which to measure everything. There are certain things, in my mind, that we're not deviating from. Unless somebody shows me something positively otherwise. I'm not deviating from the fact that it started in the bedroom. That it was going to be a strangulation, or smothering originally. That Janet gets the knife. That Janet strikes the first blow. That at that point the violence starts with the bat. That in the living room is where the kid gets nailed. Because, without that you can speculate that it might've happened in the bedroom; you don't know, the bedroom's all messed up, the kid's found in the bedroom—why not try to bop Janet, hit the kid by accident, Janet runs away?

"Now, my baseline is Janet stabbing Billy. You have chest wounds on Bill, back wounds on Bill, you have a broken arm with Kerry, and you have head wounds to Janet and Ryan. So 'Janet stabbed Bill' is the whole key for us.

"One of the big problems we have is what could possibly incite Bill Fontanille to do that, right? Well, the two knife wounds to the chest, to the heart area, could piss off the average person. It was a commonsense explanation for why someone other than the husband could have been very much enraged."

On Tuesday, December 12, the day after Rosemarie's "reading," Vincent Lamia received a call from Dale Guillot, chief of security at Nicholls State University, who informed him that Bob Blazier, communications professor at Nicholls, knew Janet and Kerry well and had "information about 'kinky sex.' " Chief Guillot had taken the liberty to schedule Vince a meeting for Thursday, December 14.

Also on December 12, Vince returned to the Detective Bureau to meet with Sergeant Sam Churcherillo to review Kerry Myers's polygraph examination of September 27, 1984. Specifically Vince was looking for the "questions in which deception was indicated." As noted by Vince, they were:

Test # 1

1.   did you strike Janet on the day she was killed?
2.   did you kill Janet?

3. on the day Janet was killed, was Billy at your house when you arrived at 4:00 P.M.?
4. did you conspire with Billy to do Janet any bodily harm?

Test #2

5. prior to calling the police, did you know Janet was dead?
6. prior to calling the police, did you see Janet?
7. did you place more than the one (1) call to the Sheriff's Office?
8. did you change any clothes prior to the emergency unit arriving?
9. to the best of your memory, did you tell the complete truth to the Grand Jury?

"Anyone can see where a husband just starts pee-laying on the wife— but his child? And if that's the case, if all he did was hit the child, even accidentally, then why doesn't Bill just come out and say the truth? There's got to be one thing that accounts for everything," W.J. is saying.

"That was for Billy to have hit the child, but accidentally, and the killing of Janet being absolutely intentional, premeditated. A conspiracy to commit murder.

"There's obviously no animosity most of the night. The thing demonstrating that is the fact that they're sitting down talking, having water, toweling off for ten hours. There's physical evidence to show that beyond *any doubt.* We're getting into concepts, reasons, plausible explanations for two people's conduct . . . and that's the one thing that triggers it: because, without Janet stabbing Bill, you can't logically put that bat into Bill's hand.

"So, yes, that's a strategy decision. By now I've got Kerry dead in the water. Because he's already the natural suspect, he's the husband. Husbands have been killing wives since the beginning of marriage. There's just no doubt. The case against Kerry was very strong circumstantially.

"Rosemarie puts the knife in Janet's hands. That's what she does for me," W.J. continues. "Now I'm able to put everything in place. Janet with the knife explains everything in my mind. It's like the one piece in a jigsaw puzzle upon which all the others fit. Once that's there . . . 'Ah! Now I can come up with something that makes sense to me *and* explains the evidence in a reasonable fashion.'

"Now, according to Rosemarie, they both swing the bat. But it's too bizarre for me to do it like that. And it's risky. It's going to be much more difficult to convict Billy of murder—of anything, frankly—if we're going to concede that Kerry Myers was the guy with the bat. Because then we're gonna have to prove that Billy *probably* hit her too, or he at least certainly *watched.* And we miss on him? Kerry goes to jail for life and Bill Fontanille walks. In my opinion, we can't make that concession, take that risk. The jury has to at least *think* this guy was capable of swinging that bat.

"While I, in fact, feel like he swung the bat—*and* Kerry swung the bat—I think it's much more important from a strategy standpoint than from a factual standpoint. It's borne out by the physical evidence—Bill is spattered from tip to toe. So it's not like it's a reach. And it accomplishes the big thing with making him the more culpable person in the eyes of the jury.

"Now Rosemarie sees something very significant about that closet in the bedroom. That's too way out for me, so I don't use it. And I don't have a problem with that. There are certain things that just don't fit, or I find difficult to reconcile. But then that's the nature of this case. There's nothing that absolutely fits with everything."

In midmorning on Thursday, December 14, in the Nicholls State Campus Police Office, Vince Lamia interviewed "Mr. Robert D. Blazier," who told him a great deal about the KVFG, Gary Landry, Janet Cannon, and Kerry Myers passion play. However, Vince made the drive back to New Orleans mostly empty-handed.

Blazier told him he had no knowledge of any "sex club" or any information concerning "kinky" sex by either Kerry or Janet. Bob Blazier added that he "did hear after Janet's murder that she and Kerry were involved in some 'kinky' sex stuff (i.e. wife swapping/open marriage, etc.), but it was just rumor—idle talk at parties, etc."

Finally Blazier told Vince he knew Ray Roy very well and that "he was a very 'moralistic' person."

"Billy Fontanille is not a stupid person." W. J. LeBlanc is again reflecting on the conspiracy. "And the only person he really ever gave a shit about is himself. So Bill's not gonna sit there like that—there's no reason why he had to sit and not tell the truth if it's Kerry. If it's *only* Kerry. If all he did was watch. And if it's only a spontaneous thing where he's involved—I don't see the stories coming out like they came out. Especially when Bill's the one sitting in jail for fourteen months awaiting trial and looking at the electric chair while his buddy is setting the world on fire on the outside, new house, new boat, new life. When absolutely the truth gets him a better deal than what he's sitting in jail risking.

"These are the kinds of things, the strongest evidence, in my opinion, that lend themselves to a conspiracy. While I think the physical evidence and circumstantial evidence all support, within certain limits, conspiracy, it's much more common sense and logic in the parties actions *afterwards.* Look at their actions if it was spontaneous but they were both involved. And you know what? *None* of it makes any sense.

"That's why it always, always comes back to the baseline. The only thing that takes into account *everything* is Janet stabbing Bill in response to a conspiracy to kill her. If not conspiracy, we have to assume that this person is going to go all over the earth, with these retarded stories, and versions, and silences, and testimonies, *when the truth shall set you free.* Unh-unh. I'll never buy that."

On a morning in mid-December, W.J. went downstairs for his morning docket and learned that Judge Eason's precarious health had taken a bad turn and he was in the hospital with an acute diabetic condition which would soon lead to the amputation of the jurist's left leg at the knee.

Consequently, the baseball bat murder, one of the most highly publicized murder cases in modern Louisiana history, was without a judge. As is procedure in occurrences of a judge's absence, an ad hoc judge, Cleveland Marcel, was appointed for thirty days with the possibility that the appointment could be extended as warranted.

Considering the uncertainty of his length of service and the complexity of the case, plus the added responsibility on the presiding judge to be, in all likelihood, the trier of fact in the State versus Kerry Myers, Judge Marcel himself transferred the case to Division B, the domain of the Right Honorable Judge E. V. Richards.

"The worst-case scenario from the beginning," W.J. is explaining, "was that Kerry Myers would walk in with Wiley Beevers as we're getting ready to pick the jury for William Fontanille and say, 'Judge, we want a jury trial. And we now have a motion to sever.' All the way I think it's a ploy, *nobody waives* a jury on a murder charge. So I'm *really* thinking that once the case gets transferred to Division B.

" 'When is the shoe gonna drop? When is he gonna do it?' Howie and I talk about it all the time, constantly. Because all Beevers has to say is, 'If that's your only reason for consolidating the case, judge, then we want a jury trial.'

"At that point it puts the judge on the spot—having to decide whether or not under *Bruton* that they're in fact antagonistic defenses. I think he'd have to find that they are and sever them."

On Tuesday, December 19, Vince telephoned and reached Ms. Cronin at her home in Georgia. However, that's as far as his luck ran; she still had not heard from her brother.

"I think Chuck's holding back on something. I think he knows more than what he's saying," Dub explains. "See, I know Chuck, personally. We met in the seventh grade at Livaudais and then we were at Shaw together, too.

"So I just want to get in real deep with Chuck—on what happened that day; prior to that day; after that day. There's a lot of information I think he can give us."

On Wednesday, December 27, Vincent Lamia was able to get Gary Landry on the phone in Florida. Mr. Landry, now a Republican Party functionary, was little more than self-serving in his memories (Janet continued to contact him after she was married) and thus not of much help.

"Fairly early on, the two biggest obstacles have been taken care of: putting the bat in Billy's hand, and recent evidence of a very bad marriage," Dub is saying. "I have the beginnings of the prosecution. I have the overall general approach to the prosecution. But it could take months to prove.

"We had a scenario. The only question is, do we give the jury a scenario? And again, that's the whole basic deal—do you give 'em a theory, or don't you? We don't have to. But juries like to know. Yet there are risks both ways. Your theory better exclude all reasonable hypotheses of innocence or you could be in deep shit; and you'd better not lay it out too early and give the other side a chance to come up with an explanation."

On Tuesday morning, January 16, Vince placed a phone call to a hospital in Houston and was able to leave a message for Nurse Gabriel LaMarche to call him collect upon her arrival at work.

Vince also spoke again with Sandy Cronin, who advised him that her brother would be working in Washington, D.C., for the following two weeks and that she should be able to get a message to him to call.

Then, only moments later, Vince received a phone call from Ms. LaMarche, who promptly gave him cause to induce a number of grins and chuckles out of Dub at that evening's debriefing—she was a bona fide, cooperative, information-possessing fact witness.

Finally, and surprisingly enough, on Wednesday, January 17, Chuck Cronin called Vince. However, he would not give his phone number and informed the investigator that his memory of the events had dulled and that he did not wish to come to Jefferson Parish to testify. Cronin then said that he would call W.J. the next day at 10:00 A.M. or 2:30 P.M.

Dub recalls that the phone call never came. Not that day. Not the next week. Not the next month. There are people *still* waiting for a return phone call from one Chuck Cronin.

"Chuck's on the run," W.J. says. "No question in my mind he's sticking and moving out there . . . just common sense tells us that this guy is running because there's something he doesn't want to tell the State. What does he have to hide?

"He even quits calling his sister once he figures out that's how we're trying to track him down. If we had a little more time, I'd've taken a shot at flying out to one of these job sites to pin him down. But at this point I feel like the case is pretty much coming together and I decide I don't want to open up that can of worms anyway, quite frankly. I don't know if either one of the stories is true.

"The one good thing about it, though, I know if we can't get him, they couldn't get him. So Bill can't avail himself of that this time around, when it's even more important, when we're trying to claim they're in it together and they're making *no* attempt to get Chuck Cronin. We're the ones that are looking for Chuck Cronin. What does that tell your common sense?"

"After she died, we'd go out on our fishing trips together, or go out drinking together," Mike Price is saying. "I'd be talking to him and the subject would come up and he'd start trying to make her into this saint and I'd say, 'Kerry, now, you know Janet was a good girl, we liked her, we loved her and I'm sure you loved her, but you know y'all fought all the time.' 'Oh, no, we never fought.' "

"Janet comes around and confronts Bill in that foyer area—Rose says Kerry strikes the first blow from behind," Dub is saying. "Kerry picks up the bat, hits her from behind. I have no problem with the way the scenario goes down—what Rosemarie gives me. Now, I have to modify it. I can't use that about Kerry using the bat first. Not that it isn't substantial. Certain things can be corroborated by the evidence that I can argue, and certain things not.

"It was probably a half-type swing. Probably, 'Kerry, you asshole, do something!' So here's this little blow to the back of the head that didn't do nearly enough to her. Bill grabs the bat away from Kerry, knocks the fuck out of her this time. Now she's starting to run away and she veers against the wall and he just starts beating the piss out of her. Boom, she falls to the floor. Continual beating, here comes the kid. Bam. Kerry scoops up and runs the baby to the back and then the big confrontation.'

"I'm not saying Ryan getting hit *has* to be accidental. That's a talking child. Bam! Bam! 'Mommy, Mommy.' Bam! So much for him. And then back to it. No way I can prove it. Of course, I can't disprove it either, which as theories go in this case puts it on a very short list.

"I think that's what triggered the second thing; that they thought he was dead to begin with. It was a blow of tremendous force, radiating skull fractures. Blood coming through the nose and ears.

"Janet's a rage killing, all right. Ryan's was not. His was just sort of an inconvenience kind of thing. Kerry cares for his kid; not his wife. The kid's put away and Fontanille continues for a couple more blows. I think Kerry is screaming at him as he's coming out of the bedroom and down the hall, 'I'm gonna kill you, you motherfucker! You killed my son.' I think Bill meets his ass around the other side before he can get to the knife.

"I think Kerry's arm is broken very early."

"My main role during the investigation is 'Defender of the Theory,' " W.J. explains. "I'm the repository of all the facts, the things we *do know.* 'You play devil's advocate and I'll tell you why it can't be like that, because of the theory.'

"The closest Vince and I get to a problem—and it's fairly persistent—is that maybe one or the other walks in during the beating. Especially Billy—he comes in at the end, tries to intervene, and then maybe helps try to cover.

" 'Vince, if that's the case then we're trying somebody unjustly—because he's not guilty of murder, at that point all he can be is an accessory after the fact.' Or vice versa.

"To me the *kid's* being there is the *weakest* link in the conspiracy theory." Dub now plays devil's advocate with himself. "Why take that very real chance that the kid's gonna get in the way—as he did—and the whole thing falls apart? But if it's supposed to be that Kerry comes home at an exactly prearranged time so that he finds the body—well, Kerry's a little leery of this despondent lunatic in his house with his kids; so he comes home a little too early and the blood's flying and you've got a minor Armageddon here.

"But you have to think conceptually of all the reams of information that you have. And what we're really talking about is with all the information there is, there are so many different directions, and combinations of directions, that the information can take you.

"You would never be able to eliminate possibilities unless you were able to say, 'This is,' for lack of a better word, 'the baseline.' These are our constants by which we have to see whether or not variables are consistent with the concept.

"And I'm the guy who's got the lock-box key to the constants, the *theory:* Janet stabbed Bill and there was a plan, real or *fantasized,* to kill their wives."

With the "fuck club" lead appearing all but dead in the water, and no luck at all finding any bartender who'd worked at Bronco's in '83 and '84 who could positively identify either Bill or Kerry—although one "advised Myers looked familiar"—in the second week of January, Vince began what seemed to be not that difficult a task: locating the EMTs who, in their ambulance, had arrived almost simultaneously with Deputy DeWilde at the Myerses' home that late night and subsequently treated Ryan and Kerry and taken them to West Jefferson Hospital.

Unfortunately, besides confirming their names as Walter Cardin and a Pat Guyote, and that they were no longer employed at West Jefferson, Vince found that any further information from the hospital would have to come by way of a subpoena.

After several promising but false starts and as many dead ends, on Thursday, January 18, Vince dialed a number for a residence in Vicksburg, Mississippi, and was able to catch a "Mrs. Walter Cardin" who told the detective that her husband worked for an ambulance service in Monroe, Louisiana, and that he wouldn't be home until the evening. She also gave Vince her husband's work number.

On Pat Guyote, the trail was even more herky-jerky. It wasn't until he started running different combinations of spellings and surnames through the Department of Motor Vehicles computer the trail started to turn up past addresses, telephone numbers, previous places of employment, and the full name she now goes under, Patricia Guyote Murphy. However, the computer could not produce *her*.

Dub very much wanted to interview her and Cardin.

The following day, January 18, W.J. received notice that half of his wish was coming through, as Walter Cardin returned Vince's phone call and an appointment was set for the detective to meet with the paramedic the following week at his residence in Vicksburg.

"Bill had utilities," Dub says. "I had Vince run a check on it and the utilities had not been turned off. They weren't turned off until he moved out. But usage was inordinately low.

"You read Bill's statement, it makes it appear that he was living there without utilities. So once we verified this wasn't the case, I was just going to stay away from it and argue it from his own statement. On cross-examination I was just going to go back to his statement and read, you know, 'Is it true you were living in a house with no utilities?' 'Yes.' The jury's gonna think, 'Anyone living in a house with no utilities must be *nuts.*' "

On Monday, January 22, Vince gave it another shot and called Sandy Cronin, who advised him that her brother Chuck was living at an "unknown hotel/motel in Clinton, Maryland."

The following day, Tuesday, almost made up for all of the investigatory detours, wild goose chases, blind alleys, and dead-cold "hot leads" when shortly after his drive up to Vicksburg, Vince filled five pages of notes before hauling his very excited ass back to Gretna to tell Dub about the mother lode they'd finally uncovered.

"When Vince told me about Cardin, it was a *very* big deal," W.J. says with his usual full measure of reflective animation and glee. "I knew if this guy had *that* kind of recall, he was gonna be a *great* witness."

Mr. Cardin does indeed have heightened powers of observation, comprehension, and retention; among all of the vivid details of that night he recalled—Kerry dressed in "button-down, light shirt, vertical stripes; dress pants darker than shirt. DeWilde frisked Kerry quickly"—his most compelling memory and question then and all the years since was: "Why it took so long for Myers to ask about his kids."

Mr. Cardin also informed Vince that Pat Murphy could be reached through a former boyfriend, whose name and place of employment Cardin provided.

"The day I spoke to Walter Cardin was a *major* turning point to me," Dub says as he remembers that he wasted little time in interviewing Walter Cardin personally.

"I could actually put the jury right there. Because I'm doing it with him as we talk. It's 'Okay, you're in the ambulance, now. What are y'all talking about?

" 'Now think, you're walking him down the driveway. What is he saying?' 'He's telling me about the attack.' I said, 'I know that. Tell me, what's he telling you about the attack?' 'All right, let me think.' Then. 'He came home at four o'clock . . . blah-blah . . . managed to get into the kitchen and get a knife.' *'Whoa! What?'* 'He managed to get into the kitchen and get a knife.' 'You're absolutely certain?' 'Oh, yeah. I remember it now. That's what he definitely said.'

"That's how it came out. We were talking with him, reliving it, putting him back there, jogging his memory with actual conversation, and that's when it came out, and boy, when I heard that it was like *boom!*"

W.J. stops in his excitement, listens to a mockingbird and a cardinal having a sing-off in the oak outside, and then further explains his view of the discovery of Cardin:

"You've got to understand that Walter Cardin had been subpoenaed the first time around—but when he called in they told him he was on standby. And that was it. Nobody ever bothered to call him back.

"To me, Walter Cardin was 'knife in the kitchen.' That was critical."

"It was pretty bad, it was swollen. He was limping pretty badly the next day and when people asked him what happened he said, 'Oh, I tripped on the steps or something.' And I'm standing right there, and he *knows* I was there and saw what happened."

Mike Price is remembering a time when he'd been with Kerry on an errand at his new house not long after Kerry had finally been let go by Air-Dreco. Mike witnessed Kerry and his very new wife, the former Debra Blakely, get into an argument, which quickly became loud, profane, and abusive and carried on to the outside of the front door, which Debbie slammed shut on Kerry's foot and ankle.

"I went home that evening and told Monique, not to her surprise, of course: 'My God, it's starting all over again!' "

"When I brought the Cannons in," begins Dub, "I had to take the unusual step of prefacing my remarks with, 'I understand you don't feel like your son-in-law is involved. And I can appreciate that—I don't agree with it, but I appreciate that. But what I would like to do is talk to you about William Fontanille. Anything that can help build a case against Fontanille.' That's how I was able to get Jane Spiers to speak to me. That's how I was able to get Lorraine and Charles Cannon to speak to me.

"Tammy DuBuc, for instance. In her letter which was very critical of the DA's Office, she implied there were things that weren't told. So I send Vince out to talk to her. To see if she can shed some light. It's obvious she's pro-Fontanille. I said, 'Go find out if you can scare up any dirt on Kerry.'

"With the pro-Kerry people, we would see whether or not we could find anything to trash Bill. We worked both sides like that. We could be anything anybody wanted us to be."

"One of Janet's sisters called me at Channel 6," Logan Banks is saying. " 'Can you do something about what is going on with Kerry? We know he didn't have anything to do with it. *Bill Fontanille is a bastard! Bill killed her!*' Which I thought was really kind of peculiar. I said, 'I can't. I can't. I'm too close to it.' "

On January 26, the Louisiana supreme court finally denied the appeals based upon the Speedy Trial Act which had been left hanging since that frenzied first week of November. W.J. could now move to set a trial date. After consultation with Dr. Lee, Dub gave John Mamoulides two dates for Dr. Lee, March or May.

"You take March," District Attorney Mamoulides told W.J.

"That's gonna be cutting it kinda close."

"Do it in March," Mamoulides repeated. He added: "This thing has gone on long enough. The people out there want to see something done. They want to know."

"Yes, sir," Dub said and hurried off to reset the date with Dr. Lee.

"I ask Vince to get with Vieira," Dub says. "The things I want are: the exact spot the baby was found; when were the photographs taken, exactly; in what sequence were they shot on the roll. Because one of the big arguments was that here's this child who has obviously not been *un*cared for for ten hours. I don't want to then start making that argument and have one of them introduce testimony that in fact the child had been screaming, had been cared for and had been brought back to the house by a neighbor or a relative and placed down there to re-create the position where the child was found. I need to nail down a time and condition and sequence, leaving nothing to chance. Close defense doors.

"I also need to get with Vieira on preparing him for trial. You never put words in your witness's mouth, but you need to know what he's gonna say and how he's gonna say it. Especially when he's already testified on it once; then you can work with that and make the presentation more effective.

"Also, I have to put Carol Dixon on or they will. Much as I said I don't want to. A, I take a lot of the sting out by putting her on myself just to show the normal chain of events; and B, the fact that, in the end, the few conclusive results she *did* get were the same as Dr. Lee."

On Tuesday, February 6, Vince finally located and met with Patricia Murphy at Highland Park Hospital across Lake Pontchartrain. The drive was well worth it.

While Ms. Murphy's recall was much more selective in its retention overall than that of her former partner Walter Cardin, the fragmentary images, impressions, and remembered dialogue from that early morning in February 1984 are exceptionally vivid and anecdotal. Vince was kept busy with his pen and notebook. Of the many things Ms. Murphy remembered and told Vince, he especially bore down with his pen when she quoted Kerry as having said he "came home at 2:30 & caught neighbor & wife together. An argument ensued between all three. 'Damn him & her—I came home & caught them. Got into it.' "

"That could've been handled a little differently, and I think it really could've been . . . better," Mike Maunoir says diplomatically. He and W. J. LeBlanc are discussing the problem with Bob Masson's not being able to remember in what sequence and in what form he had used Mrs. LeJeune's first, erroneous, statement concerning her seeing the man walking with the bat on Thursday afternoon in his baiting of Bill after the tape recorder had been turned off that early Saturday morning of his arrest.

"Oh, could've nailed him!" W.J. says. "Could've nailed him with it if it had been handled differently. But it's still very significant to showing guilty knowledge. Of course, it isn't as effective a prosecutorial tool as it could be if Masson could remember that he *actually* even *told* him that."

"That's the kind of thing that detectives usually use to solve a case, to help break somebody. Bob had the ball and didn't really run," Mike has to agree.

"He blew it," W.J. says in a tone as close to real contempt as one will hear from him professionally. "Remember the cross-examination in the James Hearing, when Noriea asked Bob if he ever told him he had an eyewitness looking through the window? That was a primitive and juvenile attempt to bait—'We've got somebody who was looking through the window.' How stupid. Because . . . they're in there ten hours, if that would've happened the police'd been beating the door down! The minute Masson did that, he lost him. He lost any hope of really shaking him up with that stuff."

"That wasn't a good attempt," Mike Maunoir says.

By January and early February, with much of the known and provable facts of their case beginning to reveal themselves, a much more informed and serious game of scenario playing became the rule between the prosecution team, particularly Vince and W.J., for whom, on the point of a before-the-fact conspiracy as opposed to a spontaneous combustion of rage and violence, agreement is the exception.

"The really weird thing," W.J. is saying, "is that both of them describe this hallway encounter that happens at about the same point in time with the two of them that precipitates the end. And the only thing I can ever logically come up with—that they just don't mention because it's too incriminating—is that Billy was going back to finish the job on Ryan and that's why they had the second altercation in that hallway. Because you almost have to say it defies logic and common sense to think that that hallway thing doesn't happen—that can't be a made-up part of the story. It doesn't do anything. They don't *need* the wrestle-in-the-hall story. The hallway scene has always been the strangest part to me," W.J. often says, contradicting his own theories unabashedly, demonstrating that upon what really happened in that house, Dub has the vision and objectivity to not be closed off to anything—as long as it's not in front of a jury.

"But that accounts for all the wounds. How else do they explain the wounds?"

"But if it's like they say and the last thing they do is fight, the question is, what the hell caused it? And it almost makes sense to think that they hear this tapping, and he goes, 'My son's alive, we've got to call help.' 'You're not calling them for help. Jackshit! You can call for an ambulance, but it's gonna be to take another body outa here. He knows me, he can talk—he can't live.' So it's like, 'Waddaya mean?'

" 'I'm gonna go finish the job right now,' they have this big fight in the hall; there's this standoff. Then, it's 'Look, I'm just getting out of here, all right? You're gonna have to take care of your kids in some kind of way. But I'm just getting the fuck outa here.' "

On Saturday, February 9, Vince and Dub interviewed Dr. Gus Gutnisky, the neurosurgeon who treated Ryan. While Vince took the most detailed, orderly, carefully transcribed notes that are in his notebook, W.J.'s specific needs were more limited in scope:

"Dr. Gutnisky could not rule out Ryan being able to tap on the door with his foot," W.J. recalls. "It's possible that it may have been spasmodic. I wouldn't have thought it could happen—that it probably *couldn't* have happened—but he couldn't rule out that it was not spasmodic. Very unlikely, but possible. And we *know* that he moved head to toe at least once, he couldn't have originally lain as he was found because no one could've shut the door, plus you don't vomit from your feet!" W.J. explains, referring to the fact that there were two pools of vomit and blood on the bedroom carpet where Ryan had been—the distance between these two stains appears to be approximately the same number of inches little Ryan was.

"So that's another little thing that doesn't make any sense to me, that tapping," W.J. continues. "I wished it would. But it doesn't. It just doesn't make any sense. Here's a doctor who tells me that it *could've* been spasmodic: I don't think that it's spasmodic, he doesn't think it's spasmodic, the odds are really against spasmodic, but you can't talk in terms of odds when you're talking about testimony. Yet, here's these two bastards that talk about the tapping of the foot. And where in the shit does that come from when it probably didn't happen? Independent of each other!

"Almost makes you believe it. But the trouble with this whole case is that there are so many little things like that that just don't add up. Like, 'That's funny, he never left his room.' That's totally bizarre, especially if he's gonna say that he hears the tapping coming from the master bedroom. Why would he say that afterwards? None of it makes any sense."

"I believe the sex happened. Because I know Janet," Tammy says. "She loved to flirt and she liked Bill a lot. Always. Kerry was always denying that Janet liked Billy. Because Janet and Bill used to always be talking— whenever we'd all get together, those two would always end up sitting and talking. They liked each other.

"Susan knew it. She always felt jealous of Janet. That's one of the reasons she left him. Because she never could understand why Janet always ran to Billy with her problems. Like that night at the Halloween party, Susan said, 'Of all the people there, why'd she have to come and get my husband to comfort her back in the bedroom?' At social gatherings, Janet hung all over Billy."

"The only other way than conspiracy is—say for instance, Fontanille is a victim of circumstance," Vince says. "And that he subsequently conspires with Myers after the killing. This is what I'm going to say. We're buddies. I think you're crazy. I'm sorry I slept with your wife. But I'm gonna get out of here and this is what we're gonna tell the police to protect you.' And he sticks with that scenario until it starts to cave in and then all of a sudden he realizes he's committed to a fantasy and he's got to stick with the cards he's dealt all the way to the end. That's the only other alternative."

"We have to deal only with the facts," W.J. says. "Explain that statement at the hospital, that spontaneous statement. Is that something you make up?

"Unh-unh. And also, I think the meekest, mildest person in the world when stabbed in the chest with a butcher knife is gonna react regardless. I don't care whether you're talking about a little effeminate homosexual, which he was not—you get stabbed in the chest with a butcher knife, you're gonna react. But even if not. Even if Kerry's the guy with the bat the entire time, that doesn't mean that Bill wasn't part of the plan to kill her."

"There is no reason to an irrational act," Vince says as if he's reading it off a chiseled stone tablet somewhere in his mind's eye.

"The idea I get from Janet was that she flirted with everybody," Vince continues. "That she pissed off maybe a few of the girls because she was a flirt and a tease, and her behavior around Bill wasn't unusual because her behavior around other people was the same. So if you come in without any facts and laid down a scenario, I'd tell you husband. Because my experience in other cases, domestics, I know how these things are, and the spouse is the first one you have to eliminate. You always take the easiest scenario, which would've been the husband and wife, and then try and make it work. But, of course, Bill being there—when he's not really logically necessary for this crime to have happened—is a *fact,* and he *stays* there, and he lies, and that messes up all the logic."

"You got it." W.J. jumps on that. "And here, even the people that knew Fontanille best didn't come up first and say, 'Oh, no. He couldn't have done that.' They said, *'He did it.'* And I don't think these people were overreacting when they said, 'Billy's on a rampage,' I think they were basing that on their own personal experiences, that he was one weird motherfucker and that he snapped," W.J. concludes.

"It's a feeling that he was capable of murder sort of after the fact, after there was a murder they feel that, prior to the murder they just knew he's a strange, volatile person," Vincent says as he is agreeing on this point. "But he's still a friend. He's still a member of the group. They play softball together. They're concerned about him, even though he's a strange individual. It's not till after the murder that they really see what potential that they feel was there. 'Jesus!' "

"I ran into Billy in a bar up in Hammond," Ron Dupuy remembers. "I hadn't seen him for a while and soon it was like old times. We picked up a couple of girls and went back to my place.

"The next morning, being kind of hungover, we decided just to blow off the day, get some more beer and just hang out. We barbecued. And then we started driving around drinking beer and Billy starts talking about the case. He wants me to ask him questions like a prosecutor would so he could practice. So that's what we did for the longest time. Nothing really significant came out of it as far as what really happened that night; I didn't know the right questions to ask, and who knows if he would've told me the truth if I had.

"But while we were doing that he said something that really opened my eyes as to the atmosphere, the ambience, inside that house while this thing was going on. I'd said something about how strange it must've been sitting there going through that, and Bill said: 'Yeah, all the lights were off, just the TV, we're sitting there in the dark—man, it was so surrealistic. You know, just like a Hitchcock movie.'

"And a little later he happened to mention one particular Hitchcock movie, *Strangers on a Train.* I didn't think much of it because it was one I've never seen.

"Also, whenever I asked him why he stayed in that house so long— basically, I said, 'Bill, Kerry Myers could never hold you hostage, I know it and you know it.' The reason he kept giving for staying was, 'I was worried about Janet and the baby.' Several times over the course of the day he said it, and it was always exactly that way, 'I just couldn't leave, I was worried about Janet and the baby.' Never plural, as in 'Janet and the babies' or 'kids.'

"Then when I commented that, 'Bill, I know you, you don't have one-night stands.' He laughed and very clearly led me to understand that his and Janet's affair had been going on since the spring or summer before.

"But the thing I'll always remember about that day was him saying, 'Ron, it was so surrealistic, it was like we were in a Hitchcock movie.' "

"That Wednesday night, before the basketball game, when Bill came over to be picked up, Janet pulled him aside while Kerry's in the back getting into his basketball clothes," Brother Jonas is saying. "Now, this is what Bill told me. So she says, 'Kerry's freaking out. He's accusing me of you and I having sex. Don't say nothing to him—but he hit me today.' "

"Remember we said early on that this murder was very indicative of a rage, an emotional killing, it was very, very characteristic of homosexuals when they murder, in its violence and its savagery." Vince has the floor in the command center.

"It wasn't your typical murder. It had a personal touch to it. For something to be planned, it was very sloppy. Knowing the means and the education of the people involved, it just seemed to me that it could've been a lot neater than the way it was done.

"And there's a complete lack of symmetry in this. This guy comes back into their lives and three days later she's brutally murdered. There's a reason for everything. So there must be a reason for lack of symmetry, and that was it—was there or was there not a relationship between Janet and Bill? Single biggest question mark of the scenario game in my view.

"From a practical standpoint, from an investigator's experience standpoint, when things lack symmetry, there're breaks, then there are reasons for these breaks. And usually if you can find out why these breaks in symmetry exist—as far as motive is concerned—if you can find out the reasons for the breaks in symmetry, usually you have your crime solved.

Remember, the solving of a crime is more of a process of elimination than identification. You eliminate all the possibilities, hopefully you'll end up with a conclusion.

"Yet I think we can fool ourselves by trying to analyze every individual aspect of the case—I think by doing so, that's where we're gonna fail. I think you've got to look at the total Bill Fontanille, the total Janet Myers, and total Kerry Myers relationship. You've got to look at the total Bill Fontanille as it relates to his relationship with Susan and his child. And the mental state he was in at the time. Remember he did some pretty weird things. There was definitely a metamorphosis going on with Bill Fontanille.

"So if you just look at Bill Fontanille without looking at the total picture, maybe you can't find logic for what happened. But if you look at Billy Fontanille in terms of his relationship with Susan, and possibly his hate for Susan. And his relationship with Susan and his child—his child wasn't born perfect, and the problem with custody in the divorce, him taking the child—and you still might say that in and of itself is not enough either, but look what it did to him. You ask anybody. He changed."

Vince pauses for a moment and then answers his own argument:

"Yet, still, to me it's not a conspiracy because maybe it was in Kerry Myers's mind that okay this is what we're going to do and it may not have ever been in Billy Fontanille's mind. Kerry Myers may have had no intention whatsoever to kill Susan Fontanille as far as the conspiracy is concerned. I just don't think it was a conspiracy. I don't think Kerry Myers could've pulled it off—to be honest with you."

"Look," W.J. begins in defense of the theory, "I don't have any problem at all with the notion that Kerry Myers told Billy Fontanille, 'Hey, start popping your ass up over at the house so that's she's used to seeing you for when we do this deal.' But that they were not in it together beforehand flies into the face of everything. All right. It flies in the face of the evidence as we know it. It flies in the face of their stand of silence. There ain't no way that that's spontaneous and they're both maintaining the postures that they did over all these years. Not to mention the statements that they made. Not to mention Bill Fontanille's statement 'He's gonna tell you we had a plan' . . . not to mention a dozen other things. Frankly, I just don't see it at all."

"But with all the violence in the marriage, Kerry did not *need* to conspire to kill his wife. It was going to happen sooner or later whether Bill's there or not. So what's Fontanille there for? Wrong place at the wrong time?" Vince asks.

"Uh-huh, it's too much of a reach. You've got to ignore too many things about his behavior while he's there in the house, forever, which to me is one of the two or three most implausible aspects, one of the keys—why does Billy stay in that house? Plus everything he's said or done in all the years afterwards. Also, to buy that, you've got to believe that Fontanille had an affair with her. And I don't see Janet, with her C-section scar still pink and prominent, on the very first day that her doctor has released her to have marital relations, seducing some ball buddy of her husband in the house with two kids there knowing that Kerry's pattern is to pop home at any time."

"As a prosecuting team, we can't be torn apart, we have to go with our facts," Vince offers. "If you look at the facts, the undeniable objective facts, and then you try to apply a scenario to the facts, it paints a picture for you—but you can go out on a limb, it's human beings involved, all kind of emotions and feelings set in. Like if you talk to women, they may have a completely different set of emotions about this than men. I think if you ran a poll, most of the women think the husband killed her."

"There's ample on both sides," W.J. answers. "Ample evidence to support both of them—to me, in my mind, more so for Kerry than for Bill. But look, once we got into it we've always said the case against Kerry is stronger than the case against Bill. Especially prior to that night. It's unbelievable that we could've even proceeded on the notion without Kerry involved in the equation."

"That afternoon, when they'd had sex, Bill said she had her head against the window of Ryan's room, they were watching out the window, and he mounted her with her pants down," Brother Jonas Robertson says. "She just pulled her leotards down—that they did it 'doggie-style,' therefore there was a little bit of comfort there of not getting completely naked and romping and raving exposing the pink scar. Plus there's a lot of paranoia over Kerry coming home, so as this chemistry was happening, Janet expressed her fears and Bill convinced her. He said they were very much afraid of Kerry coming home and catching them."

"They can't *both* be guilty of murder if there is *not* an agreement." W.J. is adamant about the matter.

"If Bill was told to park around the corner, couldn't it just as logically been Kerry that told him to park around the corner? In fact, isn't it *more* logical that it was Kerry, when you've got Kerry's car in the driveway?

"If you just look at the statement given at the hospital. If you just read what he said to the doctor. And some other things—remember when Masson talks to him that night, what's that conversation he has with his mother? He tells his mother he still doesn't know what went on. But he *knew* what went on. He had told the doctor. He had told the nurses. He had told everybody. He told John Taylor immediately that there's two dead people, that his best friend just killed his wife and son. Then he tells his mother, 'I still don't know what happened over there'?"

"It's definitely a puzzle," Vince agrees. "And there are just so many things about Fontanille, that if he were not guilty, it seems that the truth will out. And there's a reason that the truth can't will out in there. Either he is definitely involved, or he's one of the greatest fools that ever walked the face of the earth."

"I don't think he's a fool. And I don't disagree that ultimately Kerry Myers would have killed Janet on his own," W.J. says. "I think that would support the theory that Kerry Myers is the instigator. He's the mastermind behind this whole thing. He's the one with the most to gain and he brings in Billy Fontanille, and Fontanille being the weirdo bastard that he is, may very well have conjured up in his own mind that Kerry was going to be able to knock off Janet. And that then he would have something over Kerry to get him to help him get rid of Susan, the way he was gonna help him get rid of Janet. I don't find that inconsistent at all. Hell, it's a lot like that Hitchcock movie, *Strangers on a Train.*"

"If he isn't really going to do it? If he knows in his mind that it's just a mental exercise, Bill would've loved it. No doubt. Oh, yeah."

Ron Dupuy is responding to the question: what would Bill Fontanille's reaction be to Kerry Myers's asking him to help plan how they could kill their wives?

"The planning, the talking—he'd've eaten it up. That's the kind of things he loves. As long as he kept it straight in his mind that it really wasn't ever going to happen. Particularly when you add the irony that he's also having an affair with the girl he's supposed to be planning to murder; and even more especially since in a very real way he'd be fucking over Kerry Myers, who he has always said didn't deserve to have a wife like Janet; Bill used to talk about how he hated the way Kerry treated Janet, the violence and all.

"And, knowing him, he probably believed he could take it all the way to the last minute and with his dominance stop anything if it got out of control."

"As an investigator I have to take the more pragmatic approach," Vince is saying.

"What if Janet was playing one against the other? From what we know of her, there's that very real possibility—but do we know it? Is it a fact? And if it is, can we prove it? Never.

"But it's like what we've been saying from the beginning, '*Somebody* should be telling the truth.' With that house, the size and layout of it, why didn't they admit seeing the body? If just one would have said, 'Yeah, I saw the body.' That would have changed the whole complexion of this whole case. The whole thing would've fit for him. So why are they *both* lying?"

"I met Bill shortly after he got out of jail and came to live with Jonas," begins Kerri Nickel, a slender, stylish, *very brave,* doe-eyed, toasted-honey-brown-haired young woman who is now a flight attendant for a major airline.

"I thought he was really cute, he was one of these muscle-bound guys. I first saw him at the church in the weight room. He was kind of a to-himself-type person; he wouldn't leave Jonas's house for anything at first, except to go to church once in a while, after that he'd go right back to his room and hide away. He just always looked guilty. I didn't know what was going on until after he told me what had happened, why he was in jail.

"We got close, real close. We kind of dated, but not seriously. He was just mainly to himself. He was always shut up in his room. He was kind of sneaky. He wouldn't tell anybody where he'd be going. We dated about a month and a half. Actually, I went to his room and watched TV. We got *close*. We had a brief relationship. Very brief. I felt *really used.*

"I'd be there baby-sitting the kids and Bill would be in his room right next door, but he would never come over and watch me take care of the kids. In the nursery there's a door that goes between the bathroom and his room and sometimes I'd open that door and we'd talk. He would never break Jonas's rule. He would not come across that threshold.

"I had a real crush on him; so I'd go knock on the door sometimes, and he'd open it. Or I'd call him on the phone and ask him to come to the door so we could talk. There was like all this 'friction' between me and him; he told me it was 'sexual tension' between us.

"One night I was baby-sitting for Jonas, and he came up to the back door and we started talking and before he leaves he grabs me and kisses me. And that just blew my mind. I did not expect that. And then from then— you know, we kept the relationship in the back room. I don't think Jonas even knew about it.

"Our first conversations were about my old boyfriend who I was just breaking up with. Bill was a good friend. A listener. Always flexing his muscles. And very quiet. Eyes always up and down, up and down. He hardly ever looked me in the eye.

"We only had sex three or four times. It was no big deal. At least not to him. He was very . . . passive when it came to that, I guess, I don't know. He would do his breath mint and just lay there. We would never really go all the way through it; sometimes he'd just stop short of—whatever— because he felt guilty, he felt nervous. Well, that's what he said.

"We did it once, we came close to it three or four times. Not kinky. Definitely not kinky. I think it was just to make sure he felt masculine; he wanted to feel like he still had it, I guess. For sexual gratification he used people, he manipulated people. He didn't have to manipulate me, I was this naive kid. I was basically still a teenager or close to it then.

"It was hard to tell—it was hard to read what he wanted, because he would never come out and say it. Like I said, he was very stoic. And I never knew what to do around him, I never knew what to say. It wasn't the sex act that he was looking for. Okay, I should say he tried—we did it one time, the very first time I was back in his room . . . but after that he always cut it short. He would be cold and distant. If I got too close, he'd back off.

"He would tease and play with me the way a cat plays with a mouse."

"It's too easy for him to say 'I parked around the corner because I was gonna go fuck Janet Myers,' " W.J. says adamantly.

"If in fact that was what he was gonna do, or if he was gonna go talk to her. But he doesn't park around the corner to go get the baseball bat! Or to break it off!"

"He couldn't achieve one." Kerri Nickel is crying. "The first time was perfectly normal heterosexual making out leading to intercourse. After that he had problems. I just don't think he really wanted to do it; he would make me think he would, but then he would—you know, nothing would happen, if you know what I mean? It seemed to me—when he got that way after the first time—it seemed like he just wasn't interested in me anymore until he wanted to try it again.

"Sometimes he'd let me hug him and sometimes he wouldn't let me get near him. There were times when he didn't want to be touched period. He would actually flinch or grimace.

"I tried. I wanted to keep it going. He'd be cool, distant. Almost like he didn't . . . like nothing ever meant anything to him."

"I don't have a problem with Kerry swinging the bat," W.J. is saying as he reflects on the "bat man" issue.

"I told you, I firmly believe they both swung the bat. I just do. Dr. Lee will say, without equivocation, that they're both right there by her when it happened. So I personally have no problem with it; but how the hell do you even begin to get into that? I can't."

However, it in no way stops his speculation upon the subject while playing the scenario game, then and now.

"Consider this—we have the coagulation of blood to indicate two beatings—what if the first beating happens exactly like I think it happened, quiet killing, Janet stabbing Billy, then rage. Accidental blow to Ryan. Fight. Negotiations. Kerry walks down the hall. Sees Ryan. Opens up the door, sees Sarah. Goes back into the den. Gives her a look like Peggy Cowan says he gave her when she was in the coffin: pure fucking hatred. And he just picks up that bat and starts whaling at her—'You bitch. You fucking bitch!'

"It could account for the relative lack of spatter, because you don't have that blood flowing anymore. It's still liquid but the heart ain't pumping it out—could account for the reason why you have so much less on him."

* * *

"The problem with putting too much of the battered-wife deal on Kerry is that the more guilty you make him, psychologically, the less guilty you make Bill." W.J. is explaining one of the ironies, if not a flat-out moral dilemma, peculiar and perhaps unique to the baseball bat murder.

"Consequently, I'm only going to use the friends' testimony of old violence if I have to in rebuttal. In the event they put on their 'Camelot marriage defense,' then I trot out all those people.

"We have enough on Kerry to bury him, we need more on Billy. I'm thinking, shit, all the blood would indicate that Bill was stabbed earlier than when Kerry said because he's got all this blood out there that I know ain't coming from his fingers.

"I'm really starting to worry, because the case against Kerry is becoming airtight to the point that by comparison Billy's starting to appear less guilty."

On February 28, the dice the State had to roll on William Fontanille suddenly became loaded ones—in the State's favor. After determining that Dr. George Neri, the treating physician for Bill at Jo Ellen Smith, was now chief of emergency at a hospital in Newburgh, New York, Vince called and within a few minutes knew that a fourth megaton bomb was now securely within the prosecution's armory.

Dub was a very happy man again. And the scenario game can be played again without that edge of tension.

"To me it is supportable by the evidence to put Bill as the bat man—even though frankly I think they probably both were. But I'm trying the case in front of a jury, the jury is gonna be more likely to convict a person of murder that they *think* is the one who committed the murder. The bat man. Principals notwithstanding, juries see the trigger man, the bat man, as the murderer.

"So, since I'm trying Bill Fontanille in front of a jury, not Kerry Myers, then that's who I'm putting as the bat man. Because I've got a judge who knows what principals mean. If I put Kerry Myers as the bat man, the jury might walk Bill Fontanille.

"Kerry's gone. Whether the judge believes that Kerry actually did it or not, I know I have enough to sink Kerry. As a principal or otherwise. It's funny how it all turned around. Early on my big concern was how the hell do I poke holes through this 'happy marriage' shit—but, man, as we start overturning these rocks and all this stuff starts crawling out, I know I had this guy, and I'm worrying about the other one."

On March 3, W.J. and Vince flew to Houston, Texas, and interviewed Gabriel LaMarche, the emergency room nurse at Jo Ellen Smith Hospital

the night of the murder. When they flew back the following day, they had
at least a bazooka round to fire at Nick in close-quarter support of Dr.
Neri.

"What if that is true? Bill's conspiracy statement at the hospital," W.J.
begins.

"What if that is *exactly* true? What if Bill was the one to tell Kerry—
what if he is incredibly psychotic—what if he says, 'Yeah, I'm gonna do it.'
And then afterwards tells Kerry, 'You crazy motherfucker, it was only a
game!' Or, what if he *tells Janet about it?* Wow, I mean, that makes more
sense to me than anything."

Dub's random thought about the plot of one of Hitchcock's classic films,
Strangers on a Train—the appearance of a conspiracy between two men
to kill a wife and mother respectively, but only one of them has any
intentions of actually doing it—intrigued him to the degree that he personally called around the TV stations and cable companies to see if the movie
had aired within a period of six months prior to the murder: he felt a little
foolish asking Vince or Mike to run down as whimsical a lead as that. He
learned that it *had* been broadcast as a late-night movie only weeks before
the murder of Janet Myers. However, he told no one of this, because it was
useless information which he would have no predicate for introducing at
trial, and anyway he already had a scenario he could sell to a jury—but
still?

"If you ask me, that's the only possible scenario for the delayed beating.
It's got to happen with both of them there—and that's the only way that
could happen. That makes so much sense and that is so incredibly bizarre.
But I can live with that. It's very consistent with everything. And it puts
a whole new twist on the 'he's gonna tell you we had a plan' statement Bill
made to John Taylor and Torchy Adams at the hospital.

"Look at the dilemma that the person who didn't actually go through
with it is in—he can't tell, because then he would have to say yes, we
talked about killing our wives, but I was only fudging. Who's gonna believe
him? That gives both men, whoever you think *didn't* do the initial beating,
the impetus to participate and to also keep shut up about it for all these
years."

"Like Billy, Kerry was from a broken family," Mike Price is saying as he
continues to try to explain what is seemingly unexplainable. However, this
time, perhaps he does just that.

"You see, his parents' personal problems—well, one of them had been
having a lot of fun playing the field. And Kerry was young when it happened.

"Kerry finally told me about it. He said that Mr. Cliff came home and
caught her in bed with some guy while Kerry was in the hallway. And

that's when he took the kids away from her. He'd caught her before, the infidelities are what broke up the marriage, but she'd had custody of the three kids. Well, not after that time. Clifford Jr. was old enough to handle it, Kerry was ten or eleven, and it made a difference. Kerry said he actually saw her in bed with this guy.

"He'd talk to girls more about it. Kerry kind of had a modus operandi when he dated girls. When that rush of puppy love wore off a little bit, he started trying to play on their sympathy."

"Kerry was bitter towards his mother because he believed she destroyed the marriage," Connie Cassard is saying.

"He always told me that he would *not* end up like his parents; he *would not* be divorced. In his book, that was just 'No.' He harped a lot on that. He really did.

"Kerry also used to tell me that his daddy and mother used to physically fight—his real mother, Marguerite, and Mr. Cliff. He used to see them physically fight. He said there was a lot of that going on in the house. That's why I've always said this is history repeating itself."

"When did Bill give his statement?" Nick Noriea begins. "When did Kerry give his? I have reason to believe that Kerry was given Bill's statement before he gave his statement—*now* whattaya know about *that?*

"I still have a lot of friends with the police department. And sometimes these guys get cocky, drinking at the bar, and I know too many police officers—a lot of which are now working in the Jefferson Parish Sheriff's Office, by the by.

"That's how I got it. The source was good enough for me; from a high-rank officer over there, to a high-rank officer on this side: 'Hey, you wanna hear about fuck-ups? Our guy Masson *gave Fontanille's statement to Myers.*' Mirror images my ass!' "

"You almost have to believe a lot of their stories, it's almost too bizarre not to. There's too much to make up there."

W.J. is again musing upon some of the extreme oddities of the baseball bat murder.

"I've always been struck by the fact that Maureen Rilette said it was a medium jog—the man she saw going down the street at one forty-five that morning. That it was not in dire haste.

"And the amber glass with A type blood bothers the hell out of me. Where does it come from? Does it come from being smashed? Does it come from being bled on? And by whom? Ryan? And it was found in the hall? Of course, it could've been kicked there in a struggle. But still, no matter where it was before, it makes no sense with what we know.

"Take the love seat: there is an obvious indentation just crusted with blood—well, we say blood, I suppose it could've been chocolate pudding, because the sumbitches took a zillion pictures of it but didn't take one sample to prove it was blood. But every expert that has looked at the pictures says it has to be blood, but they can't testify to it because it wasn't tested. But it's blood, and the only person bleeding from the back is Bill, so we know he must've sat there for a fairly long period of time, judging by the amount of what appears to be blood and the indentation that looks like it's made by somebody's ass. Therefore, while we can't prove it, we know Bill was bleeding early on and he sat in that love seat—although *both* men absolutely steer us away from either of them *ever* sitting there. The only places they swear they sat were the big sofa, the floor by the big sofa, and the recliner chair. *Why don't they want us to know that Bill sat there?*

"And what makes it all the more confusing is that all of the broken bric-a-brac on the love seat is on *top* of the bloodstain. And Billy ain't gonna sit on all that broken glass and ceramic shit. So we can only assume that they're telling the story not only in mirror images, but they are also changing the time and sequence of events—*in concert.*

"But then again, if Billy's stabbed in the beginning, then how come there's not blood all over the kitchen? This is the sumbitch that said he went into the kitchen twice!"

"I've never ever once believed that Bill committed this crime," Madeleine Landrieu is saying. "I've always known that he had more to do with it than he is saying, and there are more pieces to the puzzle that he is not articulating to us either purposefully or that he has blocked out, but I never ever believed that he was capable of this kind of violence. I've always found him to be very quiet and reserved.

"I do a lot of driving with Bill during the final weeks and days before the trial. We drive by to where his car was parked—he shows me exactly where his car was parked—and then we drive the route that he remembers taking to his parents' home and then the route to Jo Ellen Smith—to get an accurate timing of it.

"One of the major things I'm doing that weekend is working with Bill in the event that he testifies. Trying to prepare him for it. [Nick refuses to make that decision until necessary.]

"So I spend a lot of time preparing Bill for his testimony, working with him. And what is very clear to me—if you notice, when you speak to Bill, he darts his eyes. And I'm working with him on a significant amount of eye contact. I get up close to Bill, and talk to him—even as we sit and drive with me in the passenger seat, I *make* him look at me. 'Bill, *look at me.*' I'm almost making him look at me so long that it gets uncomfortable for him—it would be uncomfortable for anybody to keep eye contact that long. But I'm almost trying to take him to a dramatic extreme so that he will get very used to it.

"I remember saying to him, 'Bill, every one of your responses and every one of your body signs tell me that you feel guilty about this, and I know you do.' And we start talking about his sense of guilt.

"I say 'Bill, I sense that a lot of the guilt I see in your eyes and in your face and in your responses to me account for the fact that you think had you not had an affair with Janet, she would not be dead. And you're ridden with that.'

"He looks at me and says, 'Yes!' I say, 'Well, you know what? You *are* guilty of that. You are guilty of having an affair with a married woman. You are guilty of putting her in a situation to cause a violent explosion. But you're *not* guilty *of her murder.* And unless you distinguish those two in your mind, the jury won't be able to either. So when they read guilt on your face, they're not going to pay as close attention to you as I am, and that guilt will be, "He did it." '

"I remember him looking at me saying, 'But, I did it. *I am guilty of that.*' Now, he also has a lot of other guilt with it—'Could I have saved her? Should I have saved her? What should I have done differently?'

"I'm convinced that a lot of his guilt feelings and what shows in his responses to questioning is simply that—that he feels guilty about the affair."

"I couldn't believe it when she called me." Tammy DuBuc is remembering the time, about a week before the trial, when Lorraine Cannon, some four years late, telephoned to invite her over for a visit in order finally to accept her offer to talk and explain what she knew.

"I'm really nervous, because I'm thinking Kerry put her up to it. Some kind of setup. That was my first thought. So I called her back and asked if it was for her and her husband, or if Kerry told her to do it, and she assured me it had nothing to do with Kerry and the trial.

"I was still very scared; I mean I was *very* nervous when I got there. I looked around and I didn't see any other cars but theirs, but I was still scared when I first walked in. He opened the door, Mr. Cannon. I said, 'I'm Tammy.' He said, 'Oh, *you're Tammy,*' like that. I'm thinking, 'Oh, Lord, this is really gonna be something!'

"But then I went in and Mrs. Cannon was very nice. He hardly said a word—he just kind of sat there and gave me this grin that looked like . . . like, I could read his mind—and he's sitting there thinking, 'This girl is *so* stupid, I can't believe she believes all this stuff.' That's the feeling I got from him. Just sitting there with this goofy grin on his face the whole time.

"But she sat there and talked, and was very nice. And I told her everything I could think of about the violence. She never once got angry or raised her voice. Most of the time she would blame Janet, like, 'She was trying to make him jealous.'

"But always, after every story, immediately, 'Did he slap her or punch her?' I'm thinking, 'What's the difference?' I mean, I found that very strange. Then it dawned on me that there was a difference to her because maybe there was a lot of that that went on in that family. And then she would always turn everything I said to look like it was Janet's fault.

"The other thing, she constantly blamed Curtis and Mike and Billy for Kerry and Janet's problems. Because they used to 'always take Kerry out to games; keep him out late at night when they knew that whenever he got home that Janet was going to be mad. They did it on purpose to get her aggravated at him because they knew that they'd get into a fight,' she said.

" 'I don't know about that.' But she said they used to do that constantly; she really blamed them for a lot of Janet and Kerry's fighting.

"Then she kept on asking me, 'Well, why did Susan leave Bill? She divorced him, so he *must've* been beating on her.' I kept telling her, 'He never did that. Why would you think that?' I said, 'They had other problems—there *are* other problems in a marriage.' 'But she left him, so he had to've been doing something really serious for her to leave him.'

"And what was really strange about it was Mrs. Cannon and Susan used to work together. As a matter of fact, they used to car-pool—they were pretty good friends until all this happened.

"But she kept saying, 'Well, why was she so scared of him? Why'd she have to leave the house?' I'm going, 'She wasn't scared of him. They just had problems.' 'Well, she must've been afraid of him or she wouldn't have divorced him.' And I'm trying to explain, 'You don't have to be afraid of somebody to divorce him. Not *everybody* has *that* problem.' But just real strange comments like that, I never could quite figure those out.

"We parted well—but I don't think she believed a word I told her. Ever. But what I'll always remember was every time, after every story, 'Well, was it a slap or a punch? Was it a slap or a punch?' I really think that tells it all.''

"Where's that motive? Other than not wanting to leave a witness, that's the only possible motivation there could be. Beyond something incredibly psychotic."

Dub is addressing one of the thorniest elements of the baseball bat murder: the extensive bruising about the lower torso of Ryan. The contusions on his lower back were so severe that a kidney specialist was consulted shortly after his arrival at the hospital.

"Dr. Gutnisky, the neurosurgeon that treated Ryan, brings that up, and

I say, 'Look, unless specifically asked about that, don't volunteer it.' He goes, 'Okay, no problem.'

"Then when I have a chance to digest this . . . ' I have no *idea* how I would work that in, or even account for it.' So I figure if they're gonna do it—which I can't imagine why either would—I'll deal with it then. But I'm not going to bring it up. Because I don't know what to make of it. I still don't know what to make of it. I don't know why there was never pictures taken of Ryan, frankly.

"But . . . it's pretty hard to believe that Ryan was hit by accident—which of course everybody in this case has always chosen to accept on faith."

"I just don't know how they can block out the facts of saying, 'Hey, Kerry was involved in her murder!' What is it that they are so brainwashed by him?" Peggy Cowan gets angry when she speaks on this subject: the Cannons' never-wavering faith and belief in their son-in-law.

"Her father said, there in the funeral parlor, he would not rest in peace *ever* until he knew exactly who did this. Kerry was sitting right there when Mr. Cannon said, 'If I ever find out, or if it ever comes out, which one hurt my baby, if it is any different than we believe, I will kill the bastard.' "

"Not too long before the trial, Kerry asked me to meet with him at his attorney's office. When I get there they asked me to recount the story of the broken door-glass to them so that they could call me as a witness," Mike Price is saying. "And when I told them what I saw, Kerry throwing her down the steps, grabbing her around the neck, slamming her head onto the car, the whole thing, Kerry looked at me with the most incredulous look—'That's not the way I remember it, Mike.' I looked at him and said, 'Well, that's the way it happened.' 'No, I just held on to her until you came out and held her so I could go to work.'

"Wiley's sitting there—Kerry was going on with the story as he wanted it to be—and Wiley started saying, 'Don't you remember it *this* way? Isn't this the *right* way that you'll remember it?' Soliciting me to go along with what he said.

"At that point I realized that what they wanted was for me to commit perjury. I said, 'Kerry, I will not lie for you.'

"I readily admit—the first grand jury hearings, the second grand jury hearings, I did slant things I said in Kerry's favor. I mean, there's no defense for it, but I did it and I'm not sorry that I did it. At the time I thought I was doing what was right."

"The Cannons *knew*." Peggy Cowan has very real anger in her voice, even as it lowers in volume and is pointedly deliberate. "The Giardinas aren't the only people who saw her with bruises and things, *I saw them.*

Not only me, her *parents* saw them. Oh yes, indeed! Janet told me she went home one night—she and Kerry had gotten into an argument—she went home to her mother and they told her to go back home and work out her own problems!

"Janet said that Lorraine told her, 'Men are just that way. Sometimes those things happen, everyone gets angry at times and that's that. Your place is with your husband.'

"Now, this was when she was pregnant with Sarah when she went home and they sent her back. That's why they will never publicly doubt Kerry, because they'd be admitting—even to themselves—that they sent her back to be murdered."

"People ask me often if I feel threatened by Bill, or frightened by Bill—never. It never crosses my mind," Madeleine Landrieu says.

"The incident with Susan—the tearing up of the house. Anybody could do that—it never caused me any concern. My brothers beat walls too. Susan and I talked, and she's always been convinced that he didn't do this. Because what I've always thought is key is that when Bill develops conflict in his life, he withdraws, he becomes silent, he'll sit by himself, he doesn't want to talk to anybody, he becomes nonverbal.

"That's why his marriage broke up, essentially; because he would not confront issues. He would just cloak himself within his shield until he got over it and then come out and never discuss it.

"Kerry, on the other hand, is violent; and Kerry deals with confrontations confrontationally. So there has never been any doubt in my mind about Kerry's guilt in this event. And that Bill was an unfortunate bystander whose involvement became a tangled web because of his low self-esteem. I have no doubt—no doubt in my mind—that that night as they sat there, Kerry told Bill, 'You son of a bitch, had you not slept with her I never would've done this.' And quite frankly, Bill believed it, and that's why I think Bill sat there with Kerry, perhaps trying to figure out a way to get them both out of it, perhaps trying to do—whatever. Because I think at that time in Bill's mind, Bill considered himself responsible. *Very much responsible.*"

Regarding the seemingly indisputable fact that Bill was in close proximity to Janet while she was being beaten, Ms. Landrieu pauses in thought and then, choosing her words very carefully, offers:

"I think . . . there may have been a second beating. That Janet was already . . . if not dead than half dead at that point and Kerry said, you know, something like, 'It's your fault and if you don't believe it, come on and I'll show you just how dead she really is,' and the beating started again and Bill was there when that was happening. I wouldn't find that really difficult to believe. I *don't* find that difficult to believe."

* * *

"I found Mike to be a complex individual. I found him to be very, very introspective. Especially as it relates to his relationship with Kerry." W.J. is speaking about his interviews with the fair-haired all-American kid next door and fellow Shaw alumnus, namely Mike Price, the most visible, publicized, out-front, and loud zealot and sworn-to-the-last-bunker defender of the honor and innocence of Kerry Myers.

"He was deeply hurt—a very real sense of betrayal by Kerry. At the first meeting he is very cautious. Then I start explaining some things to him, evidence that we have: the transcript of the 911 tape, and the whole tape itself—he had been subpoenaed for the first trial and the conspiracy, so he had never heard it. He also didn't know that Kerry hadn't passed the polygraph test. That, I feel, devastated him more than anything else—finding out Kerry had failed the polygraphs.

"Once he starts finding out this stuff, it's like, 'I don't fucking believe this. I don't fucking believe this!' This whole new world is opening up. An ugly world where he realizes what a fool he's been played by Kerry. Mike's just struggling within himself. But being very cooperative after that."

"I didn't want Kerry to be guilty—bottom line, *I didn't want Kerry to be guilty*," Mike Price is now admitting. "It was much easier for me that Billy be guilty.

"I went in there hostile—I mean, I'll tell ya, I walked in there *very* hostile. W.J. and I went back and forth—sparring back and forth. Everything he said, I had a 'but' for. Then one of the buts was: 'But Kerry passed a lie detector test.' And he and Vince looked at each other with this astonishment and then they both started laughing. And they just laughed and they laughed. I'm sitting there wondering, what in the hell?

"Finally they stopped and W.J. said, 'He told you he *passed* a lie detector?'

"I said, 'No, he told me he passed *two* lie detector tests.'

" 'Hold on a second,' W.J. said, and he started rifling through stuff and he pulls out the polygraph, the report, transcripts, the 911 tape, everything. The lie about the polygraph cut out my heart. The 911, man! That blew my mind. I was stunned. I mean, I really was speechless as I listened to it, and when it was over with and they showed me a couple more things, I just sat there for moment and then I said, 'The son of a bitch *lied to me,* he's been lying to *me*—for six years.'

"From that point on, I totally lost all respect for Kerry. It was the next day that he called me and I had that meeting with him and Wiley when they wanted me to lie for them."

* * *

With the loss of faith, Mike can finally tell the full story of perhaps the worst of the dozens of fights between Kerry and Janet he has personally witnessed. "The truth is there was violence, extreme violence there. I feared—and Monique feared—for Janet's life.

"We were sitting in the trailer watching TV and we hear—and it wasn't unusual, I mean every six or seven hours there was a fight: you'd hear na-na-na-na crash, da-da-da-da crash—like, you know, the cartoons on TV where they run up and down, then you hear a crash, well, this is what's going on inside the trailer.

"Monique was watching something stupid on TV, it was some women's show, and I just turned around to watch the trailer, figuring this was more interesting, more along my line of fun.

"The next thing I know—it was almost like déjà vu of the day we met her—trailer door swings open, the body comes hurtling out, scrhhhh! hitting the shells, Kerry pulls the glass storm door closed and he's in the process of closing the front door, and she grabs this handful of shells and rocks and hums 'em.

"I went, 'Ding, ding, round one.' I just knew this was problems. Kerry *leapt* off the doorjamb—it's like three steps, maybe three feet high—down into the shells, grabbed her by the face, and *slammed* her head down on the car—and she's screaming bloody murder.

" 'Help, Mike! Help!'

"I'm watching, man; I'm thinking, 'Yep, he's gonna kill her this time.' And she's steady screaming, 'Please, help me, Mike! Please!'

"So Monique's looking at me—we'd been dating almost about the same amount of time Kerry and Janet had—and she says, 'Don't do it. Don't go out there.'

"By this time he's got her by the neck and is twirling her around in the shell drive. I say, 'Can't let him kill her. I don't give a shit if she dies or not, but he's my friend. I don't want him going to jail.' That's exactly what I said, 'I don't want him going to jail.'

"I went out and said, 'Kerry, this ain't worth it. Send the bitch home. Get her out of your life, *this ain't worth going to jail for.* Let her go!' "

"I didn't think I'd ever hear those words come out of Mike's mouth." Monique is remembering the night her husband came home after his meeting with W. J. LeBlanc. " 'That SOB *did it.* I oughta *kill him* for the way he's used me all these years!'

"The first thing he said as he came in the door, 'I'll be damned, *he did it.*'

"He was so angry, all of this was spilling out of his mouth, and it was just such a difference to hear this coming from him—I mean, this thing had been *between* us for six years."

"He couldn't have hurt me any worse if he'd tried," Mike Price says.

"There's nothing else in this world that Kerry could've done to make me feel the way I did that night.

"Then I started thinking back to the first morning in the hospital when Kerry told me about coming home at two o'clock and then changed it. I sat right here and said to Monique, 'The son of a bitch was lying to me from the very *first sentence*!' "

BOOK IV

"Only when we learn whatever bond exists between these people, will we know what actually happened that evening and why."

—Judge E. V. Richards

17
Pretrial

Like I said once before, time to write in your journal is scarce. It has been awhile . . . many things have happened . . . so I'll catch up.

You just turned seven months old. A few weeks ago you realized that crawling wasn't quite as hard as you thought. You have been crawling all over and have been taking a few bumps and bruises now and then. I suppose it won't be long before I pack the walker away. . . .

Christmas 1981 was your first, and although you didn't understand it all, I believe you had fun. The Christmas tree didn't enchant you as much as I anticipated, but the ribbons and the wrapping paper held your interest. "Santa Claus" was generous to you with clothes and toys from the family. Santa Claus brought a Jack-in-the-box and some blocks to our house.

This was one of the poorest Christmases financially that Dad and I can remember. But we made it. Having you here for Christmas made everything worthwhile.

—Journal of Janet Cannon Myers

*   *   *

"He's gotta do it," W. J. LeBlanc again says to Howat Peters—but in a whisper this time. The two prosecutors fiddle needlessly with their ties, suit coats, and files as they stand behind the DA's end of the long table and wait for Judge E. V. Richards to take the bench on Wednesday morning, March 14, 1990, for the first pretrial motion in *State of Louisiana* v. *Kerry Myers and William Fontanille,* second degree murder.

"No way Wiley's gonna let E.V. try his man," Dub adds.

"Yeah, but maybe not today," says Peters. He is squatly built, perpetually rumpled, round-faced, a decade or so older than W.J. "He's probably gonna take us to the wire first."

Shortly thereafter the tall, stately-mannered Judge Richards ascends to take his seat, whereupon all others take theirs, except for the immaculately tailored W. J. LeBlanc. He keeps his feet through the perfunctory present-at-the-bar announcements by himself, Wiley Beevers, and Nick Noriea, and then addresses the court.

"There are a couple of motions set today in this case, one a motion for continuance filed on behalf of Kerry Myers by Mr. Beevers. I believe pursuant to discussion, the court is going to defer ruling until Monday."

"That's correct," begins the judge. "It's my understanding from conversation with Mr. Beevers, writs were applied either to the fifth circuit or the supreme court asking that the trial scheduled for Monday be stayed until a ruling is made. I think it is premature to consider whether or not the case should be continued. I'm going to reserve ruling until Monday."

"If there's any ruling, I'll immediately notify the court, the district attorney, and cocounsel," the silver-maned and hawk-nosed Wiley Beevers drawls in response.

The trial that Judge Richards and Wiley are referring to, and the reason the latter is seeking a continuance of Fontanille-Myers, has nothing to do with the pursuit of justice in the murder of Janet Cannon Myers. Rather it is a civil litigation between Wiley's wife and her ex-husband involving a substantial amount of money.

The other pretrial motion isn't to be tabled for a later date: it is another motion to sever by Nick Noriea on behalf of his client William Fontanille, this time with a bit of a rare twist—Nick, in his capacity as defense counsel, wants to take the stand and testify.

Consequently, after some legal wrangling over the issue of briefs being "filed timely" or not, Nick Noriea nimbly climbs up into the box and, after being duly sworn in as a witness in case number 87-3280, Division B of the 24th Judicial District Court, State of Louisiana, testifies in part to the following:

"Your Honor, I've represented William Fontanille for over four and a half years, since the original indictment. During the course of this litigation it has always been the State's position that William Fontanille was a murderer. The State sought the death penalty against Fontanille in 1986 with Kerry Myers as a star witness. At that time we retained an expert and prepared our entire cross-examination to show that Kerry Myers was a murderer. That continues to be what we're doing.

"We have four experts who will testify, according to the information that they have, that Kerry Myers was the murderer. Fontanille's testimony indicates that he clearly was not responsible for what was done. All the evidence shows that they are the only two people that were in the house that night and, accordingly, are the *only* two people in the *entire* world that would be in a position to commit the crime. So the exculpation of

Fontanille himself and his experts during the course of the trial will point the finger at Kerry Myers. Accordingly, all the State's evidence that I have seen points the finger in the direction of Fontanille, and we have to cross-examine that. . . . I'm not really sure what the State is going to try to do with respect to Kerry Myers, because they can't call him as a witness in this case. But our entire case is predicated on showing Kerry Myers was the murderer."

Then, in an even rarer occurrence in a criminal case, Mr. Noriea's adversarial cocounsel, Wiley Beevers, proceeds to cross-examine him.

"Mr. Noriea, have you made or has your client made an election at this time as to whether or not he will testify at a trial on the merits if and when the same goes to trial?"

"If the trials are together—he's probably not going to be able to testify unless they're severed," Nick answers.

"No further questions," Wiley pronounces.

Judge Richards looks to W.J. and asks, "Mr. LeBlanc, do you have any questions?"

"No, judge," Dub says, not entirely masking his bemused contempt for what he feels is nothing less than a judicial farce.

Then, as expected by all, the ever dignified and courtly Judge Richards rules no to the single most important judicial issue of the baseball bat murder case. The judge uses a three-pronged rationale for denying severance. The first is of the professional courtesy genre: that Judge Eason had chosen to put back together what he himself had once set asunder, and "I'm unaware of any facts that have arisen since that decision to justify tampering with that decision."

Secondly the judge states, "Mr. Myers has waived trial by jury, as I understand. So the jury in this case will be concerned only with whether or not the State has met the burden of proof beyond a reasonable doubt that Mr. Fontanille committed this offense. As a practical matter there is a severance."

And the third consideration is that "from the review of the testimony in the first trial and review of the statements of both defendants, I can't find they're antagonistic defenses. The fact of the matter is that as I appreciate both defendants' positions, they don't know how Mrs. Myers was killed."

Not too long thereafter, once some purely lawyerly bookkeeping is handled, the first of one of the most extraordinary series of pretrial hearings in any courtroom anywhere comes to an end with W. J. LeBlanc more than a little concerned that the judge has so clearly stated his second consideration, what Dub knows is the linchpin in the argument for severance.

"With the judge enunciating that particular reason—that the two triers-of-fact in essence severs the trial—we just *know* the next time we see Beevers in court he's gonna be saying, 'We exercise our right to a jury trial

and here's a motion to sever.' And after all this time, after all this preparation, all this planning, we're gonna be put in the damnable position of
having to try Fontanille before Myers!''

"This is your motion for continuance?" Judge E. V. Richards asks of
Wiley a little after nine, Monday morning, March 19, 1990.

Mr. Beevers proceeds to inform the court that as of this moment his
wife's trial has not been stayed. He continues, "This weekend in preparation for *that* trial I have worked over thirty hours and would respectfully
ask the court to reconsider or to consider my motion for continuance on
behalf of Mr. Myers."

Judge Richards, the very essence of reasonable manner and erudite
articulation, tells Myers's defense counsel that he'd "had a long conversation" with his counterpart in the civil case, Judge Allen, upon which he
learned that Mr. Beevers's participation as attorney is only for his intervention for attorney's fees, and that another attorney is, in fact, responsible for the major portion of the representation of Mrs. Beevers.

Judge Allen also assured Judge Richards "that considering the nature of
the two cases, if the trial of the case in his court becomes an impediment
to trying the case in this court, that he will on his own motion continue
that case."

"I don't *want* that case continued!" Wiley barks with all the proprietary
emphasis of a Mississippi blue-tick suddenly aroused from a lazy snooze.

Wiley then pleads his case from every angle. He tells the court, "If I have
to withdraw from my participation in that case, Your Honor, it would hurt
me *very* deeply." And that while another attorney might try that case, "I
am more familiar with that case than anybody on the face of this earth. . . .
I hate to sound melodramatic, but I *live* with this case day and night."

Mr. Beevers then makes the rather astonishing admission that "I have
not prepared for the Myers trial in that regard, Your Honor, and I have
discussed the ethical problem that I might have should this case go to trial
and I have explained to my client that under the Code of Professional
Responsibility, as I read it, that it might become incumbent upon me to ask
the court to allow me to withdraw from representation of him. Mr. Myers
has indicated that he does not wish that nor do I wish that."

However, Wiley says he has already "prepared a motion to withdraw as
attorney for Kerry Myers" in the event that a continuance is denied, even
though it is with "great reluctance," and that never has he, "as long as I
have been practicing law, been put in this position and have never stood
before the bar and asked the court to consider my personal business before
my client."

After again explaining how "Judge Allen, by his statement, relieved a lot
of decision-making for me," Judge Richards says, "With that in mind,
you're going to have to convince me more that you can't be ready for Mr.

Myers's trial by next week for me to grant a continuance."

"Well, deny my motion," Wiley suddenly retorts in a tone of condescending, brusque dismissal, and adds, "I do not know whether I'll take writs on it but I intend to guard that trial date in domestic court."

"I am going to deny your motion for continuance, but again I do hope that you'll be able to do that," Judge Richards says. "If I can accommodate you in any way in helping hold that day preparing for this one, I will certainly be happy to do it. I do know at this stage Mr. Myers waived a trial by jury."

Here it comes, both Dub and Howie are thinking.

"That's correct," is, however, all that comes from Wiley's pursed, thin mouth.

"I don't know if you will participate in voir dire, since the jury is not going to try the issues in the case," Judge Richards adds. "So that will give some additional time in preparation of this case. I haven't heard enough evidence at this point to justify considering letting you withdraw from the case. I certainly would be very reluctant to do that. I'm not going to do that at this point."

"In light of the court's ruling, Mr. Myers and I will confer and we'll do whatever we need to," Wiley yodels over his shoulder as he turns from the bench en route to an indignant beeline from the proceedings.

"When's the sumbitch gonna do it? When's he gonna drop that shoe?" Howie says.

"I don't know. But what's he up to with this withdrawal shit? I mean, man, what is going on with him? He's always been goofy, but this is something else," W.J. answers.

First thing Wednesday morning, March 21, Judge E. V. Richards nods in the direction of Wiley Beevers.

"Your Honor, I have filed another motion to continue and also a motion to withdraw as counsel of record," Myers's defense counsel informs the court, and then announces that, in connection with his motions, he is offering the court a copy of the Rules for Professional Conduct, and that he too wants to take the stand and testify.

"All right, sir," Judge Richards says evenly, amicably, as he watches Wiley Beevers now climb up into his witness box!

Once duly sworn in, Mr. Beevers proceeds to testify in open court to, in part, the following: that over and above the "some thirty hours the previous weekend [spent] answering one writ in connection with my wife's case" he now has "three other writs" which require "a response by March the 26th."

Then, at the end of a tedious recitation of the sequence and condition of the many continuances in the long history of the baseball bat murder case, Mr. Beevers states:

"I feel it is incumbent upon me to call to the court's attention, as well as my client's attention, that I do not feel like I am adequately prepared to go to trial in this case. I have discussed it with my client fully, openly, and with his knowledge, he has informed me that if I am unable to secure a continuance to adequately prepare for trial—and I call the court's attention that this is a murder two case, carrying a life imprisonment—that he would discharge me."

"Mr. Beevers, does your testimony cover the motion to withdraw based on irreconcilable differences?" Judge Richards asks and then adds, "Have you touched on the differences?"

"I have not, Your Honor," Wiley says. "Based on my conversation with my client, it was decided that we would present the motion to continue first, and hopefully that we would not get to the motion to withdraw based on irreconcilable differences. If the court denies this motion, then we will proceed with that."

W. J. LeBlanc again is able to only somewhat mask his contempt for what he is certain is only a ploy as he bores in hard when he is given the opportunity to cross-examine defense counsel: "Mr. Beevers, this matter was previously set for motions, on a motion to quash on October 31st, 1989, in Judge Eason's court. Do you recall that day?"

"Absolutely."

"Do you recall saying that day that you were ready for trial and that regardless of the court's ruling, you did not want to do anything to disturb the November 6th trial date?"

"I also remember asking for—"

"Do you recall saying that, Mr. Beevers? And then—you know the rules—yes or no, then you can *explain* it *any way* you want."

"I also asked for a stay of that November 6th trial."

"Do you recall at that time, in open court, saying that?"

"I do," admits Wiley. Soon thereafter he is off the stand and back behind counsel table as E. V. Richards addresses him directly.

"I know that you have been pressed with trial of the other case involving your wife. I do know, however, that that case was stayed and it is not going to trial. I do know that you have at least this week and probably a good part of next week to prepare for the trial of this case. I'm impressed with your abilities as a lawyer, I'm impressed with the fact that this is not a new case."

While acknowledging the validity of Wiley's domestic problems and observing that he knew him to be a good attorney, the judge states: "This is not the first time that it's been set for trial. The trial preparation that you have to go through, you would have at least gone through once before when the trial was set, so I'm not convinced that you cannot be prepared to try this case competently and adequately on Monday. So, for those reasons, I'm going to—again, with some reluctance for your personal situation—deny the motion for continuance."

In short order and again quite brusquely Wiley Beevers announces, "I would like to proceed, with the court's permission, with my next motion, which is a motion to withdraw, and call as my first witness Kerry Myers."

"All right, sir."

Then, for the second—and many believe the last—time in his life, Kerry Myers takes the stand in open court and testifies "on his oath" that, while he and his attorney have had occasion to discuss trial strategy at great length, at the present time they have "irreconcilable differences in the way we feel this case should be tried."

Kerry then affirms that his attorney has fully explained the ramifications of Judge Richards's being the trier of fact in his case. In fact, he testifies that that is the very reason he and his attorney have agreed they cannot disclose the "nature and extent of these irreconcilable differences," but that they are there and that he wishes to discharge his counsel.

"I have no further questions, Your Honor," Wiley soon says.

W. J. LeBlanc rises immediately, but deliberately, and then in like fashion asks of his fellow Archbishop Shaw High School alumnus:

"What are these irreconcilable differences, Mr. Myers?"

Wiley is up in a silver flash, yodeling, "Your Honor, I object to that and this is one of the problems that we have in this case. He is not at liberty to disclose to the district attorney the irreconcilable differences that may occur. That is between me and my client. I can understand an in camera inspection by the judge, but he doesn't get to know what the trial strategy is and I do not have to reveal, nor does this man have to reveal, what those differences are, because it's calling upon him to give testimony in this hearing that he would not—that the district attorney may not be able to get in an open hearing."

"I agree, Mr. Beevers," Judge Richards begins. "But, by the same token, you have to appreciate that I can't rule on your assertion that there are irreconcilable differences unless I know what the irreconcilable differences are."

"Your Honor, that's my entire point," says Dub in the subdued, colloquially-matter-of-fact mode he affects in almost all discourse in open court, as it is now his turn on the board of this rather crucial game of legalistic tit for tat, since what is at stake is the severance of the trials and thus the prosecution's odds of convicting *both* Kerry Myers and William Fontanille for the murder of Janet Myers.

"If you look at what the case law says when you talk about withdrawing based upon irreconcilable differences"—having done his homework, the always prepared Dub continues his argument—"just to say, we have irreconcilable differences doesn't come anywhere close to meeting their burden. And if he doesn't want to come out and say it, there's not going to be a basis in the record for the motion to withdraw."

Then, with an almost unconscious, however engaging, little-boy shrug, W.J. the grown-up prosecutor deftly switches gears and announces that he'll just move along with his questioning.

"If I might reply, Your Honor," Wiley asks, but doesn't wait for an answer. "This is a unique situation in that you, the judge who's going to rule on this motion, is also going to be sitting as the trier of fact as to his guilt or innocence," Wiley says and gestures toward the all but forgotten defendant sitting up in the witness box.

"But by your choice, Mr. Beevers." One would not think that Judge Richards would need to remind defense counsel of the remedy so readily at hand—*if* he truly only wants what he says he wants.

"But, judge," W.J. quickly interjects, "that's not unique. That's as if they are saying that you are precluded from the level of sophistication to exclude inadmissible evidence when you make your decision. That's absurd, that happens all the time."

"Well, again, Mr. Beevers—"

"I want to respond to his—" Wiley cuts off Judge Richards, who then cuts off Wiley and the wrangling entirely when he changes his mind concerning whatever he was about to say and instructs: "Let's go on with the cross-examination."

W. J. LeBlanc is only too happy to oblige. "Mr. Myers, how long has Mr. Beevers been your attorney?"

"Over two years."

"And, I believe you stated on direct that you've discussed trial strategy with him many times, is that correct?"

"Yes."

"And, you've never had any irreconcilable differences until, what's this, five days before the trial, is that right?"

"In the whole course of this thing, we've always had two different objectives, I guess you might say," Kerry responds, flashing that peculiarly detached, exceedingly self-important, condescending arrogance.

"But it's never been to the point where you felt it necessary to file anything in court or to discharge your attorney." W.J. does not feel the need to rise—or stoop, depending upon point of view—to Mr. Myers's current level of self-projection. "Isn't that right?"

"Up to this point, I would say that's correct."

"So only after the motion to continue was denied and now it looks like you're going to trial on Monday did you suddenly come up with this irreconcilable difference, is that correct?"

"No, it didn't suddenly come up, it was always a matter that we had a basic disagreement on certain aspects."

"But you've never filed anything in court or taken any action in any event?"

"I don't file anything, sir."

As much as he surely feels the urge to strangle that empty, infuriating smugness, Dub resists even the appearance of it, but before he can verbally cut it off at the throat, Wiley Beevers is on his feet somewhat belatedly saying, "I object, Your Honor. I was going to call to the court's attention that Mr. Myers does not file anything in court, that I as his counsel do it."

After a spat of verbal sparring between W.J. and Wiley, E. V. Richards, loathe to lose even the tiniest bit of control within his courtroom, moves the argument along, and Dub soon continues with the defendant.

"You didn't take any steps on your own or through another attorney to discharge Mr. Beevers as a result of these *preexisting* irreconcilable differences, is that right?"

"I'd say that is correct now, sir."

"And you still refuse to go into what these irreconcilable differences are?"

"That's correct."

"I have no further questions," Dub announces and returns to his seat.

"I have none, Your Honor," Nick Noriea advises.

"Thank you, Mr. Myers," Judge Richards says to Kerry, who wastes little time in stepping down and away from the witness stand.

Wiley Beevers then says, "Coupled with my previous testimony, I have nothing else to offer in support of the motion."

"Mr. Beevers, as I said before," begins the judge, "it's impossible for me to rule on whether or not the irreconcilable differences that exist are sufficient to allow me to grant your motion, I don't know what they are."

"I understand, Your Honor."

"I can't, based on what's in the record now, grant your motion to withdraw. I will, of course, allow Mr. Myers to retain another counsel to assist you, but I'm not going to allow you to withdraw at this point. I don't know why I should."

"From the earliest time I became familiar with the facts, I've always looked forward to the opportunity to cross-examine them, especially Billy." W. J. LeBlanc is remembering, in part, how he arrives at the decision that if Bill and Kerry testify, he will take the former and Howie the latter.

"I'm really looking forward to going one-on-one with him. I've also always thought Kerry'd be an easy mark. Kerry doesn't make a good witness. When he was on the stand during that motion to fire Beevers, man, it was involuntary—shooting the eyes—to look back to Beevers after each question."

Dub then explains his thoughts on the final structure and presentation of the baseball bat murder case. "I think it's very important the jury understands right from the start that this is a bizarre case. I also think it's important they recognize right from the start that these two guys being tried together are both lying. So my decision is to literally give them the guy's stories right like they are. The one thing I *don't* want to do in my opening statement is to indicate *how* I'm going to show it proves a murder. I want the last word on that. I don't want them to be able to argue any type of explanation.

"It doesn't bother me that the jury won't have any idea of what's going on when I finish my opening statement. Because, to me, the critical point for the jury to understand what's going on isn't until the very end of my rebuttal.

"So then the question becomes, 'All right, we've got all these witnesses. What's the best order to put 'em in?' That's always your big question in a case. Here, I know I want to *end* with Dr. Lee. I think that's very important.

"So, after the opening statement where I've given them these two very conflicting stories, bam! Right away, the coroner to establish the brutal nature of this—very important to put the coroner on first. Because, right off the bat, you're gonna get into these horrific pictures—I want to dispel any sympathy that the jury's gonna have for Kerry and Billy. Shock 'em right from the start. I want them to *know*. I want them to *think* about it *every night*. That these two guys are capable of this. I don't want them thinking, 'No, they look pretty clean-cut.' You know, 'Those are two good-looking guys down there, could they really be involved?' I want the horror and brutality to come through right from the very start.

"From there we go right to the scene with Maureen Rilette. They've just heard about this horribly beaten-to-death woman, and the very next thing they hear is this woman who's awakened at one forty-five in the morning and hears, 'Get out of here! Get out of here!' She looks out and sees this guy jogging her way. So now we know that somebody was running away from this house.

"Then Chuck DeWilde comes on and will say that he was called at such and such a time. When he went to the house he was met by this bloodied and bruised and broken man and sees the body. Goes through the whole description, the kid, the silence, the blood. Suck them right inside this nightmare from the get-go.

"Then Vieira, because he's got to identify all of the pictures he took so we can actually get them in the jury's hands as well. So they can start seeing all this blood, so they can start visualizing in their minds this scene to go along with the schematic of the house we've had DeWilde trace us through.

"Then the next important thing is Bob Masson, the case officer going through what he did that night, but most importantly to introduce the statement taken from Fontanille—and now they're gonna go 'Ahh!' Now they know because they hear his version of the story on tape, they now know where that came from in the opening statement—that came right out of Bill Fontanille's mouth. They didn't know that before.

"And then, while directing Masson, trying to minimize as much as possible, 'Why didn't you do this?, why didn't you do that?,' trying to take some of the sting out of the weak points. I want to get in the statement and description at the hospital, which is important because Bill does not say he's wearing a baseball cap in his taped statement, he says he's wearing the baseball cap before. But unless he's gonna testify, there's no other way to get that in. But it's in Masson's report initially that he told him that at the hospital. Then we go to the changing of the story. Then we put Miz LeJeune on to talk about the story.

"Then Martin Childs, who tells Kerry's side of the story. Then we call Kerry Myers to the stand. Knowing that he will take his Fifth Amendment privilege, we then seek to introduce his prior sworn testimony on the grounds that since he is exercising his right not to testify he is technically 'unavailable to testify,' therefore admissible under our interpretation of case law. Boom. We get his testimony and cross-examination from the '86 trial read into the record for the jury. Every word.

"So now the jury has completely heard the other version. So now they know again—'Goddam, that's where these stories come from. These guys are saying the same thing but just reversing their roles!'

"Then Joe Koehler, and the 911. We've gone from immediately after the murder, to investigation, to statement by Fontanille by arrest, to now statement by Myers, subsequent testimony by Myers, and now we're back to the murder. The 911 tape.

"Remember how Connick used the tape effectively by leading off with it—we're gonna do it in reverse. By putting on the 911 tape *after* I've trashed his ass, the people have a whole different reaction—'Ahh, this sniveling bastard.' 'Oh, that faking son of a bitch.' 'That put-on bastard.' I think the inception at that point is critical.

"Now to the EMTs. With Walter Cardin being extremely damaging to Kerry Myers. Because of the kitchen and knife scenario. Dr. Gutnisky. Gabe LaMarche, John Taylor, Noel Adams, Dr. Neri. Then Dr. Lee, and that's the end of my case against Fontanille. And I've got Peggy Cowan for Kerry in rebuttal.

"Then we take the jury to the house—probably the single most significant element, getting the jurors to see how small that area is and thinking, 'They never saw the body in ten hours of running and fighting and rolling around? No way, Jack!' But that's gonna be the judge's decision—the second most important decision he'll have to make in this case, after Kerry's guilt or innocence. It's totally within his discretion. There is no 'right' to visit a crime scene.

"So, that's my plan.

"Now, Mike Price, Curtis Jordan, et cetera, the friends? They're witnesses only for rebuttal. If Billy takes the stand, denies different things— I'll set him up to tell lies. To tell a whole string of lies. Facts that I know that's not really relevant. But relevant enough that I can put it on if he opens the door—like the whole scenario with the job. The lying about the job. I can't put Mike on the stand to testify about that in my case in chief. Can't do it, it's really not relevant. What does that really show? But I can question Bill about it—'Didn't you say this? Didn't you do this? Didn't you say that?' Then he denies it. Mike Price goes on. Boom. It's a lie.

"Howie's going to do the close. Noriea's going to argue what he wants. And then I'm going to give them *the theory*."

"I'm looking for another hung jury." Nick Noriea is remembering his basic strategy heading into trial. "I'm pretty sure Richards will convict Kerry. And then with the expense and all, and after *two* hung juries, they might just decide not to prosecute. That's what I'm really wishing for.

"But more practically, I'm hoping for a hung jury so I can then go through Dr. Henry Lee's testimony with a fine-tooth comb for round three when Bill's on trial by himself with the jury knowing that the husband's already been convicted of murder two and there won't be the pressure that *somebody's* gotta pay for Janet's death."

"All right. Mr. Beevers, it's my understanding that on Mr. Myers's behalf, you have waived a trial by jury in this case?" Judge Richards says in open—and quickly filling up—court a little after nine o'clock Monday morning, March 26, 1990.

"That's correct, Your Honor."

"All right, I'd like to talk to Mr. Myers a bit about that from the witness stand. Would you step up here, please, sir?"

Then, yet again, for the third time in his thirty-three and one-half years of life to that point, Kerry Myers finds himself climbing into the witness stand, whereupon Judge Richards examines him categorically as to his intention to waive a jury trial—a right only a defendant can waive.

"All right," the judge then says, "you had indicated in previous motions filed that there may be some differences between you and your attorney by way of trial strategy in this case, and I want to be certain that this is not one of your differences, because the right to a trial by jury is something that only you can waive."

"Yes, sir."

"And if you and your attorney disagree, you win that argument."

"No, sir, that's my decision."

"All right, all right, thank you, that's all."

Kerry Myers again quickly gets himself down and out of the witness box.

"All right, does the defense have any comment on the State's motion to have the jury go to the scene of the alleged crime?"

"Your Honor." Wiley is the quickest to the trigger this time. "I feel like it's incumbent upon the State to start off at least and lay the predicate that the scene is materially unchanged, it remains as it was then, at least to some degree."

"Are you prepared to do that, Mr. LeBlanc?" Judge Richards asks.

Before Dub can respond, Nick is saying, "Your Honor, I note an objection to returning to the scene, because I've personally been to the house since then, and it's a lot different in terms of the carpet, wallpaper, et cetera, furnishings . . . I think it would, could be misleading to a jury. And the *competence of the Jefferson Parish Sheriff's Office is exemplified* in the hundred and forty photographs they have, and the diagram they presented. I'm sure they're going to bring all that in this trial. And for a jury to see a house that is materially changed from photographs that *accurately depict* the scene would be confusing to a jury."

"What's material to this case," Dub says as he cuts to the essence of the State's argument on the issue, "is the fact that there are allegations, or versions given by both defendants that indicate that they did not see either the injured child, Ryan Myers, or the deceased in this particular case, Janet Myers, throughout the ten-hour period when they went from room to room in that house. And it's the State's contention that that's ridiculous and that the only way a jury, or the court, as a trier of fact, is going to be able to make that determination for its own is to actually go back to the scene."

After some protracted wrangling and lawyerly maneuvering—during which Wiley Beevers doesn't again open his mouth on the subject—E. V. Richards brings it to a halt when he surprises and worries the prosecution by stating, "I'm going to require that the State lay a predicate, subject to cross-examination, before I rule on that motion."

Shortly thereafter, the judge is addressing the first thirty-six prospective triers of fact on Bill Fontanille: "I want to welcome you ladies and gentlemen to court this morning, and I'll ask the clerk to first swear the panel with regard to their qualifications to be a juror in Jefferson Parish."

Since none of the thirty-six potential jurors is not a citizen of the United States, a resident of the parish, under eighteen years of age, or unable to read and write English, and none admits to being interdicted mentally or under indictment for a felony or convicted of a felony for which he or she has not been pardoned, Judge Richards is soon addressing them again:

"All right, during the next portion of the proceedings, which is called voir dire, the attorneys and I will ask you some questions about yourself.

Please do not be offended by those questions; they're not intended to embarrass you, but simply a means for us to learn something about your suitability to serve on this particular jury. Also during the next portion of the proceedings, some of you will be excused from service on this jury. Please do not be offended by that. Excusal from service on a particular jury is in no way a reflection on you individually."

When the somewhat lengthy hi-this-is-who-I-am introductory part of the voir dire process is over, Judge Richards begins the customary and important explanation of the trial at hand:

"In this case there are two defendants, Mr. Kerry Myers and Mr. William Fontanille. They're both charged with criminal conspiracy and second degree murder. Kerry Myers has waived his right to a jury in this case, therefore—"

"Your Honor, Your Honor." Nick is up and waving his arms like a traffic cop outside the Super Dome after a Super Bowl. "May we approach the bench?"

Looking somewhat flabbergasted, Judge Richards says, "All right."

Once there, Nick, with respectful deference in his manner, reminds the judge, "Conspiracy is not in this case, it's just second degree murder."

"It's just second degree murder, judge," W.J. agrees.

"So I would ask that you admonish the jury and I make a motion to discharge all these jurors, because they're not charged with conspiracy," says Nick.

Without hesitation Judge Richards says, "I'm going to grant his motion."

When the lawyers return to the single long table they and the defendants share, Nick addresses the bench: "Your Honor, just for the record, I make a motion that that was an inaccurate charge, and I ask that all the jurors be excused."

"All right. Mr. Noriea, you're correct, it's an error on my part. Neither Mr. Fontanille nor Mr. Myers is charged with criminal conspiracy, they're charged only with second degree murder."

Turning to the jury box, the judge continues, "And because of the fact that I told you ladies and gentlemen that, I'm going to grant the defendant's motion and excuse you from service on this jury. So thank you very much. I'll ask you to please get your cards from the deputy and take them back to the fifth floor."

As the twelve prospective jurors—*nine* of them *men*—pick up their cards and make their confused exit, the judge says, "Would counsel approach the bench?"

Then, when they are again gathered before him, E. V. Richards says, "I just want—this is ridiculous, I don't know how this got out here. What happened to the conspiracy charge? There was a conspiracy charge at one point."

"Yeah," goes Dub, "it's still hanging out there, judge, but this is just the murder trial."

"All right."

"I'm sorry I had to do that," Nick says.

"Oh, no—" starts the Judge.

"No, no, you had to," goes W.J..

"You're absolutely correct," Judge Richards assures.

Just about midafternoon of that Monday, after lengthy examinations by the State and the defense, where W.J. displays his near photographic memory—addressing panelists by their names without notes—and his uncanny knack for making friends with jurors, and Nick plumbs each female panelist for any law enforcement bias, Judge Richards summons the attorneys to the bench. "If this lady tells me what she told me in the first place, that she has three small kids and nobody to take care of them, I'm going to excuse her.

"Mrs. Scully, could I ask you to step up here, please?"

The prospective juror had indeed said what the judge thought she had, and she is excused. Another female juror is challenged "for cause" by W.J., and she too is brought before the bench, but after a gentle, careful examination by Judge Richards it is determined that her only problem is with colitis—under stress she might need to get to a rest room quickly—and is otherwise acceptable by the court.

"Do you have any other challenges for cause?"

"No other challenges for cause," Dub says.

"Does the defense have any challenges for cause?"

"No, sir," replies Nick.

"All right, what does the State say about Mrs. Henry?"

"She's fine."

"What does the defense say?"

"We'll take her."

"All right, she's juror number five. What does the State say about Ms. Tassin?"

"She's fine."

"What does the defense say about Ms. Tassin?"

"She's okay, judge."

"She's number six. What does the State say about Mr. Sylvester?

"We'll excuse Mr. Sylvester," W.J. says.

"All right, the State excuses Mr. Sylvester. What does the State say about Mrs. Waguespack?"

"She's fine."

"What does the defense say about Mrs. Waguespack?"

"She's fine."

"All right, she's juror number seven. What does the State say about Mrs. Varisco?"

"We'll excuse her, judge," Dub says of the lady who has three attorneys in her immediate family, one of whom does extensive criminal work.

"All right, the State excuses Mrs. Varisco. What does the State say about Ms. Roberts?"

"Who are we on, judge?" Nicks asks as he studies his chart and silently tries to recalculate the gender numbers and his remaining challenges now that three women have been removed. One of whom he'd already counted on in his mind.

"Ms. Roberts."

"She's fine."

"All right, she's juror number eight. What does the State say about Ms. Theriot?"

"She's fine," W.J. says, and when he gets a quizzical look from the bench, adds, "Well, judge, look, there was a method to my madness. I just didn't think Nick would want her on either."

"What does the defense say about Ms. Theriot?"

"She's fine."

"She's juror number nine. What does the State say about Mr. Gustavson?"

"He's fine."

"What does the defense say about Mr. Gustavson?"

"I'll be easy. He's okay."

"He's number ten. What does the State say about Mrs. Stackel?"

"She's fine."

"What does the defense say about Mrs. Stackel?"

"Yes, I'm easy," Nick, again, is able to say while keeping a straight face.

"All right, she's number eleven. All right, we've got eleven jurors."

Another panel of twelve is soon brought in and the process is repeated for the third-and-one-half time; in the end the State runs out of challenges, a Brenda Capella becomes the twelfth juror, and Ms. Gayle Floyd and Ms. Lorraine Kogos are the two alternates.

Eleven women, one man, with two more women in reserve. Nick—who over one trial and by now countless mock jury studies has never had a single female juror vote guilty as charged against Bill, always either not guilty or guilty of a lesser charge than murder one or two—has the jury he wants.

Quite arguably, one of the two or three most pivotal events in the entire history of the baseball bat murder occurs that Monday afternoon during voir dire, yet it has absolutely nothing to do with jury selection.

"Go on, you've got to do it," Anita Price says again to her daughter-in-law, Monique Price.

"But why me?" Monique asks her for perhaps the twelfth time over the past several days.

"Because I can't be involved. If I go up there and talk to him, everybody will start talking for sure. Go on! He has to know, it's important."

"But you know more about it than I do."

"That is not so, you've heard as much about it as I have."

"I don't even know what to say," Monique says about as plaintively as this independent-minded lady ever gets. But the relentless pressure from her very strong-willed mother-in-law for her to approach W. J. LeBlanc and inform him of the stories that Ernie Barrow has been telling some members of the Price family for several years is in fact beginning to wear her down.

"You don't have to tell him the details, just tell him that somebody'd better talk to Ernie, that you have reason to believe he has important knowledge concerning Kerry and Janet."

"I just don't want to do it. He's going to think I'm an idiot. I don't even know him."

"Mike says he's a very nice man. Now go on. It's got to be done, and I can't be seen as the one doing it. You've been left out of this thing. It has to be you. He's not going to bite you."

"All right!" Monique finally says. Consequently, during the break between the last two panels of voir dire, Monique Price approaches W. J. LeBlanc and finds him very accessible, to the point that, following her own feelings concerning Kerry Myers and the murder of his wife, she delivers the message Miz Anita had all but dictated to her and then adds, "Ernie says Janet came to see him about a divorce."

"I'm not anxious to testify in this matter," Ernie Barrow says with great understatement, which is his wont and is often the secret of his effectiveness as a born cracker-barrel, Dixie-style storyteller.

"The first one to ever ask me to talk to 'em was Bill Hall. I went over one afternoon and they started asking me questions, and I answered as best I could. But nobody ever really asked me about Janet's consulting me— and I probably wouldn't have answered 'em anyway. Because I felt like that was between Janet and I. Until Howat Peters calls me. Where they got that information, I don't know. Probably Mrs. Price—but we have a good relationship, and I'm not worried about that; it is what it is.

"The only thing I'm concerned about is the relationship I enjoyed with Janet, and I certainly feel like she's entitled to my confidence in that and I'm not gonna turn it loose until a judge turns to me and says, 'You tell it.'

"So I go over there and meet with 'em and Howat asks me had she ever consulted with me about a divorce. At that moment in time I'm very reluctant to say anything about it. I say, 'Yes, I can tell you that. But I'm not going to tell you much more than that, because there's a problem here.'

"He says, 'I recognize that problem.' Then I go on to give them the basics of what had transpired, knowing they can't do anything with it until a judge allows them to.

"So I come back here and I call Howat back, I say, 'I want to tell Wiley what I've told you. I know Wiley, and I feel like I owe that much to him and Kerry.' He goes, 'I'll tell him.'

"So he does. And soon enough, Wiley calls me. He says he understands I've told the DA about a visit I'd had with Janet. I tell him, 'Yeah.' He says, 'Can you tell me?' I say, 'Wiley, I see it that I've got a problem.' He says, 'I think you've got a problem too.'

"I say, 'And until that problem is solved, I don't want to talk about it to anybody.' So he says, 'All right.'

"Then Howat calls me back, they're gonna subpoena me and call me as a witness. I say, 'Well, the issue of lawyer-client privilege is gonna have to be addressed before I say anything. And I wanna do it from the stand.'

"Then Wiley calls me again and he goes through the conflict situation. He says, 'I don't think the judge can let you testify.'

"I go, 'Well, that's up to him. But if that judge says, "You testify," Wiley, guess what? I'm gonna testify.' "

"I'm sitting there almost in disbelief," W.J. says, remembering that Tuesday-afternoon meeting with Ernie. "As a matter of fact, if not for him suddenly becoming our star witness, I want to blast him by saying, 'Ernie, what the fuck's going through your mind, man? You've got this kind of information you've withheld for all these years!' He's told everybody and their grandma about it, but not the people he should've told. And I mean with us he's very reluctant to say anything."

But, "It is impossible to overstate the importance of Ernie. Once Ernie falls into my lap, I start looking at the witness order I'd already worked out and decide to put him up there the last thing, case in chief, in the event that Beevers decides to rest without any evidence. I don't think he'll do that—but just to avoid against it, and the possibility of never getting to drop my biggest bomb. I also no longer need Peggy Cowan; she's *very* relieved.

"So, at this point, the last night of preparation before going into opening statements the next day, the actual start of the trial, I know in my mind I've got Kerry Myers cold. Because once we get this, everything else about their marriage is irrelevant; Ernie lays to rest any question regarding unhappy marriage. That's his ass, and Wiley knows it."

18
Trial

May 11th, 1982—Once again I have a little time to write. In the past few months you have started to grow up. You aren't a baby anymore, rather a toddler. You have six teeth now and ready to cut more. . . . You have mastered saying "DA-DA" and "MA-MA," (in that order) and you are preparing for those first steps of walking. You stand up all on your own and when you get shaky you resolve yourself to crawling. Just in the past week you have learned to point to certain objects as I name them (ie. light bulb, sun, Bugs Bunny). Lately you have been learning at a pace that I can hardly keep up with, but you are adorable. So many people think so. Your personality is bright and happy, and you usually charm the pants off of most people you come in touch with.

—Journal of Janet Cannon Myers

* * *

"Are we ready for the jury?"

"The State's ready, judge," W.J. answers.

Nick, however, replies by saying, "Judge, since I don't think the jury should be present during Mr. Myers's opening statement, I'd ask the court if they could give their opening statement before we bring the jury in, so that I don't make an opening statement after the State, and the jury's running in and out."

Before the first witness is even called in the third trial of the baseball bat murder, the complications inherent with the judge being the trier of fact on one defendant while, simultaneously, the jury is the trier of fact on a codefendant begin to present themselves.

"All right. Mr. Beevers, do you intend to make an opening statement?" Judge Richards inquires.

"No, Your Honor. As a practical matter, Mr. Noriea and I have discussed it by and between ourselves this morning, and we had elected the order in which we would proceed on cross-examination that Mr. Noriea would go first and I would go last."

"I have an opening statement, Your Honor," Nick says.

"Counsel, before we bring the jury in, I want to caution you that objections are going to be heard at the bench. We're going to cut down histrionics in front of this jury. So if you have an objection, let me know, and then approach the bench and we'll hear the objection at the bench."

Soon the jury is led in; the indictment is read. The statute defining second degree murder in the State of Louisiana is read to the panel by Judge Richards, who then gives the jury a brief explanation of the order that this particular trial will follow and the purpose and weight (none) of opening statements, and that one be given is only a requirement placed upon the State.

W. J. LeBlanc rises deliberately, tugs absentmindedly upon his suit coat and tie, walks within the anticipatory silence to the center of the jury rail, and begins the opening statement of the trial he'd been craving for some three years, perhaps the biggest trial of his career:

"Good morning, ladies and gentlemen. As you all know by now, the defendants, William Fontanille and Kerry Myers, are charged with the second degree murder of Janet Myers. And you also know by now the burden of proving that is upon the State, and we have to prove each and every element beyond a reasonable doubt, that the defendants killed Janet Myers, with the specific intent to kill, or inflict great bodily harm, or they were principals to that killing.

"Now, how will we do that? From testimony that you will hear from that chair over there, the witness stand, as well as by various items of evidence that will be admitted.

"And what will that show? Well, on February 24th, 1984, the early-morning hours of that particular day, Janet Myers, a beautiful young woman, Kerry Myers's wife, was pronounced dead. Brutally bludgeoned in her living room at 2232 Litchwood Lane, in Harvey. Her two-and-a-half-year-old son lay critically injured in another bedroom, suffering from multiple skull fractures. Her six-week-old daughter Sarah in another bedroom unharmed.

"How did that happen? Well, you'd have to go back about ten years before that. That's when William Fontanille and Kerry Myers met at Archbishop Shaw High School here in Marrero. They became friends, not particularly close friends at that time, but later they did. They graduated from Shaw, moving on to college. Mr. Fontanille, Southeastern, and Mr. Myers, first to LSU, then to Nicholls State, where he met Janet Cannon, soon to be his wife, Janet Myers.

"After college they come back to the West Bank, they renew their friendship, they start playing ball together, become pretty close friends, close enough so that William Fontanille stands in Kerry and Janet's wedding.

"Now around July of 1983, William Fontanille's world started to come apart. He was unemployed, couldn't hold down a job, his wife left him. He went into a rage, inflicted great amounts of damage in his home, holes in the wall, appliances. Withdrew from all of his friends. Nobody really saw him much after November of 1983.

"Around Christmastime he exercises his visitation right with his son Matthew, doesn't return the child when he's supposed to, setting off a frantic search by his wife. The child was returned later unharmed.

"February 21st, 1984, it was a Tuesday. Bill Fontanille shows up at the Myerses' residence, out of the blue, talks about his marriage, his unhappiness.

"Two days later Janet Myers is dead, ending a very unhappy and troubled marriage between Kerry and Janet.

"Ladies and gentlemen, what happened? Well, the evidence is going to show that on that particular day, Kerry Myers came home from work a little early, about four in the afternoon. And when he opens the door into his house, he hears his name yelled out, he looks up, William Fontanille's coming at him with a baseball bat, swings at him, he throws his arm up, gets hit, breaks his arm. They run into the den, where a fight ensues. Chairs, knickknacks being broken over the head, a struggle that goes on for hours. Of course, you can't fight for hours. The evidence is going to show that they rest, that they watch television, that they get each other water, that they get towels to wipe off some of the blood.

"At some point during the night they have to go to the bathroom—then another confrontation occurs. This time, they're fighting in the hall over a knife, and they rest again, laying down in the hall, each with control of the knife.

"Janet Myers is laying dead in the living room, Ryan Myers is unconscious in the master bedroom, Sarah Myers is in her bedroom. Kerry Myers *sees no one.*

"At some point, he gets control of the knife and stabs William Fontanille as he rushes out the house, hollering for him to 'get out of here!' 'get out of here!' and then he calls the police. Again, *never* seeing his wife and children." W.J. then pauses just long enough to put an end to one story, then: "The evidence will *also* show that at about four o'clock on that day, William Fontanille arrived at 2232 Litchwood to retrieve a baseball bat. Kerry Myers answered the door, invited him in, whereupon he immediately stabbed William Fontanille in the back three times. William Fontanille ran into the den, where he saw a baseball bat; he picked up the baseball bat and defended himself against Mr. Myers, breaking his arm. They throw knickknacks at each other, they rest, they watch TV, they get water, they get towels to wipe off the blood, and they sit.

"A while later, several hours later, they get up to go to the bathroom, another confrontation with the knife, ends up in the hall down near the bedrooms. They wrestle over the knife, both having control of the knife. At some point Mr. Fontanille feels that Mr. Myers's grip on the knife had relaxed, so he gets up and runs out the house. Again, *never* seeing Janet Myers dead in the living room, or *either* of the children.

"Now, items of evidence that you're going to see are going to be photographs from the scene, there's going to be a lot of blood in them, both in the den, and naturally where Janet was killed. There are going to be lots of bloody clothes that Kerry Myers wore, that William Fontanille wore, and that Janet Myers wore.

"You're also going to see that there were three different blood types. Kerry Myers has O blood, William Fontanille has B blood, and Janet Myers has A blood.

"You're going to see that on every piece of exposed clothing that William Fontanille wore that day, there is Janet's blood, from the top of his head to the tip of his toes. On the baseball cap, on the sweater, on the blue jeans, and on the tennis shoes.

"You're also going to see that Kerry Myers had Janet's blood on him. On his pants, and on his handkerchief, which is found in the kitchen sink.

"You're going to see photographs where Janet was found, you're going to see where Ryan was found. You're going to see where Sarah was found. You're going to see where the famous ten-hour fight took place—and you're also going to see where it's one *gigantic plot*.

"Ladies and gentlemen, I would ask for your very close attention to all of the evidence presented, and most importantly for your common sense when you retire to deliberate a verdict.

"Thank you."

"Mr. Noriea, do you care to make a statement?"

Nick indeed does. And while it's not exactly a warmed-up opening statement from 1986, its thrust, with a few novel twists, is basically the same. There is a point-by-point explanation of Bill's version of events and how the physical evidence that is available better suits Bill's story than Kerry's; and of course the constant theme that whatever piece of evidence *wasn't* preserved, tested, or photographed properly could've been *the* evidence that might've proved beyond any doubt that Bill's version is the one true baseball bat murder gospel. Therefore, with so many, many, many of these blunders of omission, and the understanding that all doubt about an unproved fact must be resolved in Bill's favor, there is more than enough for reasonable doubt and surely nowhere near an exclusion of every reasonable hypothesis of innocence.

Early on and sprinkled throughout, however, are concessions to and good use of the great changes in the case between then and now.

"I've been involved in this case now for—for I guess five years. We've already been through one trial in 1986 where Kerry Myers was a star witness against Bill, and the jury couldn't reach a verdict. And we're back here again as a result of some evidence testing that took place before the 1987 indictment."

Of course, on that issue, W.J. is up and heading to the bench. "Objection Your Honor . . . I hate to interrupt defense's opening statement . . . but he can't tell 'em anything about the first trial's verdict!"

Judge Richards sustains it but the jury heard it and thats all Nick was trying to accomplish.

Then later, much later: "But, I asked you about one reasonable hypothesis of innocence, and one of the versions that the State gave you in their opening statement is a version that's consistent with what evidence they did take, and that is that Kerry had killed his wife. He knew Bill was going over there to pick up the baseball bat because he had called Janet, he had left it there the day before. Ryan, the little boy, was playing with it when he left Wednesday, and when he wanted to take it from Ryan, Ryan started to cry. So Bill said, 'Well, I'll just get it later,' so he came back the next day. Bill called Janet to make sure and Janet says, 'It's fine, come on over.' "

"I'm going to object, Your Honor, and I do it very reluctantly," pronounces Wiley Beevers. "May we approach the bench?"

At the bench conference, Wiley pleads his point. "Your Honor, the basis of the objection is that Mr. Noriea is saying what Mr. Fontanille would say, and he's getting before this jury Bill Fontanille's testimony in effect, in his opening statement, that he has not affirmatively waived, and he's forming, himself, accreditations that I can't cross-examine on. I think that's improper opening statement."

"Mr. Beevers, the jury's not going to make a determination of your client's guilt," Judge Richards offers.

"But you're sitting there and you're listening to what he's telling you that Bill Fontanille's going to testify to, and he may not even call him. This is once again the danger. And I respect—Your Honor, as to what the jurors hear, even though he's making it to the jury, *you're* hearing it."

Although Dub participates in the ensuing verbal tussle, his intellect and emotions are more involved with trying to adjust to the now certain knowledge that Nick will *not* be putting Bill on the stand.

"In the first trial, Bill testifies about going back to the house twice on Thursday," W.J. remembers. "The second time to get his bat that he'd left the first time. But in Nick's opening statement he says that Bill goes on Thursday to get the bat he'd left on Wednesday, right then and there I *know* he ain't taking the stand.

"And I don't think it's a simple misspeak when that's the whole critical issue of the case—it's not simply a case of switching days . . . it's switching days, it's switching reasons—oh, man, if he comes back and says in rebuttal that he simply misspoke the day? I'd jam it up his ass sideways."

Nick's conclusion of his opening statement isn't gimmicky, or even too laden with hyperbole: "I'd ask you to keep in mind, bear in mind, that we had no control over what happened at the crime scene. We had no control of what was left at the crime scene. We had no control over the method of analysis that was done by the police before the first trial. That we played no part in.

"That Bill is a victim—and he's more of a victim than any of us can ever imagine because of what's taken place the last six years and one month of his life. Thank you."

"Mr. LeBlanc, are you ready for your first witness?" the judge asks.

"Yes, Your Honor," Dub answers.

"I call Jane Spiers, Your Honor," says Howie Peters.

"Your Honor, for the record," Nick offers, "I'd just like to ask, is this a witness that's in the Fontanille case or the Myers case?"

"She's in both cases," answers Howie to his old friend. "But she's—may we approach the bench?"

"Yeah."

At the bench conference a testy W.J. barks, "Judge, for the record, there's *no difference* between the Fontanille and the Myers case."

"Judge, just for the record too," begins Nick, "I agreed to stipulate, as I said before, to the identity of the victim, and I don't want to be present when the family has to testify about the identity of the victim."

Howie, in some detail, and with long but amicable seesaws with Nick, basically argues that Mrs. Spiers is not only going to identify the victim in the judge portion of the trial, but is going to offer testimony pertaining to Janet's expressed attitude to her concerning Bill Fontanille—that it will be close to hearsay, but, under the circumstances, isn't and is admissible.

The battle of legal-eagle wills ebbs and flows at further length because, of course, what is really at issue—again—is not so much what the witness will *testify* to as it is *to whom* she will testify it, the judge, jury, or both.

While the identification of the victim before the triers of fact is a legal necessity, and even though over the course of the argument at the bench it is expressed by an increasingly irritated W.J. that the State is putting the witness on the stand only because Myers's defense counsel has not agreed to stipulate as to identity and that Wiley then agrees to do so, the truth of the issue is that both the State and Wiley have a mutual interest in *other* testimony from Mrs. Spiers. Nick knows it and doesn't care what Mrs. Spiers has to say so long as *none* of it is said in the presence of the jury.

In the end, Nick wins. Therefore, for the first time, before the first witness is sworn in, all proceedings come to a halt as the jury is gathered up and in single file led out. "We'll recess for about fifteen minutes," Judge Richards announces.

After the recess and out of the presence of the jury, under a very brief direct examination by the soft-edged Howat Peters, Jane Spiers, the stout, middle-aged sister of Janet Myers, identifies Kerry Myers as the husband of Janet, and, from a family snapshot and then a crime scene photograph, she identifies the pretty, smiling lady holding Ryan at the age of one in the former as being the same as the horribly disfigured remains in the latter.

Beevers then cross-examines Mrs. Spiers out of the presence of the jury. In doing so, over strenuous objections by the State directed at the inadmissibility of hearsay testimony that are silenced by Judge Richards—"It's an exception to the hearsay rule. It's a statement made by the decedent"—Wiley is able to elicit, in part, the following testimony from Janet's older sister:

"She told me that [Bill] had been to her house. And I talked to her on the phone that Wednesday . . . she told me that she was getting ready to fold a batch of clothes. And that—they had uh—they had a large sofa, a small sofa, and a recliner. And she said that she, she couldn't—he had come and sat on the sofa, on the small sofa where she was sitting getting ready to fold her clothes, and she couldn't understand why he sat there, and she said that it made her nervous."

Of course, to the annoyance of the prosecution, Judge Richards also allows Mrs. Spiers to testify (to him only) concerning her views on the marriage of Janet and Kerry:

"What, if anything, did she have to say in that conversation in reference to having resumed sexual intercourse?" Wiley leads.

"She told me that when she went to the doctor and he told her that she could resume her activities, of course that meant, you know, having relations with Kerry, that she was a little bit embarrassed because her and Kerry had had relations the night before. And she said to me, 'I'm pretty sure he probably already knew that I had intercourse.' "

She then goes on to assure the court that she wasn't aware of any problems in the marriage. Wiley also directs her into describing a close, nurturing, "clingy" relationship between Ryan Myers and his father since the murder.

"All right, thank you, Mrs. Spiers," says the judge, and then, "All right, counsel, are we ready for the jury?"

"Yes, Your Honor," Dub replies. Shortly thereafter, the jury is fetched back in and, almost half a day late, the prosecution is back on its game plan as Dr. Richard Tracy, the pathologist who performed the autopsy on Janet Myers some six years before, takes the stand.

As is called for in the plan, the doctor's testimony, directed by Howie, is, if anything, more graphic and stomach-churning than it was in 1986, as he describes in great, emotionless detail each wound and then winds up his direct examination with a conclusion upon the cause of death for Janet Myers:

"An open vein can suck air into the blood vessels. This air then travels to the heart and fouls the pump, what we call an air embolism. And this was the ultimate cause."

Nick Noriea, as in the first trial, is again able to elicit from Dr. Tracy—over the heated objections of cocounsel—that the condition of Janet's nails would not be inconsistent with her having scratched someone in a struggle, and that a review of Bill's medical records does not indicate any such scratches or "abrasions and contusions" present on his person. Nick this time, however, gets a little lagniappe:

While asking the pathologist if he could say from which direction the bat was swung, Nick demonstrates a left-handed chopping motion with the bat and elicits that—because of the directionality and pattern of the lacerations to Janet's face—that would most likely be the "orientation" of the path of the "blunt instrument."

Concerning the length of time that Janet might've lived after such a beating, Nick elicits, "That's just impossible to guess. No way to figure it out."

"Could it have been longer than two hours, or less than two hours?" Nick presses. "Well, what's the maximum she could have survived with these injuries?"

"Hours, maybe many hours."

Then the jury is trooped off to lunch before Wiley cross-examines Dr. Tracy, wherein his primary evidentiary goal seems to be the revelation that fingernail scrapings should've been taken from Janet Myers, but weren't; and, for whatever reason, the certainty with which the coroner could say that the *only* wounds to the victim's hands had been caused by nibbling cockroaches. Upon accomplishing the latter, Wiley produces the first moment of melodrama of the day and the trial:

"Would it have been helpful in your autopsy to know that she might have been wearing a wedding ring that had bent from some force, in helping you to determine whether or not she sustained a blow to the left hand?"

"A blow that would bend the ring might very well not show at the time of autopsy, that's right," Dr. Tracy replies.

"I'm going to show you what I will refer to as Kerry Myers 1, and ask the court's leave to mark it later with an evidence tag, and ask you to assume for the sake of argument that that is the wedding ring that Janet Myers was found wearing at the time of her death, and ask you if in your opinion that would indicate that she sustained a blow to the left hand as well."

Wiley, with a demeanor of great reverence, hands Janet Myers's misshapened, seemingly bloodstained wedding ring to the pathologist.

"It would have to be a guess, but it would certainly be consistent."

"Okay. So based on what you know, and the assumption that I have given you, and asked you to take as being a fact for the sake of this hypothet, would it be safe to say that she sustained not only blows to her head, but her hands as well?"

"It's a reasonable assumption."

On redirect, the prosecution asks Dr. Tracy if he can offer any actual determination of whether the bat was swung lefthanded or righthanded. He said he could not.

"On this case, every morning I would wake up with my adrenaline flowing, because I was so fascinated by it," Cheryl Hickman of Channel 4 remembers.

The adrenaline kick came in handy with the physical requirements of the task this time around. "Getting there early so you could lay claim to a good seat was a major priority, because it was *packed*.

"They tried to reserve a place for the press. You would try to claim a seat on the aisle, because you had to come and go and you wanted to be able to get in and out; we tried to put the artist on the inside. It was tight.

"When the jury was excused at different times, we might be allowed up into the jury box, but most of the time we were down in the pew they tried to reserve for us, but people wouldn't read the signs. Or other people who were following the trial felt like they could impose and take our seats. It was an event."

"All right. Is the State ready for the next witness?"

"Yes, we are, Your Honor," Howat Peters replies. "But before we do that, we'd like to offer State exhibits 50 and 51, which are photographs identified by Mrs. Spiers, into the record."

"All right."

"And also State exhibits 52 through 62. Fifty-two is the autopsy day record and the protocol," Howie adds. "And the others are photographs of the autopsy. I'd like to offer those also at this time."

Thus does the shock of the instant juxtaposition of incredulous horror with a cold functionality which is always present in some mixture when such things are viewed, occur as planned when the jurors individually view the autopsy pictures of the former Janet Cannon Myers.

"All right, I believe all members of the jury had an opportunity to examine the exhibits. Is the State ready for your next witness?"

"Yes, Your Honor," says Howat. "Carmen Gomez."

Since the judge is surprisingly resistant to the State's strong wish to have the triers of fact visit the crime scene—further throwing Dub's order-of-witnesses plan into disarray—Howie then directs the owner of 2232 Litchwood Lane through a brief history of the house since she and her husband had bought it brand-new in 1976; an identification of Kerry Myers as her former tenant; and confirmation that other than cosmetic changes such as painting, new carpet, drapes, et cetera, there have been no alterations of the house at any time since the murder.

Under extensive cross-examination by first Nick, then Wiley, and then the judge, too, the court learns little else of any import on the issue.

After a brief recess, Maureen Rilette takes the stand and testifies to her memory of hearing "Get out of here" and looking at the digital clock beside her bed, reading the time as 1:45 A.M., before going to her window and seeing an individual that fit Bill Fontanille's general description jogging toward Patricia Street from the direction of the Myerses' house. As in the '86 trial, her time upon the stand is brief—although lengthened somewhat by the jury's having to hoist up and file out so that Wiley Beevers could cross-examine her—but important and still unimpeachable.

"Your Honor, the State would call Deputy Charles DeWilde to the stand," W. J. LeBlanc soon announces.

If cops were clocks, Chuck DeWilde would be a trainman's pocket watch, ever steady, ever durable, emanating trust and common sense. Likewise is his testimony to his by now well-known participation and observance at the crime scene that early morning, even through a very thorough cross by Nick, and then a blistering, prolonged, at times mean-spirited grilling by Wiley.

The State then brings three other sheriff's deputies to the stand that afternoon, all of whom are deployed in the Crime Scene Division and are basically "chain of custody" witnesses:

Sergeant Don Carson testifies that he collected hair and body-fluid samples from the victim when he was the officer in attendance at the autopsy. He further explains how the prosecution's schematic of the house came to be, avows that he was its original creator, and says he has only days before gone back to the scene to verify the accuracy of the dimensions.

Deputy Ronald Ainsworth takes the stand for the introduction into evidence of the "hair samples, saliva samples, whole blood samples" he "picked up and secured" from Robert Masson which came from the person of William Fontanille on March 2, 1984, while he was incarcerated at the Jefferson Parish Correctional Center; and photographs he took of Kerry depicting his injuries, at the Detective Bureau on March 9.

Deputy Jerry Stapler identifies and explains his involvement with the taking of certain photographs and the securing and transporting of additional items of evidence which were collected in the weeks just after the murder.

All of it is very routine stuff, normally expeditiously dispensed with; however, since all three are crime scene technicians they are up there an inordinate amount of time and have to sit through more than just a smattering of sarcasm and abuse from both defense attorneys—in and out of the presence of the jury.

Nothing of any real consequence or advantage accrues to either party, but tedious court time passes and the first day of the trial comes to a nit-picking close.

"Don't ask me why, because I can't tell you, but I'm depressed as hell and sure that we're gonna lose, and that the whole day had been a total disaster." W.J. is remembering that first evening and night after the first day of the trial.

"But then I remember Vince telling me, 'Dub, you always feel like that— after *every* first day.' And it's true. While we're off schedule, nothing had actually gone badly for us. I just for some reason have this after-opening-day-blues syndrome."

Although the Thursday, March 29, proceedings begin on time, and everybody works hard until past six in the evening, the State is able to bring to the stand only two witnesses: now Sergeant William Vieira, and now high school math teacher Robert Masson.

Officer Vieira's direct examination by Howat Peters, eliciting an explanation of what a crime scene technician's responsibilities are at a crime scene, how this crime scene was in fact processed, and the identification of some 140 photographs and dozens of pieces of physical evidence, takes up all of the morning.

Therefore, immediately after Howie says, "Your Honor, I tender the witness at this time," Nick says, "We're going to be a while, judge."

"Your Honor, may we approach the bench?" W.J. asks.

Shortly thereafter, Judge Richards addresses the jury: "Ladies and gentlemen, we're going to take a little longer lunch break than we normally do, because I think we're going to stay a little bit later . . . so you might want to keep that in mind in ordering your lunch. But, again I caution you not to discuss the case and do not make up your mind until you've heard all the evidence."

Just shortly after one o'clock, the jury is again seated in the box and the judge says, "All right, Mr. Noriea."

Nick proceeds not to belie his estimate of the duration of his relentless trashing of the handling of the crime scene. However, with the much-better-prepared Vieira and perhaps because it's the second time around and the two combatants have formed some kind of bonding not really that unusual in adversaries who have faced off before, Nick's trashing lacks much of the personal, biting sting it might otherwise have. It is just long, and repetitive, and really only old news for everyone involved except the judge and jury. But it comes to an end, and E. V. Richards turns and says, "Mr. Beevers, I assume you're going to have questions?"

"You betcha, Your Honor," Wiley yodels with anticipation.

William Vieira, however, has benefited from old transcripts, his, and the tutelage of the prosecution, and he makes judicious use of a forthright "Yes, sir," "No, sir," "I don't know," and the biggie, "I only do what the homicide detective tells me to do," so it is not the one-sided feeding frenzy Wiley has bragged to all within the Myers camp it would be.

Then, just the knowledge of which witness comes next sparks a legal brouhaha that far overshadows in import any of his actual testimony—although, in the end, that is not without its measure of pyrotechnics.

"Judge, may we approach the bench?" Nick asks.

"Yes, sir."

At the bench, Nick begins the argument. "Robert Masson's next—he took a statement from Bill, which is admissible, in my opinion, in Bill's trial. Three weeks later, he took a statement from Kerry which is completely inadmissible as hearsay before the jury."

Then follows a protracted and furious six-way cacophony of legal-beagle huff-and-tussle—even Madeleine jumped into the middle of it—which takes up about forty minutes, half of which are spent in chambers, where Judge Richards reviews the transcripts of Myers's statement to Masson and the 911 tape.

While there are many voices in the debate, the basic arguments, distilled, are—

Nick: "It's hearsay and I can't cross-examine Kerry Myers on it. Judge, I can't cross-examine Kerry Myers's statement. I can cross-examine this police officer for six hours and he is going to say what he said to inculpate Bill Fontanille, but I can't ask Myers one question. I mean, if Kerry says something that exculpates him, it's got to implicate Bill. And if it doesn't inculpate Bill, then why does the State want the jury to hear it? And without a conspiracy the statements are even less admissible. *Man,* this is *better* for the State than the *first* trial, because I could at *least* cross-examine Kerry Myers."

W.J.: "Judge, the only way it's not admissible is if you have antagonistic defenses. And that would have required a severance. It's no different than two codefendants in a joint trial. Statements by both are admissible."

In the end, in open court, Judge Richards announces one of the truly crucial rulings of the trial and the whole case to date:

"I'm going to grant Mr. Noriea's motion for exclusion of Mr. Myers's statement given to Detective Masson," Judge Richards says, and then adds, "Again, as I told you, Mr. Beevers, I'm not going to rule on your motion at this point. I'll take that matter up in the morning. You had indicated you wanted tonight to think about it, so I'll rule on it in the morning."

"Yes, Your Honor."

"So, judge . . ." Nick begins a question which perhaps highlights the uniqueness and problematic realities of a dual-judge-and-jury trial as well as any other. "Procedurally, with the jury, the State will direct Detective Masson on his knowledge of the entire case, with the *exception* of the statement made by Myers to him? And I can cross-examine him on *that*, then the jury will be excluded and the State can continue direct of Robert Masson and then Mr. Beevers can cross-examine him on *that*—out of the presence, obviously, of the jury—is that correct?"

"That's correct," says the judge.

"Thank you, Your Honor," Nick says.

"All right, with that, are we ready for the jury?"

"Yes, Your Honor," comes in chorus. The jury files in, and then Robert Masson is on the stand.

He is still there—saying nothing new—when W.J. says, "I have no further questions, Your Honor."

And the judge says, "Mr. Noriea, before you start. It's past six o'clock, it's a good time to recess. I want to again instruct you ladies and gentlemen not to discuss the case among yourselves, or with anyone else. . . ."

And so ends day two of the trial.

"Are we ready for the jury?"

"Yes, Your Honor," says W. J. LeBlanc. "The State waives polling, Your Honor."

"Waive polling, Your Honor," Nick Noriea says.

"Good morning, ladies and gentlemen," Judge Richards welcomes the jury. Robert Masson is reminded that he is under oath, and Nick begins his cross.

"Detective Masson, how long were you a homicide detective for the Jefferson Parish Sheriff's Office?"

"Approximately ten years."

"Over the years, how many murder cases had you investigated?"

"I really don't know the exact number. I can only estimate."

"Over a hundred?"

"Probably in the neighborhood of a hundred I have either handled personally or assisted in, possibly more."

In 1986, with MacDonell, Dixon, and Vieira to beat up on, Nick was surprisingly easy on Bob Masson. Perhaps with the pent-up frustration of now so many years spent working on something he believes would have been settled to the good long before if this man had only done his job properly, and with Vieira holding up well, Nick is not so inclined this time. However, while his grinding, relentless, almost two-hour-long elicitation of a litany of every conceivable thing not done or piece of evidence not taken is a grilling of no mean proportions, it is never actually mean-spirited, or personally vicious. It is also, in the end, only old news.

"Thank you. No further questions," Nick announces.

"'No redirect," Dub says.

"Mr. Beevers, I believe you have some questions."

"Yes, sir."

The judge then sends the jury out, and in due time Dub rises and begins a second direct examination of Robert Masson.

"Mr. Masson, when you testified previously on direct examination, I believe that you omitted your taking of any statement from Kerry Myers; is that correct?"

"That is correct."

"I'll stipulate he took the statement on March 14, and that it is contained on there," says Wiley, to the absolute astonishment of every attorney in the courtroom—and there are many, as the trial has become an event and it has become customary for more and more of them to step in and observe whenever they have free moments. (By stipulating, Beevers has effectively negated his client's standing on future appeals as to any Constitutional issues in exception to the judge's ruling.) "If you will give me a copy of the transcript to make sure that's the one previously furnished, I'll stipulate it into evidence, Your Honor." Then, "Your Honor, I will stipulate that's a transcript of the statement that was taken."

"All right, sir."

"We'll mark that S-170," says Wiley.

"It'll be received in evidence," the judge says.

"At this time, I would like to play S-170," says Dub.

"All right, sir. Do you have a copy of the transcript?"

"Yes, Your Honor."

Then Kerry Myers's taped statement from March 1984 is played out of the presence of the jury.

At its conclusion, W.J. informs the court, "That's all the direct that we didn't cover yesterday. I was thinking we could break for lunch."

Judge Richards is of like mind.

At one-twenty in the afternoon, Wiley Beevers begins his cross-examination of Robert Masson.

"Now, after Kerry Myers gave you his statement on the 14th day of March, 1984, did you become aware that there was some rather apparent inconsistencies between Bill Fontanille's statement which was taken on the 25th of February and Kerry Myers's statement which was taken that night and also on the 14th of March?" Wiley asks with a warbling mouthful early on.

"There was some inconsistencies and some things were consistent."

"Now, how long was that house at Litchwood available to you to go back and do additional crime scene investigation?"

"At least through March 5th. I didn't check on it after that."

"So, after these inconsistencies became apparent, you didn't check to see if—the inconsistencies I'm talking about are from Kerry Myers's March 14th statement—you didn't go back to the house to seek any additional evidence?"

"No, sir."

"Bill Fontanille, is it not a fact, in his statement says that Kerry Myers picked up the TV controls and changed the channel?"

"That's what Mr. Myers said."

"Mr. Myers said Mr. Fontanille picked it up?"

"Yes. Mr. Fontanille said Myers picked—I don't believe he referred to his remote control. I think he just said he turned on the television. I don't recall him saying that. He may have; I don't recall that."

"If you had gone back and gotten that remote control and done a fingerprint analysis on there, might that not have given you indication that maybe Fontanille had not given a correct statement?"

"It could have, but I believe it would have been inconclusive because I knew Mr. Fontanille had been at the residence on other occasions."

"But he never told you that he changed the TV or turned on the TV on other occasions, did he?"

"No, sir."

"So, just on that supposition you decided not to get any fingerprints off that tangible object that might have corroborated Kerry Myers's statement; is that correct?"

"Yes, sir."

"Now, in your tenure as a homicide detective, have you ever had occasion to carry a victim back to the scene of the crime, get him to accompany you back?"

"I hate to say this: no. Most of my victims were *dead*."

With that line, the nonshrinking Mr. Masson draws almost a communal guffaw and has even some folks within the Myers camp pulling for him in his public bushwhacking by Wiley.

"Now, in doing your, what I will *refer* to as *background investigation* on this matter, did you talk to all of Bill Fontanille's family?"

"I talked to his wife, Susan."

"Did you ask if he had any sisters?"

"No, sir."

"Did you ask Lorraine Cannon, or anybody, if they knew that Fontanille had been violent with his sister, Angela?"

"No, sir."

"Was it ever brought to your attention that Mr. Fontanille may have hit his sister Angela where she required medical attention in Jo Ellen Smith Hospital?"

"No, sir, that was never brought to my attention."

"Did you ask any members of his family whether or not Bill Fontanille had a propensity toward violence?"

"No, sir."

And every person in that courtroom who has siblings is thinking, each in his or her own fashion, something along the order of "Christ, if fighting with your brothers and sisters shows a propensity for violence, I hope to God I'm never on trial and have *that* come up and bite me in the ass!"

In due time, and none too soon for most involved, Wiley Beevers says, "No further questions, Your Honor."

There is no direct, and Howat Peters soon rises out of the presence of the jury and says, "We call Mr. Patrick Fanning, who represented Mr. Fontanille. We have to waive any client privilege to protect Mr. Fanning."

"That's correct," Nick says. "If there exists any attorney-client privilege, I have explained to Mr. Fontanille what that means. Of course he understands that and I'm satisfied that he knowingly and voluntarily, intelligently waives any attorney-client privilege that may exist with Pat Fanning."

"Is that true, Mr. Fontanille?" Judge Richards asks the defendant with an appropriate graveness.

"Yes," Bill Fontanille answers from behind the counsel table, where sit, in the following order, from left to right as one is facing the bench with the jury box on the left: W.J., Howie, Kerry, Wiley, Madeleine, Nick, and Bill. Vince and Mike sit directly behind Dub and Howat respectively.

The jury is brought back. Polling is waived. Pat Fanning is sworn in, and Howat Peters begins his direct examination of his fellow member of the bar and former comrade-in-arms at the New Orleans District Attorney's Office.

As far as the State is concerned, Pat is up there only to highlight Bill's changing stories apparently to fit an eyewitness's erroneous account— what Pat's agenda might be is another story entirely.

Howie asks if Pat can explain his former client's reason for wanting to change his statement to say that he had been mistaken and had actually been to the Myerses' house twice on Thursday and that was the time he left the bat.

"Mr. Fontanille had apparently been through some physical trauma and he was bleeding," Pat begins. "And I believe he took a pint of blood at the hospital and he was beat up and stitched up and that was the condition I saw him in on Sunday morning. He told me that when he got to the hospital, and shortly thereafter, he was talking to different police officers, and that the police officers who were interviewing him were very accusatory. They were telling him that they knew that he had committed this murder. He told me that the police officers lied to him to try to trick him into saying he had done it, to confess that he had killed Janet Myers."

"I'm going to object," Wiley says, already on his way to the bench for the requisite conference. "Your Honor," he continues, "this is allowing Mr. Fontanille to testify without my ability to cross-examine him. Whether it comes through him or somebody else, it is still not subject to cross-examination."

The ensuing haggle at the bench is furious but fast on this issue, and Wiley wins. Howie rephrases his question:

"Mr. Fanning, without going into what was told you, what was the change, without going into what—"

"Mr. Fontanille wanted me to go tell the investigating officer that he had, in fact, been to the home earlier on Thursday at about one o'clock, and that four or four-thirty was not the first time he was there on that day."

"I have no objection to Mr. Fanning saying *exactly* what Mr. Fontanille told him for this jury to hear," booms Nick.

"All right, sir," Judge Richards agrees.

"In light of that," goes Howie, "what was the reason for the two visits?"

"I'm going to renew my objection, Your Honor," Wiley, of course, sings out. "Because that was not the court's ruling as I appreciate it at the bench."

"I will sustain your objection to the same effect as to Mr. Myers, but not as Mr. Fontanille," Judge Richards rules.

"So, you want to know the reasons Mr. Fontanille said why he made two visits to the home on Thursday?" Pat Fanning asks, truly enjoying himself upon the witness stand with such an enormous and attentive audience in the courtroom and, via the media, throughout metropolitan New Orleans. He then launches forth.

"He went there about one o'clock, Mr. Fontanille told me, to tell Janet Myers that he no longer wanted to participate in the affair that he was having with her, that he felt bad about it because Kerry Myers had been his friend and he felt guilty about it and didn't want to continue.

"So, he went over there at one o'clock to tell her he wasn't going to have that kind of relationship with her anymore. He went back at four or four-thirty to retrieve his baseball bat which he had left earlier. When he realized that he left it there, and that he felt like Mr. Myers was suspicious of him having an affair with Janet Myers, he wanted to go back and get it so Mr. Myers would not know he had been at the house."

"Did Mr. Fontanille ever tell you that Detective Masson told him the Sheriff's Office had a witness who put him at the house on Thursday around five or five-thirty?"

"No, he didn't tell me that. No, he told me one of the police officers told him that they knew he had killed Janet Myers because they had found his fingerprints in the front room where the body was and they had a witness that had seen him do it. And he knew that those things that the police officers were telling him were not true, could not have been true—'I knew they were lying and trying to trick me into confessing something I didn't do.' That was the nature of his statement," Pat concludes.

"We call Marilyn LeJeune, Your Honor," Howat Peters soon says. Although this is her first time in the witness box at trial, Mrs. LeJeune's story of how her confusion concerning her husband's running schedule caused her to mistakenly tell the detective who first interviewed her that she had seen someone fitting Bill's description with the bat on Thursday afternoon is widely known and wholly uncontested. Neither Nick nor Wiley bothers to even cross-examine her on it; consequently her time upon the stand is short and uneventful, for all but herself, of course.

"Your Honor, the State calls Gabriel LaMarche," Howie says. And then, in the presence of the jury, begins his direct examination of the witness all parties have always known of, but never bothered, or chosen, to use, the registered nurse, now living and nursing in Houston, Texas, who, during the night shift of March 23–24, was "a staff nurse in the emergency room" at Jo Ellen Smith Hospital.

After the preliminary, establishing questions are done with, Howie asks Ms. LaMarche, "Can you tell us about when you first saw this individual?"

"To the best of my recollection, I first saw the patient in the major trauma room, which is toward the back of the emergency room directly opposite of the nurses' station."

"Did you at that time approach him and administer any aid?"

"I started taking vital signs and assessing his hemodynamic status. That means I assessed his vital signs, including pulse, blood pressure, respiratory rate, listened to his chest, looked at his wounds."

"Was he in any serious distress at that time as far as you were concerned?"

"Anyone who has been stabbed in the chest is considered in serious distress until you know the nature of their injury."

"Approximately how long did it take for you all to stabilize him?"

"He was, to my recollection, pretty stable when he came in."

"After you assessed his injuries and had the IV set up, was he in a life-threatening situation?"

"Not to the best of my recollection, no."

Soon Howie asks to approach the witness. Then he has her identify copies of the emergency room records, most particularly that portion known as "nurse's notes." He then has her explain that such notes "are narratives that the nurse writes about the patient . . . contemporaneously."

Then Howie goes for his principal agenda with this witness.

"Prior to looking at those notes, did you have any independent recollection of any statement made?"

"Yes, sir, I remember. It's part of my personality perhaps to chat with the patient and ask them, 'What happened to you? How did you get here?' And I remember the patient told me, and this is my best recollection of his exact quote, 'My best friend killed his wife and stabbed me and is going to blame the whole thing on me.' "

"Ma'am, I'm going to ask, whose medical records did I show you as State's exhibit 172 from Jo Ellen Smith Hospital?"

"William Fontanille."

"And you're certain that he did mention something about someone being killed already?"

"He told me that 'My best friend killed his wife and is going to blame the whole thing on me.' "

"I'm going to ask that you look at your nurse's notes. Do you see your nurse's notes in this matter?"

"Yes, sir."

"A number of different handwritings appear to be on these records?"

"Yes, sir."

"I'm going to ask you, can you see your nurse's notes on this page?"

"Yes, sir."

"Would you read them? That portion until the next entry. I'm going to ask you to circle it also, if you would."

" 'Note: Time two-thirty A.M. Oxygen four liters per minute, nasal cannula started in patient's nose. Patient awake, alert, oriented, complained of being afraid—afraid.' In quotation marks, ' "States his friend who stabbed him told him he had murdered his wife and is going to blame it on him." Patient states initial stab wound occurred almost ten hours PTA [prior to admission] but lay in the house with assailant too weary from fighting to move until recently.' "

"Would you highlight that?"

And she does, those very same words and phrases and whole sentences that have been on record in the Fontanille-Myers file since the early weeks of the investigation some six years earlier.

Howie then has Ms. LaMarche explain the use of the word "affect" in medical jargon, and how it pertains to the defendant.

"I recall the patient as being very calm, speaking in a very clear voice, devoid of any emotion. When we speak about affect, affect is generally defined as the mood someone portrays, and everyone to some extent displays some mood, whether it's interest or apathy, excitement or lethargy. That's defined as affect."

"And how would you describe William Fontanille when you saw him?"

"I remember the patient as having what we call 'flat affect,' which means portraying no apparent mood at all."

"You have no anger, no excitement?"

"Nothing."

"Ma'am, do you remember any other conversation or any other statement he made to you during that time as to the thing about his friend murdering his wife and blaming it on him, anything else?"

"I remember him stating he had gone to his friend's house in the afternoon and entered the house and he either found the act in process or saw what happened and began fighting with the husband. That they fought for a long time; they fought until they were both literally too tired to move and laid on the floor."

"He said he either found the act in progress or saw the act; is that correct?"

"Yes."

"What are you referring to, to the best of your memory?"

"The murder."

"So that was his statement to you at that time?"

"I do not remember exactly how he referred to it. I remember that he stated he walked in the house and saw that the murder had happened or was in the progress of happening."

"Did he indicate to you that he tried to do anything one way or the other?"

"My recollection is that he attempted to intervene."

"I tender the witness, Your Honor," Howat says.

"Ma'am, you made no note of any of that in your hospital report or anywhere else, did you?" Nick is firing as he gets up from the counsel table.

"I noted that statement that I read earlier."

"But I'm talking about your not knowing whether he attempted to intervene or just walked in the act after; you can't say with any degree of certainty?"

"I'm fairly certain," this quite credible witness says.

"You're fairly certain he said either he walked right in after it happened or right as it was happening?"

"Yes. I cannot be certain that what he told me as to whether the wife was already dead or whether he walked in and found it occurring."

With that, Nick drops it like the overflowing pot of worms it is and soon says, "Thank you. I have no further questions."

"I have a few, Your Honor," goes Wiley; and out goes the jury again before Wiley tries several approaches in an attempt to make something positive for his client out of Ms. LaMarche's testimony, but with less success than his cocounsel.

Then the jury is brought back in and Judge Richards looks to the prosecution, whereupon W. J. LeBlanc rises and says, "The state calls George Neri, Your Honor."

After he establishes that Dr. Neri is a specialist in emergency medicine, lives in Newburgh, New York, and works at St. Luke's Hospital emergency room but in February 1984 was doing the same thing at Jo Ellen Smith Hospital and just happened to be the attending physician the night Bill showed up, Dub gets down to what he needs from the witness: "Did the patient tell you how he got stabbed?"

"Yes, sir, he did."

"Would you tell us what he told you?"

"He told us that he had gone to a friend's house and that the friend had tried to kill him, attacked him with a knife, that the friend had killed his wife and child and was trying to kill him, and he was going to get blamed for it."

"Now, where is this conversation taking place?"

"In what we call the trauma room in the ER at Jo Ellen."

"Would you describe his demeanor while he's being treated?"

"Quiet, controlled, calm."

Shortly thereafter, W.J. says, "I have no further questions, Your Honor."

With his turn, Nick doesn't even touch on what Bill might or might not have said while in that emergency room, much less try to mitigate the fact that with each succeeding witness the State is making at least a pretty good case for Bill's being a liar as far as what he knew or didn't know about the murder of Janet and the attempted murder of Ryan when he reached Jo Ellen Smith Hospital.

What Nick wants is for the jury to hear more about those knife wounds.

"Can you tell how far or what is the normal distance—with respect to Bill Fontanille, when you examined that wound, were you able to depict how much of the knife that caused the stab wound was from the chest cavity, the area that you worry about blood getting into the lungs?"

"Let me answer that from a different perspective, if I may."

"Sure."

"I'm assuming it's the same weapon that caused all the wounds. When you looked at the wounds, you got a picture that there was just little wounds in the chest, that they weren't very long, and the wounds in the back were wider, indicating a knife that was small at the point, wide at the back."

"Kind of like this State's exhibit?" Nick asks as he holds up the knife already received into evidence.

"Yes, sir."

"Go ahead, please continue explaining, doctor."

"Now, the wounds on the chest were short wounds in length and a lot of times the depth is determined by taking a sterile Q-Tip and seeing how far you can go."

"That's what they say when they probe the wound?"

"Yes, sir."

"And that's what they did at Charity?"

"Yes, sir."

"And the one they probed was the one—is this close to the heart area?"

"Yes, it is."

"I show you Bill's shirt and tell me if this hole in the shirt right here is consistent with the location he was stabbed?"

"I would say so."

"I'm going to open the pocket. Did the knife go through this bottle?"

"It would appear something went through the bottle."

"Like a knife?"

"It certainly could."

"Certainly if this wasn't in his pocket, the knife would have had enough force to penetrate the chest cavity and maybe the heart?"

"Objection, Your Honor," yodels Wiley.

"Mr. Noriea, lay a foundation for the question," says the judge.

"Doctor, are you board-certified?"

"In emergency medicine."

"And the nature of board certification is expertise above and beyond what a normal doctor has?"

"Yes, sir."

"As a board-certified emergency room physician, do you feel competent to answer the question: If the knife would have gone deeper, could it have perhaps penetrated the heart? Look at the shirt with the bottle."

"Yes, sir."

"And the knife."

"The State has no objection to this line of questioning," Dub feels its helpful to point out to the court.

"In your opinion," Nick goes, "if the bottle wasn't in the pocket, would Bill Fontanille be alive or had much more serious injuries than he had at the time you saw him that morning?"

"If the knife, in fact, went through the bottle, what you're saying is correct."

Not long thereafter, Nick announces, "We have no further questions, Your Honor."

There is no redirect.

Soon, after the jury is again ushered out, Wiley rises and goes, "As a board-certified emergency room medicine doctor," making it sound as if it were some dreadful third-world disease, not a profession, "can you tell, when you look at it, whether a wound is new or old?"

"Within a certain range, yes, I mean if I see a wound twenty-four hours old. Usually you can determine if a wound is hours old—three hours old, that's not easily determinable."

"If you looked at the records there and from what you remember, were these wounds that you observed consistent with ones that had been administered ten hours prior to admission?"

"They were not *in*consistent with it. Does that answer your question?"

"No. My question is: Could you tell if these wounds had been inflicted one hour before he got there or ten hours before he got there or could you tell?"

"No, I could not tell."

"No further questions, judge."

"Thank you, doctor," Judge Richards says, and then asks, "Are we ready for the jury?"

"I think we have a matter before the jury comes in," Howie says.

"Your Honor," W.J. begins, "at this time the State would like to call Kerry Myers to the stand as a witness for the State against Mr. William Fontanille."

"Absolutely not, judge!" Wiley is beside himself, arms flailing, head wagging. "He knew we were going to be here and that's the reason we requested a severance."

"I'm doing it out of the presence of the jury to lay the necessary predicate," W.J. says as sweetly as if he were still an altar boy at St. Joseph's.

"I assume Mr. Myers now invokes the Fifth Amendment," Judge Richards says with droll understatement perfect for the moment.

"Absolutely!" Wiley might even have himself a fit right then and there in front of the rippling wall of buzzing humanity just behind him on the other side of the rail. "I stated on the record earlier that we'd offered the district attorney the ability to call Mr. Myers and the district attorney at that time declined!"

"But now he's invoking his Fifth Amendment right?" the judge tries again.

"Right," yelps Wiley.

"I ask the court to declare him unavailable for purposes of testifying today," goes Dub immediately. "And we would then seek to introduce his sworn testimony at the prior trial in this matter."

"May it please the court," goes Wiley, almost back to himself now. "He is not unavailable within the meaning of the code—he is suffering under no mental defect or anything to keep him from testifying, and we respectfully ask the court to read the section on 'unavailability' and declare him *not* unavailable."

"I have read that section [of the Louisiana Code of Criminal Procedure]," Judge Richards says, to no one's surprise. "I'd be happy to read it again. Do you have it with you or do you want me to get it?"

"If the court feels like—I do have it." Wiley is actually sputtering, which is damn difficult to accomplish with his accent. "But if you feel like you're familiar with it."

"It's Article 804, as I recall," the judge says.

"Yes, Your Honor."

"Mr. Beevers." Judge Richards leans forward just a bit, looks over his glasses at Myers's counsel, and continues, "I direct your attention to Article 804, Section A(1), which says in defining the term 'unavailable' as a witness, '*Exempt* by ruling of the Court on the ground of *privilege* from testifying concerning the subject matter of his statement.' I view it that Mr. Myers invokes his Fifth Amendment right certainly, but the ruling of this court holds that he does not *have* to testify . . ."

"May it please the court." Wiley chops the judge off. "I would respectfully object and say I do not believe the Fifth Amendment is what was
contemplated in 804 A(1)."

"I disagree and do declare he's unavailable as a witness."

"I just want to object to the previously recorded testimony for these
reasons," Nick begins calmly; he has known this moment would come for
years now, and consequently he has a whole speech to deliver.

"I'm entitled to a right to effectively cross-examine the accusers of Mr.
Fontanille as guaranteed by the Louisiana Constitution and the United
States Constitution, and that includes Kerry Myers, who refuses to testify.
The previous transcript involves a cross-examination that was geared to
the State's case in 1986. The State had called Herbert MacDonell, a blood
spatter expert from New York, who they're not calling to testify at this
trial."

Nick goes on for some several minutes, ticking off the many changes the
case has undergone since he cross-examined Kerry Myers in October 1986.
The sum total of his voluminous argument is that it is effectively an
obsolete entity, thereby rendering it a fundamental abuse of William Fontanille's right to cross-examine his metamorphosed accuser.

Not a bad argument. Just not good enough for E. V. Richards, who rules:
"Mr. Noriea, what you're suggesting is that you would like to have the
testimony of Mr. Myers as an affirmative part of your case. The Constitution guarantees are that you be entitled to examine the witness who
testified previously about these matters—as they were then. You would
have that right if new matters have arisen since then. He didn't testify
about those matters, therefore you didn't have a Constitutional right to
examine him about that. He was present in the court; everything that he
said at that hearing was subject to your cross-examination. I think that
satisfies the Constitutional guarantee. If there are new matters that have
arisen since then, of course, you're free to bring those out in your defense,
but that does not preclude the State from introducing his statement."

"Let me note my objection to the court's ruling. You're going to advise
the jury as to when this was taken and without the benefit of subsequent
scientific examinations conducted by the State."

"Well, I'll certainly advise the jury as to the date the testimony was
given, but I'm not going to advise them of any affirmative matters not
contained in the testimony. I think they're entitled to listen to the testimony as given."

"Just note my objection for the record."

The jury is brought in. Polling is waived. And Judge Richards addresses
the jury: "I want to explain to you that Mr. Myers has previously given
testimony in this matter and that his previous testimony is going to be
read to you now. Mr. LeBlanc is going to assume the position of Mr.

Connick, who was the prosecutor in that case; Mr. Noriea will cross-examine; Miss Weaker is going to assume the role of Mr. Myers and read the answers that he gave."

"Just for the record," Nick goes again, "I'd like to object to the reading of the testimony because I have not had an opportunity to cross-examine the defendant."

"Okay," E. V. Richards replies.

And then, with scripts in hand, the actors begin this most peculiar chamber piece for a theater of the horrifically absurd. Life askew imitating life in cataclysmic dysfunction as the triers of fact hear Kerry Myers in his prior billing as witness for the prosecution. Then the court recesses at 7:04 P.M., thus ending day three of the trial.

19
Spatter

You're 10 months old now and your 1st birthday is just "around the corner." I am really looking forward to that occasion.

You adore your dad and you follow him around most of the time. You and I are very close. I spend alot of time teaching you and watching you learn. You are the joy of my life and O love you very, VERY much. You make me and daddy very happy and bring brightness into our lives. Just about every night we state how thankful and grateful we are to have a wonderful little boy like you!

We Love You—Mom
—Journal of Janet Cannon Myers

*   *   *

On Saturday, March 31, while it is a full day of court, only one witness will take the stand. Just minutes after nine o'clock, Judge Richards looks to the prosecution and says, "Is the State ready?"

"Yes, Your Honor," W. J. LeBlanc replies. "The State would call Dr. Henry Lee."

With the trial now a full day behind schedule, the prosecution, because of Dr. Lee's schedule, has had to juggle the batting order yet again, bringing Henry Lee to the stand much earlier sequentially than planned. A little after six o'clock that evening, when Judge Richards sends the jury to dinner and another TV-less motel night, Dr. Lee will still be under oath with a return engagement scheduled for the following day. Contained within those some nine hours is pretty damn near everything anybody will ever be able to prove *physically* about the baseball bat murder.

"Without a doubt, it can be safely said that Dr. Henry Lee is the single most preeminent forensic scientist in the world today." W. J. LeBlanc is only saying what many others on both sides of the criminal justice scrimmage line have said before.

But then how else do you qualify a man whose résumé runs almost forty pages and which is weekly, if not daily, obsolete, but on that day included the following:

That he had investigated over five thousand homicides yet has a Ph.D. in bio-chemistry and molecular biology from New York University. That he is professor of forensics at the University of New Haven, lecturer at Yale and the People's University in Beijing. He is the only bad-guy catcher in the world to be the recipient of the Distinguished Criminalist Award from both the American Academy of Forensic Science and the International Association of Forensic Science, both organizations' highest honor. He is also charter member of the International Homicide Detectives Association.

He has written better than a dozen books, but once solved a murder case by finding and identifying the minute remains of a wife who had been passed through an industrial-grade woodchipper by her insurance-hungry husband and then scattered over acres of Connecticut countryside.

He was involved in the 1980 murder case of Scarsdale Diet doctor Herman Tarnower and the aftermath of the 1985 shoot-out between the Philadelphia police and the radical group MOVE. He testified for the defense in the William Kennedy Smith rape trial, and donated his four-thousand-dollar witness fee to a task force investigating the unsolved murders of twelve Connecticut women.

He is chief of forensics, Connecticut State Police. An athletically trim man of medium build and soft voice, with a perpetually quizzical nature and an infectious smile that more often is a full-fledged grin. A man for whom just the requisite elicitation of his most current curriculum vitae takes a goodly bite out of the morning's time.

"All right. Doctor Lee will be accepted as an expert in the field of serology, blood-spatter analysis, crime-scene reconstruction, and general forensic science," Judge Richards rules, with some understatement.

After a brief overview of what is encompassed under the general heading "forensic science"—during which the jury also is given the opportunity to adjust to Dr. Lee's quite entertaining but none the less pronounced accent and fractures of syntax—Dub wants Dr. Lee to explain to the jury just what blood spatter analysis is.

"We've all saw blood spatter before, it's sort of straightforward. We all have blood in our system circulating around our body. Those blood, it's under a pressure, circulating around our body in liquid state. Once the system interrupt, the blood will rushing out, gushing out, or dripping out. Those liquid blood are subsequently deposit either on a wall, floor, table, clothing, any target surface, would leave a pattern. Once those pattern dry, those pattern cannot be altered or changed. By study those pattern, we can reconstruct the cause and effect. For example, if you have a cup of coffee, you accidentally move your hand, the coffee fall on the kitchen floor and would leave a stain. You, by looking this coffee stain, you know somebody spilled a cup of coffee. The blood spatter interpretation basically follow that principle physics of liquid. Water, coffee, milk, blood, any liquid, if you let it free-fall, let it go sooner or later will hit the lowest point. This called gravity force. Blood spatter will not fly all over the sky, unless you supply a external energy into the blood, liquid blood. It would form so-called medium-velocity impact spatter, depends what kind of energy you supply into it."

Dr. Lee then leaves the witness stand and, with various conscripted volunteers to assist him, uses a bottle of red ink, an eyedropper, and several sheets of white paper to demonstrate the different size, shape, directionality, and surface texture of bloodstains one might expect to find at any given crime scene or accident with injury.

"The first pattern I'm going to demonstrate—maybe you can give me hand." Vincent Lamia is happy to oblige, at first. He gets up from the counsel table to take hold of the sheet Dr. Lee hands him. Vince does make a small deal out of looking at the bottle of ink and tucking his new tie beneath his shirt.

"If we let the drop of blood drop," Dr. Lee continues, "it would hit the surface, leave a pattern. If I vary the distance between the source, the liquid drop to the target, the pattern increases too. For example, I drop a drop very close, and I drop a drop about a inch away, two inches away, three inches, as I increase the distance you can see these changes in relationship. This is the first drop I drop, I can correlate that and make a determination of possible high, this drop of ink.

"Of course, must have limitation, once reach the terminal velocity, it will not increase anymore. I cannot say I climb up, what the tallest building in New York, the Empire State Building, I drop a drop of blood, the blood will cover the whole Manhattan, it won't happen. It just have a certain limitation.

"The second thing I would like to demonstrate to you is so-called medium-velocity blood spatter, that's a low-velocity," Dr. Lee says as he points to the sequentially sized fuzzy red circles on the sheet which big, handsome, now a little silly-looking Vince Lamia is still holding—but not for long.

"Just holding that straight," Dr. Lee tells him. "I will be very careful."

Vince looks at the red ink and the guess-what's-coming-next little grin on Dr. Lee and retreats a pace or two. Of course, Dr. Lee, deadpan, chides him, "Don't stand over there."

Then, to the jury, as he flicks the eyedropper with progressively more violent wrist action and arm strength, "I just let go, just now I just let it go, that's without any additional force. If I supply some force, you can see the pattern changes, if I supply some force, harder force.

"If I do that, I'm going to have an angry person," Dr. Lee says—meaning a perpetrator, yet his eyes and manner include Vince, to the detective's sheepish chagrin, since not all of the spatters have found paper.

"So you can see the pattern getting smaller," Dr. Lee explains. "It's no longer like a circular shape anymore. This have a so-called medium-velocity impact spatter. The higher the energy, the smaller the spot will be. If I fire a firearm, a gun through some liquid blood source, I'm going have a so-called mist effect, just like Windex, you spray the Windex on the window, those fine mists. So by study the size of those spatters, we can reconstruct.

"The next I'm going to show you something called direction, the angle of impact. At the scene, we can tell what is the impact angle, forty-five-degree, thirty-degree, or ten-degree. Thereby putting a sheet of paper like this—"

Dr. Lee is placing Vince and the new clean white paper target in just the right position he wants; but Nick can't resist getting in on some of the fun too, "You want to put a piece of cardboard behind it?" he asks.

"Thank you so much," Dr. Lee says with an exaggerated graciousness. Then, to the jury, "Now, if I vary the angle a little, impact angle, you going to see the change. If I do it again, now you can see the ten-degree, twenty-degree, or forty-five-degree, all varies, changes. We can calculate the length, width, use a formula, and we can reestablish the possible impact pattern.

"The next thing, what so-called a phenomenal isolate drop, or a blood trail. An isolate drop, you just see one drop like this." Dr. Lee begins to squeeze and then move the eyedropper in erratic starts and stops along a horizontal plane above the sheet being held by Vince.

"If a blood trail, you can see form like this type of nature." Some of the ink is splashing off the board, and Vince gives ground. Dr. Lee says, "Sorry about that. You suppose to hold it straight." Then, as Vince retreats further still, Dr. Lee tells the jury, "He's run away, he's leaving.

"Now, you going to see this trail formation and the blood dripping into the blood creates so-called satellite spatter."

Nick's ears perk up at that term. "Satellite?" he asks, not cognizant of the fact that technically he is joining in the State's direct examination of the State's star witness.

"Satellite, that's right," Dr. Lee agrees expansively. "That's so-called satellite, it form a main group, cause by one drop drip into another one, you have some energy that cause that."

Then to Vince, making full use of the opportunity to add levity to a lecture on bloodstains, Dr. Lee scolds, "Hold it *up*. Well, come on, *hold it,* don't just stand there."

"That's washable, huh?" Vince finally speaks up and uses his one line with perfect timing and effect.

"I don't know," the renowned scientist says. "Now the DA will buy you a new pair of jeans," even though Vince, of course, is wearing dress slacks.

"Can you lower it," one of the jurors asks, as all of them have been mentally engaged by this strange man and his exotic science, craning their necks, leaning forward in their seats, all attention focused on the demonstration.

"Yes, lower, that's it," another juror says.

"Lower, lower, okay," Dr. Lee says with a slightly different sort of grin. "If I have couple drop here, if I do that"—he suddenly slaps the paper with his hand, hard, spatters flying—"I make impact. You're going to have a impact force, and somebody stand next to it going to have impact spatter look like that. That so-called impact spatter.

"Now much easy one. If somebody have some blood on their hand, touch the surface, going to leave a smear. If their hand, going to have a so-called parallel line of smear. This smear, there are two types, where is my— Howat, you want to contribute your handkerchief?" Dr. Lee asks of his by now old friend.

"Yes, sir, certainly," Howie quickly, broadly responds, and then adds, "I got it out for you. It's clean."

"All right. Now if I have little bit of blood, the handkerchief going to leave mark, that's called *wipe,* just like when you wipe kitchen counter. However, the handkerchief going to have some now, it touch a clean surface, you going to have a different type of pattern called *swipe.* It call wipe and swipe pattern, we can tell at the scene, by examine the picture of the crime scene, or observe crime scene directly, I can tell whether or not that's a direct wipe, or a swipe.

"If we have some pattern—" Vince is shying away every time Dr. Lee even looks like he's going to do anything with that red ink. "I'm not going to ruin your jeans," Dr. Lee tells him.

Then, "It's cleanup," he announces. "I don't have any water, if some water—"

"You want some water?" Howie asks. "Get some water," Howat tells Mike Maunoir, who immediately sets off to fetch it.

"Judge," goes Nick, "may we—while they're getting the water—take the CV from the jury? 'Cause it looks like they're just holding it. I don't know if they—"

"Oh, the curriculum vitae?"

"Oh, wait," Nick goes. "They're using it as shields."

Dr. Lee is now ready to continue his act. "Some liquid, you clean it up, you going to have so-called diluted pattern. It start diluting and of course—"

"Did he say 'loading'?" Nick hates to call attention to Dr. Lee's heavy Chinese accent, but he needs to know.

"Diluted, diluted," Dr. Lee repeats, nonplussed. "D-I-L-U, diluted. After this trial, I can talk like a Cajun.

"Now, if my hand have some blood on it, if I touch, you're going to have fingerprint mark. Leave fingerprint mark. Those call imprint patterns. This just a few demonstration. I don't want to ruin—everybody try to cover their blue jeans up.

"Basically, those are the common pattern one can see at the crime scene, and one can reconstruct by study those pattern.

"Now you have your handkerchief back," Dr. Lee says as he hands Howie back his stained hankie.

"Thank you," Howie says, again broadly.

"Thank you so much," Dr. Lee responds in kind. He then returns to the witness stand. He isn't there long. After all of the demonstration sheets are identified as to type of pattern, assigned a number, and admitted into evidence—which really doesn't take as long as it might've, what with everyone almost festively pitching in—the lights go dark and in the instant silence W. J. LeBlanc is saying, "Okay, Dr. Lee, would you proceed through the slide presentation, giving whatever comment is appropriate considering your expertise?"

"Yes, sir," answers the doctor, who is back on his feet, free from the constraints of the witness box to again use the available floor space as his stage. He proceeds to take the spellbound jury through an intimate journey into the crime scene itself, a full-color you-are-there tunnel-of-horrors view into 2232 Litchwood Lane on the early morning of February 24, 1984.

First they are on the curb in front of the house, a wide-angle view from a point beyond and above the T-square junction of the sidewalk and the walkway in the foreground of the frame: "Appear to have concrete pavement. Carefully examine the photograph, I did not see any blood drippings on this concrete pavement, blood drops. In this area, no blood drops found."

They are now standing right at the L-shaped covered portico which contains the somewhat claustrophobic front entranceway of the house: "Depicts the brick wall adjacent to the entrance doorway. A contact transfer type of blood pattern can be seen, which suggests at one time a liquid blood source contact that surface and caused this transfer. That so-called directly transfer, it's not moving, or smear, or cleaning or blood spatter type of pattern, it's a direct-contact bloodstain." And this fist-sized stain at about chest height is on the *outside* brick wall, the garage wall, approximately eighteen inches *past* the front door; no sample taken, of course.

Then they are just inside that doorway, standing at the bottom of the rather narrow T which is the foyer of the house: "A printed material [Mardi Gras poster] can be seen on the floor. No bloodstain can be seen on this material. Bloodstain can be seen around this area, as matter of fact we can count it, one, two, three, four, five, six different bloodstain. Those are consistent with contact smear. It's no droplet."

Now they are down into a close-up of the tile at their feet. "Here further demonstrate those pattern, is consistent with a transfer smear, which suggest could be somebody's shoes have some bloodstain and walk out of this house, get those transfer."

Now they have turned around inside the foyer and are looking at the closed white-painted front door through which they just came: "Blood smear pattern can be seen near this lock mechanism, and those smear appears to be in motion, which suggests somebody may have some liquid blood on their hand, touch the surface, cause that motion . . ."

At the end of the Kodachrome trip through the baseball bat murder, W.J. calls for the lights and has Dr. Lee retake the witness stand and deliver a concise—however detailed and comprehensive—discourse upon the history, science, methodology, and vocabulary of serology in general and the various means of typing blood, saliva, perspiration, and tissue. Dr. Lee performs in such a fashion that lay people not only can understand but find the information interesting enough to be attentive.

With that done, the lights are brought down again and Dr. Lee is out of the box, moving, pointing, performing as he discusses each piece of preserved physical evidence as it comes up in living-and-dying-color out of the hushed darkness that is the packed courtroom, pointing out patterns of blood deposits, interpreting the patterns and textures where he can, and explaining the various tests he ran and what their results indicate as to whose blood type was where on whom.

Then the lights are up and it's back to the witness stand—for the moment, anyway.

"Dr. Lee, the slides that consist of the items of physical evidence that you tested, are any of these the same items of physical evidence that we're speaking about?" Dub asks.

"Yes, those are same piece of physical evidence with my initial on it."

"I see that they have little yellow tags or spots on there—could you explain what that is. I don't think that they were actually on the slides."

"To the jury?"

"Yes, please."

"May I stand up, sir?"

"Yes, sir," answers Judge Richards.

Dr. Lee comes down from the box yet again, picks up the baseball cap, and proceeds over to the jury for some up-close show and tell.

"This one of the item I examine. Have a yellow little sticker, those are the spot I tested. As I indicate this morning, because serological testing, those are consumable, destructive test. Once I remove the stain, it's no longer going to be there for your viewing, so that area indicate the area I did test, one, two, three, four, five, six, seven, eight, a total I think nine spot of area above show the presence of blood, human blood."

"Dr. Lee, if you would, once the jury gets finished with the hat, if you would explain about the jeans as well?" W.J. cues.

"This is pair of blue jeans I tested, as I indicate in my testimony, a large bloodstain can be seen here in the back. Brushing pattern can be seen here in this location, which indicative this portion of the pants contact a liquid blood and moving in certain fashion, so cause this back-and-forth brushing pattern.

"Large amount of blood spatter on both leg. Of course, you see a lot of different markings, different color of inks. Different cuttings, those are all test performed by different individuals. The one mark in red, for example, one hundred one, one hundred two, one hundred four, one hundred eleven, one hundred eight, those are testing I performed in my laboratory. Those are the spatter pattern, some goes frontwards, some goes upwards, all different direction."

"Dr. Lee, how many blood spatter stains were you able to detect on each leg?"

"A lot, believe me, a lot. I think on the right side approximately five hundred or to one thousand, and in total, probably thousands of blood, individual bloodstain. I counted roughly so I cannot give you a exact number, say, one thousand two hundred thirty-one, it's about a thousand bloodstains."

"And some of them naturally are very small, is that correct?"

"Some are really tiny small, you will have to use a magnifying glass to look at them. For example, those tiny small bloodstain, really tiny little bloodstain. Those bloodstain are probably less than one thousandths of a cc, it's really tiny small stain." Then, "You want me to pass this around?"

"Yeah, you can pass it around," Dub says.

The first couple of jurors on the down-court end of the first row recoil in repugnance from the now six-years-old and of course unwashed evidence.

"They don't want to touch it, so all right," says Dr. Lee.

"Well, they may not want to, but it is evidence," W.J. argues.

At the requisite bench conference, Howie observes, "I think that little girl on the end is going to get sick if she has to touch it."

"Nobody wants to fool with those things," says Nick.

"Judge, they don't have to actually touch it or anything, but they have to view the evidence," W.J. asserts.

"Of course they do," Judge Richards concurs. "Why don't you pass it around to them so they don't have to put their hands on it."

"That's fine, judge," says Dub.

"If you want, why don't you lay them on here?" Howie offers up a piece of leftover cardboard—which immediately solves the problem and business goes on.

"The gray slack, when look at it first under natural light, very difficult to see anything." Dr. Lee is explaining Kerry's dress slacks. "Appear to be lack of bloodstain. Under close examination, use oblique lighting and strong UV lighting, you can see bloodstain."

There is sudden bustle in the jury box.

"Judge—" begins W.J.

"I didn't hear what she said," goes Judge Richards.

"A sticker came off in my hand," one of the jurors says.

"You can keep that sticker," Dr. Lee tells her.

"I can keep it? Okay. It's number twenty-seven," Ms. Tassin asks as if it were a Kewpie doll won at an amusement park.

"Twenty-seven, later I will find the spot," Dr. Lee assures her.

"Okay," she replies.

Piece by piece, W.J. leads Dr. Lee through every item of physical evidence, eliciting whatever the doctor can tell about each. Finally, well after reconvening from the lunchtime recess, W.J. asks: "Now, Dr. Lee, can you provide us with a summary of your findings?"

"Yes, sir. Base on my study of the crime scene photographs provide to me, the physical evidence itself, the residence is a so-called *primary* crime scene. The incident we're talking about took place in that scene. Victim apparently was hit with a blunt object, consistent with the baseball bat, in the living room.

"However, some of the bloodstain on her sneaker suggest at one time she was in upright position. Also possible indication the incident may start someplace else and subsequently get to living room. The plant stand was pushed and fall down on the ground by her hand, probably in a defense gesture, and give transfer with some bloodstain.

"High likely her hand at one time touch the wall, those finger mark could result from her hand, a transfer. As you can see here, four finger marks which consistent with little finger, the ring finger, and the index finger. The thumb probably did not show on this photo. It consistent with a, could be left hand. With the fine marking on it, it's indicate it's a small hand. The hand move down to this location, so you have the tip of the finger now, the second contact, it's coming down and have the tip of the finger, and those tip apparently pretty close to each other. Of course, the exact distance I cannot come here report to you. I was not at the crime scene, nor a scale was provide to me.

"However, I can tell those are consistent with tip of the finger, and subsequently slide down. Initial contact, secondary contact, and slide down this way. Now, from that point the hand moved to other side, you can see this smear movement, so it consistent with coming down, which indicative a individual maybe support him- or herself, and coming down from top right side towards the left side, which consistent with the victim's body location.

"Blood spatter in this location suggest she was hit repetitively in that location. Which cast-off pattern, medium-velocity spatter pattern project from down upwards, shows the blood source was in the lower point," Dr. Lee says as he begins to point out the phenomena of a multiplicity of categories of bloodstain contained within the overall eruption pattern of Janet Myers's blood across about a dozen feet of the living-room wall.

"Arterial pattern" is also present. "Which suggest the internal pressure was disrupt, the blood pressure force the blood coming out. Force this blood, project up on the wall.

"Judging by this blood spatter pattern, and blood imprint pattern, and arterial bleeding pattern, suggest *Janet Myers received some injury prior to her falling down,* because all those blood spatter are defined. Each individual we can see clearly, which suggests all those blood spatter deposit on the wall on top, *after the handprint.* Some blood spatter are—in fact, we can see on top of those handprint.

"Her hand did move in a semicircle type of fashion," Dr. Lee says, as he is now addressing the "bloody arc" on the carpet to Janet's right side. "From lower point upwards. The plant stand [on her left side] already is knocked down, fall on top, fall down, some of the plant material subsequently deposit on her body.

"In the kitchen, a individual may use the phone, report something, so cause those blood transfer on phone. The handkerchief and the multicolor hand towel with some blood smear, the running water and the reddish color like liquid in the plastic cup, all those support the *individual was clean in that location.* The diluted bloodstain on the kitchen counter further support the individual *was clean* in that location."

Oddly enough, since in both men's stories they have one or the other going into the kitchen *after* being injured, Dr. Lee points out, "No blood dripping can be seen on the kitchen floor, the hallway between the dining room to the family room, which *preclude* a injured person was have bleeding, come down and walking in those area."

Dr. Lee then addresses the den area. "*Large* amount of a blood smear, blood droplet, in the family room, supporting a *vertical* blood source have *dripping* the blood, deposit in the two main locations behind the sofa chair, and near the bookstand. Whether or not that group connected, I cannot give you clear indication.

"However, the furniture, the lamp, lampshade, everything suggest there's some altercation happen in that room. Drinking glasses was used. The sofa chair I did not observe heavy crusty bloodstain. The bat clearly indicates was not in a vertical position, no pool of blood was observed in that area, which suggests the bat was *not* have large amount of *liquid* blood on the surface and at the *same time* in a *vertical position.*"

As to the somewhat crucial bloodstain patterns observed on the tile floor of the foyer area, and the glass-shelved knickknack cabinet which is photographed askew from the back wall of the T-shaped foyer from the hall direction, Dr. Lee instructs, "Suggest could be a injured person dripping, leading from one location to another. The glass cabinet was at one time pushed and moved to a different location. Whether or not this blood dripping directly towards the living room, I have no information, no picture provide me to establish. The general direction appears to be leading in that direction. I did *not* see any dripping come *out* of the house onto the walkway."

Concerning the location where he considers the event to have begun, and where young Ryan was found, the master bedroom, Dr. Lee explains, "Large amount of bloodstain observed on the bedroom floor, carpet surface, which suggest a blood source bleeding and have a direct contact on that area."

As to his conclusions upon the crime scene as a totality, Dr. Lee testifies: "It's a disorganization type of scene because from one location, move to another location. Medium-velocity bloodspatter were produced by force. Judging look at a clothing, some of the medium-velocity bloodstain indicates person or persons wear those clothing, has to be in a close proximity near the blood source, because the medium-velocity bloodstain will not travel six to eight yard or feet, and all across the next room. Has to have direct contact and direct deposit.

"As far that exact mechanism of this contact of deposit, because lack of additional information, I cannot give you exact way how it deposit. However, the medium-velocity has to be near that blood, liquid blood source."

About some of the type A bloodstains found on clothing, Dr. Lee is also emphatic: "The blood contact smear has to be a direct contact and cause this transfer."

"Dr. Lee, talking about that for a moment . . ." W.J. chooses to interject at this point. He has his witness address a specific area of Bill Fontanille's clothing. "The blue sweater with the stain that was on the sleeve, is that a transfer stain?"

"Yes, sir."

"Aren't there two types of transfer stains?"

"Yes, sir."

"Would you explain to the jury what you feel like that particular stain is on that particular sweater?"

"Primary transfer is a direct transfer from a blood source. Secondary transfer is a deposit of blood on another surface, subsequently a clean surface contact that surface, cause that transfer, secondary transfer. Secondary transfer usually is much weaker and lighter and consistent with a smear. A primary transfer is more defined and heavier type of pattern.

"Those on the sleeve, on the right sleeve, those three parallel line, appear to be consistent with a primary transfer."

"Meaning from the initial blood source of that particular type, doctor?" Dub wants to drive the point home.

"Which suggest it's from a primary source," Dr. Lee obliges.

"I have no further questions, Your Honor," W. J. LeBlanc announces.

Nick has prepared a long time for the opportunity to cross-examine Dr. Henry Lee. Of the doctor's dozen-plus books and scores of published essays, Nick Noriea has read and possesses most. Through working with his experts Judith Bunker and Ray Grimsbo, Nick has gained further respect for Dr. Lee's ability and integrity, which, ironically enough, has led Nick to believe that, as in the first trial, the State's expert witness will also be the most effective witness for the defense of William Fontanille, but for diametrically opposite reasons.

For some six years now, through his taped statement for the police record, his three appearances before a grand jury, and his testimony in the first trial, the defense of Bill Fontanille has become entrenched behind two basic structures of fortification. The first is that Bill's version of the two all but identical stories is, granted the benefit of reasonable doubt, most likely the "truer one"; and since they are essentially divergent at only two points, the beginning and ending, the jury needs to be persuaded that Bill's timing of his five stab wounds is more consistent with what the physical evidence, limited though it may be, can support. And that in any case, the physical evidence certainly did not exclude every reasonable hypothesis of innocence, which is the extra burden the State carries in the baseball bat murder trial.

And the second, of course, is that Bill couldn't have killed Kerry's wife for the simple reason that Kerry *had.*

The first line of defense, that Bill was in fact most likely stabbed in the back as he entered the house "around four or four-thirty," Nick wastes little time getting to.

"Now, let's assume Bill Fontanille was walking in the door, Kerry stabbed him in the back . . ." Nick is saying and enacting.

"That's a real knife, counselor," Dr. Lee says with an expansive graveness, and then looks to the jury and adds. "I don't want him mad at me."

"This!" Nick, in his zeal, is demonstrating several different thrusts with the knife placed into evidence earlier. "This? And or this?"

"Yes, sir," Dr. Lee says.

"As he's going past there, and the knife was yanked out, it will produce that type of blood pattern, is that correct?" Nick now asks his question.

"Not necessary," Dr. Lee tells him.

"But it *could?*"

"It could be, it could be not," the doctor, smiling, offers with finality as he nods at the picture Nick is gesturing with, a crime scene photo depicting a rather cryptic, expressionistic grouping of *projected* bloodstains on the Sheetrock corner formed by the south wall of the foyer hooking 90 degrees left and becoming the east wall of the living room, against which Janet had gone to die.

Nick forges on, physically and narratively, as with picture, knife, and his athletic body he queries and demonstrates how a bloody knife and bloody hand in rapid motion might account for what *could* be medium-velocity impact spatter. "This type of pattern is certainly one of the patterns that's consistent with Bill being stabbed in the back by Kerry with this knife?"

"Where Kerry going to be?" Dr. Lee asks.

"Behind him," Nick explains with deliberateness. With animation he details the event, "Turned around. Open the door, he passes—and then?" He gives a final knife thrust with a flourish.

"So this has to be skinny guy hiding in the corner?" Dr. Lee effortlessly steals Nick's moment.

"Not a skinny guy hiding in the corner," Nick feels forced to respond defensively, with visible exasperation. "He lets Bill pass in front of him. In other words, he doesn't hide, the guy opens the door, as he opens the door, he turns this way." Nick continues his pantomime. "Bill passes by him, he's got the knife right here, he's standing right there. As soon as Bill gets by him, he jumps behind him and he starts stabbing him in the back."

"Okay, I cannot say it's not possible. Anything in this world is possible. I have to go back to the scene, that's why the disadvantage of me sitting here to tell you exactly what happened."

"I agree one hundred percent"—Nick's all over that—"but this blood-stain pattern is consistent with the scenario that I just gave to you?"

"Could be one of the explanations," Dr. Lee grants.

Good enough for Nick; so he moves on. Soon he engages Dr. Lee in a discourse concerning the "trail pattern" across the width of the foyer T.

"From the photograph," Nick asks with a full-color eight-by-ten glossy in hand, "can you tell the directionality of that bloodstain pattern?"

"Very difficult," Dr. Lee says and then explains to the jury: "If from the crime scene, or a close-up photo of individual bloodstain, I can tell you definitively which direction goes. With a two-dimensional picture, very difficult . . . to say from this way go that way, and from that way goes to this way.

"However," the doctor pronounces with a gesture indicating the carpet area of the living room between where the hall tiles end and where Janet was found, "if you have a liquid source you should *continue see* the pattern, you cannot disappear, vanish in the middle of the whole thing. So *lack* of bloodstain means the trail *not* go this direction," Dr. Lee con-cludes—before adding an indication just how astute, and hooked, a base-ball bat murder scenario game player he has become: "The *presence* of the bloodstain suggest the bloodstain *was* from one direction to the other."

Nick addresses the volley. "This blood pattern that's depicted right—it is just as likely that the person that was bleeding was traveling from the front door into the house, is that correct?"

"That's sort of *inconsistent,*" Dr. Lee tells him. "Because I counted approximately nine or ten tile into the house, start seeing those blood drips."

"Right, right." Nick booms his agreement to Dr. Lee's observation, disregarding the outright contradiction which preceded it, and continues with picture in hand, "If the initial stab wounds are administered according to that first photograph we looked at, one, two, three, four, five, six, seven tiles into the house, you wouldn't expect that blood drip pattern to start until *after* the knife was pulled out, and the blood exited from the wound, is that correct?"

"That's correct."

"And the blood wouldn't squirt out from the wound because it would first have to saturate the clothes, then drip to the floor?"

"That's correct."

"So there would be a time differential from the time the stabbing took place and the initial drops dropped, is that correct?"

"That's excellent," Dr. Lee says with a tone that over the last couple of exchanges has come to sound a bit like a teacher's to a very proud pupil.

"And plenty of those drops would drop from the sweater onto the bottom of the pants as he ran, and cause what you call satellite spatters, is that correct?"

"That's correct."

"In the hundreds?"

"I don't know how many of them."

"Well, well—"

"A lot of them."

"Okay. But obviously the more blood that drops from these back wounds is going to produce more satellite spatters, and a likelihood of producing a thousand drops or small spots of blood that you talked about before is not inconceivable from these type of back wounds dripping, is that correct?"

"Depends how high it drop from. As I indicated this morning, the distance between a source to target is very crucial to produce such a so-called satellite spatter."

"But the terminal velocity of blood is twenty-five feet per second, correct?"

"That's a free fall, in other words—"

"With no force or—"

"No causing nothing, you just let it go."

"So if blood gets enough to where it falls off a back, that blood is in a free fall?" Nick asks.

"Depends how you're standing. The blood may be running down along the pants and come to the cuff region and come down," Dr. Lee counters coyly.

"There's a sufficient amount of gravity to break the surface tension of the blood, permitting it to free-fall," Nick asks with patience. "Correct?"

"That has to be nothing in between, you have to leave the blood drop in the air. That's called a free fall."

"Correct," the pupil agrees.

"If you have a clothing contact the blood," Dr. Lee further explains, "that's no longer a free fall anymore."

"That's spatter?"

"Right," Dr. Lee says.

Another good enough. Then Nick directs his cross into the den, stopping just inside the big entrance at the northeast corner.

"That pattern is consistent with blood dripping from Bill, is that correct?" Nick asks about a photograph depicting numerous, sometimes overlapping pools of blood, the size of which from just the picture indicates that the source was approaching the point of terminal velocity—perhaps anywhere from the upper thigh to the chest of an average-sized individual, in this instance.

"Excellent!" Another atta-boy from the good doctor. "The blood grouping result consistent with a B type of person. As I indicate this morning from my slide, which shows the individual was in that location for quite a while. Blood just continue coming down, form this group."

Nick then goes to the large area of bloodstain in the southeast corner of the den, right in front of the near end of the askew love seat.

"That too is a type of pattern that's produced by Bill bleeding from these stab wounds in his back, is that correct?" he asks.

"If those are type B, which consistent with contribute by a person with type B . . . in this case we only talk about few people, therefore must be consistent with Mr. Fontanille."

Good, and we move on. To the rear area of the den, behind the recliner, where there is more blood than in any other place in the house except the killing wall and carpet in the living room. What is so problematic about this area of the crime scene is that the blood evidence is so inconsistent with the mirrored details of the two men's stories, which ring so true just because they are so detailed and so overlaid. There is a confusing multiplicity not only of categories of bloodstains, but also of sequences of deposit. There is blood wiped, swiped, smeared, dripped, pooled, spattered, directly transferred, and even "scuffed through," and many of these deposits are on top of at least one other category. The most graphic illustration is another large grouping of pooled, overlapping circles of blood which were deposited by a dripping source at a 90-degree angle to the floor and also some feet above it. A source which remained stationary for some period of time. And these pools were deposited on top of several other categories of bloodstains. The smaller satellite spatter which results from blood splashing into blood can be observed on top of other deposits still.

One area of this plethora of enigmatic gore draws particular attention from Nick. Holding up a photo depicting the area at the back end of the long sofa and more or less between it and the recliner, where there are blood deposits of varying categories, Nick asks:

"That would be consistent with Bill sitting on the floor and producing these type of stains, smear stains?"

Dr. Lee replies, "I think *inconsistent* with this fashion. I think probably if sitting on the floor, I should see a large pool of blood on the floor, which I did not see."

Oops! And move on. To the misshapen lampshade on the floor. "That bloodstain pattern could be produced when the baseball bat came in contact with the lamp shade, is that correct?" Nick asks.

"Except at point of impact, that area, *lack* of blood," Dr. Lee says, pointing out that the large indentation on the shade, obviously the point of impact with some forceful object, isn't bloodied at all, which of course it should be if, as Nick is implying, it was struck by the bat while Bill was indeed swinging it in his own defense supposedly right after it had been used violently against a very liquid blood source, Janet Myers's face.

"This lack of blood, which suggest preclude the bat have a lot of wet blood when do that," Dr. Lee tells the jury.

Pointing to the ill-defined spatter that *is* observable on the shade, away from the indentation, Nick asks: "Well, the blood on the lampshade . . . that *was* produced by castoff from a bloody object?"

"I cannot tell you because the lampshade, it's not a even surface. It's like a what call a folding surface [accordion-like], depends on the angle . . . I have to examine the lampshade . . . the only thing I can relate to you is the contact area, I cannot see any blood."

Not liking what he's netting with that line, Nick brings back the photograph best depicting the large areas of blood deposits behind the recliner and almost covering, in one pattern or another, the entirety of the floor space in the west end of the den. The single blood sample taken by Vieira from this area somehow became contaminated inside its plastic vial and has shown inconclusive results from every test done since, including Dr. Lee's.

"Would it be important for you to know what type of blood was where S-4 is, or do you have any opinion as to the blood type of S-4?"

"Of course it's important for me to know the exact blood type of each pattern," Dr. Lee agrees and then explains to the jury, "For example, if the entranceway, that blood spatter, if in *fact* that blood spatter, I would like to *know*. Is that somebody consistent with a B? If I know that's type B, then I can say consistent with Mr. Fontanille. If it's not type B, could be type A, could be type O, the wall help me to reconstruct."

Pointing out that from S-2 and S-3, the State's evidentiary photographs of two of the three large pooling patterns in the den, blood samples were taken and determined to be type B, Nick asks, "If Bill was stabbed running out of this hallway to the front door, in this direction, there is no way that his blood could have been shed where S-2 is? And where S-3 is?"

"S-2 have a large amount of blood dropping. S-3 here have a lot, S-4 have a lot," Dr. Lee begins his reply. "First of all, I do not know the blood swatch they collect, *which* spot of S-2, *which* spot of S-4, that's a *lot of bloodstain* in that location. Whether or not they collect single drop, or collect a multiple drop, that again going to make a difference. However, here do give me a B reading, here give me a B reading, here inconclusive. Inconclusive means I have no way to tell you. Could be B, could be other type. However, here, as you can see, had hundreds of bloodstain deposit on top of other bloodstain, which indicative quite a bit of activity happens in this location. In practical sense, just no way to collect every single drop to group it."

"If there's testimony to the effect that Bill was stabbed back here," starts Nick as he gestures at the floor plan indicating a path from the back of the hallway by the master bedroom taking a beeline up the hall and then hooking a left out of the house, "and within ten seconds to two minutes after the first stab wound and the final stab wound he took this path out, isn't it impossible for these bloodstain patterns at S-2 and S-3 to have taken place—for the stabbing to have taken place in that way?"

"If according to your scenario, that's a direct route, he did not make any turns, of course that *preclude* S-2, S-3, S-4," Dr. Lee says, testifying to the obvious.

"But if he doesn't stand above S-2 for some time, he's not going to produce that pattern." Nick wants to underscore the obvious for the jury.

"Exactly right," Dr. Lee accommodates him.

"So he would have to go—he would have to get stabbed and run here and stand here, correct?" Nick wants to tack this obvious point to the wall. "At least a long time to drop the blood, then run over here and drop some more blood, and then run out of the house, is that correct?"

"Have five wounds." Dr. Lee patiently starts to explain the perhaps not-so-obvious. "Come out of—blood come out together, that's pretty good amount of blood. If just single stab wound, of course, you only have single source. If you have five separate source all dripping the bloodstain, now you going to have a multiple drop of bloodstain."

"But the *absence* of multiple bloodstains coming out this way after five stab wounds are inflicted indicates that didn't take place like that, is that correct?"

"That would suggest it's not. Of course, I wasn't at the scene, I do not know exactly what looks like. Only can read the picture."

"Okay, so let's read the picture. Let's try this one. Let's assume Bill comes in, as I described before, and he's beginning to get stabbed right here in the back, and he proceeds into this room, and eventually stops at this spot and other spots, by the love seat—those back stabs that took place, let's say there's three of them—then right here would be consistent to produce this type of stain pattern in S-2, and this type of stain pattern in S-3, is that correct?"

"It could be, except I did not see anything in between. Here again, lack of some pattern which give me a incomplete picture. However, I cannot rule out that's a possibility either."

Very good; and move on. "This is a photograph that we have seen before of the recliner," Nick is soon saying, brandishing another crime scene glossy.

"Yes, sir."

"You don't see what would appear to be any blood deposited from a back injury or bleeding down?"

"I did not see any heavy crusting like I indicate this morning, which preclude somebody have a large amount of blood come out of wound and sit on this chair," Dr. Lee says of the recliner which each man swears the other sat in.

"So someone who has blood-soaked clothes like Bill had," Nick continues, wanting to peg down another gimme for the jury, "you wouldn't expect that he sat in this recliner?"

"If blood soak the clothes, I would not," Dr. Lee obliges. "I think this is not consistent with the indication he sit directly on the recliner."

Very good. And then Nick moves on to his pet theory—and virtually his and his blood spatter expert Judith Bunker's alone—that the bloody left handprint on the wall above Janet is Kerry's. That at some point early in the beating, he leaned over to inspect the damage he'd done and supported himself with his hand to the wall. Not a particularly good idea, because the absolute best response he is able to elicit from the doctor is "This, this *highly* unlikely."

But Nick persists in chewing on it, and at least he thinks he should be able to slam the crime scene processing a bit more with the bloody handprint. "Let me ask you a question," he starts. "You've investigated crime scenes where the police have come in and literally taken out a section of the wall, have you not?"

"Yes, sir, but I hate those police officer, take the wall scene, and carpet, everything, put in my office, I have no room on my desk."

Nick laughs along with everyone else and then quickly moves on to engage Dr. Lee in a discourse on Bill's jeans and the presence of so many bloodstains which appear to be of the medium-velocity type, be they cast-off spatter, satellite spatter, or impact spatter, and to come from all directions, particularly the spatter patterns on the lower legs of the jeans.

"In other words," Nick is saying, "if blood would drip all the way to the floor, it would hit the floor and bounce back [satellite spatter]."

"Bounce back, yes, sir." Dr. Lee nods and then adds, "But that bouncing back will not bouncing six feet tall, no, no."

"It wouldn't go higher than say ten or twelve inches at the most?" Nick hadn't read so much of Dr. Lee's literary output for nothing.

"It's very low," the doctor agrees.

"I'm talking about at the bottom of the jeans?" Nick sharpens the focus upon the increasingly obvious.

"Yes, sir," Dr. Lee accommodates.

"The bloodstain spatters at the top of the pants are also consistent with the type of satellite spatter that you explained this morning, is that correct?"

"Yes, sir."

Then Nick wants to talk about Kerry's dress shirt. "Now, how much blood was on the middle back, or do you know?"

"Large amount, quite a bit."

"Can you stand up for a second," Nick asks—and then responds quickly to the hamming of Dr. Lee, "I'm not going to hit you."

"Thank you very much. Anybody going to represent me?"

"I'll handle it," Nick says, even as he begins to handle the person of Dr. Lee. "If I get stabbed by you in the chest, and I come in contact with you like this, and you fall down—"

"Fall down," Dr. Lee repeats as these two grown-up men in business suits do just that in improvisational pantomime.

"Fall down, and if we laid on the ground for some time, will the bleeding of my wounds produce somewhat similar to the type of pattern that you saw on Kerry's back?" Nick finishes his question as he's climbing up from Dr. Lee's back and the floor of the courtroom.

"Some may be, some may be not. On the back, as I can see, as I indicate to you this morning, this long smear—it's not by holding someone," the doctor explains from the floor and then adds, "You want to give me a hand?"

"No," Nick tells him. "I was going to ask you something."

"All right," Dr. Lee says in mock submission.

"Go ahead, go ahead, you can proceed," Nick plays too.

"I'd rather work with her than you," Dr. Lee says as he gets up, referring to court reporter Martha Duley. Then, addressing the quite pronounced, striking image of a long, almost ruler-straight streak of bloodstain shooting down the spine from out of the very large morass of bloodstains which is greatly muddled and dispersed across the shoulders and upper back because of dilution from water, Dr. Lee explains, "This long smear could not produced by somebody holding. Can you see that?"

"What—that's a swipe?" Nick offers.

"Swipe," the doctor confirms.

"Okay, is that Bill's blood back here?" Nick asks, prompting a rather remarkable series of exchanges between the State's star witness and Bill Fontanille's defense counsel regarding Kerry's dress shirt.

"I did not group that," Dr. Lee says. "Here a lot of blood spatter, so-called *medium-velocity* blood spatter in the back, which could *not* produce by just a mere contact. Can you see a lot of small spatter?" Dr. Lee asks Nick, before adding pointedly, with slight shift in tone, much the sound of a hint being offered, "Those *small* spatter, those spatters *has* to come from a energy source."

Nick doesn't get it. He labors on trying to reconstruct for the jury the image of Bill, bleeding from his chest wounds, lying on top of Kerry, both holding on to each other and the knife, bleeding through his sweater and that being mostly responsible for the bloodstains on Kerry's back. Which of course is right within his game plan of demonstrating to the jury where the physical evidence more closely supports Bill's story.

After several more patient moments of Nick's narrowed scope, Dr. Lee volunteers: "All those smaller one is *inconsistent* with by somebody holding." The doctor says it with even more the sound of a teacher to a favored pupil, who won't be favored much longer if he doesn't catch on.

"Oh, I understand that," Nick goes. "But, in the process, if we loosen up, some of my blood may drip and cause a satellite spatter when it comes in contact with another portion of my sweater."

"This would *not*—those are energy source," Dr. Lee says, now not certain if the pupil has indeed gone Eureka or if Nick has a broader agenda at the moment. In the end he decides to just come out and hit him in the head with it and be done.

"Could be *somebody* raise a *bat* or something."

Got it! Soon Nick asks, "*That's* what I wanted to ask you. If some of Janet's blood was deposited on Kerry's shirt, that came about during a beating with the baseball bat, that would be medium-velocity impact spatter, correct?"

Finally! "Yes, sir, correct," Dr. Lee announces.

"And subsequently another blood type, either Kerry's or Bill's blood type, completely covered over that and saturated like this?"

"I would not be able to find it," the doctor affirms and also prompts Nick.

Again, "*That's* what I was going to ask you. Likewise, show the jury the water patterns that you talked about in this shirt. They were *washing* patterns, did you say?"

"Yes, sir."

"There was some—is that consistent with Kerry washing up after the blood has been deposited on this shirt?"

"Is consistent with."

"So really," Nick goes, "you can't say too much about this shirt, except it's full of blood, you can't tell too much about that, can you?"

"I can tell a *lot,*" the doctor tells Nick.

"Okay?" And Nick lets the witness have the reins concerning Kerry's dress shirt, during which the jury and the judge learn that, aside from all of the easily seen myriad of bloodstains on it, "eighty medium-velocity blood spatter are on the pocket."

Excellent; and Nick soon has Kerry's slacks under scrutiny.

"You mentioned in your report a transfer stain on the left thigh, is that correct?" Nick asks the witness.

"That's correct."

"Can you come over by the jury again?" Nick says. Soon the lights are out and Dr. Lee has Kerry Myers's slacks on the screen for the triers of fact to see exactly what he's talking about.

"The first frame shows the upper portion of the pants. This is zipper area, this is left side. Transfer pattern is here."

"That all contains A blood, is that correct?" Nick asks.

"A antigenic substances, which consistent."

"With type A blood?"

"Yes," Dr. Lee confirms.

"Now, how did—what kind of transfer is that?" Nick wants to know. "Would that be consistent with a bloody left hand doing something like this?" Nick is wiping his left hand on his left thigh.

"Could be, could be left hand, could be right hand."

Good enough; he'll take it. Plus another shot at damage control on Bill's jeans. "Now, the jeans are literally covered with blood," Nick is saying. "And I think you detected about eight spots that contained A."

"Right, on the right side."

"Lower right leg?"

"Right. The whole area approximately five hundred stain front. On the left side, approximately three hundred. I only group few of them."

"But the majority of the ones that you did group has shown to be Bill's blood. This is Bill's blood?"

"Right. The large amount, those big stain consistent with Bill, however, I did not cut the whole area to group. Whether or not some other material in there, I have no idea."

"Okay. But all—any of the A blood you found is very near the bottom of the pants?"

"Yes, sir."

Nick will take that. Then after beating up again on Kerry's shoes, underwear, and shirt, Nick comes to what he hopes is his exit line:

"This theory of events, getting stabbed right when you come in the door and going in this direction, is more likely than this version, getting stabbed in the back and the chest for the first time here down the hall and then going in this direction?"

"Those two version of scenario, let's say we call this version one." Dr. Lee is using his slides to illustrate the events assuming Bill's story is more consistent with the physical evidence. "Step in this location, continue to that, we did see some bloodstain on wall," Dr. Lee says as he addresses the Sheetrock corner on the living-room side of the foyer. "Except I have no information the blood type. If blood type is A, then we exclude the possibility of this version. If blood type is O, we exclude that version. Unless the blood type is B—*however,* I did not see any dripping goes to that direction. I see some blood drop in this region, and a casing, display glass shelf. Casing was moved, and the direction of the movement is from hallway towards the living room. And here, it consistent with the version one"— Dr. Lee now has a slide from the den on the screen—"which reads quite a bit of blood, and the one collected, it lists that one, shows a type B. Here also, the one shows type B, which whether or not this group connected, because lack of information, I cannot say this is definite one pattern.

"On the version two, I did see some blood smear"—a slide of the hallway looking north is up on the screen—"and the baseball hat, but I did not see any large amount of dripping in this location. So both version is a possibility, but I have to agree with you, this version more consistent with the evidence show."

"The more likely version is number one?" Nick wants to see how specific Dr. Lee will get.

"Again, I say some indication, except the glass display case moved in the wrong direction."

Nick knows he has reached the limit of forensic support for his cause that he is going to get out of Henry Lee, or any of the handful of other really top-echelon criminalists. In fact, Nick has gotten at least as much from Dr. Lee as he has gotten from Dr. Lee's former pupil, Ms. Judith Bunker, who is standing by back at the Holiday Inn.

"Thank you, I have no further questions."

W. J. LeBlanc stands and asks only one question on redirect: "Dr. Lee, would you say it's a fair statement that based upon what you have seen of the crime scene, that neither version one nor version two really depicts the facts as you appreciate them?"

"Yes, sir."

"I have no further questions."

Much as they did upstairs in the command center that Saturday evening in the spring of 1990, the prosecution team is again sitting around chewing on the event that was Dr. Lee's testimony.

"In terms of what he knows, what the physical evidence tells him he can say, Dr. Lee will always hedge it in testimony," W.J. is saying. "But in terms of speculation, there's a lot he can say. While mostly he says, 'You can't tell what the fuck happened,' there are certain things he *can* say. He can *eliminate* certain things."

"Dr. Lee believes that Kerry Myers killed his wife." Vince hedges not at all as he recalls what Dr. Lee told him. "And he's got some very good points. He arrives at the conclusion by a combination of the physical evidence, which is limited—like he said, if I'd been on the scene I could say with one hundred percent certainty—but based on what he knows right now and his feelings about the relationship and what he knows of the physical, and what he's able to prove and disprove, he'll say that Kerry Myers is the bat man.

"Of course," Vince continues, "for the record he'll lead you all the way to that point, and then you say, 'So, what you're saying, Dr. Lee, is that Kerry Myers killed her.' He'll give you that smile like 'Of course,' but only say, 'Draw your own conclusions.' Because he's a scientist."

Of the several different approaches one might choose to take in cross-examining Dr. Henry Lee on Sunday morning after witnessing the expert's virtuoso, crowd-winning performance all day Saturday, a posture of condescending contempt for a weakened foe would logically seem to be last on the list, but the ever mercurial Wiley Beevers takes exactly that tack.

For whatever reason—Mr. Beevers never deems it necessary to explain himself; however, it can only be assumed it is seedless fruit from the political cover-up and conspiracy tree the Myers and Cannon camp have been cultivating for years—Wiley chooses first to pick a fight over what reports, statements, and trial testimony the State might have supplied to Dr. Lee before he began his reexamination of all the evidence. After several questions eliciting exactly what Dr. Lee had been given to review and that he had none of it with him, Wiley asks:

"Now, in consideration of this evidence and your coming down here to testify, why would you *not* have brought the reports that you based your findings on?"

For all of his self-effacing graciousness and Oriental regard for good manners, Dr. Lee is someone it is best not to insult if you expect to keep your dignity for long.

"I did not base my findings on other people report," the doctor flares. "I base my finding on my direct examination of the physical evidence, review of the photographs, *nothing* to do with *other* people report."

"Well, if you weren't going to use it to base your findings or conclusions on, why would you read it?"

"*Read*—you can read a book, newspaper, read anything; you don't have to have reason to read to base on my findings. It's a separate issue to find any particular finding. I only stand behind *my* scientific finding, not other people finding," the doctor punches out before tossing off flippantly, "Therefore, I did not consider other people report."

After more thrusts and posturing along that line with only a sound spanking to show for it, Wiley abruptly spins his guns around.

Dripping sarcasm, Wiley hands over one of the many crime scene photographs and says, "Let's go to the den and I'll ask you if we would have been fortunate to have—if Dr. Henry Lee happened to be in New Orleans and Marrero on the day that this happened and you happened to be over at the Sheriff's Office and they carried you to the scene, how many blood samples would Dr. Henry Lee have taken out of that corner?"

But, in short, the best he gets out of the estimable doctor for his blowhard effort is:

"Let me give you an answer—a lot of time if at the scene I can resolve the issue, I don't even take *any* blood samples."

Several more harassing, badgering attempts to get Dr. Lee to bad-mouth the Sheriff's Office net Myers's defense counsel only this: "I cannot sit here and judge the investigator. Maybe he have some understanding I don't know. If I know more likely from one person, it's no sense to take six hundred sample. It still one blood type."

It wasn't long, of course, before Wiley addressed the scenario issue of the afternoon prior. "As far as the theory, the last statement you made yesterday is that what they referred to as scenario one and scenario two were consistent with what you found."

"Some area consistent; some area inconsistent. Both scenario not totally correct."

"Having testified in court many times, you're familiar with the concept 'beyond reasonable doubt,' are you not?"

"I'm scientist, not lawyer. I stay away from law."

"I try to also, but unfortunately I can't. If I defined for you that beyond a reasonable doubt is some percentage somewhere eighty percent or above, as opposed to being a preponderance of the evidence being just fifty-one percent, can you say beyond a reasonable doubt that either one of those scenarios did not happen?"

"I'm going to object." W.J. is up on his feet. "That's an improper question."

"The objection is sustained," rules the judge.

"Okay, let me ask you this." Wiley tries again. "What degree of certainty can you assign to the likelihood of scenario one occurring?"

"Let me answer your question a different way." Dr. Lee begins yet again to address that which is the essence of this scenario-postulating: either Bill was stabbed in the afternoon as he entered the house, as he claims, or he was stabbed in the back and chest at the very end when Kerry chased him down the hall and out of the house, as Myers claims.

"I yesterday testified on my findings, scientific findings, A type antigen found on certain clothing, B type antigen found on other clothes or other objects, and what medium-velocity spatter consist of, where they locate, what low-velocity, where the smear. I did not create those scenarios, so you should ask him instead of me."

"Now, you rendered the opinion as to one was more consistent than the other."

"No, I said both scenario have problems."

"So?"

"It's not fit totally."

"Some things fit both scenarios, don't they?"

"What?"

"Some of the facts that you have."

"Yes, some facts do fit and some fact is not the fact."

That was a stinger; Wiley seemed not the least bit bothered by it, however. "So it is going to be your position in reference to all of these blood clumpings—that somebody referred to them as—that you're unable to give an opinion as whether or not you would have taken more or less samples?"

"Wait a minute!" Dr. Lee isn't smiling. "I did not say that. You said that for me."

"I don't think so."

"You're the lawyer; you put word in my mouth. I did not say that. I say I cannot make judgment for him. I may take more sample; may take less sample."

"Okay, based on these photographs, were you able to come to a conclusion as to whether or not if you would have been on the scene, you would have taken more or less samples out of each area in that house?"

"Yeah, my answer I may take more sample; I may take less sample."

"You would take less than one sample?"

"If I'm at the scene, if I can find out who did it, why I take a lot of blood sample."

Perhaps it's the titter from the gallery that tells Wiley he's barking up an empty tree. "Did you read Kerry Myers's statement?" he suddenly asks.

"Probably not. I don't recall that."

"Did you read Fontanille's statement?"

"I think I read portion of it. I falling to sleep."

"Did you read any of the trial testimony?"

"No."

"In your experience as a forensic criminalist, do head wounds bleed a lot?"

"No, sir, not necessarily."

"But sometimes they do."

"Sure, sometimes they do."

"I want you to assume for the sake of this question that Mr. Fontanille has Mr. Myers around the neck on the right side, and they are bending over in a struggle, and Mr. Fontanille takes glass objects and hits Mr. Myers in the head with them."

"So you have one hand holding somebody's neck?"

"And taking stuff and hitting him over the head."

"Where he got the stuff?" Dr. Lee wants to know.

"Right on the counter right here."

"So you say next to counter?"

"Around in the area of the love seat is where the glass was and what-have-you."

"How distance between love seat and shelf? Can you go pass by there? If you cannot, of course, eliminate this possibility unless somebody have a long arm can reach."

"Or the love seat maybe didn't fit here."

"So you're asking me some questions I can't give answer."

"If you'll wait a minute, maybe we'll get the answer. You found a large pool of blood in the right corner of that love seat in the photograph?"

"I see a group of droplets; it's not large clump."

"About how many blood drops are there?"

"Approximately twenty."

"Approximately twenty?"

"Yeah. And if this photo is correct, you can see the love seat is right against that area. I don't think any way somebody can get behind that love seat."

"If you look at that love seat, that love seat sticks out in the passageway, doesn't it, doctor?"

"Of course. So therefore preclude someone hand holding somebody, and get on shelf and grab things. How can get to kitchen?"

"With all due respect, the hypothetical was that he had him with the left hand."

"Left hand, all right, not right hand anymore."

"It was never the right hand."

"Leave right hand."

"He reaches up and takes something, hits him in the head, and he's bending over and he stands there for a while. Now, that blood could have come from Kerry Myers where he's bending over after Fontanille hit him in the head with the pottery, couldn't it?"

"Sure."

"So we can't presuppose that all of that blood is Fontanille's, can we?"

"May be Fontanille, may be Myers."

"Maybe both?"

"May be both, may be Janet."

Oops! But, apparently, Wiley doesn't even hear it. He continues on, "In the area of S-4 [behind the recliner], I believe the testimony is one blood sample was taken out of that area and that's inconclusive?"

"Yes, sir."

"How many blood spots, spatters, drops, or anything else did you observe in that area?"

"I say approximately five hundred or more."

"And we do not know whose blood that is?"

"No we don't. Remember, I say I'm not black magic."

"You don't have any idea how it got there either, do you?"

"I know I have idea. It's vertical droplet ninety-degree angle from up and down from a blood source. I already tell you; I tell Mr. Noriea; that's what I reconstruct. As far as whose blood I cannot tell you."

"You cannot say that this is inconsistent with Myers's statement that he was bending over bleeding from the head, can you?"

"I did not say that."

"Well, I'm asking you now, sir, and I don't mean to be argumentative with you. I'm asking you now, is that inconsistent with Kerry Myers's statement in that he had been cut in the head and Fontanille held on to him for a long time and he was bending over like this?"

"Not going to be totally consistent; not going to be totally inconsistent."

Eventually even Wiley figures out he's gotten all he can out of that line of questioning and moves on.

"When you testified about Mr. Fontanille's pants, I believe your testimony was that there were three hundred medium-velocity impact blood spatters on one leg and five hundred on the other?"

"Yes, sir."

"How far does blood fly when it has a medium-velocity impact?"

"How far depends what the size of the blood spatter. The smaller stain will not fly as far as the larger stain."

"The size of the impact stains that were found on Mr. Fontanille's pants, were you able to formulate an opinion as to how close he was standing to the A source when he received those splatters?"

"If you remember my testimony, there are multiple deposit from different angle, different direction. Some are consistent with droplets from up and down; some are consistent from lower point projection up; some were left; some were right; some deposit on top of others, which means they not deposit all those blood spatter in one single event."

"Would it be fair to say that from what you observed—let's assume for the sake of argument that the bat is the blood source of A—that those medium-velocity impact spatters would be consistent with being within reach of this baseball bat?"

"What do you mean? Swinging the bat?"

"Right."

"More likely I will see medium-velocity spatter on somebody back and somebody shirt, less on somebody's pants."

It's as if Wiley doesn't even hear him, and he wades in for more, his focus only on Bill's jeans. "Well, the question is: Do you think those blood spatters got on his pants, assuming that he was wearing those pants, from him swinging this baseball bat at the source A blood?"

With an air of patience greatly strained, Dr. Lee again attempts to explain that the significant spatter-type patterns produced by the act of swinging that bat are somewhat higher up and on another garment, namely Kerry's dress shirt.

". . . if you raise the bat up and down, you're going to have cast-off pattern. If you're going to have a direction like a cast-off, it's not going to be the lower extremity of somebody's pants." There, at the bottom of the jeans where Wiley is pointing, Dr. Lee explains, with all due deliberateness, "What you're going to get is a splash pattern . . . impact and splash up and not going to have a cast-off like you raised the bat."

Finally catching on, Wiley asks, "Would any of the blood spatters on Billy Fontanille's pants be consistent with her laying down and him hitting her while she's laying down?"

"It is also equally consistent with somebody else using the bat and he standing next to her."

Even though apparently Wiley has gotten the drift, he still manages to ask the wrong question. "Now, if somebody else was standing next to him and you had their pants—"

"I'm going to find the same bloodstain."

Perhaps Dr. Lee's answering him before he'd finished his question is the reason Wiley blindly, but still self-importantly, flings his next question: "Did you find any medium-velocity impact bloodstains on Kerry Myers's pants that were consistent with him hitting Janet with this baseball bat?"

"I did find forty bloodstains on Mr. Myers's pants. I did find some cleaning thing, wiping the blood pattern on his shirt and his pants."

"That was not the question."

"That's my answer, forty medium-velocity blood spatters."

"Where?"

"Majority is on left side."

"Now, in your report, did you say that there was a smear pattern on the left thigh of his pants?"

"Consistent with Janet's type," Dr. Lee confirms, with devastating elaboration.

Having led himself deeply into this perilous territory, Wiley can't just hop back out; he'll have to get out the same way he went in, rashly and still brashly: "Were you able to formulate an opinion as to whether or not that was a primary transfer or secondary transfer?"

"I cannot form opinion what goes on there before this cleaning action."

"Would that be consistent, that stain, smear, whatever you want to call it, be consistent with a baseball bat that had her blood on it and two men are fighting and it goes across his leg? Yes, or no, then you may qualify."

"No, it's not. If the baseball bat, I'm going to see heavy crusty stain transfer, but this one is kind of diluted appearance which appears to be some wiping-type action. What the original pattern look like, I don't know."

"If Kerry Myers has been sitting there and somebody has taken a coffee cup that has got coffee in it or tea or a candleholder that's got water in it and crack him in the head, there can be all types of water on him, can't it?"

"Sure."

"So that does not necessarily mean because there is some wiping action on his pants that this is an attempt to cover up anything, does it?"

"I did not say cover up."

"You said that."

"I said clean. That doesn't mean cover."

With nary a flinch, Wiley charges on in his attempt at a managed, rehabilitative retreat; to Kerry's shirt, in fact. He really must at least mitigate if not reconcile the damage done by testimony implying that Kerry had also tried to clean blood off his shirt.

"When you looked at Kerry's shirt, I believe you testified that you found an area of diluted blood; did you not?"

"Yes, sir, I did."

"That could be consistent with somebody hitting him over the head with an object that had some liquid in it?" Wiley says with affected reasonableness.

"Sure," the doctor grants him.

"In other words," Wiley intones, "the water didn't have to be applied after the blood, does it?"

"No, water has to be applied after the blood, not before."

"Why do you say that?"

For all of those in the courtroom who have ever had to deal with kids and ketchup, Dr. Lee's explanation is instantly imprinted on the mind's eye:

"You can see the pattern in here which shows a dark periphery area. If the water already present on the shirt, you drop the blood, you're going have even dilution," the doctor says as he points out the lighter-in-the-center, interlocking blotches which cover almost the entirety of the shoulders and upper back of Kerry Myers's dress shirt.

"But, nowhere on Kerry Myers's shirt did you find any A antigen that would be consistent with Janet Myers?" Finally Wiley has found the only weapon he really has concerning the forensics of Kerry's shirt.

"I only grouped few stains and some of result give me no antigen detection or inconclusive. Some other very small."

"But—"

"I did not find any A antigen," the doctor gives him.

"And you had that thing and you could have tested it until the sleeve fell off if you wanted to?" Wiley takes the gift and then abuses it.

"No. Because I have a lot of other responsibility. I cannot just work on one shirt for all my life."

"I take it by that you mean that it was your decision that you had done enough testing on it."

"Because professional judgment this was clean. Once it clean you're going to have mixture going to make determination difficult, therefore, I chose not to."

Dropping that line quickly, Wiley decides to try the same approach back on Kerry's slacks. "Now, you testified that on Kerry's pants you found medium-velocity impact spatters, but they did not contain A antigen?"

"I did not group those small medium-velocity impact blood spatter; I group *larger* stain."

"So you cannot state to any degree of certainty that Kerry Myers's pants had any medium-velocity impact spatters that contained A antigen; is that correct?"

"I have no idea of those medium-velocity blood spatter, the blood type, but I do know I found A antigen on certain areas."

"So, to your professional certainty, you cannot state that Kerry Myers's shirt had any medium-velocity blood spatters that contained A antigen; is that correct?"

"In my professional opinion I did find medium-velocity blood spatters. Whose type, I do not know."

With an attitude suggesting he believes he has successfully extricated himself from the area of danger, Wiley proceeds to run by Dr. Lee every hypothesis he can think of that might explain the presence of medium-velocity impact spatter of *any* blood type on Kerry's shirt, pants, and shoes.

Upon the theory of the bat being "sufficiently wet" with blood and then striking a forearm "with force sufficient enough to break the arm in four or five places," thereby depositing spatter on the shirt, no matter the repetitive badgering of "let's assume," the very best Wiley gets from Dr. Lee is:

"Maybe, but highly unlikely."

Upon the theory that Kerry Myers's being hit over the head "repeatedly with a ceramic object after his head has been laid open" could account for the impact spatters on his pants, no matter its rephrasings, Wiley gets the best and the worst of it at the same time:

"It will definitely produce some," Dr. Lee agrees, and then adds, "but will not produce a cast-off pattern."

"Did you find a cast-off type?"

"From the left shoulder, yes."

And upon the theory of impact spatter depositing on Kerry's shoes when his arm is hit with the bloody bat, Wiley evokes of the doctor exactly what it deserves: "If you put his shoes next to his arm, maybe."

In between and along with his theorizing, Wiley is either starting little fires that singe the fire starter or stamping others out.

"When we find medium-velocity blood spatters on Kerry's clothing, that does not necessarily mean that he was standing anywhere next to Janet Myers when she was hit with that baseball bat?" Wiley asks.

"Except A type of bloodstain found."

"But that wasn't the medium-velocity impact bloodstain, was it?"

"I don't know because it shows a dilution medium."

"You can't say that smear was ever medium-velocity impact?"

"I cannot."

"Sir, if you would—"

At last letting his exasperation take voice, Dr. Lee cuts him off: "I thought I answer your question six million times!"

"Well, I don't think—I apologize, Your Honor," goes Mr. Beevers. "Those A bloodstains on the left thigh area were never reported by you to be medium-velocity impact blood spatters of a type consistent with Janet Myers, were they?"

"I did not."

"Now, when you examined Kerry Myers's shoes—you testified in your report that there was A antigen found, I believe, on the left shoe in two places; is that correct?"

"Yes, sir."

"How many spots, drops, splatters, satellite drops, or anything else were you able to detect?"

"Ten on the left shoe; forty on the right shoe."

"Now, whose blood was on the right, or what antigen was it?"

"The few spot I tested it's B."

"It wasn't A?"

"No."

"On the left shoe how many did you test?"

"I tested three spot."

"Three spots out of the ten that were there?"

"Yes, sir."

"And what were your findings?"

"Two spot containing A antigen."

"Were you able to classify these spots the way you did on your paper?"

"Yes, sir."

"What type of spots were they?"

"It's consistent with a medium-velocity type of pattern."

"That photo does not show you the blood spot itself, does it?"

"It show blood spot itself."

"That is what you refer to as the blood spot right there?"

"Right."

"Why wouldn't a sticker be up there next—"

"If I stick it there I can't group. I contaminate my own blood source, you never put the sticker on the bloodstain."

"Now, this drop on the left shoe was dropped?"

"It's not dropped."

"It's not dropped?"

"Definitely not vertical drop."

Soon Wiley actually asked: "Just when somebody is getting swung at, they don't always keep their feet on the floor, do they?"

"Ask him." Dr. Lee nods at the stone-faced Kerry Myers. "I don't know."

"But can you say to a forensic certainty that that blood did not come off of that bat?"

"What I'm saying, I found A antigen, it's not a drop; it's a medium-velocity blood spatter. Beyond that point, I cannot tell you."

And then Wiley conducts a protracted engagement of attrition over the foyer blood trails leading out, leading in, leading to the living room, stabbing and chasing down the hallway and out, stabbing and fighting up the hallway:

"He could still be stabbed into the lower back area and it can be soaked through these three layers of clothes and he doesn't have to bleed on the floor, does he?"

"It could be."

"Now, in response to Mr. Noriea's question when he had Mr. Fontanille's pants—"

"Not going to be more allowed cross-examination," Dr. Lee suddenly says, turning to Judge Richards. "Better make—I have flight to catch and better make some other arrangement."

"What time," Judge Richards asks.

"One o'clock."

"It's twelve-thirty now," observes the judge.

"I apologize, Your Honor," goes Wiley.

"We'll recess for fifteen minutes," announces Judge Richards.

After making arrangements for Dr. Lee to stay over to accommodate Kerry Myers and the court, Wiley is right back trying to find some way favorable to his client to explain type A blood being on Kerry's shoes. One such effort produced one of the trials more humorous lines, even as tragic as it also was.

"If there is an A source of blood being Ryan Myers's head," Wiley is saying, "and it's lacerated or he's bleeding from the ears or there's wounds to his head and he's placed in the ambulance with Mr. Myers, could that be a possible source of A blood on his shoes?"

"Have to have medium-velocity force applied to it," Dr. Lee explains, categorically, again.

"You don't know what happened in there," Wiley tells him.

"Somebody beat the baby up I don't know," replies Henry Lee.

Then, much, much later, "So let's assume for the sake of this discussion," Wiley is saying, "that this baseball bat has A blood on it and there's a struggle that occurs over the baseball bat."

"Yes, sir."

"Now, if somebody testified that they were holding the bat and they're bending over and Mr. Fontanille's back here, and they're fighting over it, getting hit in the head, and it brushes up against their pants, and later there is introduced a wet towel, people are drying their hands off, they're drying their pants off, they're holding on to their arm where it's hurt, that could give rise to that smear that you found on the pants; could it not?"

"I think hour ago I already give you the answer: Could be."

"Could be?"

"Sure. My answer still the same after one hour."

Then, finally, in search of an exit line, Wiley says, "In reference to the handkerchief that was found on the scene and you testified that was H type antigen on it?"

"On the mucus, yellow mucus."

"Did anybody tell you that in that family prior to this incident that people had had the flu?"

"No."

"Now, that handkerchief, merely because it's on the scene, does that indicate that only the person whose nasal mucus is on there, that doesn't indicate that they're the only one that used that handkerchief?"

"I'm testifying here, counselor," Dr. Lee feels it necessary to remind Wiley Beevers. "If you remember I said a handkerchief I found some bloodstains on those, human blood A antigen found. I found some yellow mucus material of H antigen which consistent from an O person. As far as who gets the flu, I don't know."

"No further questions."

Even though it really doesn't matter—after more than a day and a half of Dr. Lee on the stand, whoever comes next doesn't have a prayer of being able to fill that hole and gain any collective focus—Carol Dixon, now Carol Dixon Weed, largely due to first the tutelage and preparation of Howie Peters and then his adroit direct examination, handles a bad situation rather well.

She manages to be just a bit more than the even wash W.J. felt would be the best she'd be able to contribute. But in the long run all of her test results which had not been inconclusive turned out to be the same as Dr.

Lee's, and the knowledge of that gives her the confidence to come across as a fairly credible witness and a plus—a marginable plus, to be sure, but certainly not the negative W.J. feared she could be.

When she is excused, the State resubmits its motion to visit the crime scene "based upon the previous testimony that's been put on."

Wiley Beevers states, "I have no position."

Nick, of course, has a whole speech to deliver in presenting his argument in opposition to the motion.

Judge Richards then rules in favor of the State with the proviso that the visit should attempt to duplicate the daylight condition that existed at around five o'clock Thursday afternoon on February 23, 1984.

Thus ends the fifth day of the trial.

Dr. Gustavo Gutnisky, the New Orleans neurosurgeon who treated Ryan Myers, is first up for the State on Monday morning, April 2, 1990.

Since he is a well-respected local physician known to all of the attorneys involved, his being admitted to testify as an expert witness in the field of neurosurgery is immediately stipulated to by Nick and Wiley.

Dr. Gutnisky's involvement with the medical treatment of Ryan Myers after the murder of his mother is well known, and nothing new in that regard is forthcoming now. However, unlike Paul Connick in the first trial, W.J. has cause to elicit the following and not just assume that Nick will do it for him in cross: "Dr. Gutnisky, did you also have occasion to see Kerry Myers on that particular day as well?"

"Yes, I did."

"Would you describe your neurological findings, insofar as he's concerned?"

"I was asked to see him by the orthopedic surgeon, he did have a broken arm. But, as far as my part is concerned, he did have some bruises on the forehead, but he was—in other words, intact. He was well oriented, and he did not have any signs of any severe head injury."

"Skull fractures, concussion, or anything of that matter?"

"No, no skull fractures."

"What about a concussion—did he have a concussion?"

"Well, at that time when I saw him, no, he was fully awake. I guess he could have had a concussion many hours prior to me seeing him, but at the time I saw him, no."

Nick's cross is very brief; the jury is taken out. Shortly thereafter at least four attorneys' breaths come to a collective catch the moment Wiley Beevers begins his cross-examination of the neurosurgeon. Is he really going to open that can of worms? And if so, why on earth would *he* want to?

"Dr. Gutnisky, did you examine the *whole* body of Ryan Myers?"

"No, I did not," the doctor answers. "I just limited myself to the neurological exam, to his level of consciousness and whether there was any evidence of a head injury."

"Okay, I have the same medical records, or hopefully I have the same medical records that were tendered to us by the State," Wiley goes. "And I call your attention to this page right here, which I have gone through and previously marked. I ask you to come down to this area right here, and see if you can help me interpret what that says?"

"Okay, which area?"

"This area right here, Dr. Gutnisky?"

"It says—this is again, this is on Ryan Myers."

"Yes, sir."

" 'Abdomen soft, bowel sounds'—and I don't know whether he says 'B.S. non-tender,' and question marks. 'Extremities contuse, bilateral with abrasions—' "

"Okay," Wiley says quickly. "So apparently somebody examined this child when he's in there, and not only does he have head injuries, but—bilaterally, would that mean on both knees?"

"Yes."

"And on both knees there are contusions?"

"That's what it sounds like, yes, abrasions."

"Is there any indication on there whether those contusions were fresh or whether—"

"No."

"So, we know that not only does he have head injuries, but we've got at least contusions on both kneecaps that are significant enough to be noted in the medical records, is that correct?"

And, basically, that's it; Wiley soons moves on to haggle over exactly when Kerry Myers might've been given Demerol for pain. Ryan was obviously abused by one of the three adults in that house that day well beyond the "accidental" almost fatal blow to his head, and all Wiley wants is another possible source for the type A blood found on Kerry's clothes!

"The State waives polling."

"Waive, Your Honor."

"All right. Who's your next witness, Mr. LeBlanc?"

"Your Honor, the State would call Lieutenant Vince Lamia to the stand."

Vince's purpose in the box is purely procedural, therefore quite brief. His sole function is to testify that he was the police officer who brought Bill Fontanille's, Kerry Myers's, and Janet Myers's clothing up to Herbert MacDonell in Corning, New York, and that in doing so, the chain of custody had not been broken.

Nick, in a two-minute cross-examination, brings out that it was the clothes of Bill Fontanille that Professor MacDonell had focused his examination on. Wiley chooses not to cross-examine Vince at all, saving the jury another trek in and out.

"May we proceed, Your Honor?" Howat Peters soon asks.

"Yes, sir."

"I call Joe Koehler, Your Honor," Howie announces.

Mr. Koehler, now living in Slidell, Louisiana, and working for Conoco Oil, was, of course, the night commander of the Communications Division when Kerry Myers called the police. His purpose on the stand for the State also is singular, but crucial: laying a predicate for the admissibility of the 911 tape; he himself had made a cassette copy off the big continuously running multitrack recorder which is at the heart of the Communications Center.

Nick, this time around, cross-examines the witness even more briefly, only wanting to establish that the "punched time card" with the exact time of the phone call had been lost. Then, and only for the record so as not to preclude its being an appellate issue, he states his objection to the tape coming in, because Nick very much wants the jury to hear that tape. Wiley stipulates to the tape's authenticity and its admissibility as evidence in the case against his client—he also actually *wants* the tape played.

"At this time," Howie says, "in connection with the testimony of the witness, I offer State's exhibit 198 and 199 into evidence."

"Those will be received . . ." Judge Richards says.

"And I ask that 198 be played for the jury, Your Honor."

"All right, sir."

"We also have copies of 199 for them to follow along on."

"Counsel, want to see the copies?" the judge asks the defense, referring to the prepared transcript of the tape.

"I have no objections, Your Honor," Wiley says.

"Yes, we have copies, Your Honor," answers Nick.

"Are you ready, Your Honor?" Howie asks.

"Yes, sir," the judge says; and with that the tape is played in the presence of the jury. Almost immediately, the new Mrs. Myers wails at full throttle and then swoons and is carried from the courtroom.

When the tape is finished, "I tender the witness," Howat Peters says into the silent vacuum which is now the courtroom.

The jurors file out of the tense and now buzzing courtroom; then: "The State calls Walter Cardin," Dub announces.

After establishing that he was one of the two emergency medical technicians who responded to the ambulance call at 2232 Litchwood Lane in the early hours of February 24, 1984, Dub directs Mr. Cardin step by step, moment by moment, through the events immediately upon and after their arrival, making sure to highlight certain points.

"We followed the patrol car into the address. We parked in the street, parallel to the front door of the house. When we arrived on scene, my partner remained in the ambulance. We were told from dispatch that there was a stabbing, that the perpetrator may still be on scene, or he could be lying on the ground down the street. My partner remained in the unit and was basically flicking her headlights to see if she could see anything down the street. I got out of the ambulance and followed Deputy DeWilde to the door. . . ."

Mr. Cardin continues on to describe the scene at the door, the shotgun being taken and placed aside by DeWilde, Kerry Myers being "pivoted" to him, whereupon he had Myers sit down by the front wheel of the brand-new car in the driveway. There he checked and inquired after the extent of his wounds and determined that "he did not appear to have any life-threatening injuries."

Cardin further testifies, "The deputy summoned me in and when I went in—there was a railing, when I looked back to my left I could see the deceased's body. I summoned my partner, then I went to the body. I quickly did an assessment to see if there was any indication for us to try to resuscitate her. By this time my partner had arrived, we looked at each other, she was the senior medic and she was in charge. My impression was she had been dead for several hours and resuscitation would be of no benefit. I then went back out to the car where I had left Mr. Myers."

After several more minutes of administering to Kerry Myers, Walter Cardin says, "We got to the ambulance and I seem to remember either we were up in the ambulance, or getting up into the ambulance—at this point he made a mention of his children. My partner was with me."

A little later, "In the ambulance he said that this fellow and him had fought for several hours, he knew him. I remember there was something specifically said about a baseball bat being returned or retrieved. And they fought for all this time with the bat, fistfight, wrestled, that this other individual had been depressed over the recent breakup of his marriage and that he had perhaps a mental problem—I'm trying to recall all these events."

"Now, Mr. Cardin, who is present in the ambulance at this time?" Dub offers a memory jogger.

"Myself and Mr. Myers."

"Did he ever mention anything about a knife at any point?"

"Yes, he did. He said they fought for all this length, period of time, and that finally he was able to escape from him into the kitchen, get a knife, and stab him. And at this point, after he stabbed him, he was able to get him out of the house, and that's when he had called for help."

"No further questions, Your Honor," Dub soon says.

"Now, at this time, did you make any notes or anything about what you heard?"

"No, sir, I did not."

For the better part of half an hour, Wiley hammers away, demanding exact details over and over again, virtually trying everything from how much has he followed the story in the press to how much personal interest he might feel toward the case, to get Mr. Cardin to waver. But in the end all his effort nets him is the following:

"I recall very specifically that I was told that quote, 'I got a knife from the kitchen,' or 'I went in the kitchen, got a knife, and I was able to stab the other man.' At no time did he indicate to me the other man's name."

"No further questions."

"Redirect?" the judge asks of the State.

Dub rises and asks, "Did he ever inquire about his infant child?"

"No, sir."

"I have no further questions, Your Honor."

W. J. LeBlanc stands and says, "Your Honor, the State would call Patricia Murphy."

Using the same process as he had with her former partner, W.J. directs Ms. Murphy, now a cardiac ICU nurse, through her memories of that night, but this time highlighting events only she witnessed, independent of Walter Cardin, filling in the scene with more visual images and dialogue.

"Okay. Now, tell us if you would if you have any occasion to have any conversation with Mr. Myers? Is he in the ambulance at this point?" Dub asks.

"He is in the ambulance and he is on the stretcher to the left as you enter the unit. When I got into the ambulance with Ryan, Mr. Myers was laying on his back and he kept turning his head to the right looking at little Ryan. And he asked me, 'Is he okay? Is he okay?' And then he asked me where I found the child and I told him the master bedroom, and he looked back across again and he said, 'That's funny, because they never came out of their rooms.' "

And then: "He started to get extremely upset and made the comment, 'Damn him.' And I said, 'Pardon me?' And he was talking, 'They did this to my child.' At the time it didn't make a whole lot of sense. The rest of the conversation was a lot of goings-on about the situation which had occurred over the past hours."

"To the best of your recollection, would you tell us what he related to you about what had happened over that previous night?"

"What he elaborated was that someone was in the house and held them hostage, beat his wife, his son, and he was unable to communicate with anyone."

And then there comes the conversation she remembers having with Kerry Myers in the emergency room at West Jefferson when she was lending the staff a hand because it was a very busy night:

"I went into the room where they had Mr. Myers and was helping the nurse to get all the preparations ready for his patient exam, and he made a reference to, 'Damn him and her.' And then he was talking, he talked about coming home from work, finding his *neighbor,* at this time, *and his wife in bed together.* He was upset at this point, an altercation ensued, and that was the last of the elaboration."

"Is that the—the sum total of what the conversation was that you recall?" W.J. manages to say, even though every ounce of him is silently screaming, "I can't fucking believe she said that!"

"To the best of my knowledge," Ms. Murphy adds in closing.

At the moment Dub is a murderous lunatic on the inside, yet, perhaps from pure muscle memory, he is soon able to say: "I have no further questions, Your Honor, I tender."

"I've got a few, Your Honor," Wiley says, and he gets up and proceeds to conduct a rambling cross-examination.

Back at the counsel table, however, W.J. and Howie aren't hearing a word of testimony, they are looking at each other in a combination of shock and rage waiting for the explosion they know will have to come. In the at least three interviews conducted with Ms. Murphy in preparation for her testimony, she never said anything about anybody being in any bed with Kerry Myers's wife. W.J. is so angry he has to get out and collect himself while deciding how best to handle it.

"I'm not in the courtroom for sixty seconds at any time Beevers did anything," Nick is remembering. "I tell Madeleine, 'You're gonna sit here when Beevers does his case and I'm leaving. 'Cause if I sit through all this testimony, when I go to argue this case, I'm not going to remember whether the jury was in the court or out. I can distinguish firsthand recollection from what you tell me they said.'

"But I forgot something in the courtroom. So I walked back in to get it, and it was right when Murphy was saying this. I said to Madeleine, 'Did you hear that? How much other stuff is going on like this that you're missing?' She said, 'Nick, that's the first thing.' "

Completely oblivious to it all, Wiley is well into his cross-examination, hammering repetitively at the most minor of details in his attempts to impeach Ms. Murphy. Suddenly Nick and Howie are at the bench.

"I've got a problem," Nick starts. "And the reason why I'm not explaining this to Howat—"

"W.J., I know he would want to be here for this."

"And I really don't know how to handle this," Nick continues. "And I probably walked in at the wrong time to hear it, but I heard a direct quote that Kerry said he found his wife in bed with a neighbor. Now, that's not Bill, 'cause Bill's not a neighbor, at least that's one of the inferences, and if Bill walked in on a fight, that another participant in the fight left, I think that's *Brady* material [anything that might tend to exculpate the defendant must be disclosed to the defense] that I've not gotten until this moment, when I heard it in court, and I heard her tell she told the police that night. That poses—I don't know what to do. I don't want to cause a mistrial, but if ever *Brady* versus *U.S.* says you're entitled to that kind of stuff, that's the position I'm in now."

Nick is actually sputtering, for perhaps the first time in his life. If he is not exactly at a loss for words, they're damn sure difficult for him to get together and get out.

"I don't know how to handle it," Nick repeats. "I ask that you at least keep this witness under subpoena, because I may want to call her in my case just for that limited quote. I mean, I don't know how to do it, that's—in my opinion, that's clearly *Brady* material. This is the first moment I've heard it, so—"

"I wouldn't think it's necessarily that . . ." Howie hems and haws as best he can under the circumstances.

Soon W.J. joins the frenetic jawboning before the bench. Of course, the whole thing has be explained to Wiley. And the judge assures, "I heard it." Eventually it is determined that a transcript of exactly what she said will be produced as soon as possible and that Ms. Murphy will indeed remain under subpoena and be available for Nick to question, and that what they *really* ought to do is take a recess.

A very pissed-off W.J. bursts out of the courtroom doors. Pat Murphy is the first person he sees standing directly across the hall. He stops dead in his tracks and gives her a stare which all but melts the impetuous and now very scared young lady into the floor, then turns on a heel and goes upstairs. Because she is still under cross-examination, and not his witness at the moment, the rules say that's all he can do, he isn't allowed to speak to her. But while there is no communication, that look tells her all she needs to know.

"Ms. Murphy, have you ever been under any psychiatric treatment?"

When court reconvenes out of the presence of the jury, from the spin of Wiley's first question, it appears Myers's defense counsel wants to determine if being impetuous and carried away by the drama of it all is Patricia Murphy's *only* problem.

"No, sir."

"Have you ever been admitted for treatment for any alcohol or substance abuse?"

"No, sir."

With her sanity and faculties confirmed, Wiley then starts back with his relentless, grinding-out-every-detail form of cross. After better than an hour, however, his gleanings are few, and not terribly helpful to his cause:

"Okay, so after he's in this exam room, you walk in, what's the first thing that Kerry says?"

"The first thing—Kerry was already speaking and I didn't hear most of that conversation. The first thing that I heard was that he came home and found them together."

"Now, you had previously testified, it I'm not mistaken, and I quote, 'He talked about his coming home from work finding his neighbor at this time and his wife in bed together,' okay. Now, you said in response to my last question, he came home and found them together."

"Right."

"Okay. Now, did Kerry Myers say—exactly what was Kerry's words in reference to that?"

"I would like to clarify that. The words were that he came home from work and found them together."

"Now, your earlier statement, that he came home and found them in bed together was not what Kerry Myers said, was it?"

"I cannot be absolutely sure, that's why I'd like to clarify that."

"Ms. Murphy, you're not sure exactly what Kerry Myers said, and I'm talking about in specific words, when you walked into that exam room, are you?"

"As far as to that statement, yes."

"Okay, then tell me whether or not he said he found them *in bed* together, or he found them in the house together?"

"He came home and found them *together*."

Finally, "No further questions."

"Redirect?" asks Judge Richards.

Dub is already on his feet. He doesn't have many questions.

"Now, ma'am, we've spoken about this case on two or three different occasions, is that correct? At any point did you ever tell me that Kerry came home and found them in *bed* together?"

"I'm going to object and ask to approach the bench," Wiley is pontificating. "Well, we don't have a jury in here. I'm sorry, Your Honor, I'm so used to having a jury here."

"All right, sir."

"He's attempting," Wiley says, "I believe, to impeach his own—no, let me withdraw that objection and let him go."

"I thought that you would," W.J. says. "Your Honor, I feel like I have an ethical responsibility to bring this to the court's attention."

"Well, I do, too," Judge Richards says. "And the reason for it is Mr. Noriea's comment in the beginning, that the testimony of this witness may involve some *Brady* material and it was not revealed to the defendants, and I think the question is appropriate."

"Thank you, Your Honor," W.J. says and then returns to Ms. Murphy. "Did you ever tell me, ma'am, on any of the occasions in which we spoke, that Kerry Myers said that he found them in bed together?"

"Not that I recall."

"Thank you, Your Honor," Dub says. "I just wanted to clear that up for the record."

"All right, Ms. Murphy, you're excused for the day, but I'm going to ask you to be back in court at nine o'clock tomorrow morning," Judge Richards tells the witness.

"All right, counsel, are we ready for the jury?"

"Yes, Your Honor," Dub says.

"Yes, sir," says Nick.

The jury is brought back in, and W. J. LeBlanc says, "Your Honor, the State will call Officer John Taylor."

The State brings John Taylor, of the New Orleans Police Department, to the stand for a reason much different from that in Bill Fontanille's first degree murder trial. In fact, while W.J. has him briefly run through his participation in the events of that infamous morning, he is there only to testify to what he had not been allowed to testify to in 1986: exactly what he had heard Bill Fontanille say at Jo Ellen Smith Hospital that early morning.

"What else did he tell Deputy Adams that you recall?" W.J. asks.

"I believe the last thing he had said to him, that he had been told by Myers that Myers was going to tell the police that they had talked about killing each other's wife and that Myers told him, 'I didn't think you would go through with this.' "

"Objection, Your Honor," immediately goes Wiley. "We need to approach the bench.

"At this time on behalf of my client, I'm going to object to this coming in," Wiley begins when all are present at the bench. "And I'm going to ask you to disregard it, 'cause that portion of the statement has been ruled to be inadmissible as part of the conspiracy. That part of the statement is conspiratorial in nature and that portion of it can't come in. It's just that simple, that they talked about what they were going to do and that they conspired—"

"Judge—I'm sorry, I didn't mean to cut you off, Wiley," Dub says.

"Go ahead," says Wiley.

"Were you finished?"

"Go ahead, I'm through."

"All right," W.J. says. "Judge, I would just respectfully suggest that that was never ruled like that. That the court's ruling in the James Hearing was that the statements made—"

"Look, you all can fight about your case," goes Nick. "But put it in my case. You all talk about it, but just go ahead and put it in my case. That's fine, no objection to it."

"I'm going to ask you and Ms. Landrieu to stay at the bench conference," Judge Richards says.

"Judge," goes Dub, "I believe, unless I am not aware of the previous court's ruling, but I believe that the ruling Mr. Beevers is referring to was that the court ruled it was inadmissible as the State did not prove a prima facie case."

"They didn't rule on the admissibility of it," says Nick, begging the fine point, even though he and W.J. want the same thing. "That was admissible, as I understand it, and it was offered as an explanation of why the police were going to arrest him, and it was admissible."

"It was not," Dub says.

"Well, it would be inadmissible if there were conspiracy charges," says the judge.

"Right, right," goes Nick.

"That's exactly right," says W.J.

"But that's not the case here," Judge Richards reasons.

"Right," goes Howie.

"The objection is overruled."

"Please note my objection just for the record, Your Honor," Wiley says.

"All right, sir."

Nick then did a perfunctory cross-examination simply to have Officer Taylor highlight that the statement by Bill was to inform the police that that was what Kerry Myers had *told him* he was going to tell police, that it was a preemptive strike, if you will.

Wiley declines to cross-examine.

"The State would call Deputy Noel Adams," W.J. announces. Of course, Noel "Torchy" Adams, the first Jefferson Parish deputy to speak with Bill when he joined Officer Taylor at Jo Ellen Smith, who had made handwritten notes of Bill's first statement which he had included in his official report, is also put up there for only one reason:

"That's when he said that Kerry had told him he had killed his wife," Torchy Adams testifies, "and that he had killed his son, and that he was going to blame it on him, Bill Fontanille. He went on later to say that he was going to tell the police when they arrived that they had planned to kill each other's wives, but that he had no idea that Bill would come over and actually carry out the plan."

"I have no further questions, Your Honor."

Nick again conducts a very brief cross, mainly pertaining to Bill's bloody clothes having been placed in a plastic hospital bag.

Judge Richards then looks to Wiley, who says, "I've got some." And the jury is led out again. Whereupon Wiley asks exactly four innocuous questions, taking up all of maybe two minutes, and then says, "No further questions, Your Honor." And the jury comes back again.

"The State calls Ms. Pat Murphy," W.J. announces.

For the jury, Dub conducts a much less animated—however more effective—Ms. Murphy through a retelling of her story of that night, concluding with: "What did he tell you?"

"I went into the examining room to assist a nurse, and he was already engaged in some conversation. And the next clear statement I heard was, 'Damn him and her, I caught—I found them together."

"Did he have any other comment or elaborate at all?"

"No."

"Did you have occasion to report that to anyone, ma'am?"

"Yes, I did. I immediately walked out of the exam room and found the first deputy that was standing in the hall."

"Did you have any other involvement in this particular emergency call?"

"No."

"I tender the witness," W.J. says.

Since she more or less recants the "neighbor" and the "in the bed" portions of her absolute memory, there isn't much of any value accruing to Bill Fontanille that Nick gains in his cross, except more trashing of Kerry Myers, of course:

"What I can definitely recall is that he 'caught them, found them together.' The location of where they were found is not—I can't be definite—he was upset at this point, and an altercation ensued. He did not elaborate as to what type of altercation."

"I have no further questions."

"All right."

"The State would call Ernest Barrow," Howat Peters announces.

"May we approach the bench?" Wiley immediately asks. At the bench conference, he says, "I ask that it be conducted out of the presence of the jury. It has to do with the question of whether a privilege existed."

"I am going to go into the substance of what was asked with Ernie Barrow," Dub explains. "Sometime before her death, she came to Ernie and related certain information."

"Well, obviously certain stuff that she might have said is not going to be admissible," Judge Richards says. "Let's get to that point and then make your objection. I don't know what he's going to ask."

"I can tell you right now we're not seeking any privileged—no privileged information and no hearsay statements by the victim," Dub says.

"None of the substance," goes Wiley. "None of the questions that she asked him, none of the answers that he gave her."

"Sorry, Jack," goes W.J.

"Let's see where we go with it," says the judge.

The 1990 baseball bat murder trial soon has another lawyer climbing into the witness box. Howie does the direct examination:

"Mr. Barrow, what is your occupation?"

"I'm an attorney-at-law."

"How long have you been an attorney?"

"Eighteen years."

"You maintain offices in Gretna, Louisiana?"

"Yes, sir, I do."

"Do you know Kerry Myers?"

"Yes, sir."

"Look around and see if you see him."

"Yes."

"You see him?"

"Yes, Kerry Myers is right there."

"I'd ask that the record reflect the witness has identified Kerry Myers." Then, "How long have you known him?"

"Since he and Janet were married, I guess maybe a little before that."

"Did you know Janet Myers?"

"Yes, sir."

"How long did you know Janet Myers?"

"I've known Janet since 1963—whatever—how many years that is, about twenty-seven, twenty-eight years."

"How did you come to know Janet? Is she related to you?"

"Janet Myers I think is my wife's first cousin."

"Did you have occasion to meet with Janet Myers approximately two months before she died?"

"Yes, I did."

"Was she pregnant at that time?"

"Yes, she was. It looked like she was almost at the end of the pregnancy, very, very large."

"Did you have occasion, without going into what, if anything, she said to—did you have occasion to speak with her?"

"Yes, I did." And there is total silence in the courtroom; even the air doesn't move.

"I'm going to ask you, what did you tell her?"

"I'm going to at this time object," starts Wiley. "Your Honor, because with all due respect, that is attorney-client privilege. It's not affirmatively waived and it certainly cannot be waived by her death."

"We have no objection to the testimony," goes Nick.

"The objection is overruled," the judge says.

"Note my objection," says Wiley.

Ernie turns around and addresses Judge Richards in pure legalese terms—the gist of which is that Ernie wants to make double sure that the judge has indeed relieved him of the burden of confidentiality to the deceased.

"That's correct," Judge Richards assures him.

"What did you tell her?" Instantly there is again an absence of all sound.

"I gave her advice regarding her domestic situation."

"What do you mean by domestic situation?"

"She wanted to know what would happen if she were to be separated from her husband." Exhaling and a humming bustle from the audience.

"What kind of information did you provide?"

"I gave her an estimate on child support; I gave her estimates on alimony; I gave her the concept of community property and what was community property and what wasn't community property. She indicated at that time that there wasn't a whole lot of problem with community property; she wasn't that interested in the community property idea. What she was interested in was how she would survive in the event something happened, and that's exactly the way she put it."

"Did you ever talk to Janet Myers again after you gave her that information?"

"No."

"I tender the witness, Your Honor."

Nick is up: "Mr. Barrow, did you ever give this information to the Jefferson Parish Sheriff's Office about Janet seeking advice about possible separation and divorce?"

"No one ever asked me that particular question."

"When was the first time someone inquired about that information?"

"Last week."

"Thank you. I have no further questions," Nick says.

"I've got some, Your Honor," goes Wiley. Out goes the jury.

"Mr. Barrow, you were asked to institute separation proceedings?" Wiley asks.

"No, I was not."

"Did Janet Myers tell you that she was contemplating a separation?"

"No."

"Did she tell you whether she was seeking this advice for herself or someone else?"

"She did say she was seeking the advice for herself."

"Did Janet Myers tell you that she was unhappy?"

"No."

"Had you ever talked to Janet about proceeding with legal proceedings?"

"We never discussed about legal proceedings. However, I did feel like we were in an attorney-client relationship."

"Did she ever define to you what she meant by 'If anything happens'?"

"No, not as a pure definition. She indicated to me that by that she meant if she and Kerry were to separate."

"Isn't that what you interpreted what she said to mean?"

"That's correct."

"So she never did tell you whether she was happy or unhappy in the marriage, did she?"

"Not in those words."

"She never did tell you whether Kerry was happy or unhappy?"

"No."

"She never did tell you if either one of them were happy or unhappy in the marriage?"

"That's correct."

"No further questions."

"No redirect," Howie tells the court.

"The next witness we have out of the presence of the jury is Charles Cannon," announces W. J. LeBlanc.

Then, "Mr. Cannon, what is your relationship to Janet Myers?"

"Janet Myers was my daughter," the white-haired, frail, nasal-toned, very nervous, tall, hollow-chested man answers with a bit of a bite.

"And you are here under subpoena by Mr. Myers; is that correct?"

"No, State subpoena. The State subpoenaed me."

"Could we check the record, Your Honor," Dub asks. "In the event there's some mistake."

Wiley speaks up. "My appreciation is that the State subpoenaed him. I did, too."

"Mr. Cannon." W.J. turns back to the witness. "Do you recall having a conversation with Mr. Myers approximately one week after the death of your daughter?"

"Where at now?"

"At your home, sir."

"Yes."

"In your den area relative to what had happened the night of the murder? Do you recall that, sir?"

"Yes, approximately."

With Mr. Cannon obviously digging his heels into sand, Dub asks pointedly, "Do you recall Mr. Myers telling you that he went to the phone to call the police?"

"I'm going to object to the form of the question," Wiley says. "He's starting to lead."

"I have permission to lead under the new evidence code," Dub explains. "He has been subpoenaed by the defendant and I'm entitled to lead as identified with an opposing party."

"Just because somebody's subpoenaed by one side certainly does not mean he's identified with that side," Wiley argues.

"You need to lay a further predicate," Judge Richards says.

"Mr. Cannon, were you upset when your son-in-law was indicted?" W.J. asks.

"Yes."

"Do you feel like he had anything to do with Janet's murder?"

"No."

"You Honor, I think that it's very clear that we've got a son-in-law now on trial for murdering his daughter and he doesn't feel like he had anything to do with it," W.J. offers.

"That doesn't identify him with us," answers Wiley.

"It certainly doesn't identify him with us!" W.J. bites back hard and loud and in Beevers's face; he's had about enough.

"I think that, coupled with the fact he was subpoenaed as a defense witness, indicates that identification with the defendant," rules Judge Richards.

"Please note my objection, Your Honor."

"Getting back to this conversation, Mr. Cannon, do you recall Mr. Myers giving you a chronology of the events from the time that William Fontanille left the house?"

"That night?"

Charles Cannon is crawfishing badly, and it isn't pleasant to watch. This very simple, tunnel-minded man knows somehow he's done something wrong, but he's not exactly sure what it is. He knows it has something to do with a meeting he had with W. J. LeBlanc during the last recess, when the assistant district attorney asked him to verify a conversation he'd related to a grand jury some years before, and he did so because he didn't think he had any reason not to—until he mentioned the conversation to Wiley Beevers, whose reaction to it is why he's backpedaling as best he can now.

"That night, you spoke to him that night, when you're talking about William Fontanille and him fighting."

"Well, he told me he was not—that was not at my home; that was at the hospital. Well, I went to see him that Saturday morning and he told me that him and Fontanille fought and Billy beat the hell out of him, and that when he ran, Billy ran out the house, he went and called the 911 number, and then he went looking for his daughter—I mean, his wife rather. And after he found his wife he went and was looking for his son, and then he went back on the phone."

"Did he say he found his son?"

"No, he did not say. He said he went looking for him."

The old man is aging and crumbling by the word.

"Isn't it true that he said that he found his son in the master bedroom?" W.J. feels he *must* do it, it's worth it.

"No, he said he was going to look for him."

"I'm going to object." Wiley is up. "He's already asked that question and answered. He said without qualification that he did say he went and looked for his son. Now he's cross-examining his own witness and I don't think that means he's identified."

"The objection is overruled."

"May I approach the bench with counsel, please," Dub is saying.

"Judge," he says at the bench, "I have a grand jury transcript of Mr. Cannon's testimony. And I'd like you to review it in camera and I'd also like you then to instruct the witness on perjury charges, on what perjury is."

"I want to see it," Wiley says.

"You're not entitled to it," W.J. informs him.

"If it's going to be used to cross-examine," Wiley argues.

"The court is being asked to look at it," Howie says.

"The reason for this is I have talked to Mr. Cannon on numerous occasions, as recently as this afternoon, so that there would be no mistake. Now he's deviating from it. I'd like you to take a look at it and see if you are of the same opinion."

"I know *I* can look at it," Judge Richards says.

"I want to look at it," Wiley keeps jawing. "I have got the right if he's going to use it to cross-examine."

"I ask the court to review the entire part beginning from that segment on, because there's another area that I'd like you to go into," W. J. LeBlanc says.

Judge Richards reads the transcript. Then he asks W.J., "What are you going to do with that testimony?"

"I'm going to ask the witness about Kerry Myers's statement to him. I'm not intending to impeach him with it by referring to it, because I cannot do that," Dub says, reminding one and all that grand jury testimony cannot be used for that purpose.

"Let me see where we go with it," Judge Richards rules.

"I'd like the court to caution the witness as asked for previously," Dub reminds.

Then Judge Richards, in open court, addresses the witness. "I do want to caution you that anything you say while you're under oath, either here or in former proceedings, is subject to the penalty of perjury if false statements are made. I want you to be careful and aware that you are obligated to tell the truth in both proceedings."

Everybody in the courtroom who hasn't yet figured out that something extraordinary is in fact happening does so now—and it'd take a damn good blade to cut this tension.

"I intend to," Mr. Cannon says. "I'm trying to."

Then, through constant objections from Wiley, W.J. examines his witness: "Is it your testimony, Mr. Cannon, that Kerry never told you that he found his son in the master bedroom? Please answer."

"Now, that Kerry Myers found Ryan when he went to look for him? Is that what you're asking?"

"Sir, I'm asking you if Kerry ever told you that when he went looking for Ryan, that he found him in the master bedroom."

"Well, I will say this: If I did say that, I don't remember now."

With that, for a fraction of time, there is silence within the silence. Then W. J. LeBlanc breaks it: "As far as the stabbing—do you ever recall having a conversation about when Kerry got stabbed?"

"Right."

"Did he say that once he got in the kitchen and got the knife, that Fontanille caught him in the kitchen?"

"Right."

"And at that point, he took the knife from him and stabbed him in the stomach?"

"That's right."

"Mr. Myers told you that."

"Mr. Myers told me that."

"He went into the kitchen?" Dub politely hammers away.

"When Billy left he went to the kitchen to get the knife, yes." Mr. Cannon is answering in a plaintive, palms-up befuddlement as to what it is that he's doing wrong.

"And Billy and Kerry had this altercation in the kitchen?" goes Dub.

"Right," Charles Cannon says, his head swiveling along with the up-turned hands, shrugging for someone to tell him what's going on and why it is that it's so quiet and everyone's staring at him.

"And he took this knife from him and stabbed him in the stomach?"

"Right . . ." Mr. Charlie repeats into the vacuum.

Then, after a beat of that silence, W. J. LeBlanc blithely announces, "I have no further questions." Then he turns and, within that silence in which all are now looking at him, Dub smiles just ever so slightly—that trademark wisp of a grin which his detractors call a smirk—and walks back to his seat.

"I have a few, Your Honor," Wiley then says.

His few questions take a while. And if rehabilitating a witness includes trashing his age ("sixty-six"), his health ("High-blood-pressure medicine. Oh, quite a bit, yes. Heart; I had prostate"), his hearing problem ("Once in a while"), and his faculties ("Now, do you know how many Valium or can you estimate how many Valium you had taken in the twenty-four hours before?" "One. I just take one Valium in the morning every day"), Wiley Beevers does a bang-up job.

Soon Judge Richards is addressing the jury:

"I want to explain to you what's going to happen. We're not going to hear any more testimony today. It's about five-fifteen. We're going to go to the scene of the crime on Litchwood. No testimony is going to be offered at that house. What you'll be allowed to do is simply walk through the house, familiarize yourself with the location, see anything you want to see."

"We were set up by the judges' parking—the station wants both five-o'clock and six-o'clock live shots," Cheryl Hickman remembers.

"The parking lot's behind us, because that's where the van is that's going to come get the jury. It just so happens—they come to me and I'm doing my live shot and I get maybe a dozen words out and the jurors are in the van and the van starts to pull off. So I have the wonderful thing of saying, 'Well, Bill, in this van right back here, these are the jurors, they're leaving to go to the house *now*.' So that really added to some of the drama—'We're right here . . . on top of it.'

"Then we dashed over to the house and just did make it and get the truck set up and everything in time for the six-o'clock live."

The WWL truck is not alone; all of the stations are represented, as that block on Litchwood Lane becomes the media circus it had not been the night some six years before when it all began.

The five attorneys position themselves—tightly, very tightly—along the west wall of the foyer, the top of the T, and watch as the jurors and Judge Richards walk through the front door, take two or three steps, and then, almost to a person, look to their left over the wrought-iron rail and do, each in his or her own way, some form of a double take. Some do the double take and then actually shake their heads no.

Thus ends the sixth day of the trial.

"At this point, I'm saying he's gotta put Kerry on the stand," W.J. is remembering. "It's their only shot; it ain't much of a shot. But with the way the case is going—I mean, all of a sudden, where a week before all the other lawyers and the media are saying, 'No way, they'll never get a conviction,' now they're starting to say, 'Hey, they just might win this thing and put 'em both away'—so knowing that, I'm positive Beevers is going to put his man up in the box.

"He's got to after Monday. In terms of really poking holes in the story, sure, Ernie gives you a motive, but two disinterested witnesses really jam it up his ass. One is Walter Cardin—Pat Murphy to a degree, but she was so squirrelly—but Cardin, very, very damaging in my opinion; and Mr. Cannon, without even realizing, was very, very damaging—if you have any doubt as to whether or not Walter Cardin heard what he heard, the bastard said the same thing to his father-in-law. Plus he tells him he went and found Ryan in the bedroom! Chrissakes, the sumbitch is in the ambulance before he even asks about his kids and then won't tell DeWilde where they are!"

* * *

First thing Tuesday morning, W. J. LeBlanc tells the court:

"Your Honor, at this time the State would offer a stipulation that the chain of custody of the evidence is in, in addition to the testimony of the witnesses already presented, is complete from the time of the collection of the evidence until the presentation in the courtroom here today."

"Your Honor, we'd agree to that," Nick begins, "that the evidence was transported, but we're not agreeing that there was no contamination that took place in between."

"So stipulated, Your Honor," Wiley says.

"All right, sir."

"Your Honor, at this time the State would offer into evidence all previously identified State's exhibits," says Dub.

"All right. Those exhibits will be received in evidence."

"Thank you, Your Honor. At this time I'd ask that the jury be allowed sufficient time to examine all of the State's evidence," Dub says.

"Ladies and gentlemen, let me suggest that when you've finished looking at the documents that are being passed around in the jury box, it might be easier if you stepped down and came over to look at these other items. You can do that whenever you want to."

While technically no recess has been called, because the evidence is out and the triers of fact are examining it and therefore the court remains in session, just about everybody else leaves the courtroom to take a break.

"When the jury is up examining all the pictures," remembers Lisa Comeaux, who has traveled from North Carolina to attend the trial as a supporter of Bill Fontanille, "Kerry leaves and Bill starts to but Nick tells him, 'You get back up here right now. As long as they're in here'—he nods at the jury—'you're gonna sit here.'

"Bill turns around and walks right back, saying, 'I can understand that. It's not like I have better things to do.' "

The jurors apparently also feel they have nothing more important to do at the time, since they take a full two hours to examine the evidence, all 140-plus crime scene photographs, all of the clothes, the charts, reports, and scaled drawings.

"All right, has each member of the jury had an opportunity to see all of the evidence presented by the State?

"Does the State have anything further?"

"No, Your Honor. At this time the State rests," W. J. LeBlanc announces.

Shortly thereafter, out of the presence of the jury, Nick asks, "Your Honor, I asked Mr. Beevers—I've had three witnesses waiting here since early this morning—if we could perhaps take those three witnesses before he argues for his motion for acquittal, as he's entitled to argue in a judge trial."

"Specifically reserving my right to introduce my evidence and make my argument and my motion at that time," Wiley says, "I have no objection."

"All right, sir. Are we ready for the jury?"

Nick fully believes he's already gotten from Dr. Lee the most that any truly credible expert witness can give him with what there is to work with. And that even though his experts, especially Judith Bunker, could take the stand and perhaps offer some other possible explanation of the physical evidence, particularly the clothes, the moment they became hard pressed in cross-examination, they all would have had to agree on the most crucial question of all: that the blood spatter on Bill's clothes is more consistent with his being close to Janet while she was being struck with the baseball bat.

Consequently, Nick calls only three people to the stand in his defense of Bill Fontanille, none of whom is an expert witness. And of the three, what two of them have to say is old news even to the more casual observers of the phenomenon that has become the baseball bat murder.

Joseph Giardina, owner and operator of Zee Medical, can add nothing more to the already well-known stories of Janet's brief employment there almost exactly ten years before: the bruises, the black eye, and her candor in saying that they were from fighting with her husband. With Brian Baras the only twist is that finally a name, face, and personality is put to the publicly nebulous "friend" who stopped and picked Janet up after Kerry had pushed her out of the car on I-10.

The State chooses not to cross-examine either; and there really isn't much Wiley can wring out of events that old, except to point out that they are in fact ancient history.

Nick's third witness is another story entirely.

"I would call Peggy Senat," Nick Noriea announces.

Who? To the vast majority of those in the courtroom, whatever this bubbly little lady has to say will definitely be new news.

After establishing that she has lived across the street from 2232 Litchwood Lane for fourteen years, and that for two and a half of those years the occupants of 2232 had been Kerry and Janet Myers, Nick asks, "During that period of time, did you view any unusual events that occurred between Kerry and Janet at their house?"

"One specific time."

"Why don't you tell us what you recall."

"I was out in the yard—"

"Explain it to the jurors, 'cause they have to hear you, okay?" Nick tells her.

"Okay. I was out in the front yard and I heard verbal abuse back and forth, and Mr. Myers was getting ready to get in his car, and Janet hollered to him, 'If you leave and I call the police and tell them what I know, your ass'll be under the jail.' And he just turned around and walked right back in the house."

20
Verdicts

August 2nd—1982 . . .

So where has my little boy gone? You made 1 year on July 6th. It is hard to believe. We had your birthday on Saturday, July 3rd. The weather was good, so we had it outside. Over 40 people showed up to celebrate such an occasion.

You are walking very well now. You even dance to the music. Dad says that's due to me since I dance constantly and you watch. Your hair is growing more and more—your eyes are still blue and your vocabulary is "MOMMA" "DADDY," "DUCK" and a new one, Balloon." . . .

You are the joy of my life. Everyday I love you more and more. Nothing can compare to how I feel about you. Your dad adores you. You come first with him. And you adore him. You are his shadow.

We are very proud of you being you. We constantly concern ourselves with your care, both physical and emotional. Your happiness is our PRIORITY. And we love you dearly. My life would be empty without you.

Ryan is our "Blessed Little Angel."

More Later
Your Mom
—Journal of Janet Cannon Myers

*   *   *

Wiley Beevers has long told the Myerses that there just isn't enough evidence for any trier of fact to convict Kerry Myers of anything. He has in fact guaranteed it. He has always told them that when the State rests its case and he asks for a directed verdict of acquittal, all of this nightmare will vanish. The just by-product of their troubles will be to see the jury send Bill Fontanille to prison for the rest of his life.

For any of this to even have a chance of coming true, save for the last, Wiley Beevers is going to have to make one of the best speeches of his life on Tuesday afternoon, April 2, 1990—and there are those who should know who think he does.

"Your Honor, in connection with this case, at this time, I would like to make a motion for acquittal under the provisions of the Code of Criminal Procedure, 778.

"778 says, as the Court is familiar with, that upon the State resting, the court on its own motion, or on motion of counsel, shall enter a verdict of acquittal if the State has failed to prove any element of the crime. And in this case the court has previously indicated that it would give the charge that mere presence at the scene of a crime does not constitute one criminally culpable.

"We would submit to you that all that the State has proven in this case is that Kerry Myers came home on the 23rd day of February, 1984, and found Janet Myers in his house and that Bill Fontanille was already there.

"We call the court's attention to Mr. LeBlanc's opening statement in which he said that there was one of two theories that was going to be presented as to what happened. He didn't say exactly which one that he intended to prove. Certain things have been proven and testified to, which we don't think are really controverted, and that is that Janet Myers had A blood, Bill Fontanille had B blood, and Kerry Myers has O blood. Ryan Myers has A blood.

"Also the evidence has shown that the clothes that Bill Fontanille had when he went to Jo Ellen Smith were covered with blood. The baseball cap had A blood on it—all the way down to his shoes it was A blood, approximately one thousand medium-velocity impact blood spatters.

"When you listen to Dr. Lee testify, on all of Kerry Myers's clothing there was two traces of A blood. One was on the left thigh area in which he characterized, he, Dr. Lee, characterized that as a secondary transfer, which he said would be consistent with a baseball bat being brushed across Kerry's left thigh. And that it had the presence of water or a wiping action. And two drops of blood on the left shoe. He also testified that there were, on Kerry's shirt, some forty medium-velocity blood spatters which were not typed. And in reference to my question, he replied directly that he could not say that they were A type blood or any other type of blood.

"An interesting thing about Dr. Lee and all his charts, he never did have a chart or a slide presentation to show any of these medium-velocity impact splatters on Kerry Myers's shirt. He testified that he had the ability in his laboratory to blow up, enhance, any type of photograph to any degree that he thought he needed to. But he never did present the court with any picture of any medium-velocity impact spatters, even though he didn't even type them."

Wiley then begins a check-off of each witness the State presented, and his interpretation of how his or her testimony did or did not fit the evidence at hand. The majority of it is didactic, not eloquent, and his deductive logic at times is skewed.

However, at a point where he is summarizing and interpreting Bob Masson's testimony and involvement, Wiley gets off one effective shot: "A total lack of evidence at the scene has deprived Kerry Myers of the ability to present evidence that would refute the direct statements."

Given the limited options his client's story has hog-tied him with, Wiley can't really be faulted for *having* to offer a transparently skewed argument: "Then we get down to the heart of the thing, you listen to the operator tape, the 911 tape that was introduced into evidence. That tape is consistent with the scenario that Kerry Myers gave Marty Childs when he went to the hospital. It doesn't differ one iota between the two. The 911 statement, Marty Childs's statement, the statement given to Masson, are all consistent."

And: "I don't think it's that inconsistent or illogical to get somebody out of your house and call the police before checking on your family. From the time they are small children, people are inculcated in American society to call the police if anything bad happens to you. Maybe it's not what we would do today, six years later sitting in this courtroom, but maybe that was the best thing that Kerry Myers had, or knew at the time. Just because we disagree with it, does that mean he's a principal to murder?

"It was very interesting to observe the people going through the crime scene yesterday . . . when they got to the end of that corner where the wall is, they'd stop at point C and they'd look down this wall, and then look that way, and then look that way. Now all of that is real good, but those people didn't have a man after them with a baseball bat, sort of getting their attention."

For the tenuous terrain he must defend to the last, he perhaps was strongest where he had to be, at the close: "Has the State proven anything beyond a reasonable doubt that Kerry Myers had anything to do with Janet's death? The answer is no. When he gets off the telephone, he goes to Janet's body. We heard that on the 911 tape. We don't know what he did. He's an irrational man in there seeing about his wife who has just been beat to death. Can two drops of blood get on his shoes from that? What has Kerry done? What is the act that a rational trier of fact can impute criminal intent to kill his wife on? *What has he done?*

"The fact that there are inconsistencies in this evidence may be totally due to the lack of competence of the Jefferson Parish Sheriff's Office in collecting evidence.

"Each time this evidence or these photographs are useless, that does two things. It deprives the State of a piece of evidence with which to put Billy Fontanille in the penitentiary for killing Janet Myers, but it also deprives Kerry Myers of a piece of evidence to exculpate himself.

"Judge, I just do not see anything here except inconsistencies and suppositions that the State can rely on to any degree. I think no rational trier of fact can come to the conclusion, looking at this evidence, and listening to these tapes, that Kerry Myers did anything in this case, except go home.

"I further submit to you that if this matter had been properly investigated, there would have been more than ample evidence to be consistent.

"The State has not ruled out all reasonable hypothesis of innocence, Your Honor, and I ask you to grant a motion for acquittal for Kerry Myers."

It is often said that sometimes seconds can seem like hours; while the moment Wiley put a period on another misapplied vowel is of that nature, it is more appropriately milliseconds to minutes, since there really isn't much more than a beat before Judge Richards evenly enunciates:

"Counsel, the court, considering all of the evidence that's been presented against Kerry Myers to this point, does not agree that the evidence is insufficient to sustain a verdict of guilty. And for that reason, the motion for acquittal is denied."

Whooosh! goes all of that collective breath which during those heartbeats between Wiley's last words and the judge's had been sucked up along with all sound into a vortex of imploding silence. As it comes rushing out, though, the sound which quickly comes to dominate all others is the wailing "Oh! My God! Oh, my God! No! Kerry! Oh, my God!" of a hysterical Debbie Myers. She sounds, strangely enough, not at all unlike Kerry had with almost exactly the same words on the 911 tape.

The shock of it is clearly visible on the faces and in the voices of the Myerses and Cannons, indicating just how high Wiley had taken them in their expectations.

With something akin to pandemonium going on behind him, his client jerking his head around, his eyes darting in panic, Wiley Beevers never takes his eyes away from a dead-on stare at the judge. Finally, he says, "To which ruling I respectfully object, Your Honor."

"All right, sir," and then Judge Richards says with empathy, "Mr. Beevers, do you want to commence your case today, or would you rather wait until in the morning?"

"Your Honor, I would appreciate commencing it in the morning," Wiley says.

Thus ends the seventh day of the trial.

It's somewhat ironic that the defense of Kerry Myers begins with Dr. Morris "99.9 percent" Kerstein, the State's H-bomb in Billy's first degree murder trial, whose "medical certainties" have been contradicted by several other trauma specialists with even better credentials—which is why W.J. decided not to go the hematocrit route again. His opinion didn't stick in '86 when he had the power of the State behind him, and it fares even less well here. His message fell not on deaf ears, but on disinterested ones.

The second witness for Kerry Myers is Dr. Agatha Zeilinger, a senior clinical social worker in the child and adolescent unit at the West Bank Center for Psychotherapy.

"When did you first see Ryan?" Wiley asks after going through with the requisite establishing questions.

"The first time I saw him was on September 22, 1987."

"Who brought Ryan to see you in 1987?"

"Ryan was brought to the clinic by his father."

"And what was the purpose that was stated to you for him being brought there?"

"The father felt that the child was suffering from some anxiety and some depression, that he was fearful, that he had sleep problems, that he was clinging to the father, that his attention and concentration in school were not good despite the fact that he was a very bright child, and the father was very concerned about the symptoms. He wanted some treatment for his child."

"Did you have occasion to do a clinical evaluation of Ryan Myers at that time?"

"Yes, sir, I did."

"And did you make a diagnosis of any problems?"

"The diagnosis was an overanxious disorder with sign of posttraumatic stress syndrome as indicated by his sleep problems, by his nightmares, and by his fears that something terrible would happen to him."

Wiley elicits that Dr. Zeilinger then undertook the treatment of Ryan, which lasted from September 1987 until November 1988 and included a total of twenty-five sessions. And that during those months of treatment, Dr. Zeilinger observed that "Ryan and his father interacted very affectionately with one another. The child would sit on his father's lap, put his arms around him, hold his hand. The father would read to him in the waiting room while they were waiting for me."

It isn't long into his direct examination before Wiley's true agenda with this witness becomes apparent.

"In the course of therapy, would Ryan on occasion say things to you which you thought were important?"

"At this time we'd interpose an objection to testifying what the child might or might not have said," Howie says.

After arguments, Judge Richards rules, "The objection as to the statement by Ryan is overruled insofar as it is part of Dr. Zeilinger's diagnosis and treatment. Of course, anything about the facts of the case would be inadmissible."

"In the course of your treatment of Ryan, were you able to come to a conclusion as to whether someone close to him or someone who was not close to him had traumatized him?"

"Yes, sir."

"What is your opinion as to—let's get down to it: did you form an opinion as to whether or not his father, Kerry Myers, had traumatized him?"

"Yes, sir, I had some deduction that Mr. Kerry Myers had not traumatized his son, based on what the child had said."

"Did the child have some fears of being reinjured?"

"The child had nightmares about injuries coming to him, but they were vague, pervasive type of anxiety; he was a tense child; he is a delicate child, was very fearful; he seemed to me to be a very depressed child."

And then: "Dr. Zeilinger, what was related to you that formed the basis of your opinion that Ryan distinguished between his father and the person who hurt him?"

"He said it was a man with a baseball bat. He said that the man was tall and strong and has flat hair, and that he was much stronger than his mother, and he made the distinction. He said, 'A bad guy hit me, bad guy hit me,' tall and stronger than his mother and had flat hair."

"Now, did Ryan also relate some other things to you that formed the basis of your opinion that Kerry was not the one that traumatized him?"

"He did refer to other things. At one point he did say that the man was dressed like 'my father,' but he made the distinction it was not his father. He talked about they sat down in the dining room, the mother and the man, and started talking. The man had a bat, a baseball bat, saying that he was going to play baseball, but he lied, 'he told me to keep a secret,' and I have a question mark there. He did not know what the secret was. He told me that he would hit me because I did not keep the secret."

"Now, Dr. Zeilinger, have you formed an opinion as to whether or not Ryan Myers was traumatized by his father or someone else based on these twenty-five sessions of therapy?"

"My opinion was based on what the child had said, based on what I had seen, the interaction, trusting interaction of the child with the father through a long period of time—there was no possibility that the father himself would hit Ryan."

"No further questions, Your Honor," Wiley announces.

"I have a few, Your Honor," Howie says.

Immediately Howie begins a cross intended to demonstrate to the court that Dr. Zeilinger is far from being an objective observer, since she obviously has a professional and social attachment to the new Kerry Myers family.

"Had you ever talked to Mr. Beevers before today?"

"Yes, sir."

With some prodding, Howie establishes that the first time she met with Mr. Beevers was the Monday prior, March 26, the first day of jury selection, and that Kerry was with him.

Then, some time later, Howie asks, "Ma'am, the first time you saw Ryan Myers was when his father brought him in September of 1987, is that correct?"

"Yes."

"Are you aware of the fact that his father was indicted for murdering Ryan's mother approximately a month following that?"

"No, sir, I was not aware of that. It was not a case that had ever come to my attention before."

"Let me ask you this: What is the Stockholm syndrome?"

"What is it?"

"Stockholm syndrome. Is there such a thing like that? Have you ever heard of that?"

"No, I haven't heard of it. It's not one of the symptoms that is characterized or that is described in the manual we use."

With but a look and a roll of the eyes, Howie makes sure the judge notes his genuine surprise that this little old lady who received all of her degrees in Europe, who speaks with a very heavy Germanic accent, and who has been in the field of psychological social work for forty-two years has never heard of the Stockholm syndrome, the widely disseminated theory, based on studies done on POWs and concentration-camp survivors of the Second World War, that torture victims actually come to identify with their tormentors.

Howie then directs Dr. Zeilinger to examine a letter from her files which was written by two of her associates, a board-certified psychiatrist and a clinical psychologist, upon the occasion of Ryan's first visit to the Center for Psychotherapy in 1984 "for evaluation of psychological findings following the head injury." After which, while treatment was strongly recommended, Ryan did not come back to the clinic for three years, or until just before his father had every reason to believe he was about to be indicted for the murder of his wife.

"They talk about the reason for his lack of knowledge in the area of his mother's murder is probably due to two facts. That is what they found?" Howat asks.

"Yes, sir."

"What are those two facts that your colleagues found regarding his mother's murder?"

"One was the use of psychological defenses known as denial, which frequently follows a traumatic event."

"That's a concept that you accept? Denial?

"A defense, very definitely."

"It exists, you agree that it exists?"

"Such defenses do exist and are part of all our responses in human behavior."

"That people do deny things they don't want to believe?"

"That is clinically accepted."

"And it's a situation where you deny something because you just don't want to remember or believe that it happened to you?"

"Yes."

"What is the next of the two factors? One is denial. What is the other one?"

"The next of the two is physiological—"

"Would you tell what physiological 'sequelae' means?"

"Sequelae means continuation; physiological refers to the body. So that 'the continuation of the physiological consequences' would be an appropriate explanation."

"Would you continue reading."

" '. . . of his head trauma which may result in a certain form of amnesia.' "

"What is amnesia?"

"Amnesia means forgetting things."

"I have no further questions," Howie announces.

Next up for Kerry is his so loyal but shaken father-in-law, Charles Cannon.

"Mr. Charlie," Wiley begins, "I believe that you testified earlier that Janet Myers was your daughter."

"Right."

"And I call your attention to the time frame of approximately 1980, and ask you if you remember her having an occasion to be employed at Zee Medical?"

"I do."

"At the time, how many automobiles were in the Kerry Myers family?"

"One."

"Back at that time, did you have the occasion or some occasion to drive Janet to work at Zee Medical?"

"I did."

"Can you approximate how many times a week you would drive Janet to work?"

"Two to three times a week."

"Sometimes could it have been as many as three or four times a week?"

"Possibly, yes."

"Did you ever see your daughter, when you were driving her to Zee Medical, have a black eye?"

"No."

"Do you know what type of clothes she would wear on the occasions when you would drive her to Zee Medical?"

"Sometimes she wore a sundress with the little straps."

"Did you ever see any bruises or anything on the arms of Janet Myers?"

"No."

"When you would drive her to Zee Medical, did you ever see her wear any sunglasses that would cover her eyes?"

"No."

"If you had seen your daughter with a black eye or bruises on her arms, would you have inquired as to the source of them?

"I'm sure I would."

"Did you ever make any such inquiry?"

"No, I didn't see anything, so I never did ask her."

"No further questions," Wiley says.

"Does the State have any questions?"

"No, Your Honor," answers Dub.

Wiley next puts Marguerite O'Toole, Kerry's natural mother, on the stand to mouth wonderful things about Janet and Kerry's marriage, and then abruptly announces: "At this time the defendant Kerry Myers, rests."

"Rebuttal?" Judge Richards asks the prosecution.

"No, Your Honor, no rebuttal," answers W. J. LeBlanc.

"We will recess till one o'clock."

"Ladies and gentlemen," Judge Richards addresses the courtroom at large. "Before we bring the jury back in, I want to explain to you that the attorneys are going to begin closing argument and it's important that they be able to present their cases to the jury without distraction. There are probably too many people in the courtroom, so it's going to be important that the back door stays closed and there's no disturbance in the courtroom. If it becomes a problem, I'll clear the courtroom. Keep the noise level down.

"Are we ready for the jury, counsel?"

Within minutes, Howat Peters is in front of the jury to deliver the first of the State's two opportunities to tie up its case in a tidy package which the jurors can mentally take with them as they go to deliberate; the defense only gets one.

For all the heralded—and damned—protection afforded the accused under the United States Constitution, there is at least one time when the prosecution decidedly is granted the upper hand: closing arguments in a criminal case. The State leads off with a mandated closing argument, summing up all the evidence it believes it has proved, which is delivered as an address to the jury by a member of the prosecution team. Then the defense is given the opportunity, if it so desires, to deliver its closing argument, a last chance to refute the State's evidence against the defendant. However, the State is then allowed another address to be delivered to the trier of fact, known as rebuttal, in which the prosecution can amplify or diminish any points it feels needs attention before the jury begins deliberation. In other words, the State always gets last licks.

"Good afternoon, ladies and gentlemen," begins Howat Peters. "This case has gone on a good bit of time. And I don't plan to take as long as I probably will take. I ask you to bear with me. Mr. LeBlanc and I thank you for your attention. We can see you listening, and that's important, it's the only place that this can be done is in the courtroom. I want to thank you for that.

"There are a few other things I'd like to tell you about before I really get into the argument, and one of those things is basically that I'm going to tell you just my appreciation of what went on in the courtroom. The same thing is going to go on for Mr. Noriea and the same thing for Mr. LeBlanc down the line. It's what we appreciate the evidence has been and what we appreciate the evidence to show. It really doesn't matter what I think; it doesn't matter what Mr. LeBlanc thinks. What the witnesses said is what matters, what you think the witnesses said. There's only one place in the courtroom that you can get evidence; that's from the witnesses. That's the evidence in the case. That's the evidence in every case. That's how it comes in.

"You can't decide the case on emotion, whether you like some lawyer or dislike some lawyer, or you like or dislike the defendant. None of that matters. We're to the point now where you've got to make your decision based upon the law the judge gives you and the evidence, and that's the only thing that counts. If you don't do that, then you've not lived up to your oath.

"The other thing is that during the course of the trial—okay, y'all have been very serious, and that's good. And I notice, I can't help it, but I notice or feel that you think there are times when we're not. I know this goes for Mr. Noriea as well and Mr. LeBlanc, there are times in the courtroom where you see us smile, see us kid, we'll laugh, and you don't take it that way. It looks like it; but I ask you not to, okay? It looks like a big game, we don't care—that's not the case, okay? But, for lack of a better way to explain it, it's being human. If you want to say we are human, some people have doubts about that on occasion, when we get down to it—if you think about the violence and you think about the senselessness of this whole thing, and that's all you think, we couldn't do our job. That goes on for both sides, so that's why we laugh, that's the only way we can get through some of this, because for y'all this is a one-time thing; for us it's not. And I just don't want you to think it's a big game, that it doesn't mean anything to us."

Howie then begins a thorough summary of each witness and the evidence presented with that witness, highlighting little memory joggers for the jury, the key points which the State believes directly or circumstantially go to prove that William Fontanille was a principal in the murder of Janet Myers. Then:

"You know what I'm asking you for. I'm asking you to find him guilty of second degree murder. That's just the way it is. That's why I'm here. I'm here to ask you to do that. I'm going to ask you to do one thing besides that, and it's more important. That's what all of this is about. When the judge gives you the instructions and you go to deliberate, do justice, okay? 'Cause if you do justice, you're going to find Bill Fontanille guilty of second degree murder. Thank you for listening."

After a brief recess, it's Nick's turn:

"Ladies and gentlemen, I would just like to thank you for your time and attention. I guess, ten days, you feel like y'all have been in jail, because I don't think you can do a lot of the things you want to do—and that serves to indicate the importance of why we're here.

"This has gone on for a long, long time. It's over six years now, February 24th, 1984—and in the early-morning hours of that day you saw the end of one tragedy and the beginning of another. The Sheriff's Office went to the house with a suspect in mind. They got to a home and found poor dead Janet and they were confronted by an 'hysterical' husband, and they had a suspect. The suspect was at Jo Ellen Smith.

"From that time forward to through this trial, the State hasn't proved Bill Fontanille had something to do with that tragedy. A lot of people are of the type of personality that if they get something in their head, they are going to continue with the belief—just continue with that belief and do things to try to corroborate that belief, look for things that support that conclusion—and not have an open mind about what really did happen that day.

"When Detective Masson went to his house to pick him up and said, 'Come with me, you're going to make a statement,'' Bill was cooperative. He had been stabbed five times. You all saw the stab wounds. And he made a statement, and you heard the tape recording of the statement. And in the stress of the moment, the uncertainty, not knowing what his future would be because he was a victim of circumstances, he did the best he could.

"The prosecution wants you to think that failing to state with specificity on the preciseness of what happened in the past three days, Tuesday, Wednesday, and Thursday, means that he should get a life sentence for murder.

"Now that doesn't quite add up. Four years ago, the same prosecution, different prosecutors, asked twelve people like yourself to—"

"Excuse me." Dub is on his feet. "May we approach the bench?

"Normally I do not like to interrupt closing arguments," W.J. says. "But I really think that is well beyond the scope."

"Don't tell them what the other jury did," Judge Richards says somewhat firmly to Nick.

"I did not tell them what the other jury did," Nick says.

"*Do not* tell them what the other jury did," the judge repeats, with emphasis.

"I don't want him to mention the other trial," W.J says.

"He already did," Judge Richards points out.

"I understand that. As long as—"

"Don't tell them what the other jury did." The judge ends the discussion with that second repeat of the admonishment.

"At that time, Kerry Myers was a star witness," Nick says when he turns back to address the jury, which is all he'd wanted to point out to begin with. He then launches into his very, very thorough trashing of everything done and not done by the Sheriff's Office which if it had been done differently could be the very thing that would conclusively prove that Bill's version of the events of that night is, aside from minor metaphysical inconsistencies, most nearly the truth.

Except for his not having Herb MacDonell to kick around—and his having too much respect for Dr. Lee to do anything but use the doctor's own words to appear to support his interpretation—Nick's 1990 closing is all but interchangeable with his closing of 1986. But not quite. There is, after all, something new to wield in slashing away at reasonable doubt: "the neighbor."

"Myers says, 'Looks like somebody's trying to call me,' " Nick begins, working this brand-new development. "Who's calling at two in the morning unless Pat Murphy, the emergency ambulance technician, heard *right*. 'I came home this afternoon and found my wife in bed with a neighbor.' Five minutes after the start of the call, which was maybe seven to ten minutes after Kerry was screaming outside, 'Get out of here, you son of a bitch, get out of here!'

"I just wonder if the neighbor heard what was going on and was concerned about Janet. He would be in a position to hear the screams, especially if an altercation between he and Kerry took place before Janet was beaten, when he hears 'Get out of here, you son of a bitch!' and he lives four or five houses or wherever in the neighborhood—I'm wondering if he called just to see if Janet was okay. If Kerry answers the phone, he just hangs up. If Janet answers the phone, he asks, 'Janet, are you okay? I know what happened earlier this afternoon and I was afraid something bad might happen.'

"The State has the burden of proof. I'm just sharing some of my thoughts with you about what I have heard about this case. It makes sense if Kerry walked in and Janet was in the bedroom with a neighbor, for whatever reason, and you hear of Kerry's violent tendencies. They get in an argument; they get mad at each other, and the neighbor said, 'Look, I'm going—I'll see y'all later.' The neighbor leaves, then they get in an argument about 'what is he doing back here, are you crazy, look how you're dressed and you're going to bring this guy back here in the bedroom. What are you looking for?' A fight starts, continues for a while, instead of popping her—Bill's statement said Ryan liked to play with the baseball bat—here comes Ryan walking in with *the baseball bat . . . ?*"

Nick then reminds the jury that the day before, Kerry "walks in from work, the air ran out of the new tires on his car, so he stops and sees Janet on the love seat with Bill . . . and then Bill's coming over to pick up his bat . . . ?"

There are those within that courtroom who hear all of this and see Nick's apparently whole-hearted eleventh-hour grasping at this sudden third-party involvement in a case this old as a move of desperation, a show of weakness.

There are also those who know that what Nick says is in fact a broader, veiled sketch of what he really *does* believe happened that Wednesday and Thursday. Just substitute "Bill" every place he says "neighbor," and move that "Janet, are you okay?" phone call up to about midafternoon and have it placed from a pay phone at a convenience store. Leave everything else in, most especially Janet and Kerry arguing over his suspicions of her and Bill and the neighbor/Bill beating a hasty retreat and Ryan just happening to walk up dragging the "bastard's bat. He just wants to come back and get his bat? I'll show you what he can do with his bat!" Wham! Wham! Wham!

Nick's closing is perhaps stronger than in 1986: "What has the State proven to you beyond a reasonable doubt? They proved to you that Janet was murdered and they proved to you that sometime that evening Bill got to the house. That doesn't make him a murderer. That doesn't make him a principal.

"Ladies and gentlemen, this is the last time that I'll speak with you. I'll never say another word, at least not in this courtroom, and I'd ask that you take the evidence that you have, what was proven to you beyond a reasonable doubt, then you take the law from the judge, and square those two, presumption of innocence, proof beyond a reasonable doubt, exclude every reasonable hypothesis of innocence. When you square those, you square it with your conscience so that ten years from now you won't have a conscience that's still worried about did I do the right thing then. When you square it with your conscience, then you come out with your verdict, and you can look him in the eye and say, 'This is justice.' "

After a brief recess, it is W. J. LeBlanc who stands before the jury. "Good afternoon. It's been a long trial. This is it. This is the end. I'm not going to be up here any longer than I have to be. There are just a few things that I need to talk to you about.

"First, do not confuse the issues here. You're not deciding guilt or innocence of Kerry Myers, just William Fontanille, and, while I agree probably for the first time in my career with Mr. Noriea in that Kerry Myers is guilty of second degree murder, you're not to concern yourself with that. That in no way exculpates his client. Why? Because of something called principals. Yes, that's Kerry's handkerchief that he's trying to wash out with Janet's blood in it, and yes, he's trying to wash all that blood off his shirt, but does that in any way affect the guilt or innocence of William Fontanille?

"Mr. Noriea tried to make it look like we have been on a witch-hunt against Bill Fontanille since the day of the murder, and that the State's theory of the case has changed radically. From day one, from the day that William Fontanille changed his story to try and fit the evidence that he thought was against him, he's been a suspect. The only thing that's changed is that when we got additional evidence we indicted his buddy, because they're both involved. That's the only thing that's changed in this case. We have never once at any point thought that William Fontanille was not involved in this murder, never once.

"We're trying to seek the truth. We're trying to achieve justice. Yes, Kerry Myers testified for the State the first time, but when we found out that there was evidence that he was involved in this murder, we indicted him, and that's what today is all about, justice for the murderers of Janet Myers.

"Now, you know a very common defense tactic is to trash the crime scene investigation. Mr. Peters told you if they took twenty samples, they would want forty. If there's a thousand blood samples, and they tested and took nine hundred and ninety-nine, they'd be up here swearing that the untested one was going to prove that their client was innocent.

"Let us just go through the area of blood that Mr. Noriea brought up and let's take a look at the scene. What would have happened if the State would have been able to have—let's look at S-4, the inconclusive area, all of it in the back of the den in the recliner area. Think about it. If that's B blood, what is Mr. Noriea going to say? They're going to claim, 'Well, of course, you've got Bill's blood. Bill's blood is there; Bill's blood is here. He was stabbed in the back; that's his blood. That's consistent with his story.'

"If it's Kerry's blood, 'Well, of course, they had this big fight; Bill was defending himself; he was hitting him over the head; they had a big tussle. You're going to have it all over the den. That's consistent with Bill's story.'

"If it's Janet's blood, they would have said, 'Well, that was obviously there before Bill got there. That's where the fight started when Kerry killed his wife, chased her into the den, and it's consistent with Bill's story.'

"The same thing with the fingerprints on the bat, the palm print on the knife. What testimony do we have? Both of the statements are that everybody's got the bat, everybody's got the knife. If it came out as Bill's fingerprints, 'Well, of course, Bill had the bat, he had to defend himself.'

"If it's Kerry's fingerprints, 'Oh, well, you know, he grabbed the bat to try and keep Bill from killing him.' The same thing with the knife. They both claim they had control, and if Janet's fingerprints happened to be on it, the other one was killing her before they got there. You see, the State can't win. The crime scene can't win. It makes no difference. I'll tell you why it makes no difference, because you have their statements, you know what happened because of their statements, and we'll talk about the statements in a couple of minutes.

"One of the other things that we want to talk about is Dr. Lee. You know, Mr. Noriea agrees with Dr. Lee when it's convenient for him to agree with Dr. Lee and he doesn't mention anything else. He'll say he talked to Dr. Lee and Dr. Lee said this was consistent with Bill being stabbed in the back and vertical droppings. But if you remember when he laid out Bill's entire theory, his entire hypothesis of innocence, he asked if his version here is consistent with the evidence. Dr. Lee said, 'No,' he didn't say possibly, he didn't say highly unlikely; he said, 'No.'

"Now, if you recall, this is where you have the blood actually dripping down [on the left, just inside the front door, on the Sheetrock and the garage-door molding]. Dr. Lee said that this is where there's a blood source, and it's there long enough for it to be actually dripping down. Well, how does it get there? Let's look at Bill's statement.

"He tells what happened when he comes in and what happened in the den and then at the end of the hall. And as he comes out, he's never pinned up against there. Why would he deny that? Is it because Janet's body is right there and there was this big altercation in this area here? Y'all went to the scene. I don't have to tell you how close everything is. Do you mean to say, you're not able to see her? That is simply not reasonable.

"Let's talk about a couple of other things Mr. Noriea didn't bring up. . . ."

Dub then begins what the State believes is a systematic debunking of Nick's pet theories and major efforts toward establishing reasonable doubt. Because of Howie's earlier, more detailed traversal, W.J. is able to hit hard at selective targets, doing the maximum amount of damage to the other side's maximum resources.

He decides, on his feet and in midcourse, that he will "stoop" to offer rebut to the new "neighbor scenario." To buy any part of that, he tells the jury, "you've got to make the conclusion that Janet Myers, after having a cesarean section six weeks before, is now sleeping with three men within twenty-four hours. Kerry Myers says he has relations with her Wednesday night when he gets home from playing ball; Bill Fontanille said he went over there on Wednesday afternoon and then, not seeing them since November of '83, they have an affair. That was Wednesday afternoon. Then she sleeps with Kerry Wednesday night, *and* she had a mystery neighbor come over Thursday morning. Now, is that a reasonable hypothesis of innocence, *trashing a dead woman's reputation*? I don't think so."

Point by point he goes; and, in due course he gets down to *Scenario*

Game. The game he has played for so many years as primarily an intellectual and investigatory exercise he must now play for real before the jury, choosing one and only one scenario to play for keeps. If it's the right one, Bill goes to jail; the wrong one, and W.J. will never forgive himself for losing the really big one, for choking when it's gut-check time.

"There's been a lot of talk these past few days about scenarios. Well, let me give you a scenario for your consideration, and before I do that, let me preface that by telling you this is not what the State has to prove. What we have to prove is whether William Fontanille killed Janet Myers or whether he was a principal when Kerry Myers killed Janet Myers. We don't have to prove how. We don't have to prove why, although we would all like to know that. That's just not what the law requires us to do.

"Let's take a look at the statements that were made by William Fontanille at the hospital. . . . '[Kerry's] going to tell you we had a plan to kill our wives, but he didn't think I'd go through with it.' Well, if you're going to make up something, why not make up, 'Well, he caught me with his wife,' or 'You know, he suspected us of having an affair.' You're not going to come up with something like 'We had a plan to kill our wives but he didn't think I'd go through with it.' Why would he say that?

"Let's take a look at what evidence there might be to support a plan. Let me tell you, they're not charged with having a plan to kill their wives. They're not. That's not what we have to prove. I'm just attempting to lay out a *scenario* for your consideration that just might fit the evidence and just might be what happened in this case.

"Let's go back to the master bedroom. Mr. Noriea told you it was all messed up, and I agree, it's all in disarray, you've got everything all messed up. Well, if you plan to kill somebody, you're not going to try and kill them with a baseball bat. That's too sloppy. What if it's just supposed to be a strangulation? What if it was supposed to be like a burglary, and it started in the bedroom, but Janet, being the fighter—you remember, she was a fighter—she got away, and what if she got in the kitchen and she grabbed that knife and what if *she* stabbed Bill Fontanille, and not Kerry Myers, she stabbed him in the chest? Oh, yeah, that's just speculation.

"Look at where he's got those chest wounds, on his left side. If you're a right-handed person coming with a knife, you're going to be stabbing somebody on this [the left] side. If you're a left-handed person like Kerry Myers and you stab somebody in the chest, you're going to stab them on this [the right] side.

"So now this plan has gotten out of hand. Bill looks around and he grabs this bat, and he starts whaling away, just going after her, getting blood all over everything, all over that house, all over his clothes, some of it on Kerry. What goes wrong? Ryan. Ryan comes in. Ryan gets nailed with the bat, skull fracture, incredible force. The baby gets scooped and dumped in the bedroom, and now the real fight starts. Then they're going to start wrestling. They're going to have everything coming at them. But then you fight yourself out. How long can you fight? Professional fighters are exhausted after three-minute rounds. We still have ten hours to account for. What are they doing for ten hours?" W.J. begins to lay crime scene photos on the rail as he goes: "They're not watching TV. They're trying to figure a way out of this mess now. They are drinking water; they're toweling off; they're trying to figure a way to get out where neither one of them has to go to jail. Because, let's face it, they've got stab wounds; they've got head wounds; they've got a child for all intents and purposes they think is dead. Janet's got to be dead. What are they going to say?

"Well, if we can't blame it on me, if we can't blame it on you, we've got to blame it on somebody else. Now, what evidence supports that? Let's pull out the drawers, let's mess up the room; let's make it look like there was somebody that Janet walked in on, this burglary. When I call the police, what I'll do is I'll tell them somebody broke into my house and tried to kill me and give them a bogus story.

"But there's a problem with that—at some point in time they have another confrontation. It might have happened when they went to check on Ryan and Ryan is out, he's comatose, but he's *alive*. That's the second trigger; that's when you're having additional confrontations. That's when William Fontanille runs out of that house and Kerry Myers's hollering after him.

"What does Kerry do? Kerry goes to the phone. Does he say, 'Help, please send me an ambulance here, my wife and child are critically injured, this madman Bill Fontanille, he came in here early this afternoon and held me at bay, he beat my poor wife to death, my child, me, I'm bleeding'? No. 'Please, somebody broke in my house and tried to kill me.'

"You heard it, it goes on and on, never mentioning the name. Well, as they seek to elicit more information he realizes that it's just not going to work, so he dumps on him. He's now going to blame it on Fontanille and try to absolve himself. That part I agree with Mr. Noriea.

"What happens three-quarters of the way through the phone call? Is it the neighbor—no, it's Bill Fontanille. Fontanille calls. How do you know that's Bill Fontanille? Why didn't he go straight to the hospital? Here's a guy right close to West Jefferson Hospital. No, he decides to drive to his house. He gets on that phone and he calls Kerry Myers 'cause he wants to know what are you going to tell the police, but he can't get through. So what does he do? He goes to the hospital and he proceeds to tell every single person that he sees what happened. The best defense is a good offense. He tells you, 'He's going to tell you we had a plan to kill our wives, but he didn't think I'd go through with it.' That way he can say, 'Didn't I tell you that's what he was going to say? Didn't I tell you he would try to put the blame on me?'

"What did he tell Dr. Neri? He told Dr. Neri the guy that stabbed me killed his wife and child. How did he know that? Then he tells LaMarche, 'My friend killed his wife and is going to blame it on me'—John Taylor—'You're going to find two dead bodies in that house'—the whole nine yards. 'He's going to tell you we had a plan,' he told the same thing to Noel Adams. Did you notice how Mr. Noriea never questioned anybody about those statements, never mentioned those statements in his closing argument?" W.J. then reminds them not only of the infamous conspiracy statement, but of the fact that Bill had said that "his friend had killed his wife and son," and "There're two dead people over there," yet within hours disavows ever having said any of it.

"What do those statements that he made Friday undisputedly tell you?" Dub continues. "Two conclusions. One, here's the bat man; he's the killer, and folks, when you look at our little spatter ink blots and the clothes, you'll know that he's the man that swung the bat. But at the very least, it tells you that he directly aided Kerry Myers, because at this point he's denying any knowledge of that. And the only reason why he would be is because he was involved.

"Folks, the simple truth is that William Fontanille and Kerry Myers are killers, and any way you swing the bat, be it left-handed or right-handed, this was simply a case of murder between friends.

"When you go into the back to deliberate—the judge is going to read you the law, and I'd ask you to go back there and return the only verdict that is going to be consistent with both the law and the evidence, and that's going to allow you to follow your oath. The only verdict in this case is guilty of second degree murder." W.J. pauses long enough to look each juror in the eye; then, "Thank you so much for your attention."

Dead silence.

It is ten minutes after five when, at a bench conference, it is determined that under no circumstances will a verdict of the jury be received by the judge before Wiley delivers his closing argument. Consequently, there is no reason that the jury cannot begin deliberations now.

When the attorneys are back at the counsel table, Judge Richards addresses the jury: "Ladies and gentlemen, it is my duty to instruct you on the law that applies to your deliberations. I remind you that although both Kerry Myers and William Fontanille are on trial, you are to decide the guilt or innocence of William Fontanille . . ."

Judge Richards will speak on for almost ten minutes, most of it reading, as he presents the jurors their charges—which are specific, exhaustive, boring, and very important.

Deliberations begin at 5:25 P.M.

Deliberations that evening do not last long, however.

Just shortly after the panel has been led out, W.J. informs the court that the State is submitting Howat Peters's closing argument in the Fontanille case as the closing argument before the bench in the Myers case. And that after Mr. Beevers delivers his closing, Howie will then reply for the prosecution.

"Your Honor gave the indication that it will be in the morning," Wiley says. "I was prepared to go forward then."

After some discussion, Judge Richards rules that he is going to dismiss the jury early for the night and recess the court until nine the following morning, at which time the jury will begin deliberations again and Wiley Beevers will present his closing argument.

The jury is then brought back into the courtroom and given an explanation of what is going to happen by Judge Richards, who then recesses all proceedings at 6:24 P.M.

Thus ends the eighth day of the trial.

The first order of business in the morning is the jury's request for copies of the men's statements. Judge Richards informs them that under Louisiana law, they are allowed any "object, photograph, any evidence of that sort," but *not* "any written document, any statement, or any transcription."

Betty Henry, who to everyone's surprise has been selected as jury foreperson, now speaks up.

"I'd like to talk to you. I have a couple of questions."

"All right, approach the bench."

"We can't come to a full agreement on what is manslaughter. We're not sure," Mrs. Henry says.

"I'm going to have to call the lawyers up here and you can ask that question of them, and then I'll try to answer it for you," Judge Richards explains.

"Okay."

"Would counsel approach the bench?"

When all are gathered, the judge says, "Mrs. Henry has indicated that the jury may have some confusion about the charge on manslaughter. And what I will do, without objection—if the jury requests it, I will reread the charge on manslaughter." Judge Richards looks to Mrs. Henry. "If that would solve your problem."

"We don't know what we're doing," she answers. "I just want it clarified."

"Well, judge," Dub says, "I'd ask that you read all of the responsive verdicts, just so that they'll know just what their choices are. That's the State's request."

Everyone agrees. But then Nick has a question about the exact wording of one sentence in the jury charges, which sets off a lengthy debate, the result being that all agreements are off and if any part of the charges are to be read to the jury everything else is also going to be read. If the jury requests it. It does. And the charges are reread in their entirety—with some special emphasis being put on the three responsive verdicts to the charge of second degree murder: guilty as charged, guilty of manslaughter, and the magic eraser, not guilty.

"Thus, in order to convict the defendant William Fontanille of second degree murder," the judge begins, "you must find, one, that the defendant, William Fontanille, killed Janet Myers; and two, that the defendant, William Fontanille, acted with a *specific intent* to kill or to inflict great bodily harm.

"A responsive verdict to the crime of second degree murder is manslaughter. Manslaughter is the killing of a human being when the defendant has the specific intent to kill or inflict great bodily harm, but the offense is committed in a *sudden passion,* or *heat of blood* immediately caused by provocation sufficient to deprive an average person of his self-control and cool reflection. Provocation shall not reduce homicide to manslaughter if the jury finds that the offender's blood had actually cooled, or that an average person's blood would have cooled, at the time the offense was committed.

"Recall that specific criminal intent is that state of mind which exists when the circumstances indicate that the offender *actively desired* the prescribed criminal consequences to follow his act or *failure to act*."

Soon the jury is sent back to resume its deliberations.

"We were by the window at the end of the hall, just standing and talking quietly," Lisa Comeaux Grubic says, recalling part of that Thursday morning spent with Bill.

"It was only when we'd gone back in during deliberations, when the jury came out with the questions, that all of a sudden, whatever the aura was, was gone, like a light had flipped out and there was this human being standing there. That was when I reached out for his hand, he had tears in his eyes," Lisa remembers.

" 'Are you scared?'

" 'Yes. Very scared.'

" 'What do you think's going to happen?'

" 'It's not looking real good right now. *Manslaughter.* That carries twenty-one years! If they come back out and they find me guilty, they won't have to waste another penny—because I'll just die right here. My heart will stop and I'll just die.'

" 'It might not be so bad.'

" 'You know, I'm always going to have to live with the fact that I was guilty of having slept with her, and because of that she's dead—and I will always have to live with that in my mind.'

" 'How can you even stand being in the same room with Kerry?'

" 'I've kind of worked through that. I don't hate Kerry. I guess I should. But I don't. I feel really sorry for Janet and Ryan, but I don't hate Kerry.'

" 'I can't even stand to look at Kerry.'

" 'I just wish it was all over.'

"He seemed more human," Lisa remembers. "He was scared, and he admitted that to me. I was holding his hand for a while. He was very upset and at one point he started to actually cry. Nick handed him a tissue."

With the jury now back in the deliberation room, mulling the choices the judge has reiterated, court reconvenes that morning with the bailiff concerned about seating in the overcrowded courtroom. He wants to let the press sit in the now empty jury box.

Judge Richards asks Wiley Beevers if he has any objections to the press being in the box while he gives his closing argument to the court. Wiley has none.

"Your Honor." Myers's defense counsel begins what is in effect his second closing argument. "Just a short reply to some of the comments that were made by both Mr. Howat Peters and Mr. W. J. LeBlanc, that need, in my opinion, correcting.

"One is a vigorous inquiry into the sufficiency of the evidence does not necessarily mean that anybody's trying to trash the police, or do anything except call attention to what may or may not be in evidence.

"The prosecution has said that if they had taken fifty blood samples, we'd want fifty-one, or if it was nine hundred and ninety-nine we'd want a thousand. Well, that's nothing but speculation; the trier of fact is called upon to make a reasonable determination as to what is a reasonable amount of evidence to be taken from a crime scene under these circumstances.

"The inscrutable Chinaman, Dr. Lee, said that he wasn't going to help us, and that he wasn't going to say whether or not one blood sample was enough, or how many he would have taken had he been on the scene, or anything else. He just wouldn't comment.

"The question is, that for each piece of evidence that was not taken, or was taken and bungled, that could have been inculpatory to one and exculpatory to another. The piece of evidence that they did not take could have been the evidence that would surely show that my client did not act as a principal or kill Janet Myers.

"There's no doubt the State has put the hat on the man that swung the baseball bat. Billy Fontanille had blood from the top of his head, A blood, it was either Janet's or Ryan's, from the top of his head to the bottom of his shoes. And Dr. Lee said that that was consistent with that baseball bat contacting a liquid blood source of type A, Janet or Ryan.

"It hasn't been really questioned whether or not he did that. I think no rational trier of fact can come to any other conclusion than that Billy swung the bat. Right-handed, left-handed, it doesn't make any difference, he did it.

"When you go through the State's witnesses, you have to ask what they proved and what they didn't prove."

From this point on, Wiley refries the already refried hash as he begins another witness-by-witness, theory-by-theory trek in pale duplicate to that traversed in his argument for motion for acquittal.

It does eventually ramble to an end. He also manages to get two more "Chinaman" slurs in, which endears him to no one within the sound of his voice—after all, Dr. Lee has endeared himself to *everyone*.

In an "abundance of caution," Dub and Howie decide that they will offer rebuttal. Howie does it emphatically, with organization and brevity. And not a bad close at all.

"Your Honor, you've been sitting in this courtroom for a long time on this case, so I'm going to finish up.

"You have been able to watch the defendant, and your only interest is in one, as far as the finder of fact. Have you seen any emotion from the defendant? Have you seen any emotion? This is not evidence, but this is your assessment. Have you seen any emotion when his wife's clothes were shown? Any emotion when they talked about his child? Any emotion when they talked about his baby? Any emotion when they showed the pictures of his wife's blood all over the place? Some *terrible facts* in this case. No emotion at all.

"Also something that just stuck out over my dealings with this case is there's no animosity between the two of them. They don't glare at each other, they don't stare at each other.

"Your Honor, we have proven that they did it together. You only need be concerned, for your purposes right now, with this one defendant. And I submit to you that we've proved he committed second degree murder of his wife, and ask you to return that verdict. Thank you."

"Court will now recess until the jury reaches a verdict."

It is almost one o'clock that afternoon when Bill, Tammy DuBuc, earth mother, his staunch supporter, and Angela, his sister, get the word that the jury is about to come in with a verdict. They've been killing time away from the center of the storm in the annex building behind the courthouse.

"When we get back to the courtroom, they take Billy in the back entrance through the judge's chambers," Tammy remembers. "Angela and I are out in the hall with what seems like a thousand people. It's jammed so tight you can't move. And they've already closed and locked the courtroom doors. We can't get in.

"One of the deputies knocks on the door and they open it and I see him pointing at Angela and I—we are over against the wall, and Angela is hysterical at this point. One of the guards come out and get the two of us and bring us in and then they lock the doors back because they can't fit anybody else in.

"They take us up front on the other side, right by the jury. Paul Connick is sitting there, and he stands up and lets Angela sit down in his seat and I kneel down on the floor right next to the bench where she is—she has her head down in her lap through the whole thing; she's trembling. I'm pretty much the same, just kind of holding on to her."

"The room is absolutely stacked to the walls," Channel 4 reporter Cheryl Hickman remembers. "The judge comes in—at this point my heart's doing about a mile a minute, just pounding, and there is this tremendous air of expectation in the courtroom, the air thick."

"Counsel, I understand the jury has reached a verdict," Judge Richards says to the lawyers assembled at the bench. "Before they come into the courtroom, I'm going to hand the court's verdict to the clerk, and ask her to hold that until after the verdict of the jury."

Then, "Are we ready for the jury?"

"Yes, Your Honor."

"Yes, sir."

"The jurors came in and it's obvious they're not real happy," Ms. Hickman continues. "They did not look pleased with what they were going to do. There was some sniffling. They kept their eyes straight ahead."

"Does the State waive polling for their attendance?" Judge Richards asks.

"Yes, Your Honor," W. J. LeBlanc says.

"Does the defense waive polling?"

"Yes, Your Honor," Nick Noriea answers.

"Mrs. Henry, you appear to be the foreperson of the jury, is that correct?"

"Yes, sir."

"Do you have a verdict?"

"Yes, sir, we do."

"Would you hand it to the clerk, please?"

Soon, the judge says, "I ask the clerk to read the verdict."

The clerk, Dorothy Lawson, reads, " 'Verdict. We the jury find the defendant, William Fontanille, guilty of manslaughter—' "

It is as if one giant, many-throated thing gasps at once. People swivel their heads around within the sea of faces, not knowing how to react, looking for clues from their neighbors. Confusion. What does this mean? He's the bat man. *Manslaughter?* The gasps and buzzing never reach a crescendo, because everyone is aware that while Bill Fontanille is slowly shaking his head and is the picture of stunned incredulity, Kerry Myers, his face as rigid as ever, no movement of any kind, frozen, staring straight ahead, is still to learn his fate.

Each juror places his or her verdict on a supplied slip, which goes to the judge, who then, with counsel at the bench looking on, verifies the count.

"Okay," says Nick.

"All right, the court finds that the required number of ten votes concurred in the verdict, and the court orders the verdict received and recorded by the clerk. I'll now ask the clerk to read the court's verdict with reference to Mr. Myers."

Mrs. Lawson reads, " 'The verdict of the Court: I, Judge Ernest V. Richards, find the defendant, Kerry Myers, guilty of second degree murder.' "

The gasp this time is of larger proportions than the one earlier. It is a thing of much energy, finding release from different people in different ways. But again there is that wailing which rises above all, and even among those bodies packed together, Debbie Myers finds room not only to wail but to swoon and collapse into the arms of her mother and sister, sobbing.

The court, however, still has a few moments of business left. "The court orders the verdicts, both verdicts—"

"Remain seated," Mrs. Lawson calls out.

Soon there is a lull in the strange mixture of sounds, and Judge Richards continues, "The court orders both verdicts received and recorded."

Then, after the judge thanks and excuses the jury, there comes another lull in the wavelike action of the assemblage.

"Mr. Fontanille and Mr. Myers, I'm going to set sentencing for May the 3rd, and I'm going to order that you be remanded to the custody of the sheriff to await sentence on that date."

With handcuffs on and shackles bonding them together, they are led out of the courtroom and down the hall amid this circus of humanity which parts for their passing.

After the verdict, in the ebullience of victory, in chambers a discussion develops upon the speculation that perhaps the carrot of a reduction in sentence might get Billy to tell what really happened. In an off-the-record but nonetheless serious vein, Judge Richards remarks that the truth might indeed be worth some time taken away from the maximum sentence of twenty-one years.

Howat Peters then leaves the courthouse to meet Leslie Hill, the reporter for WDSU-TV Channel 6—by the end of the trial they have become an item. That evening Ms. Hill just happens to run the judge's offer as a scoop on the news.

Cheryl Hickman, feeling somewhat blindsided, calls W.J. and the judge and learns that while Judge Richards is very disturbed that the sanctity of chambers has been breeched, he confirms that the subject was discussed and that, of course, as in almost all cases less than murder, the judge has discretionary authority in sentencing.

* * *

At an impromptu victory celebration at Chris's Steak House, with Sheriff Harry Lee picking up the tab, the prosecution team is feted in full festive and raucous fashion throughout the afternoon and evening. W.J. gets his back slapped along with the constant offers to freshen his drink—"The impossible win! The cocky little sumbitch did it!" is the general tenor of the plaudits coming his way.

Dub can party with the best of them—but he was emotionally drained and he had an early-morning appointment, so he leaves the celebration early.

His and Howie's appointment that following morning is with *The Breakfast Edition* on Channel 6. Also scheduled on the show is Jane Spiers, Janet's sister. The prosecutors and the sister are not on at the same time, of course. So it is while Dub is standing off in the wings as Jane is being interviewed and ripping the DA's Office that James Spiers, Jane's husband and Janet's brother-in-law, approaches him and says very quietly, "None of them will ever admit it, but I just want you to know that you proved it to me, and to say thanks."

No other "well done" will ever mean as much to W. J. LeBlanc as that concession from the camp of the opposition.

Wiley Beevers does not like to give up.

On Thursday morning, May 3, 1990, Wiley brings a "new" witness to take the stand. Judge Richards, in his discretion, allows him to do so.

The witness is Dr. John Joseph LaMartina. He was the staff emergency room physician at West Jefferson Hospital who administered the initial treatment to Kerry Myers that early morning of February 24, 1984.

It seems that after hearing something in the media to the effect that the water dilution patterns on Kerry's clothing played a role in the circumstantial establishment of guilt, Dr. LaMartina contacted Wiley to tell him that much water could have and probably did get splashed all over Kerry's clothing while he and a nurse's aide cleaned and prepared his wounds for treatment and suturing.

He takes the stand that morning and furthermore swears to Kerry's mental state: "He was sobbing. I would say in a mental state of anguish, severe mental anguish, severe mental suffering. He was not in control of his consciousness. He was just out of control, talking, telling me the whole story, everything that happened. And I can't imagine—there's *no way he could have been lying to me.* This story, it wasn't a prepared thing, he wasn't in control of his emotional state at that particular time. And so the story he related to me I'm sure was true."

The story the doctor goes on to relate is just about exactly the story as first reported by and for years carried by the media. Every detail which is forthcoming has appeared in print or broadcast at one time or another.

When pressed for any independent recollections, the doctor has none. It is, however, apparent that the doctor believes that what he is saying is the truth.

Dr. LaMartina is on the stand a long time; Beevers leads him thoroughly on direct, then Howie cross-examines him with many, many objections and much wrangling; Nick has him for a spell, then Beevers again on redirect. Unfortunately, not one single word of it adds to the meager body of knowledge which can be taken as fact in the baseball bat murder case.

"I have no further testimony," Wiley advises the court.

"Does the State have anything to offer?"

"No, Your Honor," W. J. LeBlanc says.

"Well, the court finds first that the defendant has failed to make a showing that the evidence that was introduced today could not have been obtained with diligent effort prior to or during trial.

"This is a doctor who was the emergency room treating physician. The statements that were made to him were made by Mr. Myers. He certainly knew of those statements that he made to the doctor. The doctor has been in the same place since 1980. His name is on the medical records. His name was available to the defendant, the defendant knew of the character of the statements that he had made, and he could have had the doctor here to testify if he had so desired.

"The court further finds that the testimony probably would not have changed the judgment of guilt, and so for that reason the motion for a new trial is denied."

"Please note my objection, Your Honor."

"All right, sir."

Some procedural bookkeeping needs attention, then Judge Richards looks to Kerry Myers, handcuffed and dressed in ratty prison orange, sitting by himself in the first row of the empty jury box, and says:

"All right, Mr. Myers, do you have anything to say before I impose sentencing?"

"Just one brief thing, Your Honor," Kerry Myers answers.

"All right."

"Should I stand?"

"Stand up, please," Wiley Beevers directs his client.

"Your Honor, all I'd like to say is that Janet and my children and myself are victims of that man," Kerry says as his full arm is outstretched and pointing directly at Bill. But his voice is not angry, only the posturing.

"And I am innocent and I've always been innocent." A pause, then, "That's all I'd like to say."

"We're ready for sentencing, Your Honor," Wiley Beevers says.

"All right, Mr. Myers, you've been convicted of the crime of second degree murder. The law provides only one penalty for that crime. Accordingly I now sentence you to serve a term of life imprisonment at hard labor, this is without benefit of parole, probation, or suspension of sentence. And I order that you be remanded to the custody of the Department of Corrections to commence serving that sentence."

"Your Honor, we would now give you oral notice of intent to appeal, and will supplement the record with a written notice," Wiley intones.

"All right, sir," says Judge Richards, then, "Mr. Noriea, are you ready to take up your motions?"

Nick doesn't have any witnesses, but, of course, he does have motions, and these motions have to be handled in due process, particularly when the State chooses to present argument in opposition to a motion for a new trial based on six specific grounds.

To watch W.J. and Nick have another go at each other is not why all of these citizens and the media are crammed into the courtroom. Most of them are here for one reason and one reason alone: Will Bill tell? For three weeks any number of people throughout greater New Orleans have waited to find out if his fear of prison is greater than his fear of revealing whatever it is he doesn't want his world to know about him.

The expectation of the onlookers is palpable; you can see it, and of course you can hear it in hushed tones of anticipation as they wait for the two attorneys, who, quite candidly, did not learn to like each other at all during these many months, to stop lawyering for a spell and let the show begin. Finally:

"Does the State have any argument in connection with the other motions?"

"No, Your Honor," W.J. says.

"All right, those two motions are denied," Judge Richards rules. "Again, Mr. Noriea, Mr. Fontanille has a right to a twenty-four-hour delay before the imposition of sentence. Do you want me to reschedule the sentencing?"

"No, Your Honor," answers Nick.

"You waive the twenty-four-hour delay?"

"Yes, sir."

Howat Peters, also caught up in the excitement of will he or won't he, says, "Judge, I think Mr. Fontanille would just like to briefly say something to you."

"Yes, sir," answers the judge, who, if the truth be told, is as intellectually and emotionally ensnared by this seemingly unsolvable puzzle as anyone else who's ever been involved with it.

"Judge Richards," Bill begins softly, haltingly. "I've given up the last six years of my life, and I don't expect you to understand that, to know what it feels like. The people closest to me will never know how horrible those six years have been. But what makes this unbearable now, judge, is the fact I didn't kill Janet Myers. It's no longer an issue, and for six years that's been the only issue of my life. It had become my identity, judge."

There is a pause, and the courtroom literally holds its breath. Then, "This didn't turn out the way it was supposed to, it didn't turn out right." Another pause, a very small shrug. "It wasn't supposed to happen this way. That's all I have to say."

Epilogue

August 13, Sunday, 1978

He says he doesn't believe in "outsiders," but until today I had the impression that he'd kill me if he ever found out I was having some sort of an affair. Now he says he'd have to consider the person, situation, etc., just what I don't need to hear. If he really cared, he'd want to murder me and the other guy. . . . I'd love to have the thought he'd care enough to stop me!

—Diary of Janet Cannon
at Nicholls State University

*   *   *

It has been almost three years since that May morning when Judge Ernest V. Richards sentenced William Fontanille to the maximum of twenty-one years and Kerry Myers to the legislatively mandated life without benefit of parole, probation, or suspension of sentence.

Save for the extraordinary, in spite of Nick Noriea's Mr. Optimist pronouncements to the contrary, all appellate levels of relief have been exhausted for both men. Kerry Myers resides at Angola State Penitentiary, one of the more infamous state prisons in America. He works as a computer graphics designer for the prison print shop, which is the official printer for the State of Louisiana, producing everything from contracts to pamphlets, full-color slick magazines, and the award-winning prison newspaper the *Angolite*.

Bill Fontanille's home is a medium-security correctional institute near the Louisiana-Texas border, with a name that makes it sound more like a trade school than a state pen. But life there is only relatively superior to life at Angola; there are still men on horseback with shotguns for each row of inmates planting or tilling or harvesting the crops that sustain the larder and provide surplus assets for the state. During Bill's first year there, he worked on the blue jeans assembly line, sewing pant-leg inseams for the clothing factory the prison operates. He currently works in the library. And works out.

During the research to produce this book, a number of things turned up that were not known theretofore. This is reasonable, since a biographical researcher casts a broader net than does the criminal justice system, which concerns itself only with those things which are necessary to prosecute a crime.

The vast majority of such gleanings have, of course, already been incorporated into the body of the book—but not all. Some facts came rather late in the process and were also considered to be of such a nature that their evidentiary weight, to whatever degree we choose to grant them such, is best viewed *after* the criminal justice system has, within its strictly defined limitations, rendered its final verdicts in the baseball bat murder. And, as promised, when it is now *almost* time for you to begin *your* deliberations.

"My God, all these years and no one's ever asked me that." Dr. Richard Tracy, the pathologist, has turned quite ashen. "Worse yet, I never asked myself!"

Dr. Tracy, who did the autopsy of Janet Myers, is holding a copy of his own autopsy report and protocol and several autopsy photos. The question the doctor has been asked is: Other than the air embolism causing coronary arrest, was there any anatomical reason for Janet Myers to have died? In other words, if at any time during the possibly two hours she lived before that arbitrary air bubble hit her heart she had been taken to an average emergency room, could she have lived?

The answer, in the short of it, is a most troubled "probably."

While her scalp and facial tissues were grossly lacerated—apparently because she turned her head side to side, the glancing, choppy blows of the bat did more cutting and tearing than pulverizing—the skull itself had far less fracturing than did Ryan's. There was an area of the right forehead which had a "spiderweb" fracture, but the skull at that point is "thin and easily" fractured and the damage was not considered of itself to be dangerous to life. The one fracture to the back of her lower skull is fairly small and "certainly not life-threatening" under normal conditions.

There was no swelling of the brain whatsoever; the thing that came so close to killing her son was not evident on her, even though she most likely lived long enough to suffer the onset of the fluid buildup that is one of the major causes of death with head injuries.

From the original autopsy report: "The brain itself has no area suggestive of contusion. The midbrain and pons have no softenings or hemorrhages and no blood is present in the ventricular system . . . no appreciable grooving is present in the cerebellar tonsils or uncal gyri."

One of the other major killers with head injury is pulmonary edema: for some as yet not completely understood reason, massive head injuries very often are accompanied by fluid developing rapidly in the lungs and more or less drowning the victim. While there was some of this activity in its early stages, at the time of her autopsy there was only a "light pink, frothy watery fluid and small amounts of viscid bloodstained mucoid material. Some blood pools into the dependent posterior lungs in a manner suggesting aspiration through the airway." This could have been successfully addressed at any reasonably staffed and equipped emergency room.

And the heart itself, which was fouled by a bubble, was "contracted, firm, and of average color."

Cutting to the quick of this pathology, no matter who swung the bat, both men *let her die.*

Lena Rieffel worked with Janet in the ladies' wear section of D. H. Holmes at the Belle Promenade mall for a year and a half before her murder. She is still there now, even though it's no longer D. H. Holmes, but rather a Dillard's. It seems in all these years no one has ever questioned any of Janet's coworkers at any job other than Zee Medical, where she worked briefly four years before the murder. That was a sin of omission. Ms. Rieffel has quite a story to tell, which is corroborated by a coworker.

"Janet was pregnant, she was starting to show, and she had a miscarriage," Miz Lena begins. "Well, in a couple of days she came back to work. I'm working by the mall side, which is right across the aisle from her department. And a customer comes up to me and says, 'I need help in Juniors, can you help me?' Janet worked in Juniors—I said, 'Well they have a lady over there.' She said, 'No, they don't have anybody over there.'

"I said, 'Let me go see.' So I walked over there. I called for her and couldn't find her. Finally I went into the office. I knocked on the door. She's sitting there at the desk with her head down and she was crying—just uncontrollable. So I said, 'What's wrong?' 'Oh, no, it's all right,' she said.

"I said, 'Well, you have a customer out here, you want me to take care of it?' She said, 'No, I'll do it.' I said, 'What is wrong?' And she wouldn't tell me. I went on out and waited on the customer, and a little while later she did come out.

"But she was crying very hard, like somebody had died. I remember I said, *'What's wrong?'* She couldn't even answer me.

"Then this happened another time. It was maybe a week or so later, the same thing again, and I told her, 'You *have* to tell me what's going on.' I don't know, I thought somebody really might've died. And that's when she got up from the desk and she showed me, she said, 'This is what he did to me. Kerry!'

"See, when she miscarried the baby, he blamed her. He said he knew it was a little girl—that's what he wanted was a little girl, and it was all her fault. Well, she raised up her clothes, she showed me, all up in here [lower torso and pelvic region] was black-and-blue. In other words, he hit her where it couldn't show.

"She had like a little jumper on, blouse and little cotton jumper on, she just raised it up—because we were back there in the ladies' little office, with the door closed. And these were real big *ugly* bruises and that's seeing them two weeks *later,* because it happened right after the miscarriage.

"She said the reason he did that was because nobody could see it—but he told her, he said, 'It's your fault.' And this happened one more time.

"Then when she got pregnant with Sarah right quick after the miscarriage, things got better, but still she had crying spells. But she never did tell me about anything else, and she carried this baby full-term. But I think she was putting a face on. I think there was a black cloud—to me it was a black cloud that she was hiding. It was something in the back that I couldn't explain. But I knew it was there. She never seemed happy. Only time she would smile was when she was with a customer.

"She had this black thing in the back of her, you know; I've seen him a couple of times come in and he'd sort of argue with her, and he'd leave," Miz Lena concludes.

Apparently the nature of violence in the relationship of Janet and Kerry had at some point reached another dimension or plateau. What Ms. Rieffel saw and heard suggests premeditated, purposeful, and symbolic beatings of Janet, and that the battering had reached the stage where guilty knowledge required efforts to conceal the resulting wounds.

In the later years, at the very time when friends and family thought the marriage had improved and the violence was almost nonexistent, it was in fact far worse than in those early turbulent years when Janet and Kerry had been so public about their problems.

"See, what the problem was—I couldn't remember what day it was when I saw them arguing," Marilyn LeJeune is explaining as Peggy Senat is working fussily over a Mardi Gras Ball gown and costume—which is Mrs. Senat's business; she has a complete workshop set up in the closed-in garage across the street catty-corner to 2232 Litchwood Lane.

"But then Peggy's the one that reminded me."

"That I did," Peggy says. "I knew it was the same day, because it was the day both you and Karen came over about the same time. Karen Bucksbarg is the one to talk to, but she won't, they moved out of the neighborhood so they wouldn't have to be bothered by the police and all the questions and subpoenas."

"So when Peggy says that," Ms. LeJeune continues, "I go, 'Yeah, that *was* the same day as the murder.' "

"And I told her right then she ought to tell the police, too," reminds the feisty Peggy Senat.

"But I can't swear, because I didn't see their faces." Ms. LeJeune begins to tell her story. "It was well before three o'clock the day of the murder, I was walking here to Peggy's to sew something and there was arguing going on in the garage over there. I don't know who it was. I will tell you there was a man and a woman. They were in the shadow inside the garage, I was out in the sun, and I did not look to see. I hear the loud voices. They were arguing; standing close together arguing. I do not know who. That's all I know, and after the mixup I made about the day I saw Billy, I wasn't going to tell the police this when I can't even say who it was arguing in there. I didn't know them well enough to recognize the voices.

"But this much I'll take the oath on, there was a man and a woman standing in that garage arguing loudly between two-fifteen and three, because the kids get home on the school bus at three and I'm always there for that."

This information is particularly interesting since—if we are to assume that it was Janet and Kerry arguing in *their* garage—aside from the fact that Kerry's been proved to have told yet another lie, it also explains why Kerry so often referred to events happening at "two o'clock" in his 911 phone call: that's when he came home, not the two or three hours later in the afternoon as he claims.

Did the fighting between Janet and Kerry *begin* that early?

"I'm going to tell you something that has bothered me and my parents ever since the wake and funeral," Peggy Cowan begins, somewhat dramatically.

"It was at the wake. My mama, my daddy, and me were standing with the Cannons, Miz Lorraine and Mr. Charlie, and Clifford Myers walks over with Kerry following right behind him and when he got to us he said, 'Man, look at my boy, all beat to hell. He was so beat up and messed up that night that he had to call me to ask what to do, that's when I told him to call the police.'

"Now, he never said it again—although Janet's aunt told us she'd heard him say the same thing—and it didn't really seem important at the time, because it wasn't until years later that the 911 tape was released, and then it hit us—that son of a bitch called his father before he called the police. He never could do anything without his father, so that's where that's at.

"Absolutely, we heard it plain as day, me, my mama, and my daddy— 'course the Cannons heard it, but they'll never admit it. But we've talked about it in my family ever since.

"And you know what I believe—that call waiting wasn't from Fontanille, that was Mr. Myers calling back to see if Kerry was handling it right."

"For no apparent reason, Janet went from one mood to another," Mike Price is saying. "A classic example: we were at the ballpark. We were playing in a tournament, one of the last we all played together in, the fall before the murder.

"She was sitting in the stands, Ryan was about two, we'd been there all day long. All the kids were tired, they were dirty, and hot. It was six-thirty, seven in the evening, the girls were just sitting in the stands talking, having the best time—it was really heartwarming to see our wives all together and enjoying themselves.

"But Ryan whined about something and Janet just went *nuts:* she grabbed the kid and shook him, really shook him, like child-abuse shaking. Kerry yelled at her not to hurt him. The storm cloud quickly passed over her, and, fortunately, it was the last game and they went right home. Normally, we all sat out, drank beer, and partied after the games—they just got in the car and went home.

"Janet's temperament, her psychological background, the fact that violence has to be learned so therefore along with everything else we know, we can't say she wasn't an abused child herself, all that would make you say, 'Yeah, there's a very good chance that it happened.' Monique and I often talked about this—before the murder.

"Believe me, *believe* me when I say this—her temperament could lead to that very easily. If something hit her wrong, she was perfectly capable of picking up a baseball bat and whacking Ryan or picking up a knife and stabbing someone."

Dr. Aris Cox, perhaps the only forensic psychiatrist in these parts, has a private practice in uptown New Orleans but also does extensive work for the State Department of Corrections and various law enforcement agencies. During the middle years of the baseball bat murder case, after Bill's first trial, with the State spinning its wheels, Dr. Cox was asked to read the statements, testimonies, and a transcript of the "911 tape" to see if he could make any sense of it. Beyond being circumstantially certain a rat was loose, Dr. Cox was not able to shed any new light on what could've happened. He was, however, fascinated intellectually with the case; he remains so to this day. Consequently he has been most obliging with his time.

After he had become familiar with the pattern of violence and sex we were finding, the forensic psychiatrist remembered that there had been some speculation about the presence of kinky sex or wife swapping and he asked if we'd uncovered anything the police hadn't.

When he was told that we also hadn't found even the whiff of the alleged "fuck club," Dr. Cox shook his head and said: "No, don't look for a group or club. Look for individual couples. Because soon the level of thrill has to be increased; almost always where I have found this violence-sex relationship, there have been other couples. No groups, nothing even organized, just isolated, independent couples. They're out there. They have to be."

A certain college professor—who for reasons both litigious and humane will remain anonymous—has an interesting story to tell. One night, at a point about midway between the birth of Ryan and Janet's pregnancy with Sarah, this college professor, involved in an extramarital relationship, chose a quiet, out-of-the-way restaurant on the West Bank for a rendezvous. Upon their entry into this little place where they were sure they wouldn't run into anyone who knew them, the professor and his lady friend, a professional woman from across the river in New Orleans, immediately bumped into Janet and Kerry, whom the professor knew well enough not to be alarmed at his discovered indiscretion.

Soon the two couples joined for drinks and dinner. After eating, over another drink or two, the couples started talking about what they had planned for the rest of the evening and Janet and Kerry began urging that they all return to their home on Litchwood to continue the get-together. Both the professor and his companion remember that Janet and Kerry were being particularly insistent about it, but that all they really wanted to do was get on with their date.

Janet then asked the other woman to accompany her to the ladies' room. Once in there, to the astonishment of the other woman, in words and inflections the professor's friend swears she could not have mistaken the meaning of, Janet, in short, and in particular, said: "If y'all come over, I *guarantee* you'll have the *time of your lives!*"

This woman was soon kicking the professor under the table in an attempt to let him know she wanted to get the hell out of there. The professor remembers he'd already smelled something adrift, but that he was still somewhat shocked when they were alone and his lady friend told him what Janet said and what she believed Janet meant.

"Unmistakably, no room for doubt on my part, it was an invitation for multiparticipatory sex, swapping and games and such," this necessarily anonymous lady remembers.

Greg D'Argonne is a hospital administrator in Denver. Years ago he had grown up in Terrytown with close connections to the "Billy Circle" and at one time considered himself one of Bill's closest friends. He also, later, was a member of the now infamous softball team at the time when Janet and Kerry started dating.

"Diggie," as he is still affectionately called among the "circle," witnessed, or was a participant in, many of the events and relationships that already have been presented within the body of this work. However, one story he has to tell is unique and decidedly interesting in light of the fact that, even though the State never found it, *Rosemarie Kerr remains adamant about the existence of pornography within the parameters of the baseball bat murder:*

"Susan was a really sweet girl," Greg D'Argonne says. "I remember after they first got married, one night we're over their house and Billy gets this phone call and goes and takes it in the back room. He stays back there a long time and Susan just started unloading. She was telling us—my wife, Lisa, and I—she's telling us that Billy is starting to watch porno movies and stuff and he wanted to start acting out these things, very violent sex and stuff. We thought, 'God, this is *slightly bizarre!*'

"Susan was surprisingly candid, but it was like she was saying, 'What do I do here?' It just all kind of came tumbling out,"

It must be added that the former Susan Fontanille denies this story.

"I was alone, I was hurting, she wasn't getting what she needed from her marriage—and the grief, she'd lost a sister, I'd lost a wife. We could share that. It was a time of weakness for both of us, and we reacted to it, to each other."

Kerry Myers is confirming a fact that for years has been only a tantalizing rumor. A rumor that, from the earliest weeks of the investigation onward, kept popping up in the notes of investigators asking the circle of friends if Kerry Myers could have been having an affair with another woman. Consistently the notation would be various phrasings whose common gist was: "If he were, it would've been with Joan," referring to Joan Cannon Switzer, Janet's oldest sister.

"Yes. The affair happened, and it's not something I'm proud of, but the intentions were good," Kerry continues, and then says emphatically: "But I swear it was long after Janet was killed."

It must be noted, however, that a co-worker of Joan Switzer swears that Kerry often took Joan to lunch and would also come by at closing time and Joan would then tell her fellow employees to go on, that she would lock up, leaving her and Kerry alone, and that this activity was definitely *before* Janet's murder.

"There's extreme anger and resentment here. She *wants* them to get hurt. She wants them to *hurt each other—she's paying the pain back!*"

The voice of Rosemarie Kerr comes tumbling forth like assorted hot nuts from an old-timey vending machine. It is late summer, 1991; we're sitting on the back porch of her cottage in the tiny community called Harmony Grove, nestled so quaintly within an ancient, secluded, primitive, entirely enchanting valley amid the foothills northwest of San Diego.

"There was a lot of pornography going on," Rosemarie continues, eyes closed, rapidly rubbing the tips of her fingers across a note written by Janet Myers.

" 'But we hid it good, we hid it good,' that's coming from *her*. 'We want to hide that. That's one of the things we want to hide the most. We're *ashamed*'—something is hidden! It could've been a brown paper bag—*box*! It feels like the color brown. . . . I'm bringing in somebody . . . somebody who has it—this person is *still around*. It's a male vibration—*he's an older man!* I can't quite see his face . . . an outdoor, robust, rustic sort of man—you know the guy that has the ox? I can't remember his name—okay! *Paul Bunyan!* It would be like a miniature version of him. . . ."

"Have you ever noticed that both Kerry and his dad talk like they're such prudes: 'How can you let Ryan and Sarah watch HBO?' or something?" Debra Myers continues.

"Always preaching about 'smut,' and all. Well, you want to know what Kerry wants me to bring up in the custody battle? That his father is 'addicted to *pornography*'!" He's got a big *brown box* just full of hardcore stuff in his bedroom *closet*. Kerry said it had always been like that."

"Hell, yes, I'll admit that right up front. . . . I was a Marine, I like a 'stag' film as much as the next guy. What's wrong with that?" Clifford Myers is saying, after he's been questioned about the alleged pornography.

"We used to call 'em 'smokers'; the guys'd all get together and look at this eight-millimeter stuff. Hell, back when I was selling electrical supplies, before I retired, I used to *sell it* to the guys going out working on the oil rigs. This guy named Mike used to get 'em for me, I'd show 'em to the toolpusher for nothing, and then he'd recommend it to his crew. Some years I'd make several thousand extra bucks . . . it was a good little business there, came in handy.

"But, so what . . . men have been going to 'smokers' since long before you and me."

"I believe with all my heart the boy is innocent," begins Clifford Myers, who because of the allegedly "unfit" behavior of Kerry's second wife, Debra Myers, has experienced a bitter but successful custody battle over Ryan and Sarah and a complete break with his son.

"The boy just doesn't have any common sense. And the lying. And the 'I know everything.' For all his smarts, the boy's an idiot. He would not listen to me, said for me to back off and let him handle it. And look where he is. And all because he'll believe any girl he thinks loves him before his family and friends. His whole brain is in his pecker.

"Well, the boy ain't got any of my genes in him."

Whoa! Stop. What are you talking about, Cliff?

"In 1955, the Marines called me back to active duty and I was gone fourteen weeks. When I come home, Marguerite's six weeks pregnant with Kerry—I know the man, a friend of mine."

Does Kerry know this?

"When he used to get his grandma mad, she'd sometimes say, 'Ah, you're not one of us, anyway.' He'd come to me all upset and I'd tell him don't worry about what she says. The other kids all know it. Maybe Kerry knows, but he's never let on to me."

"That's it! That's the psychological smoking gun," Dr. Aris Cox responded when he learned how marital infidelity had figured in Kerry's background. He had witnessed his father catch his mother with another man, and he probably guessed the truth of his own paternity; probably Janet had told him she was going to leave him, and probably he thought she was having an affair and that maybe Sarah wasn't his. History was indeed repeating itself.

"Before, we could never account for that *amount* of rage, instant hatred—but this had been festering and growing for twenty years. It all flashed together . . . every time he smashed that bat into her face, he was also smashing it into his mother's."

It is almost eight years to the month after Janet's murder. It is my third visit to the sprawling rural prison in De Quincy, Louisiana, my third visit with Bill Fontanille. Many, many hours, days, weeks, and now years of sporadic but intense communications between us precede the following monologue, perhaps the *ultimate play in the scenario game.* In the end, having worked his way through the incremental layers of varnished untruths he'd been stripping away, he all but summoned us to bear witness to the final "truth." Therefore, in his own words, William Fontanille:

"The last time we talked you said that perhaps I'm an emotional masochist. I told you you were wrong because that implied I enjoyed pain, or guilt actually is what we were talking about. I've thought a lot about that since we've spoken, and I still say I don't enjoy it—but I *need* it.

"I've *got* to have that guilt. Sometimes I'll even bring it up, I'll make myself feel it—because what it tells me, being in a place like this, is that I'm still not that lost. That I still maintain some of my humanity. Feeling that guilt, man . . . I'm human! I need it; I pray to God I don't lose it. If I can still feel some remorse, some guilt, I'm still okay. I'm not one of *them,*" Bill says as he gestures toward his fellow inmates.

When told that Kerry feels no guilt, Bill says, "Kerry doesn't feel this because he doesn't *believe* he's the *cause* of Janet's death. He was telling me right then and there, '*You're* the reason Janet died. *You made me do it.*'

"He was crying and sobbing—and maybe he was sobbing because his wife was *dying*. You know what I'm saying?—he didn't *want* his wife to die; something *else* made him do that, *it wasn't his fault*. He wasn't right—I mean, I don't know why he didn't plead insanity, because that night he was *insane*. There's no doubt in my mind, he was insane! I almost feel like he was . . . I don't know the word I'm looking for . . . *he was mourning his wife*! Remember how Jack Nicholson looked in *The Shining*? That crazed look. That was Kerry that night. That night, he was insane."

There is a pause, the sounds of the prison intrude for a moment, then:

"And it being Kerry, too. If I'd slept with Monique and the same thing would've happened with Mike—I probably would've gone right through Mike and no one would've ever . . . but it being Kerry, you wanna . . . you wanna help Kerry, everybody always felt like we had to take care of Kerry—and of all people to hurt, that's the one I hurt, that way, *Kerry*. And I don't know what I was thinking. I don't know if my main focus was to help Kerry . . . or to get Kerry to forgive me for what I had done; for whatever reason I just wanted to *be there with him*. I wanted to be there when the police came, so I could say, 'Yeah, but it's *my fault*.' You know, 'He *had to do it*. Don't think badly of him.'

"I wanted to say, 'Kerry's a *good* person, he's my friend, he's great to be around. Don't think because of what happened tonight that this is Kerry Myers.'

"But that never happened, because of course I wasn't there when the police came. The police were never going to come with me in the house— he was either going to kill me, or I was gonna . . . he was never going to let the police come to the house. He was never going to call an ambulance. . . ."

Again there is silence, a moment of small talk, and then Bill says it's okay now, he's relaxed, he's ready to begin the story as the tape recorder runs. . . .

"I went to the Cronins' house early that morning, and Chuck and I discussed everything. I told Chuck I was feeling bad about it; that I was gonna go talk to Janet and tell her that whatever happened was never going to happen again, and apologize. Do whatever I had to do to make her feel better about herself. I guess I stayed at Chuck's till about noon, then I went to Janet's.

"And there's no doubt that if I'd said, 'Pack up the kids, let's go,' she'd've gone . . . there's no doubt. None, at all.

"Basically we just stood in the foyer holding each other. We stood there for a long time, maybe an hour. I couldn't tell her 'Leave,' because I was having a tough enough time supporting myself. And I wouldn't have anyway. I wasn't in love with Janet. I wasn't over Susan. I had feelings for her. I *liked* Janet; Janet and I were . . . close. I always felt something for

Janet because she was never accepted by the group; Mike never liked her, Curtis was a total jerk around her, I mean, he would say things right in front of this girl, so for that reason I was always . . . I *liked* Janet. I guess I went overboard to make her feel welcome, at get-togethers and things. She saw it, and felt it, and reciprocated; certainly if we're in a group she's gonna come sit with me rather than sit with Curtis Jordan and Mike Price. Always there was a closeness. That's why it's ludicrous for her sister to say she was scared of me, or didn't like me, that's just bull!''

Then, after a moment: "Before the basketball game Wednesday night, she told me that Kerry asked why we were sitting so close together. He cast aspersions in that direction, you know, and she said, 'Don't tell him anything.' That's no problem because I *wasn't* going to say anything to him. And he never brought anything up to me."

Soon Bill is addressing his being very distracted and nervous at the basketball game Wednesday night before the murder: "It was partly because of what Janet had warned me about, plus the situation I was in at the time—it was probably a combination of both, I'm not going to discount one over the other, but that was a large part of it, I mean I'd just slept with my friend's wife!"

The sex itself: "It was mutual, the feeling—the connection of loneliness; it wasn't a case of one leading the other. It was spontaneous. I mean, I'm talking for the first time about things that were going on in my life; and she was doing the same. When I told her about me and Susan breaking up and how I felt that was a personal failure, she was supportive in the sense that 'This is happening to me, too. It just happens, and no one's at fault.' That's what we were doing; just sitting there supporting each other, I guess, and then . . . a touch, a kiss—

"If you want to explore the differences between Janet and myself in that encounter, there's probably a lot. I'm thinking physical . . . I'm sure it was much more to her than that. I can't see her *risking everything* just to have a fling with *me*. Because no matter what Mike and them tell you, Janet was *not* promiscuous. What I'm trying to say is I'm sure she could have restrained herself, if it was just a physical thing, I think it was much more than that."

About Chuck Cronin's story to the grand jury that Bill had told him Janet had thrown herself at him, Bill says: "I don't doubt I probably said it that way first, you know, macho guy talk."

There is a very long pause before: "It's hard to imagine what happened that afternoon has led to so many lives . . . ruined.

"I can imagine the impact on Kerry when he heard it. Him seeing the bat there, and her getting angry enough to tell him, maybe to taunt him.

"But the only thing he said to me was that I was his friend. I was his friend and he didn't want to hurt me—he never talked about Janet and I getting together, nothing like that. It *never* came up. And we talked about—I mean we talked about ball games we'd played in together, places we'd gone together, down memory lane. Just . . . good friends. You've gotta know, Kerry *needs* friends, he's *got* to have them. I don't know, I guess he was reaffirming our friendship, and I was doing the same thing."

"You can go back to the initial thing, when he and I were on the floor together, he was sobbing—was he sobbing for Ryan? I don't know, there was something he was crying about, there was something that caused him great sadness."

Then: "The guilt was driven home, I'm a pretty shallow person, I don't know if I could've gotten that deep into my psyche on my own, I think Kerry's the one that drove it home. That's what I remember, 'You—you— you *caused* this.' Like I said, the first stone was cast right then and there."

Soon: "I called her from a pay phone, and before I could even finish saying I'd better come back and get my bat, she said, 'Yes, come!' "

On parking around the corner on Patricia Street only to find Kerry's car at the house when he walked up: "I could've walked back and got the car—but I just didn't want to make that long walk back, I was just going to get my bat. I wasn't going over there to confront Kerry, 'Hey, I slept with your wife.' I was going to get my bat.

"And actually I was relieved when I saw his car there. I figured if there was anything, let's get it over with right now. I was ready to take whatever verbal abuse, or whatever physical abuse he was going to put on me. If he'd've punched me in the mouth, I wouldn't've done anything. I deserved it.

"Kerry answered the door. I walked in and I walked past him and that's when he stabbed me three times—I didn't realize I was stabbed, I thought I was punched—and I turned and saw the knife in his hand. And he's blank, totally blank, there's nothing in his face; that's when I ran into the TV room. The bat was against the love seat. So I picked it up, he came at me, I swung it . . . twice maybe, I don't know. He got inside the arc of the bat, I dropped the bat and went for his hand with the knife. We struggled and fought, knocked things over, eventually came to rest in the middle of that room, and by this time he's in an emotional upheaval. He's *sobbing*, and screaming and crying, *'See what you did, you made me do it. You made me do it.'* Over and over, I mean, he must've said that a hundred times, over and over. Just struggling for air—to get air—he was just sobbing. The only thing I can compare it to is a baby, a baby crying when it can't get enough air and you know they have that little moment where they're quiet and then go right back—wah! That's what he was like.

"At that point I had the knife. I was in control—as far as the physical situation, I was in control. I knew I could've gotten out of the house anytime I wanted to. I didn't have to ask Kerry's permission.

"By this time I've realized I'm stabbed—and never having been stabbed, and seeing TV shows and reading books where somebody gets stabbed they immediately die right then and there, I'm very concerned about it. Once the struggle's over—he's calmer—the first thing I say is, 'We've gotta call an ambulance.' That's when he said, 'No, not now,' or 'We can't' or 'You don't understand' or something of that nature. I said, 'What don't I understand?' And he says, 'What I did to Janet.'

"I'd already asked about Janet, as a matter of fact I think I even called her—after he said she was in the front room, I yelled, 'Janet!' And then it all starts clicking in my head, here we are screaming and fighting and—*what*, she's just sitting in the living room? Is she *knitting* or what, you know? That doesn't make sense.

"Because, again, it hasn't really clicked with me, when he was saying, 'See what you made me do,' I thought he was talking about what he *did to me*. 'You made me do *this* to you,' okay? Nothing's really clicking yet—then it's all starting to go . . . she's *in* the living room, but she *hasn't* come out during the fight, I *called*, she *still* hasn't come out, you know . . . and then he told me he beat her.

"I said, 'Well, we've got to go see her.' That's when we threw the knife up on the thing, and we went in—this is after five now, about fifteen minutes maybe since I'd arrived, it's starting to get dark—when we walked into that room, it was real shadowy, it's like she was in a shadow.

"Again, when I looked at her the first time, you could see she was beaten—but it didn't look anything like the pictures at trial, okay? Again, maybe I never thought that she was . . . she was in a position to die from all this.

"I'm going to tell you something that I wasn't going to tell you because you might think I was crazy—*but I thought she was conscious!* Maybe that could just be a perception because I saw her breathing, I saw her laying there—I thought her *eyes* were *open*. But then I only looked at her like click-click. Maybe it was just the way it seemed to me, but that's the way I've always pictured it, that *she was conscious*. But she looked *much worse* in the pictures than what I remember seeing—in fact, the pictures shook me when I saw them, they really did."

A pause, before: "And then he comes in. He's got the bat in his hands, *he hits her again*, and *he hits her again*. . . . I back away. And that's when—he looks like, I don't know, his arms reaching up to the heavens or something, and this *sound*, this screaming, it's like—what can I compare it to? Oh . . . you ever see like an old werewolf movie when they're like . . . at the moon? He's more yelling at the moon like, 'Why is this happening to me?' The epitome of the primal scream.

"He's looking up and everything, and then he just drops the bat, and he sinks to his knees next to her [on her right side]—and, again, I walked over and *picked him up*. It was like picking up a rag, there was nothing to him. I just picked him up and said, 'We've got to call an ambulance.' And my arm's around him and we walk back towards the kitchen when he grabs my arm and says, 'Don't do it. I need some more time before we do anything.' I said, 'Sure, whatever you need.' "

Bill then quickly puts all that in perspective. "Kerry was my *friend,* Janet was my friend's *wife,*" he explains.

When does the bat get back into the den where the police find it? "Not while I was there."

Soon he continues the narrative: "Then we sat in the TV room and we talked—you know, 'You're my friend! You're my friend. I'm sorry, I didn't want to hurt you.' He said that a lot. And 'We've been friends for so long.' I think he asked me, 'Are you still my friend?' I said, 'Yeah, man, I'm your friend.'

"This went on for maybe an hour and a half, two hours, we're just sitting there, and I finally said, 'Kerry, we really need to call an ambulance.' He said, 'Yeah.' He got up and he went in there and called an ambulance, or I thought he called the ambulance, and he came back and we sat and we waited and waited, got up a couple of times and went into the front bedroom to look out the window, there wasn't any ambulance.

"He said he needed more time, 'Just give me some more time.' I said, 'Whatever you want. I'll give you anything you want, man.' Again, more time passed, an hour and a half, two hours, it was around nine-thirty, ten this time, that's when I said, 'Well, I'm going to take control. I'm going to call an ambulance.' He said, 'Yeah.' I said, 'I'm gonna go see Janet, first.' He went and called the ambulance. I went in. That's when I realized she was dead. Again, I don't know—I touched her arm, I remember the feeling, it's horrible, and you *know immediately.* Even though I'd never touched a dead body, I knew at just the touch: *she's dead!*

"I think I let out some some sort of 'Oh, my God!' or something—and there he was, over me, and I just came up and I grabbed him. I was bent down, like in a catcher's stance, I'd just touched her. It was a surge of rage, I came out of the squat and I grabbed him around the throat and literally drove him down the hall. At that time—I think what I was doing was asserting my control. I kind of want to say, 'I would've killed him. I wanted to kill him,' and maybe that's true too, but I think I said, 'All right, you bastard, now we're going to do things my way!'

"It was because she was dead. I hadn't thought far enough ahead to think about 'Oh, she's dead now we're *both* in trouble,' not yet. It was because she was dead; and I might've been just as mad at myself because we sat there and talked while this girl died!

"I couldn't strangle myself, so I'm going to strangle the other person. I guess that's when the guilt set in—I mean, we sat down and talked about softball games and she's sitting in there dying! She may have even heard us talking for all I know!

"Yeah . . . I came up and I grabbed him, and I drove him back, but he had the knife in his hand—he got me twice—we struggled some more, back down the hallway to where we came to rest down there and we both had the knife—we lay there for a while. This time, I never let go of the knife. I held on to it the whole time. It had finally dawned on me that he probably wasn't going to just let me leave. That's why when I finally was able to leave I left on my own—there was no more 'Kerry, let's do this, Kerry, let's do that.' I'm getting out whenever I can. Just the second I felt that he fell asleep, that's when I got out of the house and ran.

"Again, he came into the room with that knife—I didn't know what he had on his mind—whether the knife was meant for Janet, or was meant for me. I caused that altercation. The two stab wounds I got there, I caused. I went after him—maybe he wouldn't have stabbed me. . . ."

On the two chest wounds: "I don't know, maybe I was getting used to being stabbed now: I didn't die from them, I'm not going to die from these either. Because I was stabbed two more times but I still felt as strong as—you know, I didn't feel myself losing anything. Now, I think from the first three I actually did—it may have been something that I was making myself feel, you know. Oh, I'm stabbed, I'm dying. Ahhh! I'm losing strength, I'm losing consciousness, but I wasn't—now with these two, I didn't feel any different."

Then Bill addresses the conspiracy-to-kill-both-their-wives issue and how it was birthed: "At some point I think I'd told him that I was his friend, I would do anything to help him. Now, how he took that, what he thought it to mean, I don't know.

"My rage had subsided. All I wanted to do was get out of the house. And I think I even said it before, too, when we were sitting in the TV room, 'I will do anything to help you through this, you've gotta pay, but I will help you. That's what friends are for.'

"So he told me when we were back in the hall, 'Now that you're helping me, we're a team . . . we're in this together . . . blah, blah, da de da.' But we *never* ever, ever, *ever* discussed covering up Janet's murder—it was never brought up, never. When we were laying back there we started talking some more, that's when I told him my problems with Susan, hadn't seen Matthew in so long.

"We were there and just talking about it and he's saying we're going to get Matthew, and I'm saying, 'Yeah, yeah,' he goes, *'Really, man, we're gonna go do it!* I'm telling you, we're gonna get Matthew. Don't worry about Susan. You want Matthew? We're gonna get Matthew.'

"I guess he was looking for, 'Well, you and me, we're buddies now, we're in this, we're a team, we'll right all these wrongs—we'll go get Matthew. We'll take Matthew.' I said, 'That's not going to work, I don't think Susan's going to allow that.' It was all him talking. We were never going to go over there."

On Ryan's "foot tapping": "It was not so much tapping, as moving, something moving against carpet, it could've been his hand, foot, I don't know, I just said foot. You could hear something going across the carpet.

"What he kept telling me was, don't open the door. He had told me earlier—I asked him where Ryan was, we heard the baby crying—Ryan was in his room; that he'd told Ryan to go to his room and not come out . . . so, when we first heard that sound, he said, 'Don't open the door. Ryan's in there, I don't want him to come out and see this.' "

On his statements, his thought processes: "Here I'm being interviewed by a cop, I know Janet's dead, what am I going to say? 'Yeah, I was in there and . . .' 'How ya know she's dead?' 'Well, I'm standing over her and he hit her in the head.' 'Why didn't you do something?' 'I wanted to help him.' You just *know* you *don't* say these things. You just don't say it.

"I'm not going to be accused of Janet's death—I know that, because *Kerry killed Janet*—I mean, how can he make it anything *other* than that? The police are going to get there, they're going to see Kerry, they're going to see Janet, 'I killed my wife.' Maybe he'll tell 'em *why* he killed his wife. He's going to tell them I was there, for sure. But Kerry killed Janet—you can't make anything other than what it was.

"The only thing I was trying to say—again, I honestly thought that I helped him, and I didn't want *them* to think that I helped him, or to know that I helped him. So when they asked me, 'Well, did you see her?' 'No, I didn't see her.'

"The first thing, when we walked into the hospital, [NOPD Officer John Taylor] said, 'Ah, another drug deal.' I said, 'I don't use drugs.' 'Ah, man, who'd you kill? Or who tried to kill you over some dope?'

"I was trying to tell him what my friend did, but I *really* wanted somebody to contact Susan, just in case this idiot was going over there— because I still don't know what he's thinking. I had Herman call over there.

On his interview by Masson at Charity Hospital: "I've always told people that I felt he was alluding to maybe I had killed Janet—but I felt that he was alluding that I *helped* kill Janet; maybe that was my subconscious.

"Because he was questioning me kind of hard and here I am I'm a victim, but he wasn't questioning me like a victim. He was questioning me like I was a suspect. But I'm not thinking he's questioning me as a murder suspect, but as a *murderer's helper* suspect."

When reminded that it isn't against the law *not* to be a hero: "You could make a case that by my sitting there aiding Kerry, I was helping him commit murder. I thought that anything I said would be used against me—I wasn't going to tell them, 'Yeah, I knew Janet was dead, I tried to help the guy who killed her.'

How did you help him? "I helped him by talking to him. I helped him by not calling the police. I didn't call the police right then and there—if I'd've called the police right then and there, *none of this would be happening now*. So I helped him. *I was helping him.* He said, 'I need more time,' I said all right.

"The thing is, I really felt then that I *was* aiding and abetting"—which carries a twenty-year sentence in Louisiana. "I honestly felt like I aided and abetted Kerry Myers that night; I felt like I aided and abetted in the murder of Janet Myers. I honestly felt I helped him, so to help myself I wasn't going to tell 'em. I honestly didn't think she was going to die, *but* I *knew* she was dead *before* I talked to the police."

On the changed statement: "I think I purposely left it out the first time I said it, but then I didn't see how it could hurt me, and I wanted to tell the truth, so I told them. The only things I *didn't* want to say were things that could hurt me, and that couldn't hurt me, so . . .

"My biggest fear was anybody finding out I helped Kerry. I wasn't afraid to go to trial for Janet's murder, I was afraid of being implicated in *helping* the guy murder her, that was my biggest fear—I know *I didn't murder anyone.*

"From the get-go there were two emotions working, one, this take-care-of-Kerry thing, that's strong; we've also got 'Uh-oh, I'm responsible for this.'

"Can you understand why I couldn't say it that night? And then once I did say what I said, I'm married to it. Looking back, I can say it was wrong. But I had to stay with that. That was it; it's all I have. I mean, how do you say that? That's a lot to say: again, I don't think I could've said it—even though I don't think I said it very well just now—I couldn't have said it *then* as well as I said it just now.

"A lot of what I did was *because* it was Kerry, I wouldn't have done the same thing for someone else, but because it was Kerry—if it was somebody else, 'I ain't giving you no time, we're gonna call for an ambulance now, we're going to call the police now.' But because it's Kerry, it's *make sure he's all right.*"

"He had to go to the bathroom," Kerry Myers is saying. It is the middle of March 1993, and we're in a very small "call-out" room at Angola State Penitentiary; it could very well be our last visit together.

"And he forced me to walk with—ahead of him. Just like he was going to force me to walk ahead of him when he said he was going to leave. Now, it was already dark, okay . . . I didn't see her body. Did I even look? I knew she was in there . . . I knew she was in that room, from what I'd heard. Could I have seen her if I'd looked? I don't even remember—I honestly don't remember. Did I know she was in there? Yes, I did because I heard her. Did I *want* to look? Was I *afraid* to look? Because I *didn't* believe him? Or I was *afraid* to believe him? Based on what was happening that night, maybe I *wanted* to shut it out. *I don't remember.* Was it the darkness? Was it my physical state and my mental, emotional state all combined? Did I not *want* to look? *I don't know.*

"I mean, I *knew* she was in there because I heard her. He even basically *told* me she was in there, because he said she was in there and he tied her up. But did I believe him? The whole night I struggled with that. Do I believe what this guy is telling me? *Can* I believe it as true? *Are* they all dead? Am I sitting here for *nothing*? Should I be getting up *trying* to do *something*? Or . . . are they all right and if I do get up and do something and I die, is it *everybody* dies? Is this the situation? *I don't know* what the situation is. Yes, I'm scared—I felt . . .''

There is a pause, though not a long one; Kerry Myers speaks rapidly, however, with the enunciation skills of an ex-broadcaster.

"Again, I've explained this to you before, I felt ashamed of my fear . . . *to me.* Did I *paralyze* myself with fear? At times was I *more* afraid for *myself*—I thought a lot about my family—but while I was fighting, and while I was confronted, was I more afraid for myself? Probably. Because I was *directly* involved—it was happening to *me.*

"I possibly even *colored*—as I look back, I can't tell you where, or how, or what—but I possibly colored some of the events in my own mind to where I didn't make myself look like I was *so* afraid, or I was *so* fearful, or acted *less* like a man, because I heard all these things from the very beginning: you know, 'Why didn't you do this? Why didn't you do that?'

"And I felt some shame; 'Well, why *didn't* I do this?' Well, 'My God, don't I *know* what was happening to me?' You know? And these things start sticking—it's like, 'Well, I couldn't!' Yeah, I was scared, but . . . but 'I couldn't.' I start thinking, 'Could I? Maybe. I don't know.' It's an emotional thing, a psychological thing, that I've always . . . I didn't lie about it, but I . . . but I *may have* . . . it was like a bad dream that I just wanted to wake up from!"

Some several minutes later and many words expended further along the lines of external stimuli producing inward doubt, Kerry Myers takes a rather long pause, then looks up, his eyes dead-on, large, so very plaintive, and asks:

"Is it possible . . . is it—could I, *could* I have done this and blocked it all out?"

Then, perhaps two hours later, still in that little room with only a small table and two chairs, Kerry is saying, "I don't know . . . I've thought about it, I've thought about some of the things I've read . . . based on what I know about them, what I've read about them, what I've been told about them . . . it has to be a deep emotional conflict that I've dealt with all this time."

What he is talking about is an explanation for his failed polygraph exams. "It's in my mind, it's—what you've told me today"—the coroner now saying Janet probably could have lived—"even further emphasizes it: *Did* I act irresponsibly? Did I *let* her die? *Could* I have saved her? It makes it even *worse* . . . none of this would've been necessary—*I wouldn't be in jail.*

"And I've dealt with—again—the comments . . . the under-the-breath comments, the behind-the-back comments—'Why didn't he do this or that?' 'If he was a real man . . . ?" Even my own friends, 'If it've been me, I'd've done this.' My own father, 'I'm a Marine, I'd've kicked his ass . . .' Yeah, that's fine, if that *wasn't* you. Except . . . *except* my sense of responsibility *to my family*. That I feel now, that I've always felt—that it was *my* family, it was *my* job always and everywhere to take care of them . . . *and I failed*.

"I've struggled with it, and struggled with it, and struggled with it—and knowing that I heard her and that she was alive when I walked in . . . I don't know, I mean, *I don't know*. But it doesn't go away; it's *never* going away. And I wish it *would* go away. Just like I wished the damn night would've gone away when I was there, sitting on that floor wishing it would *just go away* . . . close my eyes and go away, close my eyes and *die*, and it would be over without having to go through it anymore!

"But can you imagine what it feels like to go through these two days of intense grilling, hooked up to the machine, nervous, scared, and then be told by this lady that *I killed Janet*?"

What Kerry Myers is referring to is a very special polygraph examination he underwent in the summer of 1991, more than a year and a half after his conviction and incarceration. Special in the sense that, upon Kerry's insistence and Clifford agreeing to foot the bill, Ralph S. Whalen, Jr., arguably one of a handful of the most respected criminal defense specialists in southeastern Louisiana, who took on the Myers defense when Kerry discharged and then sued Wiley Beevers after the 1990 trial, brought down a woman polygraph specialist whose primary client is the CIA. Special in the sense that her examination is structured to go beyond just "deception indicated," indeed is actually probative and designed to be a determiner of fact.

As reported to Mr. Whalen and his client, Kerry Myers, it was the conclusion of this woman that "Myers and Myers alone struck his wife's face with a baseball bat—*but he did not hurt Ryan*."

"Study crime scene pictures," Dr. Lee had told us almost three years before, just as he was about to board a flight back to Connecticut. "Study hard. Look hard. And keep looking; it there. Picture maybe distort, not lie. Then ask everybody all the questions. Everybody who know anything about the peoples. When do that, come see me. We talk about what maybe really happen."

Dr. Henry Lee, of course, is true to his word.

"This man not swing bat—this man *dancing*," Dr. Lee says one hot New England summer afternoon as he refers to a photograph of Bill's blue jeans. "Maybe go crazy, see what he see . . . maybe he even try stop, that I don't know. But bloodstain all directions, left, right, front, back, up and down. That mean he not only move around but change levels . . . turn around but get up and down too, bend at knee . . . impact spatter project, make those stain."

The doctor is not at all surprised by Bill's apparently "final" version of what physically happened in the house that night.

The time lapse, or lapses, between beatings is absolutely consistent with what he believes the physical evidence supports.

That Janet moved her head protractedly from side to side is evidenced to him by all of the fine-line brush-pattern bloodstains on the inside of both of Janet's forearms and on the baseboard behind her head.

That Kerry was most likely the sole "bat man" certainly isn't news to Dr. Lee. "Where the type A blood and medium-velocity impact spatter on Kerry?" the doctor asks rhetorically. The answers, of course, are the left shoe, the lower left pant leg, the left thigh, and the left shirt-pocket area. "Where cast-off from bloody object go up and down?" The left top and upper back shoulder of Kerry's shirt. "All consistent with left-hand person swinging bloody object—like maybe baseball bat. No such pattern on Fontanille . . . many, many pattern on Fontanille, but none consistent with raise bat up and down."

As far as Dr. Lee is concerned, there is only one—perhaps even significant, small though it be—particularly esoteric question possibly left unaccounted for in Bill's story: the presence of maybe a dozen cast-off spatters in the southeast corner of the living room, which in almost all certainty have to be the result of someone swinging the bloody bat at least once from the *opposite* direction, in other words, facing toward the foyer and *away* from the spot where Janet came to die on the living room floor.

Dr. Lee also is not surprised to hear that Bill doesn't remember Janet looking as disfigured as she appeared in the photographs he'd seen at trial. In fact, the chance of there having been even a *third* beating gets quite favorable odds from Dr. Lee—it being the beating of a corpse, however, which is "consistent with the tiny-tiny impact spatter" on Kerry. With the heart no longer pumping, striking the now only oozing, pooling, coagulating blood would produce fewer and much smaller impact spatters.

Of course Dr. Lee just *has* to ask, "But who and why baby kidney beat up?"

Appendix

Statement of William A. Fontanille

MASSON: The following statement is being taken from William A. Fontanille, white male, date of birth 8/23/55, who resides at 2220 Northbrook, Gretna, La. Statement is being taken by Sergeant Robert Masson, Jefferson Parish Sheriff's Office Homicide Unit, on Saturday, February 25th, 1984 at the Jefferson Parish Sheriff's Office Detective Bureau. This statement begins at approximately 2:50 A.M. Mr. Fontanille, were you advised of your rights?

FONTANILLE: Yes sir, I was.

MASSON: A little bit louder.

FONTANILLE: I'm sorry, yes sir, I was.

MASSON: Did you sign a standard Rights form?

FONTANILLE: Yes sir, I did.

MASSON: Are you willing to make a statement at this time?

FONTANILLE: Yes sir.

MASSON: How much education do you have?

FONTANILLE: I have a degree in Marketing from S.L.U.

MASSON: Where are you currently employed?

FONTANILLE: I'm unemployed.

MASSON: What type of work do you do?

FONTANILLE: I work for McDermott in the shipping end of it.

MASSON: How long have you been unemployed?

FONTANILLE: Since July of 83.

MASSON: Are you married?

FONTANILLE: I'm separated.

MASSON: What is your wife's name?

FONTANILLE: Susan Fontanille.

MASSON: Where is she residing now?

FONTANILLE: She's currently living at 2221 St. Nick in Algiers with her parents.

MASSON: Do you have any children?

FONTANILLE: I have a 14 month old son named Matthew.

MASSON: Do you know Kerry Myers?

FONTANILLE: Yes sir, I do.

MASSON: How long have you known Kerry?

FONTANILLE: Probably since junior or senior year of high school.

MASSON: What high school did you go to?

FONTANILLE: Archbishop Shaw.

MASSON: Do you know his wife?

FONTANILLE: Yes I do.

MASSON: What's his wife's name?

FONTANILLE: Janet.

MASSON: How long have you known Janet?

FONTANILLE: Five to six years.

MASSON: When did you last see Kerry?

FONTANILLE: Thursday night, Friday morning, Thursday and Friday.

MASSON: Approximately what time did you see him?

FONTANILLE: I first saw him around 4:00 P.M. Thursday to around 2:00 A.M. Friday morning.

MASSON: Where did you see him?

FONTANILLE: At his home in Woodmere.

MASSON: Why did you go to his house?

FONTANILLE: I had gone over there to pick up a baseball bat that I had been using as a cane. I had left it there the previous night.

MASSON: Why did you leave the baseball bat at his house?

FONTANILLE: I had gone over to his house Wednesday night. We were gonna go play basketball together and I arrived at his home at about 7:30. I left the bat there. Two other friends picked us up. When they brought us back to Kerry's house I just got in my car and left, and just left the bat in his house.

MASSON: How many times were you at Kerry's house on Wednesday?

FONTANILLE: Twice.

MASSON: What time did you get there the first time?

FONTANILLE: Around 1:00 P.M. in the afternoon.

MASSON: How long did you stay?

FONTANILLE: Stayed till about 5:00.

MASSON: Was anyone there when you got there?

FONTANILLE: Janet was there and the two children.

MASSON: What time did Kerry get home?

FONTANILLE: He came home about 3:30, between 3:30 and 4:00 I guess, stayed for about 45 minutes, went back to the office. And then I left before he came back again.

MASSON: What took place between you and Janet?

FONTANILLE: We sat down. We were talking about my separation from my wife and she became very comforting to me. And I suppose I was very appreciative at that. And we ended up in, well, I'm gonna say, we didn't go to bed. We made love in the baby's room. We were looking out the window while we were doing what we did.

MASSON: Why were you looking out the window?

FONTANILLE: We were afraid Kerry might come home. On Wednesdays she says that she's never sure what time he'll come home.

MASSON: How many times have you been together with Janet?

FONTANILLE: Under circumstances like I just spoke of never before. Never.

MASSON: You've never had sexual relations with her before?

FONTANILLE: No sir, never.

MASSON: Whose idea was it to have sexual relations?

FONTANILLE: It was mutual, sir.

MASSON: Was Kerry aware of your intimacy with his wife?

FONTANILLE: I can only speculate and say he was. He did not say anything to me other than he did what he had to do. He didn't accuse me of anything.

MASSON: When was the last time before Wednesday that you were at the Myers house?

FONTANILLE: Tuesday.

MASSON: How often do you go over to their house?

FONTANILLE: Not very often at all. I hadn't seen either one since before Thanksgiving and I can't remember the last time I was at their house. Not that often.

MASSON: Why have you been avoiding them?

FONTANILLE: I've been embarrassed about being unemployed. I've been avoiding all my friends. Something I don't like to talk about.

MASSON: What time did you get over to the Myers house on Thursday?

FONTANILLE: Between 3:30 and 4:00, probably closer to 4:00.

MASSON: Where did you park your car?

FONTANILLE: I parked it down the block.

MASSON: In which direction?

FONTANILLE: Going away from Lapalco.

MASSON: Why did you park down the block?

FONTANILLE: I didn't want to park my car in front of the house and have Kerry drive by. I wasn't sure if he expected that Janet and I had done what we did and I didn't want to cause any trouble. I figured if I parked my car down the block, I'd just go in, get my bat and leave. And if he did just drive by without stopping he wouldn't, he wouldn't stop he'd just drive by but if he saw my car then he might suspect something. I parked my car. When I walked to the house Kerry was there already. So I figured what the heck that he can't expect anything. So I knocked on the door and went in.

MASSON: Explain what happened when you got inside the residence?

FONTANILLE: Kerry opened the door for me. I guess I took two or three steps and then he hit me from the rear. At the time it seemed like I was stabbed twenty times in the back. It, it's three wounds back there. I guess some of them were just punches. I ran into the room where they keep their television set. Leaning against the love seat was the baseball bat. I picked it up. Kerry came into the room and we looked at each other. I said, "Kerry, why are you doing this to me. I don't understand." I was, I was hysterical. I thought I was dying. He just said, "I'm doing what I've got to do." Said, "I'm doing what I've got to do." He came at me again with the knife and I started swinging the baseball bat. I don't know how many times I hit him. I know I did hit him in the arm with the baseball bat cause he later said I broke his arm. I lost control of the bat while we were struggling cause I was more concerned with keeping that knife away from me than anything else. We struggled around. I was picking up anything I could find, cup, an ashtray, anything, little glass objects that I was hitting with it. Finally, we both fell to the floor. Neither one of us could get control of the knife. We both had our hands on it. And we stayed there, I was hysterical. I just kept asking Kerry to please let me go, please let me go. He kept telling me I didn't understand, just to be quiet while he thought things out. We stayed in that position I guess for 45 minutes or so. I kept saying, "Kerry, I think I'm dying." So finally he told me if we got up he wouldn't hurt me anymore, he'd just let me be. So he got up. He sat on the sofa and I sat on the floor. And we sat there again for an hour without saying a word. Then he turned the tv set on. We watched television from around 7:00 till 11:00, 11:30, I don't know. During that time he allowed me to get up a couple of times to go get water out of the kitchen. I tried to call an ambulance while I was in the kitchen once. He stopped me from doing that. I tried to find a knife of my own in one of the drawers but again I was too afraid to do anything cause I didn't want him to pull the knife on me again. I was still, still thought I was in a lot of trouble physically. Around 10:00 or so he agreed that he wouldn't hurt me anymore and that he would call an ambulance. And he went to the phone and made, dialed, and I thought he was speaking to a hospital, apparently he wasn't. We waited and waited. He allowed me to get up twice and go to one of the bedrooms and look out the window to see if the ambulance was there, which I guess was just to keep me calmed down, I don't know. Between 11:00 and 11:30, I don't know what time it was. I know Starsky and Hutch was on tv. That's the only thing I can remember. I said, "Kerry, I got to go to the bathroom very bad." I got up and he got up behind me and I was walking toward the hall and he lunged at me again with the knife and we started struggling. We struggled down the hall. I was stabbed twice more, and apparently he was stabbed too. Although when I asked him if he was stabbed he told me he wasn't. We came to rest at the end of the hall toward the bathroom. Again each of us having control of the knife. And again it was just more of the same. I was just begging that he let me go. I was really convinced that I was in trouble now cause the two chest wounds were both fairly deep. Then he started talking about he's got problems that I don't know anything about and that I would never know. So I started telling him about my problems, how I'm separated from my wife, how I might lose the house that I just bought. I haven't seen my son since December, which shook him up quite a bit about not seeing my son. And he told me that he would help me get my son back, that we could go to my wife's parents house and get my son without hurting anyone, just scaring them. So I agreed with him. I said, "That's a real good idea." So we made plans to go there the next morning and get him. And we were gonna wait in the hall, each of us holding the knife so we couldn't do any more damage to each other until it was time for us to leave. I guess we were there in the hallway for two hours when I, when I felt that his grip on the knife was loosening up. And when it did I took off down the hall. I guess I had taken about three or four steps and I heard him coming behind me. I went out the front door. He followed me and shouted something out the front door that, I couldn't make out what it was. I was running too hard. I was too scared. I never did see Janet or the children although I did hear the infant, the little girl crying in one of the rooms. Also, when we were laying back there he was looking under the door into his bedroom, said that Ryan was in there. He didn't want Ryan to come out and see what had happened. He asked that, when he asked me, when he saw Ryan move if I would hold the door and not let Ryan out, just hold the door where he couldn't get out. There was a couple of times when he asked me to do that. That's pretty much what I remember, sir.

MASSON: Which bedroom was Ryan in?

FONTANILLE: He was in Kerry and Janet's bedroom.

MASSON: Could you see under the door?

FONTANILLE: No sir, I never did look. I never did look under the door.

MASSON: Why did he want you to hold the door?

FONTANILLE: He said that he didn't want Ryan to come out and see what had happened. So while he was looking under the door whenever Ryan moved, and he was moving cause I could hear him, he asked that I hold the door.

MASSON: Was Ryan crying?

FONTANILLE: No sir, I never heard him cry.

MASSON: Did he say anything?

FONTANILLE: No sir, I didn't hear anything like that, just heard movement.

MASSON: Can Ryan talk?

FONTANILLE: Oh, yes sir.

MASSON: Did you see the other baby?

FONTANILLE: No sir, I just heard her crying.

MASSON: Was the door to the other baby's room open or closed?

FONTANILLE: It was closed but I don't think the, the bolt was locked, you know, it was, it was shut without being locked, know what I mean.

MASSON: Did you ever see Janet at all?

FONTANILLE: No sir, I, I heard her for about the first two hours I was there, what I assumed was Janet, a wheezing noise. I, I never did see her.

MASSON: What was Janet wearing Wednesday when you saw her?

FONTANILLE: She had some type of leotards on.

MASSON: What color?

FONTANILLE: They were white, the leotards were white. And I think she was wearing shorts or something. I don't, I can't remember, sir. Oh, I take that back. She had, the top was black, the top was black and the leotards that went down her legs were white. That's what she had on. It was a strange outfit.

MASSON: What kind of car do you have?

FONTANILLE: I have an 81 Toyota Celica.

MASSON: What color is it?

FONTANILLE: Dark brown.

MASSON: How were you dressed?

FONTANILLE: On which day, sir?

MASSON: Thursday.

FONTANILLE: I had a pair of blue jeans on and a blue Izod sweater, pair of tennis shoes.

MASSON: How was Kerry dressed?

FONTANILLE: He had a tie on. About the only thing I can remember. I think he had dressed to go to work or was coming back from work. He wasn't casually dressed or anything like that.

MASSON: At any time while you were there did he check on the children?

FONTANILLE: No sir, he never left me alone.

MASSON: Did he ever walk by any of the other doors to the den?

FONTANILLE: No sir.

MASSON: Did you see any guns?

FONTANILLE: There was a rifle, a shotgun, that was on the loveseat when I came in that we both wrestled for and it ended up on the floor. Neither one of us, you know, do anything with it.

MASSON: Do you know if it was loaded?

FONTANILLE: He told me it wasn't loaded.

MASSON: Did you bring any ammunition for the gun to the house?

FONTANILLE: No sir, he had three shells that were on the, on the rack where he kept the gun cause the previous night I had tried to juggle them. So I know he had three up there. I don't know if it was loaded or not.

MASSON: Did you ever go in any of the bedrooms?

FONTANILLE: I went into the first bedroom twice during the night cause he had told me he called an ambulance and when I heard doors slam I asked if I could see if it was an ambulance. And twice he let me go in the first bedroom and look out the window. But there wasn't any ambulance. Now, I was in Janet's bedroom the day before. I got some money out of her drawer. She had asked that I go to Wendy's with her, and I said, "I don't have any money". And she was getting dressed in the bathroom in her bedroom. She said, "There's some money in that drawer." So I don't know which drawer I opened up. There was a five and some ones. I took the five and left the ones in there.

MASSON: Took it out of her dresser, a desk, or chest of drawers?

FONTANILLE: It was on the, when you walk into the doors immediately to the right. I don't know if it was a dresser or what it was. Those were the only two bedrooms I, well, to be honest with you I was in all three bedrooms cause we made love in the infant's bedroom.

MASSON: Did Janet ever talk to you about any problems she was having with Kerry?

FONTANILLE: She told me when we were speaking about my marriage, and she said they had the same little problems like everyone else has, and that there were occasions when they thought they weren't going to make it either. But you get, she was trying to comfort me I'm sure, told me you get past it and it all works out. But she did indicate that they had the same problems that any other couples had.

MASSON: What kind of baseball bat did you have?

FONTANILLE: It was an aluminum bat, softball bat.

MASSON: What color was it?

FONTANILLE: Green and silver, I believe, green and silver.

MASSON: What color handle does it have?

FONTANILLE: Black rubber handle.

MASSON: Where do you normally keep this bat?

FONTANILLE: Well, normally I just keep it in the closet in the garage at home. I been using it the last couple of weeks as sort of like a cane cause my back was hurting. So I just been taking it with me where ever I went.

MASSON: Have you ever kept it in the car?

FONTANILLE: Oh yes sir, yes sir.

MASSON: Did you have the bat with you Thursday when you went over to the house?

FONTANILLE: No sir, I did not. I had left it there the previous night.

MASSON: Did you have the bat with you Wednesday when you went to the house?

FONTANILLE: Yes sir, I was at the house twice Wednesday and I had the bat with me both times.

MASSON: When you went to the house Tuesday, did you have the bat with you?

FONTANILLE: Yes sir, I did.

MASSON: Did you go to the house Monday?

FONTANILLE: No sir, I didn't.

MASSON: What time did you get to the house Tuesday?

FONTANILLE: I, it must have been late in the afternoon, around 5:00 because Kerry was home. He was home from work already.

MASSON: How long did you stay?

FONTANILLE: Oh, till around 7:00 and then they were going out to eat or leaving to get something to eat. I thought I was keeping them so I left.

MASSON: What kind of knife did Kerry have?

FONTANILLE: It was a (INAUDIBLE) kitchen knife. I never really saw it. It was about six inches in length, I think the blade, maybe longer.

MASSON: What color was it?

FONTANILLE: I couldn't tell you, sir, I don't know.

MASSON: What kind of handle did it have?

FONTANILLE: It looked like a wooden, it felt like a wooden handle. I did grab on to it for awhile, felt like it was made out of wood.

MASSON: You mentioned some cups earlier. What color were the cups?

FONTANILLE: Well, a cup that I hit him with was either, I think it was tan and had some kind of liquid when I hit cause the liquid splattered all over. It might have been coffee or something in it. And I picked up something that was gold, and it was, cause we were, we had fell on the love seat and the love seat moved and it moved in front of the counter going to the kitchen. And they had little knickknacks up on the counter and I was just grabbing for anything I could, and just swinging, hitting him with it.

MASSON: Did they have anything on the love seat?

FONTANILLE: The, the gun was on the love seat. When I, when I walked in the baseball bat was leaning against the love seat and the gun was sitting on top of it. I think that was all that was on the love seat. And the gun somehow wound up on the floor up against the, I think over by the tv set, right across from the tv set.

MASSON: How was Janet killed?

FONTANILLE: To this day I don't know. No one's ever told me. I didn't know she was killed until this afternoon. My mother told me.

MASSON: How was the baby injured?

FONTANILLE: Again, I don't know. I do not know.

MASSON: Did you and Kerry enter any type of agreement to harm your wives?

FONTANILLE: No sir, absolutely not.

MASSON: Have you ever heard Kerry threaten his wife?

FONTANILLE: No sir, I didn't, no.

MASSON: Has she ever, Janet, has she ever spoke to you about Kerry abusing her?

FONTANILLE: Before they were married, over the last few years to be quite honest I haven't been that close with Kerry Myers. I mean we played softball together and that's been about the extension of our relationship. Before they were married he abused her. I'm pretty sure he hit her several times. I know he did damage, physical damage to a trailer they were living in when they were in college. And I know he put her out on the highway one time, dropped her off on the Interstate.

MASSON: How did she get home that time?

FONTANILLE: We were coming back from a softball game and a friend was following a car behind Kerry's and stopped and picked her up.

MASSON: How long ago were you and your wife separated?

FONTANILLE: July of 83.

MASSON: When you were separated what happened to your house?

FONTANILLE: I was very upset and I caused quite a bit of physical damage to the house. I hit some walls and tore up some furniture.

MASSON: What did you do with your wife's clothing?

FONTANILLE: I put them out for the trash man to pick up, sir.

MASSON: Did the police ever come to your house?

FONTANILLE: No sir, no sir.

MASSON: Do you have any utilities connected to your house?

FONTANILLE: At this time no.

MASSON: Who pays the house note on your house?

FONTANILLE: Right now my wife is.

MASSON: Where does she work?

FONTANILLE: She works for Texaco.

MASSON: What's her occupation?

FONTANILLE: I think she's in the, she works as a word processor. The last I spoke with her she said that's what she was doing.

MASSON: Have you ever attempted suicide?

FONTANILLE: Once I took some pills.

MASSON: What kind of pills?

FONTANILLE: Sleeping pills. I was in a very depressed mood. It was three days after my wife had left and that's the only time, I had spoken of attempting suicide to my wife but it was just to get her to just to shake her up a little bit.

MASSON: Did you ever take your son Matthew from your wife?

FONTANILLE: Once, the day before his birthday. He was at my mother's house.

MASSON: What date was that?

FONTANILLE: December 22nd. And I went over to see him and I didn't bring him back when I should have. I kept him I guess around twelve hours longer than I should have before I brought him back.

MASSON: Why did you bring him back?

FONTANILLE: Well, it wasn't right for me to take him to begin with and I knew that. And I, there's really no place I could go. I wasn't going to leave, I wasn't going to leave and go any place with him. The only thing I could have done was bring him back. I just wanted to spend some more time with him. I was feeling that he didn't know who I was. So I wanted to at least see him on his birthday. The next day was his birthday so, that's the whole story.

MASSON: How many injuries do you have?

FONTANILLE: I have one wound below my heart, one wound to the left of my heart, three in my back and I have two fingers that are stitched up.

MASSON: How long were you confined to the hospital?

FONTANILLE: All totalled about twenty hours I was at the hospital, Jo Ellen Smith and Charity. I'm due back again this morning.

MASSON: Had you been drinking before you went to the Myers house on Thursday?

FONTANILLE: No sir.

MASSON: What about Wednesday?

FONTANILLE: No sir.

MASSON: Was Janet drinking?

FONTANILLE: On Wednesday she was drinking Kalua, Kalua, I think that's what it was. She had a small glass of Kalua.

MASSON: Was she intoxicated?

FONTANILLE: No sir.

MASSON: On any of the days that you saw Kerry had he been drinking?

FONTANILLE: Not that I could tell, no sir.

MASSON: Do you know how Janet was killed?

FONTANILLE: No sir, I don't.

MASSON: Do you know who killed her?

FONTANILLE: I know it wasn't me and I know Kerry Myers was in the house when I got there. I can only assume he did it.

MASSON: Did Kerry ever make any accusations about your having an affair with his wife?

FONTANILLE: No sir, he didn't say one word other than he did what he had to do.

MASSON: Is there anything you wish to add to this statement at this time?

FONTANILLE: Other than the fact I did not do it. I had no reason. There was no motive. And despite what any evidence. I don't even know what kind of evidence could be pointing my way. The truth is the truth. And I just told the truth, sir. It's got to hold up because I didn't do it.

MASSON: Were you forced to give this statement?

FONTANILLE: No sir.

MASSON: Were you threatened in any way or coerced in any way into giving this statement?

FONTANILLE: No sir, no.

MASSON: This statement is completed at approximately 3:20 A.M. on the same date.

Statement of Kerry Myers

MASSON: The following statement is taken from Kerry Myers, white male, date of birth 9/10/56, currently resides at 796 Deerfield, Gretna, La., telephone number 393-8609. Statement is being taken by Sergeant Robert Masson, Jefferson Parish Sheriff's Office Homicide Unit. Statement begins at approximately 1:55 P.M. on Wednesday, March 14, 1984. Statement is being taken at the Jefferson Parish Sheriff's Office Detective Bureau. Also present during the interview is Mr. Jack Rau, attorney representing Mr. Myers. Mr. Myers, what is your previous address?

MYERS: 2232 Litchwood Lane, Harvey.

MASSON: And how long did you live there?

MYERS: Two and a half years.

MASSON: Are you married?

MYERS: Yes.

MASSON: What is your wife's name?

MYERS: Janet.

MASSON: Do you have any children?

MYERS: Two.

MASSON: What are their names and ages?

MYERS: Sarah, who is ten weeks now, and Ryan, who is 2½.

MASSON: Do you know a subject by the name of William Fontanille?

MYERS: Yes.

MASSON: How long have you known William?

MYERS: About 12 years.

MASSON: Are you presently employed?

MYERS: Yes.

MASSON: Where are you employed?

MYERS: Airdreco Inc.

MASSON: How much education do you have?

MYERS: Four years of college.

MASSON: What college?

MYERS: Two at L.S.U. in Baton Rouge and two at Nicholls State University. I majored in Communications.

MASSON: How long were you married?

MYERS: It will be five, would have been five years this June.

MASSON: What is the name and address of your nearest relative?

MYERS: Clifford Myers, 796 Deerfield Rd., Gretna.

MASSON: Do you remember where you met Bill Fontanille?

MYERS: High school.

MASSON: Which high school was that?

MYERS: Archbishop Shaw.

MASSON: Were you very close friends with Bill Fontanille?

MYERS: Not in high school.

MASSON: When did you start becoming close friends with Bill?

MYERS: It was after I graduated from high school and we started playing softball with a group of, group of friends who, I guess you could call it a close group of friends. I don't think anybody individually or maybe there was a few people individually closer than others. I would have to say if anybody was the least close to anybody it was, you know, Billy was the person that everybody was least close to. But it was a close knit group of friends.

MASSON: What other people are in that close group of friends?

MYERS: Mike Price, Curtis Jordan, Glen Shirts.

MASSON: When's the last time you saw Bill Fontanille?

MYERS: The Thursday night that he attacked me.

MASSON: Do you remember the date?

MYERS: I think it was February 23rd.

MASSON: Had you seen Bill the day before?

MYERS: Yes.

MASSON: What time did you see Bill on the day before?

MYERS: I saw him twice that day. I saw him late in the afternoon, about 4:30 and I saw him again that night cause we went to play basketball.

MASSON: The first time you saw Bill, was he at your house when you arrived home?

MYERS: Yes he was.

MASSON: Was there anyone else at your house?

MYERS: My wife and my children.

MASSON: On that Wednesday when you saw Bill, did he have a baseball bat with him?

MYERS: Yes.

MASSON: Can you describe the bat?

MYERS: It was a green Easton bat, baseball bat, green and silver I believe it was with a black rubber handle and a black plastic cap on the top. He played baseball with it many times.

MASSON: How long did you stay at the house the first time?

MYERS: Twenty minutes to a half hour.

MASSON: Was Bill there when you got back?

MYERS: No.

MASSON: Did you see Bill's car?

MYERS: No.

MASSON: What kind of car does he have?

MYERS: A Toyota Corrolla Hatchback, brown.

MASSON: Did he tell you how he got to your house?

MYERS: He said his sister dropped him off, said her car was being serviced and she was using his car.

MASSON: What is his sister's name?

MYERS: Angela Fontanille, I believe, been a long time since I've seen her.

MASSON: Prior to Wednesday, when was the last time you saw Bill?

MYERS: Tuesday night he came over to my house. He showed up about 6:00 Tuesday night, rang my doorbell. That was the first time I had seen him since November of 83.

MASSON: You were home at that time?

MYERS: Yes I was.

MASSON: Did you see his car at that time?

MYERS: Yes I did.

MASSON: Where did he park his car?

MYERS: In front of the house.

MASSON: Did he have the baseball bat with him at that time?

MYERS: Yes he did.

MASSON: Did he tell you why he had the bat with him?

MYERS: He said he hurt his back and he was using it for a walking cane.

MASSON: Alright, going back to Wednesday, when Bill came back to the house that night, how did he get to the house?

MYERS: He drove his car to my house.

MASSON: Where did he park his car?

MYERS: In front of my house.

MASSON: Did he have the bat with him at that time?

MYERS: He did not come in the house with the bat. He was dressed to play basketball in shorts and tennis, did not have the bat with him.

MASSON: Did he come into your house?

MYERS: Yes he did.

MASSON: How long was he at your house before he left to play basketball?

MYERS: Ten minutes.

MASSON: How'd you go play basketball?

MYERS: Mike Price and Jimmy Jordan came and picked us up in Mike's truck.

MASSON: When was the next time that you saw Bill after Wednesday night?

MYERS: After Wednesday night, when I walked into my house Thursday afternoon and he attacked me.

MASSON: Okay, why don't you describe what happened when you got home Thursday. About what time did you get home?

MYERS: I got home approximately 3:30, 3:45.

MASSON: Did you see Bill's car?

MYERS: No.

MASSON: What happened when you got into the house?

MYERS: As I walked into the house, I unlocked the door. The door was locked. I unlocked the door and walked in, more or less not paying attention to anything. I had reached around to turn and close the door behind me and take my keys out of the door. And as I did I took a step in. As I did that, took a step in, I heard my name being screamed and Bill jumped out of the living room area with a baseball bat, swinging it at me.

MASSON: What happened from that point?

MYERS: He took a couple of swings. I raised my arms up to try, try to block the swings and deflected at least one or both of them partially cause the swings were at my head. And one of them, both of them I believe hit my arms and deflected into my shoulder or possibly into my head. And broke my left arm on one of the first initial swings. As that happened, the first thing I did was stumble into the open area of the den, stumble back into the den where he continued to come at me with the bat and take a couple of swings. I don't know if he, he actually got any clean hits again with the bat at that time cause I kept trying to get close enough to grab the bat and may have inhibited a complete swing. But he probably did catch me on the arms or on, you know, somewhere about, it was a deflection for at least one, once or twice more until I got, actually got a hand on the bat and held him from rearing back and swinging at me again. And as that happened he wrapped one of the arms around my neck and started grabbing things off the counters, a candle lamp and a coffee mug and a glass candle holder or vase, candle vase. I don't know. And my table lamp, and everything he, seemed like he could reach his hands on and try to smash it over my head, and as he continued to squeeze me around the neck. And I was screaming at him, "What are you doing? What are you trying to do?" And he kept saying, "Everybody's trying to get me. You out to get me. Everybody wants to have me put away," you know, "You're just like everybody else. You want to get me." And I started screaming at him, "I don't want to, I don't want to hurt you. I don't want to do anything but I'm gonna bleed to death. You gotta stop. You're gonna kill me." And I was screaming at him, pleading with him to, to stop trying to hurt me. And eventually he stopped, he held on to me but eventually he stopped trying to, to, to injure me and he just held on to me, maybe 15, 20 minutes. And I kept asking if my family was alright because I knew my wife and my children were home. I was hearing some moans coming from the living room. And I kept asking if my wife was okay. And he kept saying she was fine, he had her tied up, that he didn't hurt her. And I asked him about my kids. And he said they were fine and they were both the rooms, and my little girl was in her room sleeping and my little boy was in the room and he closed the door and told him not to come out, and he probably, he said he probably fell asleep, you know, that he was frightened and he probably fell asleep. And he got, he became very irritated and agitated and seemed maybe confused to a bit. And he kept saying, "I've got to think. I've got to calm down. I gotta think. I gotta think of what to do." And I kept saying, "Let me go check on my family, let me, you know, leave, let me call an ambulance or you call an ambulance or something." And he kept saying, "No, I can't leave until it gets dark cause I can't go outside like this." And then finally he let me, you know, he laid me down on the floor sitting up against the arm of the sofa. And he sat in a, in a chair right next to me with the bat in his hands, threatening me not to get up or to try anything, that he had to think what to do next, and he didn't know what to do next, and he had to calm himself down and think. He sat there until it got dark basically in the chair, just looked like a time bomb, you know, just the way he kept mumbling to himself and trying to think. Occasionally I'd ask him if my family was okay and to call an ambulance, let us get some help and to leave so we can get some help. Every time I'd ask him he'd become very agitated. And when it got dark I asked him again, I said, "You said you would leave when it got dark." And he said he couldn't leave yet, he couldn't leave yet, he had to think, he wasn't sure. And then he, as it got dark he said he wanted to watch a particular program and he, Magnum P.I. And there was a remote control unit on the chair and he changed the channel. The program wasn't quite on yet but came on shortly. And it was dark. And the only light on in the house was the tv which was on the whole time. And he sat in that chair, again warned me not to move. I was bleeding from my head. My arm, at that point I knew my arm was broken and I was, I was dazed, if, if I could call it anything. My head was kind of fuzzy. And I, I thought of trying to do something to, to get out of the situation but I, at the time I, the only thing I could think of is if I did try to do something and I did it wrong that he would kill me and if my family was alright he might kill them too. At that time if I did the wrong thing he might, you know, go and kill everybody in the house if they were alright that, you know, I, I knew I couldn't do anything. And he watched that program and he changed the channel and he watched two more half hour programs. And he said he would leave after that. And again when that time came up he didn't leave. And another program, some celebrity roast came on and he, at about every, at almost every commercial he was going to get up. I begged him to, to call an ambulance and get us some help and get out of there. I kept telling him that I wouldn't, you know, if I was, I kept telling him "If I'm the only one hurt and you didn't hurt my family, I won't press any charges. The only thing I, if they ask me what happened I'll tell them, you know, I won't I won't press any charges, just get you some help." I kept telling him that it seemed like he needed help. And he kept telling, crying to a degree as he was sitting in the chair about how he'd lost his family and he couldn't see his son, and he didn't have anything anymore. And I kept asking him finally about halfway through that show or three quarters through that show said he was going to get up and call an ambulance, which I thought he did. He went into the kitchen, he got on the phone and I thought he was calling an ambulance. He said that it would take about thirty to forty-five minutes. And I kept telling him to, you know, leave before they get here cause if they find me they going to call the police. And he kept saying maybe he wanted them to find him, maybe they should find him. He didn't know what he should do or he, at that time he didn't have any place to go yet. It was too early. And a half hour passed, forty-five minutes passed, an hour passed and no ambulance ever showed up. And I kept asking him, you know, where the ambulance was. And he kept saying well, he, he, he was going to leave, he was going to leave. So finally maybe an hour and a half or so after he said he called the ambulance and the show was over already, that he was going to get up and he was going to leave. It was in the neighborhood of 10:00.

MASSON: When he was sitting in the chair, where was the baseball bat?

MYERS: In his hand. And he said he was going to leave. And he said he
          wanted to go to the bathroom before he left and that I was to
          go with him so I wouldn't try anything because he was afraid
          that I might try to do something to stop him. And as I got up he
          made me walk in front of him. He grabbed me by the shoulder,
          which made me jump suddenly the way he grabbed me, cause he
          grabbed me suddenly and I turned and he, as I turned he tried
          to stab me with a knife in the back. And we started struggling
          again. And I stumbled back into a wall, into the hall against a
          wall and he came at me. And he tried to stab me with the knife
          again and that's where I believe he partially injured me by
          puncturing in my pubic area. And I grabbed his arm, and we
          stumbled into the hall and we both fell down on the floor, which
          he fell down on top of me. And I grabbed the knife with both of
          my hands on the blade. He had the handle. And I had it by the
          blade. I was squeezing it but I also, I had also as we fell down
          I had fell on top of the knife with my body covering it. With that
          and plus me holding onto it he couldn't pull the knife out and
          he, he, we struggled for awhile like that as he kept trying to pull
          the knife away from me. And I kept screaming at him. He was
          trying to kill me again and I wasn't letting go of the knife. And
          finally he, I don't know if he got tired or whatever, he just kept
          saying, "I won't pull if you won't pull but, you know, again I
          gotta calm down and I gotta think, and I gotta think of a plan.
          I gotta", and that's when he started letting me know what he
          had in mind. That he wanted to go get his son, and that he had
          to go get his son no matter what. And he kept saying tomorrow
          was probably going to be his last day anyway, and so he was
          gonna do whatever it took to get his son, no matter what it took,
          and that he wanted my shotgun. And he wanted me to show him
          how to use it, and he wanted to know if I had any shells in the
          house. And I kept telling him no that I don't, you know, that I
          don't keep it loaded, the gun is not loaded, I don't keep a loaded
          gun, and that I don't have any, I haven't been hunting in a few
          years, I don't have any shells in the house. And he, this went on
          for like for some time, maybe an hour or two. And he started,
          you know, to calm him down I kept trying to, he kept saying he
          had to do what he had to do, he had to do what he had to do
          but it was too early, that he had to wait, he had to get there but
          right before his wife walked out to go to work so he could get
          into the house and, and get her and get his kid. And that he
          couldn't let me leave because now he knew if he let me go that

I would stop him, that I would, I would have the police on him or I would stop him, I would have them get him is what he said. Said, "You'd have them get me before I could get down the street if I let you go now. So I can't let you go." And I kept thinking he's not going to walk out of here without killing me at all. So I kept trying to appease him and think of something that he could do as an alternate cause he kept saying, "I gotta think, I gotta come up with a plan", you know. And I started suggesting maybe he can lock me somewhere in the house but that none of the doors, you know, were lockable that he could keep me in. And I suggested he lock me in the trunk of my car. And he, he thought about that for awhile and he, then he said no that wasn't good, wouldn't be good because if somebody heard you screaming in the trunk that they might, you know, before he got there, if they got up early that they may hear me and I'd still be able to stop him. Then I told him to lock me in the trunk and stick my car in the garage where nobody could hear me. And he, again he wasn't sure about that. And then finally he said that he would take my car, stick me in the trunk and take my car, cause that way it would be even better because then nobody would know whose car it was when he pulled up in front of his wife's house where she was living with her parents. And that would be the best thing. And my son, who was in the room. We were laying in the hall right next to the bedroom door, and my son who was in that room occasionally would stir, stir. He'd moan or stir or you could hear him move on the carpet or his foot would tap the door. When this happened he became very aware of it initially and, you know, kept saying, he got a little paranoid and kept saying, "I hope he don't come out. I hope he don't come out. I can't let him come out. He can't see this. I can't let him come out." And eventually he paid less attention to me. He got off of me, as he was on top of me, and I was laying flat. And he was still leaning over me but, and he was still holding onto the handle of the knife at this time but he kept leaning towards the door making sure he could grab the door handle in case he thought my son would get up and try to come out of the room. And I didn't want my son at that time coming out either. I certainly didn't want him to come out into that so I even yelled, "Ryan, stay in the room. Don't come out, lay back down and don't come out." At that time I never thought my son was hurt or anything. I just thought he might have been sleeping through it all.

MASSON: How long did this, this encounter with Bill take place?

MYERS: What?

MASSON: How long did it last, this second encounter in the hall?

MYERS: Maybe two to three hours that I, you know, two to three hours at least. He seemed to be able to tell time from the tv. And the only time I remember that he heard something on the tv and he said, "Oh, it must be about 11:00." And it seemed like it wasn't too long because he was thinking about how long he would have to wait before he left the house to go over to his wife's house. And the nearest thing I can think from there, the time as it elapsed was two, possibly three hours.

MASSON: When were you able to wrestle the knife away from Bill?

MYERS: I didn't actually wrestle the knife away. As he became more and more aware of my son's activities, seemed to become more and more increased and he became more and more paranoid about it. And the more paranoid he became about it, it seemed to me then I started to realize that possibly maybe my son shouldn't be moving, that he may have done something to my son. Because he seemed surprised to some degree and very paranoid about it that he was moving. And as I said he was still holding onto the knife but the more frequent it occurred that my son stirred or bumped his foot into the door he eventually let the knife go, the handle of the knife go. But I was still laying on it, holding onto the blade laying on top of it with my hands underneath me. And I guess if it wouldn't have been for my son I would have never been able to do anything. But every time he bumped the door, he became so paranoid it's almost like he started paying less attention to what I was doing because I was laying there and would have had to do some, some real incredible move to have gotten up at that point to hurt him. Cause it would have taken me some time to get up from my prone position.

MASSON: What happened when you got the knife away from him?

MYERS: Well, as he let it go it was laying underneath me and then gradually every, I kept trying to move and I kept trying to, I kept saying, "I'm uncomfortable", you know, I was laying on my arm and my arm was broken back here. I kept trying to move and as I moved I kept watching how he responded to where I moved. And I'd move and then I'd shift the knife further over where I could get one of my hands on the handle of the knife. The handle was facing my left side, toward my left hand. And I gradually worked the handle from the blade into, in my hand. And then

I rolled over a little bit to one side and tried to lean up against the wall. And every time he'd look at me I'd say, "I'm just trying to get comfortable. I'm just trying to get comfortable." But I was still laying. Well, finally I got myself up on one elbow and it didn't seem to really concern him. But the knife was still underneath me. I kept it more or less concealed the fact that I had the knife in my hand, the handle in my hand. And my son just, you know, seemed like every 30, 40 seconds by now he, he would stir or moan or bump into, his foot kept tapping the door. And he kept, every now and then he'd bend down and try to look under the crack of the door, look under the crack of the door, hold the handle of the door with one hand, and finally I felt I was in a position the next time he bent down I, I would try to do something and he did. And I attacked him with the knife.

MASSON: How many times did you stab him?

MYERS: Actually, I, I don't know. I know I stabbed him at, twice before he turned around. And I lunged at him again and I don't know, my arm was numb. I know the first time I just lunged, went at him as hard as I could. So it had to, it had to stab him.

MASSON: The first time you stabbed him was it in the front or in the back?

MYERS: It was in the back. It was in the lower, the way he was, proximity towards me it was in his lower left side of the back.

MASSON: You were holding the knife in which hand?

MYERS: In my left hand. I am, my arm was broken but I, I'm left handed. And I just squeezed it as hard as I could. That seemed the natural reaction. I couldn't feel anything. It was numb by then.

MASSON: Do you know what motion you used? Did you use an overhand motion or a side motion?

MYERS: It was an overhand motion. And then I lunged at him twice, and he turned around and I lunged at him again. And I don't know after he turned around. Cause he started, he turned around and he started to struggle to get up.
(BEEP TONE ON TAPE) (END OF SIDE ONE)—(BEGINNING OF SIDE TWO)
Okay, he turned around and started to struggle to get up and I went at him again, at least once or twice more. Again, I was, once I did it I think I was just, I don't know how to describe it, enraged, my adrenalin was flowing or something. I just had to get him out of my house.

MASSON: Did you tell him anything?

MYERS: I was screaming at him, "Get out of my house, get out of my house."

MASSON: During this whole time was the front door open or closed?

MYERS: It was closed.

MASSON: When did you first see blood on Bill?

MYERS: When we were struggling the first time at the bat. I was bleeding and I, my blood was just dripping everywhere. And that was the first time that I really noticed there was blood on him. Everything happened so fast in the beginning. I, all I could see mostly was the bat coming at me. And after that he had, had me around the neck and kept smashing things over my head. And I, everything got kind of glassy.

MASSON: Which room were you in when you saw the blood the first time?

MYERS: The den.

MASSON: When did you first see the blood on the bat?

MYERS: In the den about the same time as I grabbed the bat with my hand.

MASSON: Did you see any injuries on Bill?

MYERS: No, not at all.

MASSON: When did Bill first put the bat down?

MYERS: He never put the bat down that I know of until he tried to stab me. The first time that night that I knew he did not have the bat.

MASSON: Where'd he put the bat?

MYERS: I don't know, he had it when I got up and he said he was going to the bathroom. And then he tried to stab me, and then all I saw was the knife and I didn't know where the bat, he must have just left the bat where he was. I, I, he had it when I got up.

MASSON: Okay, you mention that you were hit with a vase and a candle holder. Do you remember what color they were?

MYERS: The candle lamp was, was an off white or ivory color. The, I guess the candle holder was amber. The coffee mug was gray or brown, grayish brown.

MASSON: Did any of the fight take place in the kitchen?

MYERS: No.

MASSON: On Wednesday night, did you and your friends discuss Bill's condition?

MYERS: I didn't, no. Because we were there all the time playing basketball. And when we left the gym, Mike, and, Mike, Jim, Billie and I, Mike dropped me off at my house. I went inside. Bill got in his car and left. Mike left. I don't remember really discussing, nothing in depth, maybe a comment was made while we were playing ball or something but no big in depth discussion over his condition.

MASSON: Was his separation discussed?

MYERS: I can't, I can't honestly say if it was brought up or not. Again, it was no, I was never involved in any real discussions about his condition or his life or whatever.

MASSON: Okay, after the basketball game when you got back to your house, did Bill come into your house?

MYERS: No.

MASSON: He came in earlier that night, did he have the baseball bat with him?

MYERS: Earlier that afternoon he had the baseball bat.

MASSON: Okay, but that night when he came back to play basketball did he have the bat with him?

MYERS: No. He walked in the house dressed to play basketball.

MASSON: How long did you hear the moans coming from the den? Rather from the living room?

MYERS: An hour and a half, two hours.

MASSON: Do you remember where Bill sat?

MYERS: Sat in the rocker/recliner chair right in front of me.

MASSON: What color is the chair?

MYERS: Brown.

MASSON: Where were you sitting?

MYERS: I was on the floor up against the arm of the sofa.

MASSON: Is that the three seat sofa or the love seat?

MYERS: Three seat sofa.

MASSON: Did you see any blood in the hall on the carpet or on the walls in the hall?

MYERS: No, once it got dark I couldn't see anything but as I walked in the house all I saw was him coming at me with the bat.

MASSON: Do you remember what lights were on in the house when you got home?

MYERS: None, the only thing that was on was the tv.

MASSON: Do you remember if the front porch light was on?

MYERS: No I don't. Sometimes it, it was not uncommon, excuse me, that, it was on when I came home that night because I was, I was out the Wednesday. And it's not uncommon that my wife or I had forgotten to turn it off. And it might have stayed on all day long.

MASSON: Do you remember if any of the curtains were open in the house?

MYERS: No. Not that I remember, no, none of the curtains were open.

MASSON: Do you remember how Bill was dressed?

MYERS: He had jeans on, tennis shoes, a blue button collar I guess you would call it blue oxford cloth type shirt, and a blue Izod sweater, pullover sweater.

MASSON: What kind of jeans were they? Were they faded old blue jeans or were they new blue jeans?

MYERS: They didn't look real new.

MASSON: Did you notice if he had a belt on?

MYERS: No I didn't.

MASSON: Was he wearing a hat?

MYERS: No, not that I know. He wasn't wearing a hat when he came at me.

MASSON: On the days before when he came over to the house, either Tuesday or Wednesday, was he wearing a baseball hat or any kind of hat?

MYERS: I honestly can't remember. I, I don't think he was wearing a hat the Tuesday night he first showed up but after that I honestly don't know if he was wearing a hat or not.

MASSON: What time do you leave for work in the morning?

MYERS: It varies, sometimes, depending on how early I might have had an appointment I could leave at 7:30. I might have left my house at 9:00 if I was going right over to the Harvey Canal.

MASSON: Do you remember what time you left Thursday morning?

MYERS: It was 8:45, 9:00.

MASSON: Was Janet up?

MYERS: Yeah, she was sitting in the rocker/recliner feeding Sarah.

MASSON: Is that when you last saw her?

MYERS: That's when I last saw her.

MASSON: Do you remember how she was dressed?

MYERS: Not really, I think she had shorts and leotards on and a pullover shirt. She had gotten up before me as I, while I was taking my shower and all to feed the baby and she was still sitting in the chair. And when I went to kiss her goodbye she, she said she was going to do some exercises, that she was supposed to go to dancing that night. And I know she had shorts. I think she had her leotards on.

MASSON: How were you dressed?

MYERS: I was dressed in a coat and tie.

MASSON: What color?

MYERS: Had a blue sports coat, blazer, gray shirt and gray and blue striped tie, and gray pants.

MASSON: Did you take the tie off at any time while you were in the house?

MYERS: Yes.

MASSON: What room did you take the tie off in?

MYERS: In the den, while I was leaning up against the sofa, you know, the tie was bothering me and I took the tie off.

MASSON: Did you talk to Janet on the phone during the day?

MYERS: No.

MASSON: Did you stop by the house at any time during the day?

MYERS: Yes, when I walked in and he attacked me.

MASSON: No, I mean prior to that?

MYERS: No.

MASSON: At any time while you were fighting, while the fight was going on or there was a lull in the fighting did you hear either Ryan or Sarah crying?

MYERS: Sarah cried almost constantly on and off. I, it was she'd cry and then you wouldn't hear her for five or ten minutes, then she'd cry. I never heard Ryan at all.

MASSON: When you were fighting in the hall, did you notice what doors were open and closed?

MYERS: I think Ryan's room was open but my bedroom and Sarah's bedroom door was closed.

MASSON: What about the bathroom?

MYERS: Think the bathroom door was open. I, I really can't be sure of that but I think it was open.

MASSON: Can you describe the knife?

MYERS: It was a butcher knife with a brown wooden handle that we had in our kitchen. I've seen the knife many times. My wife used it to prepare meals.

MASSON: Okay, what did you do with the knife after Bill was stabbed?

MYERS: I ran back in the house after he got out of the house, and I kept the knife in my hand while I was on the phone. And then I remembered that he said he had put a shell in my gun but he didn't know what kind of shell it was. Whether it was, or whether it was even in there right. So, I told whoever the officer or the dispatcher I was on the phone with hold on a minute and I went to pick up the gun. I opened the chamber and looked at the shell. And it looked like a 12 guage shell. Closed it back and I left, and I set the knife down on a counter if I'm not mistaken and held the gun in case he came back.

MASSON: Did you put any type of clothing or any kind of towels or anything in the kitchen sink?

MYERS: Did I, no.

MASSON: Do you know if Bill did?

MYERS: I know he got a towel when he went into the kitchen, and wet it and wiped his, I believe his, maybe some of the blood off of him and let me wipe some of the blood from around my mouth. Cause my mouth and my nose, my whole face was caked with blood.

MASSON: Do you remember where you stabbed Bill specifically?

MYERS: Only specifically I know the first time I stabbed him was in the lower left portion of his back. That is, I mean that is, I'm absolutely positive that was where I first stabbed him. And I stabbed him again in the back. I'm not really sure where it went.

MASSON: Whose shotgun was it?

MYERS: Mine.

MASSON: Where is the shotgun normally kept?

MYERS: On a gunrack in the den.

MASSON: Is it normally kept loaded?

MYERS: No, absolutely, I've never kept a loaded gun and especially with two kids in my house.

MASSON: Did you have any ammunition in your house for the gun?

MYERS: I did. I had three shells that I always kept. I didn't. I hadn't been hunting in a couple of years so I had no boxes of shells but I always kept three shells in one of the desk drawers. But I hadn't seen them in so long, I'd probably had to look for them myself to find them.

MASSON: Did you clean any blood off of yourself?

MYERS: Only part that I wiped, my face, that, once, with that towel, just wiped my face, around my mouth area because the blood was coagulating and it dripped into, some of it had dripped into my eyes.

MASSON: Did Janet wear any of your clothing at any time?

MYERS: Yes.

MASSON: Were there any specific articles that she would wear?

MYERS: She'd wear my T-shirts to sleep in. She'd wear my jerseys sometime, some of my old baseball or football jerseys. Occasionally she'd even wear my athletic socks.

MASSON: Are you right handed or left handed?

MYERS: Left handed.

MASSON: Do you do all things left handed?

MYERS: All the things, the only thing I really do right handed is play golf, only because I've never learned how to play left handed. Cause when I started learning I couldn't find left handed clubs.

MASSON: When you came into the house Thursday, did you close the door behind you?

MYERS: Yes.

MASSON: Did you lock it?

MYERS: No, I didn't get a chance.

MASSON: Was the door locked when you got home?

MYERS: Yes.

MASSON: Were the curtains in the den open or closed?

MYERS: Closed, I can remember, they possibly could have been partially open but it wasn't, you know, where I could look right out through them.

MASSON: Did you notice any damage to the walls in the hall?

MYERS: No.

MASSON: Was there any damage to the walls before Thursday?

MYERS: No.

MASSON: Okay, when you found Janet, did you touch her at all?

MYERS: I, I bent down over her and reached out and touched her on the hand just to see if she might stir or something.

MASSON: Did Janet normally wear underwear?

MYERS: Yes.

MASSON: Around the house?

MYERS: She always wore panties. Sometimes she, around the house she did not wear a bra. She wouldn't even sleep without panties on.

MASSON: Do you know a man by the name of Chuck Kussard?

MYERS: Chuck Kussard, yes.

MASSON: Where do you know Chuck from?

MYERS: I roomed with Chuck in college. Chuck also used to play ball with us in the beginning but had, he had gotten married and moved to Hammond where he was going to school. In the last few years, you know, we hadn't seen a whole lot of Chuck.

MASSON: When you were with Chuck one time, did you have an argument with Janet where you broke a glass?

MYERS: Where I broke a glass?

MASSON: Or a glass was broken?

MYERS: Yes, we were in college when we were first dating. We lived in a trailer, Chuck and I lived in a trailer. We had an argument and she went down the steps out of the trailer, and she picked up, she was mad at me and she picked up a rock and she was going to throw it at the trailer but it, we had a storm door and instead of hitting the trailer it hit the storm door and shattered the glass.

MASSON: Do you know Curtis and Debbie Jordan?

MYERS: Very well.

MASSON: Were you at a Halloween party at their house in Terrytown?

MYERS: Yes.

MASSON: When you had an argument with Janet?

MYERS: Yes.

MASSON: What was the argument about?

MYERS: I, I think she was just kind of aggravated at me because I wasn't, I wasn't feeling real well that night and I was just, I guess I wasn't in the most lively party mood and she, she was. And she just wanted me to be a little more in the party mood and dance a little more, and she was kind of aggravating me, aggravated because I was just sitting down talking instead of

MASSON: Did you leave the party?

MYERS: We walked outside. I had walked outside for awhile. She came outside a little bit after.

MASSON: Did she come get you or did somebody else come get you?

MYERS: No, she, she came outside just to see where I was.

MASSON: Did you argue over her flirting with somebody at the party?

MYERS: No, no, I did not argue. My wife was, I mean my wife liked to dance and if somebody asked her to dance, either Jimmie or Curtis or Mike or whoever would have asked her to dance, she'd have got up and danced. And the same thing with Curtis' wife or whoever. That never bothered me. My wife was not a flirt. All those people, you know, were friends and I trusted my wife.

MASSON: When you returned from the baseball game on, you were on the highway one time, did you put your wife out the car?

(TELEPHONE RING)

MYERS: We weren't married at that time. I got mad at her once.

MASSON: Did you ask her to get out of the car on the highway?

MYERS: Yeah.

MASSON: Do you know how she got home?

MYERS: I picked her back up, I think (TELEPHONE RING) or maybe she got, I'm not really sure if she got in the car with. We were all leaving a game. This was before we even got married. We were still in college. And either she got back in my car or she rode with somebody else who was right behind us, she got in one of their cars. It's been so long ago I don't even remember. I don't even remember what we argued about then. Again, that was, that was a year before we got married at least.

MASSON: Have you ever struck your wife?

MYERS: Yes, once we had an argument a few years ago after we were married. This was, wasn't long after we were married. I don't even know what it was about. It wasn't anything major between us. It was something else that had happened and we disagreed on. All I did was, was, she got I would guess somewhat hysterical. I, something, I'm trying to think. It might have been even something her mother had done to her or, you know, she was mad at. And I just slapped her in the face and grabbed her by the shoulders and told her, you know, "calm down, you gotta stop and calm down and talk to me." Other than that I've never struck her.

MASSON: Have you had any loud arguments at your house, arguments that the neighbors would know about or would be able to hear?

MYERS: We argued and yelled, possibly, I'm not going to say that nobody ever not heard anything. If the windows might have been open sure they could have heard it. I hear my neighbor, I used to hear my neighbors yelling at their kids and yelling at each other when the windows were open in spring and fall months, I guess, all the time.

MASSON: Have you ever had the police at your house to quell an argument between you and your wife?

MYERS: When we were first married we lived in an apartment and we had an argument. And we had a neighbor who used to play his stereo 3:00 and 4:00 in the morning constantly to where it vibrated the walls. And we had, a couple of times had to call the manager and the police on him. And I think he must have heard us one night and called the police on us. We had an argument

and it wasn't violent or anything we were just, it got a little
loud.

MASSON: Did either you or your wife ever call the police to quell an
argument?

MYERS: No, no.

MASSON: Okay, when you called the police, did you call the police before
or after you checked on the condition of your wife and children?

MYERS: The first thing I did when he got out of the house was pick up
the phone and call the police.

MASSON: After you checked on your wife and found her condition, why
didn't you go check on your children instead of going back to the
phone?

MYERS: Well, I was already on the phone and I wanted to get back and
be there and have that gun in my hand for protection. He said
my children weren't hurt and I could hear Sarah crying and I
knew where Ryan was, *and I saw him,* I heard him moving, you
know, and saw his foot from under the door that he was stirring.
And so my first assumption was, you know, he wasn't hurt. And
it just never occurred, I was really shook up when I saw my wife.
And I just hung there and kept trying to talk to whoever was on
the phone and make sure I, I, you know, I could protect myself
if he came back. And it seemed just maybe a couple of minutes
after I checked on her that the police showed up at the door.

MASSON: Okay, there was a call that came on your phone while you were
talking to the police. Did you ever find out who was on the
phone or whoever called?

MYERS: I heard a beep, beep in the phone, okay. We have, we had call
waiting and I heard the beep, beep. And I didn't know, I thought
it was the call waiting. I didn't know if it may be something at
the police station or or, you know, it was from their phones or
it was mine. But I never got off the phone to, to, I never, you'd
have to touch the button and disconnect one to get to the other,
no, I never.

MASSON: Is it uncommon for you to get calls at that time in the morning?

MYERS: Very.

MASSON: Is there anything else you can think of at this time you want to
add to this statement?

MYERS: Only that I don't know what happened or what made him do it.
But I do know that once he, he started from the time I walked

in. And again I, whatever happened to my wife and to my son happened before I got there. Or possibly may even happened right before I got there. As I think about it, maybe from where he came out at me. But he definitely, I really definitely believed he wasn't going, the way he was, he would not let me go. *He, he wasn't going to be stopped before he did whatever* he had *to do at* his wife's house. And he wasn't going to let anything stop him. Maybe that's, maybe that's why he killed my wife, maybe she became frightened and he thought she might even call the police. I don't know.

MASSON: Do you believe that your wife and Bill had engaged in sexual relations?

MYERS: Absolutely not.

MASSON: When was the last time that you had relations with your wife?

MYERS: Wednesday night, after the basketball game.

MASSON: Is there anything else you want to add?

MYERS: No.

RAU: Let me just ask him a couple of things. Would you say again the nature of his voice when you first came in the door?

MYERS: Panic, he screamed my name almost in panic.

RAU: Now, before you got ahold of the knife did he have any injuries at all? (INAUDIBLE)

MYERS: The only one that he had was a cut on his finger that he had to get from breaking one of the glass objects over my head. Cause he mentioned it a couple of times about his finger was cut pretty bad.

RAU: That's all.

MASSON: Statement was completed at approximately 2:45 P.M., same date.

Index